Nonlinear Partial Differential Equations: Exact Solutions, Symmetries, Methods, and Applications

Editor

Nikolay A. Kudryashov

MDPI • Basel • Beijing • Wuhan • Barcelona • Belgrade • Manchester • Tokyo • Cluj • Tianjin

Editor
Nikolay A. Kudryashov
Department of Applied Mathematics at Moscow
Engineering and Physics Institute (MEPhI)
Moscow
Russia

Editorial Office
MDPI
St. Alban-Anlage 66
4052 Basel, Switzerland

This is a reprint of articles from the Special Issue published online in the open access journal *Mathematics* (ISSN 2227-7390) (available at: https://www.mdpi.com/journal/mathematics/special_issues/nonlinear_partial_differential_equations).

For citation purposes, cite each article independently as indicated on the article page online and as indicated below:

LastName, A.A.; LastName, B.B.; LastName, C.C. Article Title. *Journal Name* **Year**, *Volume Number*, Page Range.

ISBN 978-3-0365-8096-8 (Hbk)
ISBN 978-3-0365-8097-5 (PDF)

© 2023 by the authors. Articles in this book are Open Access and distributed under the Creative Commons Attribution (CC BY) license, which allows users to download, copy and build upon published articles, as long as the author and publisher are properly credited, which ensures maximum dissemination and a wider impact of our publications.

The book as a whole is distributed by MDPI under the terms and conditions of the Creative Commons license CC BY-NC-ND.

Contents

About the Editor vii

Preface ix

Wael W. Mohammed, Meshari Alesemi, Sahar Albosaily, Naveed Iqbal and M. El-Morshedy
The Exact Solutions of Stochastic Fractional-Space Kuramoto-Sivashinsky Equation by Using $(\frac{G'}{G})$-Expansion Method
Reprinted from: *Mathematics* **2021**, *9*, 2712, doi:10.3390/math9212712 1

Sergey Misyurin, German Kreynin, Andrey Nelyubin and Natalia Nosova
Multicriteria Optimization of a Dynamic System by Methods of the Theories of Similarity and Criteria Importance
Reprinted from: *Mathematics* **2021**, *9*, 2854, doi:10.3390/math9222854 11

Nikolai A. Kudryashov
Implicit Solitary Waves for One of the Generalized Nonlinear Schrödinger Equations
Reprinted from: *Mathematics* **2021**, *9*, 3024, doi:10.3390/math9233024 31

Alexander Sboev, Danila Vlasov, Roman Rybka, Yury Davydov, Alexey Serenko and Vyacheslav Demin
Modeling the Dynamics of Spiking Networks with Memristor-Based STDP to Solve Classification Tasks
Reprinted from: *Mathematics* **2021**, *9*, 3237, doi:10.3390/math9243237 41

Elsayed M. E. Zayed, Khaled A. Gepreel, Mahmoud El-Horbaty, Anjan Biswas, Yakup Yıldırım and Hashim M. Alshehri
Highly Dispersive Optical Solitons with Complex Ginzburg–Landau Equation Having Six Nonlinear Forms
Reprinted from: *Mathematics* **2021**, *9*, 3270, doi:10.3390/math9243270 51

Chaudry Masood Khalique and Karabo Plaatjie
Symmetry Methods and Conservation Laws for the Nonlinear Generalized 2D Equal-Width Partial Differential Equation of Engineering
Reprinted from: *Mathematics* **2022**, *10*, 24, doi:10.3390/math10010024 71

Alyaa A. Al-Qarni, Huda O. Bakodah, Aisha A. Alshaery, Anjan Biswas, Yakup Yıldırım, Luminita Moraru and Simona Moldovanu
Numerical Simulation of Cubic-Quartic Optical Solitons with Perturbed Fokas–Lenells Equation Using Improved Adomian Decomposition Algorithm
Reprinted from: *Mathematics* **2022**, *10*, 138, doi:10.3390/math10010138 89

Abdulmohsen D. Alruwaili, Aly R. Seadawy, Syed T. R. Rizvi and Sid Ahmed O. Beinane
Diverse Multiple Lump Analytical Solutions for Ion Sound and Langmuir Waves
Reprinted from: *Mathematics* **2022**, *10*, 200, doi:10.3390/math10020200 101

Lewa' Alzaleq, Valipuram Manoranjan and Baha Alzalg
Exact Traveling Waves of a Generalized Scale-Invariant Analogue of the Korteweg–de Vries Equation
Reprinted from: *Mathematics* **2022**, *10*, 414, doi:10.3390/math10030414 123

Anjan Biswas, Trevor Berkemeyer, Salam Khan, Luminita Moraru, Yakup Yıldırım and Hashim M. Alshehri
Highly Dispersive Optical Soliton Perturbation, with Maximum Intensity, for the Complex Ginzburg–Landau Equation by Semi-Inverse Variation
Reprinted from: *Mathematics* **2022**, *10*, 987, doi:10.3390/math10060987 141

Oswaldo González-Gaxiola, Anjan Biswas, Yakup Yıldırım and Luminita Moraru
Highly Dispersive Optical Solitons in Birefringent Fibers with Polynomial Law of Nonlinear Refractive Index by Laplace–Adomian Decomposition
Reprinted from: *Mathematics* **2022**, *10*, 1589, doi:10.3390/math10091589 153

Aly R. Seadawy, Hanadi Zahed and Syed T. R. Rizvi
Diverse Forms of Breathers and Rogue Wave Solutions for the Complex Cubic Quintic Ginzburg Landau Equation with Intrapulse Raman Scattering
Reprinted from: *Mathematics* **2022**, *10*, 1818, doi:10.3390/math10111818 165

Oke Davies Adeyemo, Lijun Zhang and Chaudry Masood Khalique
Bifurcation Theory, Lie Group-Invariant Solutions of Subalgebras and Conservation Laws of a Generalized (2+1)-Dimensional BK Equation Type II in Plasma Physics and Fluid Mechanics
Reprinted from: *Mathematics* **2022**, *10*, 2391, doi:10.3390/math10142391 187

Elsayed M. E. Zayed, Mohamed E. M. Alngar, Reham M. A. Shohib, Anjan Biswas, Yakup Yıldırım, Salam Khan, et al.
Highly Dispersive Optical Solitons in Fiber Bragg Gratings with Kerr Law of Nonlinear Refractive Index
Reprinted from: *Mathematics* **2022**, *10*, 2968, doi:10.3390/math10162968 233

Vladimir A. Shargatov, George G. Tsypkin, Sergey V. Gorkunov, Polina I. Kozhurina and Yulia A. Bogdanova
On the Short Wave Instability of the Liquid/Gas Contact Surface in Porous Media
Reprinted from: *Mathematics* **2022**, *10*, 3177, doi:10.3390/math10173177 245

Nikolai A. Kudryashov
Optical Solitons of the Generalized Nonlinear Schrödinger Equation with Kerr Nonlinearity and Dispersion of Unrestricted Order
Reprinted from: *Mathematics* **2022**, *10*, 3409, doi:10.3390/math10183409 261

Natalia Alekseeva, Viktoriia Podryga, Parvin Rahimly, Richard Coffin and Ingo Pecher
Modeling of Gas Hydrates Dissociation in Porous Media with Water-Ice Phase Transformations Using Differential Constrains
Reprinted from: *Mathematics* **2022**, *10*, 3470, doi:10.3390/math10193470 271

Yury Poveshchenko, Viktoriia Podryga and Parvin Rahimly
On Convergence of Support Operator Method Schemes for Differential Rotational Operations on Tetrahedral Meshes Applied to Magnetohydrodynamic Problems
Reprinted from: *Mathematics* **2022**, *10*, 3904, doi:10.3390/math10203904 291

Alexander Leonov, Oleg Nagornov and Sergey Tyuflin
Modeling of Mechanisms of Wave Formation for COVID-19 Epidemic
Reprinted from: *Mathematics* **2023**, *11*, 167, doi:10.3390/math11010167 309

About the Editor

Nikolay A. Kudryashov

Nikolay A. Kudryashov is a full professor of National Research Nuclear University Moscow Engineering Physics Institute. He has a PhD in mathematical Physics (1978) and is a Dr. of Science (1985). He was the Head of the Department of Applied Mathematics (1986) and won the USSR National Prize in Science and Technology (bestowed on him by the USSR Council of Ministers) (1982). He was a Soros professor (1994), Academician of Russian Academy of Natural Sciences (2000), and Meritorious Science Worker of the Russian Federation (2002).

He is the author of 12 books and more than 500 papers published in reputed journals. He is a member of the following journals: Applied Mathematics and Computation; Mathematics; Regular and Chaotic Dynamics; Russian Nonlinear Dynamics. He is reviewer of the following journals: *Applied Mathematics and Computations*; *Communications in Nonlinear Science and Numerical Simulations*; *Mathematics*; *Regular and Chaotic Dynamics*; *Russian Nonlinear Dynamics*; *Physics Letters A*; *Chaos, Solitons and Fractals*; *Results in Physics*, *Optics*, etc.

His research interests include nonlinear mathematical models, nonlinear mathematical physics, numerical modeling, nonlinear dynamics, analytical properties of nonlinear differential equations, analytical solutions of nonlinear differential equations, Painleve analysis, and Painleve equations.

Preface

Several decades ago, two fundamental discoveries took place in nonlinear science, which largely determined the development of nonlinear mathematical models to the present day. These discoveries—the special properties of solitons and the strange Lorentz attractor—determined numerous works related to the development of methods used for the analytical and numerical study of many mathematical models described by nonlinear differential potential nonlinear equations. Unlike the first steps in the study of nonlinear mathematical models, when attention was primarily paid to the development of methods used to solve interim nonlinear partial differential equations, in recent years, much more attention has been paid to the development of methods used to study non-integrable mathematical models with analytical solutions.

This book contains the 19 accepted articles out of the 50 manuscripts submitted to the Special Issue "Nonlinear Partial Differential Equations: Exact Solutions, Symmetries, Methods and Applications, 2023, 2020" of the MDPI "*Mathematics*" journal.

This Special Issue unites 19 papers which considers the development of research methods for a number of nonlinear mathematical models in physics, epidemiology, mechanical engineering, and nonlinear optics. A characteristic feature of all the articles in this issue is that the studies presented in the papers were obtained using computer mathematics, including symbolic mathematics packages, program codes and machine learning methods.

As the Guest Editor of the Special Issue, I am grateful to the authors of these papers for their high-quality contributions, to the reviewers for their valuable comments that helped to improve the submitted works, and to the administrative staff of the MDPI publications for their support in completing this project. I am very grateful to the Section Editor Claude Zhang for attention and help to all authors of this issue.

Nikolay A. Kudryashov
Editor

Article

The Exact Solutions of Stochastic Fractional-Space Kuramoto-Sivashinsky Equation by Using ($\frac{G'}{G}$)-Expansion Method

Wael W. Mohammed [1,2,*], Meshari Alesemi [3], Sahar Albosaily [1], Naveed Iqbal [1,*] and M. El-Morshedy [4,5]

1 Department of Mathematics, Faculty of Science, University of Ha'il, Ha'il 2440, Saudi Arabia; s.albosaily@uoh.edu.sa
2 Department of Mathematics, Faculty of Science, Mansoura University, Mansoura 35516, Egypt
3 Department of Mathematics, Faculty of Science, University of Bisha, Bisha 61922, Saudi Arabia; malesemi@ub.edu.sa
4 Department of Mathematics, College of Science and Humanities in Al-Kharj, Prince Sattam bin Abdulaziz University, Al-Kharj 11942, Saudi Arabia; m.elmorshedy@psau.edu.sa or mah_elmorshedy@mans.edu.eg
5 Department of Mathematics and Statistics, Faculty of Science, Mansoura University, Mansoura 35516, Egypt
* Correspondence: wael.mohammed@mans.edu.eg (W.W.M.); naveediqbal1989@yahoo.com (N.I.)

Abstract: In this paper, we consider the stochastic fractional-space Kuramoto–Sivashinsky equation forced by multiplicative noise. To obtain the exact solutions of the stochastic fractional-space Kuramoto–Sivashinsky equation, we apply the $\frac{G'}{G}$-expansion method. Furthermore, we generalize some previous results that did not use this equation with multiplicative noise and fractional space. Additionally, we show the influence of the stochastic term on the exact solutions of the stochastic fractional-space Kuramoto–Sivashinsky equation

Keywords: stochastic Kuramoto–Sivashinsky; fractional Kuramoto–Sivashinsky; exact stochastic-fractional solutions; ($\frac{G'}{G}$)-expansion method

1. Introduction

In recent decades, fractional derivatives have received a lot of attention because they have been effectively used to problems in finance [1–3], biology [4], physics [5–8], thermodynamic [9,10], hydrology [11,12], biochemistry and chemistry [13]. Since fractional-order integrals and derivatives allow for the representation of the memory and heredity properties of various substances, these new fractional-order models are more suited than the previously used integer-order models [14]. This is the most important benefit of fractional-order models in comparison with integer-order models, where such impacts are ignored.

On the other hand, fluctuations or randomness have now been shown to be important in many phenomena. Therefore, random effects have become significant when modeling different physical phenomena that take place in oceanography, physics, biology, meteorology, environmental sciences, and so on. Equations that consider random fluctuations in time are referred to as stochastic differential equations.

Recently, some studies on the approximation solutions of fractional differential equations with stochastic perturbations have been published, such as those of Taheri et al. [15], Zou [16], Mohammed et al. [17,18], Mohammed [19], Kamrani [20], Li and Yang [21] and Liu and Yan [22], while the exact solutions of stochastic fractional differential equations have not been discussed until now.

In this study, we take into account the following stochastic fractional-space Kuramoto–Sivashinsky (S-FS-KS) equation in one dimension with multiplicative noise in the itô sense:

$$\partial_t u + ru D_x^\alpha u + p D_x^{2\alpha} u + q D_x^{4\alpha} u = \rho u \partial_t \beta, \qquad (1)$$

where r, p, and q are nonzero real constants, α is the order of the fractional space derivative, ρ is the noise strength, and $\beta(t)$ is the standard Gaussian process and it depends only on t.

The deterministic Kuramoto–Sivashinsky Equation (1) (i.e., $\rho = 0$) with $\alpha = 1$ has been studied by a number of authors to attain its exact solutions by different methods such as the modified tanh-coth method [23], the tanh method and the extended tanh method [24], homotopy analysis method [25], the $(\frac{G'}{G})$-expansion method [26], perturbation method [27], the Weiss–Tabor–Carnevale method [28], Painlevé expansion methods [29], the truncated expansion method [30], the polynomial expansion method [31–37], among many others; see also the references therein.

The motivation of this article is to find the exact solutions of the S-FS-KS (1) derived from multiplicative noise by employing the $(\frac{G'}{G})$-expansion method. The results presented here improve and generalize earlier studies, such as those mentioned in [24]. It is also discussed how multiplicative noise affects these solutions. To the best of our knowledge, this is the first paper to establish the exact solution of the S-FS-KS (1).

In the next section, we define the order α of Jumarie's derivative and we state some significant properties of the modified Riemann–Liouville derivative. In Section 3, we obtain the wave equation for the S-FS-KS Equation (1), while in Section 4 we have the exact stochastic solutions of the S-FS-KS (1) by applying the $(\frac{G'}{G})$-expansion method. In Section 5, we show several graphical representations to demonstrate the effect of stochastic terms on the obtained solutions of the S-FS-KS. Finally, the conclusions of this paper are presented.

2. Modified Riemann–Liouville Derivative and Properties

The order α of Jumarie's derivative is defined by [38]:

$$D_x^\alpha g(x) = \begin{cases} \frac{1}{\Gamma(1-\alpha)} \frac{d}{dx} \int_0^x (x-\zeta)^{-\alpha}(g(\zeta) - g(0))d\zeta, & 0 < \alpha < 1, \\ [g^{(n)}(x)]^{\alpha-n}, & n \leq \alpha \leq n+1, \ n \geq 1, \end{cases}$$

where $g : \mathbb{R} \to \mathbb{R}$ is a continuous function but not necessarily first-order differentiable and $\Gamma(.)$ is the Gamma function.

Now, let us state some significant properties of modified Riemann–Liouville derivative as follows:

$$D_x^\alpha x^\delta = \frac{\Gamma(1+\delta)}{\Gamma(1+\delta-\alpha)} x^{\delta-\alpha}, \ \delta > 0,$$

$$D_x^\alpha [ag(x)] = a D_x^\alpha g(x),$$

$$D_x^\alpha [af(x) + bg(x)] = a D_x^\alpha f(x) + b D_x^\alpha g(x),$$

and

$$D_x^\alpha g(u(x)) = \sigma_x \frac{dg}{du} D_x^\alpha u,$$

where σ_x is called the sigma indexes [39,40].

3. Wave Equation for S-FS-KS Equation

To obtain the wave equation for the SKS Equation (1), we apply the next wave transformation

$$u(x,t) = \varphi(\eta) e^{(\rho\beta(t) - \frac{1}{2}\rho^2 t)}, \ \eta = \frac{1}{\Gamma(1+\alpha)} x^\alpha - ct, \qquad (2)$$

where φ is the deterministic function and c is the wave speed. By differentiating Equation (2) with respect to x and t, we obtain

$$\begin{aligned} u_t &= (-c\varphi' + \frac{1}{2}\rho^2\varphi - \frac{1}{2}\rho^2\varphi + \rho\varphi\beta_t) e^{(\rho\beta(t) - \frac{1}{2}\rho^2 t)}, \\ D_x^\alpha u &= \sigma_x \varphi' e^{[\rho\beta(t) - \rho^2 t]}, \ D_x^{2\alpha} u = \sigma_x^2 \varphi'' e^{[\rho\beta(t) - \rho^2 t]}. \\ D_x^{3\alpha} &= \sigma_x^3 e^{(\rho\beta(t) - \frac{1}{2}\rho^2 t)}, \ D_x^{4\alpha} = \sigma_x^4 e^{(\rho\beta(t) - \frac{1}{2}\rho^2 t)}, \end{aligned} \qquad (3)$$

where $+\frac{1}{2}\rho^2\varphi$ is the Itô correction term. Now, substituting Equation (3) into Equation (1), we obtain
$$-c\varphi' + \tilde{r}\varphi\varphi' e^{(\rho\beta(t)-\frac{1}{2}\rho^2 t)} + \tilde{p}\varphi'' + \tilde{q}\varphi'''' = 0, \qquad (4)$$
where we put $\tilde{r} = \sigma_x r$, $\tilde{p} = \sigma_x^2 p$ and $\tilde{q} = \sigma_x^4 q$. Taking the expectation on both sides and considering that φ is deterministic function, we have
$$-c\varphi' + \tilde{r}\varphi\varphi' e^{-\frac{1}{2}\rho^2 t}\mathbb{E}(e^{\rho\beta(t)}) + \tilde{p}\varphi'' + \tilde{q}\varphi'''' = 0. \qquad (5)$$

Since $\beta(t)$ is standard Gaussian random variable, then for any real constant ρ we have $\mathbb{E}(e^{\rho\beta(t)}) = e^{\frac{\rho^2}{2}t}$. Now, Equation (5) has the form
$$-c\varphi' + \tilde{r}\varphi\varphi' + \tilde{p}\varphi'' + \tilde{q}\varphi'''' = 0. \qquad (6)$$

Integrating Equation (6) once in terms of η yields
$$\tilde{q}\varphi''' + \tilde{p}\varphi' + \frac{\tilde{r}}{2}\varphi^2 - c\varphi = 0, \qquad (7)$$
where we set the constant of integration as equal to zero.

4. The Exact Solutions of the S-FS-KS Equation

Here, we apply the $\frac{G'}{G}$-expansion method [41] in order to find the solutions of Equation (7). As a result, we have the exact solutions of the S-FS-KS (1). First, we suppose the solution of the S-FS-KS equation, Equation (7), has the form
$$\varphi = \sum_{k=0}^{M} b_k [\frac{G'}{G}]^k, \qquad (8)$$
where $b_0, b_1, ..., b_M$ are uncertain constants that must be calculated later, and G solves
$$G'' + \lambda G' + \mu G = 0, \qquad (9)$$
where λ, μ are unknown constants. Let us now calculate the parameter M by balancing φ^2 with φ''' in Equation (7) as follows
$$2M = M + 3;$$
hence
$$M = 3. \qquad (10)$$

From (10), we can rewrite Equation (8) as
$$\varphi = b_0 + b_1 [\frac{G'}{G}] + b_2 [\frac{G'}{G}]^2 + b_3 [\frac{G'}{G}]^3. \qquad (11)$$

Putting Equation (11) into Equation (7) and utilizing Equation (9), we obtain a polynomial with degree 6 of $\frac{G'}{G}$ as follows

$$(\frac{1}{2}\tilde{r}b_3^2 - 60\tilde{q}b_3)[\frac{G'}{G}]^6 + (-24\tilde{q}b_2 + \tilde{r}b_2b_3 - 144\tilde{q}\lambda b_3)[\frac{G'}{G}]^5$$

$$+(\frac{1}{2}\tilde{r}b_2^2 - 3\tilde{p}b_3 - 6\tilde{q}b_1 + \tilde{r}b_1b_3 - 111\tilde{q}\lambda^2 b_3 - 114\tilde{q}\mu b_3 - 54\tilde{q}\lambda b_2)[\frac{G'}{G}]^4$$

$$+(-cb_3 + 2\tilde{p}b_2 + \tilde{r}b_0b_3 + \tilde{r}b_1b_2 - 3\tilde{p}\lambda b_3 - 38\tilde{q}\lambda^2 b_2 - 40\tilde{q}\mu b_2 - 27\lambda^3 b_3$$

$$-12\tilde{q}\lambda b_1 - 168\tilde{q}\lambda\mu b_3)[\frac{G'}{G}]^3 + (-cb_2 + \frac{1}{2}\tilde{r}b_1^2 - \tilde{p}b_1 + \tilde{r}b_0b_2 - 2\tilde{p}\lambda b_2$$

$$-3\tilde{p}\mu b_3 - 7\tilde{q}\lambda^2 b_1 - 8\tilde{q}\mu b_1 - 8\tilde{q}\lambda^3 b_2 - 52\tilde{q}\lambda\mu b_2 - 60\tilde{q}\mu^2 b_3$$

$$-57\tilde{q}\lambda^2\mu b_3)[\frac{G'}{G}]^2 + (-cb_1 + \tilde{r}b_0b_1 - \tilde{p}\lambda b_1 - 2\tilde{p}\mu b_2 - \tilde{q}\lambda^3 b_1$$

$$-16\tilde{q}\mu^2 b_2 - 8\tilde{q}\lambda\mu b_1 - 14\tilde{q}\lambda^2\mu b_2 - 36\tilde{q}\mu^2\lambda b_3)[\frac{G'}{G}]+$$

$$(-cb_0 + \frac{1}{2}\tilde{r}b_0^2 - \tilde{p}\mu b_1 - \tilde{q}\lambda^2\mu b_1 - 6\tilde{q}\mu^2\lambda b_2 - 2\tilde{q}\mu^2 b_1 - 6\tilde{q}\mu^3 b_3) = 0.$$

By equating each coefficient of $[\frac{G'}{G}]^i$ ($i = 6, 5, 4, 3, 2, 1, 0$) to zero, we have a system of algebraic equations. By solving this system by using Maple, we obtain two cases:

First case:

$$b_0 = \pm\frac{30\tilde{p}}{19\tilde{r}}\sqrt{\frac{-\tilde{p}}{19\tilde{q}}}, \quad b_1 = \frac{90\tilde{p}}{19\tilde{r}}, \quad b_2 = 0, \quad b_3 = \frac{120\tilde{q}}{\tilde{r}},$$

$$c = \pm\frac{30\tilde{p}}{19}\sqrt{\frac{-\tilde{p}}{19\tilde{q}}}, \quad \lambda = 0, \quad \mu = \frac{\tilde{p}}{76\tilde{q}}, \text{ if } \frac{\tilde{p}}{\tilde{q}} < 0. \quad (12)$$

In this situation, the solution of Equation (7) is

$$\varphi(\eta) = b_0 + b_1[\frac{G'}{G}] + b_3[\frac{G'}{G}]^3. \quad (13)$$

By solving Equation (9) with $\lambda = 0$, $\mu = \frac{\tilde{p}}{76\tilde{q}}$ if $\frac{\tilde{p}}{\tilde{q}} < 0$, we obtain

$$G(\eta) = c_1 \exp(\sqrt{\frac{-\tilde{p}}{76\tilde{q}}}\eta) + c_2 \exp(-\sqrt{\frac{-\tilde{p}}{76\tilde{q}}}\eta), \quad (14)$$

where c_1 and c_2 are constants. Putting Equation (14) into Equation (13), we have

$$\varphi(\eta) = \pm\frac{30\tilde{p}}{19\tilde{r}}\sqrt{\frac{-\tilde{p}}{19\tilde{q}}} + \frac{90\tilde{p}}{19\tilde{r}}\sqrt{\frac{-\tilde{p}}{76\tilde{q}}}[\frac{c_1 \exp(\sqrt{\frac{-\tilde{p}}{76\tilde{q}}}\eta) - c_2 \exp(-\sqrt{\frac{-\tilde{p}}{76\tilde{q}}}\eta)}{c_1 \exp(\sqrt{\frac{-\tilde{p}}{76\tilde{q}}}\eta) + c_2 \exp(-\sqrt{\frac{-\tilde{p}}{76\tilde{q}}}\eta)}]$$

$$+\frac{120\tilde{q}}{\tilde{r}}(\sqrt{\frac{-\tilde{p}}{76\tilde{q}}})^3[\frac{c_1 \exp(\sqrt{\frac{-\tilde{p}}{76\tilde{q}}}\eta) - c_2 \exp(-\sqrt{\frac{-\tilde{p}}{76\tilde{q}}}\eta)}{c_1 \exp(\sqrt{\frac{-\tilde{p}}{76\tilde{q}}}\eta) + c_2 \exp(-\sqrt{\frac{-\tilde{p}}{76\tilde{q}}}\eta)}]^3.$$

Hence, the exact solution in this case of the S-FS-KS (1), by using (2), has the form

$$u_1(x,t) = e^{(\rho\beta(t) - \frac{1}{2}\rho^2 t)}\{\pm\frac{30\tilde{p}\hbar}{19\tilde{r}}$$

$$+\frac{90\tilde{p}\hbar}{19\tilde{r}}[\frac{c_1 \exp(\hbar(\frac{1}{\Gamma(1+\alpha)}x^\alpha - ct)) - c_2 \exp(-\hbar(\frac{1}{\Gamma(1+\alpha)}x^\alpha - ct))}{c_1 \exp(\hbar(\frac{1}{\Gamma(1+\alpha)}x^\alpha - ct)) + c_2 \exp(-\hbar(\frac{1}{\Gamma(1+\alpha)}x^\alpha - ct))}]$$

$$+\frac{120\tilde{q}\hbar^3}{\tilde{r}}[\frac{c_1 \exp(\frac{\hbar}{\Gamma(1+\alpha)}x^\alpha - c\hbar t) - c_2 \exp(-\hbar(\frac{1}{\Gamma(1+\alpha)}x^\alpha - ct))}{c_1 \exp(\frac{\hbar}{\Gamma(1+\alpha)}x^\alpha - c\hbar t) + c_2 \exp(-\hbar(\frac{1}{\Gamma(1+\alpha)}x^\alpha - ct))}]^3\}, \quad (15)$$

where $c = \pm \frac{30\tilde{p}}{19}\sqrt{\frac{-\tilde{p}}{19\tilde{q}}}$, $\hbar = \sqrt{\frac{-\tilde{p}}{76\tilde{q}}}$ and $\frac{\tilde{p}}{\tilde{q}} < 0$.

Second case:

$$b_0 = \pm\frac{30\tilde{p}}{19\tilde{r}}\sqrt{\frac{11}{19\tilde{q}}}, \quad b_1 = \frac{-270\tilde{p}}{19\tilde{r}}, \quad b_2 = 0, \quad b_3 = \frac{120\tilde{q}}{\tilde{r}},$$

$$c = \pm\frac{30\tilde{p}}{19}\sqrt{\frac{11\tilde{p}}{19\tilde{q}}}, \quad \lambda = 0, \quad \mu = \frac{-11\tilde{p}}{76\tilde{q}}, \quad \text{if } \frac{\tilde{p}}{\tilde{q}} > 0. \tag{16}$$

In this situation, the solution of Equation (7) is

$$\varphi(\eta) = b_0 + b_1\left[\frac{G'}{G}\right] + b_3\left[\frac{G'}{G}\right]^3. \tag{17}$$

Solving Equation (9) with $\lambda = 0$, $\mu = \frac{-11\tilde{p}}{76\tilde{q}}$, if $\frac{\tilde{p}}{\tilde{q}} > 0$, we obtain

$$G(\eta) = c_1 \exp\left(\sqrt{\frac{11\tilde{p}}{76\tilde{q}}}\eta\right) + c_2 \exp\left(-\sqrt{\frac{11\tilde{p}}{76\tilde{q}}}\eta\right). \tag{18}$$

Substituting Equation (14) into Equation (13), we have

$$\varphi(\eta) = \pm\frac{30\tilde{p}}{19\tilde{r}}\sqrt{\frac{11\tilde{p}}{19\tilde{q}}} - \frac{270\tilde{p}}{19\tilde{r}}\sqrt{\frac{11\tilde{p}}{76\tilde{q}}}\left[\frac{c_1 \exp(\sqrt{\frac{11\tilde{p}}{76\tilde{q}}}\eta) - c_2 \exp(-\sqrt{\frac{11\tilde{p}}{76\tilde{q}}}\eta)}{c_1 \exp(\sqrt{\frac{11\tilde{p}}{76\tilde{q}}}\eta) + c_2 \exp(-\sqrt{\frac{11\tilde{p}}{76\tilde{q}}}\eta)}\right]$$

$$+\frac{120\tilde{q}}{\tilde{r}}\left(\sqrt{\frac{11\tilde{p}}{76\tilde{q}}}\right)^3\left[\frac{c_1 \exp(\sqrt{\frac{11\tilde{p}}{76\tilde{q}}}\eta) - c_2 \exp(-\sqrt{\frac{11\tilde{p}}{76\tilde{q}}}\eta)}{c_1 \exp(\sqrt{\frac{11\tilde{p}}{76\tilde{q}}}\eta) + c_2 \exp(-\sqrt{\frac{11\tilde{p}}{76\tilde{q}}}\eta)}\right]^3.$$

Therefore, by using (2), the exact solution in this case of the S-FS-KS (1) has the form

$$u_2(x,t) = e^{(\rho\beta(t) - \frac{1}{2}\rho^2 t)}\left\{\pm\frac{30\tilde{p}}{19\tilde{r}}\sqrt{\frac{11\tilde{p}}{19\tilde{q}}}\right.$$

$$-\frac{270\tilde{p}\hbar}{19\tilde{r}}\left[\frac{c_1 \exp(\hbar(\frac{x^\alpha}{\Gamma(1+\alpha)} - ct)) - c_2 \exp(-\hbar(\frac{x^\alpha}{\Gamma(1+\alpha)} - ct))}{c_1 \exp(\sqrt{\frac{11\tilde{p}}{76\tilde{q}}}(\frac{1}{\Gamma(1+\alpha)}x^\alpha - ct)) + c_2 \exp(-\hbar(\frac{x^\alpha}{\Gamma(1+\alpha)} - ct))}\right]$$

$$\left.+\frac{120\tilde{q}\hbar^3}{\tilde{r}}\left[\frac{c_1 \exp(\hbar(\frac{x^\alpha}{\Gamma(1+\alpha)} - ct)) - c_2 \exp(-\hbar(\frac{x^\alpha}{\Gamma(1+\alpha)} - ct))}{c_1 \exp(\hbar(\frac{x^\alpha}{\Gamma(1+\alpha)} - ct)) + c_2 \exp(-\hbar(\frac{x^\alpha}{\Gamma(1+\alpha)} - ct))}\right]^3\right\}, \tag{19}$$

where $c = \pm\frac{30\tilde{p}}{19}\sqrt{\frac{11\tilde{p}}{19\tilde{q}}}$, $\hbar = \sqrt{\frac{11\tilde{p}}{76\tilde{q}}}$ and $\frac{\tilde{p}}{\tilde{q}} > 0$.

Special Cases:

Case 1: If we choose $c_1 = c_2 = 1$, then Equations (15) and (19) become

$$u_1(x,t) = e^{(\rho\beta(t) - \frac{1}{2}\rho^2 t)}[\pm\frac{30\tilde{p}}{19\tilde{r}}\sqrt{\frac{-\tilde{p}}{19\tilde{q}}} + \frac{90\tilde{p}\hbar}{19\tilde{r}}\tanh(\hbar(\frac{x^\alpha}{\Gamma(1+\alpha)} - ct))$$

$$+\frac{120\tilde{q}\hbar^3}{\tilde{r}}\tanh^3(\hbar(\frac{x^\alpha}{\Gamma(1+\alpha)} - ct))], \tag{20}$$

where $c = \pm \frac{30\tilde{p}}{19}\sqrt{\frac{-\tilde{p}}{19\tilde{q}}}$, $\hbar = \sqrt{\frac{-\tilde{p}}{76\tilde{q}}}$ and $\frac{\tilde{p}}{\tilde{q}} < 0$, and

$$u_2(x,t) = e^{(\rho\beta(t)-\frac{1}{2}\rho^2 t)}[\pm\frac{30\tilde{p}}{19\tilde{r}}\sqrt{\frac{11\tilde{p}}{19\tilde{q}}} - \frac{270\tilde{p}\hbar}{19\tilde{r}}\tanh(\frac{\hbar x^\alpha}{\Gamma(1+\alpha)} - c\hbar t)$$
$$+\frac{120\tilde{q}}{\tilde{r}}\hbar^3 \tanh^3(\frac{\hbar x^\alpha}{\Gamma(1+\alpha)} - c\hbar t)], \qquad (21)$$

where $c = \pm \frac{30\tilde{p}}{19}\sqrt{\frac{11\tilde{p}}{19\tilde{q}}}$, $\hbar = \sqrt{\frac{11\tilde{p}}{76\tilde{q}}}$ and $\frac{\tilde{p}}{\tilde{q}} > 0$.

Case 2: If we choose $c_1 = 1$ and $c_2 = -1$, then Equations (15) and (19) become

$$u_1(x,t) = e^{(\rho\beta(t)-\frac{1}{2}\rho^2 t)}\{\pm\frac{30p}{19\tilde{r}}\sqrt{\frac{-\tilde{p}}{19\tilde{q}}} + \frac{90\tilde{p}\hbar}{19\tilde{r}}\coth(\frac{\hbar x^\alpha}{\Gamma(1+\alpha)} - c\hbar t)$$
$$+\frac{120\tilde{q}\hbar^3}{\tilde{r}}\coth^3(\frac{\hbar x^\alpha}{\Gamma(1+\alpha)} - c\hbar t))\}, \qquad (22)$$

where $c = \pm \frac{30\tilde{p}}{19}\sqrt{\frac{-\tilde{p}}{19\tilde{q}}}$, $\hbar = \sqrt{\frac{-\tilde{p}}{76\tilde{q}}}$ and $\frac{\tilde{p}}{\tilde{q}} < 0$, and

$$u_2(x,t) = e^{(\rho\beta(t)-\frac{1}{2}\rho^2 t)}\{\pm\frac{30\tilde{p}}{19\tilde{r}}\hbar - \frac{270\tilde{p}\hbar}{19\tilde{r}}\coth(\frac{\hbar x^\alpha}{\Gamma(1+\alpha)} - c\hbar t)$$
$$+\frac{120\tilde{q}\hbar^3}{\tilde{r}}\coth^3(\frac{\hbar x^\alpha}{\Gamma(1+\alpha)} - c\hbar t)\}, \qquad (23)$$

where $c = \pm \frac{30\tilde{p}}{19}\sqrt{\frac{11\tilde{p}}{19\tilde{q}}}$, $\hbar = \sqrt{\frac{11\tilde{p}}{76\tilde{q}}}$ and $\frac{\tilde{p}}{\tilde{q}} > 0$.

Remark 1. *If we put $\rho = 0$ (i.e., Equation (1) without noise) and $\alpha = 1$ in Equations (20)–(23), then we obtain the same results stated in [24].*

5. The Influence of Noise on the S-FS-KS Solutions

Here, we discuss the influence of stochastic term on the exact solutions of the S-FS-KS Equation (1) and fix the parameters $\tilde{r} = \tilde{p} = \tilde{q} = 1$. We present a number of simulations for different values of ρ (noise intensity). We utilize the MATLAB program to plot the solution $u_2(t,x)$ defined in Equation (21) for $t \in [0,5]$ and $x \in [0,6]$ as follows:

In Figures 1–3, as seen in the first graph in each figure, the surface becomes less flat when the noise intensity is equal to zero. However, when noise appears and the strength of the noise grows ($\rho = 1,2,3$), we notice that the surface becomes more planar after minor transit behaviors. This indicates that the solutions are stable due to the multiplicative noise effects.

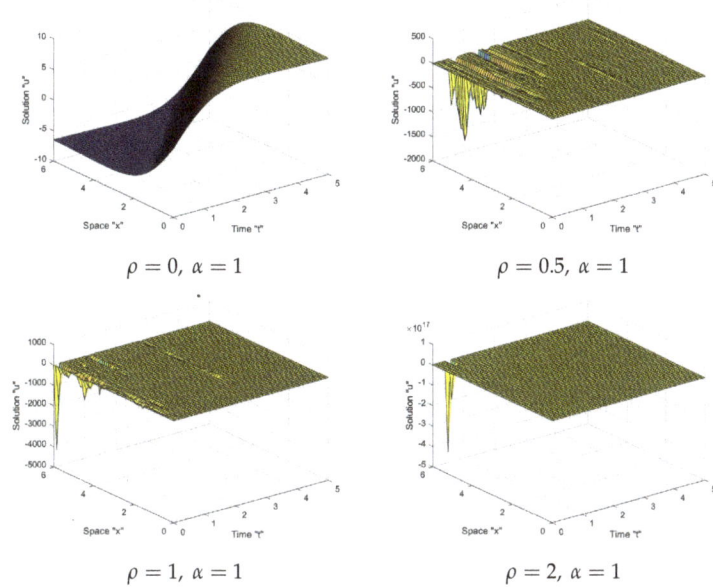

Figure 1. Graph of solution u_2 in Equation (21) with $\alpha = 1$.

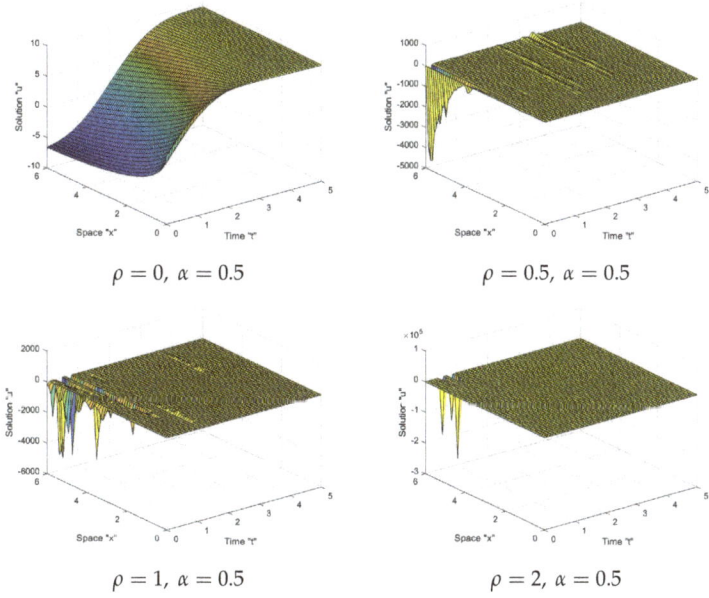

Figure 2. Graph of solution u_2 in Equation (21) with $\alpha = 0.5$.

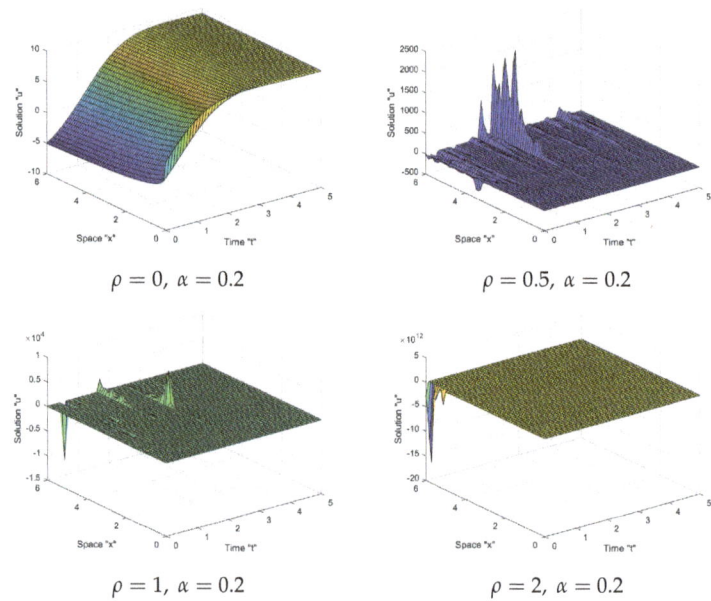

Figure 3. Graph of solution u_2 in Equation (21) with $\alpha = 0.2$.

6. Conclusions

In this paper, we presented different exact solutions of the stochastic fractional-space Kuramoto–Sivashinsky equation, Equation (1), forced by multiplicative noise. Moreover, several results were extended and improved such as those described in [24]. These types of solutions can be utilized to explain a variety of fascinating and complex physical phenomena. Finally, we used the MATLAB program to generate some graphical representations to show the effect of the stochastic term on the solutions of the S-FS-KS (1). In this paper, we considered the multiplicative noise and fractional space. In future work, we can consider the additive noise and fractional time.

Author Contributions: Conceptualization, W.W.M., M.A., N.I., S.A. and M.E.-M.; methodology, W.W.M., M.A., S.A. and M.E.-M.; software, W.W.M., M.A., S.A., N.I. and M.E.-M., formal analysis, W.W.M., M.A., S.A., N.I. and M.E.-M., investigation, M.A., S.A., N.I. and M.E.-M.; resources, W.W.M., M.A., S.A. and M.E.-M.; data curation, W.W.M., S.A. and M.E.-M.; Writing original draft preparation, W.W.M., M.A., S.A. and N.I.; writing review and editing, W.W.M., M.A., N.I., S.A. and M.E.-M.; visualization, W.W.M., M.A., N.I. and M.E.-M. All authors have read and agreed to the published version of the manuscript.

Funding: This research received no external funding.

Institutional Review Board Statement: Not applicable.

Informed Consent Statement: Not applicable.

Data Availability Statement: Not applicable.

Acknowledgments: This research has been funded by Scientific Research Deanship at University of Ha'il-Saudi Arabia through project number RG-21001.

Conflicts of Interest: The authors declare that they have no competing interests.

References

1. Gorenflo, R.; Mainardi, F. Random walk models for space—Fractional diffusion processes. *Fract. Calc. Appl. Anal.* **1998**, *1*, 167–191.
2. Raberto, M.; Scalas, E.; Mainardi, F. Waiting-times and returns in high-frequency financial data: An empirical study. *Phys. A Stat. Mech. Appl.* **2002**, *314*, 749–755. [CrossRef]
3. Wyss, W. The fractional Black—Scholes equation. *Fract. Calc. Appl. Anal.* **2000**, *3*, 51–61.
4. Yuste, S.B.; Lindenberg, K. Subdiffusion-limited $A+A$ reactions. *Phys. Rev. Lett.* **2001**, *87*, 118301. [CrossRef]
5. Barkai, E.; Metzler, R.; Klafter, J. From continuous time random walks to the fractional Fokker—Planck equation. *Phys. Rev. E* **2000**, *61*, 132–138. [CrossRef]
6. Metzler, R.; Klafter, J. The random walk's guide to anomalous diffusion: A fractional dynamics approach. *Phys. Rep.* **2000**, *339*, 1–77. [CrossRef]
7. Saichev, A.I.; Zaslavsky, G.M. Fractional kinetic equations: Solutions and applications. *Chaos* **1997**, *7*, 753–764. [CrossRef] [PubMed]
8. Zaslavsky, G.M. Chaos, fractional kinetics and anomalous transport. *Phys. Rep.* **2002**, *6*, 461–580. [CrossRef]
9. Abouelregal, A.E.; Ahmad, H. Thermodynamic modeling of viscoelastic thin rotating microbeam based on non-Fourier heat conduction. *Appl. Math. Model.* **2021**, *91*, 973–988. [CrossRef]
10. Zenkour, A.M.; Abouelregal, A.E. Effect of harmonically varying heat on FG nanobeams in the context of a nonlocal two-temperature thermoelasticity theory. *Eur. J. Comput. Mech.* **2014**, *23*, 1–14. [CrossRef]
11. Benson, D.A.; Wheatcraft, S.W.; Meerschaert, M.M. The fractional-order governing equation of Lévy motion. *Water Resour. Res.* **2000**, *36*, 1413–1423. [CrossRef]
12. Liu, F.; Anh, V.; Turner, I. Numerical solution of the space fractional Fokker—Planck equation. *J. Comput. Appl. Math.* **2004**, *166*, 209–219. [CrossRef]
13. Yuste, S.B.; Acedo, L.; Lindenberg, K. Reaction front in an $A+B \to C$ reaction—Subdiffusion process. *Phys. Rev. E* **2004**, *69*, 036126. [CrossRef] [PubMed]
14. Podlubny, I. *Fractional Differential Equations*; Academic Press: New York, NY, USA, 1999.
15. Taheri, Z.; Javadi, S.; Babolian, E. Numerical solution of stochastic fractional integro-differential equation by the spectral collocation method. *J. Comput. Appl. Math.* **2017**, *321*, 336–347. [CrossRef]
16. Zou, G. Galerkin finite element method for time-fractional stochastic diffusion equations. *Comput. Appl. Math.* **2018**, *37*, 4877–4898. [CrossRef]
17. Mohammed, W.W.; Iqbal, N. Effect of the Same Degenerate Additive Noise on a Coupled System of Fractional-Space Diffusion Equations. *Fractals* Accepted.
18. Iqbal, N.; Wu, R.; Mohammed, W.W. Pattern formation induced by fractional cross-diffusion in a 3-species food chain model with harvesting. *Math. Comput. Simul.* **2021**, *188*, 102–119. [CrossRef]
19. Mohammed, W.W. Approximate solutions for stochastic time-fractional reaction—Diffusion equations with multiplicative noise. *Math. Methods Appl. Sci.* **2021**, *44*, 2140–2157. [CrossRef]
20. Kamrani, M. Numerical solution of stochastic fractional differential equations. *Numer. Algorithms* **2015**, *68*, 81–93. [CrossRef]
21. Li, X.; Yang, X. Error estimates of finite element methods for stochastic fractional differential equations. *J. Comput. Math.* **2017**, *35*, 346–362.
22. Liu, J.; Yan, L. Solving a nonlinear fractional stochastic partial differential equation with fractional noise. *J. Theor. Probab.* **2016**, *29*, 307–347. [CrossRef]
23. Wazzan, L. A modified tanh-coth method for solving the general Burgers-Fisher and Kuramoto-Sivashinsky Equations. *Commun. Nonlinear Sci. Numer. Simulat.* **2009**, *14*, 2642–2652. [CrossRef]
24. Wazwaz, A.M. New solitary wave solutions to the Kuramoto-Sivashinsky and the Kawahara equations. *Appl. Math. Comput.* **2006**, *182*, 1642–1650. [CrossRef]
25. Abbasbandy, S. Solitary wave solutions to the Kuramoto—Sivashinsky equation by means of the homotopy analysis method. *Nonlinear Dyn.* **2008**, *52*, 35–40. [CrossRef]
26. Kheiri, H.; Jabbari, A. Application of the (G'/G)-expansion method for two nonlinear evolution equations. *Int. Nonlinear Dyn. Eng. Sci.* **2010**, *2*, 57–67.
27. Mohammed, W.W. Approximate solution of the Kuramoto-Shivashinsky equation on an unbounded domain. *Chin. Ann. Math. Ser. B* **2018**, *39*, 145–162. [CrossRef]
28. Kudryashov, N.A. Exact solutions of the generalized kuramoto-sivashinsky equation. *Phys. Lett. A* **1990**, *147*, 287–291. [CrossRef]
29. Kudryashov, N.A. On types of nonlinear nonintegrable equations with exact solutions. *Phys. Lett. A* **1991**, *155*, 269–275. [CrossRef]
30. Kudryashov, N.A.; Soukharev, M.B. Popular ansatz methods and solitary wave solutions of the Kuramoto-Sivashinsky equation. *Regul. Chaotic Dyn.* **2009**, *14*, 407–409. [CrossRef]
31. Peng, Y.Z. A polynomial expansion method and new general solitary wave solutions to KS equation. *Comm. Theor. Phys.* **2003**, *39*, 641–642.
32. Kudryashov, N.A. Solitary and periodic solutions of the generalized kuramoto-sivashinsky equation. *Regul. Chaotic Dyn.* **2008**, *13*, 234–238. [CrossRef]
33. Kudryashov, N.A. Exact soliton solutions of the generalized evolution equation of wave dynamics. *J. Appl. Math. Mech.* **1988**, *52*, 361–365. [CrossRef]

34. Khalique, C.M. Exact Solutions of the Generalized Kuramoto-Sivashinsky Equation. *Casp. J. Math. Sci.* **2012**, *1*, 109–116.
35. Zhang, S. New Exact Solutions of the KdV–Burgers–Kuramoto Equation. *Phys. Lett. A* **2006**, *358*, 414–420. [CrossRef]
36. Blomker, D.; Mohammed, W.W. Amplitude equation for spdes with quadratic nonlinearities. *Electron. J. Probab.* **2009**, *14*, 2527–2550. [CrossRef]
37. Fu, Z.; Liu, S.; Liu, S. New Exact Solutions to the KdV–Burgers–Kuramoto Equation. *Chaos Solitons Fractals* **2005**, *23*, 609–616. [CrossRef]
38. Jumarie, G. Modified Riemann–Liouville derivative and fractional Taylor series of nondifferentiable functions further results. *Comput. Math. Appl.* **2006**, *51*, 1367–1376. [CrossRef]
39. He, J.H.; Elegan, S.K.; Li, Z.B. Geometrical explanation of the fractional complex transform and derivative chain rule for fractional calculus. *Phys. Lett. A* **2012**, *376*, 257–259. [CrossRef]
40. Aksoy, E.; Kaplan, M.; Bekir, A. Exponential rational function method for space–time fractional differential equations. *Waves Random Complex Media* **2016**, *26*, 142–151. [CrossRef]
41. Wang, M.L.; Li, X.Z.; Zhang, J.L. The $\frac{G'}{G}$-expansion method and travelling wave solutions of nonlinear evolution equations in mathematical physics. *Phys. Lett. A* **2008**, *372*, 417–423. [CrossRef]

Article

Multicriteria Optimization of a Dynamic System by Methods of the Theories of Similarity and Criteria Importance

Sergey Misyurin [1,2,*,†], German Kreynin [1,†], Andrey Nelyubin [1,†] and Natalia Nosova [1,*,†]

1. Blagonravov Mechanical Engineering Research Institute of the Russian Academy of Sciences, 4 Mal. Kharitonyevskiy Pereulok, 101990 Moscow, Russia; gkreynin@mail.ru (G.K.); nelubin@gmail.com (A.N.)
2. Moscow Engineering Physics Institute, National Research Nuclear University MEPhI, 31 Kashirskoe Shosse, 115409 Moscow, Russia
* Correspondence: ssmmrr@mail.ru (S.M.); natahys@mail.ru (N.N.)
† These authors contributed equally to this work.

Abstract: The problem of multicriteria optimization of a dynamic model is solved using the methods of the similarity theory and the criteria importance theory. The authors propose the original model of a positional system with two hydraulic actuators, synchronously moving a heavy object with a given accuracy. In order to reduce the number of optimizing parameters, the mathematical model of the system is presented in a dimensionless form. Three dimensionless optimization criteria that characterize the accuracy, size, and quality of the dynamic positioning process are considered. It is shown that the application of the criteria importance method significantly reduces the Pareto set (the set of the best solutions). This opens up the possibility of reducing many optimal solutions to one solution, which greatly facilitates the choice of parameters when designing a mechanical object.

Keywords: dynamics; hydraulic drive; similarity; multicriteria optimization

1. Introduction

Artificial intelligence is now widely used in industry, applied to transporting mechanisms, such as robots and manipulators, which move and deliver various objects to specified positions. In simple loading systems, the accuracy of moving and positioning of goods can be relatively low, which makes it possible to use relatively simple devices in these cases. However, feeding a tool in processing machines requires a sufficiently high accuracy. The movement of robots can be carried out by various actuators: pneumatic, hydraulic, electric, etc.

Positioning control problems in transporting mechanisms (robots) are solved mainly in two ways: using special type regulators, such as based on fuzzy logic, neural networks, and so on or the ordinary regulators with feedback control of various type. The mathematical models of actuators, as a rule, have a rather complex structure, consisting of higher-order differential and algebraic equations.

Developing new devices requires the solving of a number of technical problems associated with the choice of their type, structure, and control system, satisfied to many requirements. In mechanical systems, hydraulic actuators are widely used. Their main advantage in relation to pneumatic and electric actuators is their high carrying capacity and low sensitivity to the load variation [1].

Mathematical models of hydraulic actuators and their control systems are well studied and fully presented in works, such as [2–5]. However, the problem of finding the best constructive solution in most cases is based of the original models not reduced to a dimensionless form. Due to the abundance of differently sized variables, the general patterns of the results obtained are often not visible, it is difficult to single out the groups of criteria to be optimized. Additionally, it is not advisable to optimize un-grouped parameters (variables) at the same time. This was noted by example in [6].

In [7], the authors turn to dimensionless models, but do not use them systematically in the search for the best solution. In this case, the dimensionless model serves only to partially simplify the general formulation of the problem and to study the properties of the original model. The transition to dimensionless parameters was used to select a special object positioning control system, which should provide an approach to a given position simultaneously with zero speed and zero acceleration in order to avoid damage to the contact point when stopping.

The principle and process of transition to dimensionless forms have been developed for a long time. Here we can note the fundamental works in this area [8,9]. The importance of the theory of similarity and analogy in understanding the essence of things was noted back in the days of Plato. In a number of philosophical works, attempts have been made to generalize approaches to equivalence in different fields of knowledge, which gives this direction additional significance. In [10], a general metric of transition to dimensionless variables was considered and introduced, but it was noted that there is no uniquely best measure of dynamic similarity, since the feasibility of any given measure depends on its intended use.

In [11], it is shown that, due to the complexity of the mathematical description of technical dynamic systems, when choosing their structure and parameters, they usually turn to very laborious interactive (dialogue) procedures. A number of tools help to avoid direct enumeration of options when using such procedures, among which the methods of dimension and similarity theory take a significant place. These methods are based on the use of dimensionless complexes of physical parameters of the system (criteria of similarity and the relationship between them) together with the translation of the mathematical description of the system into a dimensionless form [12,13]. As a result, additional opportunities open up for identifying general patterns of dynamic processes, which greatly facilitates making the final decision.

Experience shows that each specific problem of the dynamics of a mechanical system requires a special approach to the formation of a dimensionless model and similarity criteria. The structure and form of the dimensionless model depends on the accepted units of measurement of the variables included in the equations of the model, and on the expressions attached to its coefficients. These factors are initially unknown and are usually formed according to the intuition and experience of the researcher, which introduces uncertainty in the process of transition to a dimensionless model and does not guarantee high efficiency of its use. The approach proposed below to the formation of dimensionless models of a dynamic system of a hydraulic actuator is a development of the procedure started in [11].

This paper illustrates an example of finding the optimal solution for a positional system with two hydraulic actuators. This type of actuator was chosen based on the task of controlled movement of a heavy and bulky object (load). The hydraulic actuator has the highest power density. However, the presence of two actuators creates special problems in control, since the drives must operate in coordination in both position and speed. Based on this, the authors proposed an original control scheme that solves this problem based on the use of only two valves (Figure 1): one of them regulates the average speed of the moving object, and the other controls the distribution of fluid flows directed into the cavities of the hydraulic cylinders [14,15].

The study of the mathematical model is carried out in dimensionless parameters, the transition to which hydraulic actuator systems are presented in [6]. Parametric synthesis is carried out according to the principle of multicriteria optimization. During the transition of the system to a dimensionless form, three optimization criteria are identified with further application of the criteria importance method. The criteria importance method significantly reduces the optimal solutions of the system, which facilitates the selection of the best solution when designing a mechanical object.

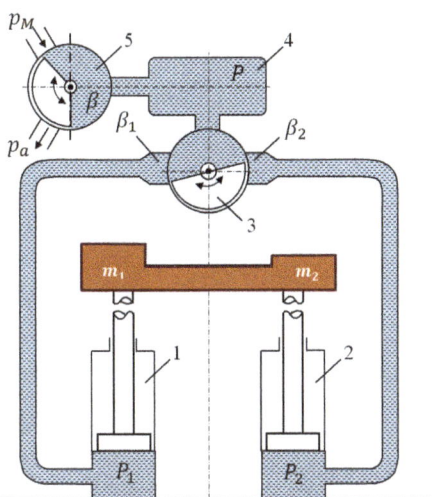

Figure 1. The model of the manipulator with two hydraulic actuators: p_M—actuator supply pressure; p_a—atmospheric pressure; P_1, P_2, P—pressure in the cavities 1, 2, 4, respectively; β, β_1, β_2—relative opening areas of the respective channels.

The parametric synthesis of a mechanical system consists in choosing the values of the parameters that make up the vector $X = (x_1, x_2, ..., x_n)$ that provide the best values of the characteristics (performance indicators) of the system that make up the vector $K = (k_1, k_2, ..., k_m)$. Thus, the problem of multicriteria (multi-objective) optimization is posed, in which X is a vector of variables, and $K(X)$ is a vector of criteria (objective functions).

To solve this problem, it is necessary to develop an adequate mathematical model of the system under consideration, using the vector X as input parameters and calculating the values of the characteristics $K(X)$ at the output. Further, it is necessary to implement a method for solving the optimization problem. In addition, in the presence of several characteristics ($m > 1$), it is required to take into account the dependencies and preferences between them.

Complex mechanical systems usually contain up to several tens of parameters n and several characteristics m. At the same time, mathematical models of dynamic systems contain complex connections and differential equations, and for calculations they require the use of numerical methods. Therefore, when solving the problem of optimizing such complex systems, the computational model usually represents a "black box", which makes it practically impossible to use local, gradient optimization methods [16,17]. Among the global optimization methods working with such complex models, genetic algorithms [18], and other variations of evolutionary algorithms, particle swarm optimization [19], and simulated annealing methods [20]. In this paper, for the global search for optimal solutions, the parameter space investigation method [21] is used, based on the construction of sequences of points uniformly distributed in the feasible area of the parameters X space [22].

In multicriteria optimization problems, as a rule, it is not possible to obtain a feasible solution that is best at once according to all criteria. Using formal mathematical and numerical methods, a set of Pareto optimal solutions can be obtained (approximated). To select the one best solution among them, it is necessary to involve additional information about the preferences regarding these criteria.

There are a priori and a posteriori methods for solving multicriteria optimization problems. In a priori methods, the question of preferences is resolved before the search for solutions is carried out. These methods include the method of identifying the "main" criterion, as well as various methods of convolution of the criteria into one aggregated performance indicator. For example, the weighted sum $F_\Sigma(X) = \sum_{i=1}^{m} w_i k_i(X)$, the product $F_\Pi(X) = \prod_{i=1}^{m} k_i^{w_i}(X)$, or the Germeier convolution $F_G(X) = min_i k_i(X)/w_i$. Before convoluting, the criteria k_i are normalized in a special way. This approach allows one to go straight to solving the optimization problem with one objective function. However, there are a number of disadvantages behind the simplicity of this approach. First of all, it is difficult for a person, no matter how expert he or she is, to set the exact values of the weights reflecting the relative importance of the criteria. In addition, there are a number of theoretical problems associated with the justification of this approach [23].

On the contrary, in a posteriori methods, optimization is performed first taking into account all the criteria, and then preferences are analyzed. Analysis of the set of obtained solutions is itself useful in solving such problems. First of all, a person, an expert working with such data of optimization results, understands the possibilities available to him or her: evaluates the areas of feasible solutions, the ranges of change in the values of the criteria. In such an analysis, visualization tools [24], and interactive interaction of an expert with a computer analytical system [25] play an important role. The more adequately the expert's real preferences are revealed, the better the solution obtained on their basis will be. The preferences are most accurately established in the process of dialogue with the analytical system, during which a person sees intermediate solutions, obtains a clearer idea of the real conditions of the problem, resource opportunities, and goals. One of the most important properties of such systems is the ability to provide explanations (justifications) of the results and conclusions obtained, interpreting them in terms of the subject area, in a language understandable for an expert [26].

It is known that the best solution should be chosen among the set of Pareto optimal ones. However, this set of solutions is usually quite large. To narrow the scope of choice, additional assumptions should be made about the preferences of experts regarding the importance and values of the criteria. For formal modeling of these preferences and obtaining conclusions on the basis of this information, the approach of the mathematical theory of criteria importance was used in this work [27,28]. This method assumes a consistent refinement of information about preferences. First, the simplest information about ordering criteria by importance is found out. Such qualitative information is easier to obtain than quantitative estimates of importance, and, therefore, more reliably describes the expert's real preferences. Next, the formal methods of the theory come into play, which make it possible to reasonably discard from consideration some of the solutions from the Pareto set, thereby narrowing the set of choices for the best solution. Then, if necessary, quantitative estimates of importance are also used, but not accurate, just in the form of intervals. Additionally, additional information about changing preferences along the criteria scale can be used.

2. Statement of the Problem and Mathematical Model of the System

The object of research in this work is a rather complex manipulator designed to lift a heavy, bulky load using two parallel and synchronously operating hydraulic actuators 1 and 2 (Figure 1). Let us describe the mathematical model of the object. The moving object has a mass $m = m_1 + m_2$, where $m_{1,2}$ are the mass loads applied to the actuators. The main working cavities are the lower cavities of the actuators; however, if necessary, the upper cavities can also be used (for example, when lowering an object). The law of motion is mainly determined by the pressures in the lower cavities, which are connected through the control valve 3, the intermediate cavity 4 (volume V) and the control valve 5 when the object is lifted to the power source (with pressure p_M), and when the object is lowered, to the drain line (with pressure p_A, usually equal to atmospheric). The ratios between the effective flow area of the valve 5 and the effective flow areas of the valve channels 3 leading to the cavities of the actuators are established depending on the formulation of the problem.

The equations of movement are:

$$m_i \ddot{x}_i = p_i F + m_i g k_i \dot{x}_i + P_{Li}, i = 1, 2; \tag{1}$$

where x is the piston displacement; p_i are pressures in the lower cavities; F is the effective piston area; m_i g, P_{Li} are weight and force load on the rod, respectively; k_i are coefficients of fluid friction in the actuator.

The changes of the pressure p_i in the lower cavities of the actuators and the pressure p in the intermediate cavity are related by dependencies:

$$\dot{p} = W\left(\beta\,sign(\Delta p)\sqrt{|\Delta p|} - \beta_1\,\alpha_1\,sign(\Delta p_1)\sqrt{|\Delta p_1|} - \beta_2\,\alpha_2\,sign(\Delta p_2)\sqrt{|\Delta p_2|}\right),$$
$$\dot{p}_i = W_i\left(\beta_i\,\alpha_i\,sign(\Delta p_i)\sqrt{|\Delta p_i|} - \dot{x}_i\right), \quad (2)$$

where $W = \left(\frac{E\,f}{F\,x_v}\right)\sqrt{\frac{2 p_M}{\rho}}$, $W_i = \left(\frac{E\,f}{F\,(x_{0i}+x_i)}\right)\sqrt{\frac{2 p_M}{\rho}}$; $\Delta p = p_M - p$ (when lifting) or $\Delta p = p_A - p$ (when lowering) of the object, $\Delta p_i = p - p_i$; β, β_1 and β_2 are channel opening degrees f, f_1 and f_2; E is the bulk modulus of the working fluid; x_v is the length of the intermediate cavity; ρ is working fluid density.

3. Transformation of the Model into a Dimensionless Form

According to the method of the similarity theory [8] Equations (1) and (2) are transformed into a dimensionless form by replacing variables with their dimensionless analogs λ, τ, σ, according to the relations $x = q_1\lambda$, $t = q_2\tau$, $p = q_3\sigma$. As a result of this replacement, as well as $m_i = c_i\,m$ (where $i = 1, 2$), $\varepsilon = E/q_3$ and simple transformations, we obtain a transformed system (3) and a system of Equation (4) of relations between the coefficients A_i of the system (3) and q_j.

$$c_i\,A_1\,\ddot{\lambda}_i = \sigma_i - c_i\,A_3 - A_4\,\dot{\lambda}_i - A_6,$$
$$\dot{\sigma} = A_5\left(\beta\,sign(\Delta\sigma)\sqrt{|\Delta\sigma|} - \beta_1\,\alpha_1\,sign(\Delta\sigma_1)\sqrt{|\Delta\sigma_1|} - \beta_2\,\alpha_2\,sign(\Delta\sigma_2)\sqrt{|\Delta\sigma_2|}\right), \quad (3)$$
$$\dot{\sigma}_i = \frac{\varepsilon}{\lambda_{0i}+\lambda}\left(\beta_i\,\alpha_i\,sign(\Delta\sigma_i)\sqrt{|\Delta\sigma_i|} - A_2\dot{\lambda}_i\right),$$

$$A_1 = \frac{m\,q_1}{q_2^2\,q_3\,F};\ A_2 = \frac{q_1}{q_2\,U};\ A_3 = \frac{m\,g}{q_3\,F};\ A_4 = \frac{k_i\,q_1}{q_1\,q_2\,F};\ A_5 = \frac{\varepsilon}{\lambda_V};\ A_6 = \frac{P_{Li}}{q_3\,F}. \quad (4)$$

where λ, τ, σ are dimensionless analogs of displacement, time and pressure in cavity 4, respectively; σ_1, σ_2 are dimensionless analogs of pressure in cavities 1 and 2.

The system (4) includes six so far unknown coefficients A_i and three, also so far unknown, scale factors q_j. This allows us to set three arbitrary values A_i, put, for example, $A_1 = A_2 = 1$ and $A_3 = mg/p_M F$. From these conditions it is possible to determine q_j, as well as three unknown coefficients A_4, A_5, A_6:

$$q_1 = \frac{m\,U^2}{p_M\,F};\ q_2 = \frac{m\,U}{p_M\,F};\ q_3 = p_M;\ A_4 = \frac{k_i\,U}{p_M\,F};\ A_5 = \frac{\varepsilon}{\lambda_V};\ A_6 = \frac{P_{Li}}{p_M\,F}, \quad (5)$$

where $U = (f/F)\sqrt{\frac{2 p_M}{\rho}}$ is the maximum achievable piston speed in the actuator with parameters f, F, p_M; $\varepsilon = E/p_M$ is the dimensionless analogue of the bulk modulus of liquid.

The final transformed model of the drive system presented below is obtained by optimizing the conversion factors:

$$c_i\,\ddot{\lambda}_i = \sigma_i + c_i\,\chi_L - \kappa_i\,\dot{\lambda}_i + \chi_{Li},$$
$$\dot{\sigma} = K_V\left(\beta\,sign(\Delta\sigma)\sqrt{|\Delta\sigma|} - \beta_1\,\alpha_1\,sign(\Delta\sigma_1)\sqrt{|\Delta\sigma_1|} - \beta_2\,\alpha_2\,sign(\Delta\sigma_2)\sqrt{|\Delta\sigma_2|}\right), \quad (6)$$
$$\dot{\sigma}_i = \frac{\varepsilon}{\lambda_{0i}+\lambda}\left(\beta_i\,\alpha_i\,sign(\Delta\sigma_i)\sqrt{|\Delta\sigma_i|} - \dot{\lambda}_i\right),$$

where $\chi_L = m\,g/p_M\,F$; $\chi_{Li} = P_{Li}/p_M\,F$; $K_V = A_5$ and $\lambda_{0i} = x_{0i}/q_i$ are the reduced initial volumes of working cavities of actuators.

The system (6) includes dimensionless parameters that are convenient to use in the optimization process by choosing them as parameters:

K_V—intermediate cavity stiffness;
λ_{0i}—stiffness of the actuators at the initial moment of movement;
χ_L—manipulator total mass load;
c_i—distributions of the total load between the actuators, additional resistance forces χ_{Li}, which can be present in the system both continuously and acting discretely;
$\kappa_i = \dfrac{k_i\,U}{p_M\,F}$—liquid friction forces;
$\alpha_i = f_i/f$—the ratios between the dimensions of the flow areas of the channels of valves 3 and 5.

Note that $\lambda_e = 0.5(1 - \cos(\omega\tau))$ is assumed to be a given basic law of motion of the manipulator from the initial position $\lambda_0 = 0$ to the final position $\lambda_e = 1$; $\omega = \pi/\tau_S$ is the conditional frequency characterizes the dimensionless time of the process τ_S. The opening of the valve channel 3 is characterized by the expression:

$$\beta = \vartheta_1\left(\lambda_e - \lambda_1\right) + \vartheta_2\left(\dot\lambda_e - \dot\lambda_1\right). \tag{7}$$

When the manipulator is operating at very low speeds, the law (7) can be replaced by the law of uniform motion, i.e., $\beta = 1$ is accepted. We will take into account the effect of the control system delay by replacing β in expression (7) by γ, where γ is the signal coming from the control system. The quantity β is determined from the first-order equation:

$$\dot\beta = \frac{1}{\tau_A}(\gamma - \beta),$$

where τ_A is the control system time constant.

If the flow areas of all channels are equal $f_1 = f_2 = f$, the mean position of the valve shutter 3 corresponds to the coordinates $\beta_1 = \beta_2 = 0.5$ that can be taken as the initial ones.

As the control law for valve 3, we take the simplest linear law, written, for example, relative to the first actuator $\beta_1 = 0.5 - \vartheta_{11}(\lambda_1 - \lambda_2)$; then $\beta_2 = 0.5 + \beta_1$.

We will take into account the effect of the delay of the valve control system (3) by replacing in the law β_1 with γ_1, where γ_1 is the signal coming from the control system, with the definition β_1 from the equation β_1, where $\dot\beta_1 = (1/\tau_B)(\gamma - \beta)$, where τ_B is the time constant of the valve control system (3).

4. The Optimization Problem

As mentioned earlier, after the transition to dimensionless parameters, three indicators (K_1, K_2 and K_3) were taken as the main criteria for optimality (objective functions) of the system, which characterize the values, respectively, of the imbalance of mass loads on actuators, power (size) of actuators and the maximum divergence of displacements of their rods (deviation from synchronicity) in the process of movement.

$$K_1 = |0.5 - c_1|,$$
$$K_2 = \frac{m\,g}{p_M\,F} = \chi_L,$$
$$K_3 = \Delta\lambda_{max}, \text{ where } \Delta\lambda = |\lambda_1 - \lambda_2|.$$

The first criterion shows that the greater its value, the greater the difference in the loads on the actuators the manipulator allows, the second characterizes the dimensions of the actuator (the higher the value of K_2, the smaller the dimensions of the actuator), an important criterion for volumetric and mass indicators. The third criterion is responsible for the synchronization of the movement of the two actuators, i.e., the smaller it is, the more uniformly (synchronously) the actuators move.

These criteria are contradictory, i.e., in the process of searching for feasible solutions in this problem, it is not possible to obtain one solution, the best one by all three criteria at the same time, and it is possible to single out a set of Pareto optimal solutions. For calculations and visualization of many solutions, a unique software MOVI was used, developed with the participation of the authors of this publication. Table 1 shows the optimized parameters of the system and the ranges of their values.

Table 1. The optimized parameters of the system and the ranges of their values.

Parameter	Range of Change	Comments
c_1	$0.3 \div 0.7$	weight load imbalance
χ_L	$-2.0 \div -0.4$	relative total operating load on actuators, simultaneously serving as a measure of their dimensions
λ_V	$0.2 \div 1.0$	the measure of the volume of the intermediate chamber
β_0	$0.3 \div 0.7$	the share of the opening of the common channel in the line leading to the actuators that relates to the first actuator
α_1	$0.25 \div 1.0$	the ratio between the flow sections of the common supply channel and the channel leading to the first actuator
α_2	$0.25 \div 1.0$	the same for the channel leading to the second actuator
κ_1	$0.05 \div 0.1$	coefficient of friction of the first actuator
κ_2	$0.05 \div 0.1$	coefficient of friction of the second actuator
ϑ_1	$25 \div 50$	position feedback ratio
ϑ_2	$0 \div 50$	speed feedback ratio
ϑ_D	$25 \div 50$	position feedback ratio
ϑ_V	$0 \div 5$	speed feedback ratio
t_A	$0.02 \div 0.04$	The time constant of the control system
t_B	$0.02 \div 0.04$	The time constant of the valve 3 control system
λ_{01}	$0.05 \div 1.0$	the measure of the initial (harmful) volume of the first actuator
λ_{02}	$0.05 \div 1.0$	the measure of the initial (harmful) volume of the second actuator
χ_{L1}	$0 \div 0.1$	additional short-term intermittent drag force acting on the first actuator
χ_{L2}	$0 \div 0.1$	additional short-term intermittent drag force acting on the second actuator
τ_S	$10 \div 50$	the mass m movement time

The load parameter c_1 is special and needs to be explained. The fact is that the imbalance of the loads c_1 and $c_2 = 1 - c_1$ characterizes a specific load, and not the design of the optimized manipulator. When designing a manipulator, we do not know in advance the load parameters and cannot optimize them. However, the maximum permissible imbalance of the loads c_1 and c_2 can already be considered a characteristic of the manipulator, which can be optimized.

Let us consider in more detail how the criteria depend on the parameter c_1. The criterion K_1 depends on c_1 explicitly: the greater the load imbalance, the better. However, K_1 values greater than 0.2 are not required in practice. Therefore, in this problem, the values of c_1 vary from 0.3 to 0.7.

The criterion K_2 does not depend on c_1 at all. A typical example of the dependence of the criterion K_3 on c_1 is shown in Figure 2.

With an increase in the load imbalance, the synchronization of the actuators monotonically deteriorates, and asymmetrically when c1 deviates from 0.5 to the lower or higher side. However, starting from certain values of c_1, this dependence is violated, and the graph begins to behave unpredictably. In Figure 2 these points are circled in red. Solutions outside these c_1 values will be considered unacceptable. To detect such cases, for each checked value of c_1, we will perform several additional calculations with the load c_1 up to 0.5.

Additionally, it is necessary to take into account the asymmetry of the dependence of K_3 on c_1. For every feasible solution we obtain, the ultimate allowable load will be either less or greater than 0.5. For a symmetric case of unbalanced loads, the values of the criteria K_1 and K_2 will be the same, but the value of the criterion K_3 may be worse. However, we can switch this manipulator to a more advantageous (from the point of view of K_3) mode ($c_1 > c_2$ or $c_1 < c_2$), depending on how the load lies. Therefore, this asymmetry is not a problem.

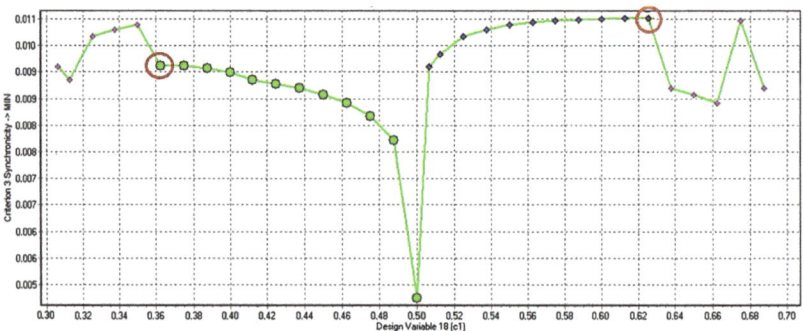

Figure 2. An example of the dependence of the criterion K_3 on the load parameter c_1. The rest of the parameters are fixed.

5. Generation of Alternative Solutions and Initial Analysis

In the software MOVI, 4000 alternative solutions were generated, the coordinates of which are uniformly distributed in the space of variable parameters [20,21]. Of these solutions, 2198 were found to be feasible in relation to the constraints of the model. Among the feasible solutions, there were 96 Pareto optimal solutions. Each solution x can be associated with a three-dimensional vector $K(x) = \left(K_1(x), K_2(x), K_3(x)\right)$, the components of which are estimates by three criteria. If the solutions are depicted as points in the three-dimensional space of criteria, then they form a cloud in a certain area, and the points of Pareto optimal solutions will be located on a part of the boundary of this cloud. In Figure 3 is shown how the projections of the cloud from the points of feasible solutions to the two-dimensional spaces of criteria are distributed. Blue rhombuses denote admissible solutions, green circles-Pareto optimal ones.

The depiction of the set of solutions in Figure 3 represent the initial, primary information for subsequent analysis and selection of the best solution. At the first stage, such images make it possible to assess in what ranges of criteria values are feasible solutions. That is, in fact, the decision maker (expert) receives primary information about the available opportunities in terms of achieving the best values of the criteria.

The first practical conclusion based on the analysis of Figure 3 is the following: a lot of feasible solutions are obtained with an acceptable value of the load imbalance K_1. Therefore, we can safely discard some of the solutions with weakly acceptable values of K_1, imposing an additional constraint on the feasibility of the solution $K_1 > 0.1$, and this leaves quite a lot of feasible solutions—821. Of these, 45 are Pareto optimal solutions. The values of the criteria for these 45 options are shown below in Table 2. The result of imposing this restriction in the criteria space is shown in Figure 4.

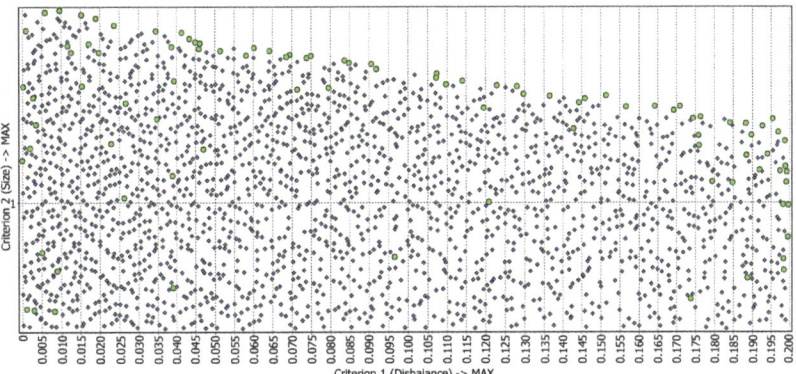

Figure 3. The set of solutions in the space of criteria: K_1 and K_2. Blue dots denote admissible solutions, green circles-Pareto optimal solutions.

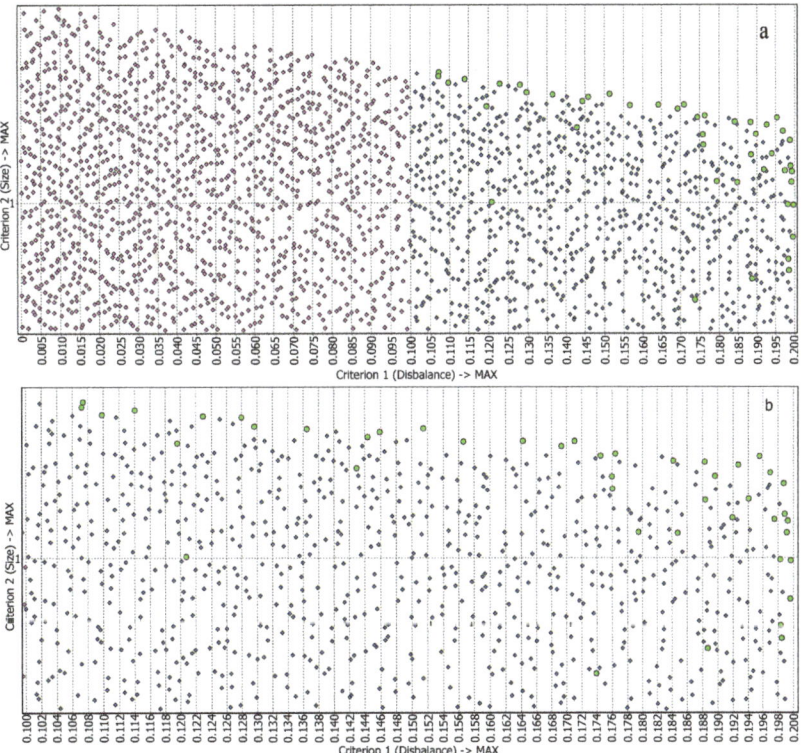

Figure 4. The set of solutions in the space of criteria: (**a**) K_1 and K_2; (**b**) K_1 and K_2 on a larger scale. Blue dots denote feasible solutions, crimson dots—infeasible ones due to the constraint $K_1 > 0.1$, green circles—Pareto optimal solutions.

We see that in the projections onto K_1 and K_2 (Figure 4a,b), the set of solutions is expectedly divided into feasible (to the right of the line $K_1 = 0.1$) and infeasible (to the left of the line $K_1 = 0.1$). Its analysis helps to verify, to make sure that the imposed constraint on the criterion K_1 led to acceptable impairments in the remaining criteria.

Further, you can also impose constraints on the remaining criteria, and then gradually increase these constraints, thereby narrowing the set of choices. This is one of the approaches, it can be classified as intuitive, informal. Its application becomes much more complicated with a larger number of criteria. To solve the problem of choosing the best solution in this work, we will apply the formal approach developed in the criteria importance theory.

6. Solving the Choice Problem by the Method of the Criteria Importance Theory

It is required to choose the best solution among the selected 45 solutions obtained at the previous stage, taking into account the constraint $K_1 > 0.1$.

To apply the methods of the criteria importance theory, the individual criteria K_1, K_2, K_3 must be brought to a homogeneous form with a common scale Z, which can be just ordinal [26]. In this problem, we will use a 10-point scale: the higher the score, the better, the higher the value (usefulness, preference) for the decision maker of such values according to the criterion. To bring the criteria to the 10-point scale Z, we use linear normalization of the criteria values and rounding. As a result, each of the 45 alternative solutions is associated with its vector score from the set $Z^3 = Z \times Z \times Z$. The values of the initial criteria and the obtained vector scores $y = (y_1, y_2, y_3)$ for all 45 options are given in Table 2. It should be noted that the requirements for minimization and maximization for the initial criteria can be different ($K_1 \to max$, $K_2 \to max$, $K_3 \to min$), while the scores on the scale Z are always the same ($y_1 \to max$, $y_2 \to max$, $y_3 \to max$).

Table 2. The values of the initial criteria and the obtained vector scores $y = (y_1, y_2, y_3)$ for 45 options.

No.	K_1, 10^{-3}	K_2	K_3, 10^{-3}	y_1	y_2	y_3	No.	K_1, 10^{-3}	K_2	K_3, 10^{-3}	y_1	y_2	y_3	No.	K_1, 10^{-3}	K_2	K_3, 10^{-3}	y_1	y_2	y_3
159	1.30	1.52	12.4	3	10	3	1267	1.76	1.32	3.7	8	8	10	2660	1.98	1.15	4.6	10	6	9
239	1.14	1.58	11.1	2	10	4	1382	1.64	1.46	7.4	7	9	7	2834	1.51	1.51	5.1	6	9	9
247	1.98	0.73	4.5	10	2	9	1615	1.69	1.44	5.2	7	9	9	2841	1.76	1.41	16.2	8	9	1
257	1.43	1.35	3.0	5	8	10	1691	1.37	1.51	4.9	4	9	9	3005	1.28	1.55	7.7	3	10	7
307	1.88	1.38	6.5	9	8	8	1734	1.90	1.32	6.3	9	8	8	3093	1.97	1.34	7.5	10	8	7
442	1.71	1.46	6.8	8	9	7	1760	1.46	1.50	5.0	5	9	9	3254	1.99	0.68	4.7	10	2	9
464	1.99	1.10	5.8	10	6	8	1847	1.96	1.40	13.8	10	8	2	3298	1.98	0.99	4.4	10	5	9
635	2.00	0.84	7.8	10	3	7	1849	1.79	1.10	3.5	8	6	10	3423	1.20	1.45	3.2	2	9	10
652	1.99	1.29	6.4	10	7	8	2010	1.84	1.38	10.0	9	8	5	3442	1.88	1.23	3.5	9	7	10
840	1.89	0.64	3.1	9	1	10	2057	1.10	1.56	8.6	1	10	6	3473	1.99	1.14	8.2	10	6	6
895	1.07	1.61	8.7	1	10	6	2112	1.75	1.40	12.2	8	8	4	3642	2.00	0.99	8.1	10	5	7
911	1.57	1.46	4.5	6	9	9	2226	1.76	1.27	6.3	8	7	8	3768	1.92	1.16	3.6	10	6	10
997	1.85	1.10	3.2	9	6	10	2236	1.99	1.17	6.5	10	6	8	3862	1.74	0.54	2.7	8	1	10
1080	1.44	1.48	3.5	5	9	10	2276	1.23	1.56	10.3	3	10	5	3900	1.93	1.37	11.8	10	8	4
1246	1.07	1.59	4.0	1	10	10	2478	1.94	1.23	3.7	10	7	10	3952	1.21	1.00	3.0	3	5	10

In fact, due to rounding, each vector score describes a certain small region in the original 3D space of the criteria. At the same time, some solutions may be in the same region, and then they will have the same vector score. For example, alternatives 307 and 1734 have the same vector score (9, 8, 8). Further, using the method of the criteria importance theory, we will solve the problem of choosing the best vector score. Choosing this vector score, we will obtain a corresponding small region in the original space of criteria, which includes one or more solutions from the 45 considered.

In the criteria importance theory, the preferences of decision makers are modeled using binary relations [26]. The non-strict preference relation R of the decision maker is introduced on the set of vector scores Z^3: the notation yRz means that the vector score y is no less preferable than z. The relation R is reflexive and transitive, it generates the relations of indifference (equivalence) I and strict preference (dominance) P:

$$yIz \Leftrightarrow yRz \text{ and } zRy,$$

$$yPz \Leftrightarrow yRz, \text{ but } zRy \text{ is not true.}$$

It is known that if the relation R is complete, then on a finite set of vector scores there is at least one optimal vector score y, such that yRz holds for all other vector scores z. There can be several optimal vector scores equivalent by the relation I. In this case, the choice of the best vector score should be carried out among the optimal vector scores.

If the relation R is incomplete, then the best vector score should be chosen among the non-dominated vector scores. A vector score y is called non-dominated with respect to P if there is no other vector score z, such that zPy holds.

Since the decision maker's preferences increase along the scale of criteria Z, the Pareto relation is defined on the set of vector scores Z^3:

$$yR^\circ z \Leftrightarrow y_i \geq z_i, \ i = 1,2,3;$$
$$yP^\circ z \Leftrightarrow yR^\circ z \text{ and } y \neq z.$$

Among the 45 vector scores under consideration, there are 10 non-dominated with respect to the Pareto relation P°. In fact, 9 vector scores remain, since variants with numbers 307 and 1734 have the same vector score (9, 8, 8). These vector scores and the corresponding alternatives are shown in Table 3.

Table 3. 10 vector scores and their the corresponding alternatives.

No.	K_1	K_2	K_3	y_1	y_2	y_3
307	0.188	1.38	0.0065	9	8	8
442	0.171	1.46	0.0068	8	9	7
1080	0.144	1.48	0.0035	5	9	10
1246	0.107	1.59	0.0040	1	10	10
1267	0.176	1.32	0.0037	8	8	10
1615	0.169	1.44	0.0052	7	9	9
1734	0.190	1.32	0.0063	9	8	8
2478	0.194	1.23	0.0037	10	7	10
3005	0.128	1.55	0.0077	3	10	7
3093	0.197	1.34	0.0075	10	8	7

At the next step of solving the choice problem by the criteria importance method, we enter information Ω about the ordering of criteria by importance into the software DASS, as shown in Figure 5 [27,29]. The criterion K_1 is more important than the criterion $K_2 (1 \succ 2)$, and the criterion K_2, in turn, is more important than the criterion $K_3 (2 \succ 3)$.

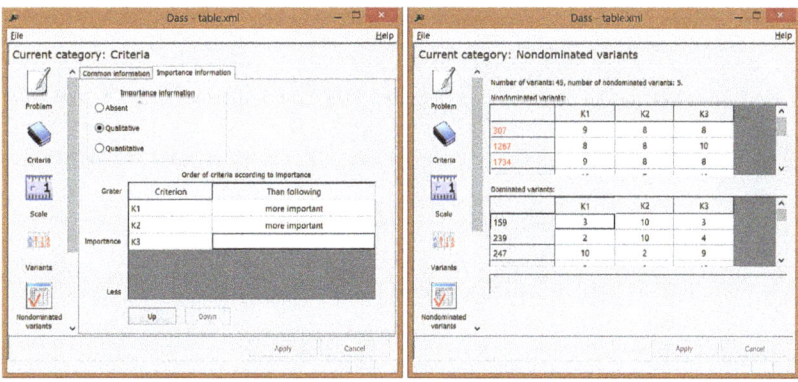

Figure 5. Non-dominated vector scores based on information about ordering criteria by importance.

As a result, there are only 4 non-dominated vector scores and the corresponding 5 alternative solutions shown in Table 4. For each of the 5 vector scores that turned out to be dominated with respect to P^Ω, it is possible to formally explain why it should be excluded from consideration. Namely, what other vector score dominates it and on the basis of what information about preferences this conclusion is made:

$$y(307) = (9,8,8)P^{1 \succ 2}(8,9,8)P^{\circ}(8,9,7) = y(442),$$
$$y(2478) = (10,7,10)P^{1 \succ 2}(7,10,10)P^{\circ}(5,9,10) = y(1080),$$
$$y(2478) = (10,7,10)P^{1 \succ 2}(7,10,10)P^{\circ}(1,10,10) = y(1246),$$
$$y(2478) = (10,7,10)P^{1 \succ 2}(7,10,10)P^{\circ}(7,9,9) = y(1615),$$
$$y(2478) = (10,7,10)P^{1 \succ 2}(7,10,10)P^{\circ}(3,10,7) = y(3005),$$

For example, the notation $(10,7,10)P^{1 \succ 2}(7,10,10)$ means that the vector score $(10,7,10)$ is preferable to the vector score $(7,10,10)$, since the first criterion is more important than the second. As we can see from the constructed chains of vector scores, in this case, in order to discard the vector scores dominated by P^Ω from the information Ω about the ordering of criteria by importance, it turned out to be enough to use only the fact that the first criterion is more important than the second.

Table 4. The 4 non-dominated vector scores and the corresponding 5 alternative solutions.

No.	y_1	y_2	y_3	Value Function Estimation
307; 1734	9	8	8	0.846
1267	8	8	10	0.802
2478	10	7	10	0.907
3093	10	8	7	0.901

The resulting 4 vector scores remain incomparable with the introduced information about the DM's preferences. Next, we will analyze them from different angles. At this stage, the value functions of these vector scores can be estimated by calculating the centroid values of the decision maker's preference parameters [28]. Figure 6 shows how to do this in the software DASS, Table 4 shows the resulting values of the value functions.

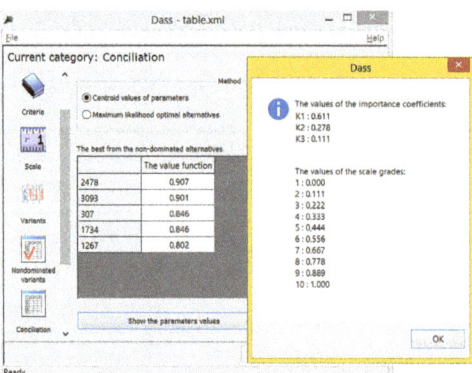

Figure 6. Estimation of value functions based on the centroid values of the decision maker's preference parameters.

Let us continue the formal solution of the choice problem by the criteria importance method. At the next step, we input in the software DASS (see Figure 7) interval information about the relative importance of the criteria: the first criterion is at least 2 times more important than the second, and no more than 4 times; the second criterion is no more than 2 times more important than the third.

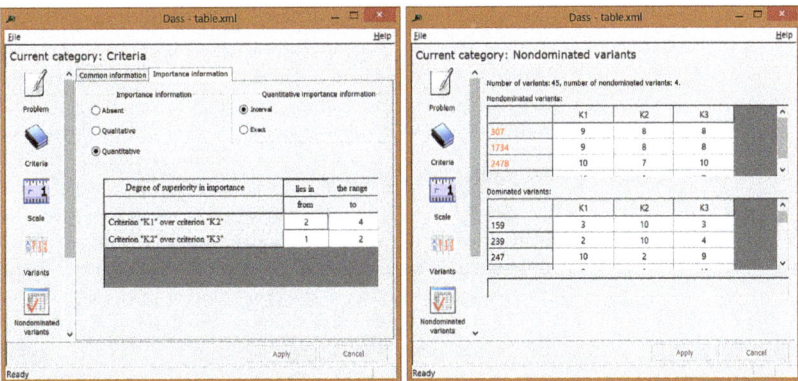

Figure 7. Non-dominated vector scores based on interval information about the importance of criteria.

With such information about the preferences of the decision maker, the vector score $y(1267) = (8, 8, 10)$ turns out to be dominated. Table 5 shows the remaining non-dominated vector scores. Their value functions have changed slightly, as the set of possible values of preference parameters has changed (narrowed) and the corresponding centroid values of these parameters have shifted.

Table 5. The remaining non-dominated vector scores.

No.	y_1	y_2	y_3	Value Function Estimation
307; 1734	9	8	8	0.978
2478	10	7	10	0.983
3093	10	8	7	0.980

At the next step in solving the choice problem, let us clarify the information on how the decision maker's preferences grow along the criterion scale Z (see Figure 8).

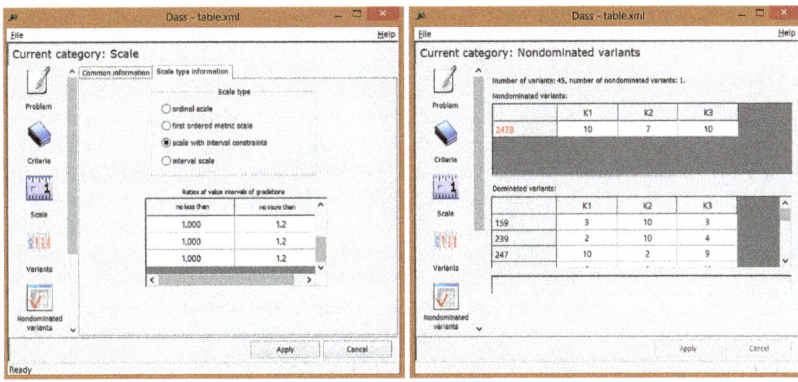

Figure 8. Non-dominated vector scores based on information on the scale of criteria.

As a result, there is only one non-dominated vector score $(10, 7, 10)$, which corresponds to the solution 2478. Additionally, in favor of this vector score, we can note the fact that the estimation of its value function was higher than others at each step of solving the problem.

The only solution was selected using imprecise information about the preferences of experts, given in the form of interval estimates. In the previous steps, the choice set was significantly narrowed down based only on qualitative assessments of preferences. The use of partial and imprecise information about the preferences, an iterative procedure for clarifying this information, as well as the ability to formally substantiate the conclusions made are significant advantages of the considered method of the criteria importance theory in comparison with other methods of multicriteria analysis.

7. Additional Visual Analysis of Alternative Solutions

After the formal analysis of the problem by the criteria importance methods, it is useful to return to the graphical representations of the solutions. Consider 4 non-dominated vector estimates and the corresponding 5 solutions listed in Table 4. Recall that they are selected after a simple ordering of the criteria by importance.

Let us see where these solutions are in the space of the initial criteria K_1, K_2, K_3. To do this, we introduce additional constraints on the values of criteria in the software MOVI. Note that the considered vector scores have the minimum values of the components y_1, y_2, y_3 equal to 8, 7, 7, respectively. In order for only solutions with estimates $y_1 \geq 8$, $y_2 \geq 7$, and $y_3 \geq 7$ to remain feasible, the following constraints should be imposed on the values of the criteria: $K_1 > 0.17$, $K_2 > 1.188$, and $K_3 < 0.0081$. The result is shown in Figure 9.

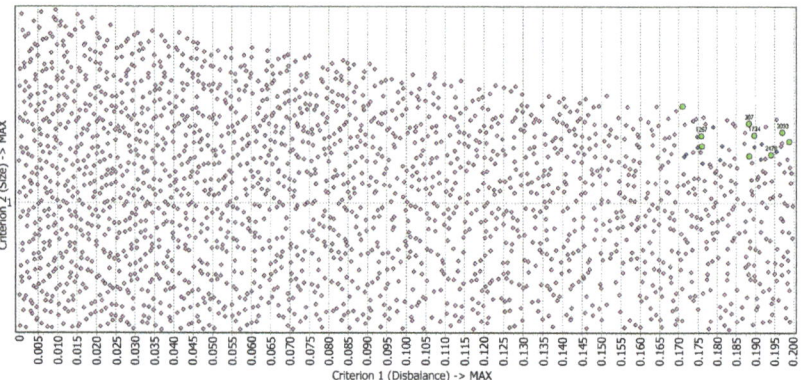

Figure 9. The set of solutions in the space of criteria: K_1 and K_2. Selected solutions are numbered at the top.

Figure 9 gives a general idea in which region of the original point cloud of all solutions the solutions we have selected turned out to be. Now, let us zoom in on the display area. In addition, we will slightly weaken the constraints on the criteria in order to exclude the rounding effect in the process of bringing the criteria to the 10-point scale: $K_1 > 0.165$, $K_2 > 1.134$ and $K_3 < 0.0088$. This extended sample contains 39 solutions, including 14 Pareto optimal solutions. The result is shown in Figure 10.

In Figure 10, the numbers of other solutions, in addition to the selected 5 solutions from Table 4, are marked. In these scaled figures, it is possible to compare different solutions in pairs. In particular, to make sure that the solution 2478, chosen by the formal method, is preferable. It is also interesting to compare the solutions 307 and 1734, which are located side by side on all three projections and have the same vector score.

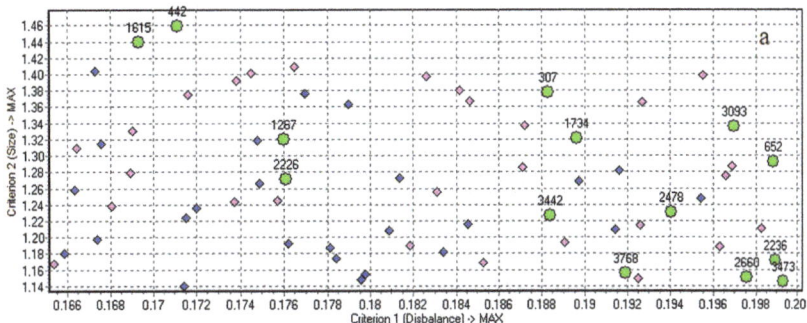

Figure 10. An extended set of solutions in the scaled space of criteria: K_1 and K_2.

8. Result and Discussion

After carrying out a numerical experiment, out of the generated 4000 solutions, only 2198 were found to be feasible in relation to the constraints of the model. Among such an abundance of solutions, it is impossible to choose the best one by examining the three-dimensional space of optimization criteria. Obtaining the set of Pareto optimal solutions allowed us to select 96 solutions. Further, the analysis of the criteria space was carried out in order to reduce the area of suitable solutions, and preferences were introduced regarding the importance and values of the criteria. Thus, we reduced the number of best solutions to 10 (Table 3), and subsequently chose one best solution. Further, the analysis of the obtained solutions is advisable to carry out using a visual analysis of solutions as shown in [11]. Here is a description of the selected solutions.

Table 6 shows the values of the optimized parameters for the selected solutions, as well as in Figures 11 and 12 are a visual representation of the dynamic characteristics. A more detailed description of the visualization principles is presented in [11].

Table 6. The optimized parameters of the system and the ranges of their values.

Parameter	Range	307	1267	1734	2478	3093
c_1	$0.3 \div 0.7$	0.688	0.676	0.690	0.694	0.697
χ_L	$-2.0 \div -0.4$	-1.378	-1.320	-1.321	-1.230	-1.336
λ_V	$0.2 \div 1.0$	0.839	0.847	0.511	0.567	0.726
β_0	$0.3 \div 0.7$	0.507	0.678	0.433	0.630	0.688
α_1	$0.25 \div 1.0$	0.779	0.964	0.800	0.801	0.676
α_2	$0.25 \div 1.0$	0.295	0.625	0.598	0.746	0.435
κ_1	$0.05 \div 0.1$	0.059	0.057	0.052	0.087	0.052
κ_2	$0.05 \div 0.1$	0.063	0.095	0.060	0.055	0.074
ϑ_1	$25 \div 50$	46.729	44.714	37.561	38.153	43.732
ϑ_2	$0 \div 50$	30.566	17.407	1.831	33.533	13.293
ϑ_D	$25 \div 50$	72.314	83.777	87.366	95.880	38.715
ϑ_V	$0 \div 5$	4.990	0.881	2.986	2.882	3.578
t_A	$0.02 \div 0.04$	0.034	0.024	0.020	0.027	0.027
t_B	$0.02 \div 0.04$	0.031	0.023	0.028	0.040	0.035
χ_{L1}	$0 \div 0.1$	0.001	0.056	0.005	0.048	0.096
χ_{L2}	$0 \div 0.1$	0.036	0.038	0.078	0.088	0.039
λ_{01}	$0.05 \div 1.0$	0.05	0.05	0.05	0.05	0.05
λ_{02}	$0.05 \div 1.0$	0.05	0.05	0.05	0.05	0.05
τ_S	$10 \div 50$	44.453	28.574	26.738	20.576	30.596

Figure 11 shows the characteristics of the movement of the system of the solution 307 with unequal mass loads on the first and second actuators ($c_1 = 0.688$, $c_2 = 0.312$):

(a) indicators of the first actuator: curves of displacement and speed (λ_1, $\dot{\lambda}_1$); in the upper part of this column I—pressure in its working cavity (σ_1);
(b) indicators of the second actuator: curves of displacement and speed (λ_2, $\dot{\lambda}_2$); in the upper part of this column II—pressure in its working cavity (σ_2);
(c) channel opening curves (β_0, β_1, β_2): changes in the mismatch criterion $\Delta\lambda$ in the movement of actuators, III—pressure in the intermediate cavity (σ).

The designations for these quantities were explained in the previous section. The curves in Figure 12 are arranged in the same order.

The values of all parameters for each solution can be viewed in Table 6. The scale for displacement λ is doubled relative to the pressure σ. The scale in speed $\dot{\lambda}$ is ten times the pressure. The β scale (flow area value) is increased five times relative to the pressure.

It follows from the graphs that under the conditions of the optimized solution 307 (Figure 11), despite the high load level of the actuators ($|\chi_L| = 1.378$), and the imbalance in loading the right and left cargo ($c_1 = 0.688$, $c_2 = 0.312$), the given laws of motion actuators are implemented with good accuracy, and the pressures in all cavities after a short-term initial disturbance quickly stabilize and are practically invisible.

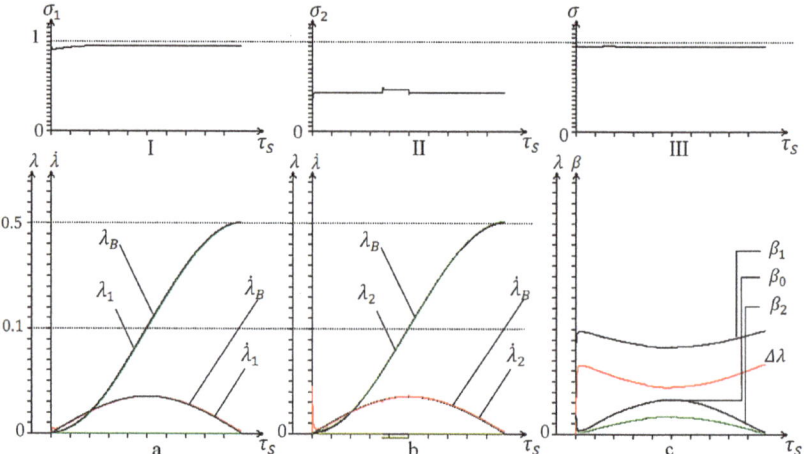

Figure 11. Estimated dynamic characteristics of the solution 307.

A short-term disturbance in the system is modeled by a variable $\chi_{L1,2}$, in Table 6 these are the variables χ_{L1} and χ_{L2}. The first actuator is supplied with an additional load $\chi_{L1} = 0.001$, and practically does not affect the positioning process, the second actuator is supplied with $\chi_{L2} = 0.036$, and we see a small jump in pressure σ_2, which also insignificantly affects the positioning process. The operation of the system under the conditions of the solution 307 is distinguished by a very low sensitivity to variations in position and speed (λ_1, $\dot{\lambda}_1$) parameters within the entire selected range.

The solution 2478 shows in Figure 12, in which unequal mass loads on the first and second actuators ($c_1 = 0.694$, $c_2 = 0.306$), short-term disturbances in the system ($\chi_{L1} = 0.048$ and $\chi_{L2} = 0.088$) are set. Despite the more significant short-term disturbances, we see pressure surges in both actuators (σ_1 and σ_2 graph), which practically does not affect the positioning process. This is primarily due to the correct choice of the remaining parameters of the optimized system. In [11], variants are presented when, for other parameters, but weaker perturbations, the system does not behave stably.

From a computational point of view, the process of generating 4000 alternative solutions in the MOVI software took the longest time—about 3 h on a personal computer. Each of these solutions had to be checked for feasibility, and, for this, the system of Equation (6) had to be solved by the Runge–Kutta method several times for different values of the parameter c1. On average, it took 15 such launches and 2.7 s to check one solution. All other calculations took almost no time and were invisible for experts working with the systems. The operation of decision rules in the DASS system in problems with up to 10 criteria takes less than a second [27]. Such problems of designing new mechanisms are one-off, individual, so it is permissible and even advisable to spend a lot of time on solutions search and careful analysis.

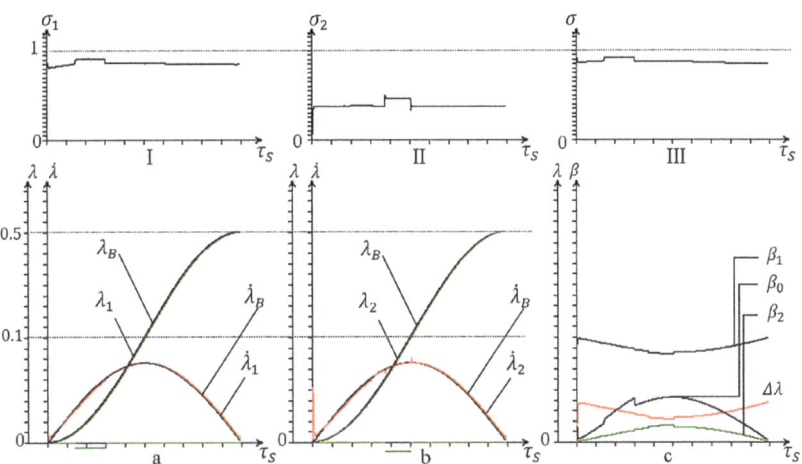

Figure 12. Estimated dynamic characteristics of the solution 2478.

9. Conclusions

The procedure used in this work is based on two important factors: a rational mathematical model and a rational optimizing method. The effectiveness of the proposed procedure is shown by the example of solving a complex dynamic problem-choosing the best option for a technical project. The first factor made possible to simplify to the limit a real computational model by reducing the number of both parameters and criteria, which are considered as a purely physical value. The second factor allowed us to enter the area of best solutions with a significant reduction in options variation. In conclusion, we note the following main stages of work:

- Developing a mathematical model of the investigated physical object;
- Transition to dimensionless parameters;
- On the basis of a dimensionless mathematical model of a physical object, multi-parameter and multicriteria optimization is carried out with the selection of the Pareto set;
- Analysis of the criteria space in order to reduce the area of suitable solutions;
- Preferences are introduced regarding the importance and values of criteria in the form of qualitative or imprecise quantitative (interval) estimates;
- Visual analysis of the received solutions.

As an additional stage, the proposed procedure can also include an optimization stage in the transition from dimensionless to dimensional values. The technical design of a robotic system with two actuators operating in accordance mode, considered as an example, shows the effectiveness of the approach proposed.

Author Contributions: Conceptualization, S.M. and G.K.; Investigation, A.N. and N.N.; Methodology, S.M. and G.K.; Project administration, N.N.; Software, A.N.; Supervision, S.M.; Visualization, A.N. and N.N.; Writing—original draft, S.M., G.K., A.N. and N.N.; Writing—review and editing, G.K. and N.N. All authors have read and agreed to the published version of the manuscript.

Funding: This research received no external funding.

Institutional Review Board Statement: Not applicable.

Informed Consent Statement: Not applicable.

Data Availability Statement: Not applicable.

Acknowledgments: The research was supported by Russian Foundation for Basic Research, project No. 18-29-10072 mk (Optimization of non-linear dynamic models of robotic drive systems taking into account forces of resistance of various nature, including frictional forces).

Conflicts of Interest: The authors declare no conflict of interest.

References

1. Pan, Q.; Zeng, Y.; Li, Y.; Jiang, X.; Huang, M. Experimental investigation of friction behaviors for double-acting hydraulic actuators with different reciprocating seals. *Tribol. Int.* **2021**, *153*, 1–14. [CrossRef]
2. Tran, X.B.; Khaing, W.H.; Endo, H.; Yanada, H. Effect of friction model on simulation of hydraulic actuator. *Proc. Inst. Mech. Eng. Part I J. Syst. Control. Eng.* **2014**, *228*, 690–698. [CrossRef]
3. Yang, G.; Yao, J.; Le, G.; Ma, D. Adaptive integral robust control of hydraulic systems with asymptotic tracking. *Mechatronics* **2016**, *40*, 78–86.
4. Li, L.; Huanga, H.; Zhao, F.; Triebe, M.J.; Liu, Z. Analysis of a novel energy-efficient system with double-actuator for hydraulic press. *Mechatronics* **2017**, *47*, 77–87. [CrossRef]
5. Misyurin, S.Y.; Kreinin, G.V. Dynamics and design of a power unit with a hydraulic piston actuator. *Dokl. Phys.* **2016**, *61*, 354–359. [CrossRef]
6. Misyurin, S.Y.; Kreinin, G.V.; Nosova, N.Y. Similarity and analogousness in dynamical systems and their characteristic features. *Russ. J. Nonlinear Dyn.* **2019**, *15*, 213–220. [CrossRef]
7. Cotsaftis, M.; Keskinen, E. Smooth High Precision Contact Posision Control of Rotating Cylinders with Hydraulic Actuators. In Proceedings of the 12th IFToMM World Congress, Besancon, France, 18–21 June 2007; pp. 738–743.
8. Mamontov, M.A. *Similarity*; Min. Oboron: Moscow, Russia, 1971; p. 51. (In Russian)
9. Kline, S.J. *Similitude and Approximation Theory*; McGrawHill Book Company, Inc.: New York, NY, USA, 1965; p. 229.
10. Shea-Blymyer, C.; Roy, S.; Jantzen, B. A General Metric for the Similarity of Both Stochastic and Deterministic System Dynamics. *Entropy* **2021**, *23*, 1191. [CrossRef] [PubMed]
11. Kreinin, G.V.; Misyurin, S.Y.; Nelyubin, A.P.; Nosova, N.Y. Visualization of the interconnection between dynamics of the system and its basic characteristics. *Sci. Vis.* **2020**, *12*, 9–20. [CrossRef]
12. Sedov, L.I. *Similarity and Dimensional Methods in Mechanics*, 10th ed.; CRC: Boca Raton, FL, USA, 1993. (In Russian)
13. Sonin, A.A. *The Physical Basis of Dimensional Analysis*, 2nd ed.; Department of Mechanical Engineering, MIT: Cambridge, UK, 2001; 57p.
14. Misyurin, S.Y.; Kreinin, G.V.; Nelubin, A.P.; Nosova, N.Y. The synchronous movement of mechanisms taking into account forces of the different nature. *J. Phys. Conf. Ser.* **2020**, *1439*, 012016. [CrossRef]
15. Jones, D.R.; Schonlau, M.; Welch, W.J. Efficient Global Optimization of Expensive Black-Box Functions. *J. Glob. Optim.* **1998**, *13*, 455–492. [CrossRef]
16. Wang, L.; Shan, S.; Wang, G. Mode-Pursuing Sampling Method for Global Optimization on Expensive Black-Box Functions. *Eng. Optim.* **2004**, *36*, 419–438. [CrossRef]
17. Michalewicz, Z. *Genetic Algorithms + Data Structures = Evolution Programs*, 3rd ed.; Springer: Heidelberg/Berlin, Germany, 1996; 388p.
18. Poli, R.; Kennedy, J.; Blackwell, T. Particle Swarm Optimization: An Overview. *Swarm Intell.* **2007**, *1*, 33–57. [CrossRef]
19. Bertsimas, D.; Tsitsiklis, J. Simulated Annealing. *Stat. Sci.* **1993**, *8*, 10–15. [CrossRef]
20. The Parameter Space Investigation Method Toolkit. Available online: http://www.psi-movi.com/ (accessed on 10 October 2021).
21. Sobol, I.M.; Statnikov, R.B. *Choice of Optimal Parameters in Multiple Criteria Problems*; Drofa: Moscow, Russia, 2006; 176p. (In Russian)
22. Podinovski, V.V.; Potapov, M.A. Weighted sum of criteria method in multi-criteria decision analysis: Pro et Contra. *Bus. Inform.* **2013**, *3*, 41–48. (In Russian)
23. Nelyubin, A.P.; Galkin, T.P.; Galaev, A.A.; Popov, D.D.; Misyurin, S.Y.; Pilyugin, V.V. Usage of Visualization in the Solution of Multicriteria Choice Problems. *Sci. Vis.* **2017**, *9*, 59–70. [CrossRef]
24. Miettinen, K.; Ruiz, F.; Wierzbicki, A.P. Introduction to Multiobjective Optimization: Interactive Approaches. In *Multiobjective Optimization*; Lecture Notes in Computer Science 5252; Branke, J., Deb, K., Miettinen, K., Słowiński, R., Eds.; Springer: Berlin/Heidelberg, Germany, 2008; pp. 27–57.
25. Hayes-Roth, F.; Waterman, D.A.; Lenat, B. *Building Expert Systems*; Advanced Book Program; Addison-Wesley Publihsing Conpany, Inc.: Reading, MA, USA, 1983; 472p.
26. Podinovski, V.V. *Ideas and Methods of the Criteria Importance Theory in Multicriteria Decision Making Problems*; Nauka: Moscow, Russia, 2019; 105p. (In Russian)

27. Nelyubin, A.P.; Podinovski, V.V.; Potapov, M.A. Methods of criteria importance theory and their software implementation. In *Springer Proceedings in Mathematics and Statistics 247, Computational Aspects and Applications in Large-Scale Networks, Nizhny Novgorod, Russia, June 2017*; Kalyagin, V., Pardalos, P., Prokopyev, O., Utkina, I., Eds.; Springer: Cham, Switzerland, 2018; pp. 189–196.
28. Nelyubin, A.P.; Podinovski, V.V. Multicriteria Choice Based on Criteria Importance Methods with Uncertain Preference Information. *Comput. Math. Math. Phys.* **2017**, *57*, 1475–1483. [CrossRef]
29. Available online: http://mcodm.ru/soft/dass (accessed on 10 October 2021).

Article

Implicit Solitary Waves for One of the Generalized Nonlinear Schrödinger Equations

Nikolay A. Kudryashov [1,2]

[1] MEPhI (Moscow Engineering Physics Institute), National Research Nuclear University, 31 Kashirskoe Shosse, 115409 Moscow, Russia; naudr@gmail.com or Nakudryashov@mephi.ru
[2] National Research Center "Kurchatov Center", 1 Akademika Kurchatova Sq., 123182 Moscow, Russia

Abstract: Application of transformations for dependent and independent variables is used for finding solitary wave solutions of the generalized Schrödinger equations. This new form of equation can be considered as the model for the description of propagation pulse in a nonlinear optics. The method for finding solutions of equation is given in the general case. Solitary waves of equation are obtained as implicit function taking into account the transformation of variables.

Keywords: generalized Schrödinger equation; solitary wave; exact solution; implicit function

Citation: Kudryashov, N.A. Implicit Solitary Waves for One of the Generalized Nonlinear Schrödinger Equations. Mathematics 2021, 9, 3024. https://doi.org/10.3390/math9233024

Academic Editor: Alberto Ferrero

Received: 16 October 2021
Accepted: 22 November 2021
Published: 25 November 2021

Publisher's Note: MDPI stays neutral with regard to jurisdictional claims in published maps and institutional affiliations.

Copyright: © 2021 by the author. Licensee MDPI, Basel, Switzerland. This article is an open access article distributed under the terms and conditions of the Creative Commons Attribution (CC BY) license (https://creativecommons.org/licenses/by/4.0/).

1. Introduction

In this paper, we consider the nonlinear partial differential equation

$$i\, q_t + q_{xx} + \alpha\, q + \beta\, |q|^n\, q + \gamma\, |q|^{2n}\, q + \delta\, |q|^{3n}\, q + \lambda\, |q|^{4n}\, q = 0, \tag{1}$$

where $q(x,t)$ is complex function, x is coordinate, t is time, n is rational number and α, β, γ, δ, λ are parameters of Equation (1). It is easy to see that Equation (1) is the generalization of the famous nonlinear Schrödinger equation which follows from Equation (1) at $\beta \neq 0$, $n = 2$, $\alpha = \gamma = \delta = \lambda = 0$. Equation (1) has been presented in recent paper [1] as an equation whose solution can be obtained using the method of transformation for dependent and independent variables. Equation (1) is the generalization of some equations describing propagation pulses in the nonlinear optics (see, for example, [2–19]).

The purpose of this paper is to present the method for finding solutions of Equation (1) and to obtain the implicit solitary wave solutions of Equation (1) using the transformations of variables.

This article is organized as follows. In Section 2, the method of finding solutions of Equation (1) is presented taking into account the traveling wave reduction. In this Section the general approach to finding exact solutions of Equation (1) is described as weel. The implicit solitary waves of Equation (1) in form of kink are given in Section 3. Implicit soliton solutions of Equation (1) are presented in Section 4.

2. Method Applied

Let us look for the exact solution of Equation (1) using the the form

$$q(x,t) = y(z)\, e^{i\,(k\,x - \omega\,t)}, \tag{2}$$

where $y(z)$ is a function describing an optical pulse profile, ω is a frequency and k is a wave number and z is a variable of x and t: $z = x - C_0\, t$.

Substituting (2) into Equation (1) and equating expressions for real and imaginary parts yields the overdetermined system of equations for function $y(z)$ in the form

$$(2k - C_0)\, y_z = 0, \tag{3}$$

$$y_{zz} + (\omega - k^2)y + \alpha y + \beta y^{n+1} - \gamma y^{2n+1} - \delta y^{3n+1} + \lambda y^{4n+1} = 0. \tag{4}$$

Provided that $C_0 = 2k$ we see that Equation (3) is satisfied. Multiplying Equation (4) by y_z and integrating over z, we obtain the first integral in the form

$$y_z^2 + (\omega + \alpha - k^2)y^2 + \frac{2\beta}{n+2}y^{n+2} - \frac{\gamma}{n+1}y^{2n+2} - \frac{2\delta}{3n+2}y^{3n+2} + \frac{\lambda}{2n+1}y^{4n+2} = C_1, \tag{5}$$

where C_1 is a constant of integration.

Solution of Equation (5) can be written in the form of quadrature

$$\int \frac{d\zeta}{\sqrt{H[y]}} = z - z_0, \tag{6}$$

where

$$H[y] = C_1 - (\omega + \alpha - k^2)y^2 - \frac{2\beta}{n+2}y^{n+2} + \frac{\gamma}{n+1}y^{2n+2} + \frac{2\delta}{3n+2}y^{3n+2} - \frac{\lambda}{2n+1}y^{4n+2}. \tag{7}$$

However integral (6) cannot be calculated in the general case.

Let us look for solution of Equation (5) in the form

$$y(z) = F(\zeta), \quad \zeta_z = F(\zeta)^n. \tag{8}$$

Using (8), we have

$$y_z = F_\zeta \zeta_z = F_\zeta F(\zeta)^n. \tag{9}$$

Substituting (8) and (9) into Equation (5), we obtain the equation

$$F_\zeta^2 + (\omega + \alpha - k^2)F^{2-2n} + \frac{2\beta}{n+2}F^{2-n} - \frac{\gamma}{n+1}F^2 - \frac{2\delta}{3n+2}F^{n+2} + \frac{\lambda}{2n+1}F^{2n+2} = 0. \tag{10}$$

Equation (10) has been previously studied in papers [1–3]. It is important to note that by using the transformation [20–23]

$$F(\zeta) = V(\zeta)^{-\frac{1}{n}}, \tag{11}$$

Equation (10) can be reduced to the equation with solutions in the form of elliptic function

$$V_\zeta^2 + (\omega + \alpha - k^2)n^2 V^4 + \frac{2n^2\beta}{n+2}V^3 - \frac{n^2\gamma}{n+1}V^2 - \frac{2n^2\delta}{3n+2}V + \frac{n^2\lambda}{2n+1} = 0. \tag{12}$$

Solution of Equation (12) can be searched for in the form [24–26]

$$V(\zeta) = V_1 + \frac{(V_2 - V_1)E}{Y^2 + E}, \quad E = \frac{(V_1 - V_3)}{(V_3 - V_2)}, \tag{13}$$

where V_1, V_2, V_3 and V_4 are the roots of the following algebraic equation

$$(\omega + \alpha - k^2)V^4 + \frac{2\beta}{n+2}V^3 - \frac{\gamma}{n+1}V^2 - \frac{2\delta}{3n+2}V + \frac{\lambda}{2n+1} = 0 \tag{14}$$

and $Y(\zeta)$ is the Jacobi elliptic sine in the form

$$Y(\zeta;k) = \text{sn}\left\{\frac{n}{2}\sqrt{a(V_4 - V_2)(V_1 - V_3)}\,(\zeta - \zeta_0);\, S\right\}, \tag{15}$$

where S is determined by the formula

$$S^2 = \frac{(V_1 - V_4)(V_1 - V_3)}{(V_4 - V_2)(V_3 - V_2)}. \tag{16}$$

Taking into account (11), the solution $F(\xi)$ can be expressed by the formula

$$F(\xi) = \left[\frac{V_1(V_3-V_2)\operatorname{sn}^2\left\{\frac{n}{2}\sqrt{a(V_4-V_2)(V_1-V_3)}(\xi-\xi_0);S\right\}+V_2(V_1-V_3)}{(V_3-V_2)\operatorname{sn}^2\left\{\frac{1}{2}\sqrt{a(V_4-V_2)(V_1-V_3)}(\xi-\xi_0);S\right\}+V_1-V_3}\right]^{-\frac{1}{n}}. \tag{17}$$

We cannot find the explicit expression for the function $\xi(z)$ using $V(\xi)$ in the general case by means of the formula

$$\int V(\xi)\, d\xi = z - z_0. \tag{18}$$

However in the case of solitary wave solutions these solutions of Equation (1) can be found as the implicit functions. To look for these solutions we use the special methods has been developing in the last few years [27–36].

3. Implicit Solitary Wave Solutions of the Generalized Nonlinear Schrödinger Equation in Form Kink

Let us look for the solution of Equation (12) using the logistic function. We assume that there exist a solution of Equation (12) in the form [37–46]

$$V(\xi) = A_0 + A_1 Q(\xi), \tag{19}$$

where $Q(\xi)$ is the logistic function [37]

$$Q(\xi) = \frac{1}{1 + e^{m(\xi - \xi_0)}}. \tag{20}$$

The function $Q(\xi)$ is the solution of the Riccati equation in the form

$$Q_\xi = m(Q^2 - Q). \tag{21}$$

The function $Q(\xi)$ satisfies the following second-order differential equation as well

$$Q_{\xi\xi} = m^2 Q(Q-1)(2Q-1). \tag{22}$$

Substituting (19) into Equation (12) and taking Equations (21) and (22) into account, yields the equality

$$\left(n^2 A_1^4 \omega - n^2 A_1^4 k^2 + n^2 A_1^4 \alpha + A_1^2 m^2\right) Q^4 + \left(4 n^2 A_0 A_1^3 \alpha - 2 A_1^2 m^2 - 4 n^2 A_0 A_1^3 k^2 + 4 n^2 A_0 A_1^3 \omega + \frac{2 n^2 A_1^3 \beta}{2+n}\right) Q^3 + \left(A_1^2 m^2 + \frac{6 n^2 A_0 A_1^2 \beta}{2+n} + 6 n^2 A_0^2 A_1^2 \alpha + 6 n^2 A_0^2 A_1^2 \omega - \frac{n^2 A_1^2 g}{1+n} - 6 n^2 A_0^2 A_1^2 k^2\right) Q^2 + \left(\frac{6 n^2 A_0^2 A_1 \beta}{2+n} - \frac{2 n^2 A_0 A_1 g}{1+n} - \frac{2 n^2 A_1 \delta}{2+3n} - 4 n^2 A_0^3 A_1 k^2 + 4 n^2 A_0^3 A_1 \alpha + 4 n^2 A_0^3 A_1 \omega\right) Q - n^2 A_0^4 k^2 + n^2 A_0^4 \alpha + n^2 A_0^4 \omega + \frac{\lambda n^2}{1+2n} - 2 \frac{n^2 A_0 \delta}{2+3n} - \frac{n^2 A_0^2 g}{1+n} + 2 \frac{n^2 A_0^3 \beta}{2+n} = 0. \tag{23}$$

We have obtained that a polynomial in solutions $Q(z)$ is equal to zero. Such thing is possible if and only if all coefficients are equal to zero. Taking into account this property in (23), we derive the conditions for the parameters of Equation (1). These conditions are the following

$$\alpha = k^2 - \omega - \frac{m^2}{n^2 A_1^2}, \tag{24}$$

$$\beta = \frac{m^2(2+n)(A_1 + 2 A_0)}{n^2 A_1^2}, \tag{25}$$

$$\gamma = \frac{\left(6 A_0^2 + 6 A_0 A_1 + A_1^2\right) m^2 (1+n)}{n^2 A_1^2}, \qquad (26)$$

$$\delta = -\frac{(2+3n) m^2 A_0 \left(2 A_0^2 + 3 A_0 A_1 + A_1^2\right)}{n^2 A_1^2}, \qquad (27)$$

$$\lambda = -\frac{(1+2n) m^2 A_0^2 \left(A_0^2 + 2 A_0 A_1 + A_1^2\right)}{n^2 A_1^2}. \qquad (28)$$

Using solution (19) and definition (18), we get the implicit function $\xi(z)$ in the form

$$(A_0 + A_1)\xi - \frac{A_1}{m} \log\left(1 + e^{m\xi}\right) = z - z_0. \qquad (29)$$

On the other hand taking into account (8) and (11), we obtain

$$\xi = \frac{1}{m} \log\left[\frac{(A_0 + A_1) y^n - 1}{A_0 y^n - 1}\right]. \qquad (30)$$

Substituting (30) into (29) yields an implicit expression for $y(z)$ in the form

$$\frac{(A_0 + A_1)}{m} \log\left[\frac{(A_0 + A_1) y^n - 1}{A_0 y^n - 1}\right] - \frac{A_1}{m} \log\left(\frac{A_1 y^n}{A_0 y^n - 1}\right) = z - z_0. \qquad (31)$$

We have obtained implicit expressions for kinks $y(\xi)$ and $y(z)$, where A_0, A_1, m and n are arbitrary. These values allow us to calculate the parameters α, β, γ, δ and λ for Equation (5) using conditions (24)–(28).

Solutions (30) of Equation (10) (on the left) and (31) of (5) (on the right) are demonstrated in Figure 1 at $A_0 = 1.0$, $A_0 = 0.5$, $n = 2$, $m = 0.02$ and $z_0 = 0.0$.

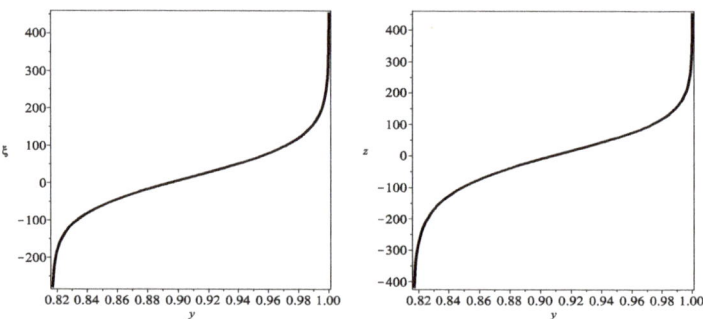

Figure 1. Solutions (30) of Equation (10) (**left**) and (31) of (5) (**right**) at $A_0 = 1.0$, $A_0 = 0.5$, $n = 2$, $m = 0.02$ and $z_0 = 0.0$.

4. Implicit Optical Solitons of the Generalized Nonlinear Schrödinger Equation

Let us obtain the exact solutions in the form of solitons. We look for the solution of Equation (12) in the form [47–51]

$$V(\xi) = A_0 + A_1 R(\xi), \qquad (32)$$

where the function $R(\xi)$ solves the following equations

$$R_\xi^2 + a R^4 + b R^3 - c R^2 = 0 \qquad (33)$$

and

$$R_{\xi\xi} + 2 a R^3 + \frac{3b}{2} R^2 - c R = 0 \qquad (34)$$

Solution of Equation (33) is as follows [47]

$$R(\xi) = \frac{4ce^{-\xi\sqrt{c}}}{4ac + b^2 + 2be^{-\xi\sqrt{c}} + e^{-2\xi\sqrt{c}}}. \tag{35}$$

Substituting expression (32) and taking into account (33) and (34) into Equation (12), we obtain the following polynomial

$$\left(n^2 A_1{}^4 \alpha - n^2 A_1{}^4 k^2 + n^2 A_1{}^4 \omega - A_1{}^2 a\right) R^4 + \left(4 n^2 A_0 A_1{}^3 \alpha - A_1{}^2 b - 4 n^2 A_0 A_1{}^3 k^2 + 4 n^2 A_0 A_1{}^3 \omega + \frac{2 n^2 A_1{}^3 \beta}{2+n}\right) R^3 + \left(A_1{}^2 c + \frac{6 n^2 A_0 A_1{}^2 \beta}{2+n} - 6 n^2 A_0{}^2 A_1{}^2 k^2 + 6 n^2 A_0{}^2 A_1{}^2 \alpha + 6 n^2 A_0{}^2 A_1{}^2 \omega - \frac{n^2 A_1{}^2 g}{1+n}\right) R^2 + \left(-2 \frac{n^2 A_0 A_1 g}{1+n} + 6 \frac{n^2 A_0{}^2 A_1 \beta}{2+n} - 2 \frac{n^2 A_1 \delta}{2+3n} - 4 n^2 A_0{}^3 A_1 k^2 + 4 n^2 A_0{}^3 A_1 \alpha + 4 n^2 A_0{}^3 A_1 \omega\right) R + \frac{\lambda n^2}{1+2n} - n^2 A_0{}^4 k^2 + n^2 A_0{}^4 \alpha + n^2 A_0{}^4 \omega - 2 \frac{A_0 \delta n^2}{2+3n} - \frac{A_0{}^2 g n^2}{1+n} + 2 \frac{A_0{}^3 \beta n^2}{2+n} = 0, \tag{36}$$

Equating the coefficients of polynomial (36) to zero, let us find the following conditions

$$\alpha = \frac{A_1{}^2 k^2 n^2 - A_1{}^2 n^2 \omega + a}{A_1{}^2 n^2}, \tag{37}$$

$$\beta = -\frac{(2+n)(4 A_0 a - A_1 b)}{2 A_1{}^2 n^2}, \tag{38}$$

$$\gamma = -\frac{\left(6 A_0{}^2 a - 3 A_0 A_1 b - A_1{}^2 c\right)(1+n)}{A_1{}^2 n^2}, \tag{39}$$

$$\delta = \frac{\left(4 A_0{}^2 a - 3 A_0 A_1 b - 2 A_1{}^2 c\right) A_0 (2+3n)}{2 A_1{}^2 n^2}, \tag{40}$$

$$\lambda = \frac{\left(A_0{}^2 a - A_0 A_1 b - A1^2 c\right) A_0{}^2 (1+2n)}{A_1{}^2 n^2}. \tag{41}$$

Solution $V(\xi)$ of Equation (12) can be written as the following

$$V(\xi) = A_0 + \frac{4 A_1 c e^{-\xi\sqrt{c}}}{4ac + b^2 + 2be^{-\xi\sqrt{c}} + e^{-2\xi\sqrt{c}}}. \tag{42}$$

At the same time, we find the function $\xi(z)$ from Equation (18)

$$z - A_0 \xi + \frac{2 A_1 \sqrt{c}}{\sqrt{ac}} \arctan\left[\frac{(4ac + b^2)e^{\xi\sqrt{c}} + b}{2\sqrt{ac}}\right] + z_0. \tag{43}$$

Solution $V(\xi)$ of Equation (12) is demonstrated in Figure 2 on the left hand side at $A_0 = 5.0$, $A_1 = -2$, $a = 2.0$, $b = 3.0$ and $c = 4.0$. Dependencies $\xi(z)$ are shown on the right hand side of Figure 2 at $A_0 = 5.0$, $A_1 = -2$, $a = 2.0$, $b = 3.0$ and $c = 4.0$ (curve 1), $A_0 = 3.0$, $A_1 = -2$, $a = 2.0$, $b = 3.0$ and $c = 4.0$ (curve 2) and at $A_0 = 1.0$, $A_1 = -2$, $a = 2.0$, $b = 3.0$ and $c = 4.0$ (curve 3).

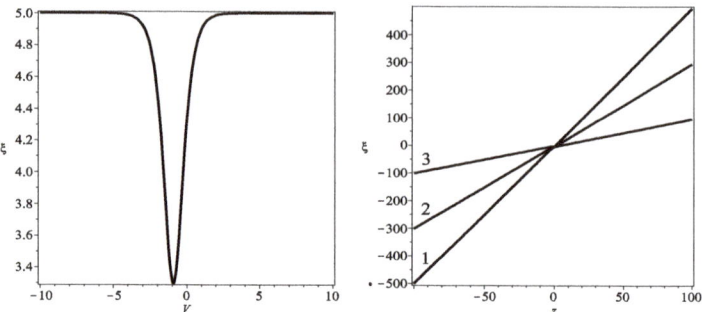

Figure 2. Solution (42) of Equation (12) at $A_0 = 5.0$, $A_1 = -2$, $a = 2.0$, $b = 3.0$ and $c = 4.0$ (**left**) and (43) of (18) (**right**) at $A_0 = 5.0$ (curve 1), $A_0 = 3.0$ (curve 2) $A_0 = 1.0$ (curve 3) and at $A_1 = -2.0$, $a = 2.0$, $b = 3.0$ and $c = 4.0$.

Taking into account Equations (8) and (11), we obtain

$$A_0 + \frac{4 A_1 c e^{-\xi \sqrt{c}}}{4ac + b^2 + 2b e^{-\xi \sqrt{c}} + e^{-2\xi \sqrt{c}}} - y^{-n}. \tag{44}$$

Solving Equation (44) gives us two expressions for $\xi(y)$

$$\xi_{1,2}(y) = -\frac{1}{\sqrt{c}} \log\left[\frac{A_1 b y^n + 2 A_1 c y^n \mp 2\sqrt{P} - b}{1 - A_0 y}\right], \tag{45}$$

where P is as follows

$$P = \left(A_1^2 c^2 + A_0 A_1 bc - A_0^2 ac\right) y^{2n} + (2 A_0 ac - bc) y^n - ac. \tag{46}$$

The dependence $\xi(y)$ is the two-valued function. Equating $\xi_1(y)$ and $\xi_2(y)$, we obtain the following formula for y^*

$$y^* = \left[\frac{2 A_0 a - A_1 b + \sqrt{4ac A_1^2 + A_1^2 b^2}}{2 A_0^2 a - 2 A_0 A_1 b - 2 A_1^2 c}\right]^{\frac{1}{n}}. \tag{47}$$

It can be seen that y^* depends on the values of A_0, A_1, a, b and c. by substituting y^* into (45) we obtain ξ^*. The dependence $\xi(z)$ can be written in the form

$$\xi(y) = \begin{cases} \xi_1(y), & \xi > \xi^*, \\ \xi_2(y), & \xi < \xi^*. \end{cases} \tag{48}$$

Substituting $\xi(y)$ into expression (43), yields the solitary wave in the form

$$z(y) = \begin{cases} A_0 \xi_1(y) + \frac{2 A_1 \sqrt{c}}{\sqrt{ac}} \arctan\left[\frac{(4ac+b^2) e^{\xi_1(y)\sqrt{c}} + b}{2\sqrt{ac}}\right] + z_0, & z > z^*, \\ A_0 \xi_2(y) + \frac{2 A_1 \sqrt{c}}{\sqrt{ac}} \arctan\left[\frac{(4ac+b^2) e^{\xi_2(y)\sqrt{c}} + b}{2\sqrt{ac}}\right] + z_0 & z < z^*, \end{cases} \tag{49}$$

where Z^* is found taking into account y^*.

Implicit solitary waves solutions $\xi(y)$ of Equation (10) (on the left) and $z(y)$ of Equation (5) are illustrated in Figure 3 at $z_0 = 0.0$, $A_0 = 5.0$, $A_1 = -2.0$, $n = 1$, $a = 2.0$, $b = 3.0$, and $c = 4.0$.

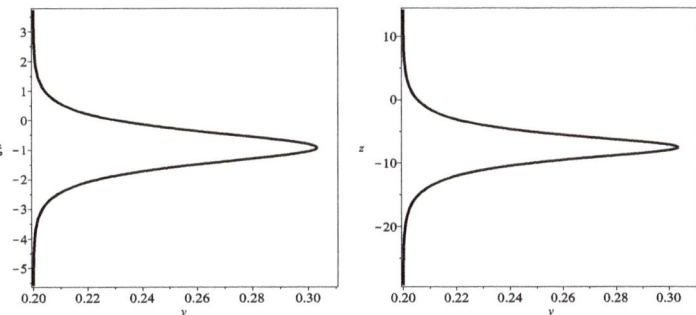

Figure 3. Implicit solitary waves solutions $\xi(y)$ of Equation (10) (**left**) and $z(y)$ of Equation (5) (**right**) at $z_0 = 0.0$, $A_0 = 5.0$, $A_1 = -2.0$, $n = 1$, $a = 2.0$, $b = 3.0$, and $c = 4.0$.

5. Conclusions

In this paper, Equation (1) has been studied. Equation (1) is the generalization of the famous nonlinear Schrödinger equation and can be used for the description of propagation pulses in optical fiber. Using the transformations for dependent and independent variables we have presented the algorithm for construction of exact solutions of nonlinear differential equations. Exact formulas for solitary waves solutions in the form of kinks and optical solitons are given as the implicit functions. The approach for finding exact solutions can be used for some other nonlinear differential equations.

Funding: This research was funded by Russian Science Foundation. Grant number 21-11-00328.

Institutional Review Board Statement: Not applicable.

Informed Consent Statement: Not applicable.

Data Availability Statement: Not applicaple.

Acknowledgments: This research was supported by Russian Science Foundation grant No 21-11-00328 "Developing biologically-inspired learning methods and schemes for spiking neural networks able to be implemented on base of memristors in order to solve heterogeneous data analysis tasks".

Conflicts of Interest: The author also declares that there is no conflict of interest.

References

1. Kudryashov, N.A. Model of propagation pulses in an optical fiber with a new law of refractive indices. *Optik* **2021**, *248*, 168160. [CrossRef]
2. Kudryashov, N.A. A generalized model for description of propagation pulses in optical fiber. *Optik* **2019**, *189*, 42–52. [CrossRef]
3. Kudryashov, N.A. Mathematical model of propagation pulse in optical fiber with power nonlinearities. *Optik* **2020**, *212*, 164750. [CrossRef]
4. Kudryashov, N.A. Solitary wave solutions of hierarchy with non-local nonlinearity. *Appl. Math. Lett.* **2020**, *103*, 106155. [CrossRef]
5. Zayed, E.M.E.; Shohib, R.M.A.; Biswas, A.; Ekici, M.; Triki, H.; Alzahrani, A.K.; Belic, M.R. Optical solitons and other solutions to Kudryashov's equation with three innovative integration norms. *Optik* **2020**, *211*, 164431. [CrossRef]
6. Arshed, S.; Arif, A. Soliton solutions of higher-order nonlinear schrodinger equation (NLSE) and nonlinear kudryashov's equation. *Optik* **2020**, *209*, 164588. [CrossRef]
7. Kumar, S.; Malik, S.; Biswas, A.; Zhou, Q.; Moraru, L.; Alzahrani, A.K.; Belic, M.R. Optical Solitons with Kudryashov's Equation by Lie Symmetry Analysis. *Phys. Wave Phenom.* **2020**, *28*, 299–304. [CrossRef]
8. Yildirim, Y.; Biswas, A.; Ekici, M.; Gonzalez-Gaxiola, O.; Khan, S.; Triki, H.; Moraru, L.; Alzahrani, A.K.; Belic, M.R. Optical solitons with Kudryashov's model by a range of integration norms. *Chin. J. Phys.* **2020**, *66*, 660–672. [CrossRef]
9. Kudryashov, N.A. Optical solitons of the resonant nonlinear Schrodinger equation with arbitrary index. *Optik* **2021**, *235*, 166626. [CrossRef]
10. Zayed, E.M.E.; Shohib, R.M.A.; Biswas, A.; Ekici, M.; Moraru, L.; Alzahrani, A.K.; Belic, M.R. Optical solitons with differential group delay for Kudryashov's model by the auxiliary equation mapping method. *Chin. J. Phys.* **2020**, *67*, 631–645. [CrossRef]
11. Zayed, E.M.E.; Alngar, M.E.M.; Biswas, A.; Asma, M.; Ekici, M.; Alzahrani, A.K.; Belic, M.R. Optical solitons and conservation laws with generalized Kudryashov's law of refractive index. *Chaos Solitons Fractals* **2020**, *139*, 110284. [CrossRef]

12. Zayed, E.M.E.; Alngar, M.E.M.; Biswas, A.; Asma, M.; Ekici, M.; Alzahrani, A.K.; Belic, M.R. Solitons in magneto–optic waveguides with Kudryashov's law of refractive index. *Chaos Solitons Fractals* **2020**, *140*, 110129. [CrossRef]
13. Kudryashov, N.A. Optical solitons of mathematical model with arbitrary refractive index. *Optik* **2021**, *231*, 166443. [CrossRef]
14. Biswas, A.; Asma, M.; Guggilla, P.; Mullick, L.; Moraru, L.; Ekici, M.; Alzahrani, A.K.; Belic, M.R. Optical soliton perturbation with Kudryashov's equation by semi–inverse variational principle. *Phys. Lett. Sect. A Gen. At. Solid State Phys.* **2020**, *384*, 126830. [CrossRef]
15. Biswas, A.; Sonmezoglu, A.; Ekici, M.; Alzahrani, A.K.; Belic, M.R. Cubic–Quartic Optical Solitons with Differential Group Delay for Kudryashov's Model by Extended Trial Function. *J. Commun. Technol. Electron.* **2020**, *65*, 1384–1398. [CrossRef]
16. Arnous, A.H.; Biswas, A.; Ekici, M.; Alzahrani, A.K.; Belic, M.R. Optical solitons and conservation laws of Kudryashov's equation with improved modified extended tanh-function. *Optik* **2021**, *225*, 165406. [CrossRef]
17. Zayed, E.M.E.; Alngar, M.E.M. Optical soliton solutions for the generalized Kudryashov equation of propagation pulse in optical fiber with power nonlinearities by three integration algorithms. *Math. Methods Appl. Sci.* **2021**, *44*, 315–324. [CrossRef]
18. Hyder, A.A.; Soliman, A.H. Exact solutions of space-time local fractal nonlinear evolution equations generalized comformable derivative approach. *Resilts Phys.* **2020**, *17*, 103135. [CrossRef]
19. Hyder, A.A.; Soliman, A.H. An extended Kudryashov technique for solving stochastic nonlinear models with generalized comformable derivatives. *Commun. Nonlinear Sci. Numer. Simul.* **2021**, *97*, 105730. [CrossRef]
20. Zayed, E.M.E.; Shohib, R.M.A.; Alngar, M.E.M.; Biswas, A.; Kara, A.H.; Dakova, A.; Khan, S.; Alshehri, H.M.; Belic, M.R. Solitons and conservation laws in magneto-optic waveguides with generalized Kudryashov's equation by the unified auxiliary equation approach. *Optik* **2021**, *245*, 167694. [CrossRef]
21. Ekici, M.; Sonmezoglu, A.; Biswas, A. Stationary optical solitons with Kudryashov's laws of refractive index. *Chaos Solitons Fractals* **2021**, *151*, 111226. [CrossRef]
22. Yildirim, Y.; Biswas, A.; Kara, A.H.; Ekici, M.; Alzahrani, A.K.; Belic, M.R. Cubic–quartic optical soliton perturbation and conservation laws with generalized Kudryashov's form of refractive index. *J. Opt.* **2021**, *50*, 354–360. [CrossRef]
23. Biswas, A.; Ekici, M.; Dakova, A.; Khan, S.; Moshokoa, S.P.; Alshehri, H.M.; Belic, M.R. Highly dispersive optical soliton perturbation with Kudryashov's sextic-power law nonlinear refractive index by semi-inverse variation. *Results Phys.* **2021**, *27*, 104539. [CrossRef]
24. Kudryashov, N.A. Exact solutions of the equation for surface waves in a convecting fluid. *Appl. Math. Comput.* **2019**, *344–345*, 97–106. [CrossRef]
25. Kudryashov, N.A. Method for finding highly dispersive optical solitons of nonlinear differential equations. *Optik* **2019**, *206*, 163550. [CrossRef]
26. Kudryashov, N.A. Highly dispersive optical solitons of the generalized nonlinear eigth-order Scrödinger equation. *Optik* **2020**, *206*, 164335. [CrossRef]
27. Kudryashov, N.A. Exact solutions of the generalized Kuramoto-Sivashinsky equation. *Phys. Lett. A* **1990**, *147*, 287–291. [CrossRef]
28. Parkes, E.J.; Duffy, B.R. An automated tanh-function method for finding solitary wave solutions to non-linear evolution equations. *Comput. Phys. Commun.* **1996**, *98*, 288–300 [CrossRef]
29. Malfliet, W.; Hereman, W. The Tanh method: I Exact solutions of nonlinear evolution and wave equations. *Phys. Scr.* **1996**, *54*, 563–568 [CrossRef]
30. Fan, E. Extended tanh-function method and its applications to nonlinear equations. *Phys. Lett. A* **2000**, *227*, 212–218 [CrossRef]
31. Fu, Z.; Liu, S.; Liu, S.; Zhao, Q. New Jacobi elliptic function expansion and new periodic solutions of nonlinear wave equations. *Phys. Lett. A* **2001**, *290*, 72–76 [CrossRef]
32. Liu, S.; Fu, Z.; Liu, S.; Zhao, Q. Jacobi elliptic function expansion method and periodic wave solutions of nonlinear wave equations. *Phys. Lett. A* **2001**, *289*, 69–74 [CrossRef]
33. Biswas, A. 1-soliton solution of the generalized Radhakrishnan–Kundu–Laksmanan equation. *Phys. Lett. A* **2009**, *373*, 2546–2548. [CrossRef]
34. Vitanov, N.K. Application of simplest equations of Bernoulli and Riccati kind for obtaining exact traveling-wave solutions for a class of PDEs with polynomial nonlinearity. *Commun. Nonlinear Sci. Numer. Simul.* **2010**, *15*, 2050–2060. [CrossRef]
35. Vitanov, N.K. Modified method of simplest equation: Powerful tool for obtaining exact and approximate traveling-wave solutions of nonlinear PDEs. *Commun. Nonlinear Sci. Numer. Simul.* **2011**, *16*, 1176–1185. [CrossRef]
36. Vitanov, N.K.; Dimitrova, Z.I.; Kantz, H. Modified method of simplest equation and its application to nonlinear PDEs. *Appl. Math. Comput.* **2010**, *216*, 2587–2595. [CrossRef]
37. Kudryashov, N.A. One method for finding exact solutions of nonlinear differential equations. *Commun. Nonlinear Sci. Numer. Simul.* **2012**, *17*, 2248–2253. [CrossRef]
38. Yildirim, Y.; Biswas, A.; Kara, A.H.; Guggilla, P.; Khan, S.; Alzahrani, A.K.; Belic, M.R. Highly dispersive optical solitons and conservation laws with Kudryashov's sextic power-law of nonlinear refractive index. *Optik* **2021**, *240*, 166915. [CrossRef]
39. Elsherbeny, A.M.; El-Barkouky, R.; Ahmed, H.M.; Arnous, A.H.; El-Hassani, R.M.I.; Biswas, A.; Yildirim, Y.; Alshomrani, A.S. Optical soliton perturbation with Kudryashov's generalized nonlinear refractive index. *Optik* **2021**, *240*, 166620. [CrossRef]
40. Zayed, E.M.E.; Alngar, M.E.M.; Biswas, A.; Kara, A.H.; Asma, M.; Ekici, M.; Khan, S.; Alzahrani, A.K.; Belic, M.R. Solitons and conservation laws in magneto-optic waveguides with generalized Kudryashov's equation. *Chin. J. Phys.* **2021**, *69*, 186–205. [CrossRef]

41. Zayed, E.M.E.; Shohib, R.M.A.; Alngar, M.E.M.; Biswas, A.; Ekici, M.; Khan, S.; Alzahrani, A.K.; Belic, M.R. Optical solitons and conservation laws associated with Kudryashov's sextic power-law nonlinearity of refractive index. *Ukr. J. Phys. Opt.* **2021**, *22*, 38–49. [CrossRef]
42. Zayed, E.M.E.; Alngar, M.E.M.; Biswas, A.; Ekici, M.; Alzahrani, A.K.; Belic, M.R. Chirped and Chirp-Free Optical Solitons in Fiber Bragg Gratings with Kudryashov's Model in Presence of Dispersive Reflectivity. *J. Commun. Technol. Electron.* **2020**, *65*, 1267–1287. [CrossRef]
43. Arnous, A.H.; Zhou, Q.; Biswas, A.; Guggilla, P.; Khan, S.; Yildirim, Y.; Alshomrani, A.S.; Alshehri, H.M. Optical solitons in fiber Bragg gratings with cubic-quartic dispersive reflectivity by enhanced Kudryashov's approach. *Phys. Lett. A* **2022**, *422*, 127797. [CrossRef]
44. Gonzalez-Gaxiola, O. Optical soliton solutions for Triki-Biswas equation by Kudryashov's R function method. *Optik* **2022**, *249*, 168230. [CrossRef]
45. Arnous, A.H. Optical solitons with Biswas-Milovic equation in magneto-optic waveguide having Kudryashov's aw of refractive index. *Optik* **2021**, *247*, 167987. [CrossRef]
46. Alotaibi, H. Traveling wave solutions to the nonlinear evolution equation using expansion method and addendum to Kudryashov's method. *Symmetry* **2021**, *13*, 2126. [CrossRef]
47. Kudryashov, N.A. Highly dispersive solitary wave solutions of perturbed nonlinear Schrödinger equations. *Appl. Math. Comput.* **2020**, *371*, 124972. [CrossRef]
48. Raza, N.; Seadawy, A.R.; Kaplan, M.; Butt, A.R. Symbolic computation and sensitivity analysis of nonlinear Kudryashov's dynamical equation with applications. *Phys. Scr.* **2021**, *96*, 105216. [CrossRef]
49. Kaplan, M.; Akbulut, A. The analysis of the soliton-type solutions of conformable equations by using generalized Kudryashov method. *Opt. Quantum Electron.* **2021**, *53*, 498. [CrossRef]
50. Malik, S.; Kumar, S.; Biswas, A.; Ekici, M.; Dakova, A.; Alzahrani, A.K.; Belic, M.R. Optical solitons and bifurcation analysis in fiber Bragg gratings with Lie symmetry and Kudryashov's approach. *Nonlinear Dyn.* **2021**, *105*, 735–751. [CrossRef]
51. Rahman, Z.; Ali, M.Z.; Roshid, H.-O. Closed form soliton solutions of three nonlinear fractional models through proposed improved Kudryashov method. *Chin. Phys. B* **2021**, *30*, 050202. [CrossRef]

Article

Modeling the Dynamics of Spiking Networks with Memristor-Based STDP to Solve Classification Tasks

Alexander Sboev [1,2,*], Danila Vlasov [1], Roman Rybka [1], Yury Davydov [1], Alexey Serenko [1] and Vyacheslav Demin [1]

[1] National Research Centre "Kurchatov Institute", 123182 Moscow, Russia; vfked0d@gmail.com (D.V.); rybkarb@gmail.com (R.R.); davydov.workbox@gmail.com (Y.D.); serenko@phystech.edu (A.S.); Demin_VA@nrcki.ru (V.D.)
[2] Moscow Engineering Physics Institute, National Research Nuclear University, 115409 Moscow, Russia
* Correspondence: Sboev_AG@nrcki.ru

Citation: Sboev, A.; Vlasov, D.; Rybka, R.; Davydov, Y.; Serenko, A.; Demin, V. Modeling the Dynamics of Spiking Networks with Memristor-Based STDP to Solve Classification Tasks. *Mathematics* **2021**, *9*, 3237. https://doi.org/10.3390/math9243237

Academic Editors: Nikolai A. Kudryashov and Cornelio Yáñez Márquez

Received: 6 November 2021
Accepted: 10 December 2021
Published: 14 December 2021

Publisher's Note: MDPI stays neutral with regard to jurisdictional claims in published maps and institutional affiliations.

Copyright: © 2021 by the authors. Licensee MDPI, Basel, Switzerland. This article is an open access article distributed under the terms and conditions of the Creative Commons Attribution (CC BY) license (https://creativecommons.org/licenses/by/4.0/).

Abstract: The problem with training spiking neural networks (SNNs) is relevant due to the ultra-low power consumption these networks could exhibit when implemented in neuromorphic hardware. The ongoing progress in the fabrication of memristors, a prospective basis for analogue synapses, gives relevance to studying the possibility of SNN learning on the base of synaptic plasticity models, obtained by fitting the experimental measurements of the memristor conductance change. The dynamics of memristor conductances is (necessarily) nonlinear, because conductance changes depend on the spike timings, which neurons emit in an all-or-none fashion. The ability to solve classification tasks was previously shown for spiking network models based on the bio-inspired local learning mechanism of spike-timing-dependent plasticity (STDP), as well as with the plasticity that models the conductance change of nanocomposite (NC) memristors. Input data were presented to the network encoded into the intensities of Poisson input spike sequences. This work considers another approach for encoding input data into input spike sequences presented to the network: temporal encoding, in which an input vector is transformed into relative timing of individual input spikes. Since temporal encoding uses fewer input spikes, the processing of each input vector by the network can be faster and more energy-efficient. The aim of the current work is to show the applicability of temporal encoding to training spiking networks with three synaptic plasticity models: STDP, NC memristor approximation, and PPX memristor approximation. We assess the accuracy of the proposed approach on several benchmark classification tasks: Fisher's Iris, Wisconsin breast cancer, and the pole balancing task (CartPole). The accuracies achieved by SNN with memristor plasticity and conventional STDP are comparable and are on par with classic machine learning approaches.

Keywords: spiking neural networks; synaptic plasticity; spike-timing-dependent plasticity; memristor

1. Introduction

A variety of problems surround the phenomena or dynamical processes that cannot be described by explicit laws expressed in differential equations. Such tasks could be solved with the help of data-driven modeling, which forms an implicit model of the process of interest by learning from the observed data. An especially relevant direction in data-driven modeling involves spiking neural networks (SNNs) [1–3], an inherent characteristic of which is the nonlinearity in the temporal dynamics of neurons receiving and transmitting spikes and the dynamics of the synaptic weights during learning. The dynamics of spiking neurons is described by nonlinear differential equations: the membrane potential of a neuron receives non-differentiable pulses when input spikes arrive and is instantaneously reset to its resting value upon emitting an output spike.

The practical relevance of SNNs involves the ultra-low power consumption these networks could exhibit when implemented in neuromorphic hardware [4,5]. For instance, the digital neuromorphic chip TrueNorth [6] spends only 26 pJ for transmitting an impulse (spike) from neuron-to-neuron. Devices in which synapses (and possibly neurons too) are implemented in an analogue fashion can be even more efficient [7]. The prospective element base for the analogue implementation of a synapse is a memristor [8,9].

This gives relevance toward developing spiking neural network models with learning based on synaptic plasticity mechanisms that model the conductance change of a memristor. A number of memristor plasticity models have been obtained so far, backed by experimental measurements, in which the drift of the conductance of a memristor depends nonlinearly on its current conductance and on the time difference between presynaptic and postsynaptic spikes [10–14]. Spiking networks with the plasticity approximating nanocomposite (NC) memristors $(CoFeB)_x(LiNbO_3)_{1-x}$ were shown to classify the MNIST handwritten digits [15]. Recently, a highly-plastic poly-p-xylylene (PPX) memristor was created [16], which makes it relevant to study the possibility of learning about SNNs, with plasticity modeling that type of memristor.

This paper considers three synaptic plasticity models: the model of the PPX memristor plasticity obtained by approximation of its experimental measurements, the existing NC memristor plasticity model [15], and the additive spike-timing-dependent plasticity, which was shown to resemble the plasticity of various types of memristors [17,18].

The aim of this paper is to numerically solve the learning dynamics of the spiking neural network model with the aforementioned plasticity mechanisms, to obtain weights established after learning, and to obtain the times of output spikes for given input spikes, which are then decoded into classes to solve a classification task.

Unlike existing works devoted to SNN learning with memristor plasticity models [15,17,19–21], which are based on frequency encoding of the input data, we use temporal encoding, in which the information is contained in the timings of input spike patterns, as it requires fewer spikes and, thus, less energy.

For the NC and PPX memristor plasticity models (described in Section 2.2), we show in Section 3.1 that a neuron memorizes repetitive spike patterns. Based on this, an algorithm for training a spiking neural network with temporal encoding is proposed in Section 2.5. The performance of the algorithm is tested in Section 3.2 on benchmark classification problems.

2. Materials and Methods

2.1. Neuron Model

Keeping in mind the prospective possibility of hardware implementation, we strive for a simple neuron model. We thus use the leaky integrate-and-fire model [22] for the neuron dynamics, in which the neuron has one state variable, the membrane potential $V(t)$, which obeys the following dynamics as soon as it is below the threshold V_{th}:

$$\frac{dV}{dt} = -\frac{V(t) - V_{rest}}{\tau_m} + \frac{I_{syn}(t) + I_{ext}(t)}{C_m}. \quad (1)$$

The neuron is considered to fire an output spike when $V(t)$ exceeds V_{th}, after which V is instantaneously reset to 0, and during the refractory period t_{ref} the neuron is unable to fire spikes.

$I_{ext}(t)$ is the external stimulation current applied during training, described in Section 2.5. $I_{syn}(t)$ is the incoming postsynaptic current, summed over currents $I_{syn,i}(t)$ coming from the neuron's input synapses:

$$I_{syn}(t) = \sum_i I_{syn,i}(t), \quad \frac{dI_{syn,i}}{dt} = -\frac{I_{syn,i}(t)}{\tau_{syn}} + w_i(t)\frac{q_{syn}}{\tau_{syn}} S_{pre,i}(t - t_{delay}). \quad (2)$$

Here, $S_{pre,i}(t)$ is equal to 1 when a presynaptic spike arrives at the i-th input synapse of the neuron, and to 0 otherwise. The arrivals of presynaptic spikes are governed by the input encoding algorithm described in Section 2.4. t_{delay} is the delay for transmitting a presynaptic spike to the postsynaptic neuron, in our simulations equal to the integration timestep $dt = 0.1$ ms. $C_m = 1$ pF, $q_{syn} = 5$ fC, $\tau_{syn} = 5$ ms. The constants V_{th}, τ_m, and t_{ref} are adjusted for each particular classification task and presented in Section 3.

The dimensionless synaptic weight $0 \leqslant w_i(t) \leqslant 1$ changes after each presynaptic and postsynaptic spike in accordance with the plasticity model, as defined in Section 2.2.

2.2. Plasticity Models

2.2.1. Additive Spike-Timing-Dependent Plasticity

For the sake of comparison, in addition to memristive plasticity models, which will be presented in the next sections, we perform numerical experiments with the conventional STDP [23] in its additive form, where the synaptic weight change Δw does not depend on the current weight w, and only depends on the time interval Δt from the arrival of a presynaptic spike to emitting the postsynaptic spike:

$$\Delta w = \begin{cases} -A^- \cdot \exp\left(\frac{\Delta t}{\tau^-}\right) & \text{if } \Delta t < 0; \\ A^+ \cdot \exp\left(-\frac{\Delta t}{\tau^+}\right) & \text{if } \Delta t > 0. \end{cases} \quad (3)$$

Here, following the existing literature [24], $\tau^+ = 20$ ms, $\tau^- = 20$ ms, $A^+ = A^- = 0.01$.

Solving the synapse dynamics is performed with the help of two more state variables for each synapse i, its presynaptic and postsynaptic eligibility traces [25] x_i and y_i:

$$\begin{cases} \dfrac{dx_i}{dt} = -\dfrac{x_i(t)}{\tau_+} + S_{\text{pre},i}(t), \\ \dfrac{dy_i}{dt} = -\dfrac{y_i(t)}{\tau_-} + S_{\text{post}}(t). \\ \dfrac{dw_i}{dt} = \max(A^- \cdot y_i(t) \cdot S_{\text{pre},i}(t), \, 1 - w_i) + \\ \qquad + \min(A^+ \cdot x_i(t) \cdot S_{\text{post}}(t), \, w). \end{cases} \quad (4)$$

2.2.2. Nanocomposite Memristor Plasticity

The plasticity model for nanocomposite memristors (CoFeB)$_x$(LiNbO$_3$)$_{1-x}$ is borrowed from the literature [15]:

$$\Delta w(\Delta t) = \begin{cases} A^+ \cdot w \cdot \left[1 + \tanh\left(-\dfrac{\Delta t - \mu_+}{\tau_+}\right)\right] & \text{if } \Delta t > 0; \\ A^- \cdot w \cdot \left[1 + \tanh\left(\dfrac{\Delta t - \mu_-}{\tau_-}\right)\right] & \text{if } \Delta t < 0. \end{cases} \quad (5)$$

The constants are kept as in the original literature [15]: $A^+ = 0.074$, $A^- = -0.047$, $\mu^+ = 26.7$ ms, $\mu^- = -22.3$ ms, $\tau^+ = 9.3$ ms, $\tau^- = 10.8$ ms.

The spike timing dependence curves for different conductance values are depicted in Figure 1A.

2.2.3. Model of Poly-p-Xylylene Memristors

PPX-based memristors, in contrast to NC-based memristors, demonstrate resistive switching driven by electrochemical metallization mechanism: conductive filaments are formed in them due to electromigration of metal ions [16]. This leads to a slightly different shape of the spike timing dependence curves.

We fitted the experimental dependences of the change in synaptic conductance on the time interval Δt between presynaptic and postsynaptic splices for PPC memristors using the following function:

$$\Delta w(\Delta t) = \begin{cases} \frac{|\Delta t|}{\tau} \alpha^+ e^{-\beta^+ \left(\frac{w_{\max} - w}{w_{\max} - w_{\min}}\right)} e^{-\gamma^+ \left(\frac{\Delta t}{\tau}\right)^2} & \text{if } \Delta t > 0; \\ \frac{|\Delta t|}{\tau} \alpha^- e^{-\beta^- \left(\frac{w - w_{\min}}{w_{\max} - w_{\min}}\right)} e^{-\gamma^- \left(\frac{\Delta t}{\tau}\right)^2} & \text{if } \Delta t < 0. \end{cases} \quad (6)$$

Here $\tau = 10$ ms, $\alpha^+ = 0.32$, $\alpha^- = 0.01$, $\beta^+ = 2.21$, $\beta^- = -5.97$, $\gamma^+ = 0.03$, $\gamma^- = 0.15$, $w_{\max} = 1$, $w_{\min} = 0$.

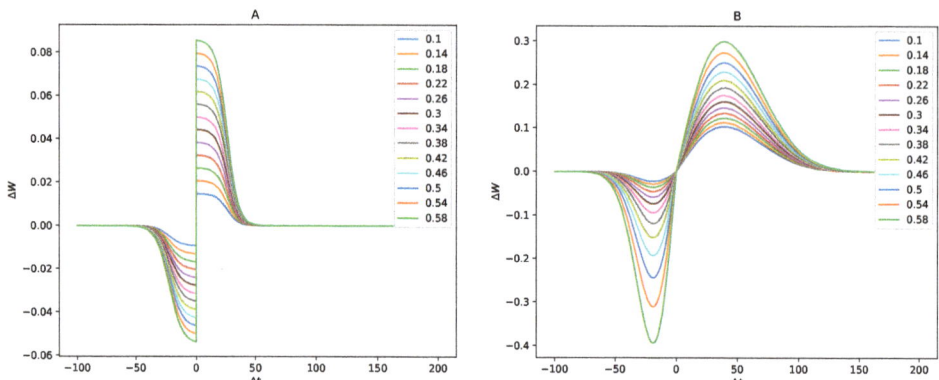

Figure 1. Spike timing dependence curves: the dependence of the change Δw in synaptic conductance on the interval Δt between a presynaptic spike and a postsynaptic spike for different current synaptic conductance values w. (**A**): for the nanocomposite memristors, redrawn from the original paper [15], (**B**): for poly-p-xylylene memristors.

The weight-dependent exponents in Equation (6) express the experimentally observed dependence of the change in synaptic conductance on the initial conductance value. Similar dependencies have already been applied in some works on memristic conductivity, in particular in [26]. Parameters $\alpha^+, \alpha^-, \beta^+, \beta^-, \gamma^+, \gamma^-$ were determined from the experimentally obtained dependencies in three stages: at the first stage, experimental dependencies were approximated by cubic splines. At the second stage, the obtained spline curves were approximated by the function above (see Equation (6)) for each set of experimental data by the nonlinear least squares method At the third stage, the best set of parameters was chosen based on the maximum possible values of R^2. The experimental data consisted of measurements of the dependence of the change in synaptic conductance on Δt for four different initial conductance values, for each of which, measurements were performed five times, after which the results were averaged. The results of the experiments and approximations are shown in Figure 1B.

2.3. Network Model Implementation

Overall, the network is defined by the following system of equations:

$$\begin{cases} \text{For each neuron } j: \\ V_j(t) = \int_{\hat{t}_j}^{t} \exp\left(-\frac{t-t'}{\tau_m}\right) \cdot \left(I_{\text{ext, for neuron } j}(t') + I_{\text{syn, for neuron } j}(t')\right) dt', \\ S_{\text{post},j}(t) = \Theta(V_j(t) - V_{\text{th}}) \cdot \Theta(t - \hat{t}_j - t_{\text{ref}}); \\ \text{For each input component } i: \\ S_{\text{pre},i}(t) = \sum_{t^i_{\text{input}}} \delta(t - t^i_{\text{input}}); \\ \text{For each input synapse } i \text{ of each neuron } j: \\ \frac{dw_{ij}}{dt} = \text{Plasticity}(w_{ij}, S_{\text{pre},i}, S_{\text{post},j}). \end{cases} \quad (7)$$

Here, the formal solution for a neuron's potential $V_j(t)$ is presented [27,28], starting from the moment $\hat{t}_j$ of its most recent spike. The initial conditions are $V_j(\hat{t}_j) = 0$, $w_{ij}(0) = w_{\text{init}}$. The times t^i_{input} of the presynaptic spikes arriving from each input i during presenting every input vector are defined in Section 2.4. I_{syn} are defined in Equation (2). Plasticity refers to one of the models (3), (5), or (6). Θ is the heaviside step function.

Solving the network dynamics is performed numerically in a piecewise manner: $V_j(t)$ is obtained over an interval during which $S_{\text{post},j}(t)$ and all $S_{\text{pre},i}(t)$ equal 0. When a postsynaptic spike occurs, w_{ij} is updated in accordance with the plasticity model, and $\hat{t}_j$ is updated to equal the current value of t. When a presynaptic spike arrives, w_{ij} is updated, and the integration continues.

Simulations are carried out with the help of the NEural Simulation Tool (NEST) library [29].

2.4. Input Preprocessing and Encoding

Before presenting input data to the SNN, it is normalized by applying L2 norm or MinMaxScale (https://scikit-learn.org/stable/modules/preprocessing.html, accessed on 13 October 2021) depending on the dataset (see Section 2.6), and then processed by Gaussian receptive fields [30–32]. The latter converts an input vector $\vec{x}$ of dimension N, a vector of dimension $N \cdot M$, where M is the number of receptive fields. Each component x^i is transformed into M components $g(x^i, \mu_0), \ldots, g(x^i, \mu_M)$, where $g(x^i, \mu_j) = \exp\left(\frac{(x^i - \mu_j)^2}{\sigma^2}\right)$.

Here, $\mu_j = X_{\min}^i + (X_{\max}^i - X_{\min}^i) \cdot \frac{j}{M-1}$ is the center of the j-th receptive field, $X_{\max}^i$ and $X_{\min}^i$ are the maximal and minimal values of the i-th component among all vectors of the training set, which are 1 and 0, respectively, if MinMaxScale normalization is applied. M is chosen to be 20 in all experiments.

After preprocessing, the vector obtained is encoded into a pattern of spikes to present to the input synapses of the network. Each component x^i of the preprocessed vector is represented by one spike arriving at he i-th input synapse at time $t_{\text{input}}^i = t_h(1 - x^i)$, relative to the beginning of presenting that input vector, where t_h is the duration of presenting one vector. That way, the particularities of a class of input vectors are characterized by a few of the earliest input spikes, which, in turn, correspond to the receptive fields typical to that class.

2.5. Learning Algorithm

To solve multi-class classification tasks, on the base of local plasticity tasks, the learning algorithm should be designed so that each neuron learns specifically the class it is assigned to. To achieve that, we use a learning algorithm in which neurons memorize their classes induced by a reinforcing signal (see Algorithm 1).

The network consists of as many neurons as there are classes in the classification problem; the neurons are connected with each other by non-plastic inhibitory synapses with fixed weights w_{inh} (see Figure 2).

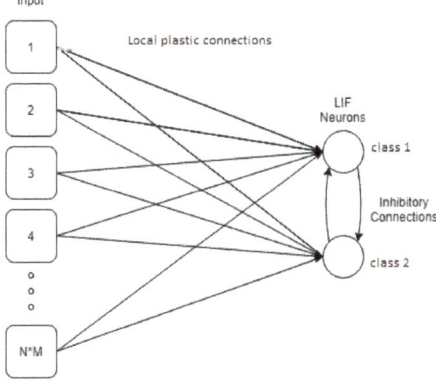

Figure 2. The spiking neural network topology.

At the training stage, the neurons receive spike patterns encoding vectors of classes of the training sample. The neuron that corresponds to the class of the input sample being fed at the moment is stimulated by setting a high positive I_{ext} for a short period, starting from $x_i^{\min} + t_{\text{shift}}$, where $x_i^{\min}$ is the beginning of presenting an input vector. The value of I_{ext} is chosen such that it causes an immediate output spike. The spike induced by such a stimulation will lead to amplification, according to the rule of local plasticity, of those inputs that receive spikes at earlier moments of time. To decrease the probability of excitation of other neurons and prevent their synaptic weights from growing while giving examples of classes that are not assigned to them at the learning stage, the threshold is set so that only the trained neuron spikes in response to reinforcing signal. The class of the example is determined by the neuron that generated the spike earliest.

Algorithm 1 Learning algorithm

Input: matrix of preprocessed input objects X, vector of object classes Y, neuron parameters, plasticity parameters, initial distribution of weights
Parameter: N_epochs, t_h, h
Output: network weights

1: Initialize neural network: neurons, synapses and initial weights.
2: Define input spike patterns with the duration t_h.
3: **for** each x_i in X **do**
4: search for a minimal value of $x_i^{\min}$.
5: define the time since the beginning of the reinforcing signal as $x_i^{\min} + t_{\text{shift}}$, where t_{shift} is a reinforcing signal temporal shift.
6: define the termination time of the reinforcing signal as $x_i^{\min} + t_{\text{shift}} + 2 * dt$, where dt is the simulation timestep.
7: Set an amplitude for the reinforcing signal.
8: **end for**
9: **for** k in N_epochs **do**
10: Set input spikes at the generators.
11: Set teacher current impulse times at the generators.
12: Simulate a training epoch.
13: For the next sample, times of input spikes and teacher current impulse times are shifted on a time period equal to the epoch simulation time.
14: **end for**
15: **return** weight distribution, output spike times.

2.6. Datasets

Two benchmark classification problems are considered: Fisher's Iris and Wisconsin breast cancer.

The dataset of Fisher's Iris consists of 150 flowers, described by four traits: the length and width of the sepal and petals in centimeters. The specimens belong to three different classes of 50 specimens each, corresponding to three species: *Iris setosa*, *Iris virginica*, and *Iris versicolor*. The first class is linearly separable from the second and third, while the second and third are not linearly separable.

The breast cancer dataset collected at the University of Wisconsin consists of 569 samples, 357 of which are classified as "benign" and 212 as "malignant". Each sample in the dataset represents cell characteristics from a digitized image of a fine needle aspiration breast biopsy. The input vector of length 30 is composed of the mean value (among all cells), the standard deviation, and the extreme values of each of the 10 cell nucleus characteristics—radius, texture, perimeter, area, smoothness, compactness, concavity, concave points, symmetry, and fractal dimension.

Pole balancing [33] is originally a reinforcement learning task. However, creating a reinforcement learning algorithm for SNNs with memristive plasticity will be included in future work. As a preliminary step for that, we here consider it as a classification task.

In this task, the objective is to hold a massive pole attached to a moving cart by a hinge for a given number of episodes (at least 195 out of 200) by changing the position of the carriage. The environment is characterized by four parameters: coordinate and speed of the carriage, as well as angle of deviation from the vertical and angular velocity of the pole (x, $\dot{x}$, ϕ and $\dot{\phi}$). The control action which the network should predict applies a force of 1 N to the carriage in the left or right direction.

To convert this task into a classification problem, we collected a reference set of environmental states and control actions with the help of an artificial neural network, with one hidden layer of two neurons to the task. This network was trained using the RL algorithm Policy Gradient (https://github.com/norse/norse/blob/master/norse/task/cartpole.py, accessed on 24 October 2021) until the average number of episodes (carriage movements), during which the pole remained in an acceptable position, was equal to 198 (out of 200 episodes). After the artificial neural network was successfully trained, it was run in the CartPole environment without training, and the decisions it made at each step and their corresponding environment states were recorded. A total of 100 runs were performed, which resulted in the collection of 1949 input-output pairs. The collected set of pairs was used to train the spiking neural network.

3. Results

3.1. Memorizing Repeating Patterns

The first experiment was aimed at testing the underlying effect necessary for learning with temporal encoding. This effect was shown previously [34] for STDP: if a neuron gets a repeating spike pattern among Poisson noise, the neuron will gradually become selectively sensitive to this pattern. The times of spikes emitted by the neuron in response to the pattern will gradually become closer to the beginning of its presentation.

We tested this effect by feeding a single neuron with a single vector from the Fisher's Iris dataset, interspersed with random Poisson spike sequences. When a repeating spike pattern is presented to a neuron, the synaptic weights change, so that the neuron generates spike earlier, related to the start of pattern presentation (Figure 3). The spike time eventually established depends on the value of the neuron threshold. At the same time, the neuron gradually stops spiking during presenting Poisson noise. Plasticity modeling PPX memristors is less robust to noise due to the high value of its time window constant τ.

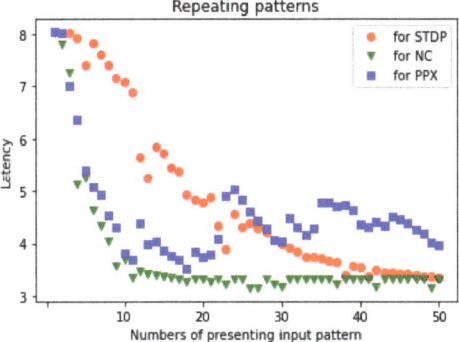

Figure 3. Reduction over time of the delay between the start of the repetitive input spike pattern and the output spike of the neuron.

In the next section, the learning algorithm based on the pattern memorization effect confirmed here for all three plasticity models is tested on benchmark classification datasets: Fisher's Iris, Wisconsin breast cancer, and CartPole.

3.2. Classification with SNN

For each dataset, the learning algorithm was applied three times: with STDP, with NC plasticity, and with PPX plasticity. The plasticity model constants were kept unchanged as originally defined. The neuron model and input encoding constants were adjusted when necessary. As a result, the neuron membrane time constant τ_m was found to be 13 ms. The neuron refractoriness period is $t_{ref} = 300$ ms, so that after emitting a spike, it cannot spike again up until the end of the inter-pattern interval $t_h = 400$ ms. The initial weight of excitatory synapses is $w_{init} = 0.5$. The inhibitory weight $w_{inh} = -4$.

The parameters adjusted separately for each task are shown in Table 1 along with the accuracies of solving respective classification tasks. Accuracy is measured by the F1-macro score, since the classes are almost equal by the numbers of input vectors. Mean, minimum, and maximum values are presented over the splits of five-fold cross-validation.

Table 1. Spiking network parameters and F1-score for different classification tasks.

Task	Plasticity	V_{th}, mV	σ	t_{shift}, ms	F1, % mean	min	max
Fisher's Iris	STDP	5	0.005	0	97	93	100
Fisher's Iris	NC	5	0.005	0	97	93	100
Fisher's Iris	PPX	3	0.005	0	97	93	100
Breast cancer	STDP	8	0.005	3.2	94	89	97
Breast cancer	NC	8	0.005	3.2	93	88	96
Breast cancer	PPX	6	0.005	3.2	93	89	96
CartPole	STDP	5	0.01	1.2	66 (199/200)	65	68
CartPole	NC	6	0.01	1.2	63 (199/200)	62	65
CartPole	PPX	5	0.01	1	60 (197/200)	60	68

4. Discussion

The fact that the results were obtained with similar neuron and synapse model parameters indicates a possible applicability of the proposed learning algorithm to other problems, while the parameters reported here could form the initial working range. Still, selecting the network and encoding parameters individually can achieve greater accuracy. For example, for the Wisconsin breast cancer and CartPole tasks, the timing of the reinforcing signal had to be shifted in the positive direction.

The simplicity of the neuron model considered contributes towards the prospective possibility of hardware implementation of the proposed learning algorithm. However, other nonlinear forms of the neuron's response function could be studied in further work.

5. Conclusions

This paper demonstrates the possibility of solving classification tasks using spiking neural network models with synaptic plasticity models that approximate the plasticity of nanocomposite and poly-p-xylylene memristors. The proposed learning algorithm was tested on several benchmark classification tasks: Fisher's Iris, Wisconsin breast cancer, and the pole balancing task. The network hyperparameters were similar for all tasks, which shows the robustness of the approach.

In the future, we plan to test the proposed algorithm on more benchmarks, and analyze more variants of memristive plasticity models.

Author Contributions: Conceptualization, A.S. (Alexander Sboev) and V.D.; funding acquisition, R.R.; investigation, D.V. and Y.D.; methodology, D.V., R.R., and A.S. (Alexey Serenko); project administration, A.S. (Alexander Sboev) and R.R.; resources, V.D.; software, D.V. and Y.D.; supervision, V.D.; writing—original draft, D.V., Y.D., and A.S. (Alexey Serenko); writing—review & editing, A.S. (Alexander Sboev), R.R. and A.S. (Alexey Serenko). All authors have read and agreed to the published version of the manuscript.

Funding: Developing the network model and the learning algorithm and running numerical simulations were supported by Russian Science Foundation grant no. 21-11-00328. Obtaining experimental measurements of memristor conductivity changes in which the memristor plasticity models are based, in Sections 2.2.2 and 2.2.3, was supported by Russian Science Foundation grant no. 20-79-10185.

Institutional Review Board Statement: Not applicable.

Informed Consent Statement: Not applicable.

Data Availability Statement: Not applicable.

Acknowledgments: This work was carried out using computing resources of the federal collective usage center Complex for Simulation and Data Processing for MEGA-Science Facilities at NRC "Kurchatov Institute", http://ckp.nrcki.ru/, accessed on 13 October 2021.

Conflicts of Interest: The authors declare no conflict of interest. The funders had no role in the design of the study; in the collection, analyses, or interpretation of data; in the writing of the manuscript, or in the decision to publish the results.

References

1. Paugam-Moisy, H.; Bohte, S.M. Computing with spiking neuron networks. In *Handbook of Natural Computing*; Rozenberg, G., Back, T., Kok, J., Eds.; Springer: Berlin/Heidelberg, Germany, 2012; pp. 335–376. [CrossRef]
2. Tavanaei, A.; Ghodrati, M.; Kheradpisheh, S.R.; Masquelier, T.; Maida, A. Deep learning in spiking neural networks. *Neural Netw.* **2019**, *111*, 47–63. [CrossRef] [PubMed]
3. Taherkhani, A.; Belatreche, A.; Li, Y.; Cosma, G.; Maguire, L.P.; McGinnity, T. A review of learning in biologically plausible spiking neural networks. *Neural Netw.* **2020**, *122*, 253–272. [CrossRef] [PubMed]
4. Davies, M.; Srinivasa, N.; Lin, T.H.; Chinya, G.; Cao, Y.; Choday, S.H.; Dimou, G.; Joshi, P.; Imam, N.; Jain, S.; et al. Loihi: A neuromorphic manycore processor with on-chip learning. *IEEE Micro* **2018**, *38*, 82–99. [CrossRef]
5. Indiveri, G.; Corradi, F.; Qiao, N. Neuromorphic architectures for spiking deep neural networks. In Proceedings of the 2015 IEEE International Electron Devices Meeting, Washington, DC, USA, 7–9 December 2015; pp. 4.2.1–4.2.4.
6. Merolla, P.A.; Arthur, J.V.; Alvarez-Icaza, R.; Cassidy, A.S.; Sawada, J.; Akopyan, F.; Jackson, B.L.; Imam, N.; Guo, C.; Nakamura, Y.; et al. A million spiking-neuron integrated circuit with a scalable communication network and interface. *Science* **2014**, *345*, 668–673. [CrossRef]
7. Rajendran, B.; Sebastian, A.; Schmuker, M.; Srinivasa, N.; Eleftheriou, E. Low-Power Neuromorphic Hardware for Signal Processing Applications: A review of architectural and system-level design approaches. *IEEE Signal Process. Mag.* **2019**, *36*, 97–110. [CrossRef]
8. Camuñas-Mesa, L.A.; Linares-Barranco, B.; Serrano-Gotarredona, T. Neuromorphic spiking neural networks and their memristor-CMOS hardware implementations. *Materials* **2019**, *12*, 2745. [CrossRef]
9. Saïghi, S.; Mayr, C.G.; Serrano-Gotarredona, T.; Schmidt, H.; Lecerf, G.; Tomas, J.; Grollier, J.; Boyn, S.; Vincent, A.F.; Querlioz, D.; et al. Plasticity in memristive devices for spiking neural networks. *Front. Neurosci.* **2015**, *9*, 51. [CrossRef]
10. Ismail, M.; Chand, U.; Mahata, C.; Nebhen, J.; Kim, S. Demonstration of synaptic and resistive switching characteristics in W/TiO_2/HfO_2/TaN memristor crossbar array for bioinspired neuromorphic computing. *J. Mater. Sci. Technol.* **2022**, *96*, 94–102. [CrossRef]
11. Ryu, J.H.; Mahata, C.; Kim, S. Long-term and short-term plasticity of Ta_2O_5/HfO_2 memristor for hardware neuromorphic application. *J. Alloys Compd.* **2021**, *850*, 156675. [CrossRef]
12. Sboev, A.G.; Emelyanov, A.V.; Nikiruy, K.E.; Serenko, A.V.; Sitnikov, A.V.; Presnyakov, M.Y.; Rybka, R.B.; Rylkov, V.V.; Kashkarov, P.K.; Kovalchuk, M.V.; et al. Self-adaptive STDP-based learning of a spiking neuron with nanocomposite memristive weights. *Nanotechnology* **2019**, *31*, 045201. [CrossRef]
13. Prudnikov, N.V.; Lapkin, D.A.; Emelyanov, A.V.; Minnekhanov, A.A.; Malakhova, Y.N.; Chvalun, S.N.; Demin, V.A.; Erokhin, V.V. Associative STDP-like learning of neuromorphic circuits based on polyaniline memristive microdevices. *J. Phys. D Appl. Phys.* **2020**, *53*, 414001. [CrossRef]
14. Lapkin, D.A.; Emelyanov, A.V.; Demin, V.A.; Berzina, T.S.; Erokhin, V.V. Spike-timing-dependent plasticity of polyaniline-based memristive element. *Microelectron. Eng.* **2018**, *185–186*, 43–47. [CrossRef]
15. Demin, V.; Nekhaev, D.; Surazhevsky, I.; Nikiruy, K.; Emelyanov, A.; Nikolaev, S.; Rylkov, V.; Kovalchuk, M. Necessary conditions for STDP-based pattern recognition learning in a memristive spiking neural network. *Neural Netw.* **2021**, *134*, 64–75. [CrossRef]

16. Minnekhanov, A.A.; Shvetsov, B.S.; Martyshov, M.M.; Nikiruy, K.E.; Kukueva, E.V.; Presnyakov, M.Y.; Forsh, P.A.; Rylkov, V.V.; Erokhin, V.V.; Demin, V.A.; et al. On the resistive switching mechanism of parylene-based memristive devices. *Org. Electron.* **2019**, *74*, 89–95. [CrossRef]
17. Serrano-Gotarredona, T.; Masquelier, T.; Prodromakis, T.; Indiveri, G.; Linares-Barranco, B. STDP and STDP variations with memristors for spiking neuromorphic learning systems. *Front. Neurosci.* **2013**, *7*, 2. [CrossRef]
18. Du, N.; Kiani, M.; Mayr, C.; You, T.; Bürger, D.; Skorupa, I.; Schmidt, O.; Schmidt, H. Single pairing spike-timing dependent plasticity in BiFeO$_3$ memristors with a time window of 25 ms to 125 µs. *Front. Neurosci.* **2015**, *9*, 227. [CrossRef]
19. Qu, L.; Zhao, Z.; Wang, L.; Wang, Y. Efficient and hardware-friendly methods to implement competitive learning for spiking neural networks. *Neural Comput. Appl.* **2020**, *32*, 13479–13490. [CrossRef]
20. Wang, Z.; Joshi, S.; Savel'ev, S.; Song, W.; Midya, R.; Li, Y.; Rao, M.; Yan, P.; Asapu, S.; Zhuo, Y.; et al. Fully memristive neural networks for pattern classification with unsupervised learning. *Nat. Electron.* **2018**, *1*, 137–145. [CrossRef]
21. Pedretti, G.; Milo, V.; Ambrogio, S.; Carboni, R.; Bianchi, S.; Calderoni, A.; Ramaswamy, N.; Spinelli, A.; Ielmini, D. Memristive neural network for on-line learning and tracking with brain-inspired spike timing dependent plasticity. *Sci. Rep.* **2017**, *7*, 1–10. [CrossRef]
22. Burkitt, A.N. A review of the integrate-and-fire neuron model: II. Inhomogeneous synaptic input and network properties. *Biol. Cybern.* **2006**, *95*, 97–112. [CrossRef]
23. Bi, G.Q.; Poo, M.M. Synaptic modification by correlated activity: Hebb's postulate revisited. *Annu. Rev. Neurosci.* **2001**, *24*, 139–166. [CrossRef]
24. Diehl, P.U.; Cook, M. Unsupervised learning of digit recognition using Spike-Timing-Dependent Plasticity. *Front. Comput. Neurosci.* **2015**, *9*, 99. [CrossRef]
25. Morrison, A.; Diesmann, M.; Gerstner, W. Phenomenological models of synaptic plasticity based on spike timing. *Biol. Cybern.* **2008**, *98*, 459–478. [CrossRef]
26. Querlioz, D.; Dollfus, P.; Bichler, O.; Gamrat, C. Learning with memristive devices: How should we model their behavior? In Proceedings of the 2011 IEEE/ACM International Symposium on Nanoscale Architectures, San Diego, CA, USA, 8–9 June 2011; pp. 150–156. [CrossRef]
27. Gerstner, W. A framework for spiking neuron models: The spike response model. *Handb. Biol. Phys.* **2001**, *4*, 469–516.
28. Gerstner, W.; Kistler, W.M. *Spiking Neuron Models: Single Neurons, Populations, Plasticity*; Cambridge University Press: Cambridge, UK, 2002.
29. Kunkel, S.; Morrison, A.; Weidel, P.; Eppler, J.M.; Sinha, A.; Schenck, W.; Schmidt, M.; Vennemo, S.B.; Jordan, J.; Peyser, A.; et al. NEST 2.12.0. 2017. Available online: https://doi.org/10.5281/zenodo.259534 (accessed on 13 October 2021).
30. Gütig, R.; Sompolinsky, H. The tempotron: A neuron that learns spike timing-based decisions. *Nat. Neurosci.* **2006**, *9*, 420–428. [CrossRef]
31. Yu, Q.; Tang, H.; Tan, K.C.; Yu, H. A brain-inspired spiking neural network model with temporal encoding and learning. *Neurocomputing* **2014**, *138*, 3–13. [CrossRef]
32. Wang, X.; Hou, Z.G.; Lv, F.; Tan, M.; Wang, Y. Mobile robots' modular navigation controller using spiking neural networks. *Neurocomputing* **2014**, *134*, 230–238. [CrossRef]
33. Barto, A.G.; Sutton, R.S.; Anderson, C.W. Neuronlike adaptive elements that can solve difficult learning control problems. *IEEE Trans. Syst. Man Cybern.* **1983**, *SMC-13*, 834–846. [CrossRef]
34. Masquelier, T.; Guyonneau, R.; Thorpe, S.J. Spike Timing Dependent Plasticity finds the start of repeating patterns in continuous spike trains. *PLoS ONE* **2008**, *3*, e1377. [CrossRef]

Article

Highly Dispersive Optical Solitons with Complex Ginzburg–Landau Equation Having Six Nonlinear Forms

Elsayed M. E. Zayed [1,†], Khaled A. Gepreel [1,2,†], Mahmoud El-Horbaty [1,†], Anjan Biswas [3,4,5,6,7,*,†], Yakup Yıldırım [8,†] and Hashim M. Alshehri [4,†]

- [1] Mathematics Department, Faculty of Sciences, Zagazig University, Zagazig 44519, Egypt; eme_zayed@yahoo.com (E.M.E.Z.); k.gepreel@tu.edu.sa (K.A.G.); mahmoudelhorbaty8@gmail.com (M.E.-H.)
- [2] Mathematics Department, Faculty of Sciences, Taif University, Taif 21944, Saudi Arabia
- [3] Department of Applied Mathematics, National Research Nuclear University, 31 Kashirskoe Hwy, 115409 Moscow, Russia
- [4] Mathematical Modeling and Applied Computation (MMAC) Research Group, Department of Mathematics, King Abdulaziz University, Jeddah 21589, Saudi Arabia; hmalshehri@kau.edu.sa
- [5] Department of Applied Sciences, Cross-Border Faculty, Dunarea de Jos University of Galati, 111 Domneasca Street, 800201 Galati, Romania
- [6] Department of Mathematics and Applied Mathematics, Sefako Makgatho Health Sciences University, Ga-Rankuwa 0204, South Africa
- [7] Department of Physics, Chemistry and Mathematics, Alabama A&M University, Huntsville, AL 35762 4900, USA
- [8] Department of Mathematics, Faculty of Arts and Sciences, Near East University, Nicosia 99138, Cyprus; yakupyildirim110@gmail.com
- * Correspondence: biswas.anjan@gmail.com
- † These authors contributed equally to this work.

Abstract: This paper retrieves highly dispersive optical solitons to complex Ginzburg–Landau equation having six forms of nonlinear refractive index structures for the very first time. The enhanced version of the Kudryashov approach is the adopted integration tool. Thus, bright and singular soliton solutions emerge from the scheme that are exhibited with their respective parameter constraints.

Keywords: solitons; refractive index; Kudryashov

1. Introduction

The physics and technology of optical solitons in telecommunications industry has totally revolutionized the modern world of quantum communications. The dynamics of soliton propagation through a variety of waveguides [1–3], as well as the modern study of meta-optics covers it all. Later, the concept of highly dispersive (HD) optical solitons [4–8] that was conceived during 2019 has theoretically addressed a growing problem in the modern telecommunications industry. This is the low count of chromatic dispersion (CD) that is a key element in sustaining the much needed balance between it and the self-phase modulation (SPM). HD solitons provide additional sources of dispersion to maintain this key balance between CD and SPM for the smooth propel of solitons through optical fibers for trans-continental and trans-oceanic distances. These additional sources of dispersion are from inter-modal dispersion (IMD), third-order dispersion (3OD), fourth-order dispersion (4OD), fifth-order dispersion (5OD), and sixth-order dispersion (6OD). These lead to the concept of HD solitons although, technically, dispersive effects would dominate the soliton propagation. Another shortcoming would be the drastic slow-down of solitons with such a collective dispersive count.

When HD solitons first came into existence, it was on the platform of nonlinear Schrödinger's equation (NLSE) [9–12]. After the concept of HD solitons was first reported, several works from this area have flooded a variety of journals over the last couple of years [13–17]. This, in fact, includes addressing of solitons with eighth-order dispersion.

The current paper is addressing, for the first time, HD solitons on a different platform, namely the complex Ginzburg–Landau equation (CGLE) [18–26]. There are six forms of nonlinear refractive index structures that are considered. The integration scheme is the enhanced Kudryashov approach that reveals bright and singular optical solitons for each of these six nonlinear forms. These are exhibited and their respective parameter constraint conditions are also displayed. The detailed analysis are pen-pictured after a quick intro to the model.

Governing Model

The perturbed HD–CGLE that is considered for the very first time in this paper is indicated below

$$iq_t + ia_1 q_x + a_2 q_{xx} + ia_3 q_{xxx} + a_4 q_{xxxx} + ia_5 q_{xxxxx} + a_6 q_{xxxxxx} + F(|q|^2) q$$
$$= \alpha \frac{|q_x|^2}{q^*} + \frac{\beta}{4|q|^2 q^*} \left\{ 2|q|^2 \left(|q|^2\right)_{xx} - \left[\left(|q|^2\right)_x\right]^2 \right\}$$
$$+ \gamma q + i \left[\lambda \left(|q|^{2m} q\right)_x + \mu \left(|q|^{2m}\right)_x q + v|q|^{2m} q_x \right], \tag{1}$$

where $q = q(x,t)$ denotes the wave profile and q^* represents the complex conjugate of the field $q = q(x,t)$, while t and x represents temporal and spatial variables, sequentially. a_j ($j = 1,2,\cdots,6$) are the coefficients of IMD, CD, 3OD, 4OD, 5OD, and 6OD. The first term is linear temporal evolution and $i = \sqrt{-1}$. γ gives the detuning effect. λ is the coefficient of self–steepening. μ is the coefficient of higher-order dispersion. v is the coefficient of nonlinear dispersion. β and α are the coefficients of nonlinear term. Lastly, $F(|q|^2)$ stands for nonlinear form.

Equation (1) is a generalized version of the perturbed CGLE [27–31]

$$iq_t + iaq_{xxx} + F(|q|^2) q = \alpha \frac{|q_x|^2}{q^*} + \frac{\beta}{4|q|^2 q^*} \left\{ 2|q|^2 \left(|q|^2\right)_{xx} - \left[\left(|q|^2\right)_x\right]^2 \right\}$$
$$+ \gamma q + i \left[\delta q_x + \lambda \left(|q|^{2m} q\right)_x + \mu \left(|q|^{2m}\right)_x q + v|q|^{2m} q_x \right]. \tag{2}$$

This paper studies the perturbed HD–CGLE (1) with six nonlinear forms using the integration methodology. The current paper is structured as: In Section 2, the perturbed HD–CGLE (1) is analyzed. In Section 3, the integration methodology is presented. In Sections 4–9, we arrive soliton solutions with the proposed models. The results of the paper are discussed in Section 10.

2. Mathematical Preliminaries

We presume the traveling wave transformation

$$q(x,t) = \phi(\xi) e^{i(-\kappa x + wt + \theta_0)}, \quad \xi = x - ct, \tag{3}$$

where $\phi(\xi)$ is the amplitude of the traveling wave, κ is the frequency, c is the velocity, w is the wave number and θ_0 is the phase constant. Substituting (3) into (1) gives the real part

$$a_6 \phi \phi^{(6)} + \left(5 a_5 \kappa + a_4 - 15 a_6 \kappa^2\right) \phi \phi^{(4)}$$
$$+ \left(15 a_6 \kappa^4 - 10 a_5 \kappa^3 - 6 a_4 \kappa^2 + 3 a_3 \kappa + a_2 - \beta\right) \phi \phi''$$
$$- \alpha (\phi')^2 - \phi^2 \left[a_6 \kappa^6 - a_5 \kappa^5 - a_4 \kappa^4 + a_3 \kappa^3 + (\alpha + a_2) \kappa^2 - a_1 \kappa + \gamma + w\right]$$
$$- \kappa (v + \lambda) \phi^{2m+2} + F(\phi^2) \phi^2 = 0, \tag{4}$$

and the imaginary part

$$[6a_6\kappa - a_5]\phi^{(5)} + \left(6a_6\kappa^5 - 4a_4\kappa^3 - 5a_5\kappa^4 + 2a_2\kappa + 3a_3\kappa^2 - a_1 + c\right)\phi'$$
$$+ \phi^{2m}\phi'(2m\lambda + 2m\mu + \lambda + v) + \phi'''\left(-20a_6\kappa^3 + 10a_5\kappa^2 + 4a_4\kappa - a_3\right) = 0. \quad (5)$$

Equation (5) yields the velocity

$$c = -6a_6\kappa^5 + 4a_4\kappa^3 + 5a_5\kappa^4 - 2a_2\kappa - 3a_3\kappa^2 + a_1, \quad (6)$$

and the frequency

$$\kappa = \frac{a_5}{6a_6}, \quad (7)$$

and the constraint conditions

$$2m\lambda + 2m\mu + \lambda + v = 0, \quad -20a_6\kappa^3 + 10a_5\kappa^2 + 4a_4\kappa - a_3 = 0. \quad (8)$$

Equation (4) can be written as

$$\phi\phi^{(6)} + \Delta_1 \phi\phi^{(4)} + \Delta_2 \phi\phi'' + \Delta_3(\phi')^2 + \Delta_4 \phi^2 + \Delta_5 \phi^{2m+2} + F\left(\phi^2\right)\phi^2 = 0, \quad (9)$$

where

$$\Delta_1 = \frac{5a_5\kappa + a_4 - 15a_6\kappa^2}{a_6}, \quad \Delta_5 = -\frac{\kappa(v+\lambda)}{a_6}, \quad \Delta_3 = -\frac{\alpha}{a_6},$$

$$\Delta_2 = \frac{15a_6\kappa^4 - 10a_5\kappa^3 - 6a_4\kappa^2 + 3a_3\kappa + a_2 - \beta}{a_6},$$

$$\Delta_4 = -\frac{a_3\kappa^3 - a_5\kappa^5 + a_6\kappa^6 - a_4\kappa^4 + (a_2+\alpha)\kappa^2 + \gamma - a_1\kappa + w}{a_6}. \quad (10)$$

3. Enhanced Kudryashov Method

The integration approach permits the formal solution

$$\phi(\xi) = \sum_{g=0}^{N} \sigma_g [R(\xi)]^g, \quad \sigma_g \neq 0, \quad (11)$$

where N is the order of the pole, σ_g ($g = 0, 1, 2, \cdots, N$) are arbitrary constants and $R(\xi)$ satisfies the ordinary differential equation

$$R'^2(\xi) = R^2(\xi)[1 - \chi R^{2p}(\xi)] \ln^2 K, \quad 0 < K \neq 1, \quad (12)$$

along with the analytical solution

$$R(\xi) = \left[\frac{4A}{4A^2 \exp_K(p\xi) + \chi \exp_K(-p\xi)}\right]^{\frac{1}{p}}. \quad (13)$$

Here χ, p and A are non-zero real constants and $\exp_K(p\xi) = K^{p\xi}$. Plugging (11) along with (12) into (9) yields the coefficients σ_g ($g = 0, 1, 2, \cdots, N$). Substituting the coefficients σ_g ($g = 0, 1, 2, \cdots, N$) together with (13) into (11), we arrive the analytical solution of the model Equation (1).

4. Kerr Law

The Kerr law of nonlinearity is considered as

$$F(\phi^2) = e\phi^2, \quad e \neq 0, \quad (14)$$

where e is an arbitrary constant. Therefore, Equation (1) turns into

$$iq_t + ia_1 q_x + a_2 q_{xx} + ia_3 q_{xxx} + a_4 q_{xxxx} + ia_5 q_{xxxxx} + a_6 q_{xxxxxx} + e|q|^2 q$$
$$= \alpha \frac{|q_x|^2}{q^*} + \frac{\beta}{4|q|^2 q^*} \left\{ 2|q|^2 \left(|q|^2\right)_{xx} - \left[\left(|q|^2\right)_x\right]^2 \right\}$$
$$+ \gamma q + i \left[\lambda \left(|q|^{2m} q\right)_x + \mu \left(|q|^{2m}\right)_x q + v|q|^{2m} q_x \right], \qquad (15)$$

while Equation (9) simplifies to

$$\phi \phi^{(6)} + \Delta_1 \phi \phi^{(4)} + \Delta_2 \phi \phi'' + \Delta_3 (\phi')^2 + \Delta_4 \phi^2 + \Delta_5 \phi^{2m+2} + e\phi^4 = 0. \qquad (16)$$

Setting $m = 1$, Equation (16) collapses to

$$\phi \phi^{(6)} + \Delta_1 \phi \phi^{(4)} + \Delta_2 \phi \phi'' + \Delta_3 (\phi')^2 + \Delta_4 \phi^2 + (\Delta_5 + e)\phi^4 = 0. \qquad (17)$$

Balancing $\phi \phi^{(6)}$ and ϕ^4 gives rise to

$$2N + 6p = 4N \Longrightarrow N = 3p. \qquad (18)$$

<u>Case 1</u>: With the help of $p = 1$, Equation (11) turns into

$$\phi(\xi) = \sigma_0 + \sigma_1 R(\xi) + \sigma_2 R^2(\xi) + \sigma_3 R^3(\xi), \quad \sigma_3 \neq 0, \qquad (19)$$

where $\sigma_0, \sigma_1, \sigma_2$ and σ_3 are arbitrary constants. Substituting (19) along with (12) into (17) causes the coefficients to

$$\sigma_0 = \sigma_1 = \sigma_2 = 0, \quad \sigma_3 = 24\varepsilon\chi\sqrt{\frac{35\chi}{\Delta_5 + e}}\ln^3 K, \qquad (20)$$

and the constraint conditions

$$\Delta_1 = -83 \ln^2 K, \quad \Delta_3 = -\frac{\Delta_2 - 7564 \ln^4 K}{3},$$
$$\Delta_4 = \left(3\Delta_2 - 16698 \ln^4 K\right) \ln^2 K, \quad \chi(\Delta_5 + e) > 0, \quad \varepsilon = \pm 1. \qquad (21)$$

Plugging (20) together with (13) and (21) into (19), the straddled soliton is formulated as

$$q(x,t) = 24\varepsilon\chi\left(\ln^3 K\right)\sqrt{\frac{35\chi}{\Delta_5 + e}} \left[\frac{4A}{4A^2 \exp_K(x - ct) + \chi \exp_K(-(x - ct))}\right]^3$$
$$\times e^{i(-\kappa x + wt + \theta_0)}. \qquad (22)$$

By the aid of $\Delta_5 + e > 0$ and $\chi = 4A^2$, the bright soliton is indicated below

$$q(x,t) = 24\varepsilon\left(\ln^3 K\right)\sqrt{\frac{35}{\Delta_5 + e}} \operatorname{sech}^3[(x - ct)\ln K] e^{i(-\kappa x + wt + \theta_0)}. \qquad (23)$$

By the usage of $\Delta_5 + e < 0$ and $\chi = -4A^2$, the singular soliton is considered as

$$q(x,t) = 24\varepsilon\left(\ln^3 K\right)\sqrt{-\frac{35}{\Delta_5 + e}} \operatorname{csch}^3[(x - ct)\ln K] e^{i(-\kappa x + wt + \theta_0)}. \qquad (24)$$

Case 2: With the help of $p = 2$, Equation (11) transforms to

$$\phi(\xi) = \sigma_0 + \sigma_1 R(\xi) + \sigma_2 R^2(\xi) + \sigma_3 R^3(\xi) + \sigma_4 R^4(\xi) + \sigma_5 R^5(\xi) + \sigma_6 R^6(\xi), \ \sigma_6 \neq 0, \quad (25)$$

where σ_i $(i = 0, 1, \cdots, 6)$ are arbitrary constants and $R(\xi)$ changes to

$$R'^2(\xi) = R^2(\xi)\left[1 - \chi R^4(\xi)\right] \ln^2 K, \ 0 < K, \ K \neq 1. \quad (26)$$

Inserting (25) along with (26) into (17) yields the coefficients

$$\sigma_0 = \sigma_1 = \sigma_2 = \sigma_3 = \sigma_4 = \sigma_5 = 0, \ \sigma_6 = -192\varepsilon\chi\sqrt{\frac{35\chi}{\Delta_4 + e}} \ln^3 K, \quad (27)$$

and the parameter constraints

$$\Delta_1 = -332 \ln^2 K, \ \Delta_3 = -\frac{4\Delta_2 - 121024 \ln^4 K}{3},$$

$$\Delta_4 = \left(12\Delta_2 - 1068672 \ln^4 K\right) \ln^2 K, \ \chi(\Delta_5 + e) > 0, \ \varepsilon = \pm 1. \quad (28)$$

Putting (27) together with (13) and (28) into (25), the straddled soliton is structured as

$$q(x,t) = -192\varepsilon\chi\left(\ln^3 K\right)\sqrt{\frac{35\chi}{\Delta_4 + e}}\left[\frac{4A}{4A^2 \exp_K[2(x-ct)] + \chi \exp_K[2(x-ct)]}\right]^3$$

$$\times e^{i(-\kappa x + wt + \theta_0)}. \quad (29)$$

By the aid of $\Delta_5 + e > 0$ and $\chi = 4A^2$, the bright soliton is formulated as

$$q(x,t) = -192\varepsilon\left(\ln^3 K\right)\sqrt{\frac{35}{\Delta_5 + e}}\operatorname{sech}^3[2(x-ct)\ln K]e^{i(-\kappa x + wt + \theta_0)}. \quad (30)$$

By virtue of $\Delta_5 + e < 0$ and $\chi = -4A^2$, the singular soliton is indicated below

$$q(x,t) = 192\varepsilon\left(\ln^3 K\right)\sqrt{-\frac{35}{\Delta_5 + e}}\operatorname{csch}^3[2(x-ct)\ln K]e^{i(-\kappa x + wt + \theta_0)}. \quad (31)$$

5. Power Law

The power law of nonlinearity is structured as

$$F(\phi^2) = e\phi^{2n}, \ e \neq 0, \quad (32)$$

where e is an arbitrary constant. Thus, Equation (1) simplifies to

$$iq_t + ia_1 q_x + a_2 q_{xx} + ia_3 q_{xxx} + a_4 q_{xxxx} + ia_5 q_{xxxxx} + a_6 q_{xxxxxx} + e|q|^{2n} q$$

$$= \alpha\frac{|q_x|^2}{q^*} + \frac{\beta}{4|q|^2 q^*}\left\{2|q|^2\left(|q|^2\right)_{xx} - \left[\left(|q|^2\right)_x\right]^2\right\}$$

$$+ \gamma q + i\left[\lambda\left(|q|^{2m} q\right)_x + \mu\left(|q|^{2m}\right)_x q + v|q|^{2m} q_x\right], \quad (33)$$

while Equation (9) collapses to

$$\phi\phi^{(6)} + \Delta_1 \phi\phi^{(4)} + \Delta_2 \phi\phi'' + \Delta_3 (\phi')^2 + \Delta_4 \phi^2 + \Delta_5 \phi^{2m+2} + e\phi^{2n+2} = 0. \quad (34)$$

Setting $n = m$, Equation (34) transforms to

$$\phi\phi^{(6)} + \Delta_1\phi\phi^{(4)} + \Delta_2\phi\phi'' + \Delta_3(\phi')^2 + \Delta_4\phi^2 + (\Delta_5 + e)\phi^{2m+2} = 0. \tag{35}$$

Balancing $\phi\phi^{(6)}$ and ϕ^{2m+2} yields $N = \frac{3}{m}$. Setting

$$\phi = [U(\xi)]^{\frac{3}{m}}, \tag{36}$$

Equation (35) turns into

$$\begin{aligned}
& -9(m-1)(2m-3)(4m-3)(5m-3)(m-3)U'^6 \\
& + 135m(m-1)(2m-3)(4m-3)(m-3)UU''U'^4 \\
& - 9\Delta_1 m^2(m-1)(2m-3)(m-3)U^2U'^4 \\
& - 180m^2(m-1)(2m-3)(m-3)U^2U'^3U''' + \Delta_4 m^6 U^6 \\
& - 405m^2(m-1)(2m-3)(m-3)U^2U''^2U'^2 + 18\Delta_1 m^3(2m-3)(m-3)U^3U''U'^2 \\
& + 3m^5 U^5 U^{(6)} + 45m^3(2m-3)(m-3)U^3 U^{(4)} U'^2 + 3m^4[3\Delta_3 - (m-3)\Delta_2]U^4 U'^2 \\
& - 12\Delta_1 m^4(m-3)U^4 U'''U' + 180m^3(2m-3)(m-3)U^3 U''U'''U' \\
& - 18m^4(m-3)U^4 U^{(5)} U' + 45m^3(2m-3)(m-3)U^3(U''')^3 \\
& - 9\Delta_1 m^4(m-3)U^4(U'')^2 - 45m^4(m-3)U^4 U^{(4)} U'' + 3m^5\Delta_2 U^5 U'' \\
& + m^6(\Delta_5 + e)U^{12} - 30m^4(m-3)U^4(U''')^2 + 3m^5\Delta_1 U^5 U^{(4)} = 0. \tag{37}
\end{aligned}$$

Balancing $U^5 U^{(6)}$ and U^{12} leads to

$$6N + 6p = 12N \implies N = p. \tag{38}$$

Case 1: By virtue of $p = 1$, Equation (11) collapses to

$$U(\xi) = \sigma_0 + \sigma_1 R(\xi), \quad \sigma_1 \neq 0, \tag{39}$$

where σ_0 and σ_1 are arbitrary constants. Plugging (39) along with (12) into (37), we arrive the coefficients

$$\sigma_0 = 0, \quad \sigma_1 = \frac{\epsilon \ln K}{m}\left(\frac{9(4m+3)(5m+3)(2m+3)(m+3)(m+1)\chi^3}{\Delta_5 + e}\right)^{\frac{1}{6}}, \tag{40}$$

and the parameter constraints

$$\Delta_1 = -\frac{(20m^2 + 36m + 27)\ln^2 K}{m^2}, \quad \chi^3(\Delta_5 + e) > 0,$$

$$\Delta_3 = -\frac{\left(\begin{array}{c}64m^5 + 480m^4 + 1512m^3 \\ +2592m^2 + 2187m + 729\end{array}\right)\ln^4 K}{3m^4} - \frac{(m+3)\Delta_2}{3},$$

$$\Delta_4 = -\frac{3\left(\begin{array}{c}64m^5 + 480m^4 + 1512m^3 \\ +2052m^2 + 1215m + 243\end{array}\right)\ln^6 K}{m^6} + \frac{3\Delta_2 \ln^2 K}{m}. \tag{41}$$

Inserting (40) together with (13) and (41) into (39), the straddled soliton is modeled as

$$q(x,t) = \left\{ \frac{4\epsilon A \left(\frac{9(4m+3)(2m+3)(5m+3)(m+1)(m+3)\chi^3}{\Delta_5 + e} \right)^{\frac{1}{6}} \ln K}{m[4A^2 \exp_K(x-ct) + \chi \exp_K(-(x-ct))]} \right\}^{\frac{3}{m}}$$

$$\times e^{i(-\kappa x + wt + \theta_0)}. \tag{42}$$

By the usage of $\Delta_5 + e > 0$ and $\chi = 4A^2$, the bright soliton is structured as

$$q(x,t) = \left\{ \frac{4\epsilon \ln K}{m} \left(\frac{9(4m+3)(2m+3)(5m+3)(m+1)(m+3)}{\Delta_5 + e} \right)^{\frac{1}{6}} \times \operatorname{sech}[(x-ct)\ln K] \right\}^{\frac{3}{m}}$$

$$\times e^{i(-\kappa x + wt + \theta_0)}. \tag{43}$$

With the help of $\Delta_5 + e < 0$ and $\chi = -4A^2$, the singular soliton is indicated below

$$q(x,t) = \left\{ \frac{4\epsilon \ln K}{m} \left(-\frac{9(4m+3)(2m+3)(5m+3)(m+1)(m+3)}{\Delta_5 + e} \right)^{\frac{1}{6}} \times \operatorname{csch}[(x-ct)\ln K] \right\}^{\frac{3}{m}}$$

$$\times e^{i(-\kappa x + wt + \theta_0)}. \tag{44}$$

<u>Case 2</u>: By virtue of $p=2$, Equation (11) becomes

$$U(\xi) = \sigma_0 + \sigma_1 R(\xi) + \sigma_2 R^2(\xi), \quad \sigma_2 \neq 0, \tag{45}$$

where σ_0, σ_1 and σ_2 are arbitrary constants. Putting (45) along with (12) into (37) causes to the coefficients

$$\sigma_0 = \sigma_1 = 0, \quad \sigma_2 = \frac{2\epsilon \ln K}{m} \left(\frac{9(4m+3)(2m+3)(5m+3)(m+1)(m+3)\chi^3}{\Delta_5 + e} \right)^{\frac{1}{6}}, \tag{46}$$

and the constraints

$$\Delta_1 = -\frac{4(20m^2 + 36m + 27)\ln^2 K}{m^2}, \quad \chi^3(\Delta_5 + e) > 0,$$

$$\Delta_3 = \frac{16 \left(\begin{array}{c} 64m^5 + 480m^4 + 1512m^3 \\ +2592m^2 + 2187m + 729 \end{array} \right) \ln^4 K}{3m^4} - \frac{(m+3)\Delta_2}{3},$$

$$\Delta_4 = -\frac{192 \left(\begin{array}{c} 64m^5 + 480m^4 + 1512m^3 \\ +2052m^2 + 1215m + 243 \end{array} \right) \ln^6 K}{m^6} + \frac{12\Delta_2 \ln^2 K}{m}. \tag{47}$$

Plugging (46) together with (13) and (47) into (45), the straddled soliton is considered as

$$q(x,t) = \left\{ \frac{8\epsilon A \ln K \left(\frac{9(4m+3)(2m+3)(5m+3)(m+1)(m+3)\chi^3}{e + \Delta_5} \right)^{\frac{1}{6}}}{m[4A^2 \exp_K[2(x-ct)] + \chi \exp_K[-2(x-ct)]]} \right\}^{\frac{3}{m}}$$

$$\times e^{i(-\kappa x + wt + \theta_0)}. \tag{48}$$

By the usage of $\Delta_5 + e > 0$ and $\chi = 4A^2$, the bright soliton is modeled as

$$q(x,t) = \left\{ \frac{2\epsilon \ln K}{m} \left(\frac{9(4m+3)(5m+3)(2m+3)(m+3)(m+1)}{e+\Delta_5} \right)^{\frac{1}{6}} \times \text{sech}[2\ln K(x-ct)] \right\}^{\frac{3}{m}}$$
$$\times e^{i(-\kappa x + wt + \theta_0)}. \tag{49}$$

With the help of $\Delta_5 + e < 0$ and $\chi = -4A^2$, the singular soliton is formulated as

$$q(x,t) = \left\{ \frac{2\epsilon \ln K}{m} \left(-\frac{9(4m+3)(5m+3)(2m+3)(m+3)(m+1)}{e+\Delta_5} \right)^{\frac{1}{6}} \times \text{csch}[2\ln K(x-ct)] \right\}^{\frac{3}{m}}$$
$$\times e^{i(-\kappa x + wt + \theta_0)}. \tag{50}$$

6. Parabolic Law

The parabolic law of nonlinearity is indicated below

$$F(\phi^2) = e_1\phi^2 + e_2\phi^4, \ e_2 \neq 0, \tag{51}$$

where e_1 and e_2 are arbitrary constants. Consequently, Equation (1) turns into

$$iq_t + ia_1 q_x + a_2 q_{xx} + ia_3 q_{xxx} + a_4 q_{xxxx} + ia_5 q_{xxxxx} + a_6 q_{xxxxxx}$$
$$+ \left(e_1|q|^2 + e_2|q|^4\right)q = \alpha \frac{|q_x|^2}{q^*} + \frac{\beta}{4|q|^2 q^*}\left\{2|q|^2\left(|q|^2\right)_{xx} - \left[\left(|q|^2\right)_x\right]^2\right\}$$
$$+ \gamma q + i\left[\lambda\left(|q|^{2m}q\right)_x + \mu\left(|q|^{2m}\right)_x q + v|q|^{2m}q_x\right], \tag{52}$$

while Equation (9) decreases to

$$\phi\phi^{(6)} + \Delta_1\phi\phi^{(4)} + \Delta_2\phi\phi'' + \Delta_3(\phi')^2 + \Delta_4\phi^2 + \Delta_5\phi^{2m+2} + e_1\phi^4 + e_2\phi^6 = 0. \tag{53}$$

Setting $m = 1$, Equation (53) becomes

$$\phi\phi^{(6)} + \Delta_1\phi\phi^{(4)} + \Delta_2\phi\phi'' + \Delta_3(\phi')^2 + \Delta_4\phi^2 + (\Delta_5 + e_1)\phi^4 + e_2\phi^6 = 0. \tag{54}$$

Balancing $\phi\phi^{(6)}$ and ϕ^6 causes to $N = \frac{3}{2}$. Setting

$$\phi(\xi) = [U(\xi)]^{\frac{3}{2}}, \tag{55}$$

Equation (54) collapses to

$$315[U']^6 + 36\Delta_1 U^2 U'^4 - 1350 U U'' U'^4 + 720 U^2 U'^3 U''' + 1620 U^2 U''^2 U'^2$$
$$- 144\Delta_1 U^3 U'' U'^2 - 360 U^3 U^{(4)} U'^2 + 48[3\Delta_3 + \Delta_2] U^4 U'^2 + 192\Delta_1 U^4 U''' U'$$
$$+ 288 U^4 U^{(5)} U' - 1440 U^3 U''' U'' U' - 360 U^3 (U'')^3 + 144\Delta_1 U^4 (U'')^2$$
$$+ 96\Delta_2 U^5 U'' + 720 U^4 U^{(4)} U'' + 480 U^4 (U''')^2 + 96\Delta_1 U^5 U^{(4)} + 96 U^5 U^{(6)}$$
$$+ 64 e_2 U^{12} + 64(e_1 + \Delta_5) U^9 + 64\Delta_4 U^6 = 0. \tag{56}$$

Balancing $U^5 U^{(6)}$ and U^{12} gives rise to

$$6N + 6p = 12N \implies N = p. \tag{57}$$

Case 1: By the usage of $p = 1$, Equation (56) permits the solution (39). Substituting (39) along with (12) into (56) gives rise to the coefficients

$$\sigma_0 = 0, \ \sigma_1 = \left(\frac{135135\chi^3}{64e_2}\right)^{\frac{1}{6}} \ln K, \tag{58}$$

and the parameters

$$\Delta_1 = -\frac{179 \ln^2 K}{4}, \ \Delta_3 = \frac{37295 \ln^4 K}{48} - \frac{5\Delta_2}{3},$$

$$\Delta_4 = -\frac{98115 \ln^6 K}{64} + \frac{3\Delta_2 \ln^2 K}{2}, \ \Delta_5 = -e_1, \ \chi^3 e_2 > 0. \tag{59}$$

Plugging (58) together with (13) and (59) into (39), we arrive the straddled soliton

$$q(x,t) = \left\{\frac{4A\left(\frac{135135\chi^3}{64e_2}\right)^{\frac{1}{6}} \ln K}{4A^2 \exp_K(x-ct) + \chi \exp_K(-(x-ct))}\right\}^{\frac{3}{2}} e^{i(-\kappa x + wt + \theta_0)}. \tag{60}$$

Setting $e_2 > 0$ and $\chi = 4A^2$, Equation (60) transforms to the bright soliton

$$q(x,t) = \left\{(\ln K)\left(\frac{135135}{64e_2}\right)^{\frac{1}{6}} \text{sech}[(x-ct)\ln K]\right\}^{\frac{3}{2}} e^{i(-\kappa x + wt + \theta_0)}. \tag{61}$$

If $e_2 < 0$ and $\chi = -4A^2$, Equation (60) yields the singular soliton

$$q(x,t) = \left\{(\ln K)\left(-\frac{135135}{64e_2}\right)^{\frac{1}{6}} \text{csch}[(x-ct)\ln K]\right\}^{\frac{3}{2}} e^{i(-\kappa x + wt + \theta_0)}. \tag{62}$$

Case 2: By the aid of $p = 2$, Equation (56) holds the solution (45). Substituting (45) along with (12) into (56) leads to the coefficients

$$\sigma_0 = \sigma_1 = 0, \ \sigma_2 = \left(\frac{135135\chi^3}{e_2}\right)^{\frac{1}{6}} \ln K, \tag{63}$$

and the constraints

$$\Delta_1 = -179 \ln^2 K, \ \Delta_3 = \frac{37295 \ln^4 K}{3} - \frac{5\Delta_2}{3},$$

$$\Delta_4 = \left(6\Delta_2 - 98115 \ln^4 K\right) \ln^2 K, \ \Delta_5 = -e_1, \ \chi^3 e_2 > 0. \tag{64}$$

Inserting (63) together with (13) and (64) into (45), the straddled soliton is formulated as

$$q(x,t) = \left\{\frac{4A\left(\frac{135135\chi^3}{e_2}\right)^{\frac{1}{6}} \ln K}{4A^2 \exp_K[2(x-ct)] + \chi \exp_K[-2(x-ct)]}\right\}^{\frac{3}{2}} e^{i(-\kappa x + wt + \theta_0)}. \tag{65}$$

If $e_2 > 0$ and $\chi = 4A^2$, Equation (65) becomes the bright soliton

$$q(x,t) = \left\{ (\ln K) \left(\frac{135135}{e_2} \right)^{\frac{1}{6}} \operatorname{sech}[2 \ln K(x-ct)] \right\}^{\frac{3}{2}} e^{i(-\kappa x + wt + \theta_0)}. \tag{66}$$

When $e_2 < 0$ and $\chi = -4A^2$, Equation (65) turns into the singular soliton

$$q(x,t) = \left\{ (\ln K) \left(-\frac{135135}{e_2} \right)^{\frac{1}{6}} \operatorname{csch}[2 \ln K(x-ct)] \right\}^{\frac{3}{2}} e^{i(-\kappa x + wt + \theta_0)}. \tag{67}$$

7. Dual Power Law

The dual power law of nonlinearity is considered as

$$F(\phi^2) = e_1 \phi^{2n} + e_2 \phi^{4n}, \quad e_2 \neq 0, \tag{68}$$

where e_1 and e_2 are arbitrary constants. Hence, Equation (1) simplifies to

$$iq_t + ia_1 q_x + a_2 q_{xx} + ia_3 q_{xxx} + a_4 q_{xxxx} + ia_5 q_{xxxxx} + a_6 q_{xxxxxx}$$
$$+ \left(e_1 |q|^{2n} + e_2 |q|^{4n} \right) q = \alpha \frac{|q_x|^2}{q^*} + \frac{\beta}{4|q|^2 q^*} \left\{ 2|q|^2 \left(|q|^2 \right)_{xx} - \left[\left(|q|^2 \right)_x \right]^2 \right\}$$
$$+ \gamma q + i \left[\lambda \left(|q|^{2m} q \right)_x + \mu \left(|q|^{2m} \right)_x q + v |q|^{2m} q_x \right], \tag{69}$$

while Equation (9) collapses to

$$\phi \phi^{(6)} + \Delta_1 \phi \phi^{(4)} + \Delta_2 \phi \phi'' + \Delta_3 (\phi')^2 + \Delta_4 \phi^2 + \Delta_5 \phi^{2m+2} + e_1 \phi^{2n+2} + e_2 \phi^{4n+2} = 0. \tag{70}$$

Setting $n = m$, Equation (70) decreases to

$$\phi \phi^{(6)} + \Delta_1 \phi \phi^{(4)} + \Delta_2 \phi \phi'' + \Delta_3 (\phi')^2 + \Delta_4 \phi^2 + (\Delta_5 + e_1) \phi^{2m+2} + e_2 \phi^{4m+2} = 0. \tag{71}$$

Balancing $\phi \phi^{(6)}$ and ϕ^{4m+2} gives $N = \frac{3}{2m}$. Setting

$$\phi(\xi) = [U(\xi)]^{\frac{3}{2m}}, \tag{72}$$

Equation (71) turns into

$$-9(2m-3)(2m-1)(4m-3)(10m-3)[U']^6$$
$$+ 270m(2m-3)(2m-1)(8m-3)(4m-3)UU''U'^4$$
$$- 36m^2(2m-3)(4m-3)(2m-1)\Delta_1 U^2 U'^4$$
$$- 720m^2(2m-3)(2m-1)(4m-3)U^2 U'^3 U'''$$
$$- 1620m^2(2m-1)(2m-3)(4m-3)U^2 U''^2 U'^2$$
$$+ 144\Delta_1 m^3 (2m-3)(4m-3)U^3 U'' U'^2$$
$$+ 360m^3(2m-3)(4m-3)U^3 U^{(4)} U'^2 - 48m^4[(2m-3)\Delta_2 - 3\Delta_3]U^4 U'^2$$
$$+ 1440m^3(2m-3)(4m-3)U^3 U''' U'' U' - 192\Delta_1 m^4(2m-3)U^4 U''' U'$$
$$- 288m^4(2m-3)U^4 U^{(5)} U' + 360m^3(2m-3)(4m-3)U^3(U'')^3$$
$$- 144\Delta_1 m^4(2m-3)U^4(U'')^2 - 720m^4(2m-3)U^4 U^{(4)} U''$$
$$+ 96m^5\Delta_2 U^5 U'' - 480m^4(2m-3)U^4(U''')^2 + 96m^5\Delta_1 U^5 U^{(4)}$$
$$+ 96m^5 U^5 U^{(6)} + 64m^6 e_2 U^{12} + 64m^6(e_1 + \Delta_5)U^9 + 64m^6\Delta_4 U^6 = 0. \quad (73)$$

Balancing $U^5 U^{(6)}$ and U^{12} leads to

$$6N + 6p = 12N \Longrightarrow N = p. \quad (74)$$

<u>Case 1</u>: By the usage of $p = 1$, Equation (73) satisfies the solution (39). Putting (39) along with (12) into (73), we arrive the coefficients

$$\sigma_0 = 0, \ \sigma_1 = \frac{\ln K}{m}\left(\frac{9\chi^3(8m+3)(4m+3)(10m+3)(2m+3)(2m+1)}{64e_2}\right)^{\frac{1}{6}}, \quad (75)$$

and the constraints

$$\Delta_1 = -\frac{(80m^2 + 72m + 27)\ln^2 K}{4m^2}, \ \Delta_5 = -e_1, \ \chi^3 e_2 > 0,$$

$$\Delta_3 = \frac{\left(\begin{array}{c}2048m^5 + 7680m^4 + 12096m^3 \\ +10368m^2 + 4374m + 729\end{array}\right)\ln^4 K}{48m^4} - \frac{(2m+3)\Delta_2}{3},$$

$$\Delta_4 = -\frac{3\left(\begin{array}{c}2048m^5 + 7680m^4 + 12096m^3 \\ +8208m^2 + 2430m + 243\end{array}\right)\ln^6 K}{64m^6} + \frac{3\Delta_2}{2m}\ln^2 K. \quad (76)$$

Inserting (75) together with (13) and (76) into (39), we arrive the straddled soliton

$$q(x,t) = \left\{\frac{4A\left(\frac{9\chi^3(8m+3)(4m+3)(10m+3)(2m+3)(2m+1)}{64e_2}\right)^{\frac{1}{6}} \ln K}{m[4A^2 \exp_K(x-ct) + \chi \exp_K(-(x-ct))]}\right\}^{\frac{3}{2m}}$$

$$\times e^{i(-\kappa x + wt + \theta_0)}. \quad (77)$$

By virtue of $e_2 > 0$ and $\chi = 4A^2$, Equation (77) simplifies to the bright soliton

$$q(x,t) = \left\{ \frac{\ln K}{m} \left(\frac{9(8m+3)(4m+3)(10m+3)(2m+3)(2m+1)}{64e_2} \right)^{\frac{1}{6}} \times \text{sech}[(x-ct)\ln K] \right\}^{\frac{3}{2m}}$$
$$\times e^{i(-\kappa x + wt + \theta_0)}. \tag{78}$$

By the aid of $e_2 < 0$ and $\chi = -4A^2$, Equation (77) collapses to the singular soliton

$$q(x,t) = \left\{ \frac{\ln K}{m} \left(-\frac{9(8m+3)(4m+3)(10m+3)(2m+3)(2m+1)}{64e_2} \right)^{\frac{1}{6}} \times \text{csch}[(x-ct)\ln K] \right\}^{\frac{3}{2m}}$$
$$\times e^{i(-\kappa x + wt + \theta_0)}. \tag{79}$$

Case 2: With the help of $p = 2$, Equation (73) presumes the solution (45). Plugging (45) along with (12) into (73) yields the coefficients

$$\sigma_0 = \sigma_1 = 0, \ \sigma_2 = \frac{\ln K}{m} \left(\frac{9\chi^3(8m+3)(4m+3)(10m+3)(2m+3)(2m+1)}{e_2} \right)^{\frac{1}{6}}, \tag{80}$$

and the conditions

$$\Delta_1 = -\frac{(80m^2 + 72m + 27)\ln^2 K}{m^2}, \ \Delta_5 = -e_1, \ \chi^3 e_2 > 0,$$

$$\Delta_3 = \frac{\left(\begin{array}{c} 2048m^5 + 7680m^4 + 12096m^3 \\ +10368m^2 + 4374m + 729 \end{array} \right) \ln^4 K}{3m^4} - \frac{(2m+3)\Delta_2}{3},$$

$$\Delta_4 = -\frac{3\left(\begin{array}{c} 2048m^5 + 7680m^4 + 12096m^3 \\ +8208m^2 + 2430m + 243 \end{array} \right) \ln^6 K}{m^6} + \frac{6\Delta_2}{m} \ln^2 K. \tag{81}$$

Substituting (80) together with (13) and (81) into (45), we attain the straddled soliton

$$q(x,t) = \left\{ \frac{4A \left(\frac{9\chi^3(4m+3)(8m+3)(2m+3)(10m+3)(2m+1)}{e_2} \right)^{\frac{1}{6}} \ln K}{m[4A^2 \exp_K[2(x-ct)] + \chi \exp_K[-2(x-ct)]]} \right\}^{\frac{3}{2m}}$$
$$\times e^{i(-\kappa x + wt + \theta_0)}. \tag{82}$$

With the help of $e_2 > 0$ and $\chi = 4A^2$, Equation (82) changes to the bright soliton

$$q(x,t) = \left\{ \frac{\ln K}{m} \left(\frac{9(8m+3)(4m+3)(10m+3)(2m+3)(2m+1)}{e_2} \right)^{\frac{1}{6}} \times \text{sech}[2\ln K(x-ct)] \right\}^{\frac{3}{2m}}$$
$$\times e^{i(-\kappa x + wt + \theta_0)}. \tag{83}$$

By the aid of $e_2 < 0$ and $\chi = -4A^2$, Equation (82) collapses to the singular soliton

$$q(x,t) = \left\{ \frac{\ln K}{m} \left(-\frac{9(8m+3)(4m+3)(10m+3)(2m+3)(2m+1)}{e_2} \right)^{\frac{1}{6}} \right\}^{\frac{3}{2m}}$$
$$\times \text{csch}[2\ln K(x-ct)]$$
$$\times e^{i(-\kappa x + wt + \theta_0)}. \tag{84}$$

8. Polynomial Law

The polynomial law of nonlinearity is modeled as

$$F(\phi^2) = e_1\phi^2 + e_2\phi^4 + e_3\phi^6, \; e_3 \neq 0, \tag{85}$$

where e_1, e_2 and e_3 are arbitrary constants. Therefore, Equation (1) simplifies to

$$iq_t + ia_1q_x + a_2q_{xx} + ia_3q_{xxx} + a_4q_{xxxx} + ia_5q_{xxxxx} + a_6q_{xxxxxx}$$
$$+ \left(e_1|q|^2 + e_2|q|^4 + e_3|q|^6\right)q = \alpha\frac{|q_x|^2}{q^*} + \frac{\beta}{4|q|^2 q^*}\left\{2|q|^2\left(|q|^2\right)_{xx} - \left[\left(|q|^2\right)_x\right]^2\right\}$$
$$+ \gamma q + i\left[\lambda\left(|q|^{2m}q\right)_x + \mu\left(|q|^{2m}\right)_x q + \nu|q|^{2m}q_x\right], \tag{86}$$

while Equation (9) collapses to

$$\phi\phi^{(6)} + \Delta_1\phi\phi^{(4)} + \Delta_2\phi\phi'' + \Delta_3(\phi')^2 + \Delta_4\phi^2$$
$$+ \Delta_5\phi^{2m+2} + e_1\phi^4 + e_2\phi^6 + e_3\phi^8 = 0. \tag{87}$$

Setting $m = 1$, Equation (87) transforms to

$$\phi\phi^{(6)} + \Delta_1\phi\phi^{(4)} + \Delta_2\phi\phi'' + \Delta_3(\phi')^2 + \Delta_4\phi^2 + (\Delta_5 + e_1)\phi^4 + e_2\phi^6 + e_3\phi^8 = 0. \tag{88}$$

Balancing $\phi\phi^{(6)}$ and ϕ^8 gives

$$2N + 6p = 8N \Longrightarrow N = p. \tag{89}$$

Case 1: By virtue of $p = 1$, Equation (88) holds the solution (39). Putting (39) along with (12) into (88) causes to the coefficients

$$\sigma_0 = 0, \; \sigma_1 = \left(\frac{720\chi^3}{e_3}\right)^{\frac{1}{6}} \ln K, \tag{90}$$

and the constraint conditions

$$\Delta_1 = -\frac{1}{24\chi^2}\left[\frac{e_2}{e_3^4}\left(720\chi^3 e_3^5\right)^{2/3} + 840\chi^2\ln^2 K\right], \; \chi^3 e_3 > 0,$$

$$\Delta_2 = \frac{1}{6\chi^2 e_3^4}\left[\begin{array}{c}6e_3^2\chi(90\chi^3 e_3^5)^{1/3}(e_1 + \Delta_5) + 10\left(\ln^2 K\right)e_2(90\chi^3 e_3^5)^{2/3}\\ -3\chi^2 e_3^4(\Delta_3 - 518\ln^4 K)\end{array}\right],$$

$$\Delta_4 = -\frac{3\ln^2 K}{2\chi^2 e_3^4}\left[\begin{array}{c}\frac{2}{3}e_3^2\chi(90\chi^3 e_3^5)^{1/3}(e_1 + \Delta_5) + \left(\ln^2 K\right)e_2(90\chi^3 e_3^5)^{2/3}\\ +\frac{1}{3}\chi^2 e_3^4(\Delta_3 + 450\ln^4 K)\end{array}\right]. \tag{91}$$

Plugging (90) together with (13) and (91) into (39) gives rise to the straddled soliton

$$q(x,t) = \left\{ \frac{4A\left(\frac{720\chi^3}{e_3}\right)^{\frac{1}{6}} \ln K}{4A^2 \exp_K(x-ct) + \chi \exp_K(-(x-ct))} \right\} e^{i(-\kappa x + wt + \theta_0)}. \tag{92}$$

When $e_3 > 0$ and $\chi = 4A^2$, Equation (92) becomes the bright soliton

$$q(x,t) = \left\{ \left(\frac{720}{e_3}\right)^{\frac{1}{6}} \ln K \operatorname{sech}[(x-ct)\ln K] \right\} e^{i(-\kappa x + wt + \theta_0)}. \tag{93}$$

If $e_3 < 0$ and $\chi = -4A^2$, Equation (92) turns into the singular soliton

$$q(x,t) = \left\{ \left(-\frac{720}{e_3}\right)^{\frac{1}{6}} \ln K \operatorname{csch}[(x-ct)\ln K] \right\} e^{i(-\kappa x + wt + \theta_0)}. \tag{94}$$

<u>Case 2</u>: When $p = 2$, Equation (88) permits the solution (45). Substituting (45) along with (12) into (88) yields the coefficients

$$\sigma_0 = \sigma_1 = 0, \quad \sigma_2 = 2\left(\frac{720\chi^3}{e_3}\right)^{\frac{1}{6}} \ln K, \tag{95}$$

and the parameter conditions

$$\Delta_1 = -\frac{1}{24\chi^2}\left[\frac{e_2}{e_3^4}\left(720\chi^3 e_3^5\right)^{2/3} + 3360\chi^2 \ln^2 K\right], \quad \chi^3 e_3 > 0,$$

$$\Delta_2 = \frac{1}{6\chi^2 e_3^4}\left[\begin{array}{c} 6e_3^2\chi\left(90\chi^3 e_3^5\right)^{1/3}(e_1 + \Delta_5) + 40\left(\ln^2 K\right) e_2\left(90\chi^3 e_3^5\right)^{2/3} \\ -3\chi^2 e_3^4(\Delta_3 - 8288\ln^4 K) \end{array}\right],$$

$$\Delta_4 = -\frac{6\ln^2 K}{\chi^2 e_3^4}\left[\begin{array}{c} \frac{2}{3}e_3^2\chi\left(90\chi^3 e_3^5\right)^{1/3}(e_1 + \Delta_5) + 4\left(\ln^2 K\right) e_2\left(90\chi^3 e_3^5\right)^{2/3} \\ +\frac{1}{3}\chi^2 e_3^4(\Delta_3 + 7200\ln^4 K) \end{array}\right]. \tag{96}$$

Inserting (95) together with (13) and (96) into (45) gives the straddled soliton

$$q(x,t) = \left\{ \frac{8A\left(\frac{720\chi^3}{e_3}\right)^{\frac{1}{6}} \ln K}{4A^2 \exp_K[2(x-ct)] + \chi \exp_K[-2(x-ct)]} \right\} e^{i(-\kappa x + wt + \theta_0)}. \tag{97}$$

Setting $e_2 > 0$ and $\chi = 4A^2$, Equation (97) transforms to the bright soliton

$$q(x,t) = \left\{ 2\ln K\left(\frac{720}{e_3}\right)^{\frac{1}{6}} \operatorname{sech}[2\ln K(x-ct)] \right\} e^{i(-\kappa x + wt + \theta_0)}. \tag{98}$$

If $e_2 < 0$ and $\chi = -4A^2$, Equation (97) simplifies to the singular soliton

$$q(x,t) = \left\{ 2\ln K\left(-\frac{720}{e_3}\right)^{\frac{1}{6}} \operatorname{csch}[2\ln K(x-ct)] \right\} e^{i(-\kappa x + wt + \theta_0)}. \tag{99}$$

9. Triple Power Law

The triple power law of nonlinearity is structured as

$$F(\phi^2) = e_1\phi^{2n} + e_2\phi^{4n} + e_3\phi^{6n}, \quad e_3 \neq 0, \tag{100}$$

where e_1, e_2 and e_3 are arbitrary constants. Thus, Equation (1) turns into

$$iq_t + ia_1 q_x + a_2 q_{xx} + ia_3 q_{xxx} + a_4 q_{xxxx} + ia_5 q_{xxxxx} + a_6 q_{xxxxxx}$$
$$+ \left(e_1|q|^{2n} + e_2|q|^{4n} + e_3|q|^{6n}\right)q = \alpha\frac{|q_x|^2}{q^*} + \frac{\beta}{4|q|^2 q^*}\left\{2|q|^2\left(|q|^2\right)_{xx} - \left[\left(|q|^2\right)_x\right]^2\right\}$$
$$+ \gamma q + i\left[\lambda\left(|q|^{2m} q\right)_x + \mu\left(|q|^{2m}\right)_x q + \nu|q|^{2m} q_x\right], \tag{101}$$

while Equation (9) reduces to

$$\phi\phi^{(6)} + \Delta_1 \phi\phi^{(4)} + \Delta_2 \phi\phi'' + \Delta_3 (\phi')^2 + \Delta_4 \phi^2$$
$$+ \Delta_5 \phi^{2m+2} + e_1 \phi^{2n+2} + e_2 \phi^{4n+2} + e_3 \phi^{6n+2} = 0. \tag{102}$$

Setting $n = m$, Equation (102) changes to

$$\phi\phi^{(6)} + \Delta_1 \phi\phi^{(4)} + \Delta_2 \phi\phi'' + \Delta_3 (\phi')^2 + \Delta_4 \phi^2$$
$$+ (\Delta_5 + e_1)\phi^{2m+2} + e_2 \phi^{4m+2} + e_3 \phi^{6m+2} = 0. \tag{103}$$

Balancing $\phi\phi^{(6)}$ and ϕ^{6m+2} yields $N = \frac{1}{m}$. Setting

$$\phi(\xi) = [U(\xi)]^{\frac{1}{m}}, \tag{104}$$

Equation (103) becomes

$$-(2m-1)(m-1)(4m-1)(3m-1)(5m-1)[U']^6$$
$$+ 15m(2m-1)(m-1)(4m-1)(3m-1)UU''U'^4$$
$$- \Delta_1 m^2(2m-1)(m-1)(3m-1)U^2 U'^4 - 20m^2(2m-1)(m-1)(3m-1)U^2 U'^3 U'''$$
$$- 45m^2(2m-1)(m-1)(3m-1)U^2 U''^2 U'^2 + 6\Delta_1 m^3(2m-1)(m-1)U^3 U'' U'^2$$
$$+ 15m^3(2m-1)(m-1)U^3 U^{(4)} U'^2 - m^4[(m-1)\Delta_2 - \Delta_3]U^4 U'^2$$
$$+ 60m^3(2m-1)(m-1)U^3 U''' U'' U' - 4\Delta_1(m-1)m^4 U^4 U''' U'$$
$$- 6(m-1)m^4 U^4 U^{(5)} U' + 15m^3(m-1)(2m-1)U^3(U'')^3 - 3\Delta_1 m^4(m-1)U^4(U'')^2$$
$$- 15m^4(m-1)U^4 U^{(4)} U'' + m^5 \Delta_2 U^5 U'' - 10m^4(m-1)U^4(U''')^2 + m^5 \Delta_1 U^5 U^{(4)}$$
$$+ m^5 U^5 U^{(6)} + m^6 e_3 U^{12} + m^6 e_2 U^{10} + m^6(e_1 + \Delta_5)U^8 + m^6 \Delta_4 U^6 = 0. \tag{105}$$

Balancing $U^5 U^{(6)}$ and U^{12} gives

$$6N + 6p = 12 \implies N = p. \tag{106}$$

Case 1: When $p = 1$, Equation (105) admits the solution (39). Inserting (39) along with (12) into (105) leads to the coefficients

$$\sigma_0 = 0, \quad \sigma_1 = \frac{\ln K}{m}\left(\frac{(2m+1)(m+1)(4m+1)(3m+1)(5m+1)\chi^3}{e_3}\right)^{\frac{1}{6}}, \tag{107}$$

and the parameter constraints

$$\Delta_1 = -\frac{1}{m^2 e_3^4 (2m+1)(m+1)(3m+1)\chi^2}$$
$$\times \left\{ m^2 e_2 \left[\chi^3 e_3^5 (2m+1)(m+1)(4m+1)(3m+1)(5m+1) \right]^{2/3} \right.$$
$$\left. + 480 e_3^4 \chi^2 (m+1)(m+\frac{1}{3})(m^2+\frac{3}{5}m+\frac{3}{20})(m+\frac{1}{2}) \ln^2 K \right\},$$

$$\Delta_2 = \frac{1}{m^4 (2m+1)(m+1)(3m+1)\chi^2 e_3^4} \left\{ -(3m+1)(2m+1)m^4 \Delta_3 e_3^4 \chi^2 \right.$$
$$+ 4m^2 (m^2+m+\frac{1}{2}) e_2 \left(\ln^2 K \right) \left[(2m+1)(m+1)(4m+1)(3m+1)(5m+1)\chi^3 e_3^5 \right]^{2/3}$$
$$+ m^4 (3m+1)(2m+1) e_3^2 \chi (e_1+\Delta_5) \left[(2m+1)(m+1)(4m+1)(3m+1)(5m+1)\chi^3 e_3^5 \right]^{1/3}$$
$$\left. + (3m+1)(2m+1)(m+1)(64m^4+96m^3+72m^2+24m+3) e_3^4 \chi^2 \ln^4 K \right\},$$

$$\Delta_4 = -\frac{\ln^2 K}{m^6 (m+1)(3m+1)\chi^2 e_3^4}$$
$$\times \left\{ m^2 (2m+1) \ln^2 K e_2 \left[\chi^3 e_3^5 (2m+1)(m+1)(4m+1)(3m+1)(5m+1) \right]^{2/3} \right.$$
$$+ m^4 (3m+1)(e_1+\Delta_5) e_3^2 \chi \left[\chi^3 e_3^5 (2m+1)(m+1)(4m+1)(3m+1)(5m+1) \right]^{1/3}$$
$$\left. + (3m+1) e_3^4 \chi^2 \left[\Delta_3 m^5 + (m+1)(4m+1)^2 (2m+1)^2 \ln^4 K \right] \right\}, \quad \chi^3 e_3 > 0. \tag{108}$$

Substituting (107) together with (13) and (108) into (39), we arrive the straddled soliton

$$q(x,t) = \left\{ \frac{4A \left(\frac{(2m+1)(m+1)(4m+1)(3m+1)(5m+1)\chi^3}{e_3} \right)^{\frac{1}{6}} \ln K}{m[4A^2 \exp_K(x-ct) + \chi \exp_K(-(x-ct))]} \right\}^{\frac{1}{m}}$$
$$\times e^{i(-\kappa x + wt + \theta_0)}. \tag{109}$$

If $e_3 > 0$ and $\chi = 4A^2$, Equation (109) reduces to the bright soliton

$$q(x,t) = \left\{ \frac{\ln K}{m} \left(\frac{(2m+1)(m+1)(4m+1)(3m+1)(5m+1)}{e_3} \right)^{\frac{1}{6}} \right.$$
$$\left. \times \operatorname{sech}[(x-ct) \ln K] \right\}^{\frac{1}{m}}$$
$$\times e^{i(-\kappa x + wt + \theta_0)}. \tag{110}$$

When $e_3 < 0$ and $\chi = -4A^2$, Equation (109) changes to the singular soliton

$$q(x,t) = \left\{ \frac{\ln K}{m} \left(-\frac{(2m+1)(m+1)(4m+1)(3m+1)(5m+1)}{e_3} \right)^{\frac{1}{6}} \right.$$
$$\left. \times \operatorname{csch}[(x-ct) \ln K] \right\}^{\frac{1}{m}}$$
$$\times e^{i(-\kappa x + wt + \theta_0)}. \tag{111}$$

Case 2: If $p=2$, Equation (105) presumes the solution (45). Plugging (45) along with (12) into (105) gives rise to the coefficients

$$\sigma_0 = \sigma_1 = 0, \quad \sigma_2 = \frac{2\ln K}{m}\left(\frac{(2m+1)(m+1)(4m+1)(3m+1)(5m+1)\chi^3}{e_3}\right)^{\frac{1}{6}}, \quad (112)$$

and the parameter conditions

$$\Delta_1 = -\frac{1}{m^2(m+1)(2m+1)(3m+1)\chi^2}$$

$$\times \left\{\frac{m^2 e_2}{e_3^4}\left[\chi^3 e_3^5(2m+1)(m+1)(4m+1)(3m+1)(5m+1)\right]^{2/3} \right.$$

$$\left. + 120\chi^2(m+1)(m+\tfrac{1}{3})(m^2+\tfrac{3}{5}m+\tfrac{3}{20})(m+\tfrac{1}{2})\ln^2 K\right\},$$

$$\Delta_2 = \frac{1}{m^4(2m+1)(m+1)(3m+1)\chi^2 e_3^4}\left\{-(3m+1)(2m+1)m^4\Delta_3 e_3^4\chi^2\right.$$

$$+ 16m^2(m^2+m+\tfrac{1}{2})e_2\ln^2 K\left[(2m+1)(m+1)(4m+1)(3m+1)(5m+1)\chi^3 e_3^5\right]^{2/3}$$

$$+ m^4(3m+1)(2m+1)e_3^2\chi(e_1+\Delta_5)\left[(2m+1)(m+1)(4m+1)(3m+1)(5m+1)\chi^3 e_3^5\right]^{1/3}$$

$$\left. + (2m+1)(3m+1)(1024m^4+1536m^3+1152m^2+384m+48)(m+1)e_3^4\chi^2\ln^4 K\right\},$$

$$\Delta_4 = -\frac{12\ln^2 K}{m^6(m+1)(3m+1)\chi^2 e_3^4}$$

$$\times \left\{\tfrac{4}{3}m^2(2m+1)\ln^2 Ke_2\left[\chi^3 e_3^5(2m+1)(m+1)(4m+1)(3m+1)(5m+1)\right]^{2/3}\right.$$

$$+ \tfrac{1}{3}m^4(3m+1)(e_1+\Delta_5)e_3^2\chi\left[\chi^3 e_3^5(2m+1)(m+1)(4m+1)(3m+1)(5m+1)\right]^{1/3}$$

$$\left. + \frac{(3m+1)e_3^4\chi^2}{3}\left\{\left[\Delta_3 m^5+16(m+1)(4m+1)^2(2m+1)^2\ln^4 K\right]\right\}, \chi^3 e_3 > 0.\right. \quad (113)$$

Inserting (112) together with (13) and (113) into (45) causes to the straddled soliton

$$q(x,t) = \left\{\frac{8A\left(\frac{(2m+1)(m+1)(4m+1)(3m+1)(5m+1)\chi^3}{e_3}\right)^{\frac{1}{6}}\ln K}{m\{\chi\exp_K(-2(x-ct))+4A^2\exp_K(2(x-ct))\}}\right\}^{\frac{1}{m}}$$

$$\times e^{i(-\kappa x+wt+\theta_0)}. \quad (114)$$

Setting $e_3 > 0$ and $\chi = 4A^2$, Equation (114) simplifies to the bright soliton

$$q(x,t) = \left\{\frac{2\ln K}{m}\left(\frac{(2m+1)(m+1)(4m+1)(3m+1)(5m+1)}{e_3}\right)^{\frac{1}{6}}\right\}^{\frac{1}{m}}$$

$$\times \text{sech}[2\ln K(x-ct)]$$

$$\times e^{i(-\kappa x+wt+\theta_0)}. \quad (115)$$

Article

Symmetry Methods and Conservation Laws for the Nonlinear Generalized 2D Equal-Width Partial Differential Equation of Engineering

Chaudry Masood Khalique [1,2,*,†] and Karabo Plaatjie [1,†]

[1] Department of Mathematical Sciences, International Institute for Symmetry Analysis and Mathematical Modelling, Mafikeng Campus, North-West University, Private Bag X 2046, Mmabatho 2735, South Africa; 25451308@student.g.nwu.ac.za

[2] Department of Mathematics and Informatics, Azerbaijan University, Jeyhun Hajibeyli Str., 71, Baku AZ1007, Azerbaijan

* Correspondence: Masood.Khalique@nwu.ac.za
† The authors contributed equally to this work.

Abstract: In this work, we study the generalized 2D equal-width equation which arises in various fields of science. With the aid of numerous methods which includes Lie symmetry analysis, power series expansion and Weierstrass method, we produce closed-form solutions of this model. The exact solutions obtained are the snoidal wave, cnoidal wave, Weierstrass elliptic function, Jacobi elliptic cosine function, solitary wave and exponential function solutions. Moreover, we give a graphical representation of the obtained solutions using certain parametric values. Furthermore, the conserved vectors of the underlying equation are constructed by utilizing two approaches: the multiplier method and Noether's theorem. The multiplier method provided us with four local conservation laws, whereas Noether's theorem yielded five nonlocal conservation laws. The conservation laws that are constructed contain the conservation of energy and momentum.

Keywords: generalized 2D equal-width equation; exact solution; Weierstrass elliptic functions; Kudryashov's method; conservation laws; Noether's theorem

1. Introduction

It is well established that numerous physical phenomena of the real world are modeled by the nonlinear partial differential equations (NPDE). Therefore, finding the exact solutions of the NPDEs plays a vital role in the understanding of these physical phenomena. NPDEs appear in various fields of sciences, which include the fields of biology, quantum mechanics, economics, optical fibers, fluid dynamics, chaos theory and plasma physics, just to mention a few. For instance, the Ginzburg–Landau equation [1] was used to describe superconductivity and was postulated as a phenomenological model which could describe type-I superconductors without examining their microscopic properties; the Fokas–Lenells equation [2] is an important model that is used in solitary wave theory and optical fibers phenomena; the Black–Scholes equation [3] is mostly used in finance—for example, it may be used as the governing model for the price evolution of a European call; the nonlinear elastic circular rod equation [4] was used to analyze the solitary strain waves in the nonlinear elastic rod that produce some results on the effect of the geometrical and physical parameters of the rod on the waves—just to name a few. Scholars and researchers have dedicated most of their time to investigating some of these models, and for this reason, there are a number of solution methods suggested in the literature. These solution methods include, amongst others, Bäcklund transformations [5–7], the extended simplest equation method [8], the extended Jacobi elliptic function technique [9], power series technique [10], tanh method [11], Lie symmetry technique [12–18], bifurcation method [19] and (G'/G)−expansion method [20].

Conservation laws have vast applications in the study of differential equations (DEs) and are known as the fundamental laws of nature as they play a huge role in physics, applied mathematics and other fields of science such as chemistry, biology, geology and engineering. There are techniques brought forward in the literature which aid in deriving conserved vectors which include the classical Noether's theorem, the multiplier method, the Ibragimov's new theorem and the partial Lagrangian method [21–31]. It should be noted that Noether's theorem can only be applied to DEs which have a Lagrangian formulation. However, many DEs exist that do not have a Lagrangian and as a result Nother's theorem cannot be used to derive their conservation laws. In such a situation the general method of multipliers can be invoked to construct conservation laws. Thus, the general multiplier method provides us with the conservation laws of a DE irrespective of whether or not the DE comes from a variational principle.

The nonlinear third-order PDE given by

$$u_t + 2\alpha u u_x + u_{txx} = 0 \tag{1}$$

is known as the equal-width (EW) equation and was first introduced by Morrison et al. [32] as the mathematical model that describes nonlinear dispersive waves, for example, the waves created in shallow water channel. Several works has been conducted on this equation. For instance, in [33], the authors presented some closed-form solutions and conservation laws for this equation. The authors of [34] invoked the Petrov–Galerkin method utilizing quadratic B-spline spatial finite elements to derive solutions for this equation. In [35], the extended simple equation method along with the exponential expansion method were employed to derive its exact solutions.

The modified equal-width (MEW) equation reads

$$u_t + 2\alpha u^2 u_x + u_{txx} = 0 \tag{2}$$

and models the simulation of one-dimensional wave propagation in nonlinear media with dispersion processes. More work that has been performed on MEW equation can be found in [35–38] and the references therein.

In [39], the authors studied the general form of the equal width (GEW) equation with power law nonlinearity that reads

$$u_t + a u^p u_x - \mu u_{txx} = 0 \tag{3}$$

and presented exact solitary wave solutions. In addition, analytical expressions of three invariants of motion for these solitary wave solutions were derived. Recently, the traveling wave solution of the GEW Equation (3) was found in [40] by using the Lie symmetry method along with the sine-cosine method.

The generalized equal width-Burgers equation

$$u_t + a u^p u_x - \delta u_{xx} - \mu u_{txx} = 0 \tag{4}$$

describes the propagation of nonlinear and dispersive waves with certain dissipative effects. The exact solitary wave solutions of (4) were derived in [39].

Recently, Equation (2) was generalized to the two-dimensional modified equal-width equation, which reads [41]

$$u_t + u^2 u_x - \mu(u_{txx} + u_{tyy}) = 0, \tag{5}$$

where μ is a real constant. Firstly, Lie symmetries were computed, and thereafter, one-dimensional and two-dimensional subalgebras were obtained. These were then utilized to perform the symmetry reductions of (5) to ordinary differential equations.

In this work, we further generalize (5) to the two-dimensional equal-width (2D-EW) equation with power law nonlinearity, viz.,

$$u_t + u^n u_x + \alpha u_{txx} + \beta u_{tyy} = 0 \tag{6}$$

with α, β and n being nonzero constants. In this work, we provide the exact solutions of the 2D-EW Equation (6). The classical symmetry method was employed to obtain point symmetries of this model, and thereafter, symmetries were used to reduce (6) to some nonlinear ordinary differential equations (NODEs). Various solution methods were then utilized to construct solutions of these NODEs, which consequently provides us with the exact solutions of the 2D-EW Equation (6). Moreover, the obtained solutions were described graphically for certain parametric values. Finally, we derive both local and nonlocal conservation laws for this model by invoking two distinct approaches.

2. Symmetries, Reductions and Solutions

In this section, we firstly compute Lie symmetries of the 2D-EW Equation (6) and thereafter perform symmetry reductions to obtain various NODEs. By employing different techniques on these NODE, we then construct closed-form solutions of the Equation (6).

2.1. Lie Symmetries

We consider the one-parameter group of transformations

$$\bar{t} \to t + a\tau(t,x,y,u), \quad \bar{x} \to x + a\xi(t,x,y,u),$$
$$\bar{y} \to y + a\phi(t,x,y,u), \quad \bar{u} \to u + a\eta(t,x,y,u) \tag{7}$$

with a small parameter a, for which the corresponding vector field is

$$\mathcal{Z} = \tau \frac{\partial}{\partial t} + \xi \frac{\partial}{\partial x} + \phi \frac{\partial}{\partial y} + \eta \frac{\partial}{\partial u}. \tag{8}$$

The vector field $\mathcal{Z}$ is a Lie symmetry of Equation (6) whenever

$$\mathcal{Z}^{[3]}(u_t + u^n u_x + \alpha u_{txx} + \beta u_{tyy})\Big|_{(6)} = 0. \tag{9}$$

Here $\mathcal{Z}^{[3]}$ is the third prolongation of (8); see for example [14]. Expanding Equation (9) and separating the various derivatives of u lead to the determining equations:

$$\tau_u = 0, \ \tau_x = 0, \ \tau_y = 0, \ \tau_{tt} = 0, \ \xi_t = 0, \ \xi_u = 0, \ \xi_x = 0,$$
$$\xi_y = 0, \ \phi_t = 0, \ \phi_u = 0, \phi_x = 0, \ \phi_y = 0, \ n\eta + u\tau_t = 0. \tag{10}$$

Solving the above equations, we end up with

$$\mathcal{Z} = (C_1 t + C_2)\frac{\partial}{\partial t} + C_3 \frac{\partial}{\partial x} + C_4 \frac{\partial}{\partial y} - \frac{C_1}{n} u \frac{\partial}{\partial u}, \tag{11}$$

where $C_1, \ldots, C_4$ are arbitrary constants. Thus, we see that the Lie symmetries of the 2D-EW Equation (6) are

$$\mathcal{Z}_1 = \frac{\partial}{\partial t}, \ \mathcal{Z}_2 = \frac{\partial}{\partial x}, \ \mathcal{Z}_3 = \frac{\partial}{\partial y}, \ \mathcal{Z}_4 = nt\frac{\partial}{\partial t} - u\frac{\partial}{\partial u}. \tag{12}$$

Here, the symmetries $\mathcal{Z}_1$, $\mathcal{Z}_2$, $\mathcal{Z}_3$ represent the translation symmetries, whereas $\mathcal{Z}_4$ is the scaling symmetry.

2.2. Symmetry Reductions Using $\mathcal{Z}_1, \mathcal{Z}_2, \mathcal{Z}_3$

We use the symmetry $\mathcal{Z} = \mathcal{Z}_1 + a\mathcal{Z}_2 + b\mathcal{Z}_3$, ($a, b$ constants) to reduce the 2D-EW Equation (6) to a NODE. The characteristic equations of symmetry $\mathcal{Z}$ give the invariants

$$f = x - at, \quad g = y - bt, \quad u(t,x,y) = \Gamma(f,g),$$

which reduce (6) to the NPDE

$$a\Gamma_f + b\Gamma_g - \Gamma^n \Gamma_f + \alpha a \Gamma_{fff} + \alpha b \Gamma_{ffg} + \beta a \Gamma_{fgg} + b\beta \Gamma_{ggg} = 0. \tag{13}$$

Equation (13) has two translation symmetries $\zeta_1 = \partial/\partial f$, $\zeta_2 = \partial/\partial g$. Symmetry $\zeta = \zeta_1 + \nu \zeta_2$ produces the invariants

$$z = g - \nu f, \quad \Gamma(f,g) = \Psi(z)$$

and these invariants transform the NPDE (13) to the NODE

$$(a\nu - b)\Psi'(z) - \nu \Psi^n \Psi'(z) + (a\alpha\nu^3 - \alpha b\nu^2 + \beta\nu a - \beta b)\Psi'''(z) = 0, \tag{14}$$

which we rewrite as

$$A\Psi'(z) - \nu \Psi^n(z)\Psi'(z) + B\Psi'''(z) = 0, \tag{15}$$

where $A = a\nu - b$, $B = a\alpha\nu^3 - \alpha b\nu^2 + \beta\nu a - \beta b$ and $z = (a\nu - b)t - \nu x + y$.

2.3. Solution of (6) Using Kudryashov's Method

We engage Kudryashov's method [42] to construct the closed-form solution for the 2D-EW Equation (6). To do this, we start by removing the power n in the NODE (15) using the transformation

$$\Psi(z) = F^{1/n}(z). \tag{16}$$

Thus, the NODE (15) becomes

$$(1 - 3n + 2n^2)BF'(z)^3 + 3n(a-n)BF(z)F'(z)F''(z) + n^2 BF(z)^2 F'''(z)$$
$$- n^2 \nu F(z)^3 F'(z) + An^2 F(z)^2 F'(z) = 0. \tag{17}$$

Next, we assume that the NODE (17) has the solution of the form

$$F(z) = \sum_{k=0}^{J} C_k V^k(z), \tag{18}$$

where C_k is the unknown constants to be determined and the function $V(z)$ satisfies the Riccati equation

$$V'(z) = V^2(z) - V(z), \tag{19}$$

whose solution is

$$V(z) = \frac{1}{1 + \exp(z)}. \tag{20}$$

By using the balancing procedure [35] on Equation (17), we obtain $J = 2$. Hence, (18) becomes

$$F(z) = C_0 + C_1 V(z) + C_2 V^2(z). \tag{21}$$

Inserting the value of $F(z)$ from (21) into (17) and using (19), we obtain an equation which splits into nine algebraic equations:

$n^2 v C_0^3 C_1 - A n^2 C_0^2 C_1 - B n^2 C_0^2 C_1 = 0,$

$4 B C_2{}^3 - n^2 v C_2^4 + 2 B n^2 C_2{}^3 + 6 B n C_2{}^3 = 0,$

$2 n^2 v C_2^4 - 7 n^2 v C_1 C_2^3 + 12 B n^2 C_1 C_2^2 - 6 B n^2 C_2^3 + 30 B n C_1 C_2^2 - 24 B n C_2^3 - 24 B C_2^3$
$+ 12\, B C_1 C_2^2 = 0,$

$2 n^2 v C_0^3 C_2 - n^2 v C_0^3 C_1 + 3 n^2 v C_0^2 C_1^2 + A n^2 C_0^2 C_1 - 2 A n^2 C_0^2 C_2 - 2 A n^2 C_0 C_1^2$
$+ 7 B n^2 C_0^2 C_1 - 8\, B n^2 C_0^2 C_2 + B n^2 C_0 C_1^2 - 3\, B n C_0 C_1^2 = 0,$

$3 n^2 v C_0 C_1^3 - 2 n^2 v C_0^3 C_2 - 3 n^2 v C_0^2 C_1^2 + 9 n^2 v C_0^2 C_1 C_2 + 2 A n^2 C_0^2 C_2$
$+ 2 A n^2 C_0 C_1^2 - 6 A n^2 C_0 C_1 C_2 - A n^2 C_1^3 - 12 B n^2 C_0^2 C_1 + 38 B n^2 C_0^2 C_2$
$+ 2 B n^2 C_0 C_1^2 + 12 B n C_0 C_1^2 - 18 B n C_0 C_1 C_2 - B C_1^3 = 0,$

$7 n^2 v C_1 C_2^3 - 6 n^2 v C_0 C_2{}^3 - 9 n^2 v C_1^2 C_2^2 + 2 A n^2 C_2^3 + 12 B n^2 C_0 C_2^2$
$+ 12 B n^2 C_1^2 C_2 - 18 B n^2 C_1 C_2^2 + 2 B n^2 C_2^3 + 36 B n C_0 C_2^2 + 18 B n C_1^2 C_2 \qquad (22)$

$12 B n C_2^3 - 66 B n C_1 C_2^2 + 6 B C_1^2 C_2 - 36 B C_1 C_2^2 + 24 B C_2{}^3 = 0,$

$6 n^2 v C_0 C_2^3 - 15 n^2 v C_0 C_1 C_2^2 - 5 n^2 v C_1^3 C_2 + 9 n^2 v C_1^2 C_2^2 + 5 A n^2 C_1 C_2^2 - 2 A n^2 C_2^3$
$+ 30 B n^2 C_0 C_1 C_2 - 12 B n^2 C_0 C_2^2 + 2 B n^2 C_1^3 - 21 B n^2 C_1^2 C_2 + 5 B n^2 C_1 C_2^2$
$+ 30 B n C_0 C_1 C_2 - 96 B n C_0 C_2^2 + 3 B n C_1^3 - 39 B n C_1^2 C_2 + 42 B n C_1 C_2^2 + B C_1^3$
$+ 36 B C_1 C_2^2 - 18 B C_1^2 C_2 - 8 B C_2^3 = 0,$

$6 n^2 v C_0^2 C_2^2 - 9 n^2 v C_0^2 C_1 C_2 - 3 n^2 v C_0 C_1^3 + 12 n^2 v C_0 C_1^2 C_2 + n^2 v C_1^4 + 6 A n^2 C_0 C_1 C_2$
$+ A n^2 C_1^3 - 4 A n^2 C_0 C_2^2 - 4 A n^2 C_1^2 C_2 + 6 B n^2 C_0^2 C_1 - 54 B n^2 C_0^2 C_2 - 9 B n^2 C_0 C_1^2$
$+ 24 B n^2 C_0 C_1 C_2 + 8 B n^2 C_0 C_2^2 + B n^2 C_1^3 - B n^2 C_1^2 C_2 - 15 B n C_0 C_1^2 + 66 B n C_0 C_1 C_2$
$+ 3 B C_1^3 - 24 B n C_0 C_2^2 + 3 B n C_1^3 - 3 B n C_1^2 C_2 - 6 B C_1^2 C_2 = 0,$

$15 n^2 v C_0 C_1 C_2^2 - 6 n^2 v C_0^2 C_2^2 - 12 n^2 v C_0 C_1^2 C_2 - n^2 v\, C_1^4 + 5 n^2 v C_1^3 C_2$
$+ 4 A n^2 C_0 C_2^2 + 4 A n^2 C_1^2 C_2 - 5 A n^2 C_1 C_2^2 + 24 B n^2 C_0^2 C_2 + 6 B n^2 C_0 C_1^2 - 12 B C_1 C_2^2$
$+ 10 B n^2 C_1^2 C_2 - 54 B n^2 C_0 C_1 C_2 - 8 B n^2 C_0 C_2^2 - 3 B n^2 C_1^3 + B n^2 C_1 C_2^2 + 6 B n C_0 C_1^2$
$+ 84 B n C_0 C_2^2 - 78 B n C_0 C_1 C_2 - 6 B n C_1^3 + 24 B n C_1^2 C_2 - 6 B n C_1 C_2^2 - 3 B C_1^3$
$+ 18 B C_1^2 C_2 = 0.$

Using Maple, we attain the solution of the above algebraic equations in the form

$$C_0 = 0, \quad C_1 = \frac{2A}{v}(n^2 + 3n + 2), \quad C_2 = -\frac{2A}{v}(n^2 + 3n + 2), \quad B = -n^2 A. \qquad (23)$$

Thus, corresponding to the above values, we obtain the solution for the 2D-EW Equation (6) in the form

$$u(t, x, y) = \left\{ \frac{2}{v} A(n^2 + 3n + 2) \left(\frac{\exp(z)}{\{1 + \exp(z)\}^2} \right) \right\}^{\frac{1}{n}}, \qquad (24)$$

where $z = (av - b)t - vx + y$. Figure 1 demonstrates the wave profile of solution (24) for the values $a = 2$, $b = 6$, $v = 8$, $n = 1$, $A = 1$ and $t = 0$.

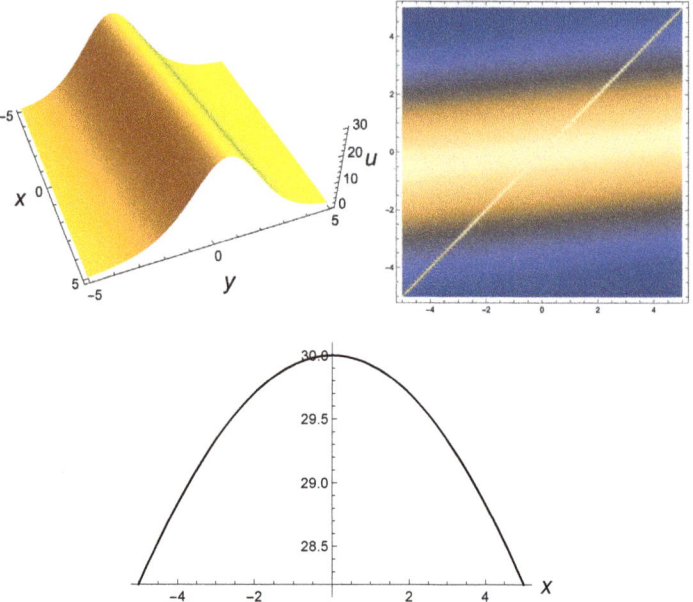

Figure 1. The 3D and 2D wave profile of solution (24).

2.4. Solitary Wave Solution of (6)

We now seek the solitary wave solution for 2D-EW Equation (6). To achieve this task, we focus on the NODE (15). Integrating this NODE twice and taking the constants of integration to be zero, we obtain

$$\Psi'^2 - \frac{2v}{B(n+1)(n+2)}\Psi^{n+2} + \frac{A}{B}\Psi^2 = 0. \tag{25}$$

Using the transformation $\Psi(z) = V^{1/n}(z)$, the NODE (25) becomes

$$V'^2 - \frac{2n^2 v}{B(n+1)(n+2)}V^3 + \frac{n^2 A}{B}V^2 = 0, \tag{26}$$

whose solution is

$$V(z) = \frac{A(n+1)(n+2)}{2v}\text{sech}^2\left(\sqrt{-\frac{An^2}{4B}}(z \pm K)\right),$$

where $K = (\sqrt{A(n+1)(n+2)}\,C_1)/2$ and C_1 is an integration constant. Thus, the solution 2D-EW Equation (6) is

$$u(t,x,y) = \left\{\frac{A(n+1)(n+2)}{2v}\text{sech}^2\left(\sqrt{-\frac{An^2}{4B}}(z \pm K)\right)\right\}^{1/n}, \tag{27}$$

where C_1 is the integration constant and $z = (av - b)t - vx + y$. In Figure 2, we give the illustration of the solution (27) for the values $v = 0.9$, $A = 0.18$, $a = 0.2$, $b = 0.2$, $n = 1$, $K = 0$ and time $t = 0.1$.

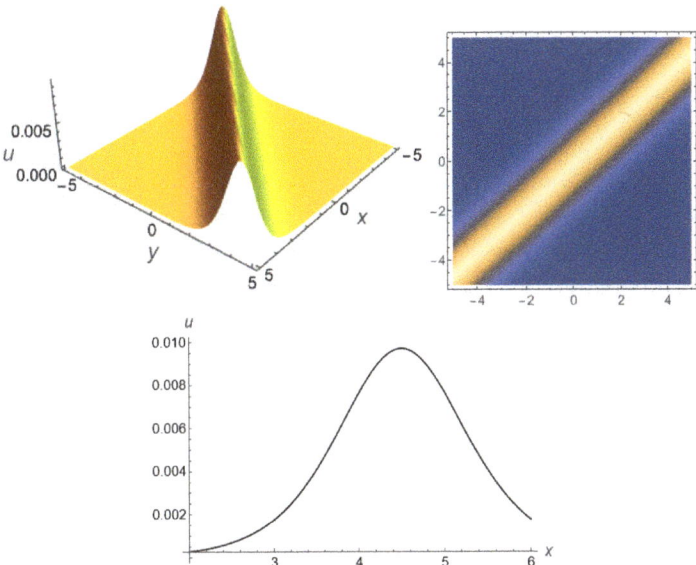

Figure 2. The 3D and 2D solution profiles of (27).

2.5. Solutions of (6) for $n = 1$

2.5.1. Solution via Direct Integration

We now seek the solution for 2D-EW Equation (6) for $n = 1$ via the direct integration. Substituting $n = 1$ into (15) and integrating the resultant equation twice gives

$$\Psi'^2 = \frac{\nu}{3B}\Psi^3 - \frac{A}{B}\Psi^2 - \frac{2c_1}{B}\Psi - \frac{2c_2}{B}, \tag{28}$$

where c_1, c_2 are arbitrary constants. To gain the solution for the NODE (28), we assume that κ_1, κ_2, κ_3 are the real roots of the cubic polynomial

$$\Psi^3 - \frac{3A}{\nu}\Psi^2 - \frac{6c_1}{\nu}\Psi - \frac{6c_2}{\nu}$$

with $\kappa_1 > \kappa_2 > \kappa_3$. Then, Equation (28) can be written as

$$\Psi'^2 = \frac{\nu}{3B}(\Psi - \kappa_1)(\Psi - \kappa_2)(\Psi - \kappa_3),$$

whose solution [43,44] is

$$\Psi(z) = \kappa_2 + (\kappa_1 - \kappa_2)\mathrm{cn}^2\left\{\sqrt{\frac{\nu(\kappa_1 - \kappa_3)}{12B}}(z - z_0), \mathcal{R}^2\right\}, \quad \mathcal{R}^2 = \frac{\kappa_1 - \kappa_2}{\kappa_1 - \kappa_3},$$

where z_0 is a constant and (cn) is the Jacobi cosine function. Consequently, the solution for the 2D-EW Equation (6) is

$$u(t, x, y) = \kappa_2 + (\kappa_1 - \kappa_2)\mathrm{cn}^2\left\{\sqrt{\frac{\nu(\kappa_1 - \kappa_3)}{12B}}(z - z_0), \mathcal{R}^2\right\}, \tag{29}$$

where $z = (av - b)t - vx + y$. Figure 3 depicts the solution (29) graphically for the parametric values $\kappa_1 = 1$, $\kappa_2 = -54$, $\kappa_3 = -64$, $B = 15$, $v = 1.2$, $b = 0.2$, $\nu = 0.6$, $a = -4$, $z_0 = 0$ and $t = -15$.

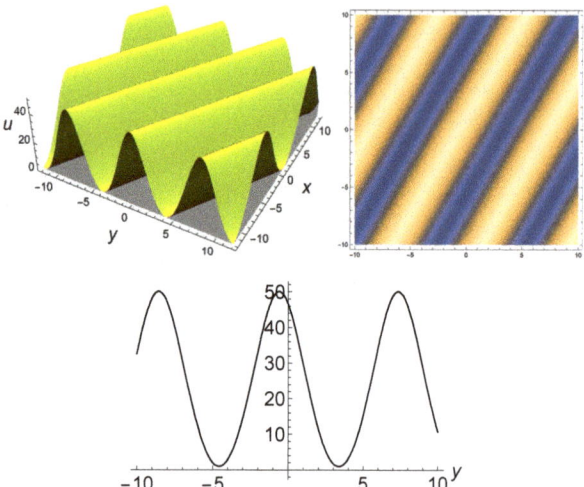

Figure 3. The 3D and 2D solution profiles of (29).

2.5.2. Solution via Weierstrass Elliptic Function Method

We begin by writing Equation (28) in the form

$$\Psi'^2(z) - k_1\Psi^3(z) - k_2\Psi^2(z) - k_3\Psi(z) - k_4 = 0, \qquad (30)$$

where the coefficients k_1, k_2, k_3, k_4 are expressed as $k_1 = \nu/(3B)$, $k_2 = -A/B$, $k_3 = -2c_1/B$, $k_4 = -2c_2/B$. Now, using the transformation

$$\Psi = \mathcal{V} - \frac{k_2}{3k_1}, \qquad (31)$$

Equation (30) reduces to

$$\mathcal{V}'(\xi) = 4\mathcal{V}^3(\xi) - g_2^2\mathcal{V}(\xi) - g_3^2, \quad \xi = \sqrt{\frac{k_1}{4}}\, z, \qquad (32)$$

whose general solution [45] is given by

$$\mathcal{V}(\xi) = \wp\left(\xi; g_2^2; g_2^3\right) - \frac{k_2}{3k_1}, \quad \xi = \sqrt{\frac{k_1}{4}}\, z, \qquad (33)$$

where $\wp$ is the Weierstrass elliptic function and g_2^2, g_3^2 are the invariants that are given by

$$g_2^2 = \frac{4k_3}{k_1} - \frac{k_2^2}{3k_1^2}, \quad g_3^2 = \frac{4k_4}{k_1} - \frac{4k_2 k_3}{3k_1^2} + \frac{8k_2^3}{27k_1^3}.$$

Thus, going back to our original variables, we obtain the solution of the 2D-EW equation as

$$u(t, x, y) = \wp\left(\sqrt{\frac{k_1}{4}}\, z; g_2^2; g_2^3\right) - \frac{k_2}{3k_1} \qquad (34)$$

where $z = (a\nu - b)t - \nu x + y$. Figure 4 illustrates the solution (34) with the parameters assigned to be $k_1 = 4$, $k_2 = 0$, $k_3 = 1$, $k_4 = 2$, $a = 3$, $\nu = 0.1$, $b = 9$ and $t = 0$.

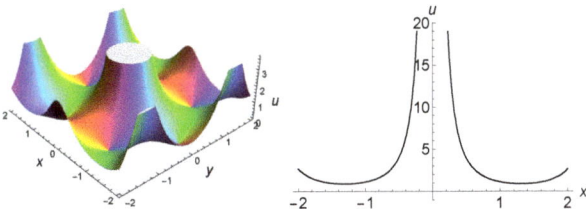

Figure 4. The 3D and 2D solution profiles of (34).

2.5.3. Solution via the Extended Jacobi Elliptic Function Method

We now construct exact explicit solutions of the 2D-EW Equation (6) in terms of the Jacobi elliptic functions [9]. We apply this method to NODE (15) for the case when $n = 1$. For this case, the NODE (15) becomes

$$A\Psi'(z) - \nu \Psi(z)\Psi'(z) + B\Psi'''(z) = 0. \tag{35}$$

The equations that are used are the first-order ODEs

$$H'(z)^2 = (1 - H(z)^2)(1 - \omega + \omega H(z)^2) \tag{36}$$

and

$$H'(z)^2 = (1 - H(z)^2)(1 - \omega H(z)^2) \tag{37}$$

whose solutions are the Jacobi elliptic cosine and the Jacobi elliptic sine functions, respectively, given by

$$H(z) = \operatorname{cn}(z|\omega) \tag{38}$$

and

$$H(z) = \operatorname{sn}(z|\omega), \tag{39}$$

where $0 \leq \omega \leq 1$.

Cnoidal wave solutions

We now consider the solution of the NODE (35) in the form

$$\Psi(z) = \sum_{j=-M}^{M} A_j H(z)^j, \tag{40}$$

where A_j is the undetermined constants and M is the integer greater than zero, obtained by the balancing procedure. Using the balancing procedure on NODE (35), we obtain $M = 2$. Thus, (40) becomes

$$\Psi(z) = A_{-2}H(z)^{-2} + A_{-1}H(z)^{-1} + A_0 + A_1 H(z) + A_2 H(z)^2. \tag{41}$$

Using the above value of Ψ in (35) and invoking (36), we obtain the following algebraic equations:

$12\alpha a v^3 A_{-2} - 12\alpha a v^3 \omega A_{-2} - 12 a v \beta \omega A_{-2} + 12 a v \beta A_{-2} + 12 \alpha b v^2 \omega A_{-2} - 12 \alpha b v^2 A_{-2}$
$+ 12 b \beta \omega A_{-2} - 12 b \beta A_{-2} - \nu A_{-2}^2 = 0,$
$2\alpha a v^3 A_{-1} - 2\alpha a v^3 \omega A_{-1} - 2 a v \beta \omega A_{-1} + 2 a v \beta A_{-1} + 2 \alpha b v^2 \omega A_{-1} - 2 \alpha b v^2 A_{-1}$
$+ 2 b \beta \omega A_{-1} - 2 b \beta A_{-1} - \nu A_{-2} A_{-1} = 0,$
$16 \alpha a v^3 \omega A_{-2} - 8 \alpha a v^3 A_{-2} + 16 a v \beta \omega A_{-2} - 8 a v \beta A_{-2} + 2 a v A_{-2} - 16 \alpha b v^2 \omega A_{-2}$

$$+ 8\alpha bv^2 A_{-2} - 16b\beta\omega A_{-2} + 8b\beta A_{-2} - 2bA_{-2} - vA_{-1}^2 - 2A_{-2}A_0v = 0,$$
$$2\alpha av^3 \omega A_{-1} - \alpha av^3 A_{-1} + 2av\beta\omega A_{-1} - av\beta A_{-1} + av A_{-1} - 2\alpha bv^2 \omega A_{-1} - A_{-1}b$$
$$+ \alpha A_{-1}bv^2 - 2A_{-1}b\beta\omega + A_{-1}b\beta - A_{-1}A_0v - A_{-2}A_1v = 0,$$
$$\alpha av^3 A_1 - 2\alpha av^3 \omega A_1 - 2av\beta\omega A_1 + av\beta A_1 - av A_1 + 2\alpha bv^2 \omega A_1 - \alpha bv^2 A_1$$
$$+ 2b\beta\omega A_1 - b\beta A_1 + bA_1 + vA_0 A_1 + vA_{-1}A_2 = 0,$$
$$8\alpha av^3 A_2 - 16\alpha av^3 \omega A_2 - 16av\beta\omega A_2 + 8av\beta A_2 - 2av A_2 + 16\alpha bv^2 \omega A_2 - 8\alpha bv^2 A_2$$
$$+ 16b\beta\omega A_2 - 8b\beta A_2 + 2bA_2 + vA_1^2 + 2vA_0 A_2 = 0,$$
$$2\alpha av^3 \omega A_1 + 2av\beta\omega A_1 - 2\alpha bv^2 \omega A_1 - 2b\beta\omega A_1 + vA_1 A_2 = 0,$$
$$12\alpha av^3 \omega A_2 + 12av\beta\omega A_2 - 12\alpha bv^2 \omega A_2 - 12b\beta\omega A_2 + vA_2^2 = 0.$$

Solving the above system, using Mathematica, we obtain

$$A_{-2} = \frac{12(1-\omega)(av-b)(\alpha v^2+\beta)}{v}, \quad A_0 = 4(av-b)\left\{\frac{((2\omega-1)(\alpha v^2+\beta)+1)}{v}\right\}, \quad (42)$$
$$A_{-1} = 0, \quad A_1 = 0, \quad A_2 = \frac{12\omega(b-av)(\alpha v^2+\beta)}{v}.$$

Therefore, the solution to the 2D-EW Equation (6) is

$$u(t,x,y) = \left\{\frac{12(av-b)(\alpha v^2+\beta)}{v}\right\}\left\{\frac{1-\omega}{\text{cn}^2(z|\omega)} - \omega\text{cn}^2(z|\omega)\right\} \quad (43)$$
$$+ 4(av-b)\left\{\frac{((2\omega-1)(\alpha v^2+\beta)+1)}{v}\right\},$$

where $0 \leq \omega \leq 1$ and $z = (av-b)t - vx + y$.

Snoidal wave solutions

Substituting (41) into (35) and making use of (37), we obtain an algebraic equation, which splits and yields the algebraic equations:

$$12\alpha bv^2 A_{-2} - 12\alpha av^3 A_{-2} - 12av\beta A_{-2} + 12b\beta A_{-2} + vA_{-2}^2 = 0,$$
$$vA_{-2}A_{-1} - 2\alpha av^3 A_{-1} - 2av\beta A_{-1} + 2\alpha bv^2 A_{-1} + 2b\beta A_{-1} = 0,$$
$$8\alpha av^3 \omega A_{-2} + 8\alpha av^3 A_{-2} + 8av\beta\omega A_{-2} + 8av\beta A_{-2} - 2av A_{-2} - 8\alpha bv^2 \omega A_{-2}$$
$$+ 2vA_{-2}A_0 - 8\alpha bv^2 A_{-2} - 8b\beta\omega A_{-2} - 8b\beta A_{-2} + 2bA_{-2} + vA_{-1}^2 = 0,$$
$$\alpha av^3 \omega A_{-1} + \alpha av^3 A_{-1} + av\beta\omega A_{-1} + av\beta A_{-1} - av A_{-1} - \alpha bv^2 \omega A_{-1} - \alpha bv^2 A_{-1}$$
$$+ vA_{-1}A_0 - b\beta\omega A_{-1} - b\beta A_{-1} + bA_{-1} + vA_{-2}A_1 = 0,$$
$$av A_1 - \alpha av^3 \omega A_1 - \alpha av^3 A_1 - av\beta\omega A_1 - av\beta A_1 + \alpha bv^2 \omega A_1 + \alpha bv^2 A_1 + b\beta\omega A_1$$
$$+ b\beta A_1 - bA_1 - vA_0 A_1 - vA_{-1}A_2 = 0,$$
$$8\alpha bv^2 \omega A_2 - 8\alpha av v^2 \omega A_2 - 8\alpha av v^2 A_2 - 8av\beta\omega A_2 - 8av\beta A_2 + 2av A_2 + 8\alpha bv^2 A_2$$
$$+ 8b\beta\omega A_2 + 8b\beta A_2 - 2bA_2 - vA_1^2 - 2A_0 vA_2 = 0,$$
$$2\alpha av v^2 \omega A_1 + 2av\beta\omega A_1 - 2\alpha bv^2 \omega A_1 - 2b\beta\omega A_1 - vA_1 A_2 = 0,$$
$$12\alpha av v^2 \omega A_2 + 12av\beta\omega A_2 - 12\alpha bv^2 \omega A_2 - 12b\beta\omega A_2 - vA_2^2 = 0.$$

The solution of the above system, using Mathematica, is

$$A_{-2} = \frac{12(av-b)(\alpha v^2+\beta)}{v}, \quad A_0 = (b-av)\left\{\frac{(4(\omega+1)(\alpha v^2+\beta)-1)}{v}\right\} \quad (44)$$
$$A_{-1} = 0, \quad A_1 = 0, \quad A_2 = \frac{12\omega(av-b)(\alpha v^2+\beta)}{v}.$$

Therefore, the solution for 2D-EW Equation (6) is

$$u(t,x,y) = \left\{ \frac{12(av-b)(av^2+\beta)}{v} \right\} \left\{ \frac{1}{\text{sn}^2(z|\omega)} + \omega \, \text{sn}^2(z|\omega) \right\} \\ + (b-av)\left\{ \frac{(4(\omega+1)(av^2+\beta)-1)}{v} \right\}, \qquad (45)$$

where $0 \leq \omega \leq 1$ and $z = (av-b)t - vx + y$.

2.6. Solution of (6) for $n=2$ Using $\mathcal{Z}_4$

We use the symmetry $\mathcal{Z}_4$ to reduce then 2D-EW Equation (6) for $n=2$. This symmetry has the invariants

$$r = x, \ s = y, \ u(t,x,y) = \frac{1}{t^{1/2}} \mathcal{P}(r,s) \qquad (46)$$

and they reduce Equation (6) to the NLPDE

$$\alpha \mathcal{P}_{rr} + \beta \mathcal{P}_{ss} - 2\mathcal{P}^2 \mathcal{P}_r + \mathcal{P} = 0. \qquad (47)$$

Equation (47) has two translation symmetries

$$W_1 = \frac{\partial}{\partial r}, \ W_2 = \frac{\partial}{\partial s}.$$

Consider the symmetry $W = W_1 + cW_2$. This gives the invariants

$$\mathcal{P}(r,s) = \mathcal{Q}(z), \ z = s - cr,$$

which reduces Equation (47) to the NODE

$$\beta \mathcal{Q}'' + \alpha c^2 \mathcal{Q}'' + 2c\mathcal{Q}^2 \mathcal{Q}' + \mathcal{Q} = 0. \qquad (48)$$

Power series solution

We find the solution of NODE (48) using the power series expansion method [10]. To obtain the power series solutions, we use the hypothesis

$$\mathcal{Q}(z) = \sum_{j=0}^{\infty} A_j z^j, \qquad (49)$$

where A_j, $j = 0, 1, \ldots$ are constants to be determined. From (49), we have

$$\mathcal{Q}'(z) = \sum_{j=0}^{\infty}(j+1)A_{j+1}z^j, \ \mathcal{Q}''(z) = \sum_{j=0}^{\infty}(j+1)(j+2)A_{j+2}z^j. \qquad (50)$$

Substituting the values of $\mathcal{Q}, \mathcal{Q}', \mathcal{Q}''$ from (49) and (50) into the NODE (48), we obtain

$$(\beta + \alpha c^2) \sum_{j=0}^{\infty}(j+1)(j+2)A_{j+2}z^j + 2c\left(\sum_{j=0}^{\infty} A_j z^j\right)^2 \left(\sum_{j=0}^{\infty}(j+1)A_{j+1}z^j\right) \\ + \sum_{j=0}^{\infty} A_j z^j = 0 \qquad (51)$$

and this simplifies to

$$(\beta + c^2 \alpha) \sum_{j=0}^{\infty}(j+1)(j+2)A_{j+2}z^j + 2c \sum_{j=0}^{\infty} \sum_{i=0}^{j} \sum_{k=0}^{i}(j-i+1)A_k A_{i-k} A_{j-i+1}z^j \\ + \sum_{j=0}^{\infty} A_j z^j = 0. \qquad (52)$$

Hence, by inspecting the coefficients for $j = 0$ and $j \geq 1$, we have

$$A_{j+2} = -\frac{1}{(\beta + \alpha c^2)(j+2)(j+1)} \left\{ 2c \sum_{i=0}^{j} \sum_{k=0}^{i} (j-i+1) A_k A_{i-k} A_{j-i+1} + A_j \right\}, \tag{53}$$

for $j \geq 0$ and A_0, A_1 are arbitrary constants. Thus, reverting to the original variables, the solution of the 2D-EW Equation (6) is

$$u(t,x,y) = A_0 + A_1(y - cx) + A_{j+2}(y - cx)^{j+2}, \tag{54}$$

where the coefficients $A_2, A_3, A_4, \ldots$ are obtained from the recursive formula (53).

3. Conservation Laws

We now derive conservation laws for the 2D-EW Equation (6) by invoking two approaches. Firstly, we employ the multiplier method, and secondly, we use the Noether's theorem.

3.1. Conservation Laws Using the Multiplier Method

We consider the zeroth-order multipliers for Equation (6), that is the multipliers $\mathcal{M}$ that depend on the variables t, x, y and u only. We obtain the multipliers by using the determining equation

$$E_u \{ \mathcal{M} (u_t + u^n u_x + \alpha u_{txx} + \beta u_{tyy}) \} = 0, \tag{55}$$

where E_u is the Euler–Lagrange operator defined by

$$E_u = \partial_u - D_t \partial_{u_t} - D_x \partial_{u_x} - D_y \partial_{u_y} - D_t D_x^2 \partial_{u_{txx}} - D_t D_y^2 \partial_{u_{tyy}} + \cdots. \tag{56}$$

Here, D_t, D_x, D_y are the total derivatives and are given by

$$D_t = \partial_t + u_t \partial_u + u_{tt} \partial_{u_t} + u_{tx} \partial_{u_x} + u_{ty} \partial_{u_y} + \cdots,$$
$$D_x = \partial_x + u_x \partial_u + u_{tx} \partial_{u_t} + u_{xx} \partial_{u_x} + u_{xy} \partial_{u_y} + \cdots,$$
$$D_y = \partial_y + u_y \partial_u + u_{ty} \partial_{u_t} + u_{xy} \partial_{u_x} + u_{yy} \partial_{u_y} + \cdots.$$

Expanding (55) and separating on various derivatives of u, we obtain

$$\beta \mathcal{M}_{tyy} + \mathcal{M}_t = 0, \; \mathcal{M}_{tu} = 0, \; \mathcal{M}_{uu} = 0, \; \mathcal{M}_x = 0, \tag{57}$$

which, upon solving, yields

$$\mathcal{M} = \mathbf{C_1} u + F(y) + G(t) \sin(y/\sqrt{\beta}) + H(t) \cos(y/\sqrt{\beta}), \tag{58}$$

where $\mathbf{C_1}$ is a constant and F, G, H are arbitrary functions of their arguments. Now, the conserved quantities of 2D-EW Equation (6) are derived using the divergence identity

$$D_t C^t + D_x C^x + D_y C^y = \mathcal{M} (u_t + u^n u_x + \alpha u_{txx} + \beta u_{tyy})$$

with C^t representing conserved density and C^x, C^y being spatial fluxes.

Case 1. The multiplier $\mathcal{M}_1 = u$ gives the conserved vector (C_1^t, C_1^x, C_1^y), where

$$\begin{aligned} C_1^t &= \frac{1}{2} u^2 - \frac{1}{6} \left(\alpha u_x^2 + \beta u_y^2 \right) + \frac{1}{3} (\alpha u u_{xx} + \beta u u_{yy}), \\ C_1^x &= \frac{1}{n+2} u^{n+2} - \frac{1}{3} \alpha u_t u_x + \frac{2}{3} \alpha u u_{tx}, \\ C_1^y &= \frac{2}{3} \beta u u_{ty} - \frac{1}{3} \beta u_t u_y; \end{aligned} \tag{59}$$

Case 2. For the multiplier $\mathcal{M}_2 = F(y)$, we obtain the conserved vector whose components are

$$C_2^t = \left(\frac{1}{3}\beta u_{yy} + \frac{1}{3}\alpha u_{xx} + u\right)F(y) - \frac{1}{3}\beta u_y F'(y) + \frac{1}{3}\beta u F''(y),$$

$$C_2^x = \left(\frac{2}{3}\alpha u_{tx} + \frac{1}{n+1}u^{n+1}\right)F(y), \qquad (60)$$

$$C_2^y = \frac{2}{3}\beta u_{ty}F(y) - \frac{1}{3}\beta u_t F'(y);$$

Case 3. Using the multiplier $\mathcal{M}_3 = G(t)\sin(y/\sqrt{\beta})$, we attain the conservation law whose components are

$$C_3^t = -\frac{1}{3}\left\{\sqrt{\beta}u_y \cos\left(\frac{y}{\sqrt{\beta}}\right) - (\alpha u_{xx} + \beta u_{yy} + 2u)\sin\left(\frac{y}{\sqrt{\beta}}\right)\right\}G(t),$$

$$C_3^x = \left\{\left(\frac{1}{n+1}u^{n+1} + \frac{2}{3}\alpha u_{tx}\right)G(t) + \frac{1}{3}\alpha u_x G'(t)\right\}\sin\left(\frac{y}{\sqrt{\beta}}\right),$$

$$C_3^y = \left\{\frac{2}{3}\beta u_{ty}G(t) - \frac{1}{3}\beta u_y G'(t)\right\}\sin\left(\frac{y}{\sqrt{\beta}}\right) + \left\{\frac{2}{3}\sqrt{\beta}u G'(t) - \frac{1}{3}\sqrt{\beta}u_t G(t)\right\}\cos\left(\frac{y}{\sqrt{\beta}}\right);$$

Case 4. Finally, the multiplier $\mathcal{M}_4 = H(t)\cos(y/\sqrt{\beta})$ gives the conserved vector (C_4^t, C_4^x, C_4^y), where

$$C_4^t = \frac{1}{3}\left\{\sqrt{\beta}u_y \sin\left(\frac{y}{\sqrt{\beta}}\right) + (\alpha u_{xx} + \beta u_{yy} + 2u)\cos\left(\frac{y}{\sqrt{\beta}}\right)\right\}H(t),$$

$$C_4^x = \left\{\left(\frac{1}{n+1}u^{n+1} + \frac{2}{3}\alpha u_{tx}\right)H(t) - \frac{1}{3}\alpha u_x H'(t)\right\}\cos\left(\frac{y}{\sqrt{\beta}}\right),$$

$$C_4^y = \left\{\frac{2}{3}\beta u_{ty}H(t) - \frac{1}{3}\beta u_y H'(t)\right\}\cos\left(\frac{y}{\sqrt{\beta}}\right) + \left\{\frac{1}{3}\sqrt{\beta}u_t H(t) - \frac{2}{3}\sqrt{\beta}u H'(t)\right\}\sin\left(\frac{y}{\sqrt{\beta}}\right).$$

3.2. Conservation Laws Using Noether's Theorem

The 2D-EW Equation (6) is a third-order NPDE and, as a result, does not have a Lagrangian. We however overcome this limitation by using the transformation $u = V_x$, and this transforms the 2D-EW Equation (6) to the variational equation

$$V_{tx} + V_x^n V_{xx} + \alpha V_{txxx} + \beta V_{txyy} = 0, \qquad (61)$$

which has a second-order Lagrangian $\mathcal{L}$ given by

$$\mathcal{L} = -\frac{1}{2}V_t V_x - \frac{1}{(n+1)(n+2)}V_x^{n+2} + \frac{1}{2}\alpha V_{tx}V_{xx} + \frac{1}{2}\beta V_{ty}V_{xy}, \; n \neq -1, -2, \qquad (62)$$

because $E_u \mathcal{L} = 0$ on the Equation (61). Here, the Euler operator E_u is given by

$$E_u = \frac{\partial}{\partial V} - D_t\frac{\partial}{\partial V_t} - D_x\frac{\partial}{\partial V_x} + D_t D_x\frac{\partial}{\partial V_{tx}} + D_x^2\frac{\partial}{\partial V_{xx}} + D_x D_y\frac{\partial}{\partial V_{xy}}.$$

The determining equation for Noether symmetries is

$$Z^{[2]}\mathcal{L} + \{D_t(\tau) + D_x(\xi) + D_y(\phi)\}\mathcal{L} - D_t(B^t) - D_x(B^x) - D^y(B^y) = 0, \qquad (63)$$

where $\mathcal{Z}^{[2]}$ is the second prolongation of

$$\mathcal{Z} = \tau(t,x,y,\mathcal{V})\frac{\partial}{\partial t} + \xi(t,x,y,\mathcal{V})\frac{\partial}{\partial x} + \phi(t,x,y,\mathcal{V})\frac{\partial}{\partial y} + \eta(t,x,y,\mathcal{V})\frac{\partial}{\partial \mathcal{V}}$$

and (B^t, B^x, B^y) are gauge functions that depend on $(t,x,y,\mathcal{V})$. Expanding (63), we obtain an equation which is then separated by various derivatives of $\mathcal{V}$ to give the following PDEs:

$\tau_x = 0,\ \tau_y = 0,\ \tau_\mathcal{V} = 0,\ \xi_t = 0,\ \xi_y = 0,\ \xi_{xx} = 0,\ \xi_\mathcal{V} = 0,\ \phi_t = 0,\ \phi_\mathcal{V} = 0,\ \phi_x = 0,$

$\eta_{tx} = 0,\ \eta_{tx} = 0,\ \eta_x = 0,\ B^t_\mathcal{V} = 0,\ \eta_{\mathcal{V}\mathcal{V}} = 0,\ \eta_{x\mathcal{V}} = 0,\ \eta_{t\mathcal{V}} = 0,\ \eta_{x\mathcal{V}} = 0,\ \eta_{yy} = 0,$

$\eta_{y\mathcal{V}} = 0,\ \eta_{t\mathcal{V}} = 0,\ 2\eta_\mathcal{V} - \phi_y = 0,\ B^x_\mathcal{V} + \frac{1}{2}\eta_t = 0,\ \eta_\mathcal{V} + \frac{1}{2}\phi_y = 0,\ B^t_\mathcal{V} + \frac{1}{2}\eta_x = 0,$

$\phi_y + 2\eta_\mathcal{V} - 2\xi_x = 0,\ B^t_t + B^x_x + B^y_y = 0,\ \tau_t + \xi_x + n\xi_x - \phi_y - (n+2)\eta_\mathcal{V} = 0.$

Solving the above overdetermined system of equations, we obtain

$\tau = c_1,\ \xi = c_2,\ \phi = c_3,\ \eta = yg(t) + f(t),$

$B^t = F_4(t,x,y),\ B^x = -\frac{1}{2}y\mathcal{V}g'(t) - \frac{1}{2}\mathcal{V}f'(t) + F_5(t,x,y),\ B^y = F_6(t,x,y),$

where c_1, c_2, c_2 are constants, whereas f, g, F_4, F_5, F_6 are arbitrary functions of their arguments. We take $F_4 = F_5 = F_6 = 0$, since they contribute to the trivial part of the conservation laws. Thus, the Noether symmetries and their gauge functions are

$\mathcal{Z}_1 = \frac{\partial}{\partial t},\ B^t_1 = 0,\ B^x_1 = 0,\ B^y_1 = 0,$

$\mathcal{Z}_2 = \frac{\partial}{\partial x},\ B^t_2 = 0,\ B^x_2 = 0,\ B^y_2 = 0,$

$\mathcal{Z}_3 = \frac{\partial}{\partial y},\ B^t_3 = 0,\ B^x_3 = 0,\ B^y_3 = 0,$

$\mathcal{Z}_4 = f(t)\frac{\partial}{\partial \mathcal{V}},\ B^t_4 = 0,\ B^x_4 = -\frac{1}{2}\mathcal{V}f'(t),\ B^y_4 = 0,$

$\mathcal{Z}_5 = yg(t)\frac{\partial}{\partial \mathcal{V}},\ B^t_5 = 0,\ B^x_5 = -\frac{1}{2}y\mathcal{V}g'(t),\ B^y_5 = 0.$

Corresponding to each of the above Noether symmetries, we obtain the following nonlocal conserved vectors for the 2D-EW Equation (6) by invoking formulas given in [24]:

Case 1. $\mathcal{Z}_1 = \partial/\partial t$

$T^t_1 = \frac{1}{4}\alpha u_x u_t - \frac{1}{(n+1)(n+2)}u^{n+2} + \left(\frac{1}{4}\alpha u_{xx} + \frac{1}{4}\beta u_{yy}\right)\int u_t dx$

$\quad + \frac{1}{4}\beta u_t \int u_{yy}dx,$

$T^x_1 = -\frac{1}{2}\alpha u_t^2 + \left(\frac{3}{4}\alpha u_{tx} + \frac{1}{n+1}u^{n+1} + \frac{1}{2}\int u_t dx + \frac{1}{4}\beta \int u_{tyy}dx\right)\int u_t dx$

$\quad - \left(\frac{1}{4}\beta\int u_{yy}dx + \frac{1}{4}\alpha u_x\right)\int u_{tt}dx,$

$T^y_1 = \frac{1}{2}\beta u_{ty}\int u_t dx - \frac{1}{2}\beta u_t\int u_{ty}dx;$

Case 2. $\mathcal{Z}_2 = \partial/\partial x$

$T^t_2 = \frac{1}{4}\alpha u u_{xx} - \frac{1}{4}\alpha u_x^2 + \frac{1}{4}\beta u u_{yy} - \frac{1}{4}\beta u_x\int u_{yy}dx + \frac{1}{2}u^2,$

$T^x_2 = \frac{1}{n+2}u^{n+2} + \frac{3}{4}\alpha u u_{tx} - \frac{1}{4}\alpha u_x u_t + \frac{1}{4}\beta u\int u_{tyy}dx + \frac{1}{4}\beta u_t\int u_{yy}dx,$

$$T_2^y = \frac{1}{2}\beta u u_{ty} - \frac{1}{2}\beta u_t u_y;$$

Case 3. $\mathcal{Z}_3 = \partial/\partial y$

$$T_3^t = -\frac{1}{4}\alpha u_x u_y - \frac{1}{4}\beta u_y \int u_{yy}dx + \left(\frac{1}{4}\alpha u_{xx} + \frac{1}{4}\beta u_{yy} + \frac{1}{2}u\right)\int u_y dx,$$

$$T_3^x = \left(\frac{1}{n+1}u^{n+1} + \frac{3}{4}\alpha u_{tx} + \frac{1}{4}\beta \int u_{tyy}dx + \frac{1}{2}\int u_t dx\right)\int u_y dx$$
$$- \left(\frac{1}{4}\alpha u_x + \frac{1}{4}\beta \int u_{yy}dx\right)\int u_{ty}dx - \frac{1}{2}\alpha u_t u_y,$$

$$T_3^y = -\frac{1}{(n+1)(n+2)}u^{n+2} + \frac{1}{2}\alpha u_x u_t + \frac{1}{2}\beta u_{ty}\int u_y dx - \frac{1}{2}u \int u_t dx;$$

Case 4. $\mathcal{Z}_4 = f(t)\partial/\partial \mathcal{V}$

$$T_4^t = \left(-\frac{1}{4}\beta u_{yy} - \frac{1}{4}\alpha u_{xx} - \frac{1}{2}u\right)f(t),$$

$$T_4^x = \left(-\frac{1}{n+1}u^{n+1} - \frac{3}{4}\alpha u_{tx} - \frac{1}{4}\beta \int u_{tyy}dx - \frac{1}{2}\int u_t dx\right)f(t) + \left(\frac{1}{4}\alpha u_x\right.$$
$$\left. + \frac{1}{4}\beta u_{yy} + \frac{1}{2}\int u dx\right)f'(t),$$

$$T_4^y = -\frac{1}{2}\beta f(t)u_{ty};$$

Case 5. $\mathcal{Z}_5 = yg(t)\partial/\partial \mathcal{V}$

$$T_5^t = \left(-\frac{1}{4}\alpha y u_{xx} - \frac{1}{4}\beta y u_{yy} - \frac{1}{2}yu\right)g(t),$$

$$T_5^x = \left(-\frac{1}{n+1}yu^{n+1} - \frac{3}{4}\alpha y u_{tx} - \frac{1}{4}\beta y \int u_{tyy}dx - \frac{1}{2}y \int u_t dx\right)g(t)$$
$$+ \left(\frac{1}{4}\alpha y u_x + \frac{1}{4}\beta y \int u_{yy}dx + \frac{1}{2}y \int u dx\right)g'(t),$$

$$T_5^y = \left(\frac{1}{2}\beta u_t - \frac{1}{2}\beta y u_{ty}\right)g(t).$$

We note that due to the presence of arbitrary functions f and g, we obtain infinitely many conservation laws.

4. Conclusions

In this work, we investigated the 2D-EW Equation (6), which is used to model nonlinear dispersive waves. We computed Lie point symmetries of (6), and as a result, we obtained four symmetries that include the three translation and one scaling symmetries. Moreover, we performed symmetry reductions and obtained several NODEs, which were solved with the aid of various techniques. The methods included the Kudryashov's method, power series expansion method, extended Jacobi elliptic method and the Weierstrass elliptic function method. The exact solutions obtained are the snoidal wave, cnoidal wave, Weierstrass elliptic function, Jacobi elliptic cosine function, solitary wave and exponential function solutions. Furthermore, the graphical representation for certain solutions was also presented for certain parametric values in 2D and 3D, so as to give the reader a better understanding of these solutions. Finally, using two techniques, the conservation laws for the underlying equation were constructed. The techniques utilized were the multiplier method which gave four local conservation laws and the classical Noether's theorem, which gave five nonlocal conservation laws. The conservation laws that were constructed contained the conservation of energy and momentum.

Author Contributions: Conceptualization, C.M.K. and K.P.; methodology, C.M.K.; software, K.P.; validation, C.M.K.; writing—original draft, K.P.; writing—review and editing, C.M.K. All authors have read and agreed to the published version of the manuscript.

Funding: This research received no external funding.

Institutional Review Board Statement: Not applicable.

Informed Consent Statement: Not applicable.

Data Availability Statement: Not applicable.

Acknowledgments: The authors thank North-West University, Mafikeng campus, for their continued support.

Conflicts of Interest: The authors declare no conflict of interest.

References

1. Xu, G.; Zhang, Y.; Li, J. Exact solitary wave and periodic-peakon solutions of the complex Ginzburg-Landau equation: Dynamical system approach. *Math. Comput. Simul.* **2022**, *191*, 157–167. [CrossRef]
2. Mahak, N.; Akram, G. Exact solitary wave solutions of the (1+1)-dimensionional Fokas-Lenells equation. *Optik* **2020**, *208*, 164459. [CrossRef]
3. Patsiuk, O.; Kovalenko, S. Symmetry reduction and exact solutions of the non-linear Black-Scholes equation. *Commun. Nonliear Sci. Numer. Simulat.* **2018**, *62*, 164–173. [CrossRef]
4. Celik, N.; Seadawy, A.R.; Ozkan, Y.S.; Yasar, E. A model of solitary waves in a nonlinear elastic circular rod: Abundant different type of exact solutions and conservation laws. *Chaos Solit. Fractals* **2021**, *143*, 110486. [CrossRef]
5. Rogers, C.; Shadwick, W.F. *Bäcklund Transformations and Their Applications*; Mathematics in Science and Engineering Series; Academic Press: New York, NY, USA, 1982.
6. Krasil'shchik, I.S.; Vinogradov Editors, A.M. *Symmetries and Conservation Laws for Differential Equations of Mathematical Physics*; American Mathematical Society: Providence, RI, USA, 1999.
7. Igonin, S.; Van De Leur, J.; Manno, G.; Trushko, V. Infinite-dimensional prolongation Lie algebras and multicomponent Landau-Lifshitz systems associated with higher genus curves. *J. Geom. Phys.* **2013**, *68*, 1–26. [CrossRef]
8. Kudryashov, N.A. Simplest equation method to look for exact solutions of nonlinear differential equations. *Chaos Solit. Fractals* **2005**, *24*, 1217–1231. [CrossRef]
9. Wen, X.; Lu, D. Extended Jacobi elliptic function expansion method and its application to nonlinear evolution equation. *Chaos Solit. Fractals* **2009**, *41*, 1454–1458. [CrossRef]
10. Liu, H.; Sang, B.; Xin, X.; Liu, X. CK transformations, symmetries, exact solutions and conservation laws of the generalized variable-coefficient KdV types of equations. *J. Comput. Appl. Math.* **2019**, *345*, 127–134. [CrossRef]
11. Malfliet, W. Solitary wave solutions of nonlinear wave equations. *Am. J. Phys.* **1992**, *60*, 650. [CrossRef]
12. Ovsiannikov, L.V. *Group Analysis of Differential Equations*; Academic Press: New York, NY, USA, 1982.
13. Bluman, G.W.; Kumei, S. *Symmetries and Differential Equations*; Springer: New York, NY, USA, 1989.
14. Olver, P.J. *Applications of Lie Groups to Differential Equations*, 2nd ed.; Springer: Berilin/Heidelberg, Germany, 1993.
15. Ibragimov, N.H. *CRC Handbook of Lie Group Analysis of Differential Equations*; CRC Press: Boca Raton, FL, USA, 1995; Volume 2.
16. Ibragimov, N.H. *Elementary Lie Group Analysis and Ordinary Differential Equations*; John Wiley & Sons: Chichester, NY, USA, 1999.
17. Khalique, C.M.; Plaatjie, K. Exact solutions and conserved vectors of the two-dimensional generalized shallow water wave equation. *Mathematics* **2021**, *9*, 1439. [CrossRef]
18. Adeyemo, O.D.; Motsepa, T.; Khalique, C.M. A study of the generalized nonlinear advection diffusion equation arising in engineering sciences. *Alexandria Eng. J.* **2022**, *61*, 185–194. [CrossRef]
19. Zhang, L.; Khalique, C.M. Classification and bifurcation of a class of second-order ODEs and its application to nonlinear PDEs. *Discrete Cont. Dyn-S* **2018**, *11*, 777–790. [CrossRef]
20. Wang, M.; Li, X.; Zhang, J. The $(G'/G)-$ expansion method and travelling wave solutions for linear evolution equations in mathematical physics. *Phys. Lett. A* **2005**, *24*, 1257–1268.
21. Leveque, R.J. *Numerical Methods for Conservation Laws*, 2nd ed.; Birkhäuser-Verlag: Basel, Switzerland, 1992.
22. Sjöberg, A. On double reductions from symmetries and conservation laws. *Nonlinear Anal. Real World Appl.* **2009**, *10*, 3472–3477. [CrossRef]
23. Noether, E. Invariante variationsprobleme. *Nachrichten von der Gesellschaft der Wissenschaften zu Göttingen* **1918**, *2*, 235–257.
24. Sarlet, W. Comment on 'Conservation laws of higher order nonlinear PDEs and the variational conservation laws in the class with mixed derivatives'. *J. Phys. A Math. Theor.* **2010**, *43*, 458001. [CrossRef]
25. Khalique, C.M.; Abdallah, S.A. Coupled Burgers equations governing polydispersive sedimentation; a Lie symmetry approach. *Results Phys.* **2020**, *16*, 102967. [CrossRef]

26. Khalique, C.M.; Maefo, K. A study on the (2+1)-dimensional first extended Calegero-Bogoyavlenskii-Schiff equation. *Math. Bioci. Eng.* **2021**, *18*, 5816–5835. [CrossRef] [PubMed]
27. Gandarias, M.L.; Duran, M.R.; Khalique, C.M. Conservation laws and travelling wave solutions for double dispersion equations in (1+1) and (2+1) dimensions. *Symmetry* **2020**, *12*, 950. [CrossRef]
28. Ibragimov, N.H. A new conservation theorem. *J. Math. Anal. Appl.* **2007**, *333*, 311–328. [CrossRef]
29. Naz, R.; Mahomed, F.M.; Mason, D.P. Conservation laws via the partial Lagrangian and group invariant solutions for radial and two-dimensional free jets. *Nonlinear. Anal. Real World Appl.* **2009**, *10*, 3457–3465. [CrossRef]
30. Motsepa, T.; Khalique, C.M. Closed-form solutions and conserved vectors of the (3+1)-dimensional negative-order KdV equation. *Adv. Math. Models Appl.* **2020**, *5*, 7–18.
31. Jhangeer, A.; Naeem, I. Conserved quantities for a class of (1+n)-dimensional linear evolution equation. *Commun. Nonlinear Sci. Numer. Simul.* **2012**, *17*, 2804–2814. [CrossRef]
32. Morrison, P.J.; Meiss, J.D.; Carey, J.R. Scattering of regularized long-waves. *Phys. D* **1984**, *11*, 324–336. [CrossRef]
33. Khalique, C.M.; Plaatjie, K.; Simbanefayi, I. Exact solutions of equal-width equation and its conservation laws. *Open Phys.* **2019**, *17*, 505–511. [CrossRef]
34. Gardner, L.R.T.; Gardner, G.A.; Ayoub, F.A.; Amein, N.K. Simulations of the EW undular bore. *Comput. Num. Methods Engrg.* **1997**, *13*, 583–592. [CrossRef]
35. Lu, D.; Seadawy, A.R.; Ali, A. Dispersive traveling wave solutions of the equal-width and modified equal-width equations via mathematical methods and its applications. *Results Phys.* **2018**, *9*, 313–32. [CrossRef]
36. Zaki, S.I. Solitary wave interactions for the modified equal width equation. *Comput. Phys. Commun.* **2000**, *126*, 219–231. [CrossRef]
37. Saka, B. Algorithms for numerical solution of the modified equal width wave equation using collocation method. *Math. Comput. Model* **2007**, *45*, 1096–1117. [CrossRef]
38. Khalique, C.M.; Adeyemo, O.D.; Simbanefayi, I. On optimal system, exact solutions and conservation laws of the modified equal-width equation. *Appl. Mathe. Nonlinear Sci.* **2018**, *3*, 409–418. [CrossRef]
39. Hamdi, S.; Enright, W.H.; Schiesser, W.E.; Gottlieb, J.J. Exact solutions of the generalized equal width wave equation. In *Computational Science and Its Applications—ICCSA 2003*; Lecture Notes in Computer Science; Kumar, V., Gavrilova, M.L., Tan, C.J.K., L'Ecuyer, P., Eds.; Springer: Berlin/Heidelberg, Germany, 2003; Volume 2668.
40. Munir, M.; Athar, M.; Sarwar, S.; Shatanawi, W. Lie symmetries of generalized equal width wave equations. *AIMS Math.* **2021**, *6*, 12148–12165. [CrossRef]
41. Padmasekaran, S.; Asokan, R.; Kannagidevi, K. Lie symmetries of (2+1)-dimensional modified equal width wave equation. *Int. J. Math. Trends Technol.* **2018**, *56*, 2231–5373.
42. Kudryashov, N.A. One method for finding exact solutions of nonlinear differential equations. *Commun. Nonlinear Sci. Numer. Simulat.* **2012**, *17*, 2248–2253. [CrossRef]
43. Kudryashov, N.A. *Analytical Theory of Nonlinear Differential Equations*; Institute of Computer Investigations: Moskow, Russia, 2004.
44. Abramowitz, M.; Stegun, I. *Handbook of Mathematical Functions*; Dover: New York, NY, USA, 1972.
45. Kudryashov, N.A. First integrals and general solution of the Fokas-Lenells equation. *Optik* **2019**, *195*, 163135. [CrossRef]

Article

Numerical Simulation of Cubic-Quartic Optical Solitons with Perturbed Fokas–Lenells Equation Using Improved Adomian Decomposition Algorithm

Alyaa A. Al-Qarni [1], Huda O. Bakodah [2], Aisha A. Alshaery [2], Anjan Biswas [3,4,5,6,7], Yakup Yıldırım [8], Luminita Moraru [9] and Simona Moldovanu [10,*]

1. Department of Mathematics, College of Science, University of Bisha, P.O. Box 551, Bisha 61922, Saudi Arabia; aqarny@ub.edu.sa
2. Department of Mathematics, Faculty of Science, University of Jeddah, P.O. Box 80327, Jeddah 21959, Saudi Arabia; hobakodah@uj.edu.sa (H.O.B.); aaal-shaery@uj.edu.sa (A.A.A.)
3. Department of Applied Mathematics, National Research Nuclear University, 31 Kashirskoe Hwy, 115409 Moscow, Russia; biswas.anjan@gmail.com
4. Mathematical Modeling and Applied Computation (MMAC) Research Group, Department of Mathematics, King Abdulaziz University, Jeddah 21589, Saudi Arabia
5. Department of Applied Sciences, Cross–Border Faculty, Dunarea de Jos University of Galati, 111 Domneasca Street, 800201 Galati, Romania
6. Department of Mathematics and Applied Mathematics, Sefako Makgatho Health Sciences University, Medunsa 0204, South Africa
7. Department of Physics, Chemistry and Mathematics, Alabama A&M University, Normal, AL 35762-4900, USA
8. Department of Mathematics, Faculty of Arts and Sciences, Near East University, Nicosia 99138, Cyprus; yakup.yildirim@neu.edu.tr
9. Faculty of Sciences and Environment, Department of Chemistry, Physics and Environment, Dunarea de Jos University of Galati, 47 Domneasca Street, 800008 Galati, Romania; luminita.moraru@ugal.ro
10. Department of Computer Science and Information Technology, Faculty of Automation, Computers, Electrical Engineering and Electronics, Dunarea de Jos University of Galati, 47 Domneasca Street, 800008 Galati, Romania
* Correspondence: simona.moldovanu@ugal.ro

Citation: Al-Qarni, A.A.; Bakodah, H.O.; Alshaery, A.A.; Biswas, A.; Yıldırım, Y.; Moraru, L.; Moldovanu, S. Numerical Simulation of Cubic-Quartic Optical Solitons with Perturbed Fokas–Lenells Equation Using Improved Adomian Decomposition Algorithm. *Mathematics* **2022**, *10*, 138. https://doi.org/10.3390/math10010138

Academic Editors: David Carfì and Yang-Hui He

Received: 25 November 2021
Accepted: 30 December 2021
Published: 4 January 2022

Publisher's Note: MDPI stays neutral with regard to jurisdictional claims in published maps and institutional affiliations.

Copyright: © 2022 by the authors. Licensee MDPI, Basel, Switzerland. This article is an open access article distributed under the terms and conditions of the Creative Commons Attribution (CC BY) license (https:// creativecommons.org/licenses/by/ 4.0/).

Abstract: The current manuscript displays elegant numerical results for cubic-quartic optical solitons associated with the perturbed Fokas–Lenells equations. To do so, we devise a generalized iterative method for the model using the improved Adomian decomposition method (ADM) and further seek validation from certain well-known results in the literature. As proven, the proposed scheme is efficient and possess a high level of accuracy.

Keywords: improved adomian decomposition method; optical soliton; Fokas–Lenells equations; cubic-quartic optical solitons

1. Introduction

Optical solitons, which emerge from nonlinear evolution equations, have been studied for the past few decades. The self-phase modulation (SPM) that comes from intensity-dependent refractive index of light coupled with the chromatic dispersion (CD) leads to a delicate balance, which sustains the solitons that travel down the fiber for intercontinental distances. Several models that give way to optical solitons are addressed in Mathematics, Physics and telecommunications engineering. The notion of cubic-quartic (CQ) solitons surfaced in the realm of nonlinear fiber optics for the first time in 2017, and an avalanche of results were eventually visible. Prior to this, it is the concept of pure-quartic solitons that was visible [1]. Such CQ solitons were introduced due to the sheer necessity whenever CD is low enough to be ignored and thus third-order dispersion (3OD) and fourth-order dispersion (4OD) effects are able to compensate for this depletion. This allows the sustainment of the necessary balance between the dispersion effects and SPM to be restored, allowing stable solitons to be transmitted across intercontinental distances.

Furthermore, optical solitons have painstakingly fashioned pulse transmission technology for several waveguides [2–4]. This technical feat is described at a spectacular level by several mathematical models. The Fokas–Lenells equation (FLE), which governs this dynamic, was originally launched almost a decade ago [5–7]. Since its initial introduction, this model has garnered widespread recognition in the fiber-optics community. In the past, several types of soliton solutions for this model were recovered. However, none of these studies have explored the implications of perturbation terms that emerge as a result of natural factors in soliton transmission dynamics. The FLE is examined in this study, along with a few perturbative effects.

As all previous efforts on CQ solitons have been analytical in nature, it is therefore imperative to consider such solitons from a numerical standpoint. Thus, this article employs a numerical approach to CQ solitons. However, the methodology used to present the findings in this manuscript is the enhanced form of the strongly reliant Adomian's method called the improved Adomian decomposition method (ADM) [8]. We will, therefore, suggest an efficient numerical scheme for solving CQ optical solitons associated with the perturbed FLE. The approach will be based on the improved ADM. Besides, improved ADM is a fast numerical approach for integral and functional solutions that is based on Adomian's method [9]. Validation of the suggested method will be carried out with recent analytical results in the literature. The integration method reveals promising results without the need of either linearization or any artificial boundary condition. Lastly, the improved ADM architecture has its shortcomings. It fails to capture the effect of soliton radiation that is a major detrimental factor in the soliton propagation.

The manuscript is arranged in the following manner: the perturbed FLE is described in Section 2; while the governing model is addressed via the improved ADM in Section 3. The simulated numerical results are retrieved in Section 4, and some concluding comments are reported in Section 5.

2. Governing Model

The dimensionless form of the CQ solitons with the perturbed FLE is indicated below [10]

$$iq_t + iaq_{xxx} + bq_{xxxx} + |q|^2(cq + idq_x) = i\left[\alpha q_x + \lambda\left(|q|^2 q\right)_x + \mu\left(|q|^2\right)_x q\right], \quad (1)$$

where x and t are the independent spatial and temporal variables, sequentially; while the function $q = q(x, t)$ is the complex wave profile. Additionally, starting with the left-hand side, the first component indicates the temporal evolution, whereas a and b are the coefficients of the 3OD and 4OD, sequentially; while d gives the nonlinear dispersion term and the coefficient c is the Kerr law nonlinearity. Additionally for Equation (1), λ is the self-steepening term, whereas the coefficients μ and α are for the higher-order and inter-modal dispersions, sequentially.

3. Analysis of the Method

This section introduces the efficient improved ADM to derive a numerical scheme for the CQ–FLE given in Equation (1). Initially, we offer the fundamental technique for constructing nonlinear wave solutions of the equation. In our analysis, the complex CQ–FLE given in Equation (1) will be converted to a real system using

$$q(x,t) = u_1 + iu_2. \quad (2)$$

Plugging Equation (2) into Equation (1), we have

$$i(u_1 + iu_2)_t + ia(u_1 + iu_2)_{xxx} + b(u_1 + iu_2)_{xxxx}$$
$$+ |u_1 + iu_2|^2 (c(u_1 + iu_2) + id(u_1 + iu_2)_x) = i[\alpha(u_1 + iu_2)_x \qquad (3)$$
$$+ \lambda \left(|qu_1 + iu_2|^2 (u_1 + iu_2) \right)_x + \mu \left(|u_1 + iu_2|^2 \right)_x (u_1 + iu_2)].$$

Thus, from the above equation, the following system is obtained, after splitting the real and imaginary parts as follows

$$u_{1t} + au_{1xxx} + bu_{2xxxx} + (u_1^2 + u_2^2)(cu_2 + du_{1x}) \\ = \alpha u_{1x} + \lambda((q^2 u_1^2 + u_2^2)u_2)_x + \mu(u_1^2 + u_2^2)_x u_2, \qquad (4)$$

and

$$-u_{2t} - au_{2xxx} + bu_{1xxxx} + (u_1^2 + u_2^2)(cu_1 - du_{2x}) \\ = -\alpha u_{2x} + \lambda((q^2 u_1^2 + u_2^2)u_1)_x + \mu(u_1^2 + u_2^2)_x u_1, \qquad (5)$$

where

$$u_1(x, 0) = [q(x, 0)]_R,$$

and

$$u_2(x, 0) = [q(x, 0)]_I.$$

Now, on using the Adomian's approach, the solution of the above system transforms into the following infinite series

$$u_1(x, t) = \sum_{n=0}^{\infty} u_{1n}(x, t), \qquad (6)$$

and

$$u_2(x, t) = \sum_{n=0}^{\infty} u_{2n}(x, t). \qquad (7)$$

Here u_{1n}, u_{2n}, $n \geq 0$, will be obtained recurrently. Furthermore, in an operator form, we re-express Equations (4) and (5) as follows

$$L_t(u_1) + au_{1xxx} + bu_{2xxxx} + (u_1^2 + u_2^2)(cu_2 + du_{1x}) \\ = \alpha u_{1x} + \lambda((q^2 u_1^2 + u_2^2)u_2)_x + \mu(u_1^2 + u_2^2)_x u_2, \qquad (8)$$

and

$$L_t(u_2) + au_{2xxx} - bu_{1xxxx} - (u_1^2 + u_2^2)(cu_1 - du_{2x}) \\ = \alpha u_{2x} - \lambda((q^2 u_1^2 + u_2^2)u_1)_x - \mu(u_1^2 + u_2^2)_x u_1, \qquad (9)$$

where

$$L_t = \frac{\partial}{\partial t}.$$

Further, using the inverse operator L_t^{-1} on both sides of Equations (8) and (9) yields

$$u_1(x, t) = u_1(x, 0) - L_t^{-1} au_{1xxx} - L_t^{-1} bu_{2xxxx} - L_t^{-1}(u_1^2 + u_2^2)(cu_2 + du_{1x}) \\ + L_t^{-1} \alpha u_{1x} + \lambda((q^2 u_1^2 + u_2^2)u_2)_x + L_t^{-1}\mu(u_1^2 + u_2^2)_x u_2,$$

and

$$u_2(x, t) = u_2(x, 0) - L_t^{-1} au_{2xxx} + L_t^{-1} bu_{1xxxx} + L_t^{-1}(u_1^2 + u_2^2)(cu_1 - du_{2x}) \\ + L_t^{-1} \alpha u_{2x} - L_t^{-1}\lambda((q^2 u_1^2 + u_2^2)u_1)_x - L_t^{-1}\mu(u_1^2 + u_2^2)_x u_1.$$

Next, re-expressing the above system via the Adomian polynomials, we have

$$u_1(x, t) = u_1(x, 0) - L_t^{-1} au_{1xxx} + L_t^{-1} bu_{2xxxx} + L_t^{-1} \alpha u_{1x} + L_t^{-1} A_1, \qquad (10)$$

and

$$u_2(x, t) = u_2(x, 0) - L_t^{-1} au_{2xxx} - L_t^{-1} bu_{1xxxx} + L_t^{-1} \alpha u_{2x} + L_t^{-1} A_2, \qquad (11)$$

where the terms A_1 and A_2 in Equations (10) and (11) are the nonlinear terms represented by

$$A_1 = -\left(u_1^2 + u_2^2\right)(cu_2 + du_{1x}) + \lambda\left(\left(q^2 u_1^2 + u_2^2\right)u_2\right)_x + \mu\left(u_1^2 + u_2^2\right)_x u_2, \quad (12)$$

and

$$A_2 = \left(u_1^2 + u_2^2\right)(cu_1 - du_{2x}) - \lambda\left(\left(q^2 u_1^2 + u_2^2\right)u_1\right)_x - \mu\left(u_1^2 + u_2^2\right)_x u_1, \quad (13)$$

Of which $A_1 = \sum_{n=0}^{\infty} A_{1n}$ and $A_2 = \sum_{n=0}^{\infty} A_{2n}$, where $A_{1n}, \ldots, A_{2n}, \ldots$ are the Adomian polynomials, which may be generated from all types of nonlinearity, using Adomian's specific algorithms. Plugging the solution forms in Equations (5) and (6), as well as A_1 and A_2 in Equations (12) and (13), into Equations (10) and (11) yields

$$\sum_{n=0}^{\infty} u_{1n}(x,t) = u_1(x,0) - L_t^{-1} a \sum_{n=0}^{\infty} (u_{1n}(x,t))_{xxx} + L_t^{-1} b \sum_{n=0}^{\infty} (u_{2n}(x,t))_{xxxx} + L_t^{-1} \sum_{n=0}^{\infty} A_{1n}, \quad (14)$$

and

$$\sum_{n=0}^{\infty} u_{2n}(x,t) = u_2(x,0) - L_t^{-1} a \sum_{n=0}^{\infty} (u_{2n}(x,t))_{xxx} + L_t^{-1} b \sum_{n=0}^{\infty} (u_{1n}(x,t))_{xxxx} + L_t^{-1} \sum_{n=0}^{\infty} A_{2n}. \quad (15)$$

The following recursive relations are introduced as a result of the decomposition analysis

$$u_{1,0}(x,t) = u_1(x,0), \quad (16)$$

$$u_{2,0}(x,t) = u_2(x,0), \quad (17)$$

$$u_{1,k+1}(x,t) = -L_t^{-1} a \sum_{n=0}^{\infty} (u_{1n}(x,t))_{xxx} + L_t^{-1} b \sum_{n=0}^{\infty} (u_{2n}(x,t))_{xxxx} + L_t^{-1} \sum_{n=0}^{A_{1n}} A_{1n}, \quad (18)$$

and

$$u_{2,k+1}(x,t) = -L_t^{-1} a \sum_{n=0}^{\infty} (u_{2n}(x,t))_{xxx} + L_t^{-1} b \sum_{n=0}^{\infty} (u_{1n}(x,t))_{xxxx} + L_t^{-1} \sum_{n=0}^{\infty} A_{2n}. \quad (19)$$

Thus, we determine u_1 and u_2 as follows

$$u_1 = u_{1,0} + u_{1,1} + u_{1,2} + \ldots,$$

and

$$u_2 = u_{2,0} + u_{2,1} + u_{2,2} + \ldots,$$

and the entire approximate solution for Equation (1) is derived by plugging the preceding equations into Equation (2), which is connected to Equations (16)–(19) to yield the following

$$q(x,t) = u_{1,0} + u_{1,1} + u_{1,2} + \cdots + i(u_{2,0} + u_{2,1} + u_{2,2} + \cdots). \quad (20)$$

4. Numerical Results

This section analyzes three distinct scenarios for the CQ–FLE given in Equation (1) to demonstrate how the improved ADM scheme derived in the previous Section might be applied. We analyze the CQ bright soliton of the perturbed FLE, which was recently derived by Elsayed et al. [10] that is formulated as

$$q(x,t) = A \operatorname{sech}[B(x - vt)] e^{i(-k_l x + \omega_l t + \theta)}, \quad (21)$$

where A and B are the soliton's amplitude and width, sequentially, that are structured as

$$A = \pm \frac{\Delta_0}{10} \sqrt{-\frac{30}{\Delta_1}}, \quad (22)$$

and
$$B = \frac{1}{2}\sqrt{-\frac{\Delta_0}{5}}, \tag{23}$$

along with
$$v = -\alpha - 3ak^2 + 4bk^3,$$
$$\Delta_0 = \frac{1}{b}\left(3ak - 6bk^2\right),$$

and
$$\Delta_3 = \frac{1}{b}(c + dk + \lambda k).$$

Moreover, from Equations (22)–(23), the constraint criteria for the possibility of bright solitons were given by
$$\Delta_0 < 0, \Delta_3 < 0.$$

The phase component in Equation (21) represents the soliton's velocity. θ is the phase constant. The soliton's frequency is
$$k = -\frac{a}{4b},$$
while the wave number is
$$\omega = -\frac{k\left(36ka^2 - 119abk^2 + 119b^2k^3 + 25b\alpha\right)}{25b}.$$

Consider the CQ-FLE (1) along with the parameters [10]
$$\alpha = 0.1, \ \lambda = 1, \ \mu = 1, d = 3\lambda + 2\mu.$$

In addition, the initial condition at $t = 0$ from Equation (21) follows as
$$q(x,0) = A \operatorname{sech}[B(x)]e^{i(-kx+\theta)}. \tag{24}$$

However, for the sake of numerical simulation, we consider the following three cases of the model fixed parameters:
Case 1:
$$a = 0.5, \ b = -1, \ c = 1.$$
Case 2:
$$a = 1, \ b = -2, \ c = 2.$$
Case 3:
$$a = 0.5, \ b = -0.5, \ c = 1.$$

In what follows, we report the absolute error differences between the exact solution and that of the approximate solution using the improved ADM of the three solution cases in Tables 1–3. Furthermore, we portray the respective solution cases in Figures 1–3 for various values of t over the interval $-50 \le x \le 50$. Without loss of generality, these figures are self-explanatory, as the proposed numerical method performs excellently. Additionally, an absolute agreement is noted in these figures in the bulk parts of the bell-shaped solution; only a small disparity is noted at the peak of the curves. This disparity can equally be overcome when the model's parameters are suitably chosen and, also by considering more iterates/approximants in the series summation.

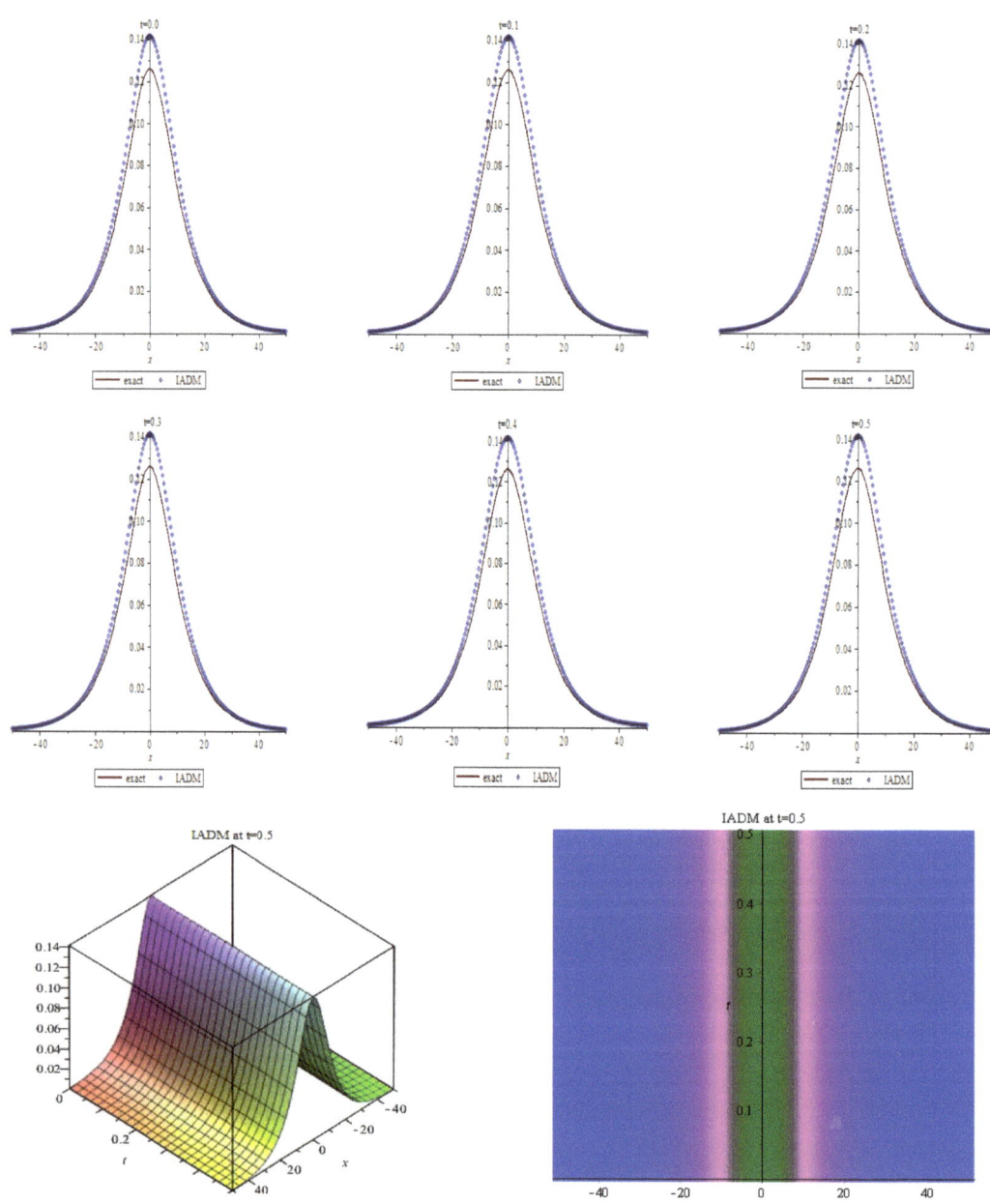

Figure 1. Comparison of the exact and improved ADM solutions for case 1 for $-50 \leq x \leq 50$.

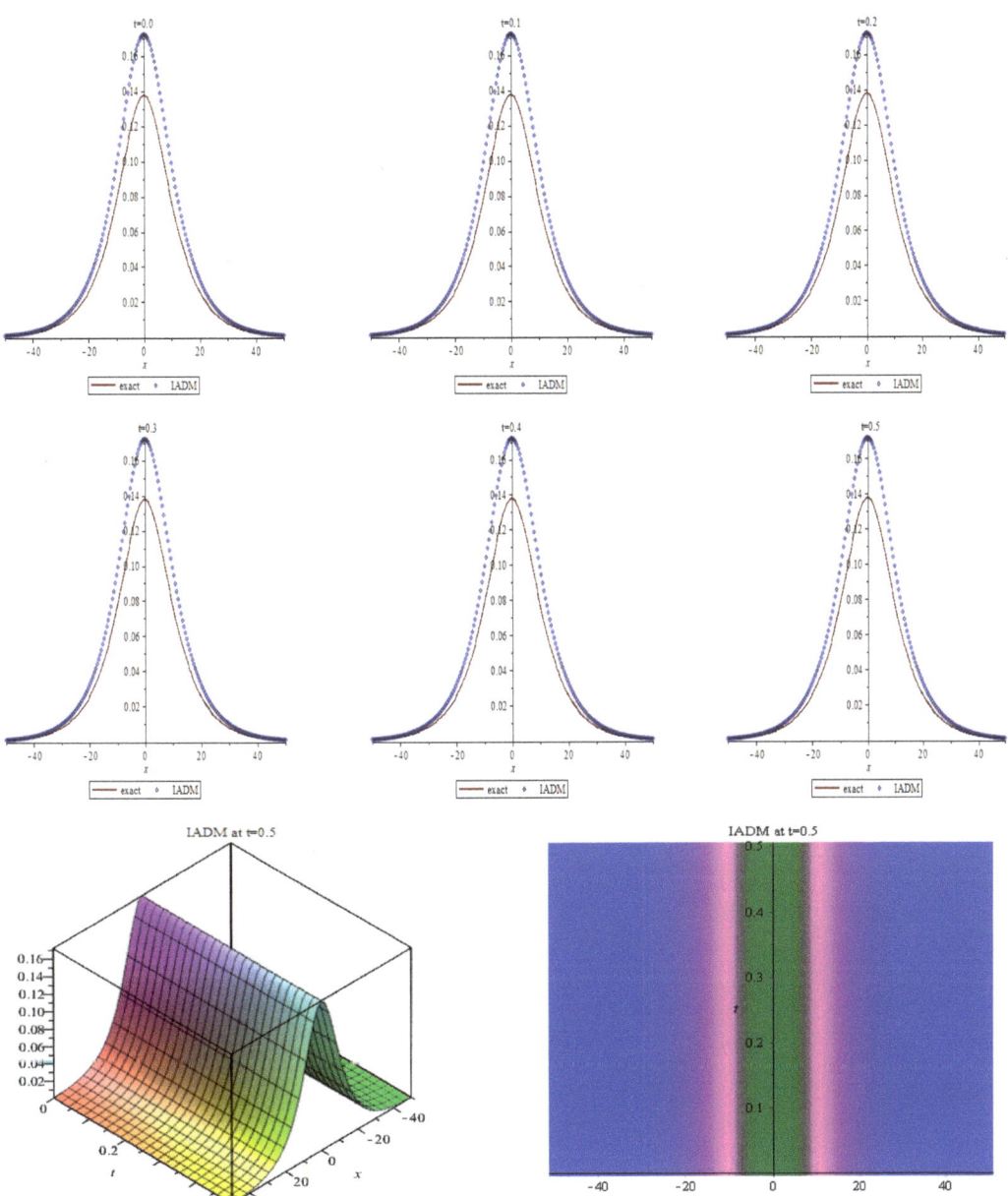

Figure 2. Comparison of the exact and improved ADM solutions for case 2 for $-50 \leq x \leq 50$.

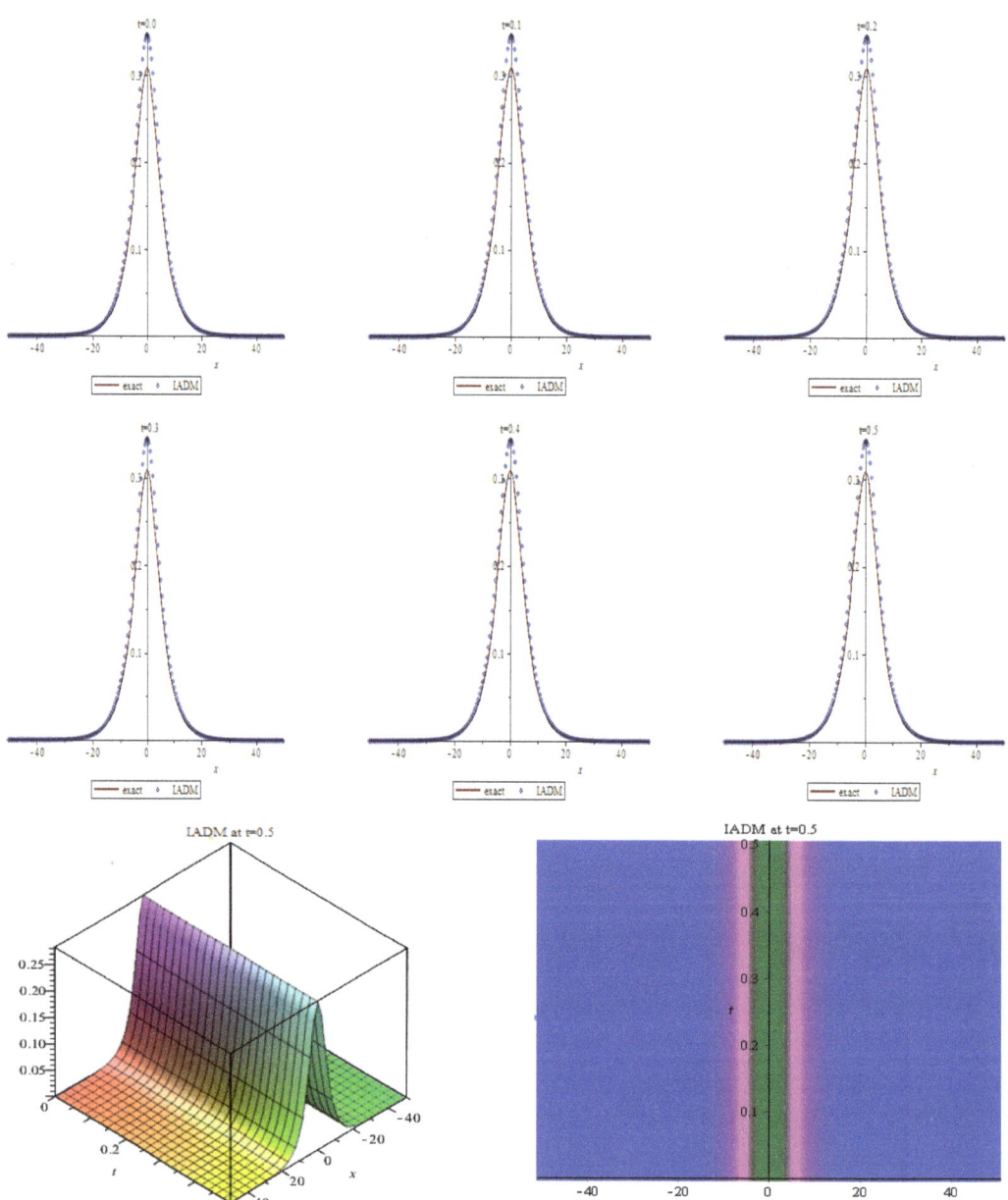

Figure 3. Comparison of the exact and improved ADM solutions for case 3 for $-50 \leq x \leq 50$.

Table 1. Absolute error for Case 1 for $x = 20$, $x = 50$.

t	Error When $x = 20$	Error When $x = 50$
0.0	0.00304922317	0.0000878266951
0.1	0.00306667344	0.0000883416821
0.2	0.00308409727	0.0000888560318
0.3	0.00310149460	0.0000893697436
0.4	0.00311886552	0.0000898828190
0.5	0.00313621000	0.0000903952578

Table 2. Absolute error for Case 2 for $x = 20$, $x = 50$.

t	Error When $x = 20$	Error When $x = 50$
0.0	0.00692281558	0.0001996291264
0.1	0.00692913128	0.0001998464016
0.2	0.00693539773	0.0002000633452
0.3	0.00694161507	0.0002002799558
0.4	0.00694778339	0.0002004962310
0.5	0.00695390283	0.0002007121745

Table 3. Absolute error for Case 3 for $x = 20$, $x = 50$.

t	Error When $x = 20$	Error When $x = 50$
0.0	0.000574951108	$4.67316035 \times 10^{-7}$
0.1	0.000570769757	$4.63918739 \times 10^{-7}$
0.2	0.000566597435	$4.60529257 \times 10^{-7}$
0.3	0.000562434066	$4.57147514 \times 10^{-7}$
0.4	0.000558279554	4.5377342×10^{-7}
0.5	0.000554133811	$4.50406915 \times 10^{-7}$

5. Conclusions

In conclusion, CQ optical solitons are a modern topic of great interest in the field of optical communications. In this paper, the effect of changing the optical parameters of such CQ solitons with perturbed FLE was studied.

The unperturbed FLE, coupled with the chromatic dispersion and spatiotemporal dispersion has been studied for the past few decades [5–7]. The initial-boundary value problems, that are referred to as the linearizable boundary conditions, for the FLE are analyzed in [5]. A class of exact combined solitary wave solutions of the FLE is constructed by adopting the complex envelope function ansatz [6]. The influences of spatiotemporal dispersion on the characteristics of combined solitary waves are also discussed in [6]. A class of chirped soliton-like solutions including bright, dark and kink solitons is derived in [8]. The associated chirp, including linear and nonlinear contributions, is also determined for each of optical pulses in [7]. When compared with [5–7], none of these studies have explored the implications of perturbation terms that emerge as a result of natural factors in soliton transmission dynamics. Therefore, the FLE is examined in this study along with a few perturbative effects that are crucial to many applications in photonics, performing essential functions in lasing, frequency conversion, and entangled-photon generation. Furthermore, these perturbative effects may be used to generate new frequency components from high power pulses, resulting in optical pulses with spectral widths much larger than the gain-bandwidth of optical fiber amplifiers. In other words, these nonlinear effects can be used to make useful devices capable of processing high-speed optical signals. Additionally, none of the works in [5–7] have addressed the implications of cubic-quartic solitons. Thus, the current paper reports cubic-quartic solitons that are the sheer necessity whenever CD is low enough to be ignored. As a result, CQ solitons compensate for this depletion. Hence, CQ solitons allow the sustainment of the necessary balance between the dispersion effects and self-phase modulation to be restored, allowing stable solitons to be transmitted across intercontinental distances. The results of the current paper are new and are elegant numerical results for cubic-quartic optical solitons associated with the perturbed FLE, where the perturbation terms are all of Hamiltonian type and the chromatic dispersion is replaced by a combination of third-order dispersion and fourth-order dispersion.

Cubic-quartic solitons with the perturbed FLE (1) have been addressed for the analytical study and revealed quite a number of interesting solitons in nonlinear optics [10], where bright and singular solitons have been yielded by a couple of integration approaches. While all previous efforts on CQ solitons have been analytical in nature [10], it is therefore imperative to consider such solitons from a numerical standpoint. Thus, the current paper focuses on the integrability of the perturbed FLE (1) for the numerical investigation using the improved ADM architecture for the very first time. Analytical solutions are possible using simplifying assumptions that may not realistically reflect reality. In many applications, analytical solutions are impossible to achieve. Hence, numerical methods make it possible to obtain realistic solutions without the need for simplifying assumptions. The improved ADM adopted in this paper leads to the emergence of bright soliton solutions and is being reported for the first time in this paper, which makes these results novel. The bright soliton solutions are very important, and these soliton solutions are used to sustain pulse transmission through optical fibers in the telecommunications industry.

A promising technique called the improved ADM, which was based on the famous Adomian's method, was utilized to derive a recurrent numerical scheme for the governing model and, furthermore, was successfully applied to the model through bright soliton solutions. The integration method firstly converts a special case of the complex-valued system into a real-valued system. Next, the integration scheme decomposes the solutions into infinite sums of components called infinite series. When compared with the famous Adomian's method, the improved ADM reveals promising results without the need of either linearization or any artificial boundary condition. The scheme is indeed reliable as it was discovered to display results with higher accuracy. The numerical computations are simpler and faster than most of the traditional techniques. Finally, the method is recommended to investigate additional evolution equations.

Author Contributions: Conceptualization, A.A.A. and H.O.B.; methodology, A.A.A.-Q.; software, A.B.; writing—original draft preparation, Y.Y.; writing—review and editing, L.M. and S.M. All authors have read and agreed to the published version of the manuscript.

Funding: This research received no external funding.

Institutional Review Board Statement: Not applicable.

Informed Consent Statement: Not applicable.

Data Availability Statement: All data generated or analyzed during this study are included in this manuscript.

Acknowledgments: The authors thank the anonymous referees whose comments helped to improve the paper.

Conflicts of Interest: The authors declare no conflict of interest.

References

1. Blanco-Redondo, A.; Sterke, C.M.D.; Sipe, J.E.; Krauss, T.F.; Eggleton, B.J.; Husko, C. Pure–quartic solitons. *Nat. Commun.* **2016**, *7*, 11048. [CrossRef] [PubMed]
2. Boutabba, N. Kerr-effect analysis in a three-level negative index material under magneto cross-coupling. *J. Opt.* **2018**, *20*, 025102. [CrossRef]
3. Eleuch, H.; Elser, D.; Bennaceur, R. Soliton propagation in an absorbing three-level atomic system. *Laser Phys. Lett.* **2004**, *1*, 391. [CrossRef]
4. Boutabba, N.; Eleuch, H.; Bouchriha, H. Thermal bath effect on soliton propagation in three-level atomic system. *Synth. Met.* **2009**, *159*, 1239–1243. [CrossRef]

5. Lennels, J.; Fokas, A.S. An integrable generalization of the nonlinear Schrödinger equation on the half-line and solitons. *Inverse Probl.* **2009**, *25*, 115006. [CrossRef]
6. Triki, H.; Wazwaz, A.M. Combined optical solitary waves of the Fokas–Lenells equation. *Waves Rand. Complex Media* **2017**, *27*, 587–593. [CrossRef]
7. Triki, H.; Wazwaz, A.M. New types of chirped soliton solutions for the Fokas–Lenells equation. *Int. J. Numer. Methods Heat Fluid Flow* **2017**, *27*, 1596–1601. [CrossRef]
8. Bakodah, H.O.; Banaja, M.A.; Alshaery, A.A.; Al Qarni, A.A. Numerical Solution of Dispersive Optical Solitons with Schrödinger-Hirota Equation by Improved Adomian Decomposition Method. *Math. Probl. Eng.* **2019**, *2019*, 2960912. [CrossRef]
9. Adomian, G. Solution of physical problems by decomposition. *Comput. Math. Appl.* **1994**, *27*, 145–154. [CrossRef]
10. Zayed, E.M.E.; Alngar, M.E.M.; Biswas, A.; Yıldırım, Y.; Khan, S.; Alzahrani, A.K.; Belic, M.R. Cubic–quartic optical soliton perturbation in polarization-preserving fibers with Fokas–Lenells equation. *Optik* **2021**, *234*, 166543. [CrossRef]

Article

Diverse Multiple Lump Analytical Solutions for Ion Sound and Langmuir Waves

Abdulmohsen D. Alruwaili [1], Aly R. Seadawy [2,*], Syed T. R. Rizvi [3] and Sid Ahmed O. Beinane [1]

[1] Mathematics Department, College of Science, Jouf University, Sakaka 72341, Saudi Arabia; adalruwail@ju.edu.sa (A.D.A.); sabeinane@ju.edu.sa (S.A.O.B.)

[2] Mathematics Department, Faculty of Science, Taibah University, Al-Madinah Al-Munawarah 41411, Saudi Arabia

[3] Department of Mathematics, COMSATS University Islamabad, Lahore Campus, Sakaka 72341, Pakistan; strrizvi@gmail.com

* Correspondence: aabdelalim@taibahu.edu.sa

Abstract: In this work, we study a time-fractional ion sound and Langmuir waves system (FISLWS) with Atangana–Baleanu derivative (ABD). We use a fractional ABD operator to transform our system into an ODE. We investigate multiwaves, periodic cross-kink, rational, and interaction solutions by the combination of rational, trigonometric, and various bilinear functions. Furthermore, 3D, 2D, and relevant contour plots are presented for the natural evolution of the gained solutions under the selection of proper parameters.

Keywords: multiwave; periodic cross-kink solutions; rational and interaction solutions; time-fractional ion sound and Langmuir waves system

1. Introduction

At the present time, various real phenomena have been formulated by integer-order nonlinear partial differential equations (NPDEs). These supermodels are studied in different domains of sciences, such as engineering, chemistry, biology, physics, optics, etc. However, it is not enough to use integer order where the nonlocal property does not appear in these forms, so different models have been systematized in fractional NPDEs to determine that kind of similarity [1]. By using numerical and computational schemes, these models give more familiar properties [2–10]. To use most of these schemes, one needs fractional operator to transform the fractional forms into nonlinear ODEs with integer orders such as conformable fractional derivative, Caputo, Caputo–Fabrizio definition, Riemann–Liouville derivatives, and so on [11–24]. These operators have been applied to estimate the numeric and exact solutions of fractional order NPDEs through different integration schemes, such as (ϕ^6)-model expansion [25], $(\frac{G'}{G})$-expansion [26], $tan(\frac{\Phi(\rho)}{2})$-expansion [27], Kudryashove scheme [28], $exp((-\frac{\Psi'}{\Psi})\eta)$-expansion [29], extended auxiliary equation technique [30], and so many others.

Here, we consider the FISLWS as follows [17],

$$i\,^{AB}D_t^\alpha m + \frac{1}{2}m_{xx} - nm = 0, \qquad (1)$$
$$^{AB}D_t^{2\alpha}n - n_{xx} - 2(|m|^2)_{xx} = 0, \quad t > 0, \quad 0 < \alpha \leq 1.$$

where $me^{-i\omega_p t}$ and n illustrate the normalized electric-field of the Langmuir oscillation and perturbation of density, respectively. Both x and t are normalized variables and $^{AB}D_t^\alpha$ is the AB fractional operator in t direction.

ABD operator is well defined as

$$^{ABD}D^{\alpha}_{a^+}F(t) = \frac{B(\alpha)}{1-\alpha}\frac{d}{dt}\int_a^t F(x)G_\alpha\left(\frac{-\alpha(t-\alpha)^\alpha}{1-\alpha}\right)dx, \qquad (2)$$

where G_α is Mittag-Leffler function, defined as

$$G_\alpha\left(\frac{-\alpha(t-\alpha)^\alpha}{1-\alpha}\right) = \sum_{n=0}^\infty \frac{(\frac{-\alpha}{1-\alpha})^s(t-x)^{\alpha s}}{\Gamma(\alpha s+1)}, \qquad (3)$$

and $B(\alpha)$ is the normalization function that satisfies $B(1) = B(0) = 1$. Thus,

$$^{ABD}D^{\alpha}_{a^+}F(t) = \frac{B(\alpha)}{1-\alpha}\sum_{n=0}^\infty \left(\frac{-\alpha}{1-\alpha}\right)^s{}^{RL}I^{\alpha s}_a F(t). \qquad (4)$$

for more properties of this operator. This leads towards the following form,

$$m(x,t) = u(\zeta)e^{i\vartheta}, \qquad n(x,t) = v(\zeta), \qquad (5)$$

$$\vartheta = ax + \frac{\beta(1-\alpha)t^{-s}}{B(\alpha)\sum_{s=0}^\infty(-\frac{\alpha}{1-\alpha})^s\Gamma(1-\alpha s)},$$

$$\zeta = bx + \frac{\gamma(1-\alpha)t^{-s}}{B(\alpha)\sum_{s=0}^\infty(-\frac{\alpha}{1-\alpha})^s\Gamma(1-\alpha s)},$$

where β and γ are arbitrary constants. This wave alteration converts Equation (1) into the following ODE.

$$\frac{1}{2}b^2 u'' + i(\gamma + ab)u' - \frac{1}{2}(a^2 + 2\beta)u - uv = 0, \qquad (6)$$

$$(\gamma^2 - b^2)v'' - 4b^2(u'^2 + uu'') = 0.$$

Here, u and v are the functions of ζ. By separating the Img part from the first part of Equation (6),

$$\gamma + ab = 0 \implies \gamma = -ab. \qquad (7)$$

and then by integrating the second part of Equation (6) by two times the w.r.t ζ, we obtain

$$v = \frac{2b^2}{-b^2+\gamma^2}u^2 = \frac{2}{a^2-1}u^2. \qquad (8)$$

Equations (7) and (8) transform Equation (6) into the following form:

$$u'' - \frac{4}{b^2(a^2-1)}u^3 - \frac{a^2+2\beta}{b^2}u = 0, \qquad (9)$$

or

$$u'' = \frac{4}{b^2(a^2-1)}u^3 + \frac{a^2+2\beta}{b^2}u.$$

The contents of this paper are arranged as follows: In Section 2, we present M-shaped rational solitons. In Section 3, we evaluate M-shaped interaction solutions. In Section 4, we find the multiwaves solution. In Section 5, we study homoclinic breather. In Section 6, we investigate periodic cross-kink solutions. In Section 7, we present results and discussions and Section 8 contains concluding remarks.

2. M-Shaped Rational Solitons

By using the following log transformation,

$$u = u_0 + 2(\ln \Phi)_\xi. \tag{10}$$

Equation (10) transforms Equation (9) into the following bilinear form:

$$u_0(-a^4 - 4u_0^2 + a^2(1-2\beta) + 2\beta)\Phi^3 + 4(-8 + (-1+a^2)b^2)\Phi'^3 - 6\Phi\Phi'(8u_0\Phi' + (-1+a^2)b^2\Phi'') - 2\Phi^2((a^4 + 12u_0^2 - 2\beta + a^2(-1+2\beta))\Phi' - (-1+a^2)b^2\Phi''') = 0. \tag{11}$$

We choose M-shaped rational solution in bilinear form for Φ, as follows [31]:

$$\Phi = (b_2 + b_1\xi)^2 + (b_4 + b_3\xi)^2 + b_5, \tag{12}$$

where $b_i (1 \leq i \leq 5)$ all are real-valued parameters to be measured. Inserting Φ into Equation (11) and collecting all powers of ξ, we obtain proper results, as follows (See Figures 1 and 2):

Set I. For $b_2 = 0$,

$$a = a, b = b, \beta = -\frac{a^4 - a^2 + 4u_0^2}{2(a^2-1)}, b_1 = ib_3, b_3 = b_3, b_4 = b_4, b_5 = b_5, u_0 = u_0. \tag{13}$$

Using this in Equation (12), and then by using Equations (8) and (10), we obtain

$$u(\xi) = u_0 + \frac{2(-2b_3^2\xi + 2b_3(b_4+b_3\xi))}{b_5 - b_3^2\xi^2 + (b_4+b_3\xi)^2}, \tag{14}$$

$$v(\xi) = \frac{2}{a^2-1}\left(u_0 + \frac{2(-2b_3^2\xi + 2b_3(b_4+b_3\xi))}{b_5 - b_3^2\xi^2 + (b_4+b_3\xi)^2}\right)^2.$$

To obtain final results, we use Equation (5):

$$m_{21}(x,t) = e^{i\left(ax - \frac{t^{-s}(a^4-a^2+4u_0^2)(1-\alpha)}{2(a^2-1)B(\alpha)\sum_{s=0}^\infty(-\frac{\alpha}{1-\alpha})^s \Gamma(1-\alpha s)}\right)}\left(u_0 + \frac{2(2b_3(b_4+b_3\Omega) - 2b_3^2\Omega)}{b_5 + (b_4+b_3\Omega)^2 - b_3\Omega^2}\right),$$

$$n_{22}(x,t) = \frac{2}{(a^2-1)}\left(u_0 + \frac{2(2b_3(b_4+b_3\Omega) - 2b_3^2\Omega)}{b_5 + (b_4+b_3\Omega)^2 - b_3\Omega^2}\right)^2, \tag{15}$$

where $\Omega = \left(bx - \frac{abt^{-s}(1-\alpha)}{B(\alpha)\sum_{s=0}^\infty(-\frac{\alpha}{1-\alpha})^s \Gamma(1-\alpha s)}\right)$.

Set II. For $b_5 = 0$,

$$a = a, b = b, \beta = -\frac{a^4 - a^2 + 4u_0^2}{2(a-1)(a+1)}, b_1 = ib_3, b_2 = b_2, b_3 = b_3, b_4 = b_4, u_0 = u_0. \tag{16}$$

Using this in Equation (12), and then by using Equations (8) and (10) in Equation (5), we obtain

$$m_{23}(x,t) = e^{i\left(ax - \frac{t^{-s}(a^4-a^2+4u_0^2)(1-\alpha)}{2(a^2-1)B(\alpha)\sum_{s=0}^\infty(-\frac{\alpha}{1-\alpha})^s \Gamma(1-\alpha s)}\right)}\left(u_0 + \frac{2(2ib_3(b_2+ib_3\Omega) + 2b_3(b_4+b_3\Omega))}{(b_2+ib_3\Omega)^2 + (b_4+b_3\Omega)^2}\right),$$

$$n_{24}(x,t) = \frac{2}{(a^2-1)}\left(u_0 + \frac{2(2ib_3(b_2+ib_3\Omega) + 2b_3(b_4+b_3\Omega))}{(b_2+ib_3\Omega)^2 + (b_4+b_3\Omega)^2}\right)^2, \tag{17}$$

where $\Omega = \left(bx - \frac{abt^{-s}(1-\alpha)}{B(\alpha)\sum_{s=0}^\infty(-\frac{\alpha}{1-\alpha})^s \Gamma(1-\alpha s)}\right)$.

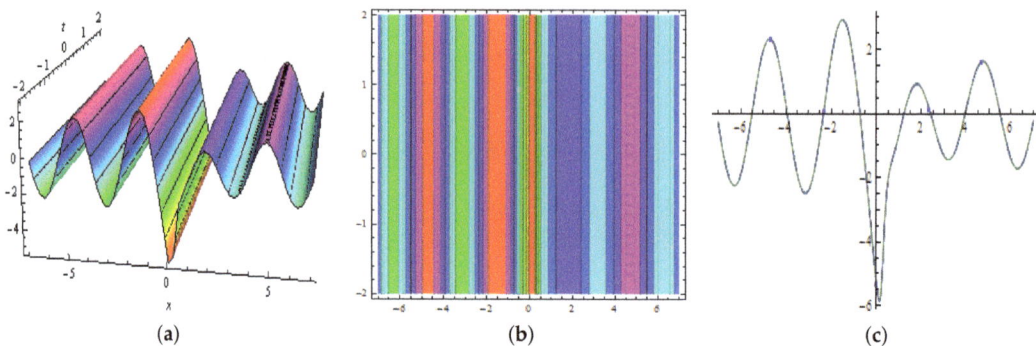

Figure 1. Plots of $m_{23}(x,t)$ in Equation (17) for $a = 2, b = 1.2, u_0 = -2, b_2 = 3, b_3 = 5, b_4 = -3, \alpha = 0.9$, respectively as three-dimensions in (**a**); contour in (**b**) and two-dimensions in (**c**)

Set III. For $u_0 = 0$,

$$a = a, b = b, \beta = -\frac{1}{2}a^2, b_1 = ib_3, b_2 = b_2, b_3 = b_3, b_4 = b_4, b_5 = b_5. \tag{18}$$

Using this in Equation (12), and then by using Equations (8) and (10), we obtain

$$u(\xi) = \frac{2(2ib_3(b_2+ib_3\xi)+2b_3(b_4+b_3\xi))}{b_5+(b_2+ib_3\xi)^2+(b_4+b_3\xi)^2}, \tag{19}$$

$$v(\xi) = \frac{8(2ib_3(b_2+ib_3\xi)+2b_3(b_4+b_3\xi))^2}{(-1+a^2)(b_5+(b_2+ib_3\xi)^2+(b_4+b_3\xi)^2)^2}.$$

To obtain final results, we use Equation (5):

$$m_{25}(x,t) = \frac{2e^{i\left(ax - \frac{a^2 t^{-s}(1-\alpha)}{2B(\alpha)\sum_{s=0}^{\infty}(-\frac{\alpha}{1-\alpha})^s \Gamma(1-\alpha s)}\right)}(2ib_3(b_2+ib_3\Omega)+2b_3(b_4+b_3\Omega))}{b_5+(b_2+ib_3\Omega)^2+(b_4+b_3\Omega)^2}, \tag{20}$$

$$n_{26}(x,t) = \frac{8}{(a^2-1)}\left(\frac{2ib_3(b_2+ib_3\Omega)+2b_3(b_4+b_3\Omega)}{b_5+(b_2+ib_3\Omega)^2+(b_4+b_3\Omega)^2}\right)^2,$$

where $\Omega = \left(bx - \frac{abt^{-s}(1-\alpha)}{B(\alpha)\sum_{s=0}^{\infty}(-\frac{\alpha}{1-\alpha})^s \Gamma(1-\alpha s)}\right)$.

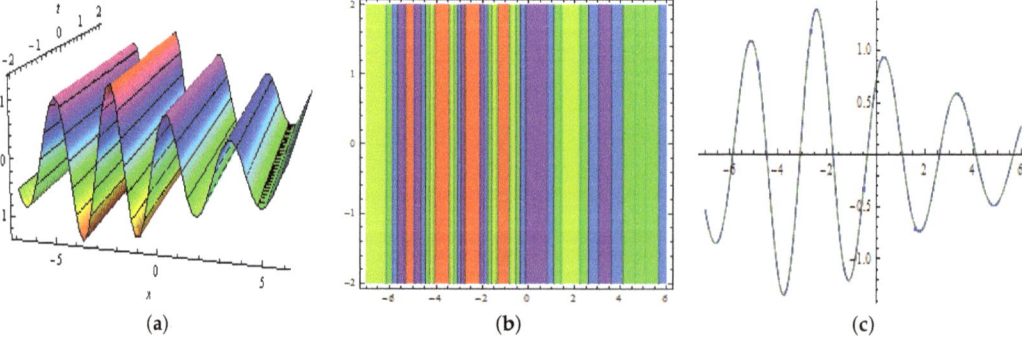

Figure 2. represented three-dimensions in (**a**); contour in (**b**) and two-dimensions in (**c**), Plots of $m_{25}(x,t)$ in Equation (20) for $a = 2, b = 0.5, b_2 = -3, b_3 = 1, b_4 = 3, b_5 = -1, \alpha = 0.8$, respectively.

3. M-Shaped Rational Soliton Interactions with

In this part, we evaluate M-shaped rational interactions with periodic and kink waves by using exponential and cos function in bilinear combinations.

3.1. One-Kink Soliton

For this, the bilinear form for Φ is as follows [31]:

$$\Phi = (b_2 + b_1\zeta)^2 + (b_4 + b_3\zeta)^2 + c\, e^{b_6 + b_5\zeta} + b_7, \qquad (21)$$

where $b_i (1 \leq i \leq 7)$, all are real-valued parameters to be measured. Inserting Φ into Equation (11) and collecting all powers of $e^{b_5\zeta+b_6}$, $e^{2(b_5\zeta+b_6)}$, $e^{3(b_5\zeta+b_6)}$, $\zeta e^{b_5\zeta+b_6}$, $\zeta e^{2(b_5\zeta+b_6)}$, $\zeta^2 e^{b_5\zeta+b_6}$, $\zeta^3 e^{b_5\zeta+b_6}$, $\zeta^4 e^{b_5\zeta+b_6}$, and ζ, we obtain proper results, as follows (See Figures 3–6):

Set I. For $b_2 = b_6 = 0$,

$$a = a, b = 2\sqrt{2}\sqrt{\tfrac{1}{a^2-1}}, \beta = -\tfrac{a^4-a^2+4b_5^2}{2(a-1)(a+1)}, b_1 = ib_3, b_3 = b_3, b_4 = b_4, b_5 = b_5, \qquad (22)$$

$$b_7 = b_7, u_0 = -b_5.$$

Using Equation (22) in Equation (21), and then by using Equations (8) and (10), we obtain

$$u(\zeta) = -b_5 + \frac{2\left(b_5 c e^{b_5\zeta} - 2b_3^2 \zeta + 2b_3(b_4 + b_3\zeta)\right)}{b_7 + c e^{b_5\zeta} - b_3^2\zeta^2 + (b_4 + b_3\zeta)^2}, \qquad (23)$$

$$v(\zeta) = \frac{2\left(b_5(b_4^2 + b_7 - c e^{b_5\zeta}) + 2b_3 b_4(-2 + b_5\zeta)\right)^2}{(-1+a^2)(b_4^2 + b_7 + c e^{b_5\zeta} + 2b_3 b_4\zeta)^2}.$$

Using Equation (5) to obtain the required solution for Equation (1),

$$m_{31}(x,t) = -\frac{e^{\Delta}\left(4\sqrt{2}a\sqrt{\tfrac{1}{a^2-1}}b_3 b_4 b_5(\alpha-1) + t^s\left(b_5(b_4^2 + b_7 - c e^{\Delta_1}) + 4b_3 b_4(-1 + \sqrt{2}\sqrt{\tfrac{1}{a^2-1}}b_5 x)\right)\Xi\right)}{4\sqrt{2}a\sqrt{\tfrac{1}{a^2-1}}b_3 b_4(\alpha-1) + t^s\left(b_4^2 + b_7 + c e^{\Delta_1} + 4\sqrt{2}\sqrt{\tfrac{1}{a^2-1}}b_3 b_4 x\right)\Xi},$$

(24)

$$n_{32}(x,t) = \frac{2}{(a^2-1)}\left(\frac{4\sqrt{2}a\sqrt{\tfrac{1}{a^2-1}}b_3 b_4 b_5(\alpha-1) + t^s\left(b_5(b_4^2 + b_7 - c e^{\Delta_1}) + 4b_3 b_4(-1 + \sqrt{2}\sqrt{\tfrac{1}{a^2-1}}b_5 x)\right)\Xi}{4\sqrt{2}a\sqrt{\tfrac{1}{a^2-1}}b_3 b_4(\alpha-1) + t^s\left(b_4^2 + b_7 + c e^{\Delta_1} + 4\sqrt{2}\sqrt{\tfrac{1}{a^2-1}}b_3 b_4 x\right)\Xi}\right)^2,$$

where $\Delta = \tfrac{1}{2}i(2ax + \tfrac{(-a^2+a^4+4b_5^2)t^{-s}(-1+\alpha)}{(-1+a)(1+a)B(\alpha)\sum_{s=0}^{\infty}(-\tfrac{\alpha}{1-\alpha})^s \Gamma(1-\alpha s)})$,

$\Delta_1 = 2\sqrt{2}\sqrt{\tfrac{1}{a^2-1}}b_5\left(x + \tfrac{at^{-s}(-1+\alpha)}{B(\alpha)\sum_{s=0}^{\infty}(-\tfrac{\alpha}{1-\alpha})^s \Gamma(1-\alpha s)}\right)$,

and $\Xi = B(\alpha)\sum_{s=0}^{\infty}(-\tfrac{\alpha}{1-\alpha})^s \Gamma(1-\alpha s)$.

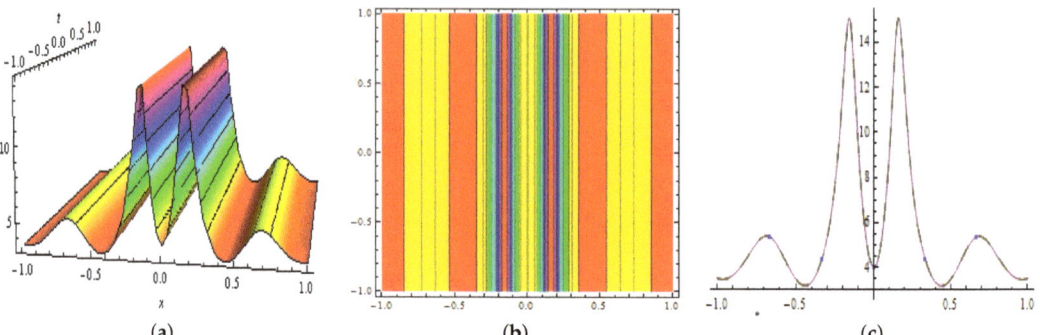

Figure 3. showed three-dimensions in (**a**); contour in (**b**) and two-dimensions in (**c**), Plots of $m_{31}(x,t)$ in Equation (24) for $a = 0.2, b_3 = 1, b_4 = 2, b_5 = -4, b_7 = -3, c = 1, \alpha = 0.6$, respectively.

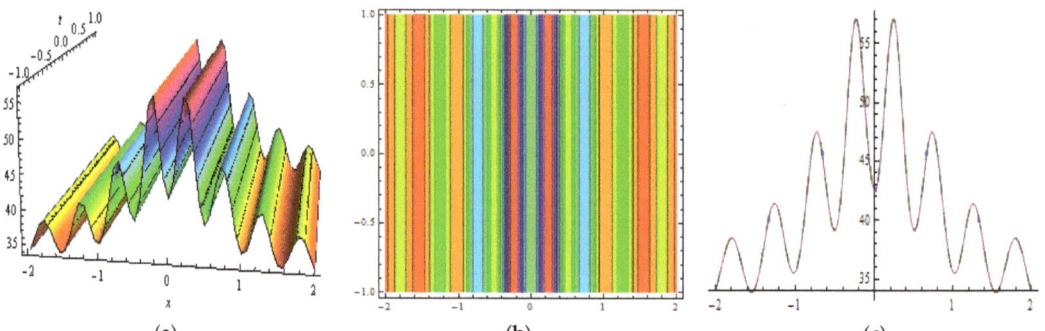

Figure 4. illustrated three-dimensions in (**a**); contour in (**b**) and two-dimensions in (**c**), Plots of $n_{32}(x,t)$ in Equation (24) for $a = 0.2, b_3 = 1, b_4 = 5, b_5 = -4, b_7 = -3, c = 1, \alpha = 0.8$, respectively.

Set II. For $b_1 = 0$,

$$a = a, b = 0, \beta = -\frac{1}{2}a^2, b_2 = b_2, b_3 = b_3, b_4 = -\frac{2b_3}{u_0}, b_5 = -\frac{1}{2}u_0, b_6 = b_6, b_7 = -\frac{b_2^2 u_0^2 - 4b_3^2}{u_0^2}, u_0 = u_0. \qquad (25)$$

Using Equation (25) in Equation (21), and then by using Equations (8) and (10), we obtain

$$u(\zeta) = u_0 + \frac{2\left(-\frac{1}{2}ce^{b_6 - \frac{u_0\zeta}{2}}u_0 + 2b_3(-\frac{2b_3}{u_0} + b_3\zeta)\right)}{b_2^2 + ce^{b_6 - \frac{u_0\zeta}{2}} - \frac{b_2^2 u_0^2 - 4b_3^2}{u_0^2} + (-\frac{2b_3}{u_0} + b_3\zeta)^2}, \qquad (26)$$

$$v(\zeta) = \frac{2b_3^4 e^{u_0\zeta} u_0^6 \zeta^4}{(-1 + a^2)\left(ce^{b_6} u_0^2 + b_3^2 e^{\frac{u_0\zeta}{2}}(8 - 4u_0\zeta + u_0^2\zeta^2)\right)^2}.$$

Using Equation (5), we obtain the required solution for Equation (1):

$$m_{33}(x,t) = e^{i\left(ax - \frac{a^2 t^{-s}(1-\alpha)}{2B(\alpha)\sum_{s=0}^{\infty}(-\frac{\alpha}{1-\alpha})^s \Gamma(1-\alpha s)}\right)}\left(u_0 + \frac{2(-\frac{4b_3^2}{u_0} - \frac{1}{2}ce^{b_6}u_0)}{b_2^2 + ce^{b_6} + \frac{4b_3^2}{u_0^2} - \frac{b_2^2 u_0^2 - 4b_3^2}{u_0^2}}\right), \qquad (27)$$

$$n_{34}(x,t) = 0, \qquad (\because b = 0).$$

Set III. For $b_2 = b_6 = 0$,

$$a = a, b = \frac{2\sqrt{-\frac{6u_0 b_5 + 4u_0^2}{a^2-1}}}{b_5}, \beta = -\frac{4u_0^2 - a^2 + a^4}{2(a^2-1)}, b_1 = \frac{\frac{1}{2}i(b_7 + b_4^2)u_0}{b_4}, b_3 = -\frac{(b_7 + b_4^2)u_0}{3b_4}, \quad (28)$$

$$b_4 = b_4, b_5 = b_5, b_7 = b_7, u_0 = u_0.$$

Using Equation (28) in Equation (21), and then by using Equations (8) and (10), we obtain

$$u(\xi) = u_0 + \frac{2\left(b_5 c e^{b_5\xi} - \frac{2(b_4^2 + b_7)^2 u_0^2 \xi}{9b_4^2} - \frac{2(b_4^2 + b_7)u_0(b_4 - \frac{(b_7 + b_4^2)u_0\xi}{3b_4})}{3b_4}\right)}{b_7 + c e^{b_5\xi} - \frac{(b_4^2 + b_7)^2 u_0^2 \xi^2}{9b_4^2} + (b_4 - \frac{(b_7 + b_4^2)u_0\xi}{3b_4})^2}, \quad (29)$$

$$v(\xi) = \frac{2\left(-6b_5 c e^{b_5\xi} + u_0(b_7 - 3c e^{b_5\xi} + 2b_7 u_0\xi + b_4^2(1 + 2u_0\xi))\right)^2}{(-1+a^2)\left(3c e^{b_5\xi} + b_4^2(3 - 2u_0\xi) + b_7(3 - 2u_0\xi)\right)^2}.$$

Now, using Equation (5), we obtain the required solution for Equation (1):

$$m_{35}(x,t) = \frac{e^\Delta\left(-4\sqrt{2}a(b_4^2 + b_7)u_0^2\Delta_1(\alpha-1) + t^s\left(6b_5^2 c e^{\Delta_2} - b_5(b_4^2 + b_7 - 3c e^{\Delta_2})u_0 - 4\sqrt{2}(b_4^2 + b_7)u_0^2\Delta_1 x\right)\Xi\right)}{-4\sqrt{2}a(b_4^2 + b_7)u_0\Delta_1(\alpha-1)t^s\left(3b_5(b_7 + c e^{\Delta_2}) - 4\sqrt{2}b_7 u_0\Delta_1 x + b_4^2(3b_5 - 4\sqrt{2}u_0\Delta_1 x)\right)\Xi},$$
(30)

$$n_{36}(x,t) = \frac{2}{(a^2-1)}\left(\frac{-4\sqrt{2}a(b_4^2 + b_7)u_0^2\Delta_1(\alpha-1) + t^s\left(6b_5^2 c e^{\Delta_2} - b_5(b_4^2 + b_7 - 3c e^{\Delta_2})u_0 - 4\sqrt{2}(b_4^2 + b_7)u_0^2\Delta_1 x\right)\Xi}{-4\sqrt{2}a(b_4^2 + b_7)u_0\Delta_1(\alpha-1)t^s\left(3b_5(b_7 + c e^{\Delta_2}) - 4\sqrt{2}b_7 u_0\Delta_1 x + b_4^2(3b_5 - 4\sqrt{2}u_0\Delta_1 x)\right)\Xi}\right)^2,$$

where $\Delta = \frac{1}{2}i\left(2ax + \frac{t^{-s}(-a^2 + a^4 + 4u_0^2)(-1+\alpha)}{(-1+a)(1+a)B(\alpha)\sum_{s=0}^{\infty}(-\frac{\alpha}{1-\alpha})^s\Gamma(1-\alpha s)}\right)$, $\Delta_1 = \sqrt{-\frac{u_0(3b_5 + 2u_0)}{-1+a^2}}$,

$$\Delta_2 = \frac{2\sqrt{2}t^{-s}\sqrt{-\frac{u_0(3b_5 + 2u_0)}{-1+a^2}}\left(a(-1+\alpha) + t^s xB(\alpha)\sum_{s=0}^{\infty}(-\frac{\alpha}{1-\alpha})^s\Gamma(1-\alpha s)\right)}{B(\alpha)\sum_{s=0}^{\infty}(-\frac{\alpha}{1-\alpha})^s\Gamma(1-\alpha s)},$$

and $\Xi = B(\alpha)\sum_{s=0}^{\infty}(-\frac{\alpha}{1-\alpha})^s\Gamma(1-\alpha s)$.

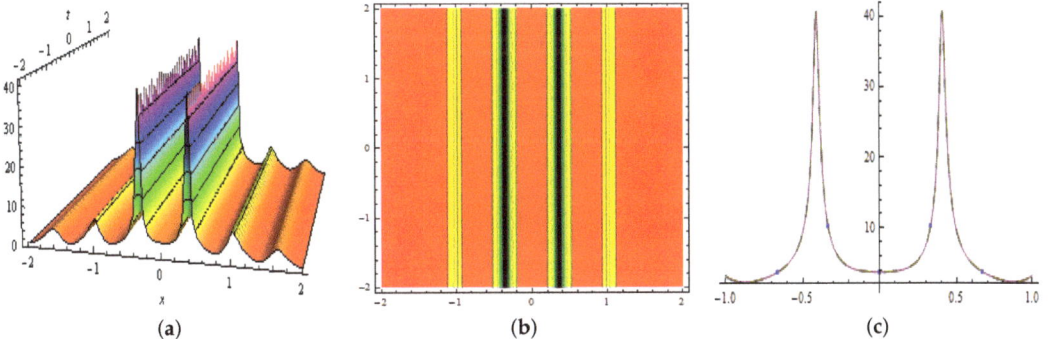

Figure 5. clarify three-dimensions in (**a**); contour in (**b**) and two-dimensions in (**c**), Plots of $m_{35}(x,t)$ in Equation (30) for $a = 0.5, u_0 = 1, b_4 = 2, b_5 = -4, b_7 = -3, c = 1, \alpha = 0.8$, respectively.

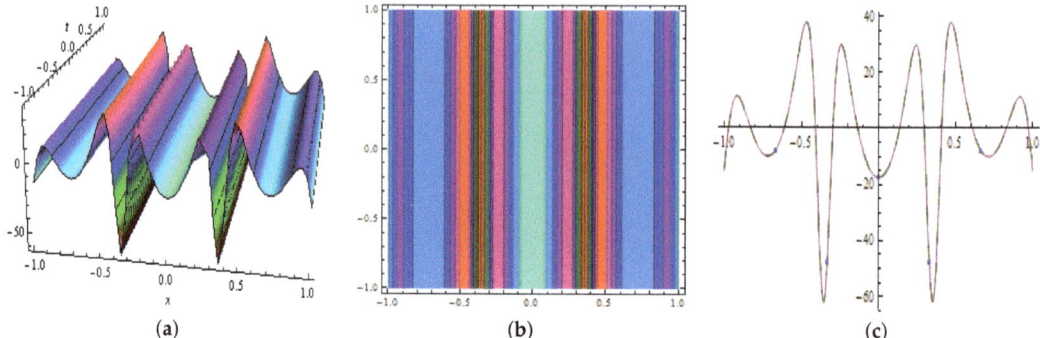

Figure 6. explain three-dimensions in (**a**); contour in (**b**) and two-dimensions in (**c**), Plots of $n_{36}(x,t)$ in Equation (30) for $a = 0.3, u_0 = 0.8, b_4 = 2, b_5 = -5, b_7 = -3, c = 0.4, \alpha = 0.8$, respectively.

3.2. Two-Kink Soliton

For two-kink interaction, the bilinear solution for Φ is as follows (See Figures 7–9):

$$\Phi = (b_2 + b_1\xi)^2 + (b_4 + b_3\zeta)^2 + e^{b_6 + b_5\xi} + e^{b_8 + b_7\zeta} + b_9, \tag{31}$$

where $b_i (1 \leq i \leq 9)$ and all are real-valued parameters to be found. Inserting Φ into Equation (11) and collecting all powers of ξ, and $e^{3(b_5\xi+b_6)}, e^{2(b_5\xi+b_6)}, e^{2(b_7\zeta+b_8)}, \zeta e^{b_5\xi+b_6}, \zeta e^{2(b_5\xi+b_6)}, \zeta e^{b_7\zeta+b_8}, \zeta e^{2(b_7\zeta+b_8)}, \xi^2 e^{b_5\xi+b_6}, \xi^3 e^{b_5\xi+b_6}, \xi^3 e^{b_7\zeta+b_8}, \xi^4 e^{b_7\zeta+b_8}, \xi^4 e^{b_5\xi+b_6}$, we obtain proper results, as follows:

Set I. For $u_0 = 0$,

$$a = a, b = 2\sqrt{2}\sqrt{\frac{1}{a^2-1}}, \beta = -\frac{a^4-a^2+16b_7^2}{2(a-1)(a+1)}, b_1 = ib_3, b_2 = ib_4, b_3 = b_3, b_4 = b_4, \tag{32}$$
$$b_5 = -b_7, b_6 = b_6, b_7 = b_7, b_8 = b_8, b_9 = b_9.$$

Using Equation (32) in Equation (31), and then by using Equations (8) and (10), we obtain

$$u(\xi) = \frac{2\left(-b_7 e^{b_6-b_7\zeta} + b_7 e^{b_8+b_7\zeta} + 2ib_3(ib_4 + ib_3\zeta) + 2b_3(b_4 + b_3\zeta)\right)}{b_9 + e^{b_6-b_7\zeta} + e^{b_8+b_7\zeta} + (ib_4 + ib_3\zeta)^2 + (b_4 + b_3\zeta)^2}, \tag{33}$$

$$v(\xi) = \frac{8}{-1+a^2}\left(\frac{-b_7 e^{b_6-b_7\zeta} + b_7 e^{b_8+b_7\zeta} + 2ib_3(ib_4 + ib_3\zeta) + 2b_3(b_4 + b_3\zeta)}{b_9 + e^{b_6-b_7\zeta} + e^{b_8+b_7\zeta} + (ib_4 + ib_3\zeta)^2 + (b_4 + b_3\zeta)^2}\right)^2.$$

Using Equation (5), we obtain the required solution for Equation (1),

$$m_{37}(x,t) = -\frac{2b_7 e^{\frac{1}{2}i\left(2ax + \frac{(-a^2+a^4+16b_7^2)t^{-s}(-1+\alpha)}{(-1+a)(1+a)B(\alpha)\sum_{s=0}^{\infty}(-\frac{\alpha}{1-\alpha})^s\Gamma(1-\alpha s)}\right)}\left(e^{b_6} - e^{b_8+2\Omega}\right)}{e^{b_6} + e^{b_8+2\Omega} + b_9 e^{\Omega}}, \tag{34}$$

$$n_{38}(x,t) = \frac{8b_7^2}{(a^2-1)}\left(\frac{e^{b_6} - e^{b_8+2\Omega}}{e^{b_6} + e^{b_8+2\Omega} + b_9 e^{\Omega}}\right)^2,$$

where $\Omega = 2\sqrt{2}\sqrt{\frac{1}{a^2-1}}b_7\left(x + \frac{at^{-s}(-1+\alpha)}{B(\alpha)\sum_{s=0}^{\infty}(-\frac{\alpha}{1-\alpha})^s\Gamma(1-\alpha s)}\right).$

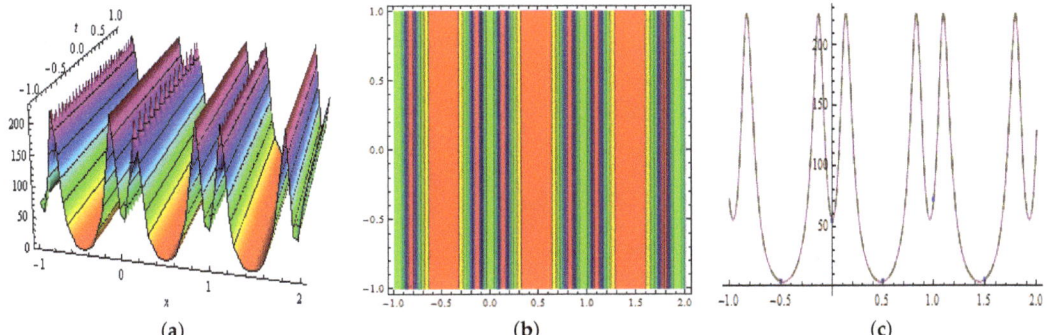

Figure 7. represented three-dimensions in (**a**); contour in (**b**) and two-dimensions in (**c**), Plots of $n_{38}(x,t)$ in Equation (34) for $a = 0.5, b_6 = 1, b_7 = -2, b_8 = 2, b_9 = -6, \alpha = 0.8$, respectively.

Set II.

$$a = a, b = 4\sqrt{\frac{2+i\sqrt{2}}{a^2-1}}, \beta = \frac{a^2 - a^4 - 8i(-2i+\sqrt{2})b_7^2}{2(a^2-1)}, b_1 = ib_3, b_2 = b_2, b_3 = b_3, b_4 = -ib_2, \quad (35)$$

$$b_5 = (1+\tfrac{1}{2}i\sqrt{2})b_7, b_6 = b_6, b_7 = b_7, b_8 = b_8, b_9 = 0.$$

Using Equation (35) in Equation (31), and then by using Equations (8) and (10), we obtain

$$u(\xi) = \frac{2\left(b_7 e^{b_8+b_7\xi} + (1+\tfrac{i}{\sqrt{2}})b_7 e^{b_6+(1+\tfrac{i}{\sqrt{2}})b_7\xi} + 2ib_3(b_2+ib_3\xi) + 2b_3(-ib_2+b_3\xi)\right)}{e^{b_8+b_7\xi} + e^{b_6+(1+\tfrac{i}{\sqrt{2}})b_7\xi} + (b_2+ib_3\xi)^2 + (-ib_2+b_3\xi)^2}, \quad (36)$$

$$v(\xi) = \frac{8}{-1+a^2}\left(\frac{b_7 e^{b_8+b_7\xi} + (1+\tfrac{i}{\sqrt{2}})b_7 e^{b_6+(1+\tfrac{i}{\sqrt{2}})b_7\xi} + 2ib_3(b_2+ib_3\xi) + 2b_3(-ib_2+b_3\xi)}{e^{b_8+b_7\xi} + e^{b_6+(1+\tfrac{i}{\sqrt{2}})b_7\xi} + (b_2+ib_3\xi)^2 + (-ib_2+b_3\xi)^2}\right)^2.$$

Using Equation (5), we obtain the required solution for Equation (1):

$$m_{39}(x,t) = \frac{b_7 e^{\tfrac{1}{2}i\left(2ax + \frac{(-a^2+a^4+8(2+i\sqrt{2})b_7^2)t^{-s}(-1+\alpha)}{(-1+a^2)B(\alpha)\sum_{s=0}^{\infty}(-\frac{\alpha}{1-\alpha})^s \Gamma(1-\alpha s)}\right)} \left(2e^{b_8+\Omega} + (2+i\sqrt{2})e^{b_6+(1+\tfrac{i}{\sqrt{2}})\Omega}\right)}{e^{b_8+\Omega} + e^{b_6+(1+\tfrac{i}{\sqrt{2}})\Omega}}, \quad (37)$$

$$n_{40}(x,t) = \frac{2b_7^2}{(a^2-1)}\left(\frac{2e^{b_8+\Omega} + (2+i\sqrt{2})e^{b_6+(1+\tfrac{i}{\sqrt{2}})\Omega}}{e^{b_8+\Omega} + e^{b_6+(1+\tfrac{i}{\sqrt{2}})\Omega}}\right)^2,$$

where $\Omega = 4\sqrt{\frac{2+i\sqrt{2}}{-1+a^2}} b_7 \left(x + \frac{at^{-s}(-1+\alpha)}{B(\alpha)\sum_{s=0}^{\infty}(-\frac{\alpha}{1-\alpha})^s \Gamma(1-\alpha s)}\right).$

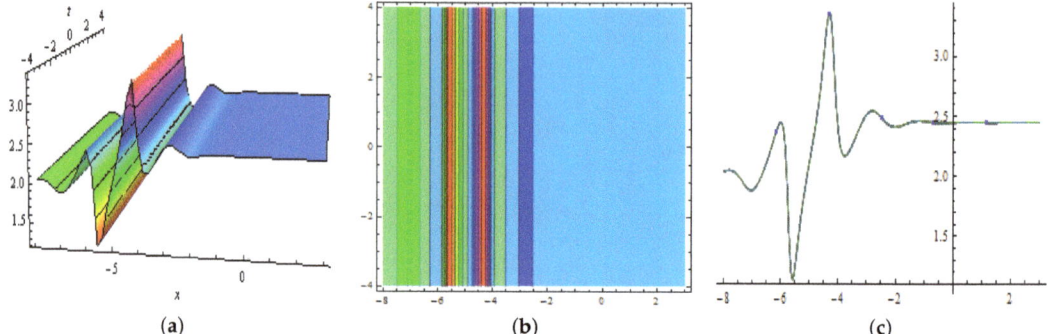

Figure 8. showed three-dimensions in (**a**); contour in (**b**) and two-dimensions in (**c**), Plots of $m_{39}(x,t)$ in Equation (37) for $a = 1.5, b_6 = 8, b_7 = -1, b_8 = 2, \alpha = 0.6$, respectively.

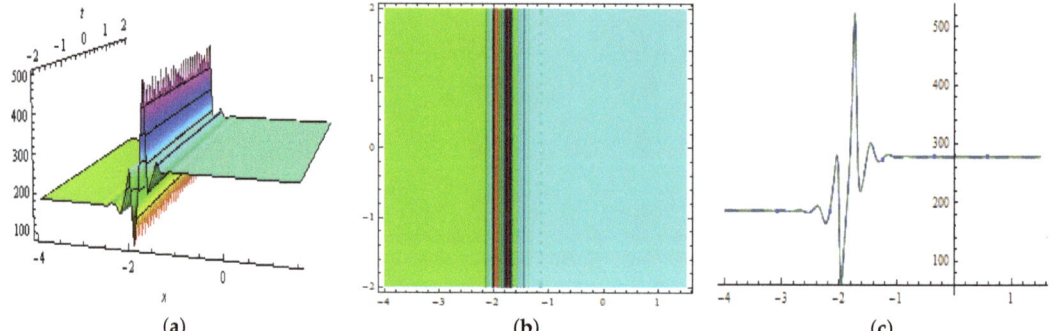

Figure 9. illustrated three-dimensions in (**a**); contour in (**b**) and two-dimensions in (**c**), Plots of $n_{40}(x,t)$ in Equation (37) for $a = 1.3, b_6 = 7, b_7 = -4, b_8 = -5, \alpha = 0.6$, respectively.

3.3. Periodic Waves

For periodic-wave interaction solutions, the bilinear form for Φ is as follows (See Figures 10 and 11):

$$\Phi = (b_2 + b_1\zeta)^2 + (b_4 + b_3\zeta)^2 + \cos(b_6 + b_5\zeta) + b_7, \tag{38}$$

where $b_i (1 \leq i \leq 7)$ and all are real-valued parameters to be found. Inserting Φ into Equation (11) and collecting all powers of ζ and $\cos(b_5\zeta + b_6), \zeta \cos(b_5\zeta + b_6), \zeta^2 \cos(b_5\zeta + b_6), \zeta^3 \cos(b_5\zeta+b_6), \zeta \sin(b_5\zeta + b_6), \zeta^2 \sin(b_5\zeta + b_6), \zeta^3 \sin(b_5\zeta + b_6), \zeta \cos(b_5\zeta + b_6) \sin(b_5\zeta + b_6), \zeta^2 \cos(b_5\zeta + b_6) \sin(b_5\zeta + b_6), \sin(b_5\zeta + b_6)^3$, we obtain proper results as follows:

Set I. For $u_0 = 0$,

$$a = a, b = 2\sqrt{2}\sqrt{\frac{1}{a^2-1}}, \beta = -\frac{a^4-a^2+4b_5^2}{2(a-1)(a+1)}, b_1 = ib_3, b_2 = b_2, b_3 = b_3, b_4 = b_4, b_5 = b_5, \tag{39}$$
$$b_6 = b_6, b_7 = -b_4^2 - b_2^2.$$

By using these parameters in Equation (38), and then by using Equations (8) and (10), we obtain

$$u(\xi) = \frac{2(2ib_3(b_2+ib_3\xi) + 2b_3(b_4+b_3\xi) - b_5\sin(b_6+b_5\xi))}{-b_2^2 - b_4^2 + (b_2+ib_3\xi)^2 + (b_4+b_3\xi)^2\cos(b_6+b_5\xi)}, \quad (40)$$

$$v(\xi) = \frac{8}{-1+a^2}\left(\frac{2ib_3(b_2+ib_3\xi) + 2b_3(b_4+b_3\xi) - b_5\sin(b_6+b_5\xi)}{-b_2^2 - b_4^2 + (b_2+ib_3\xi)^2 + (b_4+b_3\xi)^2\cos(b_6+b_5\xi)}\right)^2.$$

Now, using Equation (5), we obtain the required solution for Equation (1):

$$m_1(x,t) = \frac{2e^{i\left(ax - \frac{(-a^2+a^4+4b_5^2)t^{-s}(-1+\alpha)}{2(-1+a^2)B(\alpha)\sum_{s=0}^{\infty}(-\frac{\alpha}{1-\alpha})^s\Gamma(1-\alpha s)}\right)}(-b_5\sin(b_6+b_5\Omega) + 2ib_3(b_2+ib_3\Omega) + 2b_3(b_4+b_3\Omega))}{-b_2^2 - b_4^2 + \cos(b_6+b_5\Omega) + (b_2+ib_3\Omega)^2 + (b_4+b_3\Omega)^2}, \quad (41)$$

$$n_2(x,t) = \frac{8}{(a^2-1)}\left(\frac{-b_5\sin(b_6+b_5\Omega) + 2ib_3(b_2+ib_3\Omega) + 2b_3(b_4+b_3\Omega)}{-b_2^2 - b_4^2 + \cos(b_6+b_5\Omega) + (b_2+ib_3\Omega)^2 + (b_4+b_3\Omega)^2}\right)^2,$$

where $\Omega = 2\sqrt{2}\sqrt{\frac{1}{-1+a^2}}x - \frac{2\sqrt{2}a\sqrt{\frac{1}{-1+a^2}}t^{-s}(-1+\alpha)}{B(\alpha)\sum_{s=0}^{\infty}(-\frac{\alpha}{1-\alpha})^s\Gamma(1-\alpha s)}.$

Set II. For $b_1 = b_2 = 0$,

$$a = a, b = \frac{2\sqrt{-\frac{2}{a^2-1}u_0}}{b_5}, \beta = -\frac{a^4 - a^2 + 4u_0^2}{2(a^2-1)}, b_3 = b_3, b_4 = b_4, b_5 = b_5, b_6 = b_6, b_7 = b_7, u_0 = u_0. \quad (42)$$

By using these parameters in Equation (38), and then by using Equations (8) and (10) in Equation (5), we obtain

$$m_3(x,t) = e^{i\left(ax - \frac{t^{-s}(-a^2+a^4+4u_0^2)(-1+\alpha)}{2(-1+a^2)B(\alpha)\sum_{s=0}^{\infty}(-\frac{\alpha}{1-\alpha})^s\Gamma(1-\alpha s)}\right)}\left(u_0 + \frac{2(-b_5\sin(b_6+b_5\Omega) + 2b_3(b_4+b_3\Omega))}{b_7 + \cos(b_6+b_5\Omega) + (b_4+b_3\Omega)^2}\right), \quad (43)$$

$$n_4(x,t) = \frac{2}{-1+a^2}\left(u_0 + \frac{2(-b_5\sin(b_6+b_5\Omega) + 2b_3(b_4+b_3\Omega))}{b_7 + \cos(b_6+b_5\Omega) + (b_4+b_3\Omega)^2}\right)^2,$$

where $\Omega = \frac{2\sqrt{2}\sqrt{-\frac{u_0}{-1+a^2}}x}{b_5} - \frac{2\sqrt{2}at^{-s}\sqrt{-\frac{u_0}{-1+a^2}}(-1+\alpha)}{b_5 B(\alpha)\sum_{s=0}^{\infty}(-\frac{\alpha}{1-\alpha})^s\Gamma(1-\alpha s)}.$

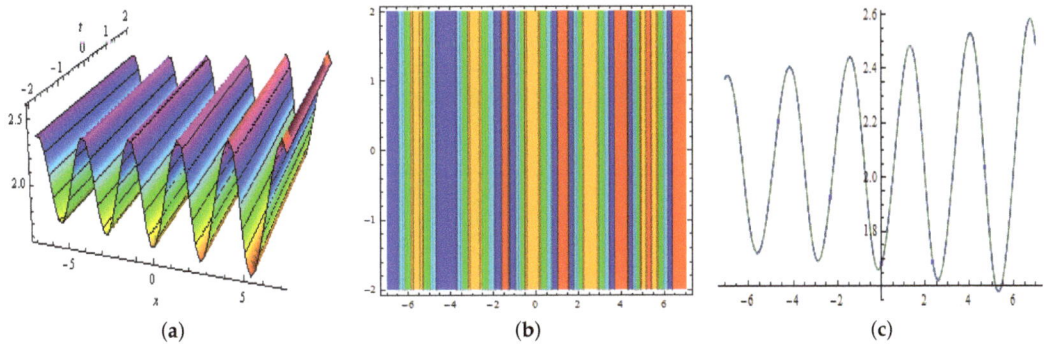

Figure 10. showed three-dimensions in (**a**); contour in (**b**) and two-dimensions in (**c**), Plots of $m_3(x,t)$ in Equation (43) at $a = 2, u_0 = -2, b_3 = 0.05, b_4 = -3, b_5 = 2, b_6 = 5, b_7 = 1, \alpha = 0.9$, respectively.

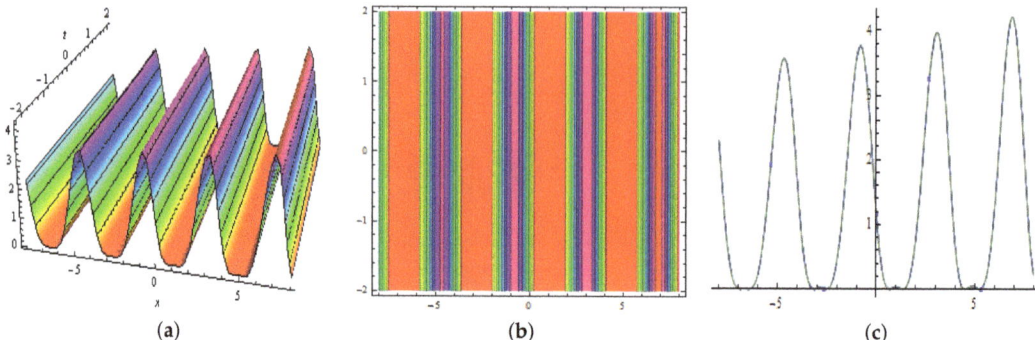

Figure 11. represented three-dimensions in (**a**); contour in (**b**) and two-dimensions in (**c**), Plots of $n_4(x,t)$ in Equation (43) at $a = 2, u_0 = -1, b_3 = 0.1, b_4 = -3, b_5 = 7, b_6 = 3, b_7 = 2, \alpha = 0.5$, respectively.

4. Multiwave Solutions

For multiwave solutions, Φ in bilinear form can be assumed as [32]

$$\Phi = z_0 \cosh(b_2 + b_1\xi) + z_1 \cos(b_4 + b_3\xi) + z_2 \cosh(b_6 + b_5\xi), \tag{44}$$

where $z_i's$ and $b_i's$ all are real-valued parameters to be measured. Inserting Φ into Equation (11) and collecting all coefficients of $\cosh(b_2 + b_1\xi)$, $\sinh(b_2 + b_1\xi)$, $\cos(b_4 + b_3\xi) \sinh(b_2 + b_1\xi)$ $\sinh(b_6 + b_5\xi)$, $\cos(b_4 + b_3\xi)$, $\cosh(b_6 + b_5\xi)$, $\sin(b_4 + b_3\xi)$, $\cosh(b_2 + b_1\xi) \sinh(b_6 + b_5\xi)$, $\cosh(b_2 + b_1\xi) \cos(b_4 + b_3\xi) \cosh(b_6 + b_5\xi)$, and $\sinh(b_2 + b_1\xi) \sin(b_4 + b_3\xi) \sinh(b_6 + b_5\xi)$, we obtain proper results, as follows (See Figures 12 and 13):

Case I.

$$a = a, b = 2\sqrt{2}\sqrt{\tfrac{1}{a^2-1}}, \beta = -\tfrac{4u_0^2-a^2+a^4}{2(a^2-1)}, b_1 = \tfrac{i\sqrt{2}u_0}{2}, b_2 = b_2, b_3 = \tfrac{\sqrt{2}u_0}{2}, b_4 = b_4, \tag{45}$$

$$b_5 = \tfrac{i\sqrt{2}u_0}{2}, b_6 = b_6, u_0 = u_0, z_0 = z_0, z_1 = z_1, z_2 = z_2.$$

By using these values in Equation (44) and then by using Equations (8) and (10), we obtain

$$u(\xi) = u_0 - \frac{\sqrt{2}u_0\left(z_1 \sin(b_4+\tfrac{u_0\xi}{\sqrt{2}}) - iz_0 \sinh(b_2+\tfrac{iu_0\xi}{\sqrt{2}}) - iz_2 \sinh(b_6+\tfrac{iu_0\xi}{\sqrt{2}})\right)}{z_1 \cos(b_4+\tfrac{u_0\xi}{\sqrt{2}}) + z_0 \cosh(b_2+\tfrac{iu_0\xi}{\sqrt{2}}) + z_2 \cosh(b_6+\tfrac{iu_0\xi}{\sqrt{2}})}, \tag{46}$$

$$v(\xi) = \tfrac{2}{a^2-1}\left(u_0 - \frac{\sqrt{2}u_0\left(z_1 \sin(b_4+\tfrac{u_0\xi}{\sqrt{2}}) - iz_0 \sinh(b_2+\tfrac{iu_0\xi}{\sqrt{2}}) - iz_2 \sinh(b_6+\tfrac{iu_0\xi}{\sqrt{2}})\right)}{z_1 \cos(b_4+\tfrac{u_0\xi}{\sqrt{2}}) + z_0 \cosh(b_2+\tfrac{iu_0\xi}{\sqrt{2}}) + z_2 \cosh(b_6+\tfrac{iu_0\xi}{\sqrt{2}})}\right)^2.$$

Using Equation (5), we obtain the following multiwave solutions for Equation (1):

$$m_{41}(x,t) = e^{i\left(ax + \tfrac{t^{-s}(4u_0^2-a^2+a^4)(-1+\alpha)}{2(a^2-1)B(\alpha)\sum_{s=0}^{\infty}(-\tfrac{\alpha}{1-\alpha})^s \Gamma(1-\alpha s)}\right)} \left(u_0 - \frac{\sqrt{2}u_0(z_1 \sin(b_4+\Lambda) - iz_0 \sinh(b_2+i\Lambda) - iz_2 \sinh(b_6+i\Lambda))}{z_1 \cos(b_4+\Lambda) + z_0 \cosh(b_2+i\Lambda) + z_2 \cosh(b_6+i\Lambda)}\right), \tag{47}$$

$$n_{42}(x,t) = \tfrac{2}{(a^2-1)}\left(u_0 - \frac{\sqrt{2}u_0(z_1 \sin(b_4+\Lambda) - iz_0 \sinh(b_2+i\Lambda) - iz_2 \sinh(b_6+i\Lambda))}{z_1 \cos(b_4+\Lambda) + z_0 \cosh(b_2+i\Lambda) + z_2 \cosh(b_6+i\Lambda)}\right)^2,$$

where $\Lambda = 2\sqrt{\tfrac{1}{a^2-1}} u_0\left(x + \tfrac{at^{-s}(-1+\alpha)}{B(\alpha)\sum_{s=0}^{\infty}(-\tfrac{\alpha}{1-\alpha})^s \Gamma(1-\alpha s)}\right).$

Case II.

$$a = a, b = \frac{2\sqrt{-\frac{1}{a^2-1}}u_0}{b_5}, \beta = -\frac{4u_0^2+a^4-a^2}{2(a-1)(a+1)}, b_1 = -b_5, b_2 = b_2, b_3 = ib_5, b_4 = b_4, b_5 = b_5, \quad (48)$$
$$b_6 = b_6, u_0 = u_0, z_0 = z_0, z_1 = z_1, z_2 = z_2.$$

By using these values in Equation (44) and then by using Equations (8) and (10), we obtain

$$u(\xi) = u_0 + \frac{2b_5(-iz_1\sin(b_4+ib_5\xi)-z_0\sinh(b_2-b_5\xi)+z_2\sinh(b_6+b_5\xi))}{z_1\cos(b_4+ib_5\xi)+z_0\cosh(b_2-b_5\xi)+z_2\cosh(b_6+b_5\xi)}, \quad (49)$$

$$v(\xi) = \frac{2}{-1+a^2}\left(u_0 + \frac{2b_5(-iz_1\sin(b_4+ib_5\xi)-z_0\sinh(b_2-b_5\xi)+z_2\sinh(b_6+b_5\xi))}{z_1\cos(b_4+ib_5\xi)+z_0\cosh(b_2-b_5\xi)+z_2\cosh(b_6+b_5\xi)}\right)^2.$$

Using Equation (5), we obtain the following multiwave solutions for Equation (1):

$$m_{43}(x,t) = e^{i\left(ax + \frac{t^{-s}(4u_0^2-a^2+a^4)(-1+\alpha)}{2(a^2-1)B(\alpha)\sum_{s=0}^{\infty}(-\frac{\alpha}{1-\alpha})^s \Gamma(1-\alpha s)}\right)} \left(u_0 + \frac{2b_5(-iz_1\sin(b_4+i\Lambda)-z_0\sinh(b_2-\Lambda)+z_2\sinh(b_6+\Lambda))}{z_1\cos(b_4+i\Lambda)+z_0\cosh(b_2-\Lambda)+z_2\cosh(b_6+\Lambda)}\right), \quad (50)$$

$$n_{44}(x,t) = \frac{2}{(a^2-1)}\left(u_0 + \frac{2b_5(-iz_1\sin(b_4+i\Lambda)-z_0\sinh(b_2-\Lambda)+z_2\sinh(b_6+\Lambda))}{z_1\cos(b_4+i\Lambda)+z_0\cosh(b_2-\Lambda)+z_2\cosh(b_6+\Lambda)}\right)^2,$$

where $\Lambda = 2\sqrt{\frac{1}{1-a^2}}u_0\left(x + \frac{at^{-s}(-1+\alpha)}{B(\alpha)\sum_{s=0}^{\infty}(-\frac{\alpha}{1-\alpha})^s\Gamma(1-\alpha s)}\right)$.

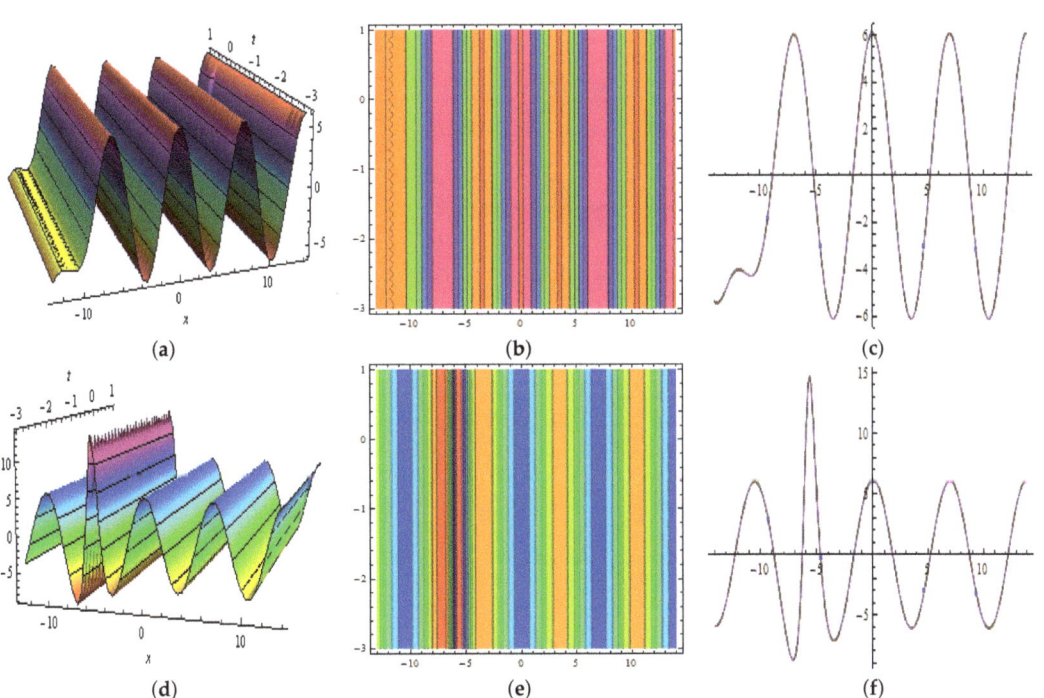

Figure 12. Showed three-dimensions in (**a**); contour in (**b**) and two-dimensions in (**c**), Graphical representation of $m_{43}(x,t)$ in Equation (50), for $a = 0.9, u_0 = 0.1, b_2 = -5, b_4 = 5, b_5 = 3, z_0 = -2, z_1 = 1, z_2 = 2, \alpha = 0.9$, respectively.

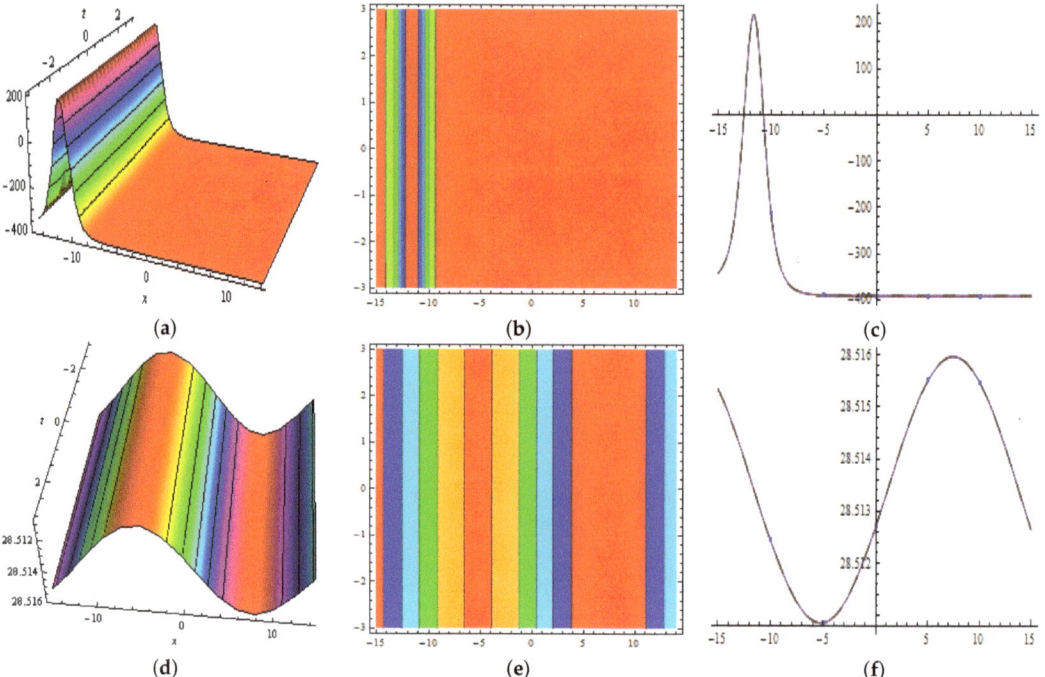

Figure 13. Represented three-dimensions in (**a**); contour in (**b**) and two-dimensions in (**c**), Graphical representation of $n_{44}(x,t)$ in Equation (50), for $u_0 = 0.1, b_2 = -5, b_4 = 5, b_5 = 3, b_6 = 10, z_0 = -2, z_1 = 1, z_2 = 2, \alpha = 0.9$, respectively.

5. Homoclinic Breather Approach

To obtain breather solutions, Φ in bilinear form can be assumed as [32]

$$\Phi = e^{-p(b_1\xi+b_2)} + z_1 e^{p(b_3\xi+b_4)} + z_2 \cos(q(b_5\xi+b_6)), \tag{51}$$

where p, q, z_1, z_2, and $b'_i s$ all are real-valued parameters to be found. Inserting Φ into Equation (11) and collecting all coefficients of $e^{p(b_4+b_3\xi)}$, $\sin(q(b_6+b_5\xi))$, $\cos(q(b_6+b_5\xi))$, $e^{p(b_4+b_3\xi)}\sin(q(b_6+b_5\xi))$, $e^{-p(b_2+b_1\xi)+p(b_4+b_3\xi)}\cos(q(b_6+b_5\xi))$, and $\cos(q(b_6+b_5\xi))\sin(q(b_6+b_5\xi))$, we obtain an algebraic system of equations, then, after solving them, we obtain proper results, as follows (See Figures 14 and 15):

Case I.

$$a = a, b = 2\sqrt{2}\sqrt{\frac{1}{a^2-1}}, \beta = -\frac{a^4-16b_5^2q^2-a^2}{2(a^2-1)}, b_1 = \frac{iqb_5}{p}, b_2 = b_2, b_3 = \frac{iqb_5}{p}, b_4 = b_4, b_5 = b_5, \tag{52}$$
$$b_6 = b_6, u_0 = 0, p = p, q = q, z_1 = z_1, z_2 = z_2.$$

By using these parameters in Equation (51) and then by using Equations (8) and (10), we obtain

$$u(\xi) = \frac{2ib_5q\left(-1+e^{b_2p+b_4p+2ib_5q\xi}z_1+ie^{b_2p+ib_5q\xi}z_2\sin(q(b_6+b_5\xi))\right)}{1+e^{b_2p+b_4p+2ib_5q\xi}z_1+e^{b_2p+ib_5q\xi}z_2\cos(q(b_6+b_5\xi))}, \tag{53}$$

$$v(\xi) = -\frac{8b_5^2q^2}{a^2-1}\left(\frac{-1+e^{b_2p+b_4p+2ib_5q\xi}z_1+ie^{b_2p+ib_5q\xi}z_2\sin(q(b_6+b_5\xi))}{1+e^{b_2p+b_4p+2ib_5q\xi}z_1+e^{b_2p+ib_5q\xi}z_2\cos(q(b_6+b_5\xi))}\right)^2.$$

Using Equation (5), we obtain the following breather solutions for Equation (1):

$$m_{51}(x,t) = \frac{2ib_5 e^\Delta q\left(-1 + e^{b_2 p + b_4 p + 4i\Omega}z_1 + ie^{b_2 p + 2i\Omega}z_2 \sin(q(b_6 + \frac{2}{q}\Omega))\right)}{1 + e^{b_2 p + b_4 p + 4i\Omega}z_1 + e^{b_2 p + 2i\Omega}z_2 \cos(q(b_6 + \frac{2}{q}\Omega))},$$

(54)

$$n_{52}(x,t) = -\frac{8b_5^2 q^2}{(-1+a^2)} \left(\frac{-1 + e^{b_2 p + b_4 p + 4i\Omega}z_1 + ie^{b_2 p + 2i\Omega}z_2 \sin(q(b_6 + \frac{2}{q}\Omega))}{1 + e^{b_2 p + b_4 p + 4i\Omega}z_1 + e^{b_2 p + 2i\Omega}z_2 \cos(q(b_6 + \frac{2}{q}\Omega))}\right)^2,$$

where $\Delta = \frac{1}{2}i\left(2ax + \frac{(-16b_5^2 q^2 - a^2 + a^4)t^{-s}(\alpha - 1)}{(-1+a)(1+a)B(\alpha)\sum_{s=0}^{\infty}(-\frac{\alpha}{1-\alpha})^s \Gamma(1-\alpha s)}\right),$

$\Omega = \sqrt{2}\sqrt{\frac{1}{-1+a^2}}b_5 q\left(x + \frac{at^{-s}(-1+\alpha)}{B(\alpha)\sum_{s=0}^{\infty}(-\frac{\alpha}{1-\alpha})^s \Gamma(1-\alpha s)}\right).$

Case II.

$$a = a, b = 2\sqrt{2}\sqrt{\frac{1}{a^2-1}}, \beta = -\frac{a^4 + 4u_0^2 - a^2}{2(a^2-1)}, b_1 = \frac{u_0}{p}, b_2 = b_2, b_3 = -\frac{u_0}{p}, b_4 = b_4, b_5 = 0, (55)$$
$$b_6 = b_6, u_0 = u_0, p = p, q = q, z_1 = z_1, z_2 = z_2.$$

By using these parameters in Equation (51), and then by using Equations (8) and (10) in Equation (5), we obtain the following solutions for Equation (1):

$$m_{53}(x,t) = -\frac{e^{\frac{1}{2}i\left(2ax + \frac{t^{-s}(4u_0^2 - a^2 + a^4)(\alpha-1)}{(-1+a)(1+a)B(\alpha)\sum_{s=0}^{\infty}(-\frac{\alpha}{1-\alpha})^s \Gamma(1-\alpha s)}\right)} u_0 \left(1 + e^{b_2 p + b_4 p}z_1 - e^{p(\Omega)}z_2 \cos(b_6 q)\right)}{1 + e^{b_2 p + b_4 p}z_1 + e^{p(\Omega)}z_2 \cos(b_6 q)},$$

(56)

$$n_{54}(x,t) = \frac{2u_0^2}{(-1+a^2)} \left(\frac{1 + e^{b_2 p + b_4 p}z_1 - e^{p(\Omega)}z_2 \cos(b_6 q)}{1 + e^{b_2 p + b_4 p}z_1 + e^{p(\Omega)}z_2 \cos(b_6 q)}\right)^2,$$

where $\Omega = b_2 + \frac{2\sqrt{2}\sqrt{\frac{1}{-1+a^2}}u_0\left(x + \frac{at^{-s}(-1+\alpha)}{B(\alpha)\sum_{s=0}^{\infty}(-\frac{\alpha}{1-\alpha})^s \Gamma(1-\alpha s)}\right)}{p}.$

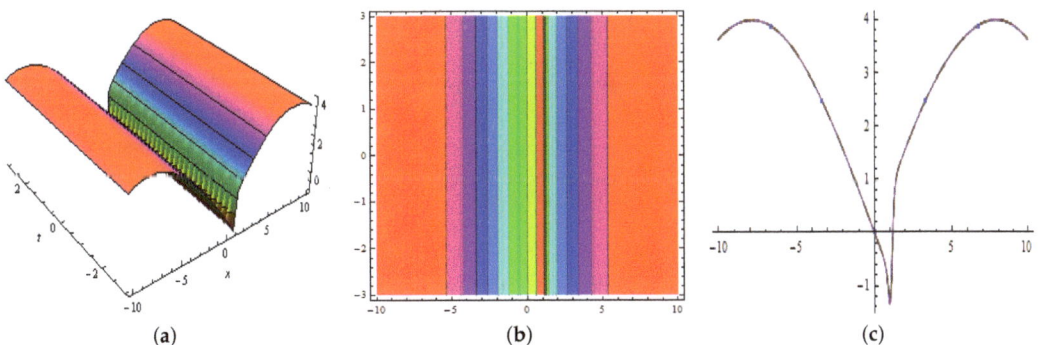

(a)   (b)   (c)

Figure 14. Cont.

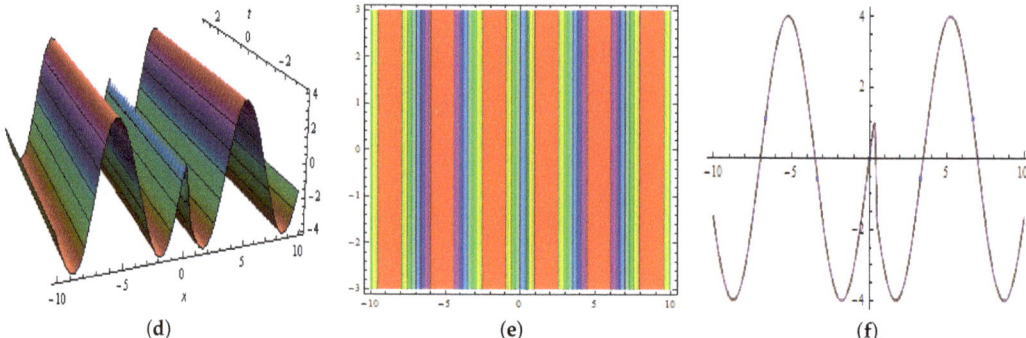

Figure 14. Explain three-dimensions in (**a**); contour in (**b**) and two-dimensions in (**c**), Graphical representation of $m_{51}(x,t)$ in Equation (54), at $b_2 = -4, b_4 = -7, b_5 = 10, b_6 = 3, z_1 = -2, z_2 = 2, p = 3, q = -0.2, \alpha = 0.8$, respectively.

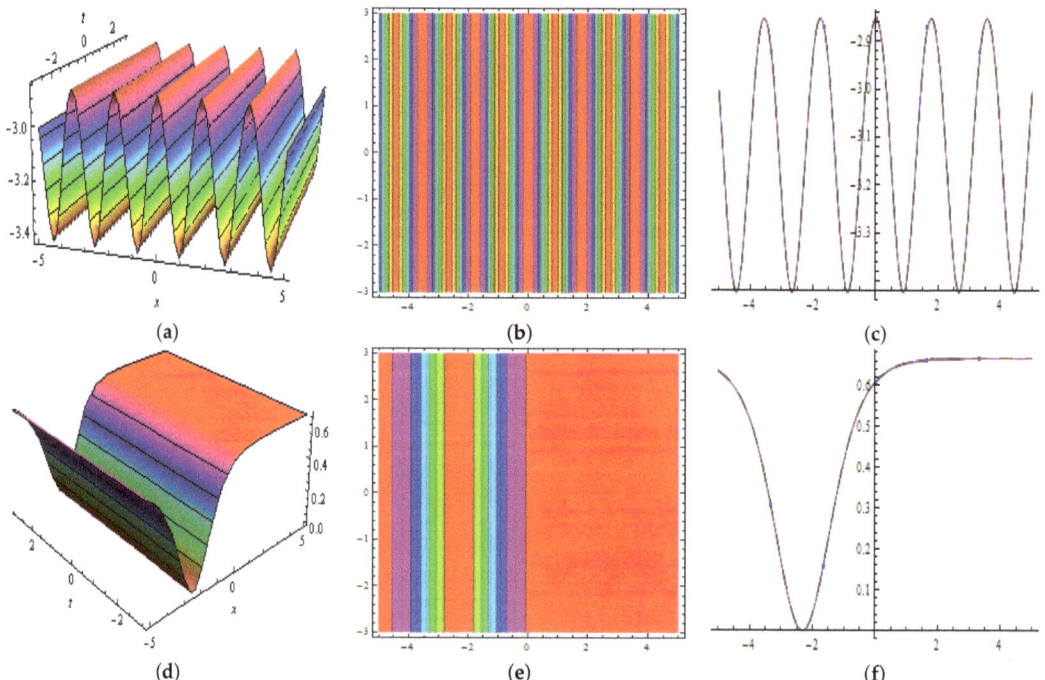

Figure 15. Clarify three-dimensions in (**a**); contour in (**b**) and two-dimensions in (**c**), Graphical representation of $n_{54}(x,t)$ in Equation (56), at $b_2 = 4, b_4 = -3, b_6 = 3, z_1 = -1.5, z_2 = 2.5, p = 1, q = -1, u_0 = 1, \alpha = 0.6$, successively.

6. The Periodic Cross-Kink Wave Solutions

For this, Φ in bilinear form can be assumed as [33]

$$\Phi = e^{-(b_1\xi + b_2)} + z_1 e^{b_1\xi + b_2} + z_2 \cos(b_3\xi + b_4) + z_3 \cosh(b_5\xi + b_6) + b_7, \quad (57)$$

where $z'_i s$ and $b'_i s$ all are real-valued parameters to be measured. Inserting Φ into Equation (11) and collecting all coefficients of $e^{b_1\xi + b_2}$, $e^{-b_1\xi - b_2}$, $e^{b_2 + b_1\xi + 2(b_2 + b_1\xi)}$, $e^{-(b_1\xi + b_2) + 2(b_1\xi + b_2)}$, $\cos(b_4 + b_3\xi)$, $\cos(b_4 + b_3\xi)\cosh(b_6 + b_5\xi)$, $e^{-(b_1\xi + b_2) + 2(b_1\xi + b_2)}\cos(b_4 + b_3\xi)$,

$e^{-(b_1\xi+b_2)+2(b_1\xi+b_2)}\sin(b_4 + b_3\xi)$, $\cos(b_4 + b_3\xi)\cosh(b_6 + b_5\xi)\sinh(b_6 + b_5\xi)$, $e^{-(b_1\xi+b_2)+2(b_1\xi+b_2)}\cos(b_4 + b_3\xi)\cosh(b_6 + b_5\xi)$, and $e^{-(b_1\xi+b_2)+2b_1\xi+2b_2)}\sin(b_4 + b_3\xi)\sinh(b_6 + b_5\xi)$, after solving them, we attain the following parameters (See Figures 16 and 17):

Case I. For $b_4 = 0$,

$$a = a, b = 8\sqrt{2}\sqrt{\frac{1}{a^2-1}}, \beta = -\frac{64b_1^2 - a^2 + a^4}{2(a^2-1)}, b_1 = b_1, b_2 = b_2, b_3 = b_3, b_5 = 0, b_6 = b_6, \quad (58)$$
$$b_7 = 0, u_0 = -2b_1, z_1 = z_1, z_2 = 0, z_3 = z_3.$$

By using these values in Equation (57), and then by using Equations (8) and (10), we obtain

$$u(\xi) = -2b_1 + \frac{2(-b_1 e^{-b_2-b_1\xi} + b_1 e^{b_2+b_1\xi} z_1)}{e^{-b_2-b_1\xi} + e^{b_2+b_1\xi} z_1 + z_3 \cosh(b_6)}, \quad (59)$$

$$v(\xi) = \frac{2}{a^2-1}\left(-2b_1 + \frac{2(-b_1 e^{-b_2-b_1\xi} + b_1 e^{b_2+b_1\xi} z_1)}{e^{-b_2-b_1\xi} + e^{b_2+b_1\xi} z_1 + z_3 \cosh(b_6)}\right)^2.$$

Now, using Equation (5), we obtain the following solutions for Equation (1):

$$m_{61}(x,t) = -\frac{2b_1 e^{\frac{i}{2}\left(2ax + \frac{(64b_1^2-a^2+a^4)t^{-s}(\alpha-1)}{(a^2-1)B(\alpha)\sum_{s=0}^{\infty}(-\frac{\alpha}{1-\alpha})^s\Gamma(1-\alpha s)}\right)}(2+e^{\Omega}z_3\cosh(b_6))}{1+e^{2\Omega}z_1+e^{\Omega}z_3\cosh(b_6)}, \quad (60)$$

$$n_{62}(x,t) = \frac{8b_1^2}{(a^2-1)}\left(\frac{2+e^{\Omega}z_3\cosh(b_6)}{1+e^{2\Omega}z_1+e^{\Omega}z_3\cosh(b_6)}\right)^2,$$

where $\Omega = b_2 + 8\sqrt{2}\sqrt{\frac{1}{a^2-1}}b_1\left(x + \frac{at^{-s}(-1+\alpha)}{B(\alpha)\sum_{s=0}^{\infty}(-\frac{\alpha}{1-\alpha})^s\Gamma(1-\alpha s)}\right)$.

Case II.

$$a = a, b = 2\sqrt{2}\sqrt{\frac{1}{a^2-1}}, \beta = -\frac{a^4-a^2-16b_3^2}{2(a^2-1)}, b_1 = ib_3, b_2 = b_2, b_3 = b_3, b_5 = -ib_3, b_6 = b_6, \quad (61)$$
$$b_7 = 0, z_1 = z_1, z_2 = z_2, z_3 = z_3.$$

Now, by using these values in Equation (57), and then by using Equations (8) and (10) in Equation (5), we obtain the following solutions for Equation (1):

$$m_{63}(x,t) = \frac{2ib_3 e^{\Lambda}\left(-2 + 2e^{2b_2+\Omega}z_1 - e^{b_2}z_2 + e^{b_2+\Omega}z_2 + e^{b_2}(-1+e^{\Omega})z_3\cosh(b_6) - e^{b_2}(1+e^{\Omega})z_3\sinh(b_6)\right)}{2 + 2e^{2b_2+\Omega}z_1 + e^{b_2}z_2 + e^{b_2+\Omega}z_2 + e^{b_2}(1+e^{\Omega})z_3\cosh(b_6) - e^{b_2}(-1+e^{\Omega})z_3\sinh(b_6)}, \quad (62)$$

$$n_{64}(x,t) = -\frac{8b_3^2}{(a^2-1)}\left(\frac{2 - 2e^{2b_2+\Omega}z_1 + e^{b_2}z_2 - e^{b_2+\Omega}z_2 - e^{b_2}(-1+e^{\Omega})z_3\cosh(b_6) + e^{b_2}(1+e^{\Omega})z_3\sinh(b_6)}{2 + 2e^{2b_2+\Omega}z_1 + e^{b_2}z_2 + e^{b_2+\Omega}z_2 + e^{b_2}(1+e^{\Omega})z_3\cosh(b_6) - e^{b_2}(-1+e^{\Omega})z_3\sinh(b_6)}\right)^2,$$

where $\Lambda = \frac{1}{2}i\left(2ax + \frac{(-16b_3^2-a^2+a^4)t^{-s}(\alpha-1)}{(a^2-1)B(\alpha)\sum_{s=0}^{\infty}(-\frac{\alpha}{1-\alpha})^s\Gamma(1-\alpha s)}\right)$,

and $\Omega = 4i\sqrt{2}\sqrt{\frac{1}{-1+a^2}}b_3\left(x + \frac{at^{-s}(-1+\alpha)}{B(\alpha)\sum_{s=0}^{\infty}(-\frac{\alpha}{1-\alpha})^s\Gamma(1-\alpha s)}\right)$.

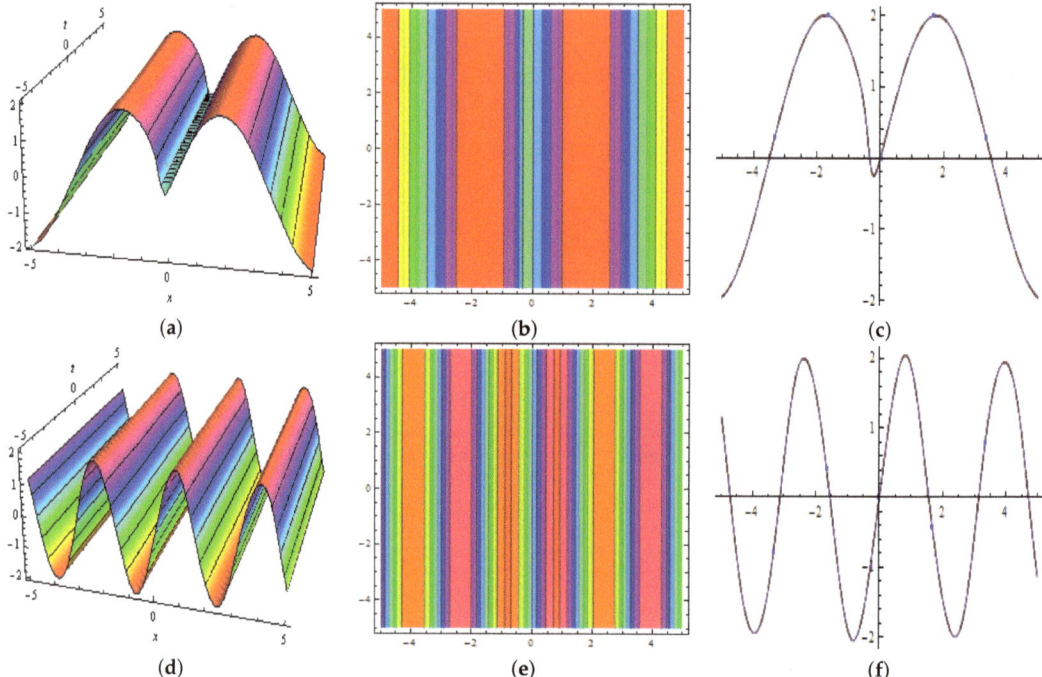

Figure 16. Showed three-dimensions in (**a**); contour in (**b**) and two-dimensions in (**c**), Graphical representation of $m_{63}(x,t)$ in Equation (62), for $b_2 = -5, b_3 = 1, b_6 = 5, z_1 = 1, z_2 = 3, z_3 = -0.5, \alpha = 0.9$, respectively.

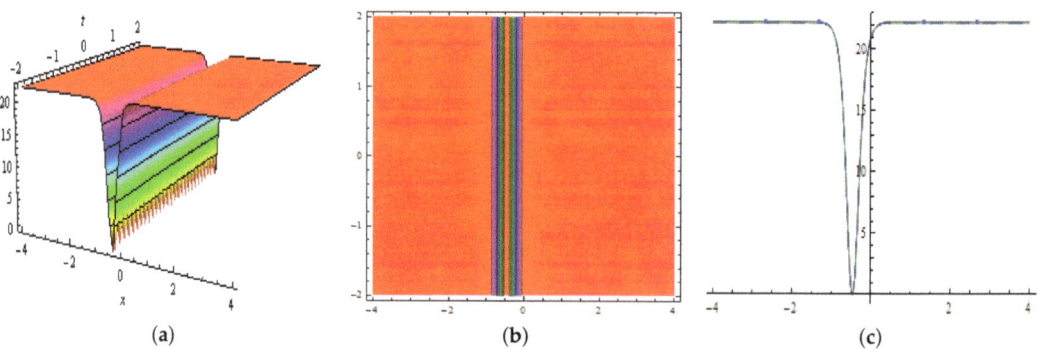

Figure 17. Cont.

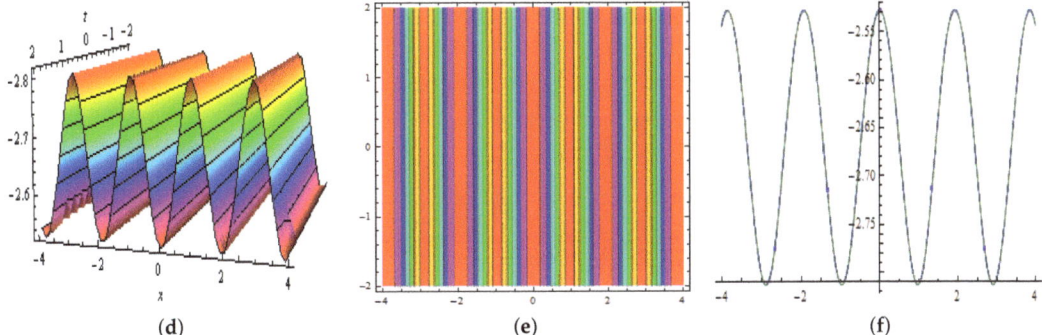

Figure 17. Represented three-dimensions in (**a**); contour in (**b**) and two-dimensions in (**c**), Graphical representation of $n_{64}(x,t)$ in Equation (62), for $b_2 = -5, b_3 = 1, b_6 = 5, z_1 = 1, z_2 = 3, z_3 = -0.5, \alpha = 0.9$, respectively.

7. Results and Discussion

The study of new imposed solutions for the ion sound and Langmuir waves (ISLWs) has huge importance among scientists. Much of the work has been carried out on ISLWs, for example, Mohammed et al. constructed new traveling wave solutions for ISLWs by using He's semi-inverse and extended Jacobian elliptic function method [34]. Shakeel et al. studied new wave behaviors for ISLWs with the aid of modified exp-function approach [35]. Seadawy et al. used direct algebraic and auxiliary equation mapping to obtain the families of new exact traveling wave solutions for ISLWs [36]. Tripathy and Sahoo studied a variety of analytical solutions for ISLWs [37]. Seadawy et al. studied a variety of exact solutions with modified Kudraysov and hyperbolic-function scheme for ISLWs [38].

Here, we obtained a variety of analytical solutions with rational and trigonometric forms for ISLWs, in which some of them are represented graphically in 3D, contour, and 2D shapes. In Figures 1 and 2, we present M-shaped solutions for m_{23} and m_{25} with contour and 2D plots, respectively. In Figures 3–6, we see the interactional phenomena with M-shaped and one-kink for m_{31}, n_{32}, m_{35}, and n_{36} at different values of the parameters. In these figures, we see M-shaped waves with multiple bright and dark solutions. In Figure 4, waves strongly increased their amplitude according to time. In Figures 7–9, we see the interactional phenomena with M-shaped and two-kink for n_{38}, m_{39}, and n_{40}. In Figure 7, multiple bright, dark, and M-size solitons appear. In Figures 8 and 9, large-sized dark and bright waves appear. Figures 10 and 11 represent the evolution of M-shaped and periodic waves for m_3 and n_4. Figures 12 and 13 represent the evolution of multiwaves solution for m_{43} and n_{44} at different values. In Figures 14 and 15, two solutions, m_{51} and n_{54}, of homoclinic breather are presented graphically, and we also see the changes in graphs by varying the value of a. In Figures 16 and 17, we present periodic cross-kink solutions m_{63} and n_{44} graphically, and we also see the change in waves into bright and dark solutions by varying the value of a. As $\alpha \in (0,1]$, in all these solutions, we can see that when $\alpha = 1$, $\sum_{s=0}^{\infty}(-\frac{a}{1-\alpha})^s$ does not converge.

8. Conclusions

In this work, we successfully derived some new analytic solutions for FISLWS with Atangana–Baleanu derivative. These exact solutions are derived in the form of bilinear, trigonometric, and exponential functions. As a result, new traveling wave solutions are gained in the form of rational, periodic, multiwaves, multi-kink, solitary waves, bright and dark solitons that are shown graphically in 3D, 2D, and contour structures. These solutions play an important role in different areas of physics, engineering, and other branches of sciences.

Author Contributions: Methodology, S.T.R.R.; Resources, A.D.A.; Supervision, A.R.S.; Writing, S.A.O.B. All authors have read and agreed to the published version of the manuscript.

Funding: This research received no external funding.

Institutional Review Board Statement: Not applicable.

Informed Consent Statement: Not applicable.

Data Availability Statement: Not applicable.

Acknowledgments: This work was funded by the Deanship of Scientific Research at Jouf University under grant No (DSR-2021-03-03106).

Conflicts of Interest: The authors declare no conflict of interest.

References

1. Dalir, M.; Bashour, M. Applications of Fractional Calculus. *Appl. Math. Sci.* **2010**, *4*, 1021–1032.
2. Özkan, Y.S.; Seadawy, A.R.; Yaşar, E. Multi-wave, breather and interaction solutions to (3 + 1) dimensional Vakhnenko–Parkes equation arising at propagation of high-frequency waves in a relaxing medium. *J. Taibah Univ. Sci.* **2021**, *15*, 666–678. [CrossRef]
3. Lu, D.; Seadawy, A.R.; Iqbal, M. Mathematical physics via construction of traveling and solitary wave solutions of three coupled system of nonlinear partial differential equations and their applications. *Results Phys.* **2018**, *11*, 1161–1171. [CrossRef]
4. Seadawy, A.R.; Ali, A.; Albarakati, W.A. Analytical wave solutions of the (2 + 1)-dimensional first integro-differential Kadomtsev-Petviashivili hierarchy equation by using modified mathematical methods. *Results Phys.* **2019**, *15*, 102775. [CrossRef]
5. Seadawy, A.R.; Cheemaa, N. Propagation of nonlinear complex waves for the coupled nonlinear Schrödinger Equations in two core optical fibers. *Phys. A Stat. Mech. Its Appl.* **2019**, *529*, 121330. [CrossRef]
6. Kudryashov, N.A. The generalized Duffing oscillator. *Commun. Nonlinear Sci. Numer. Simulat.* **2021**, *93*, 105526. [CrossRef]
7. Kudryashov, N.A. Model of propagation pulses in an optical fiber with a new law of refractive index. *Optik* **2021**, *248*, 168160. [CrossRef]
8. Kudryashov, N.A. Solitary waves of the non-local Schrödinger equation with arbitrary refractive index. *Optik* **2021**, *231*, 166443. [CrossRef]
9. Kudryashov, N.A. Almost general solution of the reduced higher-order nonlinear Schrödinger equation. *Optik* **2021**, *230*, 166347. [CrossRef]
10. Kudryashov, N.A. Periodic and solitary waves in optical fiber Bragg gratings with dispersive reflectivity. *Chin. J. Phys.* **2020**, *66*, 401–405. [CrossRef]
11. Rizvi, S.T.R.; Seadawy, A.R.; Younis, M.; Ahmad, N.; Zaman, S. Optical dromions for perturbed fractional nonlinear Schrödinger equation with conformable derivatives. *Opt. Quantum Electron.* **2021**, *53*, 477. [CrossRef]
12. Younas, U.; Younis, M.; Seadawy, A.R.; Rizvi, S.T.R.; Althobaiti, S.; Sayed, S. Diverse exact solutions for modified nonlinear Schrödinger equation with conformable fractional derivative. *Results Phys.* **2021**, *20*, 103766. [CrossRef]
13. Mohammadi, H.; Kumar, S.; Rezapour, S.; Etemad, S. A theoretical study of the Caputo–Fabrizio fractional modeling for hearing loss due to Mumps virus with optimal control. *Chaos Solitons Fractals* **2021**, *144*, 110668 [CrossRef]
14. Nisar, K.S.; Jothimani, K.; Kaliraj, K.; Ravichandran, C. An analysis of controllability results for nonlinear Hilfer neutral fractional derivatives with non-dense domain. *Chaos Solitons Fractals* **2021**, *146*, 110915 [CrossRef]
15. Kaliraj, K.; Thilakraj, E.; Ravichandran, C.; Nisar, K.S. Controllability analysis for impulsive integro-differential equation via Atangana–Baleanu fractional derivative. *Math. Methods Appl. Sci.* **2020**. [CrossRef]
16. Panda, S.K.; Ravichandran, C.; Hazarika, B. Ravichandran, Bipan Hazarika, Results on system of Atangana–Baleanu fractional order Willis aneurysm and nonlinear singularly perturbed boundary value problems. *Chaos Solitons Fractals* **2021**, *142*, 110390. [CrossRef]
17. Younas, U.; Seadawy, A.R.; Younis, M.; Rizvi, S. Construction of analytical wave solutions to the conformable fractional dynamical system of ion sound and Langmuir waves. *Waves Random Complex Media* **2020**, *32*, 1–19. [CrossRef]
18. Akram, U.; Seadawy, A.R.; Rizvi, S.T.R.; Younis, M.; Althobaiti, S.; Sayed, S. Traveling waves solutions for the fractional Wazwaz Benjamin Bona Mahony model in arising shallow water waves. *Results Phys.* **2021**, *20*, 103725. [CrossRef]
19. Dokuyucua, M.A. Caputo and Atangana-Baleanu-Caputo Fractional Derivative Applied to Garden Equation. *Turk. J. Sci.* **2020**, *5*, 1–7.
20. Seadawy, A.R. Modulation instability analysis for the generalized derivative higher order nonlinear Schrödinger equation and its the bright and dark soliton solutions. *J. Electromagn. Waves Appl.* **2017**, *31*, 1353–1362 [CrossRef]
21. Zhang, S.; Zong, Q.A.; Liu, D.; Gao, Q. A generalized exp-function method for fractional Riccati differential equations. *Commun. Fract. Calc.* **2010**, *1*, 48–51.
22. Seadawy, A.R.; Tariq, K.U. On some novel solitons to the generalized (1 + 1)-dimensional unstable spacetime fractional nonlinear Schrödinger model emerging in the optical fibers. *Opt. Quantum Electron.* **2021**, *53*, 1–16. [CrossRef]
23. Chen, C.; Jiang, Y.; Wang, Z.; Wu, J. Dynamical behavior and exact solutions for time-fractional nonlinear Schrödinger equation with parabolic law nonlinearity. *Optik* **2020**, *222*, 165331. [CrossRef]

24. Khan, S.A.; Shah, K.; Kumam, P.; Seadawy, A.; Zaman, G.; Shah, Z. Study of mathematical model of Hepatitis B under Caputo-Fabrizo derivative. *AIMS Math.* **2021**, *6*, 195–209. [CrossRef]
25. Seadawy, A.R.; Bilal, M.; Younis, M.; Rizvi, S.; Althobaiti, S.; Makhlouf, M. Analytical mathematical approaches for the double-chain model of DNA by a novel computational technique. *Chaos Solitons Fractals* **2021**, *144*, 110669. [CrossRef]
26. Farah, N.; Seadawy, A.R.; Ahmad, S.; Rizvi, S.T.R.; Younis, M. Interaction properties of soliton molecules and Painleve analysis for nano bioelectronics transmission model. *Opt. Quantum Electron.* **2020**, *52*, 1–15. [CrossRef]
27. Helal, M.A.; Seadawy, A.R. Variational method for the derivative nonlinear Schrödinger equation with computational applications. *Phys. Scr.* **2009**, *80*, 350–360. [CrossRef]
28. Gaber, A.A.; Aljohani, A.F.; Ebaid, A.; Machado, J.T. The generalized Kudryashov method for nonlinear space-time fractional partial differential equations of Burgers type. *Nonlinear Dyn.* **2019**, *95*, 361–368. [CrossRef]
29. Ghaffar, A.; Ali, A.; Ahmed, S.; Akram, S.; Junjua, M.-U.-D.; Baleanu, D.; Nisar, K.S. A novel analytical technique to obtain the solitary solutions for nonlinear evolution equation of fractional order. *Adv. Differ. Equ.* **2020**, *2020*, 308. [CrossRef]
30. Rizvi, S.T.R.; Ali, K.; Ahmad, M. Optical solitons for Biswas–Milovic equation by new extended auxiliary equation method. *Optik* **2020**, *204*, 164181. [CrossRef]
31. Ahmed, I.; Seadawy, A.R.; Lu, D. M-shaped rational solitons and their interaction with kink waves in the Fokas–Lenells equation. *Phys. Scr.* **2019**, *94*, 055205. [CrossRef]
32. Ahmed, I.; Seadawy, A.R.; Lu, D. Kinky breathers, W-shaped and multi-peak solitons interaction in (2 + 1)-dimensional nonlinear Schrödinger equation with Kerr law of nonlinearity. *Eur. Phys. J. Plus* **2019**, *134*, 120. [CrossRef]
33. Ma, H.; Zhang, C.; Deng, A. New Periodic Wave, Cross-Kink Wave, Breather, and the Interaction Phenomenon for the (2+1)-Dimensional Sharmo–Tasso–Olver Equation. *Complexity* **2020**, *2020*, 4270906. [CrossRef]
34. Mohammed, W.W.; Abdelrahman, M.A.E.; Inc, M.; Hamza, A.E.; Akinlar, M.A. Soliton solutions for system of ion sound and Langmuir waves. *Opt. Quantum Electron.* **2020**, *52*, 1–10. [CrossRef]
35. Shakeel, M.; Iqbal, M.A.; Din, Q.; Hassan, Q.M.; Ayub, K. New exact solutions for coupled nonlinear system of ion sound and Langmuir waves. *Indian J. Phys.* **2019**, *94*, 885–894. [CrossRef]
36. Seadawy, A.R.; Lu, D.; Iqbal, M. Application of mathematical methods on the system of dynamical equations for the ion sound and Langmuir waves. *Pramana* **2019**, *93*, 1–12. [CrossRef]
37. Tripathy, A.; Sahoo, S. Exact solutions for the ion sound Langmuir wave model by using two novel analytical methods. *Results Phys.* **2020**, *19*, 103494. [CrossRef]
38. Seadawy, A.R.; Kumar, D.; Hosseini, K.; Samadani, F. The system of equations for the ion sound and Langmuir waves and its new exact solutions. *Results Phys.* **2018**, *9*, 1631–1634. [CrossRef]

Article

Exact Traveling Waves of a Generalized Scale-Invariant Analogue of the Korteweg–de Vries Equation

Lewa' Alzaleq [1],*, Valipuram Manoranjan [2] and Baha Alzalg [3,4]

[1] Department of Mathematics, Faculty of Science, Al al-Bayt University, Mafraq 25113, Jordan
[2] Department of Mathematics and Statistics, Washington State University, Pullman, WA 99164, USA; mano@wsu.edu
[3] Department of Mathematics, The University of Jordan, Amman 11942, Jordan; b.alzalg@ju.edu.jo
[4] Department of Computer Science and Engineering, The Ohio State University, Columbus, OH 43210, USA
* Correspondence: lewa.alzaleq@aabu.edu.jo

Abstract: In this paper, we study a generalized scale-invariant analogue of the well-known Korteweg–de Vries (KdV) equation. This generalized equation can be thought of as a bridge between the KdV equation and the SIdV equation that was discovered recently, and shares the same one-soliton solution as the KdV equation. By employing the auxiliary equation method, we are able to obtain a wide variety of traveling wave solutions, both bounded and singular, which are kink and bell types, periodic waves, exponential waves, and peaked (peakon) waves. As far as we know, these solutions are new and their explicit closed-form expressions have not been reported elsewhere in the literature.

Keywords: generalized SIdV equation; auxiliary equation method; exact traveling waves; solitary waves—kink and bell types; periodic waves; peakon

1. Introduction

Over the years, the Korteweg–de Vries (KdV) equation,

$$u_t + 6uu_x + u_{xxx} = 0, \qquad (1)$$

has been well studied analytically and numerically [1,2]. There are a number of physical problems that can be represented by the KdV equation [3]. In the continuum limit, it is the governing equation of the string in the Fermi–Pasta–Ulam–Tsingou problem. It also describes the movement of long waves in shallow water and internal waves in a density-stratified ocean. Additionally, acoustic waves on a crystal lattice and ion acoustic waves in a plasma can be described by the KdV equation too [4]. Further, it is known to be connected to the Huygens' principle [5]. The earlier studies employed the inverse scattering transform method to solve the KdV equation [6]. It has been shown that the KdV equation has solitary wave solutions (single and n-solitary waves, where n is an integer) with remarkable conservation properties. The single solitary wave solution (also, known as soliton) of the KdV Equation (1) is of the following form:

$$u(x,t) = \frac{c}{2}\operatorname{sech}^2\left[\frac{\sqrt{c}}{2}(x - ct - x_0)\right], \qquad (2)$$

where the wave speed $c > 0$ and x_0 is the spatial location of the soliton at time $t = 0$. Recently, while searching (with the use of genetic programming) for other equations that could have a solution of the sech^2 form as in (2), some authors (see [7] and references therein) stumbled upon a scale-invariant analogue of the KdV equation given by

$$u_t + \left(\frac{2u_{xx}}{u}\right)u_x = u_{xxx}. \qquad (3)$$

Due to its scale-invariant property, the authors in [7] named it the SIdV equation. It is easy to check that this equation shares the same sech^2 solution as the KdV equation. However, the SIdV equation does not possess an infinite number of conservation properties like the KdV equation, and thus, as shown numerically in [7], its solutions after collision do not preserve their shapes or energy. However, one can show that it has one conservation property, namely,

$$\int u^2\, dx.$$

In looking for other analytical solutions other than the sech^2 form, some authors [8,9] have studied a variant of the SIdV equation of the form

$$u_t + \left(\frac{3\,u_{xx}}{u}\right)u_x = u_{xxx}. \tag{4}$$

An analytical solution of kink type was obtained in [8] by solving an associated Legendre equation. Instead, in [9], by employing the Darboux transformation along with one, two, and three-soliton solutions of the KdV equation, one, two, and three-kink solutions were found. It should be noted that Darboux transformation was also used in finding kink and bell-type solutions [10] of the negative order KdV equation of the form

$$\left(\frac{u_{xx}}{u}\right)_t + 2uu_x = 0.$$

In the literature, there have been studies of a generalized Korteweg–de Vries equation of the form

$$u_t + (f(u))_x + u_{xxx} = 0.$$

Such studies have considered various choices for $f(u)$ such as $f(u) = \frac{u^{k+1}}{k+1} + u$ (for some positive integer k), $f(u) = e^u$, and $f(u) = \frac{u^p}{p}$ ($p = 1, 2, 3, 4$) [11].

In this paper, we consider the generalized scale-invariant analogue of the Korteweg–de Vries equation proposed in [7] and given by

$$u_t + \left(3(1-\delta)u + (\delta+1)\frac{u_{xx}}{u}\right)u_x = \gamma u_{xxx}. \tag{5}$$

Here, γ and δ are nonzero real constants. Equation (5) can be thought of as a KdV-like equation with an advecting velocity given by the expression $\left(3(1-\delta)u + (\delta+1)\frac{u_{xx}}{u}\right)$. Note that when $\delta = -1$ and $\gamma = -1$, (5) reduces to the KdV Equation (1). When $\delta = 1$ and $\gamma = 1$, it reduces to the SIdV Equation (3). We refer to (5) as the generalized SIdV equation. One can think of the SIdV equation as a natural extension of the KdV equation. At this juncture it should be pointed out that a recent work [12] has shown that there are strong links between the Sylvester equation and integrable systems such as the KdV and SIdV equations. Since the Sylvester equation is widely used in control theory, image restoration, and signal processing [13], one should not be surprised to find applications of the SIdV equation in these areas too. Equation (5) was recently studied in [14] using dynamical system theory, and it was shown that traveling waves of bell type and valley type exist. A study of the existence of traveling waves did consider the constant of integration associated with the general solution of (5). In fact, the bell-type and valley-type solutions were shown to exist for varying conditions of the constant of integration. However, hitherto, no exact solutions, in closed forms, have been reported for choices of δ and γ that are other than ± 1. Our goal was to look for exact traveling wave solutions of the generalized SIdV equation in closed forms even when δ and γ are not equal to ± 1.

There are many known powerful methods that can be used to find the exact solutions of nonlinear partial differential equations, such as Hirota's bilinear method [2], the inverse scattering transform method [1], the $(\frac{G'}{G})$-expansion method [15,16], the Riccati–Bernoulli sub-ODE method [17,18], the homogeneous balance method [19], and the generalized

Riccati equation mapping method [20,21]. Other recent meritorious work on finding exact solutions include [22–28]. Further, readers interested in the solutions of fractional differential equations or fractional forms of the KdV equation should consult [29–33]. The authors in [34] suggested a simple and useful method, known as the auxiliary equation method, to obtain some exact traveling wave solutions of nonlinear partial differential equations by presenting an auxiliary first-order and fourth-degree nonlinear ordinary differential equation:

$$(\phi'(\xi))^2 = \mu_2 \phi^2(\xi) + \mu_3 \phi^3(\xi) + \mu_4 \phi^4(\xi), \tag{6}$$

where μ_2, μ_3, and μ_4 are real numbers, and the prime denotes $\frac{d}{d\xi}$. In this method, the traveling wave solutions of the nonlinear partial differential equation depend on the selection of the solution $\phi(\xi)$ of the auxiliary ordinary differential equation. We applied the auxiliary equation method to the generalized SIdV Equation (5) in our quest to find exact traveling wave solutions in closed forms.

This paper is structured as follows: The auxiliary equation method is briefly described in Section 2 by showing the main steps and presenting the solutions $\phi(\xi)$ of the auxiliary ordinary differential Equation (6). In Section 3, the auxiliary equation method is applied to the generalized SIdV Equation (5) in order to construct exact bounded and singular traveling wave solutions that are kink and bell types, periodic waves, exponential waves, and peakon waves. In addition, some of the solutions obtained for the generalized SIdV Equation (5) are presented graphically in 2D and 3D plots. Section 4 presents the conclusions.

2. Description of the Auxiliary Equation Method

Let us consider a (1 + 1)-dimensional nonlinear partial differential equation with two variables x and t as

$$H(u, u_x, u_t, u_{xx}, u_{xt}, u_{tt}, \ldots) = 0. \tag{7}$$

In the following, the main steps are described:

Step 1. To find the exact traveling waves of Equation (7), we introduce the wave variable

$$u(x,t) = U(\xi), \quad \xi = x - \omega t, \tag{8}$$

where ω is a non-zero constant to be sought. By substituting Equation (8) into Equation (7), we get an ordinary differential equation as

$$G(U, U_\xi, U_{\xi\xi}, \ldots) = 0. \tag{9}$$

Step 2. We assume that Equation (9) has the finite series form solution

$$U(\xi) = \sum_{k=0}^{K} \gamma_k \phi^k(\xi), \tag{10}$$

in which γ_k ($k = 0, 1, 2, \ldots, K$) are all real numbers with $\gamma_K \neq 0$, and K is a positive integer to be determined later.

Step 3. The integer K can be computed by balancing the nonlinear terms and the highest order derivatives arising in Equation (9). We denote the degree of $U(\xi)$ by $Deg(U(\xi)) = K$ which leads to the degrees of other expressions as

$$Deg\left(\frac{d^r U}{d\xi^r}\right) = K + r, \quad Deg\left(U^p \left(\frac{d^r U}{d\xi^r}\right)^s\right) = pK + s(K + r). \tag{11}$$

Hence, the value of K can be computed in Equation (10) using Equation (11). Moreover, an analytic solution in a closed form could be obtained because the value of K is normally a positive integer.

Step 4. By substituting Equation (6) with Equation (10) into Equation (9), we get an algebraic equation involving powers of $\phi(\xi)$. Then, equating the coefficients of each power of $\phi(\xi)$ to zero yields a system of algebraic equations for $\mu_2, \mu_3, \mu_4, \omega$ and γ_k ($k = 0, 1, 2, \ldots, K$).

Step 5. After solving the set of over-determined algebraic equations with the aid of *Maple*, one ends up with the explicit expressions for $\mu_2, \mu_3, \mu_4, \omega$ and γ_k ($k = 0, 1, 2, \ldots, K$).

Step 6. Consequently, we may obtain different types of exact traveling wave solutions for Equation (7), such as solitons; kink and anti-kink, bell and anti-bell, periodic, and exponential solutions; and other solutions by substituting $\mu_2, \mu_3, \mu_4, \omega$ and γ_k ($k = 0, 1, 2, \ldots, K$) and the general solutions of Equation (6) into Equation (10).

The function $\phi(\xi)$ satisfies Equation (6). It should be pointed out that there is a general solution to the auxiliary Equation (6), and for the present work, we focus on only the solutions $\phi(\xi)$ of Equation (6) given below. Here, $\Delta = \mu_3^2 - 4\mu_2\mu_4$, $i^2 = -1$, and ε and η can be any values of -1 or 1. The solutions below are presented according to the values of μ_2 and Δ. Readers interested in other forms of solutions for Equation (6) can refer to [34–36].

i. When $\mu_2 > 0$,

$$\phi_1(\xi) = \frac{-\mu_2\mu_3\text{sech}^2\left(\frac{\sqrt{\mu_2}}{2}\xi\right)}{\mu_3^2 - \mu_2\mu_4\left(1 + \varepsilon\tanh\left(\frac{\sqrt{\mu_2}}{2}\xi\right)\right)^2},$$

$$\phi_2(\xi) = \frac{\mu_2\mu_3\text{csch}^2\left(\frac{\sqrt{\mu_2}}{2}\xi\right)}{\mu_3^2 - \mu_2\mu_4\left(1 + \varepsilon\coth\left(\frac{\sqrt{\mu_2}}{2}\xi\right)\right)^2},$$

$$\phi_3(\xi) = \frac{4\mu_2\exp\left(\varepsilon\sqrt{\mu_2}\xi\right)}{\left(\exp\left(\varepsilon\sqrt{\mu_2}\xi\right) - \mu_3\right)^2 - 4\mu_2\mu_4}.$$

ii. When $\mu_2 > 0$ and $\Delta > 0$,

$$\phi_4(\xi) = \frac{2\mu_2\text{sech}\left(\sqrt{\mu_2}\xi\right)}{\varepsilon\sqrt{\Delta} - \mu_3\text{sech}\left(\sqrt{\mu_2}\xi\right)}.$$

iii. When $\mu_2 > 0$ and $\Delta = 0$,

$$\phi_5(\xi) = -\frac{\mu_2}{\mu_3}\left(1 + \varepsilon\tanh\left(\frac{\sqrt{\mu_2}}{2}\xi\right)\right),$$

$$\phi_6(\xi) = -\frac{\mu_2}{\mu_3}\left(1 + \varepsilon\coth\left(\frac{\sqrt{\mu_2}}{2}\xi\right)\right),$$

$$\phi_7(\xi) = -\frac{\mu_2}{\mu_3}\left(1 + \varepsilon\left(\tanh\left(\sqrt{\mu_2}\xi\right) + \eta i\,\text{sech}\left(\sqrt{\mu_2}\xi\right)\right)\right).$$

iv. When $\mu_2 > 0$ and $\Delta < 0$,

$$\phi_8(\xi) = \frac{2\mu_2\text{csch}\left(\sqrt{\mu_2}\xi\right)}{\varepsilon\sqrt{-\Delta} - \mu_3\text{csch}\left(\sqrt{\mu_2}\xi\right)}.$$

v. When $\mu_2 < 0$ and $\Delta > 0$,

$$\phi_9(\xi) = \frac{2\mu_2\sec\left(\sqrt{-\mu_2}\xi\right)}{\varepsilon\sqrt{\Delta} - \mu_3\sec\left(\sqrt{-\mu_2}\xi\right)}.$$

3. Application of the Auxiliary Equation Method

In this section, we apply the auxiliary equation method to the generalized SIdV Equation (5) in order to construct exact traveling wave solutions.

We assume that the traveling wave transform of Equation (5) is in the form $u(x,t) = U(\xi)$, where $\xi = x - \omega t$ and ω is the propagating wave speed, and change Equation (5) into the ordinary differential equation

$$-\omega U U_\xi + 3(1-\delta)U^2 U_\xi + (1+\delta)U_\xi U_{\xi\xi} - \gamma U U_{\xi\xi\xi} = 0. \tag{12}$$

By integrating Equation (12) once and setting the constant of integration as g, we obtain

$$2(1-\delta)U^3 - \omega U^2 - 2\gamma U U_{\xi\xi} + (1+\delta+\gamma)U_\xi^2 - 2g = 0. \tag{13}$$

By considering the homogeneous balance between $UU_{\xi\xi}$ and U^3 in Equation (13) ($2K+2 = 3K \Leftrightarrow K = 2$), we then assume that the solution of Equation (13) has the form

$$U(\xi) = \gamma_0 + \gamma_1 \phi + \gamma_2 \phi^2, \tag{14}$$

where $\phi = \phi(\xi)$ satisfies the auxiliary Equation (6), and $\gamma_0, \gamma_1,$ and γ_2 are real numbers to be determined later.

By substituting Equations (6) and (14) into Equation (13) and collecting coefficients of polynomials of ϕ^k ($k = 0, 1, \ldots, 6$), and then setting each coefficient to zero, a system of algebraic equations is obtained for $\delta, \gamma, \gamma_0, \gamma_1, \gamma_2, \mu_2, \mu_3, \mu_4, g,$ and ω. By solving the resulting system of algebraic equations using *Maple*, we get a variety of interesting wave solutions as described below. Every solution is constructed for parameter values, satisfying a certain condition, making use of a suitable function from the functions that are given in Section 2 ($\phi_1(\xi), \phi_2(\xi), \ldots, \phi_9(\xi)$). However, at every instance, more solutions, in addition to the solutions that we construct, can be found using the functions $\phi_i(\xi)$ ($i = 1, 2, \ldots, 9$), which we did not make use of in constructing the solutions. Those details are omitted for brevity.

3.1. Traveling Wave Solutions for the Case $\delta \in \mathbb{R}$

We start by substituting the first type of solutions, namely,

$$\gamma_0 = \gamma_2 = \mu_4 = g = 0, \gamma = -\frac{2\gamma_1 \delta - \delta \mu_3 - 2\gamma_1 - \mu_3}{2\mu_3}, \omega = \frac{\mu_2(2\gamma_1 \delta + \delta \mu_3 - 2\gamma_1 + \mu_3)}{2\mu_3},$$

and noting that $\Delta = \mu_3^2 > 0$, with the solutions of Equation (6) into Equation (14), we obtain the exact traveling wave solutions of (5) as follows:

For $\mu_2 > 0$, we have

$$u(x,t) = -\frac{\gamma_1 \mu_2}{\mu_3} \operatorname{sech}^2\left(\frac{1}{2}\sqrt{\mu_2}(x - \omega t)\right), \tag{15}$$

which is a bell-shaped solitary wave solution when γ_1 and μ_3 are of the opposite signs and an anti-bell-shaped solitary wave solution when γ_1 and μ_3 are of the same sign:

$$u(x,t) = \frac{\gamma_1 \mu_2}{\mu_3} \operatorname{csch}^2\left(\frac{1}{2}\sqrt{\mu_2}(x - \omega t)\right), \tag{16}$$

which is a singular wave solution, and

$$u(x,t) = \frac{4\gamma_1 \mu_2 \exp(\varepsilon \sqrt{\mu_2}(x - \omega t))}{\left(\exp(\varepsilon \sqrt{\mu_2}(x - \omega t)) - \mu_3\right)^2}, \tag{17}$$

which is a bell-shaped solitary wave solution when $\mu_3 < 0$ and $\gamma_1 > 0$, an anti-bell-shaped solitary wave solution when $\mu_3 < 0$ and $\gamma_1 < 0$, and a singular wave solution when $\mu_3 > 0$.

For $\mu_2 > 0$, we have

$$u(x,t) = \frac{2\gamma_1 \mu_2 \operatorname{sech}(\sqrt{\mu_2}(x-\omega t))}{\varepsilon\sqrt{\mu_3^2 - \mu_3 \operatorname{sech}(\sqrt{\mu_2}(x-\omega t))}}, \qquad (18)$$

which is a bell-shaped solitary wave solution when $\gamma_1 > 0, \mu_3 < 0$ and $\varepsilon = 1$ (or when $\gamma_1 < 0, \mu_3 > 0$, and $\varepsilon = -1$), an anti-bell-shaped solitary wave solution when $\gamma_1 > 0$, $\mu_3 > 0$ and $\varepsilon = -1$ (or when $\gamma_1 < 0, \mu_3 < 0$, and $\varepsilon = 1$), and a singular wave solution when μ_3 and ε are of the same sign.

For $\mu_2 < 0$, we have

$$u(x,t) = \frac{2\gamma_1 \mu_2 \sec(\sqrt{-\mu_2}(x-\omega t))}{\varepsilon\sqrt{\mu_3^2 - \mu_3 \sec(\sqrt{-\mu_2}(x-\omega t))}}, \qquad (19)$$

which is a periodic singular wave solution.

By substituting

$$\gamma_2 = \mu_4 = 0, \gamma_0 = \frac{2\gamma_1 \mu_2}{3\mu_3}, g = -\frac{\gamma_1^2 \mu_2^3 (2\gamma_1 \delta - 3\delta\mu_3 - 2\gamma_1 - 3\mu_3)}{27\mu_3^3},$$

$$\gamma = -\frac{2\gamma_1 \delta - \delta\mu_3 - 2\gamma_1 - \mu_3}{2\mu_3}, \omega = -\frac{\mu_2(2\gamma_1 \delta + \delta\mu_3 - 2\gamma_1 + \mu_3)}{2\mu_3},$$

and noting that $\Delta = \mu_3^2 > 0$, with the solutions of Equation (6) into Equation (14), we obtain the exact traveling wave solutions of (5) as follows:

For $\mu_2 > 0$, we have

$$u(x,t) = -\frac{\gamma_1 \mu_2}{\mu_3} \operatorname{sech}^2\left(\frac{1}{2}\sqrt{\mu_2}(x-\omega t)\right) + \frac{2\gamma_1 \mu_2}{3\mu_3}, \qquad (20)$$

which is a bell-shaped solitary wave solution when γ_1 and μ_3 are of the opposite signs and an anti-bell-shaped solitary wave solution when γ_1 and μ_3 are of the same sign,

$$u(x,t) = \frac{\gamma_1 \mu_2}{\mu_3} \operatorname{csch}^2\left(\frac{1}{2}\sqrt{\mu_2}(x-\omega t)\right) + \frac{2\gamma_1 \mu_2}{3\mu_3}, \qquad (21)$$

which is a singular wave solution, and

$$u(x,t) = \frac{4\gamma_1 \mu_2 \exp(\varepsilon\sqrt{\mu_2}(x-\omega t))}{(\exp(\varepsilon\sqrt{\mu_2}(x-\omega t)) - \mu_3)^2} + \frac{2\gamma_1 \mu_2}{3\mu_3}, \qquad (22)$$

which is a bell-shaped solitary wave solution when $\mu_3 < 0$ and $\gamma_1 > 0$, an anti-bell-shaped solitary wave solution when $\mu_3 < 0$ and $\gamma_1 < 0$, and a singular wave solution when $\mu_3 > 0$.

For $\mu_2 > 0$, we have

$$u(x,t) = \frac{2\gamma_1 \mu_2 \operatorname{sech}(\sqrt{\mu_2}(x-\omega t))}{\varepsilon\sqrt{\mu_3^2 - \mu_3 \operatorname{sech}(\sqrt{\mu_2}(x-\omega t))}} + \frac{2\gamma_1 \mu_2}{3\mu_3}, \qquad (23)$$

which is a bell-shaped solitary wave solution when $\gamma_1 > 0, \mu_3 < 0$ and $\varepsilon = 1$ (or when $\gamma_1 < 0, \mu_3 > 0$, and $\varepsilon = -1$), an anti-bell-shaped solitary wave solution when $\gamma_1 > 0$, $\mu_3 > 0$ and $\varepsilon = -1$ (or when $\gamma_1 < 0, \mu_3 < 0$, and $\varepsilon = 1$), and a singular wave solution when μ_3 and ε are of the same sign.

For $\mu_2 < 0$, we have

$$u(x,t) = -\frac{2\gamma_1 \mu_2 \sec(\sqrt{-\mu_2}(x-\omega t))}{\varepsilon\sqrt{\mu_3^2 - \mu_3 \sec(\sqrt{-\mu_2}(x-\omega t))}} + \frac{2\gamma_1 \mu_2}{3\mu_3}, \quad (24)$$

which is a periodic singular wave solution.

By substituting

$$\gamma_0 = \frac{\gamma_1^2}{6\gamma_2}, g = -\frac{\gamma_1^6(\gamma_2\delta - 6\delta\mu_4 - \gamma_2 - 6\mu_4)}{864\gamma_2^4}, \mu_2 = \frac{\gamma_1^2 \mu_4}{\gamma_2^2}, \mu_3 = 2\frac{\gamma_1 \mu_4}{\gamma_2},$$

$$\gamma = -\frac{\gamma_2\delta - 2\delta\mu_4 - \gamma_2 - 2\mu_4}{4\mu_4}, \omega = -\frac{\gamma_1^2(\gamma_2\delta + 2\delta\mu_4 - \gamma_2 + 2\mu_4)}{4\gamma_2^2},$$

and noting that $\Delta = 0$, with the solutions of Equation (6) into Equation (14), we obtain the exact traveling wave solutions of (5) as follows:

$$u(x,t) = \frac{\gamma_1^2}{4\gamma_2}\left(1 + \varepsilon\tanh\left(\sqrt{\frac{\gamma_1^2 \mu_4}{4\gamma_2^2}}(x-\omega t)\right)\right)^2 - \frac{\gamma_1^2}{2\gamma_2}\left(1 + \varepsilon\tanh\left(\sqrt{\frac{\gamma_1^2 \mu_4}{4\gamma_2^2}}(x-\omega t)\right)\right) + \frac{\gamma_1^2}{6\gamma_2}, \quad (25)$$

which is a bell-shaped solitary wave solution when $\mu_4 > 0$ and $\gamma_2 < 0$ and an anti-bell-shaped solitary wave solution when $\mu_4 > 0$ and $\gamma_2 > 0$,

$$u(x,t) = \frac{\gamma_1^2}{4\gamma_2}\left(1 + \varepsilon\coth\left(\sqrt{\frac{\gamma_1^2 \mu_4}{4\gamma_2^2}}(x-\omega t)\right)\right)^2 - \frac{\gamma_1^2}{2\gamma_2}\left(1 + \varepsilon\coth\left(\sqrt{\frac{\gamma_1^2 \mu_4}{4\gamma_2^2}}(x-\omega t)\right)\right) + \frac{\gamma_1^2}{6\gamma_2}, \quad (26)$$

which is a singular wave solution when $\mu_4 > 0$, and

$$u(x,t) = \frac{\gamma_1^2}{4\gamma_2}\left(1 + \varepsilon\left(\tanh\left(\sqrt{\frac{\gamma_1^2 \mu_4}{\gamma_2^2}}(x-\omega t)\right) + \eta i\operatorname{sech}\left(\sqrt{\frac{\gamma_1^2 \mu_4}{\gamma_2^2}}(x-\omega t)\right)\right)\right)^2$$
$$- \frac{\gamma_1^2}{2\gamma_2}\left(1 + \varepsilon\left(\tanh\left(\sqrt{\frac{\gamma_1^2 \mu_4}{\gamma_2^2}}(x-\omega t)\right) + \eta i\operatorname{sech}\left(\sqrt{\frac{\gamma_1^2 \mu_4}{\gamma_2^2}}(x-\omega t)\right)\right)\right) + \frac{\gamma_1^2}{6\gamma_2}, \quad (27)$$

which is a complex-valued solitary wave solution when $\mu_4 > 0$.

By substituting

$$\gamma_0 = g = 0, \mu_2 = \frac{\gamma_1^2 \mu_4}{\gamma_2^2}, \mu_3 = \frac{2\gamma_1 \mu_4}{\gamma_2},$$

$$\gamma = \frac{-(\delta\gamma_2 - 2\delta\mu_4 - \gamma_2 - 2\mu_4)}{4\mu_4}, \omega = \frac{\gamma_1^2(\delta\gamma_2 + 2\delta\mu_4 - \gamma_2 + 2\mu_4)}{4\gamma_2^2},$$

and noting that $\Delta = 0$, with the solutions of Equation (6) into Equation (14), we obtain the exact traveling wave solution of (5) as follows:

$$u(x,t) = \frac{\gamma_1^2}{4\gamma_2}\left(1 + \varepsilon\tanh\left(\sqrt{\frac{\gamma_1^2 \mu_4}{4\gamma_2^2}}(x-\omega t)\right)\right)^2 - \frac{\gamma_1^2}{2\gamma_2}\left(1 + \varepsilon\tanh\left(\sqrt{\frac{\gamma_1^2 \mu_4}{4\gamma_2^2}}(x-\omega t)\right)\right), \quad (28)$$

which is a bell-shaped solitary wave solution when $\mu_4 > 0$ and $\gamma_2 < 0$ and an anti-bell-shaped solitary wave solution when $\mu_4 > 0$ and $\gamma_2 > 0$.

By substituting

$$\gamma_1 = \mu_3 = 0, \gamma = -\frac{3\gamma_0\delta - 4\delta\mu_2 - 3\gamma_0 - 4\mu_2}{8\mu_2}, g = \frac{1}{4}\gamma_0^3(1-\delta) + \gamma_0^2\mu_2(\delta+1),$$

$$\mu_4 = \frac{2\gamma_2\mu_2}{3\gamma_0}, \omega = -2\mu_2(\delta+1) + \frac{3}{2}\gamma_0(1-\delta),$$

and noting that $\Delta = -\frac{8\mu_2^2\gamma_2}{3\gamma_0}$, with the solutions of Equation (6) into Equation (14), we obtain the exact traveling wave solutions of (5) as follows:

For $\gamma_0\gamma_2 < 0$ and $\mu_2 > 0$, we have

$$u(x,t) = \gamma_0\left(1 - \frac{3}{2}\operatorname{sech}^2(\sqrt{\mu_2}(x-\omega t))\right), \tag{29}$$

which is a bell-shaped solitary wave solution when $\gamma_0 < 0$ and an anti-bell-shaped solitary wave solution when $\gamma_0 > 0$.

For $\gamma_0\gamma_2 > 0$ and $\mu_2 > 0$, we have

$$u(x,t) = \gamma_0\left(1 + \frac{3}{2}\operatorname{csch}^2(\sqrt{\mu_2}(x-\omega t))\right), \tag{30}$$

which is a singular wave solution.

For $\gamma_0\gamma_2 < 0$ and $\mu_2 < 0$, we have

$$u(x,t) = \gamma_0\left(1 - \frac{3}{2}\sec^2(\sqrt{-\mu_2}(x-\omega t))\right), \tag{31}$$

which is a periodic singular wave solution.

By substituting

$$\gamma_0 = \gamma_1 = g = \mu_3 = 0, \gamma = \frac{-(\delta\gamma_2 - 2\delta\mu_4 - \gamma_2 - 2\mu_4)}{4\mu_4}, \omega = \frac{\mu_2(\delta\gamma_2 + 2\delta\mu_4 - \gamma_2 + 2\mu_4)}{\mu_4},$$

and noting that $\Delta = -4\mu_2\mu_4$, with the solutions of Equation (6) into Equation (14), we obtain the exact traveling wave solution of (5) as follows:

For $\mu_4 < 0$ and $\mu_2 > 0$, we have

$$u(x,t) = -\frac{\gamma_2\mu_2}{\mu_4}\operatorname{sech}^2(\sqrt{\mu_2}(x-\omega t)), \tag{32}$$

which is a bell-shaped solitary wave solution when $\gamma_2 > 0$ and an anti-bell-shaped solitary wave solution when $\gamma_2 < 0$.

3.2. Traveling Wave Solutions for the Case $\delta \in \mathbb{R} \setminus \{\pm 1\}$

By substituting

$$g = 0, \gamma = 2(\delta+1), \omega = 4\mu_2(\delta+1), \gamma_0 = \frac{-2\mu_2(\delta+1)}{\delta-1}, \gamma_2 = \frac{-\gamma_1^2(\delta-1)}{8\mu_2(\delta+1)},$$

$$\mu_3 = \frac{-\gamma_1(\delta-1)}{3(\delta+1)}, \mu_4 = \frac{\gamma_1^2(\delta-1)^2}{48\mu_2(\delta+1)^2},$$

and noting that $\Delta = \frac{\gamma_1^2(\delta-1)^2}{36(\delta+1)^2} > 0$, with the solutions of Equation (6) into Equation (14), we obtain the exact traveling wave solutions of (5) as follows:

For $\mu_2 > 0$, we have

$$u(x,t) = \frac{-\gamma_1^2(\delta-1)\mu_2 \operatorname{sech}^2\left(\sqrt{\mu_2}(x-\omega t)\right)}{2(\delta+1)\left(\frac{\varepsilon}{6}\sqrt{\frac{\gamma_1^2(\delta-1)^2}{(\delta+1)^2}} + \frac{\gamma_1(\delta-1)\operatorname{sech}\left(\sqrt{\mu_2}(x-\omega t)\right)}{3(\delta+1)}\right)^2}$$
$$+ \frac{2\gamma_1\mu_2\operatorname{sech}\left(\sqrt{\mu_2}(x-\omega t)\right)}{\frac{\varepsilon}{6}\sqrt{\frac{\gamma_1^2(\delta-1)^2}{(\delta+1)^2}} + \frac{\gamma_1(\delta-1)\operatorname{sech}\left(\sqrt{\mu_2}(x-\omega t)\right)}{3(\delta+1)}} - \frac{2\mu_2(\delta+1)}{\delta-1},$$
(33)

which is a bell-shaped solitary wave solution when $|\delta| > 1, \gamma_1 > 0$, and $\varepsilon = 1$ (or when $|\delta| > 1, \gamma_1 < 0$, and $\varepsilon = -1$); an anti-bell-shaped solitary wave solution when $0 < |\delta| < 1, \gamma_1 > 0$ and $\varepsilon = -1$ (or when $0 < |\delta| < 1, \gamma_1 < 0$ and $\varepsilon = 1$); and a singular wave solution when $|\delta| > 1$ and γ_1 and ε are of the opposite signs, and when $0 < |\delta| < 1$ and γ_1 and ε are of the same sign.

For $\mu_2 < 0$, we have

$$u(x,t) = \frac{-\gamma_1^2(\delta-1)\mu_2 \sec^2\left(\sqrt{-\mu_2}(x-\omega t)\right)}{2(\delta+1)\left(\frac{\varepsilon}{6}\sqrt{\frac{\gamma_1^2(\delta-1)^2}{(\delta+1)^2}} + \frac{\gamma_1(\delta-1)\sec\left(\sqrt{-\mu_2}(x-\omega t)\right)}{3(\delta+1)}\right)^2}$$
$$+ \frac{2\gamma_1\mu_2\sec\left(\sqrt{-\mu_2}(x-\omega t)\right)}{\frac{\varepsilon}{6}\sqrt{\frac{\gamma_1^2(\delta-1)^2}{(\delta+1)^2}} + \frac{\gamma_1(\delta-1)\sec\left(\sqrt{-\mu_2}(x-\omega t)\right)}{3(\delta+1)}} - \frac{2\mu_2(\delta+1)}{\delta-1},$$
(34)

which is a periodic wave solution.

By substituting

$$g = 0, \gamma = \frac{2}{3}(\delta+1), \omega = -2\gamma_0(\delta-1), \gamma_1 = \frac{-2\mu_3(\delta+1)}{3(\delta-1)}, \gamma_2 = \frac{\mu_3^2(\delta+1)^2}{9\gamma_0(\delta-1)^2},$$

$$\mu_2 = \frac{-3\gamma_0(\delta-1)}{2(\delta+1)}, \mu_4 = \frac{-(\delta+1)\mu_3^2}{6\gamma_0(\delta-1)},$$

and noting that $\Delta = 0$, with the solutions of Equation (6) into Equation (14), we obtain the exact traveling wave solutions of (5) as follows:

$$u(x,t) = \frac{\gamma_0}{4}\left(1 + \varepsilon \tanh\left(\frac{1}{4}\sqrt{\frac{-6\gamma_0(\delta-1)}{\delta+1}}(x-\omega t)\right)\right)^2$$
$$- \gamma_0\left(1 + \varepsilon \tanh\left(\frac{1}{4}\sqrt{\frac{-6\gamma_0(\delta-1)}{\delta+1}}(x-\omega t)\right)\right) + \gamma_0,$$
(35)

which is a bell-shaped solitary wave solution when $|\delta| > 1, \gamma_0 < 0$, and $\varepsilon = 1$ or when $0 < |\delta| < 1, \gamma_0 > 0$, and $\varepsilon = -1$ and an anti-bell-shaped solitary wave solution when $|\delta| > 1, \gamma_0 < 0$, and $\varepsilon = -1$ or when $0 < |\delta| < 1, \gamma_0 > 0$, and $\varepsilon = 1$,

$$u(x,t) = \frac{\gamma_0}{4}\left(1 + \varepsilon \coth\left(\frac{1}{4}\sqrt{\frac{-6\gamma_0(\delta-1)}{\delta+1}}(x-\omega t)\right)\right)^2$$
$$- \gamma_0\left(1 + \varepsilon \coth\left(\frac{1}{4}\sqrt{\frac{-6\gamma_0(\delta-1)}{\delta+1}}(x-\omega t)\right)\right) + \gamma_0,$$
(36)

which is a singular wave solution when $|\delta| > 1$ and $\gamma_0 < 0$ or when $0 < |\delta| < 1$ and $\gamma_0 > 0$, and

$$u(x,t) = \frac{\gamma_0}{4}\left(1 + \varepsilon\left(\tanh\left(\frac{1}{2}\sqrt{\frac{-6\gamma_0(\delta-1)}{\delta+1}}(x-\omega t)\right) + \eta i \operatorname{sech}\left(\frac{1}{2}\sqrt{\frac{-6\gamma_0(\delta-1)}{\delta+1}}(x-\omega t)\right)\right)\right)^2$$
$$- \gamma_0\left(1 + \varepsilon\left(\tanh\left(\frac{1}{2}\sqrt{\frac{-6\gamma_0(\delta-1)}{\delta+1}}(x-\omega t)\right) + \eta i \operatorname{sech}\left(\frac{1}{2}\sqrt{\frac{-6\gamma_0(\delta-1)}{\delta+1}}(x-\omega t)\right)\right)\right)$$
$$+ \gamma_0,$$
(37)

which is a complex-valued solitary wave solution when $|\delta| > 1$ and $\gamma_0 < 0$ or when $0 < |\delta| < 1$ and $\gamma_0 > 0$.

By substituting

$$\gamma_0 = \gamma_2 = g = 0, \gamma_1 = \frac{\mu_3(\delta+1)}{6(\delta-1)}, \gamma = \frac{1}{3}(\delta+1), \omega = \frac{2}{3}\mu_2(\delta+1),$$

and noting that $\Delta = \mu_3^2 - 4\mu_2\mu_4$, with the solutions of Equation (6) into Equation (14), we obtain the exact traveling wave solutions of (5) as follows:

For $\Delta > 0$ and $\mu_2 > 0$, we have

$$u(x,t) = \frac{\mu_3(\delta+1)\mu_2 \operatorname{sech}(\sqrt{\mu_2}(x-\omega t))}{3(\delta-1)\left(\varepsilon\sqrt{\Delta} - \mu_3 \operatorname{sech}(\sqrt{\mu_2}(x-\omega t))\right)},$$
(38)

which is a bell-shaped (or an anti-bell-shaped) solitary wave solution when $\mu_4 < 0$ and a singular wave solution when $\mu_4 > 0$.

For $\Delta = 0$ and $\mu_2 > 0$, we have

$$u(x,t) = -\frac{\mu_2(\delta+1)\left(1 + \varepsilon \tanh\left(\frac{1}{2}\sqrt{\mu_2}(x-\omega t)\right)\right)}{6(\delta-1)},$$
(39)

which is a kink-shaped (or an anti-kink-shaped) solitary wave solution,

$$u(x,t) = -\frac{\mu_2(\delta+1)\left(1 + \varepsilon \coth\left(\frac{1}{2}\sqrt{\mu_2}(x-\omega t)\right)\right)}{6(\delta-1)},$$
(40)

which is a singular wave solution, and

$$u(x,t) = -\frac{\mu_2(\delta+1)\left(1 + \varepsilon\left(\tanh(\sqrt{\mu_2}(x-\omega t)) + i\eta \operatorname{sech}(\sqrt{\mu_2}(x-\omega t))\right)\right)}{6(\delta-1)},$$
(41)

which is a complex-valued solitary wave solution.

For $\Delta < 0$ and $\mu_2 > 0$, we have

$$u(x,t) = \frac{\mu_3(\delta+1)\mu_2 \operatorname{csch}(\sqrt{\mu_2}(x-\omega t))}{3(\delta-1)\left(\varepsilon\sqrt{-\Delta} - \mu_3 \operatorname{csch}(\sqrt{\mu_2}(x-\omega t))\right)},$$
(42)

which is a singular wave solution.

For $\Delta > 0$ and $\mu_2 < 0$, we have

$$u(x,t) = \frac{\mu_3(\delta+1)\mu_2 \sec(\sqrt{-\mu_2}(x-\omega t))}{3(\delta-1)\left(\varepsilon\sqrt{\Delta} - \mu_3 \sec(\sqrt{-\mu_2}(x-\omega t))\right)},$$
(43)

which is a periodic solitary wave solution when $\mu_4 < 0$ or a periodic singular wave solution when $\mu_4 > 0$. On the other hand, we can get a peakon solution for the generalized SIdV Equation (5) from Equation (39) that is given by

$$u(x,t) = -\frac{\mu_2(\delta+1)\left(1-\tanh\left(\frac{1}{2}\sqrt{\mu_2}\,|x-\omega t|\right)\right)}{6(\delta-1)}, \tag{44}$$

for when $0 < |\delta| < 1$, where the peak is located at the point $-\frac{\mu_2(\delta+1)}{6(\delta-1)}$ and for when $|\delta| > 1$, where the trough is located at the point $-\frac{\mu_2(\delta+1)}{6(\delta-1)}$, where $\mu_2 > 0, \gamma = \frac{1}{3}(\delta+1)$, and $\omega = \frac{2}{3}\mu_2(\delta+1)$.

By substituting

$$\gamma_0 = \gamma_1 = g = 0, \gamma = \frac{2}{3}(\delta+1), \omega = \frac{4}{3}\mu_2(\delta+1), \gamma_2 = \frac{-2\mu_4(\delta+1)}{3(\delta-1)},$$

and noting that $\Delta = \mu_3^2 - 4\mu_2\mu_4$, with the solutions of Equation (6) into Equation (14), we obtain the exact traveling wave solutions of (5) as follows:

For $\Delta > 0$ and $\mu_2 > 0$, we have

$$u(x,t) = \frac{-8\mu_4(\delta+1)\mu_2^2 \operatorname{sech}^2\left(\sqrt{\mu_2}\,(x-\omega t)\right)}{3(\delta-1)\left(\varepsilon\sqrt{\Delta} - \mu_3 \operatorname{sech}(\sqrt{\mu_2}\,(x-\omega t))\right)^2}, \tag{45}$$

which is a bell-shaped (or an anti-bell-shaped) solitary wave solution when $\mu_4 < 0$ and a singular wave solution when $\mu_4 > 0$.

For $\Delta = 0$ and $\mu_2 > 0$, we have

$$u(x,t) = \frac{-2\mu_4(\delta+1)\mu_2^2\left(1+\varepsilon\tanh\left(\frac{1}{2}\sqrt{\mu_2}(x-\omega t)\right)\right)^2}{3(\delta-1)\mu_3^2}, \tag{46}$$

which is a kink-shaped (or an anti-kink-shaped) solitary wave solution.

For $\Delta > 0$ and $\mu_2 < 0$, we have

$$u(x,t) = \frac{-8\mu_4(\delta+1)\mu_2^2 \sec^2\left(\sqrt{-\mu_2}\,(x-\omega t)\right)}{3(\delta-1)\left(\varepsilon\sqrt{\Delta} - \mu_3 \sec(\sqrt{-\mu_2}\,(x-\omega t))\right)^2}, \tag{47}$$

which is a periodic solitary wave solution when $\mu_4 < 0$ or a periodic singular wave solution when $\mu_4 > 0$.

3.3. Traveling Wave Solutions for the Case $\delta \in \mathbb{R} \setminus \{-1\}$

By substituting

$$\gamma_2 = 0, \gamma = \frac{1}{3}(\delta+1), g = \frac{\gamma_0^3(6\delta\gamma_1 + \delta\mu_3 - 6\gamma_1 + \mu_3)}{6\gamma_1}, \omega = \frac{-\gamma_0(12\delta\gamma_1 + \delta\mu_3 - 12\gamma_1 + \mu_3)}{3\gamma_1},$$

$$\mu_2 = \frac{\gamma_0(3\delta\gamma_1 + \delta\mu_3 - 3\gamma_1 + \mu_3)}{\gamma_1(\delta+1)}, \mu_4 = \frac{-\gamma_1(6\delta\gamma_1 - \delta\mu_3 - 6\gamma_1 - \mu_3)}{4\gamma_0(\delta+1)},$$

and noting that

$$\Delta = \frac{3\gamma_1(6\delta^2\gamma_1 + \delta^2\mu_3 - 12\delta\gamma_1 + 6\gamma_1 - \mu_3)}{(\delta+1)^2},$$

with the solutions of Equation (6) into Equation (14), we obtain the exact traveling wave solutions of (5) as follows:

For $\gamma_0\gamma_1\mu_3 > 0$ and $\delta = 1$ (and therefore $\Delta = 0$), we have

$$u(x,t) = -\varepsilon\gamma_0 \tanh\left(\frac{1}{2}\sqrt{\frac{\gamma_0\mu_3}{\gamma_1}}(x-\omega t)\right), \quad (48)$$

which is a kink-shaped (or an anti-kink-shaped) solitary wave solution with boundary values $\pm\gamma_0$ at left and right infinities.

For $\gamma_0\gamma_1\mu_3 > 0$ and $\delta = \frac{6\gamma_1-\mu_3}{6\gamma_1+\mu_3}$ (and therefore $\Delta = 0$), we have

$$u(x,t) = \frac{-\varepsilon\gamma_0}{2}\tanh\left(\frac{\sqrt{2}}{4}\sqrt{\frac{\gamma_0\mu_3}{\gamma_1}}(x-\omega t)\right) + \frac{\gamma_0}{2}, \quad (49)$$

which is a kink-shaped (or an anti-kink-shaped) solitary wave solution with boundary values 0 and $|\gamma_0|$ at left and right infinities or a kink-shaped (or an anti-kink-shaped) solitary wave solution with boundary values $-|\gamma_0|$ and 0 at left and right infinities.

For $\mu_2 = \frac{\gamma_0(3\delta\gamma_1+\delta\mu_3-3\gamma_1+\mu_3)}{\gamma_1(\delta+1)} > 0$ and $\Delta = \frac{3\gamma_1(6\delta^2\gamma_1+\delta^2\mu_3-12\delta\gamma_1+6\gamma_1-\mu_3)}{(\delta+1)^2} > 0$, we have

$$u(x,t) = \frac{2\gamma_0(3\delta\gamma_1+\delta\mu_3-3\gamma_1+\mu_3)\operatorname{sech}(\sqrt{\mu_2}(x-\omega t))}{(\delta+1)\left(\varepsilon\sqrt{\Delta}-\mu_3\operatorname{sech}(\sqrt{\mu_2}(x-\omega t))\right)} + \gamma_0, \quad (50)$$

which is a bell-shaped (or an anti-bell-shaped) solitary wave solution.

3.4. Traveling Wave Solutions for the Case $\delta = 1$

By substituting

$$\delta = 1, g = 0, \gamma_0 = 0, \gamma_1 = 0, \mu_4 = 0, \gamma = \frac{4}{3}, \omega = \frac{8}{3}\mu_2,$$

and noting that $\Delta = \mu_3^2 > 0$, with the solutions of Equation (6) into Equation (14), we obtain the exact traveling wave solutions of (5) as follows:

For $\mu_2 > 0$, we have

$$u(x,t) = \frac{\gamma_2\mu_2{}^2}{\mu_3{}^2}\operatorname{sech}^4\left(\frac{1}{2}\sqrt{\mu_2}(x-\omega t)\right), \quad (51)$$

which is a bell-shaped solitary wave solution when $\gamma_2 > 0$ and an anti-bell-shaped solitary wave solution when $\gamma_2 < 0$,

$$u(x,t) = \frac{\gamma_2\mu_2{}^2}{\mu_3{}^2}\operatorname{csch}^4\left(\frac{1}{2}\sqrt{\mu_2}(x-\omega t)\right), \quad (52)$$

which is a singular wave solution, and

$$u(x,t) = \frac{16\gamma_2\mu_2{}^2\exp^2(\varepsilon\sqrt{\mu_2}(x-\omega t))}{\left(\exp(\varepsilon\sqrt{\mu_2}(x-\omega t))-\mu_3\right)^4}, \quad (53)$$

which is a bell-shaped solitary wave solution when $\mu_3 < 0$ and $\gamma_2 > 0$, an anti-bell-shaped solitary wave solution when $\mu_3 < 0$ and $\gamma_2 < 0$, and a singular wave solution when $\mu_3 > 0$.

By substituting

$$\delta = 1, g = 0, \gamma_0 = 0, \gamma_2 = 0, \mu_3 = 0, \mu_4 = 0, \omega = \mu_2(2-\gamma),$$

and noting that $\Delta = 0$, with the solutions of Equation (6) into Equation (14), we obtain the following exponential traveling wave solution:

$$u(x,t) = \frac{4\,\gamma_1\mu_2}{\exp(\varepsilon\,\sqrt{\mu_2}\,(x-\omega t))}, \tag{54}$$

where $\mu_2 > 0$. On the other hand, we can get a peakon solution for the generalized SIdV Equation (5) from Equation (54) that is given by

$$u(x,t) = \frac{4\,\gamma_1\mu_2}{\exp(\sqrt{\mu_2}\,|x-\omega t|)}, \tag{55}$$

for $\mu_2 > 0$ and $\omega = \mu_2\,(2-\gamma)$, where the peak is located at the point $4\,\gamma_1\mu_2$.

By substituting

$$\delta = 1, g = 0, \gamma_0 = 0, \gamma_1 = 0, \mu_3 = 0, \mu_4 = 0, \omega = 4\,\mu_2(2-\gamma),$$

and noting that $\Delta = 0$, with the solutions of Equation (6) into Equation (14), we obtain the following exponential traveling wave solution:

$$u(x,t) = \frac{16\,\gamma_2\mu_2^2}{\exp(\varepsilon\,\sqrt{4\,\mu_2}\,(x-\omega t))}, \tag{56}$$

where $\mu_2 > 0$. On the other hand, we can get a peakon solution for the generalized SIdV Equation (5) from Equation (56) that is given by

$$u(x,t) = \frac{16\,\gamma_2\mu_2^2}{\exp(\sqrt{4\,\mu_2}\,|x-\omega t|)}, \tag{57}$$

for $\mu_2 > 0$ and $\omega = 4\,\mu_2\,(2-\gamma)$, where the peak is located at the point $16\,\gamma_2\mu_2^2$.

By substituting

$$\delta = 1, g = 0, \gamma_0 = 0, \gamma_2 = 0, \mu_3 = 0, \gamma = \frac{2}{3}, \omega = \frac{4}{3}\mu_2,$$

and noting that $\Delta = -4\,\mu_2\mu_4$, with the solutions of Equation (6) into Equation (14), we obtain the exact traveling wave solutions of (5) as follows:

For $\mu_2 > 0$, we have

$$u(x,t) = \frac{4\,\gamma_1\mu_2\exp(\varepsilon\,\sqrt{\mu_2}\,(x-\omega t))}{\exp(\varepsilon\,\sqrt{4\,\mu_2}\,(x-\omega t)) - 4\,\mu_2\mu_4}, \tag{58}$$

which is a bell-shaped solitary wave solution when $\mu_4 < 0$ and $\gamma_1 > 0$, an anti-bell-shaped solitary wave solution when $\mu_4 < 0$ and $\gamma_1 < 0$, and a singular wave solution when $\mu_4 > 0$.

For $\mu_2 > 0$ and $\mu_4 < 0$, we have

$$u(x,t) = \frac{\gamma_1\mu_2\operatorname{sech}(\sqrt{\mu_2}\,(x-\omega t))}{\varepsilon\,\sqrt{-\mu_2\mu_4}}, \tag{59}$$

which is a bell-shaped solitary wave solution when $\gamma_1\varepsilon > 0$ and an anti-bell-shaped solitary wave solution when $\gamma_1\varepsilon < 0$.

3.5. Traveling Wave Solutions for the Case $\delta = -1$

By substituting

$$\delta = -1, \gamma_2 = 0, \mu_4 = 0, \gamma = \frac{2\gamma_1}{\mu_3}, g = -\frac{\gamma_0^2(\gamma_0\mu_3 - \gamma_1\mu_2)}{\mu_3}, \omega = \frac{2\,(3\,\gamma_0\mu_3 - \gamma_1\mu_2)}{\mu_3},$$

and noting that $\Delta = \mu_3^2 > 0$, with the solutions of Equation (6) into Equation (14), we obtain the exact traveling wave solution of (5) as follows:

For $\mu_2 > 0$, we have

$$u(x,t) = \gamma_0 - \frac{\gamma_1 \mu_2 \operatorname{sech}^2\left(\frac{1}{2}\sqrt{\mu_2}(x-\omega t)\right)}{\mu_3}, \qquad (60)$$

which is a bell-shaped solitary wave solution when $\gamma_1 \mu_3 < 0$ and an anti-bell-shaped solitary wave solution when $\gamma_1 \mu_3 > 0$. On the other hand, it is important to mention that the bell-shaped solitary wave Equation (60) when $\delta = -1, \gamma_0 = 0, \gamma_1 = -1, \mu_2 = c$, and $\mu_3 = 2$ (and therefore $\omega = 6\gamma_0 + c$) becomes

$$u(x,t) = \gamma_0 + \frac{c}{2}\operatorname{sech}^2\left(\frac{\sqrt{c}}{2}(x-(6\gamma_0+c)t)\right),$$

which is a solution of the KdV Equation (1), and if $\gamma_0 = 0$, then we get the soliton solution Equation (2) of the KdV Equation (1).

By substituting

$$\delta = -1, \gamma = \frac{\gamma_2}{2\mu_4}, \mu_2 = \frac{\gamma_1^2 \mu_4}{\gamma_2^2}, \mu_3 = \frac{2\gamma_1 \mu_4}{\gamma_2}, g = -\frac{\gamma_0^2(4\gamma_0\gamma_2 - \gamma_1^2)}{4\gamma_2}, \omega = \frac{12\gamma_0\gamma_2 - \gamma_1^2}{2\gamma_2},$$

and noting that $\Delta = 0$, with the solutions of Equation (6) into Equation (14), we obtain the exact traveling wave solution of (5) as follows:

For $\mu_4 > 0$, we have

$$u(x,t) = \frac{\gamma_1^2}{4\gamma_2}\left(1 + \varepsilon \tanh\left(\sqrt{\frac{\gamma_1^2 \mu_4}{4\gamma_2^2}}(x-\omega t)\right)\right)^2 - \frac{\gamma_1^2}{2\gamma_2}\left(1 + \varepsilon \tanh\left(\sqrt{\frac{\gamma_1^2 \mu_4}{4\gamma_2^2}}(x-\omega t)\right)\right) + \gamma_0, \qquad (61)$$

which is a bell-shaped solitary wave solution when $\gamma_2 < 0$ and an anti-bell-shaped solitary wave solution when $\gamma_2 > 0$.

By substituting

$$\delta = -1, \gamma_1 = 0, \mu_3 = 0, \mu_4 = \frac{\gamma_2}{2\gamma}, g = 2\gamma\gamma_0^2\mu_2 - \gamma_0^3, \omega = -4\gamma\mu_2 + 6\gamma_0,$$

and noting that $\Delta = \frac{-2\mu_2\gamma_2}{\gamma}$, with the solutions of Equation (6) into Equation (14), we obtain the exact traveling wave solution of (5) as follows:

For $\mu_2 > 0$ and $\gamma\gamma_2 < 0$, we have

$$u(x,t) = \gamma_0 - 2\mu_2 \gamma \operatorname{sech}^2(\sqrt{\mu_2}(x-\omega t)), \qquad (62)$$

which is a bell-shaped solitary wave solution when $\gamma < 0$ and an anti-bell-shaped solitary wave solution when $\gamma > 0$.

In order to get a better visual understanding of the solutions that we obtained, some of the solutions for the generalized SIdV Equation (5) are presented graphically in 2D and 3D plots in Figures 1–4.

Figure 1 shows a rich array of bounded solutions from a solitary pulse ($\delta = 2$) to a kink ($\delta = \frac{1}{2}$) and to a periodic wave ($\delta = 2$) for values of δ other than either 1 or negative 1.

In Figure 2, one can see a singular solitary wave and a singular periodic wave for the δ-value of 2. If the singular solitary pulse is compared to the bounded solitary wave in Figure 1 for $\delta = 2$, the only difference is in the choice of μ_3. The singular pulse is obtained with a positive μ_3, whereas the bounded solitary pulse is found with a negative μ_3. Similarly, if one compares parameter values for the singular solitary pulse with the bounded solitary wave in Equation (23) when $\varepsilon = 1$, it can be observed that the singular pulse is obtained with a positive μ_3, whereas the bounded solitary pulse is found with a negative μ_3.

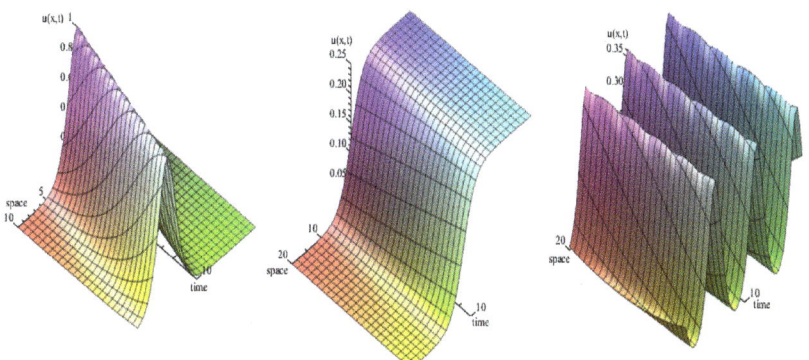

Figure 1. The exact solutions of the generalized SIdV Equation (5) over the time interval $[0, 10]$. The **left** is a bell-shaped solitary wave solution (18) when $\gamma_1 = 1, \delta = 2, \mu_2 = 1, \mu_3 = -1$, and $\varepsilon = 1$, the **middel** is an anti-kink-shaped solitary wave solution (39) when $\delta = \frac{1}{2}, \mu_2 = \frac{1}{4}, \mu_3 = 1, \mu_4 = 1$, and $\varepsilon = -1$, and the **right** is a periodic solitary wave solution (43) when $\delta = 2, \mu_2 = \frac{-1}{5}, \mu_3 = 1$, $\mu_4 = -1$, and $\varepsilon = 1$.

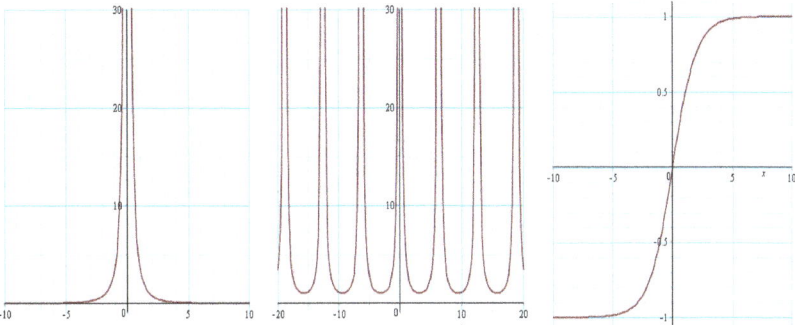

Figure 2. The exact solutions of the generalized SIdV Equation (5) at $t = 0$. The **left** is a singular wave solution (18) when $\gamma_1 = 1, \delta = 2, \mu_2 = 1, \mu_3 = 1$, and $\varepsilon = 1$, the **middel** is a periodic singular wave solution (19) when $\delta = 2, \mu_2 = -1, \mu_3 = 1, \gamma_1 = 1$, and $\varepsilon = 1$, and the **right** is a kink-shaped solitary wave solution (48) when $\delta = 1, \mu_3 = 1, \gamma_0 = 1, \gamma_1 = 1$, and $\varepsilon = -1$.

Figure 3 presents other bounded solitary pulse solutions (as opposed to the KdV soliton of the sech^2 form) of the forms of sech, sech^2, and sech^4 for δ values of either 1 or negative 1.

Figure 4 shows the peaked solutions (peakons) that we are able to find for two different δ values. Note that a peakon has a discontinuous first derivative at its peak.

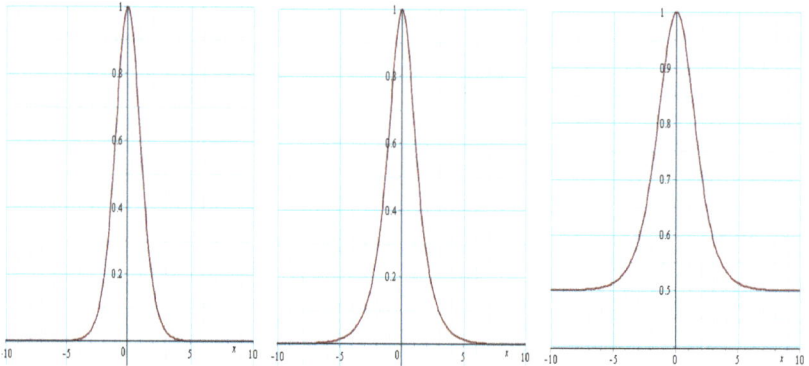

Figure 3. The exact solutions of the generalized SIdV Equation (5) at $t = 0$. The **left** is a bell-shaped solitary wave solution (51); namely, $u(x,t) = \text{sech}^4(\frac{1}{2}x - \frac{4}{3}t)$ when $\delta = 1, \gamma = \frac{4}{3}, \gamma_2 = 1, \mu_2 = 1$, and $\mu_3 = 1$, the **middle** is a bell-shaped solitary wave solution (59); namely, $u(x,t) = \text{sech}(x - \frac{4}{3}t)$ when $\delta = 1, \gamma = \frac{2}{3}, \gamma_1 = 1, \mu_2 = 1, \mu_4 = -1$, and $\varepsilon = 1$, and the **right** is a bell-shaped solitary wave solution (60); namely, $u(x,t) = \frac{1}{2} + \frac{1}{2}\text{sech}^2(\frac{1}{2}x - 2t)$ when $\delta = -1, \gamma_0 = \frac{1}{2}, \gamma_1 = -1, \mu_2 = 1$, and $\mu_3 = 2$.

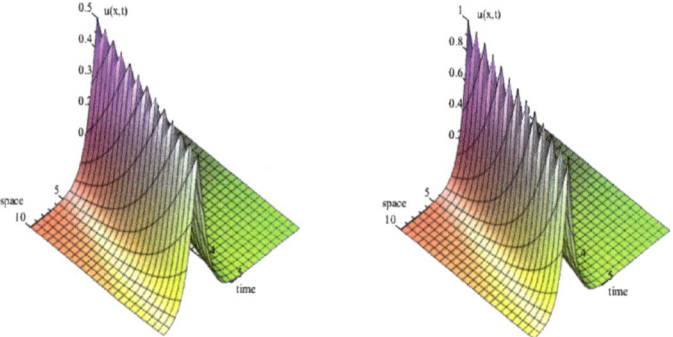

Figure 4. The exact peakon wave solutions of the generalized SIdV Equation (5) over the time interval $[0, 5]$. The **left** side shows a peakon wave solution (44)—namely, $u(x,t) = \frac{1}{2}\left[1 - \tanh(\frac{1}{2}|x - t|)\right]$ when $\delta = \frac{1}{2}$ and $\mu_2 = 1$; and the **right** side shows a peakon wave solution (55), namely, $u(x,t) = \exp(-|x - t|)$ when $\delta = 1, \gamma = 1, \mu_2 = 1$, and $\gamma_1 = \frac{1}{4}$. The peakon solution is obtained when kink and anti-kink solutions (or two exponential solutions of the opposite forms) move in the same direction with the same speed.

4. Conclusions

In this paper, we considered a generalized SIdV equation that is KdV-like, with an advecting velocity given by $\left(3(1 - \delta)u + (\delta + 1)\frac{u_{xx}}{u}\right)$. Making use of the auxiliary equation method, for different values of δ, we were able to find closed-form expressions for a variety of solutions, both bounded and singular. Interestingly, we showed that the SIdV equation (i.e., when $\delta = 1$) has solitary wave solutions of bell type of the forms of sech and sech^4 in addition to the sech^2 solution that it shares with the KdV equation (see Figure 3). Further, we even obtained peakon solutions for the SIdV equation ($\delta = 1$) and for the generalized SIdV equation when δ is any value (see Figure 4 when $\delta = \frac{1}{2}$). The solutions found in this work are new and have not been reported elsewhere in the literature. Looking ahead, one could explore to determine whether the generalized SIdV equation possesses multiple kink or bell-type solutions, as was shown for the negative order KdV equation [10]. In addition, one could build on the work in [12] and expand our knowledge to understand how one may be able to employ the SIdV equation in engineering applications such as control theory and image restoration. Our work also demonstrated the versatility of the auxiliary equation in extracting an array of interesting solutions from a KdV-like advection equation.

Author Contributions: Investigation, L.A., V.M. and B.A.; Software, L.A.; Supervision, V.M.; Writing—original draft, L.A., V.M. and B.A.; Writing—review & editing, L.A., V.M. and B.A. All authors have read and agreed to the published version of the manuscript.

Funding: This research received no external funding.

Institutional Review Board Statement: Not applicable.

Informed Consent Statement: Not applicable.

Data Availability Statement: Not applicable.

Conflicts of Interest: The authors declare no conflict of interest.

References

1. Ablowitz, M.J.; Clarkson, P.A. *Solitons, Nonlinear Evolution Equations and Inverse Scattering*; Cambridge University Press: Cambridge, UK, 1991; p. 149.
2. Hirota, R. Exact solution of the Korteweg-de Vries equation for multiple collisions of solitons. *Phys. Rev. Lett.* **1971**, *27*, 1192–1194. [CrossRef]
3. Crighton, D.G. Applications of KdV. *Acta Appl. Math.* **1995**, *39*, 39–67. [CrossRef]
4. Hershkowitz, N.; Romesser, T. Observations of ion-acoustic cylindrical solitons. *Phys. Rev. Lett.* **1974**, *32*, 581. [CrossRef]
5. Berest, Y.Y.; Loutsenko, I.M. Huygens' principle in Minkowski spaces and soliton solutions of the Korteweg-de Vries equation. *Commun. Math. Phys.* **1997**, *190*, 113–132. [CrossRef]
6. Gardner, C.S.; Greene, J.M.; Kruskal, M.D.; Miura, R.M. Method for solving the Korteweg-deVries equation. *Phys. Rev. Lett.* **1976**, *19*, 1095. [CrossRef]
7. Sen, A.; Ahalpara, D.P.; Thyagaraja, A.; Krishnaswami, G.S. A KdV like advection-dispersion equation with some remarkable properties. *Commun. Nonlinear Sci. Numer. Simul.* **2012**, *17*, 4115–4124. [CrossRef]
8. Silva, P.L.D.; Freire, I.L.; Sampaio, J.C.S. A family of wave equations with some remarkable properties. *Proc. R. Soc. A* **2018**, *474*, 20170763. [CrossRef]
9. Zhang, G.; He, J.; Wang, L.; Mihalache, D. Kink-type solutions of the SIdV equation and their properties. *R. Soc. Open Sci.* **2019**, *6*, 191040. [CrossRef]
10. Qiao, Z.; Fan, E. Negative-order Korteweg-de Vries equations. *Phys. Rev. E* **2012**, *86*, 016601. [CrossRef]
11. Tsutsumi, M.; Mukasa, T.; Iino, R. On the generalized Korteweg–De Vries equation. *Proc. Jpn. Acad.* **1970**, *46*, 921–925.
12. Xu, D.D.; Zhang, D.J.; Zhao, S.L. The Sylvester equation and integrable equations: I. The Korteweg-de Vries system and sine-Gordon equation. *J. Nonlinear Math. Phys.* **2014**, *21*, 382–406. [CrossRef]
13. Bhatia, R.; Rosenthal, P. How and why to solve the operator equation $AX - XB = Y$. *Bull. Lond. Math. Soc.* **1997**, *29*, 1–21. [CrossRef]
14. Fan, X.; Yin, J. Two types of traveling wave solutions of a KdV-like advection-dispersion equation. *Math. Aeterna* **2012**, *2*, 273–282.
15. Feng, Q.; Zheng, B. Traveling wave solutions for the fifth-order Sawada-Kotera equation and the general Gardner equation by $(\frac{G'}{G})$-expansion method. *WSEAS Trans. Math.* **2010**, *9*, 171–180.
16. Zayed, E.; Abdelaziz, M. Exact traveling wave solutions of nonlinear variable coefficients evolution equations with forced terms using the generalized $(\frac{G'}{G})$-expansion method. *Wseas Trans. Math.* **2011**, *10*, 115–124. [CrossRef]
17. Alzaleq, L.; Manoranjan, V. Exact traveling waves for the Fisher's equation with nonlinear diffusion. *Eur. Phys. J. Plus.* **2020**, *135*, 1–11. [CrossRef]
18. Yang, X.-F.; Deng, Z.-C.; We, Y.i. A Riccati–Bernoulli sub-ODE method for nonlinear partial differential equations and its application. *Adv. Differ. Equ.* **2015**, *2015*, 1–17. [CrossRef]
19. Wang, M. Exact solutions for a compound KdV-Burgers equation. *Phys. Lett. A* **1996**, *213*, 279–287. [CrossRef]
20. Alzaleq, L.; Manoranjan, V. Analysis of the Fisher-KPP equation with a time-dependent Allee effect. *IOP SciNotes* **2020**, *1*, 025003. [CrossRef]
21. Zhu, S.D. The generalizing Riccati equation mapping method in non-linear evolution equation: Application to (2+1)-dimensional Boiti-Leon-Pempinelle equation. *Chaos Solitons Fractals* **2008**, *37*, 1335–1342. [CrossRef]
22. Biswas, A. Solitary wave solution for the generalized Kawahara equation. *Appl. Math. Lett.* **2009**, *22*, 208–210. [CrossRef]
23. Kudryashov, N.A. Method for finding highly dispersive optical solitons of nonlinear differential equations. *Optik* **2020**, *206*, 163550. [CrossRef]
24. Kudryashov, N.A. One method for finding exact solutions of nonlinear differential equations. *Commun. Nonlinear Sci. Numer. Simul.* **2012**, *17*, 2248–2253. [CrossRef]

25. Parkes, E.J.; Duffy, B.R.; Abbott, P.C. The Jacobi elliptic-function method for finding periodic-wave solutions to nonlinear evolution equations. *Phys. Lett. A* **2002**, *295*, 280–286. [CrossRef]
26. Yu, J.; Sun, Y. Modified method of simplest equation and its applications to the Bogoyavlenskii equation. *Comput. Math. Appl.* **2016**, *72*, 1943–1955. [CrossRef]
27. Yu, J.; Wang, D.S.; Sun, Y.; Wu, S. Modified method of simplest equation for obtaining exact solutions of the Zakharov–Kuznetsov equation, the modified Zakharov–Kuznetsov equation, and their generalized forms. *Nonlinear Dyn.* **2016**, *85*, 2449–2465. [CrossRef]
28. Sun, Y.L.; Ma, W.X.; Yu, J.P.; Khalique, C.M. Exact solutions of the Rosenau–Hyman equation, coupled KdV system and Burgers–Huxley equation using modified transformed rational function method. *Mod. Phys. Lett. B* **2018**, *32*, 1850282. [CrossRef]
29. Veeresha, P.; Prakasha, D.G.; Singh, J. Solution for fractional forced KdV equation using fractional natural decomposition method. *Aims Math.* **2020**, *5*, 798–810. [CrossRef]
30. Baishya, C.; Achar, S.J.; Veeresha, P.; Prakasha, D.G. Dynamics of a fractional epidemiological model with disease infection in both the populations. *Chaos Interdiscip. J. Nonlinear Sci.* **2021**, *31*, 043130. [CrossRef]
31. Baishya, C.; Veeresha, P. Laguerre polynomial-based operational matrix of integration for solving fractional differential equations with non-singular kernel. *Proc. R. Soc. A* **2021**, *477*, 20210438. [CrossRef]
32. Veeresha, P.; Prakasha, D.G.; Kumar, D.; Baleanu, D.; Singh, J. An efficient computational technique for fractional model of generalized Hirota-Satsuma-coupled Korteweg-de Vries and coupled modified Korteweg-de Vries equations. *J. Comput. Nonlinear Dyn.* **2020**, *15*, 071003. [CrossRef]
33. Veeresha, P.; Prakasha, D.G.; Magesh, N.; Christopher, A.J.; Sarwe, D.U. Solution for fractional potential KdV and Benjamin equations using the novel technique. *J. Ocean Eng. Sci.* **2021**, *31*, 943–950. [CrossRef]
34. Sirendaoreji, N.A.; PrakJiongasha, S. Auxiliary equation method for solving nonlinear partial differential equations. *Phys. Lett. A* **2003**, *309*, 387–396. [CrossRef]
35. Alzaleq, L. *A Klein-Gordon Equation Revisited: New Solutions and a Computational Method*; Washington State University: Pullman, WA, USA, 2016.
36. Sirendaoreji, N.A. Auxiliary equation method and new solutions of Klein-Gordon equations. *Chaos Solitons Fractals* **2007**, *31*, 943–950. [CrossRef]

Article

Highly Dispersive Optical Soliton Perturbation, with Maximum Intensity, for the Complex Ginzburg–Landau Equation by Semi-Inverse Variation

Anjan Biswas [1,2,3,4,5], Trevor Berkemeyer [5], Salam Khan [5], Luminita Moraru [6,*], Yakup Yıldırım [7] and Hashim M. Alshehri [2]

Citation: Biswas, A.; Berkemeyer, T.; Khan, S.; Moraru, L.; Yıldırım, Y.; Alshehri, H.M. Highly Dispersive Optical Soliton Perturbation, with Maximum Intensity, for the Complex Ginzburg–Landau Equation by Semi-Inverse Variation. *Mathematics* 2022, *10*, 987. https://doi.org/10.3390/math10060987

Academic Editor: Nikolai A. Kudryashov

Received: 25 February 2022
Accepted: 17 March 2022
Published: 18 March 2022

Publisher's Note: MDPI stays neutral with regard to jurisdictional claims in published maps and institutional affiliations.

Copyright: © 2022 by the authors. Licensee MDPI, Basel, Switzerland. This article is an open access article distributed under the terms and conditions of the Creative Commons Attribution (CC BY) license (https://creativecommons.org/licenses/by/4.0/).

[1] Department of Applied Mathematics, National Research Nuclear University, 31 Kashirskoe Hwy, 115409 Moscow, Russia; biswas.anjan@gmail.com
[2] Mathematical Modeling and Applied Computation (MMAC) Research Group, Department of Mathematics, King Abdulaziz University, Jeddah 21589, Saudi Arabia; hmalshehri@kau.edu.sa
[3] Department of Applied Sciences, Cross–Border Faculty, Dunarea de Jos University of Galati, 111 Domneasca Street, 800201 Galati, Romania
[4] Department of Mathematics and Applied Mathematics, Sefako Makgatho Health Sciences University, Medunsa 0204, South Africa
[5] Department of Physics, Chemistry and Mathematics, Alabama A&M University, Normal, AL 35762-4900, USA; tberkeme@bulldogs.aamu.edu (T.B.); salam.khan@aamu.edu (S.K.)
[6] Faculty of Sciences and Environment, Department of Chemistry, Physics and Environment, Dunarea de Jos University of Galati, 47 Domneasca Street, 800008 Galati, Romania
[7] Department of Mathematics, Faculty of Arts and Sciences, Near East University, Nicosia 99138, Cyprus; yakup.yildirim@neu.edu.tr
* Correspondence: luminita.moraru@ugal.ro

Abstract: This work analytically recovers the highly dispersive bright 1–soliton solution using for the perturbed complex Ginzburg–Landau equation, which is studied with three forms of nonlinear refractive index structures. They are Kerr law, parabolic law, and polynomial law. The perturbation terms appear with maximum allowable intensity, also known as full nonlinearity. The semi-inverse variational principle makes this retrieval possible. The amplitude–width relation is obtained by solving a cubic polynomial equation using Cardano's approach. The parameter constraints for the existence of such solitons are also enumerated.

Keywords: solitons; Kudryashov; Cardano; semi-inverse; perturbation

MSC: 78A60; 35C08; 37K40

1. Introduction

One of the most important necessities with a mathematical model that describes soliton propagation across inter-continental distances is its integrability to secure an exact soliton solution. This provides the ease and convenience of conducting further analysis with such a solution structure at our disposal. Some such conveniences are the study of quasi-monochromatic solitons, the computing of the collision-induced timing jitter, the application of the variational principle, the implementation of the moment method approach, or even the application of collective variables to secure the dynamical system of soliton parameters [1–30]. Thus, it is necessary to recover the structure of a soliton. There are diverse approaches that can make this soliton solution retrieval possible. These range of approaches are visible in various works across the board. However, in specific situations, securing a soliton solution is rendered to be challenging. In fact, under such situations, the classic approach of inverse scattering transform is not applicable either, since the model fails the Painleve test of integrability. In such a situation, a modern approach of integrability has been successfully applied to recover an analytical bright 1–soliton solution. This is the application of the semi-inverse variational principle (SVP) that was proposed by J. H. He [11,12,17].

SVP was successfully implemented to a variety of problems in a wide range of physical situations. Apart from photonics, some such fields are fluid dynamics [2,9,10,12,13,23], relativistic quantum mechanics [21,24], plasma physics [4], mathematical chemistry [11], and various others [5,13–17,22,26]. In particular, the application of optics problems has been quite noticeably successful and widely visible, as reported [1–20]. The models that have been commonly studied in optics, with the implementation of SVP, are the Lakshmanan–Porsezian–Daniel model [1,7], Schrödinger's nonlinear model [20], and the Fokas–Lenells model [8]. In this context, solitons were studied with chromatic dispersion [1] as well as cubic–quartic dispersive effects [7]. The novelty of the work ushers in with an established analytical soliton solution for an arbitrary maximum intensity where all pre-existing integration approaches fail.

The current paper will address SVP, for the first time, with the complex Ginzburg–Landau equation (CGLE) [3,19,25]. This will appear with six dispersion sources that constitute highly dispersive (HD) optical solitons [6,15,16,25]. The perturbation terms appear with maximum allowable intensity, i.e., AKA full nonlinearity [3–8,15,16,22]. Three forms of nonlinear refractive index structures are addressed: cubic (or Kerr) nonlinearity [1,3,14,25], parabolic (or cubic–quintic) nonlinearity [14,25], and polynomial nonlinearity [15,16,25]. Bright 1–soliton is finally extracted, for each law, where the soliton amplitude–width relation is recoverable by solving a cubic polynomial equation using Cardano's approach [6]. The significance of the work is the retrieval of an analytical bright 1–soliton solution in spite of the fact that the perturbed CGLE is not rendered integrable by any of the pre-existing algorithms. The details are exhibited after introducing the model together with its perturbation terms.

Governing Model

The general form of CGLE without the perturbation terms reads as [25]

$$iq_t + ia_1 q_x + a_2 q_{xx} + ia_3 q_{xxx} + a_4 q_{xxxx} + ia_5 q_{xxxxx} + a_6 q_{xxxxxx} + \frac{1}{|q|^2 q^*}\left[\alpha |q|^2 \left(|q|^2\right)_{xx} - \beta\left\{\left(|q|^2\right)_x\right\}^2\right] + F\left(|q|^2\right) q = 0. \quad (1)$$

Here, $q(x,t)$ depicts the wave profile that travels down the optical fiber and is a complex valued function. The first term denotes the linear temporal evolution that has its coefficient as $i = \sqrt{-1}$. The coefficients of a_j for $1 \leq j \leq 6$ represent the six dispersion terms. Here, a_1 gives the inter-modal dispersion; a_2 accounts for the chromatic dispersion; while a_3 till a_6 yield the third-order, fourth-order, fifth-order, and sixth-order dispersion effects sequentially. Next, α and β come from the nonlinear effects that are considered in CGLE [25]. The intensity-dependent nonlinear refractive index of the fiber is governed by the real valued functional F. The current paper will consider three nonlinear forms: cubic (or Kerr) nonlinearity, parabolic (or cubic–quintic) nonlinearity, and polynomial nonlinearity.

With perturbation terms turned on, the CGLE extends to

$$iq_t + ia_1 q_x + a_2 q_{xx} + ia_3 q_{xxx} + a_4 q_{xxxx} + ia_5 q_{xxxxx}$$
$$+ a_6 q_{xxxxxx} + \frac{1}{|q|^2 q^*}\left[\alpha |q|^2 \left(|q|^2\right)_{xx} - \beta\left\{\left(|q|^2\right)_x\right\}^2\right] + F\left(|q|^2\right) q \quad (2)$$
$$= i\left[\lambda \left(|q|^{2m} q\right)_x + \theta \left(|q|^{2m}\right)_x q + \sigma |q|^{2m} q_x\right].$$

The perturbation terms stem from the self-steepening effect, the self-frequency shift, and nonlinear dispersion, which are represented by the coefficients of λ, θ, and σ, respectively. The parameter m comes from maximum permissible intensity, also known as full nonlinearity.

2. Mathematical Start-Up

The starting hypothesis to handle Equation (2) is the substitution

$$q(x,t) = g(x - vt)e^{i(-\kappa x + \omega t + \theta_0)} = g(s)e^{i(-\kappa x + \omega t + \theta_0)}. \tag{3}$$

Here in (3), the function $g(x,t)$ is the traveling wave hypothesis while from the phase, ω is the wave number, while θ_0 is the phase constant and κ represents the frequency. Inserting (3) into (2) gives way to the following set of relations. The real part gives:

$$\begin{aligned}&\left(-\omega - a_6\kappa^6 + a_5\kappa^5 + a_4\kappa^4 - a_3\kappa^3 - a_2\kappa^2 + a_1\kappa\right)g \\ &+ \left(a_2 + 2\alpha + 3a_3\kappa - 6a_4\kappa^2 - 10a_5\kappa^3 + 15a_6\kappa^4\right)g'' \\ &+ \left(a_4 + 5a_5\kappa - 15a_6\kappa^2\right)g^{(iv)} + a_6 g^{(vi)} + 2(\alpha - 2\beta)\frac{(g')^2}{g} + F(g^2)g = \kappa(\lambda + \sigma)g^{2m+1}.\end{aligned} \tag{4}$$

The imaginary part yields:

$$\begin{aligned}&\{(2m+1)\lambda + 2m\theta + \sigma\}g^{2m}g' \\ &+ \left(v - a_1 + 2a_2\kappa + 3a_3\kappa^2 - 4a_4\kappa^3 - 5a_5\kappa^4 + 6a_6\kappa^5\right)g' \\ &- \left(a_3 - 4a_4\kappa - 10a_5\kappa^2 + 20a_6\kappa^3\right)g''' - (a_5 - 6a_6\kappa)g^{(v)} = 0.\end{aligned} \tag{5}$$

In (4) and (5), the notations $g' = dg/ds$, $g'' = d^2g/ds^2$, $g''' = d^3g/ds^3$, $g^{(iv)} = d^4g/ds^4$, $g^{(v)} = d^5g/ds^5$ and $g^{(vi)} = d^6g/ds^6$ are adopted. Next, introducing the parameters

$$P_1 = -a_6\kappa^6 + a_4\kappa^4 + a_5\kappa^5 - a_3\kappa^3 - a_2\kappa^2 + a_1\kappa - \omega, \tag{6}$$

$$P_2 = a_2 + 2\alpha + 3a_3\kappa - 6a_4\kappa^2 - 10a_5\kappa^3 + 15a_6\kappa^4, \tag{7}$$

$$P_3 = a_4 + 5a_5\kappa - 15a_6\kappa^2, \tag{8}$$

and setting

$$\alpha = 2\beta, \tag{9}$$

Equation (4) transforms to

$$P_1 g + P_2 g'' + P_3 g^{(iv)} + a_6 g^{(vi)} + F(g^2)g = \kappa(\lambda + \sigma)g^{2m+1}. \tag{10}$$

Thus, with (9), the governing Equation (2) modifies to:

$$\begin{aligned}&iq_t + ia_1 q_x + a_2 q_{xx} + ia_3 q_{xxx} + a_4 q_{xxxx} + ia_5 q_{xxxxx} \\ &+ a_6 q_{xxxxxx} + \frac{\beta}{|q|^2 q^*}\left[2|q|^2\left(|q|^2\right)_{xx} - \left\{\left(|q|^2\right)_x\right\}^2\right] + F\left(|q|^2\right)q \\ &= i\left[\lambda\left(|q|^{2m} q\right)_x + \theta\left(|q|^{2m}\right)_x q + \sigma|q|^{2m} q_x\right].\end{aligned} \tag{11}$$

Next, the imaginary part Equation (5) gives the following parameter constraints

$$(2m+1)\lambda + 2m\theta + \sigma = 0, \tag{12}$$

$$v = a_1 - 2a_2\kappa - 3a_3\kappa^2 + 4a_4\kappa^3 + 5a_5\kappa^4 - 6a_6\kappa^5, \tag{13}$$

$$a_3 - 4a_4\kappa - 10a_5\kappa^2 + 20a_6\kappa^3 = 0, \tag{14}$$

and

$$a_5 = 6a_6\kappa. \tag{15}$$

Equation (13) gives the velocity. The relations (12)–(15) stay the same, irrespective of the type of nonlinearity considered.

3. Application of SVP

From Equation (10), multiplying by g' and integrating gives

$$P_1 g^2 + P_2(g')^2 - P_3(g'')^2 + a_6(g''')^2 \\ + 2\int F(g^2) g g' dg - \frac{\kappa(\lambda+\sigma)}{m+1} g^{2m+2} = K, \quad (16)$$

where K is the integration constant. The stationary integral is introduced as below

$$J = \int_{-\infty}^{\infty} \left[\begin{array}{c} P_1 g^2 + P_2(g')^2 - P_3(g'')^2 + a_6(g''')^2 \\ +2\int F(g^2) g g' dg - \frac{\kappa(\lambda+\sigma)}{m+1} g^{2m+2} \end{array} \right] dx. \quad (17)$$

The bright 1–soliton to (11) is the same as that of the homogeneous counterpart, namely with $\lambda = \theta = \sigma = 0$, whose structure is of the form:

$$g(s) = Af\{\mathrm{sec}\,hB(x-vt)\}, \quad (18)$$

where the functional form of the bright soliton, given by f, is based on the type of nonlinearity in question. The amplitude (A) and inverse width (B) of the soliton will be recovered by the coupled system of Equations (1)–(18):

$$\frac{\partial J}{\partial A} = 0, \quad (19)$$

and

$$\frac{\partial J}{\partial B} = 0. \quad (20)$$

This principle will be applied to study HD bright 1–soliton to (11) for three nonlinear forms.

3.1. Kerr Law

The refractive index structure is presented as

$$F(s) = b_0 s, \quad (21)$$

where b_0 is a real-valued constant parameter. Thus, Equation (11) reads as

$$iq_t + ia_1 q_x + a_2 q_{xx} + ia_3 q_{xxx} + a_4 q_{xxxx} + ia_5 q_{xxxxx} \\ + a_6 q_{xxxxxx} + \frac{\beta}{|q|^2 q^*} \left[2|q|^2 \left(|q|^2\right)_{xx} - \left\{ \left(|q|^2\right)_x \right\}^2 \right] + b_0 |q|^2 q \\ = i\left[\lambda \left(|q|^{2m} q\right)_x + \theta\left(|q|^{2m}\right)_x q + \sigma |q|^{2m} q_x \right], \quad (22)$$

so that (16) comes out as

$$2P_1 g^2 + 2P_2(g')^2 - 2P_3(g'')^2 + 2a_6(g''')^2 + b_0 g^4 - \frac{2\kappa(\lambda+\sigma)}{m+1} g^{2m+2} = K. \quad (23)$$

The stationary integral, in this case, is introduced as

$$J = \int_{-\infty}^{\infty} \left[\begin{array}{c} 2P_1 g^2 + 2P_2(g')^2 - 2P_3(g'')^2 \\ +2a_6(g''')^2 + b_0 g^4 - \frac{2\kappa(\lambda+\sigma)}{m+1} g^{2m+2} \end{array} \right] dx. \quad (24)$$

The solution of (22), for $\lambda = \theta = \sigma = 0$, is given as [19]

$$g(x - vt) = A\mathrm{sec}\,h^3[B(x-vt)]. \quad (25)$$

By substituting this 1–soliton solution into (24), one can obtain

$$J = \frac{16P_1}{15}\frac{A^2}{B} + \frac{144}{35}P_2A^2B - \frac{592}{35}P_3A^2B^3 + \frac{15{,}024}{1155}a_6A^2B^5 \\ + \frac{256}{693}\frac{b_0A^4}{B} - \frac{\kappa(\lambda+\sigma)}{m+1}\frac{PA^{2m+2}}{B}, \tag{26}$$

where

$$P = \frac{8m(3m+1)(3m+2)}{(2m+1)(6m+1)(6m+5)}\frac{\Gamma(3m)\Gamma\left(\frac{1}{2}\right)}{\Gamma\left(3m+\frac{1}{2}\right)}. \tag{27}$$

The coupled pair of Equations (19) and (20), for Kerr law, is given as:

$$\frac{P_1}{15} + \frac{9}{35}P_2B^2 - \frac{37}{35}P_3B^4 + \frac{939}{1155}a_6B^6 + \frac{32}{693}b_0A^2 - \frac{\kappa(\lambda+\sigma)}{16}PA^{2m} = 0, \tag{28}$$

and

$$-\frac{P_1}{15} + \frac{9}{35}P_2B^2 - \frac{111}{35}P_3B^4 + \frac{4695}{1155}a_6B^6 + \frac{16}{693}b_0A^2 - \frac{\kappa(\lambda+\sigma)}{16(m+1)}PA^{2m} = 0. \tag{29}$$

Adding (28) and (29) leaves us with

$$\frac{18}{35}P_2B^2 - \frac{148}{35}P_3B^4 + \frac{5634}{1155}a_6B^6 + \frac{48}{693}b_0A^2 - \frac{\kappa(\lambda+\sigma)(m+2)}{16(m+1)}PA^{2m} = 0. \tag{30}$$

Equation (30) can be restructured as a cubic polynomial equation in u:

$$au^3 + bu^2 + cu + d = 0, \tag{31}$$

with the following notations:

$$B^2 = u, \tag{32}$$

$$a = \frac{5634}{1155}a_6, \tag{33}$$

$$b = -\frac{148}{35}P_3, \tag{34}$$

$$c = \frac{18}{35}P_2, \tag{35}$$

and

$$d = \frac{48}{693}b_0A^2 - \frac{\kappa(\lambda+\sigma)(m+2)}{16(m+1)}PA^{2m}. \tag{36}$$

By Cardano's method, (31) and (32) solves to [6]:

$$B = \left[\left\{\left(-\frac{b^3}{27a^3} + \frac{bc}{6a^2} - \frac{d}{2a}\right) - \sqrt{\left(-\frac{b^3}{27a^3} + \frac{bc}{6a^2} - \frac{d}{2a}\right)^2 + \left(\frac{c}{3a} - \frac{b^2}{9a^2}\right)^3}\right\}^{\frac{1}{3}} \\ + \left\{\left(-\frac{b^3}{27a^3} + \frac{bc}{6a^2} - \frac{d}{2a}\right) + \sqrt{\left(-\frac{b^3}{27a^3} + \frac{bc}{6a^2} - \frac{d}{2a}\right)^2 + \left(\frac{c}{3a} - \frac{b^2}{9a^2}\right)^3}\right\}^{\frac{1}{3}} - \frac{b}{3a}\right]^{\frac{1}{2}}. \tag{37}$$

The constraint for this solution to exist is

$$a_6 \neq 0, \tag{38}$$

along with the discriminant

$$\left(-\frac{b^3}{27a^3} + \frac{bc}{6a^2} - \frac{d}{2a}\right)^2 + \left(\frac{c}{3a} - \frac{b^2}{9a^2}\right)^3 > 0. \tag{39}$$

Moreover,

$$\left\{\left(-\frac{d}{2a} + \frac{bc}{6a^2} - \frac{b^3}{27a^3}\right) - \sqrt{\left(-\frac{d}{2a} + \frac{bc}{6a^2} - \frac{b^3}{27a^3}\right)^2 + \left(\frac{c}{3a} - \frac{b^2}{9a^2}\right)^3}\right\}^{\frac{1}{3}}$$
$$+ \left\{\left(-\frac{d}{2a} + \frac{bc}{6a^2} - \frac{b^3}{27a^3}\right) + \sqrt{\left(-\frac{d}{2a} + \frac{bc}{6a^2} - \frac{b^3}{27a^3}\right)^2 + \left(\frac{c}{3a} - \frac{b^2}{9a^2}\right)^3}\right\}^{\frac{1}{3}} > \frac{b}{3a}. \tag{40}$$

Thus, the HD bright 1–soliton to (22) is introduced as (see Figure 1)

$$q(x,t) = A \operatorname{sech}^3[B(x - vt)] e^{i(-\kappa x + \omega t + \theta_0)}. \tag{41}$$

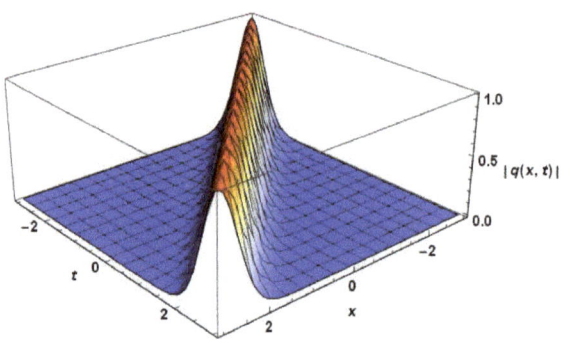

Figure 1. Profile of the HD bright 1–soliton (41) setting all arbitrary parameters to unity.

Here, the inverse width (B) is explicitly expressed via (37), provided that the constraint conditions given by (38)–(40) are maintained.

3.2. Parabolic Law

The refractive index structure is indicated below

$$F(s) = b_1 s + b_2 s^2, \tag{42}$$

where b_1 and b_2 are real-valued constant parameters. Then, Equation (11) evolves as

$$iq_t + ia_1 q_x + a_2 q_{xx} + ia_3 q_{xxx} + a_4 q_{xxxx} + ia_5 q_{xxxxx}$$
$$+ a_6 q_{xxxxxx} + \frac{\beta}{|q|^2 q^*} \left[2|q|^2 \left(|q|^2\right)_{xx} - \left\{\left(|q|^2\right)_x\right\}^2 \right] + \left(b_1 |q|^2 + b_2 |q|^4\right) q \tag{43}$$
$$= i\left[\lambda \left(|q|^{2m} q\right)_x + \theta \left(|q|^{2m}\right)_x q + \sigma |q|^{2m} q_x \right],$$

so that (16) comes out as

$$6P_1 g^2 + 6P_2 (g')^2 - 6P_3 (g'')^2 + 6a_6 (g''')^2$$
$$+ 3b_1 g^4 + 2b_2 g^6 - \frac{6\kappa(\lambda+\sigma)}{m+1} g^{2m+2} = K. \tag{44}$$

The stationary integral, in this case, is structured as

$$J = \int_{-\infty}^{\infty} \left[\begin{array}{c} 6P_1 g^2 + 6P_2 (g')^2 - 6P_3 (g'')^2 + 6a_6 (g''')^2 \\ + 3b_1 g^4 + 2b_2 g^6 - \frac{6\kappa(\lambda+\sigma)}{m+1} g^{2m+2} \end{array} \right] dx. \tag{45}$$

The solution of (43), for $\lambda = \theta = \sigma = 0$, is given as [19]

$$g(x - vt) = A\operatorname{sech}^{\frac{3}{2}}[B(x - vt)]. \tag{46}$$

By substituting this 1-soliton solution into (45), one can obtain

$$J = \pi P_1 \frac{A^2}{B} + \frac{9\pi}{16} P_2 A^2 B - \frac{153}{128} P_3 A^2 B^3 + \frac{21{,}429}{4096} a_6 A^2 B^5 \\ + \frac{16}{15} \frac{b_1 A^4}{B} + \frac{35\pi}{192} \frac{b_2 A^6}{B} - \frac{6\kappa(\lambda+\sigma) P}{m+1} \frac{A^{2m+2}}{B}, \tag{47}$$

where

$$P = \frac{2(3m+1)}{3m(3m+2)} \frac{\Gamma\left(\frac{3m}{2} + \frac{1}{2}\right)\Gamma\left(\frac{1}{2}\right)}{\Gamma\left(\frac{3m}{2}\right)}. \tag{48}$$

The coupled pair of Equations (19) and (20), for parabolic law, is:

$$\pi P_1 + \frac{9\pi}{16} P_2 B^2 - \frac{153\pi}{128} P_3 B^4 + \frac{21{,}429\pi}{4096} a_6 B^6 \\ + \frac{32}{15} b_1 A^2 + \frac{35\pi}{64} b_2 A^4 - 2\kappa(\lambda+\sigma) P A^{2m} = 0, \tag{49}$$

and

$$-\pi P_1 + \frac{9\pi}{16} P_2 B^2 - \frac{459\pi}{128} P_3 B^4 + \frac{107{,}145\pi}{4096} a_6 B^6 \\ - \frac{16}{15} b_1 A^2 - \frac{35\pi}{192} b_2 A^4 + \frac{2\kappa(\lambda+\sigma)}{m+1} P A^{2m} = 0. \tag{50}$$

Adding (49) and (50) yields

$$\frac{9\pi}{8} P_2 B^2 - \frac{153\pi}{32} P_3 B^4 + \frac{64{,}287\pi}{2048} a_6 B^6 \\ + \frac{16}{15} b_1 A^2 + \frac{70\pi}{192} b_2 A^4 - \frac{2m\kappa(\lambda+\sigma)}{m+1} P A^{2m} = 0. \tag{51}$$

Equation (51) is reducible to (31) with

$$a = \frac{64{,}287\pi}{2048} a_6, \tag{52}$$

$$b = -\frac{153\pi}{32} P_3, \tag{53}$$

$$c = \frac{9\pi}{8} P_2, \tag{54}$$

and

$$d = \frac{16}{15} b_1 A^2 + \frac{70\pi}{192} b_2 A^4 - \frac{2m\kappa(\lambda+\sigma)}{m+1} P A^{2m}. \tag{55}$$

Hence, the HD bright 1-soliton to (43) reads as (see Figure 2)

$$q(x,t) = A\operatorname{sech}^{\frac{3}{2}}[B(x - vt)] e^{i(-\kappa x + \omega t + \theta_0)}. \tag{56}$$

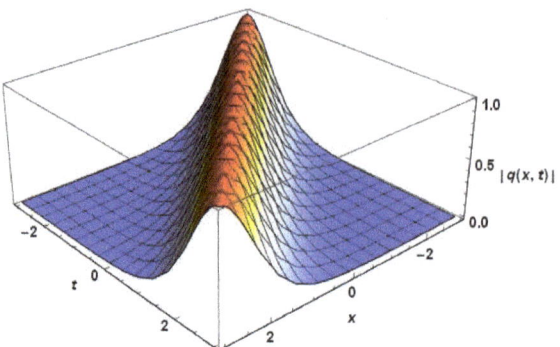

Figure 2. Profile of the HD bright 1–soliton (56) setting all arbitrary parameters to unity.

Here, the inverse width (B) is explicitly expressed via (37), providing that the constraint conditions given by (38)–(40) are maintained.

3.3. Polynomial Law

The refractive index structure extends to

$$F(s) = b_1 s + b_2 s^2 + b_3 s^3, \tag{57}$$

where b_1, b_2, and are real-valued constant parameters. Hence, Equation (11) comes out as

$$\begin{aligned} & iq_t + ia_1 q_x + a_2 q_{xx} + ia_3 q_{xxx} + a_4 q_{xxxx} + ia_5 q_{xxxxx} + a_6 q_{xxxxxx} \\ & + \left(b_1 |q|^2 + b_2 |q|^4 + b_3 |q|^6\right) q + \frac{\beta}{|q|^2 q^*} \left[2|q|^2 \left(|q|^2\right)_{xx} - \left\{\left(|q|^2\right)_x\right\}^2\right] \\ & = i\left[\lambda \left(|q|^{2m} q\right)_x + \theta \left(|q|^{2m}\right)_x q + \sigma |q|^{2m} q_x\right], \end{aligned} \tag{58}$$

so that (16) now is

$$\begin{aligned} & 12P_1 g^2 + 12P_2 (g')^2 - 12P_3 (g'')^2 + 12a_6 (g''')^2 \\ & + 6b_1 g^4 + 4b_2 g^6 + 3b_3 g^8 - \frac{12\kappa(\lambda+\sigma)}{m+1} g^{2m+2} = K. \end{aligned} \tag{59}$$

The stationary integral, for polynomial law, reads as

$$J = \int_{-\infty}^{\infty} \left[\begin{array}{c} 12P_1 g^2 + 12P_2 (g')^2 - 12P_3 (g'')^2 + 12a_6 (g''')^2 \\ + 6b_1 g^4 + 4b_2 g^6 + 3b_3 g^8 - \frac{12\kappa(\lambda+\sigma)}{m+1} g^{2m+2} \end{array} \right] dx. \tag{60}$$

The solution of (58), for $\lambda = \theta = \sigma = 0$, is [19]

$$g(x - vt) = A\operatorname{sech}[B(x - vt)]. \tag{61}$$

By substituting this 1–soliton solution into (60), one can obtain

$$\begin{aligned} J = & 3P_1 \frac{A^2}{B} + P_2 A^2 B - \frac{7}{5} P_3 A^2 B^3 + \frac{31}{7} a_6 A^2 B^5 + \frac{b_1 A^4}{B} \\ & + \frac{8 b_2}{15} \frac{A^6}{B} + \frac{12 b_3}{35} \frac{A^8}{B} - \frac{3\kappa(\lambda+\sigma) P}{m+1} \frac{A^{2m+2}}{B}, \end{aligned} \tag{62}$$

where

$$P = \frac{m}{2m+1} \frac{\Gamma(m)\Gamma\left(\frac{1}{2}\right)}{\Gamma\left(m+\frac{1}{2}\right)}. \tag{63}$$

The coupled pair of Equations (19) and (20), for polynomial law, formulates as:

$$3P_1 + P_2 B^2 - \tfrac{7}{5} P_3 B^4 + \tfrac{31}{7} a_6 B^6 + 2 b_1 A^2 \\ + \tfrac{24}{15} b_2 A^4 + \tfrac{48}{35} b_3 A^6 - 3\kappa(\lambda + \sigma) P A^{2m} = 0, \tag{64}$$

and

$$-3P_1 + P_2 B^2 - \tfrac{21}{5} P_3 B^4 + \tfrac{155}{7} a_6 B^6 - b_1 A^2 \\ - \tfrac{8}{15} b_2 A^4 - \tfrac{12}{35} b_3 A^6 - \tfrac{3\kappa(\lambda+\sigma)}{m+1} P A^{2m} = 0. \tag{65}$$

Adding (64) and (65) implies to

$$2 P_2 B^2 - \tfrac{28}{5} P_3 B^4 + \tfrac{186}{7} a_6 B^6 + b_1 A^2 + \tfrac{16}{15} b_2 A^4 \\ + \tfrac{36}{35} b_3 A^6 - \tfrac{3(m+2)\kappa(\lambda+\sigma)}{m+1} P A^{2m} = 0. \tag{66}$$

Again, Equation (66) is transformable to the cubic polynomial Equation (31) where

$$a = \frac{186}{7} a_6, \tag{67}$$

$$b = -\frac{28}{5} P_3, \tag{68}$$

$$c = 2 P_2, \tag{69}$$

and

$$d = b_1 A^2 + \frac{16}{15} b_2 A^4 + \frac{36}{35} b_3 A^6 - \frac{3(m+2)\kappa(\lambda+\sigma)}{m+1} P A^{2m}. \tag{70}$$

Hence, the HD bright 1–soliton to (58) comes out as (see Figure 3)

$$q(x,t) = A \operatorname{sech}[B(x - vt)] e^{i(-\kappa x + \omega t + \theta_0)}. \tag{71}$$

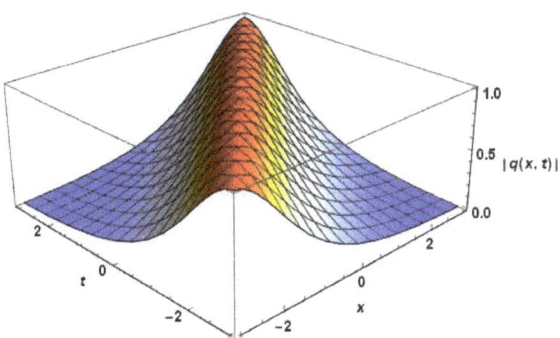

Figure 3. Profile of the HD bright 1–soliton (71) setting all arbitrary parameters to unity.

Here, the inverse width (B) is explicitly expressed via (37), providing that the constraint conditions given by (38)–(40) are maintained.

4. Conclusions

This work obtains an analytical expression of the HD bright 1–soliton to the perturbed CGLE by SVP, where the perturbation terms are considered with the maximum allowable intensity. Three nonlinear forms are addressed. Such an analytical 1–soliton solution, with arbitrary intensity parameters, in its closed form, and is not recoverable by any of the pre-existing integration algorithms.

There are some shortcomings to this approach. It is only the bright soliton that is obtainable using this approach. This scheme fails to retrieve singular or dark solitons since the stationary integral is rendered to be divergent with singular or dark solitons. The bright

1–soliton solutions that are recovered for three nonlinear forms are not exact since they are obtained by the usage of a principle, namely the SVP. Therefore, the results of this work cannot be compared with any pre-existing results since there are none. The homogenous model was first proposed during 2021 [25] and the current paper is the very first one to extend the model with perturbation terms and with full nonlinearity. The simulations, therefore, provide a visual accuracy to the proposed approach, namely the SVP.

This analytical soliton solution can take us further along with advanced studies. Some of them include the analysis of quasi-monochromatic solitons, the computing of the soliton parameter dynamics with the help of the variational principle, the study of the collision-induced timing jitter and the numerical simulation of the problem with the application of the Adomian decomposition algorithm, Laplace ADM, and variational iteration approach. More research results that can be aligned with the current findings [27–30] exist.

Author Contributions: Conceptualization, A.B.; methodology, T.B.; software, S.K.; writing—original draft preparation, L.M.; writing—review and editing, Y.Y.; project administration, H.M.A. All authors have read and agreed to the published version of the manuscript.

Funding: This research received no external funding.

Institutional Review Board Statement: Not applicable.

Informed Consent Statement: Not applicable.

Data Availability Statement: Not applicable.

Conflicts of Interest: The authors declare no conflict of interest.

References

1. Alqahtani, R.T.; Babatin, M.M.; Biswas, A. Bright optical solitons for Lakshmanan–Porsezian–Daniel model by semi–inverse variational principle. *Optik* **2018**, *154*, 109–114. [CrossRef]
2. Biswas, A.; Milovic, D.; Kumar, S.; Yildirim, A. Perturbation of shallow water waves by semi–inverse variational principle. *Indian J. Phys.* **2013**, *87*, 567–569. [CrossRef]
3. Biswas, A.; Alqahtani, R.T. Optical soliton perturbation with complex Ginzburg–Landau equation by semi–inverse variational principle. *Optik* **2017**, *147*, 77–81. [CrossRef]
4. Biswas, A.; Alqahtani, R.T. Chirp–free bright optical solitons for perturbed Gerdjikov–Ivanov equation by semi–inverse variational principle. *Optik* **2017**, *147*, 72–76. [CrossRef]
5. Biswas, A.; Asma, M.; Guggilla, P.; Mullick, L.; Moraru, L.; Ekici, M.; Alzahrani, A.K.; Belic, M.R. Optical soliton perturbation with Kudryashov's equation by semi–inverse variational principle. *Phys. Lett. A* **2020**, *384*, 126830. [CrossRef]
6. Biswas, A.; Ekici, M.; Dakova, A.; Khan, S.; Moshokoa, S.P.; Alshehri, H.M.; Belic, M.R. Highly dispersive optical soliton perturbation with Kudryashov's sextic–power law nonlinear refractive index by semi–inverse variation. *Results Phys.* **2021**, *27*, 104539. [CrossRef]
7. Biswas, A.; Edoki, J.; Guggilla, P.; Khan, S.; Alzahrani, A.K.; Belic, M.R. Cubic–quartic optical soliton perturbation with Lakshmanan–Porsezian–Daniel model by semi–inverse variational principle. *Ukr. J. Phys. Opt.* **2021**, *22*, 122–127. [CrossRef]
8. Biswas, A.; Dakova, A.; Khan, S.; Ekici, M.; Moraru, L.; Belic, M.R. Cubic–quartic optical soliton perturbation with Fokas–Lenells equation by semi–inverse variation. *Semicond. Phys. Quantum Electron. Optoelectron.* **2021**, *24*, 431–435. [CrossRef]
9. Collins, T.; Kara, A.H.; Bhrawy, A.H.; Triki, H.; Biswas, A. Dynamics of shallow water waves with logarithmic nonlinearity. *Rom. Rep. Phys.* **2016**, *68*, 943–961.
10. Girgis, L.; Biswas, A. A study of solitary waves by He's variational principle. *Wave Random Complex.* **2011**, *21*, 96–104. [CrossRef]
11. He, J.H. Semi–inverse method and generalized variational principles with multi-variables in elasticity. *Appl. Math. Mech.* **2000**, *21*, 797–808.
12. He, J.H. Variational principle and periodic solution of the Kundu–Mukherjee–Naskar equation. *Results Phys.* **2020**, *17*, 103031. [CrossRef]
13. Kheir, H.; Jabbari, A.; Yildirim, A.; Alomari, A.K. He's semi–inverse method for soliton solutions of Boussinesq system. *World J. Model. Simul.* **2013**, *9*, 3–13.
14. Kohl, R.; Milovic, D.; Zerrad, E.; Biswas, A. Optical solitons by He's variational principle in a non–Kerr law media. *J. Infrared Millim. Terahertz Waves* **2009**, *30*, 526–537. [CrossRef]
15. Kohl, R.W.; Biswas, A.; Ekici, M.; Zhou, Q.; Khan, S.; Alshomrani, A.S.; Belic, M.R. Highly dispersive optical soliton perturbation with cubic–quintic–septic refractive index by semi–inverse variational principle. *Optik* **2019**, *199*, 163322. [CrossRef]
16. Kohl, R.W.; Biswas, A.; Ekici, M.; Zhou, Q.; Khan, S.; Alshomrani, A.S.; Belic, M.R. Sequel to highly dispersive optical soliton perturbation with cubic–quintic–septic refractive index by semi–inverse variational principle. *Optik* **2020**, *203*, 163451. [CrossRef]

17. Li, X.W.; Li, Y.; He, J.H. On the semi–inverse method and variational principle. *Therm. Sci.* **2013**, *17*, 1565–1568. [CrossRef]
18. Liu, H.M. The variational principle for Yang–Mills equation by semi–inverse method. *Facta Univ. Ser. Mech. Autom. Control Robot.* **2004**, *4*, 169–171.
19. Liu, W.Y.; Yu, Y.J.; Chen, L.D. Variational principles for Ginzburg–Landau equation by He's semi–inverse method. *Chaos Solit. Fractals* **2007**, *33*, 1801–1803. [CrossRef]
20. Ozis, T.; Yildirim, A. Application of He's semi–inverse method to the nonlinear Schrodinger equation. *Comput. Math. Appl.* **2007**, *54*, 1039–1042. [CrossRef]
21. Sassaman, R.; Heidari, A.; Biswas, A. Topological and non–topological solitons of nonlinear Klein–Gordon equations by He's semi–inverse variational porinciple. *J. Franklin Inst.* **2010**, *347*, 1148–1157. [CrossRef]
22. Singh, S.S. Bright and dark 1–soliton solutions to perturbed Schrodinger–Hirota equation with power law nonlinearity via semi–inverse variation method and ansatz method. *Int. J. Phys. Res.* **2017**, *5*, 39–42. [CrossRef]
23. Tao, Z.L. Solving the breaking soliton equation by He's variational method. *Comput. Math. Appl.* **2009**, *58*, 2395–2397. [CrossRef]
24. Yan, W.; Liu, Q.; Zhu, C.M.; Zhao, Y.; Shi, Y. Semi–inverse method to the Klein–Gordon equation with quadratic nonlinearity. *Appl. Comput. Electromagn. Soc. J.* **2018**, *33*, 842–846.
25. Zayed, E.M.E.; Gepreel, K.A.; El–Horbaty, M.; Biswas, A.; Yildirim, Y.; Alshehri, H.M. Highly dispersive optical solitons with complex Ginzburg–Landau equation having six nonlinear forms. *Mathematics* **2021**, *9*, 3270. [CrossRef]
26. Zhang, J.; Yu, J.Y.; Pan, N. Variational principles for nonlinear fiber optics. *Chaos Solit. Fractals* **2005**, *24*, 309–311. [CrossRef]
27. Abdel–Gawad, H.I. Chirped, breathers, diamond and W-shaped optical waves propagation in nonself–phase modulation medium. Biswas–Arshed equation. *Int. J. Mod. Phys. B* **2017**, *35*, 2150097. [CrossRef]
28. Abdel–Gawad, H.I. A generalized Kundu–Eckhaus equation with an extra–dispersion: Pulses configuration. *Opt. Quantum Electron.* **2021**, *53*, 705. [CrossRef]
29. Abdel–Gawad, H.I. Study of modulation instability and geometric structures of multisolitons in a medium with high dispersivity and nonlinearity. *Pramana* **2021**, *95*, 146. [CrossRef]
30. Tantawy, M.; Abdel–Gawad, H.I. On multi–geometric structures optical waves propagation in self–phase modulation medium: Sasa–Satsuma equation. *Eur. Phys. J. Plus* **2020**, *135*, 928. [CrossRef]

Article

Highly Dispersive Optical Solitons in Birefringent Fibers with Polynomial Law of Nonlinear Refractive Index by Laplace–Adomian Decomposition

Oswaldo González-Gaxiola [1], Anjan Biswas [2,3,4,5], Yakup Yıldırım [6] and Luminita Moraru [7,8,*]

1. Applied Mathematics and Systems Department, Universidad Autónoma Metropolitana-Cuajimalpa, Vasco de Quiroga 4871, Mexico City 05348, Mexico; ogonzalez@correo.cua.uam.mx
2. Department of Applied Mathematics, National Research Nuclear University, 31 Kashirskoe Hwy, 115409 Moscow, Russia; biswas.anjan@gmail.com
3. Mathematical Modeling and Applied Computation (MMAC) Research Group, Department of Mathematics, King Abdulaziz University, Jeddah 21589, Saudi Arabia
4. Department of Applied Sciences, Cross–Border Faculty, Dunarea de Jos University of Galati, 111 Domneasca Street, 800201 Galati, Romania
5. Department of Mathematics and Applied Mathematics, Sefako Makgatho Health Sciences University, Medunsa 0204, South Africa
6. Department of Mathematics, Faculty of Arts and Sciences, Near East University, Nicosia 99138, Cyprus; yakup.yildirim@neu.edu.tr
7. Department of Chemistry, Physics and Environment, Faculty of Sciences and Environment, Dunarea de Jos University of Galati, 47 Domneasca Street, 800008 Galati, Romania
8. The Modelling & Simulation Laboratory, Dunarea de Jos University of Galati, 47 Domneasca Street, 800008 Galati, Romania
* Correspondence: luminita.moraru@ugal.ro

Abstract: This paper is a numerical simulation of highly dispersive optical solitons in birefringent fibers with polynomial nonlinear form, which is achieved for the first time. The algorithmic approach is applied with the usage of the Laplace–Adomian decomposition scheme. Dark and bright soliton simulations are presented. The error measure has a very low count, and thus, the simulations are almost an exact replica of such solitons that analytically arise from the governing system. The suggested iterative scheme finds the solution without any discretization, linearization, or restrictive assumptions.

Keywords: solitons; polynomial law; Laplace–Adomian decomposition; birefringence

MSC: 78A60

1. Introduction

The term highly dispersive (HD) optical soliton was conceived a couple of years ago. Later, it was studied by several authors including N. Kudryashov [1–5]. The two essential factors that make the propel of solitons through fibers and other waveguides possible are the self-phase modulation (SPM) and chromatic dispersion (CD). When CD runs low during soliton transmission, the balance between nonlinearity and dispersion is compromised. This would lead to a catastrophic situation. To avoid such a scenario, CD is compensated with other sources of dispersion, and they are sixth-order dispersion (6OD), fifth-order dispersion (5OD), fourth-order dispersion (4OD), third-order dispersion (3OD) and inter-modal dispersion (IMD). The inclusion of six dispersive effects secures HD solitons. This however has other detrimental effects although they are being ignored in the current paper. They are the presence of soliton radiation and the slowdown of solitons due to this shedding of energy. Pulse splitting or polarization-mode dispersion is another feature in the dynamics of optical soliton propagation that cannot be avoided.

This leads to the effect of differential group delay, which cumulatively would lead to birefringence. The split-pulse dynamics in birefringent fibers is the focus of attention in the current paper. The dynamics of such soliton pulses are studied when the nonlinear form is of the polynomial type. The numerical simulations are recovered by the aid of the Laplace–Adomian decomposition method (LADM) that is a manifestation of the pre-existing Adomian decomposition approach. Dark and bright solitons are addressed in this work. The low error measure leads to an almost exact replica of solitons that have been analytically recovered in the past. The results are displayed after a recapitulation of the known analytical results.

Our work is divided in several sections. In the "Governing Equation" section, we provide a brief introduction to the model given by the highly dispersive nonlinear Schrödinger equation with cubic–quintic–septic law. We also illustrate the model by taking into account the birefringence effect. In the "Description and Application of the LADM" section, we describe the Laplace–Adomian decomposition method to be applied to approximate the solution of the highly dispersive nonlinear Schrödinger equation with polynomial law. In the "Graphical Representations" section, the results of the numerical experiment are shown in tables and graphs. Finally, in the "Conclusions" section, we summarize our findings and present our final conclusions.

2. Governing Equation

The highly dispersive nonlinear Schrödinger with polynomial nonlinear form is presented below [6–16]:

$$iq_t + ia_1 q_x + a_2 q_{xx} + ia_3 q_{xxx} + a_4 q_{xxxx} + ia_5 q_{xxxxx} \\ + a_6 q_{xxxxxx} + \left(b_1|q|_2 + b_2|q|^4 + b_3|q|^6\right)q = 0. \tag{1}$$

Here, a_k ($1 \leq k \leq 6$) and b_l ($1 \leq l \leq 3$) are real-valued constants, while $q = q(x,t)$ is a complex-valued function. a_6 gives 6OD, a_5 is associated with 5OD, a_4 arises from 4OD, a_3 stems from 3OD, a_2 is related to CD, and a_1 emerges from IMD. x is the spatial variable; q stands for the soliton profile; t is the temporal variable; the first term signifies the temporal evolution, where $i = \sqrt{-1}$; and b_1, b_2, and b_3 secure the polynomial nonlinear form. Additionally, the subscript t and x denote distinct order temporal and spatial derivatives.

The main governing system derived from the model (1) is considered as [6]

$$iu_t + ia_1^1 u_x + a_2^1 u_{xx} + ia_3^1 u_{xxx} + a_4^1 u_{xxxx} + ia_5^1 u_{xxxxx} + a_6^1 u_{xxxxxx} \\ + \left(b_{11}^1 |u|_2 + b_{12}^1 |v|^2\right)u + \left(b_{11}^2 |u|_4 + b_{12}^2 |u|^2|v|_2 + b_{13}^2 |v|^4\right)u \\ + \left(b_{11}^3 |u|^6 + b_{12}^3 |u|^4|v|^2 + b_{13}^3 |u|^2|v|^4 + b_{14}^3 |v|^6\right)u = 0, \tag{2}$$

$$iv_t + ia_1^2 v_x + a_2^2 v_{xx} + ia_3^2 v_{xxx} + a_4^2 v_{xxxx} + ia_5^2 v_{xxxxx} + a_6^2 v_{xxxxxx} \\ + \left(b_{21}^1 |v|_2 + b_{22}^1 |u|^2\right)v + \left(b_{21}^2 |v|^4 + b_{22}^2 |u|^2|v|^2 + b_{23}^2 |u|^4\right)v \\ + \left(b_{21}^3 |v|^6 + b_{22}^3 |v|^4|u|^2 + b_{23}^3 |v|^2|u|^4 + b_{24}^3 |u|^6\right)v = 0. \tag{3}$$

Here, b_{j1}^1, b_{j1}^2, b_{j1}^3, b_{j2}^1, b_{j2}^2, b_{j3}^2, b_{j2}^3, b_{j3}^3, b_{j4}^3 ($j = 1, 2$), and a_k^j ($1 \leq k \leq 6$) are real-valued constants, while $v = v(x,t)$ and $u = u(x,t)$ are complex-valued functions. b_{j1}^1, b_{j1}^2, and b_{j1}^3 give the self-phase modulation; u and v stand for the soliton profiles; b_{j2}^1, b_{j2}^2, b_{j3}^2, b_{j2}^3, b_{j3}^3, and b_{j4}^3 secure the cross-phase modulation, and the first terms imply linear evolutions. a_6^j gives 6OD, a_5^j is associated with 5OD, a_4^j arises from 4OD, a_3^j stems from 3OD, a_2^j is related to CD, and a_1^j emerges from IMD.

It must be noted that in order to derive (2) and (3) from (1), for birefringent fibers, it is necessary to split $q(x,t) = u(x,t) + v(x,t)$, to substitute it into (1), and then to write the two components of the equation after neglecting the effects of four wave mixing.

Bright and Dark Solitons

The dark solitons with the present governing system of (2) and (3) are formulated as following [6]:

$$\begin{cases} u(x,t) = (A_1 \tanh(x - v_1 t))e^{i[-\kappa_1 x + \omega_1 t + \theta_1]}, \\ v(x,t) = (A_2 \tanh(x - v_2 t))e^{i[-\kappa_2 x + \omega_2 t + \theta_2]}, \end{cases} \qquad (4)$$

where the parameters are listed as [6]

$$A_1 = \pm \sqrt{ -\frac{\left(\begin{array}{c} 30\kappa_1^4 a_6^1 - 20\kappa_1^3 a_5^1 + 600\kappa_1^2 a_6^1 - 12\kappa_1^2 a_4^1 \\ -200\kappa_1 a_5^1 + 6\kappa_1 a_3^1 + 2a_2^1 + 1232 a_6^1 - 40 a_4^1 \end{array} \right)}{b_{11}^1 + b_{12}^1} }, \qquad (5)$$

$$v_1 = 5a_5^1 \kappa_1^4 - 6a_6^1 \kappa_1^5 - 2a_2^1 \kappa_1 - 3a_3^1 \kappa_1^2 + 4a_4^1 \kappa_1^3 + a_1^1, \qquad (6)$$

$$A_2 = \pm \sqrt{ -\frac{\left(\begin{array}{c} 30\kappa_2^4 a_6^2 - 20\kappa_2^3 a_5^2 + 600\kappa_2^2 a_6^2 - 12\kappa_2^2 a_4^2 \\ -200\kappa_2 a_5^2 + 6\kappa_2 a_3^2 + 2a_2^2 + 1232 a_6^2 - 40 a_4^2 \end{array} \right)}{b_{22}^1 + b_{21}^1} }, \qquad (7)$$

$$v_2 = 5a_5^2 \kappa_2^4 - 6a_6^2 \kappa_2^5 - 2a_2^2 \kappa_2 - 3a_3^2 \kappa_2^2 + 4a_4^2 \kappa_2^3 + a_1^2, \qquad (8)$$

with the following natural constraint:

$$\left(b_{j2}^1 + b_{j1}^1 \right) \left(\begin{array}{c} 30\kappa_2^4 a_6^2 - 20\kappa_2^3 a_5^2 + 600\kappa_2^2 a_6^2 - 12\kappa_2^2 a_4^2 \\ -200\kappa_2 a_2^2 + 6\kappa_2 a_3^2 + 2a_2^2 + 1232 a_6^2 - 40 a_4^2 \end{array} \right) < 0. \qquad (9)$$

In the above, A_1 and A_2 are free parameters of the dark soliton, while the velocities of the two components of the dark solitons are v_1 and v_2.

The bright solitons with the strategic governing system (2) and (3) are introduced below [6]:

$$\begin{cases} u(x,t) = (B_1 \text{sech}(x - v_1 t))e^{i[-\kappa_1 x + \omega_1 t + \theta_1]}, \\ v(x,t) = (B_2 \text{sech}(x - v_2 t))e^{i[-\kappa_2 x + \omega_2 t + \theta_2]}, \end{cases} \qquad (10)$$

where the parameters are enumerated as

$$B_1 = \pm \sqrt{ \frac{\left(\begin{array}{c} 30\kappa_1^4 a_6^1 - 20\kappa_1^3 a_5^1 + 600\kappa_1^2 a_6^1 - 12\kappa_1^2 a_4^1 \\ -200\kappa_1 a_5^1 + 6\kappa_1 a_3^1 + 2a_2^1 + 1232 a_6^1 - 40 a_4^1 \end{array} \right)}{b_{11}^1 + b_{12}^1} }, \qquad (11)$$

$$v_1 = 5a_5^1 \kappa_1^4 - 6a_6^1 \kappa_1^5 - 2a_2^1 \kappa_1 - 3a_3^1 \kappa_1^2 + 4a_4^1 \kappa_1^3 + a_1^1, \qquad (12)$$

$$B_2 = \pm \sqrt{ \frac{\left(\begin{array}{c} 30\kappa_2^4 a_6^2 - 20\kappa_2^3 a_5^2 + 600\kappa_2^2 a_6^2 - 12\kappa_2^2 a_4^2 \\ -200\kappa_2 a_2^2 + 6\kappa_2 a_3^2 + 2a_2^2 + 1232 a_6^2 - 40 a_4^2 \end{array} \right)}{b_{22}^1 + b_{21}^1} }, \qquad (13)$$

$$v_2 = 5a_5^2 \kappa_2^4 - 6a_6^2 \kappa_2^5 - 2a_2^2 \kappa_2 - 3a_3^2 \kappa_2^2 + 4a_4^2 \kappa_2^3 + a_1^2, \qquad (14)$$

with the following natural constraint:

$$\left(b_{j2}^1 + b_{j1}^1 \right) \left(\begin{array}{c} 30\kappa_2^4 a_6^2 - 20\kappa_2^3 a_5^2 + 600\kappa_2^2 a_6^2 - 12\kappa_2^2 a_4^2 \\ -200\kappa_2 a_2^2 + 6\kappa_2 a_3^2 + 2a_2^2 + 1232 a_6^2 - 40 a_4^2 \end{array} \right) > 0. \qquad (15)$$

In this context, the parameters B_1 and B_2 are the amplitudes of the two components of bright solitons that travel with velocities v_1 and v_2, respectively.

3. Description and Application of the LADM

The integration scheme is derived from the decomposition algorithm that has been reported in [17] by the aid of Laplace transform [18]. The solution of a governing model is structured as the local truncation of a convergent series of functions [19].

To address this scheme, the governing system (2) and (3) is presented below:

$$u_t = -a_1^1 u_x + ia_2^1 u_{xx} - a_3^1 u_{xxx} + ia_4^1 u_{xxxx} \\ -a_5^1 u_{xxxxx} + ia_6^1 u_{xxxxxx} + iN_1(u,v), \tag{16}$$

$$v_t = -a_1^2 v_x + ia_2^2 v_{xx} - a_3^2 v_{xxx} + ia_4^2 v_{xxxx} \\ -a_5^2 v_{xxxxx} + ia_6^2 v_{xxxxxx} + iN_2(u,v). \tag{17}$$

Equations (16) and (17) are also formulated as

$$D_t u = iN_1(u,v) + \sum_{k=1}^{3}\left(ia_{2k}^1 D_x^{2k} - a_{2k-1}^1 D_x^{2k-1}\right)u, \tag{18}$$

$$D_t u = iN_2(u,v) + \sum_{k=1}^{3}\left(ia_{2k}^2 D_x^{2k} - a_{2k-1}^2 D_x^{2k-1}\right)v \tag{19}$$

by virtue of initial conditions $v(x,0) = g(x)$ and $u(x,0) = f(x)$. Here, N_j are differential operators containing all nonlinear terms, D_x^k stands for a partial derivative of order k in terms of the independent variable x, and D_t stands for first-order derivative in terms of the independent variable t. Thus, the operators N_j are presented below:

$$N_2(u,v) = (b_{21}^2 |v|_4 + b_{22}^2 |u|^2 |v|_2 + b_{23}^2 |u|^4)v + (b_{21}^1 |v|_2 + b_{22}^1 |u|^2)v \\ + \left(b_{21}^3 |v|^6 + b_{22}^3 |v|^4 |u|^2 + b_{23}^3 |v|^2 |u|^4 + b_{24}^3 |u|^6\right)v, \tag{20}$$

$$N_1(u,v) = (b_{11}^2 |u|_4 + b_{12}^2 |u|^2 |v|_2 + b_{13}^2 |v|^4)u + (b_{11}^1 |u|_2 + b_{12}^1 |v|^2)u \\ + \left(b_{11}^3 |u|^6 + b_{12}^3 |u|^4 |v|^2 + b_{13}^3 |u|^2 |v|^4 + b_{14}^3 |v|^6\right)u. \tag{21}$$

Using the Laplace transform in the system with (18) and (19) along with the initial conditions, one secures

$$v(x,s) = \frac{1}{s}\mathcal{L}\left\{\sum_{k=1}^{3}\left(ia_{2k}^2 D_x^{2k} - a_{2k-1}^2 D_x^{2k-1}\right)v + iN_2(u,v)\right\} + \frac{g(x)}{s}, \tag{22}$$

$$u(x,s) = \frac{1}{s}\mathcal{L}\left\{\sum_{k=1}^{3}\left(ia_{2k}^1 D_x^{2k} - a_{2k-1}^1 D_x^{2k-1}\right)u + iN_1(u,v)\right\} + \frac{f(x)}{s}. \tag{23}$$

By the aid of the conventional inverse Laplace transform $\mathcal{L}^{-1}$, we arrive at the following:

$$v(x,t) = \mathcal{L}^{-1}\left[\frac{1}{s}\mathcal{L}\left\{\sum_{k=1}^{3}\left(ia_{2k}^2 D_x^{2k} - a_{2k-1}^2 D_x^{2k-1}\right)v + iN_2(u,v)\right\}\right] + v(x,0), \tag{24}$$

$$u(x,t) = \mathcal{L}^{-1}\left[\frac{1}{s}\mathcal{L}\left\{\sum_{k=1}^{3}\left(ia_{2k}^1 D_x^{2k} - a_{2k-1}^1 D_x^{2k-1}\right)u + iN_1(u,v)\right\}\right] + u(x,0). \tag{25}$$

Now, the solution functions v and u in the Adomian decomposition algorithm are extracted as

$$v(x,t) = \sum_{n=0}^{\infty} v_n(x,t), \quad u(x,t) = \sum_{n=0}^{\infty} u_n(x,t). \tag{26}$$

Additionally, the nonlinear terms in Equations (20) and (21) are decomposed in Adomian polynomials [17–19] as

$$N_2(u,v) = (b_{21}^2|v|_4 + b_{22}^2|u|^2|v|_2 + b_{23}^2|u|^4)v + (b_{21}^1|v|_2 + b_{22}^1|u|^2)v$$
$$+ (b_{21}^3|v|^6 + b_{22}^3|v|^4|u|_2 + b_{23}^3|v|^2|u|_4 + b_{24}^3|u|^6)v$$
$$= \sum_{n=0}^{\infty} B_n(u_0,\ldots,u_n;v_0,\ldots,v_n), \quad (27)$$

$$N_1(u,v) = (b_{11}^2|u|_4 + b_{12}^2|u|^2|v|_2 + b_{13}^2|v|^4)u + (b_{11}^1|u|_2 + b_{12}^1|v|^2)u$$
$$+ (b_{11}^3|u|^6 + b_{12}^3|u|^4|v|^2 + b_{13}^3|u|^2|v|^4 + b_{14}^3|v|^6)u$$
$$= \sum_{n=0}^{\infty} A_n(u_0,\ldots,u_n;v_0,\ldots,v_n), \quad (28)$$

where A_n and B_n are enumerated as follows [20]:

$$\begin{cases} B_0 = (b_{21}^1|v_0|_2 + b_{22}^1|u_0|^2)v_0 + (b_{21}^2|v_0|^4 + b_{22}^2|u_0|^2|v_0|^2 + b_{23}^2|u_0|^4)v_0 \\ \quad + (b_{21}^3|v_0|^6 + b_{22}^3|v_0|^4|u_0|^2 + b_{23}^3|v_0|^2|u_0|^4 + b_{24}^3|u_0|^6)v_0, \\ B_n = \frac{1}{n}\sum_{k=0}^{n-1}(k+1)\left(u_{k+1}\frac{\partial}{\partial u_k}B_{n-1} + v_{k+1}\frac{\partial}{\partial v_k}B_{n-1}\right), \quad n \geq 1, \end{cases} \quad (29)$$

$$\begin{cases} A_0 = (b_{11}^1|u_0|_2 + b_{12}^1|v_0|^2)u_0 + (b_{11}^2|u_0|^4 + b_{12}^2|u_0|^2|v_0|^2 + b_{13}^2|v_0|^4)u_0 \\ \quad + (b_{11}^3|u_0|^6 + b_{12}^3|u_0|^4|v_0|^2 + b_{13}^3|u_0|^2|v_0|^4 + b_{14}^3|v_0|^6)u_0, \\ A_n = \frac{1}{n}\sum_{k=0}^{n-1}(k+1)\left(u_{k+1}\frac{\partial}{\partial u_k}A_{n-1} + v_{k+1}\frac{\partial}{\partial v_k}A_{n-1}\right), \quad n \geq 1. \end{cases} \quad (30)$$

Plugging (26)–(28) into (24) and (25) yields the solution functions:

$$\sum_{n=0}^{\infty} v_n = \mathcal{L}^{-1}\left[\frac{1}{s}\mathcal{L}\left\{\sum_{k=1}^{3}\left(ia_{2k}^2 D_x^{2k} - a_{2k-1}^2 D_x^{2k-1}\right)\sum_{n=0}^{\infty} v_n + i\sum_{n=0}^{\infty} B_n\right\}\right] + v(x,0), \quad (31)$$

$$\sum_{n=0}^{\infty} u_n = \mathcal{L}^{-1}\left[\frac{1}{s}\mathcal{L}\left\{\sum_{k=1}^{3}\left(ia_{2k}^1 D_x^{2k} - a_{2k-1}^1 D_x^{2k-1}\right)\sum_{n=0}^{\infty} u_n + i\sum_{n=0}^{\infty} A_n\right\}\right] + u(x,0). \quad (32)$$

Therefore, the v_n and u_n components for the system with (16) and (17) are yielded by the following algorithm:

$$\begin{cases} u_{n+1}(x,t) = \mathcal{L}^{-1}\left[\frac{1}{s}\mathcal{L}\left\{\sum_{k=1}^{3}\left(ia_{2k}^1 D_x^{2k} - a_{2k-1}^1 D_x^{2k-1}\right)u_n + iA_n\right\}\right], \quad n \geq 0, \\ u_0(x,t) = u(x,0) = f(x), \end{cases} \quad (33)$$

$$\begin{cases} v_{n+1}(x,t) = \mathcal{L}^{-1}\left[\frac{1}{s}\mathcal{L}\left\{\sum_{k=1}^{3}\left(ia_{2k}^2 D_x^{2k} - a_{2k-1}^2 D_x^{2k-1}\right)v_n + iB_n\right\}\right], \quad n \geq 0, \\ v_0(x,t) = v(x,0) = g(x). \end{cases} \quad (34)$$

Finally, adding the components $u_n(x,t)$ and $v_n(x,t)$ along with the solution functions in (26), an approximation for the system with (16) and (17) is obtained.

Convergence of the Proposed Method

The following theorem provides a necessary condition for the convergence of the proposed technique. The results are standard and can be seen in [21].

Theorem 1. *Let N be an operator from a Hilbert Space H into H, and let u be an exact solution of Equation (1). $\sum_{j=0}^{\infty} u_j$ converges to the exact solution u, if there exists β, $0 \leq \beta < 1$, such that $||u_{k+1}|| \leq \beta ||u_k||$, for every $k \geq 0$.*

Proof of Theorem 1. We have

$$S_0 = 0,$$
$$S_1 = S_0 + u_1 = u_1,$$
$$S_2 = S_1 + u_2 = u_1 + u_2,$$
$$\vdots$$
$$S_n = S_{n-1} + u_n = u_1 + u_2 + \ldots + u_n,$$

and we show that $\{S_n\}$ is a Cauchy sequence in a Hilbert Space H. Now, for

$$||S_{n+1} - S_n|| = ||u_{n+1}|| \leq \beta ||u_n|| \leq \beta^2 ||u_{n-1}|| \leq \ldots \leq \beta^{n+1} ||u_0||,$$

for every $n, m \in \mathbb{N}, n \geq m$, we have

$$\begin{aligned}
||S_n - S_m|| &= ||(S_n - S_{n-1}) + (S_{n-1} - S_{n-2}) + \cdots + (S_{m+1} - S_m)|| \\
&\leq ||S_n - S_{n-1}|| + ||S_{n-1} - S_{n-2}|| + \cdots + ||S_{m+1} - S_m|| \\
&\leq \beta^n ||u_0|| + \beta^{n-1} ||u_0|| + \cdots + \beta^{m+1} ||u_0|| \\
&\leq (\beta^{m+1} + \beta^{m+2} + \cdots) ||u_0|| = \frac{\beta^{m+1}}{1-\beta} ||u_0||
\end{aligned}$$

From the previous inequality, we have

$$||S_n - S_m|| \to 0, \text{ as } n \to \infty, m \to \infty.$$

Hence, $\{S_n\}$ is the Cauchy sequence in the Hilbert space H; therefore, it has a limit $u \in H$, which is the exact solution of Equation (1), namely

$$u = \lim_{n \to \infty} S_n.$$

Now, we have the following theorem, of which the proof is a direct consequence of Theorem 1. □

Theorem 2. *Assume that u is the exact solution of Equation (1). Let $\{S_N\}$ be the sequence of the approximate series solutions defined by Equation (26). Then, it holds for every $t \geq 0$.*

$$\max_{a \leq x, y \leq b} |u(x, y, t) - \sum_{j=0}^{N} u_j(x, y, t)| \leq \frac{\beta^{m+1}}{1-\beta} ||u_0||.$$

From this analysis, it is evident that the Adomian decomposition method combined with the Laplace transform requires less effort in comparison with the traditional Adomian decomposition method. This method considerably decreases the number of calculations. In addition, the Adomian decomposition procedure is easily established without requiring the problem to be linearized.

4. Graphical Representations

In this section, we solve some numerical examples, and we also present the results obtained graphically as well as the absolute error committed by the LADM approximation. Additional references to the recent application of LADM to a similar mathematical model can be seen in [22–24].

4.1. Dark Soliton Simulation

To display the dark soliton numerical simulation for the governing system (2) and (3), we consider the following coefficients:

Case A: Let us consider the following:

$$\begin{cases} a_1^1 = 1.34, \ a_2^1 = 1.5, \ a_3^1 = -3.2, \ a_4^1 = -2.1, \ a_5^1 = 5.2, \ a_6^1 = 0.21, \\ b_1^1 = 6.2, \ b_{11}^2 = 3.3, \ b_{12}^2 = 0.11, a_1^2 = 0.67, \ a_2^2 = 3.1, \ a_3^2 = -0.3, \\ a_4^2 = 1.1, \ a_5^2 = -5.9, \ a_6^2 = 0.33, \ b_2^1 = 4.6, \ b_{21}^2 = 2.2, \ b_{22}^2 = 3.7. \end{cases} \quad (35)$$

Together with the initial conditions, we obtain the following:

$$f(x) = 3.04\tanh(x)e^{i[-0.22x+0.76]},$$

$$g(x) = 2.91\tanh(x)e^{i[1.13x-2.34]}.$$

The 2D and 3D illustrations for $|v|^2$ and $|u|^2$ for this case are shown in Figure 1. In Table 1, we show the absolute error committed in the numerical simulation of the present case for different values of the (x,t) pair and for $N = 15$.

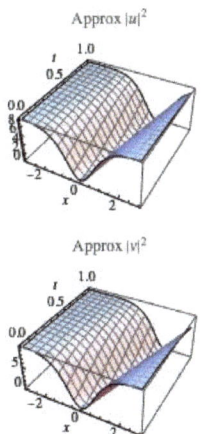
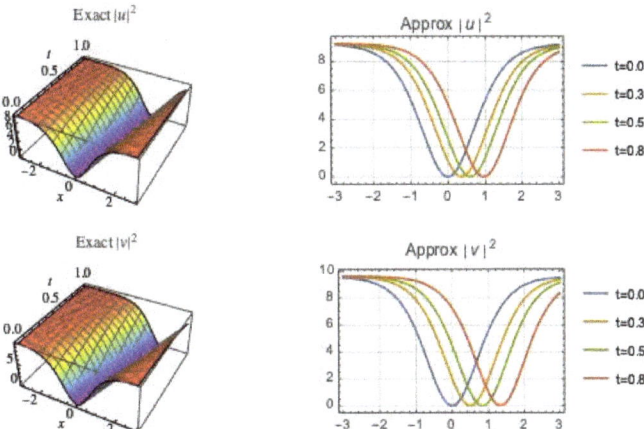

Figure 1. (**Above**) Three-dimensional illustrations of the numerical simulation and exact solution, and two-dimensional illustration of the approximation of $|u|^2$; (**Below**) three-dimensional illustrations of the numerical simulation and exact solution, and two-dimensional illustration of the approximation of $|v|^2$ for Case A.

Table 1. Case A: Absolute error for different values of (x,t) considering $N = 15$ steps.

(t,x)	−2.0	−1.0	0	1.0	2.0
0.1	4.7×10^{-8}	3.5×10^{-0}	2.3×10^{-9}	3.9×10^{-8}	5.2×10^{-8}
0.3	5.0×10^{-7}	4.6×10^{-7}	3.7×10^{-8}	4.9×10^{-7}	6.1×10^{-7}
0.5	5.2×10^{-7}	5.6×10^{-7}	4.9×10^{-7}	5.8×10^{-7}	7.0×10^{-6}
0.8	6.1×10^{-5}	4.8×10^{-5}	5.5×10^{-7}	4.3×10^{-5}	6.9×10^{-5}

Case B: Let us consider the following:

$$\begin{cases} a_1^1 = 0.33, \ a_2^1 = 0.89, \ a_3^1 = -1.4, \ a_4^1 = 0.9, \ a_5^1 = 1.1, \ a_6^1 = 0.59, \\ b_1^1 = 2.2, \ b_{11}^2 = 1.23, \ b_{12}^2 = 0.5, a_1^2 = 8.1, \ a_2^2 = 0.36, \ a_3^2 = 1.1, \\ a_4^2 = -0.27, \ a_5^2 = 3.22, \ a_6^2 = 1.06, \ b_2^1 = 2.8, \ b_{21}^2 = 0.66, \ b_{22}^2 = 2.3. \end{cases} \quad (36)$$

By the aid of the initial conditions, we obtain the following:

$$g(x) = 4.09\tanh(x)e^{i[2.09x+0.95]},$$

$$f(x) = 6.11\tanh(x)e^{i[5.5x+1.23]}.$$

The 2D and 3D illustrations for $|v|^2$ and $|u|^2$ for this case are shown in Figure 2. In Table 2, we show the absolute error committed in the numerical simulation of the present case for different values of the (x,t) pair and for $N = 15$.

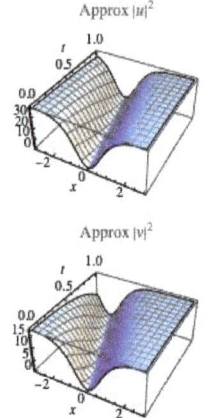
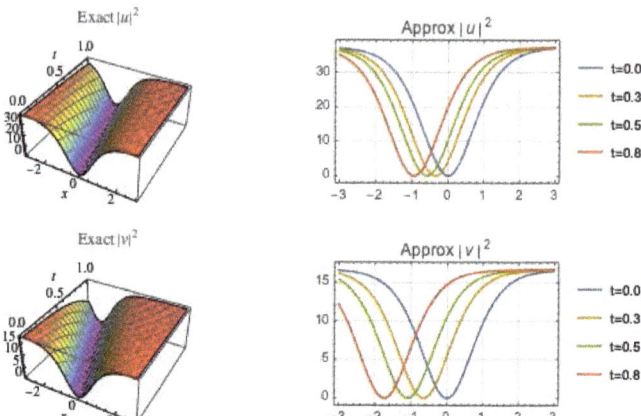

Figure 2. (**Above**) Three-dimensional illustrations of the numerical simulation and exact solution, and two-dimensional illustration of the approximation of $|u|^2$; (**Below**) three-dimensional illustrations of the numerical simulation and exact solution, and two-dimensional illustration of the approximation of $|v|^2$ for Case B.

Table 2. Case B: Absolute error for different values of (x,t) considering $N = 15$ steps.

(t,x)	−2.0	−1.0	0	1.0	2.0
0.1	3.2×10^{-8}	3.0×10^{-8}	2.1×10^{-9}	3.3×10^{-8}	3.8×10^{-8}
0.3	6.1×10^{-7}	5.1×10^{-7}	3.4×10^{-8}	5.6×10^{-7}	6.7×10^{-7}
0.5	6.8×10^{-7}	6.0×10^{-7}	2.9×10^{-7}	6.2×10^{-7}	6.9×10^{-6}
0.8	7.2×10^{-5}	6.4×10^{-5}	3.5×10^{-7}	6.6×10^{-5}	8.0×10^{-5}

4.2. Bright Soliton Simulation

To depict the bright soliton numerical simulation for the governing system (2) and (3), we consider the following coefficients:

Case C: Let us consider the following:

$$\begin{cases} a_1^1 = 0.01,\ a_2^1 = 1.23,\ a_3^1 = 0.53,\ a_4^1 = 0.11,\ a_5^1 = 0.97,\ a_6^1 = 1.6, \\ b_1^1 = 3.6,\ b_{11}^2 = 1.11,\ b_{12}^2 = 2.6,\ a_1^2 = 3.01,\ a_2^2 = 0.12,\ a_3^2 = 3.6, \\ a_4^2 = -4.7,\ a_5^2 = -2.01,\ a_6^2 = 0.2,\ b_2^1 = 0.3,\ b_{21}^2 = 6.1,\ b_{22}^2 = 2.11. \end{cases} \quad (37)$$

With the help of the initial conditions, we obtain the following:

$$g(x) = 2.74\operatorname{sech}(x)e^{i[8.34x-0.35]},$$

$$f(x) = 2.23\operatorname{sech}(x)e^{i[-3.09x-1.01]}.$$

The 2D and 3D illustrations for $|v|^2$ and $|u|^2$ for this case are shown in Figure 3. In Table 3, we show the absolute error committed in the numerical simulation of the present case for different values of the (x,t) pair and for $N = 15$.

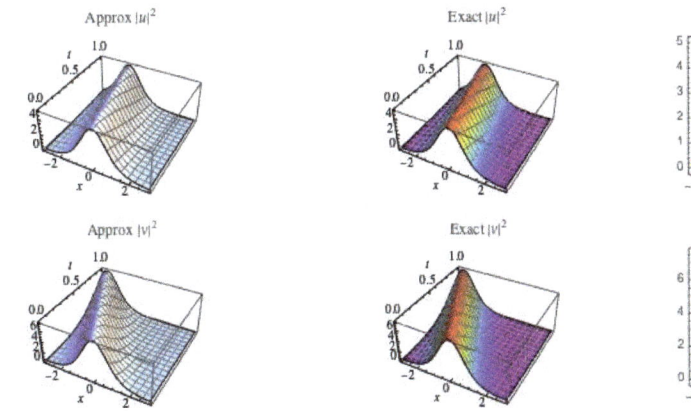

Figure 3. (**Above**) Three-dimensional illustrations of the numerical simulation and exact solution, and two-dimensional illustration of the approximation of $|u|^2$; (**Below**) three-dimensional illustrations of the numerical simulation and exact solution, and two-dimensional illustration of the approximation of $|v|^2$ for Case C.

Table 3. Case C: Absolute error for different values of (x,t) considering $N = 15$ steps.

(t,x)	−2.0	−1.0	0	1.0	2.0
0.1	4.5×10^{-8}	3.7×10^{-8}	1.8×10^{-9}	3.2×10^{-8}	4.9×10^{-8}
0.3	4.4×10^{-7}	4.7×10^{-7}	2.3×10^{-9}	4.6×10^{-7}	4.0×10^{-7}
0.5	8.8×10^{-7}	5.7×10^{-7}	3.3×10^{-8}	5.2×10^{-7}	8.3×10^{-6}
0.8	7.2×10^{-5}	3.4×10^{-5}	7.5×10^{-8}	2.9×10^{-5}	7.0×10^{-5}

Case D: Let us consider the following:

$$\begin{cases} a_1^1 = 9.0,\ a_2^1 = 4.2,\ a_3^1 = 0.33,\ a_4^1 = 0.31,\ a_5^1 = 0.08,\ a_6^1 = 0.03, \\ b_1^1 = 5.08,\ b_{11}^2 = 4.1,\ b_{12}^2 = -9.2,\ a_1^2 = 1.16,\ a_2^2 = 0.4,\ a_3^2 = -9.0, \\ a_4^2 = -2.03,\ a_5^2 = 0.1,\ a_6^2 = 0.21,\ b_2^1 = 2.1,\ b_{21}^2 = 0.7,\ b_{22}^2 = 0.33. \end{cases} \quad (38)$$

By virtue of the initial conditions, we obtain the following:

$$f(x) = 6.02\text{sech}(x)e^{i[-0.57x-36.01]},$$

$$g(x) = 5.74\text{sech}(x)e^{i[11.6x+3.08]}.$$

The 2D and 3D illustrations for $|v|^2$ and $|u|^2$ for this case are shown in Figure 4. In Table 4, we show the absolute error committed in the numerical simulation of the present case for different values of the (x,t) pair and for $N = 15$.

Table 4. Case D: Absolute error for different values of (x,t) considering $N = 15$ steps.

(t,x)	−2.0	−1.0	0	1.0	2.0
0.1	7.2×10^{-8}	4.4×10^{-8}	5.2×10^{-9}	4.2×10^{-8}	6.9×10^{-8}
0.3	6.3×10^{-7}	4.7×10^{-7}	6.3×10^{-9}	4.6×10^{-7}	5.3×10^{-7}
0.5	7.8×10^{-7}	5.9×10^{-7}	7.7×10^{-8}	5.5×10^{-7}	8.0×10^{-6}
0.8	8.3×10^{-5}	2.4×10^{-5}	9.0×10^{-7}	3.1×10^{-5}	9.1×10^{-5}

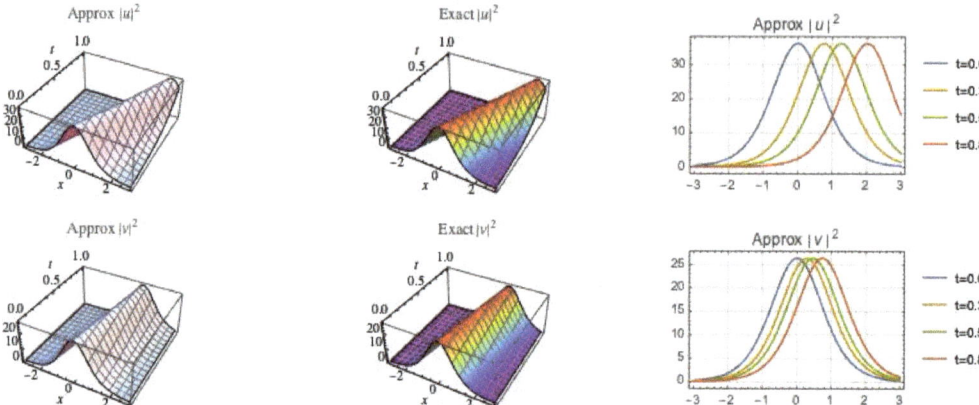

Figure 4. (**Above**) Three-dimensional illustrations of the numerical simulation and exact solution, and two-dimensional illustration of the approximation of $|u|^2$; (**Below**) three-dimensional illustrations of the numerical simulation and exact solution, and two-dimensional illustration of the approximation of $|v|^2$ for Case D.

From the physics perspective, the surface plots of HD bright and dark solitons are accurate representations of the actual pulses that travel down an optical fiber based on the studied model. The error measure is impressive and acceptable as computed. These pulses are computed in such a way that the radiation component is completely avoided so that the core soliton regime is under focus, both for bright and dark solitons. Another source to receive a visual effect to the model would be an oscilloscope, which is outside the scope of the current work since this paper focuses on a specific numerical scheme, namely the application of LADM to handle HD solitons with polynomial law of nonlinear refractive index change.

5. Conclusions

This paper is an exhibit of numerical simulations for dark and bright HD solitons with polynomial nonlinear form. The LADM scheme has made this display possible. Dark and bright soliton surface plots are included with an error measure that is impressively small. The results are thus a step towards the final goal that is to address the model in dispersion-flattened fibers. The immediate next thought, however, is the study of HD solitons with non-local nonlinearity.

The current results are going to be pretty helpful with its implementation in a photonics lab when the experimental research is conducted to take a look at the eye diagrams without the soliton radiation. The results of this paper would therefore provide a forefront view of the bright and dark HD solitons. Thus, apart from physicists and mathematicians, the results would reach the desk of electrical engineers, whose successful observations on an oscilloscope would be closer to reality. These observations would be just before rubber meets the road.

Other areas of expansion would be to address the model with the inclusion of the effect of soliton radiation. With HD solitons, soliton radiation is unavoidable and that would unavoidably be quite pronounced. Therefore, it is imperative to include its effect and to study the model with its presence. This would require the usage of *beyond all-order asymptotics and/or the theory of unfoldings* to quantify the radiation effect followed by its numerical implementation. Such studies will be taken up with time, and the results will be disseminated thereafter.

Author Contributions: Conceptualization, O.G.-G.; methodology, A.B.; software, Y.Y.; writing—original draft preparation, L.M.; writing—review and editing, Y.Y.; project administration, L.M. All authors have read and agreed to the published version of the manuscript.

Funding: This research received no external funding.

Institutional Review Board Statement: Not applicable.

Informed Consent Statement: Not applicable.

Data Availability Statement: Not applicable.

Acknowledgments: The authors thank the anonymous referees whose comments helped to improve this paper.

Conflicts of Interest: The authors declare no conflict of interest.

References

1. Kudryashov, N.A. Highly dispersive optical solitons of an equation with arbitrary refractive index. *Regul. Chaotic Dyn.* **2020**, *25*, 537–543. [CrossRef]
2. Kudryashov, N.A. Highly dispersive optical solitons of equation with various polynomial nonlinearity law. *Chaos Soliton Fract.* **2020**, *140*, 110202. [CrossRef]
3. Kudryashov, N.A. Highly dispersive optical solitons of the generalized nonlinear eighth-order Schrödinger equation. *Optik* **2020**, *206*, 164335. [CrossRef]
4. Kudryashov, N.A. Method for finding highly dispersive optical solitons of nonlinear differential equations. *Optik* **2020**, *206*, 163550. [CrossRef]
5. Kudryashov, N.A. Highly dispersive solitary wave solutions of perturbed nonlinear Schrödinger equations. *Appl. Math. Comput.* **2020**, *371*, 124972. [CrossRef]
6. Yildirim, Y.; Biswas, A.; Ekici, M.; Zayed, E.M.E.; Khan, S.; Moraru, L.; Alzahrani, A.K.; Belic, M.R. Highly dispersive optical solitons in birefringent fibers with four forms of nonlinear refractive index by three prolific integration schemes. *Optik* **2020**, *220*, 165039. [CrossRef]
7. Wazwaz, A.M. Bright and dark optical solitons for (3+1)-dimensional Schrödinger equation with cubic–quintic-septic nonlinearities. *Optik* **2021**, *225*, 165752. [CrossRef]
8. Wazwaz, A.M.; Khuri, S.A. Two (3+1)-dimensional Schrödinger equations with cubic–quintic–septic nonlinearities: Bright and dark optical solitons. *Optik* **2021**, *235*, 166646. [CrossRef]
9. Mirzazadeh, M.; Akinyemi, L.; Senol, M.; Hosseini, K. A variety of solitons to the sixth-order dispersive (3+1)-dimensional nonlinear time-fractional Schrödinger equation with cubic-quintic-septic nonlinearities. *Optik* **2021**, *241*, 166318. [CrossRef]
10. Kerbouche, M.; Hamaizi, Y.; El-Akrmi, A.; Triki, H. Solitary wave solutions of the cubic-quintic-septic nonlinear Schrödinger equation in fiber Bragg gratings. *Optik* **2016**, *127*, 9562–9570. [CrossRef]
11. Rabie, W.B.; Ahmed, H.M. Optical solitons for multiple-core couplers with polynomial law of nonlinearity using the modified extended direct algebraic method. *Optik* **2022**, *258*, 168848. [CrossRef]
12. Rabie, W.B.; Ahmed, H.M. Cubic-quartic optical solitons and other solutions for twin-core couplers with polynomial law of nonlinearity using the extended F-expansion method. *Optik* **2022**, *253*, 168575. [CrossRef]
13. Wang, M.-Y. Optical solitons with perturbed complex Ginzburg–Landau equation in kerr and cubic–quintic–septic nonlinearity. *Results Phys.* **2022**, *33*, 105077. [CrossRef]
14. Djoko, M.; Kofane, T.C. Dissipative optical bullets modeled by the cubic-quintic-septic complex Ginzburg–Landau equation with higher-order dispersions. *Commun. Nonlinear Sci. Numer. Simulat.* **2017**, *48*, 179–199. [CrossRef]
15. Kutukov, A.A.; Kudryashov, N.A. Traveling wave solutions of the coupled nonlinear Schrödinger equation with cubic-quintic-septic and weak non-local nonlinearity. *AIP Conf. Proc.* **2022**, *2425*, 340002.
16. Wang, F.; Liu, Y.C.; Zheng, H. A localized method of fundamental solution for numerical simulation of nonlinear heat conduction. *Mathematics* **2022**, *10*, 773. [CrossRef]
17. Adomian, G. *Nonlinear Stochastic Operator Equations*; Academic Press: New York, NY, USA, 1986.
18. Adomian, G.; Rach, R. On the solution of nonlinear differential equations with convolution product nonlinearities. *J. Math. Anal. Appl.* **1986**, *114*, 171–175. [CrossRef]
19. Adomian, G. *Solving Frontier Problems of Physics: The Decomposition Method*; Kluwer Academic Publishers: Boston, MA, USA, 1994.
20. Duan, J.S. Convenient analytic recurrence algorithms for the Adomian polynomials. *Appl. Math. Comput.* **2011**, *217*, 6337–6348. [CrossRef]
21. González-Gaxiola, O.; Biswas, A.; Alshomrani, A.S. Highly dispersive optical solitons having Kerr law of refractive index with Laplace-Adomian decomposition. *Rev. Mex. Fis.* **2020**, *66*, 291–296. [CrossRef]
22. González-Gaxiola, O.; Biswas, A.; Asma, M.; Alzahrani, A.K. Highly dispersive optical solitons with non-local law of refractive index by Laplace-Adomian decomposition. *Opt. Quantum Electron.* **2021**, *53*, 55. [CrossRef]

23. González-Gaxiola, O.; Biswas, A.; Alzahrani, A.K.; Belic, M.R. Highly dispersive optical solitons with a polynomial law of refractive index by Laplace-Adomian decomposition. *J. Comput. Electron.* **2021**, *20*, 1216–1223. [CrossRef]
24. Abbaoui, K.; Cherruault, Y. Convergence of Adomian's method applied to differential equations. *Comput. Math. Appl.* **1994**, *28*, 103–109. [CrossRef]

Article

Diverse Forms of Breathers and Rogue Wave Solutions for the Complex Cubic Quintic Ginzburg Landau Equation with Intrapulse Raman Scattering

Aly R. Seadawy [1,*], Hanadi Zahed [1] and Syed T. R. Rizvi [2]

1 Mathematics Department, Faculty of Science, Taibah University,
Al-Madinah Al-Munawarah 41411, Saudi Arabia; hzahed@taibahu.edu.sa
2 Department of Mathematics, COMSATS University Islamabad, Lahore Campus, Lahore 54000, Pakistan; strrizvi@gmail.com
* Correspondence: aabdelalim@taibahu.edu.sa

Abstract: This manuscript consist of diverse forms of lump: lump one stripe, lump two stripe, generalized breathers, Akhmediev breather, multiwave, M-shaped rational and rogue wave solutions for the complex cubic quintic Ginzburg Landau (CQGL) equation with intrapulse Raman scattering (IRS) via appropriate transformations approach. Furthermore, it includes homoclinic, Ma and Kuznetsov-Ma breather and their relating rogue waves and some interactional solutions, including an interactional approach with the help of the double exponential function. We have elaborated the kink cross-rational (KCR) solutions and periodic cross-rational (KCR) solutions with their graphical slots. We have also constituted some of our solutions in distinct dimensions by means of 3D and contours profiles to anticipate the wave propagation. Parameter domains are delineated in which these exact localized soliton solutions exit in the proposed model.

Keywords: NLSE; lump solitons; breathers; multiwave

MSC: 35J05; 35J10; 35K05; 35L05

1. Introduction

The analysis of the solitary wave solutions (SWs) for various nonlinear partial differential Equations (NLPDEs) play a significant role in different aspects of mathematical and physical phenomena [1–5]. Mainly natural phenomena arising in applied science, such as nuclear physics, chemical reactions, optical fibres [6–10], fluid mechanics, plasma, physics and ecology, can sometimes be modeled and described by NLPDEs [11–21]. Constructing the SWs of these equations has become a global interest in recent years. Hence, an enormous number of mathematical experts have attempted to invent various approaches by which one can obtain the exact solutions of such equations. Nowadays, some new effective techniques have been residential and well known [22]. To learn the mechanism of phenomena for the NLPDEs in physics and engineering, their SWs are calculated. There are many integration architectonics, such as Lie symmetry analysis [23], Backlund transformations [24], conservation laws, symmetry bifurcation [25], extended tanh-function, spontaneous symmetry [26], Painleve and Lie symmetries [27], CESTAC Method [28], polynomial law [29], computational architectonic, Semi inverse technique [30], HBM [31], mapping algorithm [32], (G'/G) expansion algorithm [33], Kudryashove architectonic [34], auxiliary equation scheme [35] and $\exp((-\varphi'/\varphi)\eta)$-expansion scheme [36]. The Riccati-Bernoulli sub-ODE method, optimal homotopy asymptotic approach, Exp-function algorithm, sine-cosine process, tanh-sech mechanism, extended tanh-scheme, F-expansion method, homogeneous balance technique, Jacobi elliptic function mechanism and several others have been developed to obtain SWs. A massive number of NLPDEs can be purely

solved by the abovementioned methods. However, there is no a specific approach by which we can deal with all NLPDEs. In addition, some NLPDEs cannot be effortlessly solved by most traditional methods. The proposed method, which allows us to execute tedious and sophisticated algebraic calculations, is utilized to establish solitary wave solutions, peaked wave solutions and exact wave solutions for NLPDEs.

The NLPDEs are mainly valuable zones for nonlinear optics to reveal the proliferation distinctively short pulse in ultra-fast signal routing and telecommunication and light pulse propagation in condensed matter [37–41]. There are lots of recognized model, such as the modified KP-Equation [24], Fokas Equation [23], rth Dym Equation [21], Pochhammer-Chree model [14], modified Equation [11], fractional NLSE [20], fiber Bragg gratings model [29], Einstein's vacuum field Equation [27], double-chain model [13], Wazwaz Benjamin model [12], modified Veronese Web Equation [42], (KMN)-Equation [30], Sawada Kotera Equation [31] and Fokas–Lenells model.

Recently, lump and interactional solutions (LISs) have shown significance to depict the wave features for various NLPDEs. For instance, LISs were studied by Zhou et al. with the Hirota Satsuma model [43], LIsS were found by Wang et al. with the Burgers model [44], Wu et al. worked on lump, periodic lump solutions in the KP model [45] and, similarly, Li et al. studied various lumps for BLMP model [46]. Breather soliton is a nonlinear wave in which energy is localized in space but oscillates in time, or vice versa, and has been newly reported in an optical fiber cavity. Cavity solitons (CSs) are localized pulses of light that can be wound up in nonlinear optical resonators and have sparked imperative study curiosity in the perspective of micro resonator-based frequency comb generation, and are found in a range of subfields of natural science, for instance fluid dynamics, solid-state physics, plasma physics, molecular biology, chemistry and nonlinear optics [47]. Recently, Rizvi et al. investigated breathers for NLEE [15], Seadawy et al. interpreted breather solutions for NLEE [42], Ahmed et al. studied breathers for the general $(2+1)$-rth dispersionless Equation [21], and Ahmed et al. found kinky breathers for the nonlinear model [48], among many other studies. Multiwave solutions (MS) for nonlinear models have its own worth. Seadawy et al. worked on MS for the HS-Equation [15], Ahmed et al. studied MS for the $(2+1)$-rth dispersionless Equation [21], Rizvi et al. reported MS for NLEE [42], Seadawy et al. worked on MS for the nonlinear model [48], Wazwaz analyzed rogue wave and breathers [49], etc.

In this template, we begin our analysis by taking the CQGL-equation with IRS term [22];

$$i\Delta_z + \frac{1}{2}\Delta_{tt} + \gamma|\Delta|^2\Delta = i\delta\Delta + i\beta\Delta_{tt} + i\epsilon|\Delta|^2\Delta - \nu|\Delta|^4\Delta + i\mu|\Delta|^4\Delta + T_r\left(|\Delta|^2\right)_t\Delta, \quad (1)$$

where z is the normalized propagation distance, t is the retarded time and Δ is the normalized envelope of the pulse. For a laser system, the interpretation of distinct coefficients is as follows: β shows spectral filtering or gain dispersion, μ expresses higher-order correction to the nonlinear absorption or amplification, ϵ shows nonlinear gain, ν shows a higher-order correction term to the nonlinear refractive index, T_r shows the IRS coefficient, γ displays the positive Kerr effect (or negative Kerr effect if negative) and δ is a constant gain (or loss if negative). The stated equation is a canonical model for weakly nonlinear, dissipative systems and one of the most studied nonlinear equations in the physics community. It can be used to describe a vast variety of nonlinear phenomena, such as Bose–Einstein condensation, superconductivity, strings in field theory, superfluidity, lasers and liquid crystals.

In order to solve Equation (1), we insert $\Delta = p + iq$, where $|\Delta| = \sqrt{p^2 + q^2}$. Thus, Equation (1) may be converted into real and imaginary parts:

$$\begin{cases} p^3\gamma + q^2\gamma p + p^5\nu + 2p^3q^2\nu + q^4\nu p + \delta q + p^2\epsilon q + q^3\epsilon + p^4\mu q + 2p^2q^3\mu + q^5\mu + \frac{1}{2}p_{tt} + \beta q_{tt} - q_z = 0, \\ -\delta p - p^3\epsilon - q^2\epsilon p - \mu p^5 - 2\mu p^3 q^2 - \mu q^4 p + \gamma p^2 q + \gamma q^3 + \nu p^4 q + 2\nu p^2 q^3 + \nu q^5 - \beta p_{tt} + \frac{1}{2}q_{tt} + p_z = 0. \end{cases} \quad (2)$$

The document for the upcoming sections will be detailed in a sequence: in Section 2, we will evaluate the lump solutions for the proposed model form with few graphical slots. In Section 3, there will be a concise discussion of lump one stripe solutions with some 3D and contour graphical slots. In Section 4, we will construct lump two stripe results with some suitable profiles. Section 5 consist of a Ma-breather (MB) and its relating rogue wave. Similarly, in Section 6, we will evaluate the Kuznetsov-Ma breather (KMB) with some suitable 3D and contour shapes. In Section 7, we will find the generalized breathers (GB) for proposed equation with their relating figures. Section 8 includes Akhmediev breathers (AB) along with some profiles for the concerned model. Similarly, Section 9 will detail the procedure to construct standard rogue waves. In Section 10, we will explain the methodology for finding multiwave solutions. In the same way, we will compute homoclinic breathers for the proposed equation in Section 11. There will be M-shaped solitons in Section 12. In Section 13, there will be an interaction approach for the proposed model. We will find kink cross-rational (KCR) solutions in Section 14. Section 15 includes periodic cross-rational (PCR) solutions along with some 3D and contour profiles for the concerned model. Section 16 contains the results and a discussion about our newly achieved solutions and we will make an suitable comparison with earlier work. Finally, in Section 17, we will provide some concluding annotations.

2. Lump Solution

For the lump solutions of Equation (2), we apply the subsequent ansatz [43,44]:

$$p = \frac{6}{\rho}(\ln g)_z, \quad q = \frac{6}{\omega}(\ln h)_z, \tag{3}$$

and get the proceeding form:

$$2p^2\gamma\omega g^2 h^3 g_z + 2q^2\gamma\omega g^2 h^3 g_z + 2p^4 v\omega g^2 h^3 g_z + 4p^2 q^2 \gamma\omega g^2 h^3 g_z + 2q^4 v\omega g^2 h^3 g_z$$
$$+2\omega h^3 g_t^2 g_z - \omega g h^3 g_{tt} g_z + 2\delta\rho g^3 h^2 h_z + 2p^2 \varepsilon\rho g^3 h^2 h_z + 2q^2 \varepsilon\rho g^3 h^2 h_z + 2p^4 \mu\rho g^3 h^2 h_z \tag{4}$$
$$+4p^2 q^2 \mu\rho g^3 h^2 h_z + 2q^4 \mu\rho g^3 h^2 h_z + 4\beta\rho g^3 h_t^2 h_z + \ldots + 2\beta\rho g^3 h^2 h_{ztt} - 2\rho g^3 h^2 h_{zz} = 0.$$

Now, the function g and h in Equation (4) can be considered as [43,44]:

$$g = \xi_1^2 + \xi_2^2 + a_2, \quad h = \zeta_1^2 + \zeta_2^2 + a_3, \tag{5}$$

where $\xi_1 = a_0 z + t$, $\xi_2 = a_1 z + t$., while $a_i (1 \leq i \leq 3)$ are specific real parameters. Now, using g and h into Equation (4) and solving the coefficients of the z and t implies:
Set I. When

$$a_0 = \left(-4 + \sqrt{15}\right) a_1, a_1 = a_1, a_2 = 0, \rho = \rho, \omega = \omega. \tag{6}$$

These generated parameters make the lump solution:

$$\Delta_1 = \frac{-6\left(-4+\sqrt{15}\right) R_1 + \left(-4+\sqrt{15}\right)^2 a_1^2 \left(2a_1(t+a_1 z) + 2\left(-4+\sqrt{15}\right) a_1 R_2\right)}{a_1^2 \left((t+a_1 z)^2 + \left(t + \left(-4+\sqrt{15}\right) a_1 z\right)^2\right)} + \Omega_1, \tag{7}$$

where $R_1 = a_1^2 + \left(-4+\sqrt{15}\right) a_1^2$, $\Omega_1 = \dfrac{6i\left(2a_1(t+a_1z) + 2\left(-4+\sqrt{15}\right) a_1 \left(t + \left(-4+\sqrt{15}\right) a_1 z\right)\right)}{\left(\dfrac{\left(-4+\sqrt{15}\right)^2 a_1^3}{a_1^3 - \left(-4+\sqrt{15}\right) a_1^3 + \left(-4+\sqrt{15}\right) a_1^3} + (t+a_1 x)^2 + \left(t + \left(-4+\sqrt{15}\right) a_1 z\right)^2\right) \omega}$

and $R_2 = t + \left(-4 + \sqrt{15}\right) a_1 z$.

3. Lump One Stripe Solution

To get the lump one stripe solution, we apply the transformation shown in Equation (4) [50]:

$$g = \tilde{\zeta}_1^2 + \tilde{\zeta}_2^2 + a_2 + b_0 e^{k_1 z + k_2 t}, \quad h = \tilde{\zeta}_1^2 + \tilde{\zeta}_2^2 + a_3 + b_0 e^{k_1 z + k_2 t}, \quad (8)$$

where $\tilde{\zeta}_1 = a_0 z + t$, $\tilde{\zeta}_2 = a_1 z + t.$, while $a_i (1 \leq i \leq 3)$, k_1, k_2 and b_0 are any specific real parameters. Now, using g and h in Equation (4) and solving the coefficients of the z and t:
Set I. When $a_2 = 0$:

$$a_0 = -a_1, a_3 = \frac{-6 b_0 \omega}{b_0 \omega (\nu p^6 q^2 + \nu q^4 + \gamma p^2 + \gamma q^2)}, a_5 = a_5, \omega = \omega, \rho = \rho, k_2 = 0. \quad (9)$$

These parameters exhibit the required solution to Equation (2):

$$\Delta_2 = \frac{6 \left(b_0 e^{k_1 z} k_1 - 2 a_1 (t - a_1 z) + 2 a_1 (t + a_1 z) \right)}{\rho \left(b_0 e^{k_1 z} + (t - a_1 z)^2 + (t + a_1 z)^2 \right)} + \Omega_2. \quad (10)$$

where $\Omega_2 = \dfrac{6i \left(b_0 e^{k_1 z} k_1 - 2 a_1 (t - a_1 z) + 2 a_1 (t + a_1 z) \right)}{\left(b_0 e^{k_1 z} + (t - a_1 z)^2 + (t + a_1 z)^2 - \frac{6}{p^2 \gamma + q^2 \gamma + p^4 \nu + 2 p^2 q^2 \nu + q^4 \nu} \right) \omega}.$

4. Lump Two Stripe Solution

To obtain the lump two stripe solution, we assume the subsequent transformation in Equation (4) [50]:

$$g = \tilde{\zeta}_1^2 + \tilde{\zeta}_2^2 + a_2 + b_0 e^{k_1 z + k_2 t} + b_1 e^{k_3 z + k_4 t}, \quad h = \tilde{\zeta}_1^2 + \tilde{\zeta}_2^2 + a_3 + b_0 e^{k_1 z + k_2 t} + b_1 e^{k_3 z + k_4 t}, \quad (11)$$

where $\tilde{\zeta}_1 = a_0 z + t$, $\tilde{\zeta}_2 = a_1 z + t.$, while $a_i (1 \leq i \leq 3)$, k_1, k_2, k_3, k_4, b_0 and b_1 are any specific real parameters. Now, using g and h in Equation (4) and solving the coefficients of the z and t:
Set I. When $a_1 = a_2 = a_3 = 0$:

$$a_0 = a_0, a_5 = a_5, b_1 = \frac{-5 k_3 \delta}{7 k_3^2 - 5 k_3 \delta}, \beta = \frac{b_1 \omega \left(7 k_3^2 - 5 k_3 \delta \right)}{10 b_1 k_3 \delta \rho}, \rho = \frac{-4 k_3^2 + 5 k_3}{5 k_3}. \quad (12)$$

These parameters exhibits the required solution to Equation (2):

$$\Delta_3 = \frac{6 \left(b_0 e^{k_2 t + k_1 z} k_1 - \frac{e^{k_4 t + k_3 z} k_3 (5 k_3 - 4 k_3^2)}{-5 k_3 + 11 k_3^2} + R_3 \right)}{\rho \left(b_0 e^{k_2 t + k_1 z} k_1 - \frac{e^{k_4 t + k_3 z} k_3 (5 k_3 - 4 k_3^2)}{-5 k_3 + 11 k_3^2} + R_4 \right)} + \frac{6i \left(b_0 e^{k_2 t + k_1 z} k_1 - \frac{e^{k_4 t + k_3 z} k_3 (5 k_3 - 4 k_3^2)}{-5 k_3 + 11 k_3^2} + R_3 \right)}{\omega \left(b_0 e^{k_2 t + k_1 z} k_1 - \frac{e^{k_4 t + k_3 z} k_3 (5 k_3 - 4 k_3^2)}{-5 k_3 + 11 k_3^2} + R_4 \right)}, \quad (13)$$

where $R_3 = 2 a_0 (t + a_0 z)$ and $R_4 = t^2 + (t + a_0 z)^2$.

5. Ma-Breather (MB) and Its Relating Rogue Wave

We assume g and h in Equation (4) as [44]:

$$g = 1 + \alpha_1 + e^{i(p_1 x)} + e^{-i(p_1 x)} e^{\lambda_1 t + \gamma_1} + \beta_1 e^{2(\lambda_1 t + \gamma_1)}, \quad h = 1 + \alpha_2 + e^{i(p_2 x)} + e^{-i(p_2 x)} e^{\lambda_2 t + \gamma_2} + \beta_2 e^{2(\lambda_2 t + \gamma_2)}, \quad (14)$$

where $\alpha_1, \alpha_2, p_1, p_2, \lambda_1, \lambda_2, \gamma_1$ and γ_2 are any parameters. Now, using g and h in Equation (4) and letting the coefficients of exp and cos functions be zero:
Set I. When $\gamma_1 = \beta_2 = 0$:

$$\alpha_1 = \alpha_1, \alpha_2 = \alpha_2, \mu = \frac{i p_2 - 2 \delta - 2 p^2 \varepsilon - 2 q^2 \varepsilon - 5 \beta \lambda_2^2}{2 (p^2 + q^2)^2}, p_1 = p_1, a_4 = a_4. \quad (15)$$

These parameters form the Ma-breather solution to Equation (1):

$$\Delta_4 = \frac{6e^{t\lambda_1}\left(-ie^{-ip_1z}p_1 + ie^{ip_1z}p_1\right)\alpha_1}{\left(1+e^{t\lambda_1}\left(e^{-ip_1z}+e^{ip_1z}\right)\alpha_1\right)\rho} + \frac{6ie^{\gamma_2+t\lambda_2}\left(-ie^{-ip_2z}p_2 + ie^{ip_2z}p_2\right)\alpha_2}{\left(1+e^{\gamma_2+t\lambda_2}\left(e^{-ip_2z}+e^{ip_2z}\right)\alpha_2 + e^{2(\gamma_2+t\lambda_2)}\beta_2\right)\omega}. \tag{16}$$

6. Kuznetsov-Ma Breather (KMB) and Its Relating Rogue Wave

We assume g and h in Equation (4) as [44]:

$$g = e^{-p_1(b_2z - b_1t)} + a_1\cos(p(b_2z + b_1t)) + a_2\cos(p(b_2z - b_1t)),$$
$$h = e^{-p_2(b_3z - b_4t)} + a_3\cos(p(b_3z + b_4t)) + a_4\cos(p(b_3z - b_4t)), \tag{17}$$

where p_1, p_2, b_1, b_2, b_3, b_4, a_1, a_2, a_3 and a_4 are any parameters to be found. Now, using g and h in Equation (4) and letting the coefficients of exp and cos functions be zero follows:
Set I. When:

$$p_1 = p_1, \nu = \frac{-p_1^2(\gamma^2 + \mu)}{p^2}, a_1 = a_1, \gamma = \gamma, a_3 = a_3, \rho = \rho. \tag{18}$$

These parameters form the proposed solution to Equation (1):

$$\Delta_5 = \frac{6\left(-b_2 e^{-p_1(-b_1t+b_2z)}p_1 + a_2 b_2 e^{p_1(-b_1t+b_2z)}p_1 - a_1 b_2 p \sin(p(b_1t+b_2z))\right)}{\rho\left(e^{-p_1(-b_1t+b_2z)} + a_2 e^{p_1(-b_1t+b_2z)} + a_1\cos(p(b_1t+b_2z))\right)} + \Omega_3, \tag{19}$$

where $\Omega_3 = \frac{6i\left(-b_3 e^{-p_2(-b_3t+b_4z)}p_2 + a_4 b_3 e^{-p_2(-b_3t+b_4z)}p_2 - a_3 b_3 p \sin(p(b_4t+b_3z))\right)}{\omega\left(e^{-p_2(-b_3t+b_4z)} + a_4 e^{p_2(-b_3t+b_4z)} + a_3\cos(p(b_4t+b_3z))\right)}.$

7. Generalized Breathers (GB)

In order to obtain generalized breathers we use ansatz [51]:

$$\Delta(z,t) = 2bc\left(\frac{6}{\kappa}\ln\Psi(z,t)\right)_z + m, \tag{20}$$

where b, c and m are any particular constants. Inserting Equation (20) into Equation (1), we have:

$$m^3\gamma\kappa^5\psi^5 - im\delta\kappa^5\psi^5 - im^3\varepsilon\kappa^5\psi^5 + m^5\kappa^5\nu\psi^5 + m^5\kappa^5\nu\psi^5 + 36bcm^2\gamma\kappa^4\psi^4\psi_z - 12ibc\delta\kappa^4\psi^4\psi_z$$
$$-36ibcm^2\varepsilon\kappa^4\psi^4\psi_z - 60ibcm^4\mu\kappa^4\psi^4\psi_z + 60bcm^4\nu\kappa^4\psi^4\psi_z + 12bcmT_r\kappa^4\psi^3\psi_t\psi_z + 12bc\kappa^4\psi^2\psi_z\psi_t^2 \tag{21}$$
$$-24ibc\beta\kappa^4\psi^2\psi_t^2\psi_z - 6bc\kappa^4\psi^3\psi_{tt}\psi_z + 12ibc\beta\kappa^4\psi^3\psi_{tt}\psi_z + \ldots + 12ibc\kappa^4\psi^4\psi_{zz} - 12ibc\beta\kappa^4\psi^4\psi_{zt} = 0.$$

For finding the required solutions, we use the following assumption in Equation (21):

$$\psi = \frac{(1-4c)\cosh(\sigma t) + \sqrt{2c}\cos(\rho z) + i\sigma\sinh(\sigma t)}{\sqrt{2c}\cos(\rho z) - \cosh(\sigma t)}e^{it}, \tag{22}$$

where σ, ρ and c are constants to be found. The coefficients of cosh, sinh and exp functions are defined as follows:

$$a = a, b = b, m = 0, c = \frac{1}{2}, \rho = \rho, \sigma = \sigma. \tag{23}$$

These values implies the following GB profiles of Equation (1):

$$\Delta_6 = \frac{6bie^{-it}(\cos(\rho z) - \cosh(\sigma t))\left(\frac{-e^{it}\rho\sin((\rho z))}{\cos(\rho z) - \cosh(\sigma t)} + \frac{e^{it}\rho\sin((\rho z))(\cos((\rho z)) - \cosh(\sigma t) + i\sigma\sinh(\sigma t))}{(\cos(\rho z) - \cosh(\sigma t))^2}\right)}{\kappa\cos(\rho z) - \cosh(\sigma t) + i\sigma\sinh(\sigma t)}. \tag{24}$$

8. Akhmediev Breathers (AB)

We use the following transformation in Equation (21) [52]:

$$\psi = \sqrt{p_0}\frac{(1-4a)\cosh(bz) + ib\sinh(bz) + \sqrt{2a}\cos(w_{\mod} T)}{\sqrt{2a}\cos(w_{\mod} T) - \cosh(b\xi)}, \quad (25)$$

where w_{mod} interprets the perturbation frequency (PF) with p_0 as the power. The coefficients a and b depends on w_{mod} and are defined by $2a = 1 - (\frac{w_{mod}}{w_c})^2$ and $b = [8a(1-2a)]^2$ with $w_c^2 = \frac{4p_0\gamma}{|\beta_2|}$. Setting the coefficients of trigonometric and hyperbolic functions be zero:

$$a = a, b = b, c = c, w = \sqrt{\frac{4-82}{2i\beta}}, \rho = \rho, p_0 = p_0. \quad (26)$$

These values imply the AB of Equation (1) to be as follows:

$$\Delta_7 = m + \frac{12bc\left(\sqrt{2a}\cos\left(t\sqrt{-\frac{i(4-8a)}{\beta}}\over\sqrt{2}\right) - \cosh(bz)\right)\Omega_4}{\sqrt{p_0}\kappa\left(\sqrt{2a}\cos\left(t\sqrt{-\frac{i(4-8a)}{\beta}}\over\sqrt{2}\right) + (1-4a)\cosh(bz) + ib\sinh(bz)\right)}, \quad (27)$$

where:

$$\Omega_4 = \left(\frac{b\sqrt{p_0}\sinh(bz)\left(\sqrt{2a}\cos\left(t\sqrt{-\frac{i(4-8a)}{\beta}}\over\sqrt{2}\right) + (1-4a)\cosh(bz) + ib\sinh(bz)\right)}{\left(\sqrt{2a}\cos\left(t\sqrt{-\frac{i(4-8a)}{\beta}}\over\sqrt{2}\right) - \cosh(bz)\right)^2} + \frac{\sqrt{p_0}\left(ib^2\cosh(bz) + (1-4a)b\sinh(bz)\right)}{\sqrt{2a}\cos\left(t\sqrt{-\frac{i(4-8a)}{\beta}}\over\sqrt{2}\right) - \cosh(bz)}\right).$$

9. Standard Rogue Wave (SRW) Solutions

For evaluating the SRW, we apply the subsequent assumption in Equation (21) [44]:

$$\psi = -\left(1 - \frac{4(1+2it)}{1+4z^2+4t^2}\right)e^{it}, \quad (28)$$

Setting the coefficients of exponential function, z and t be zero will follow:

$$b = b, \beta = \frac{-i}{2}, m = \sqrt{\frac{-3i\varepsilon + 3\gamma + \sqrt{20\delta\mu - 9\varepsilon^2 - 18i\gamma\varepsilon + 20i\delta\nu + 9\gamma^2}}{10(i\mu-\nu)}}, c = c, \kappa = \kappa. \quad (29)$$

These values implies the SRW to Equation (1):

$$\Delta_8 = -\frac{384bc(1+2it)z}{(1+4t^2+4z^2)\left(-1+\frac{4(1+2it)}{1+4t^2+4z^2}\right)\kappa} + \sqrt{\frac{-3i\varepsilon + 3\gamma + \sqrt{20\delta\mu - 9\varepsilon^2 - 18i\gamma\varepsilon + 20i\delta\nu + 9\gamma^2}}{10(i\mu-\nu)}}. \quad (30)$$

10. Multiwaves Solutions (MS)

For these type of results, we use the preceding transformation in Equation (2) [48]:

$$\Delta(z,t) = \psi(\xi)e^{i\theta}, \quad \xi = k_1 z - c_1 t, \quad \theta = k_2 z - c_2 t. \quad (31)$$

Using the above transformation, we obtain the real and imaginary parts of equal Equation (2), by considering the real part only:

$$\gamma\psi^3 + \nu\psi^5 + c_1 T_r \psi\psi' - \frac{1}{2}c_1^2\psi + \frac{1}{2}c_1^2\psi'' + 2\beta c_1 c_2 \psi' = 0. \quad (32)$$

Now, by way of following the assumption in Equation (32):

$$\psi = 2(\ln f)_{\xi'} \tag{33}$$

we obtain:

$$-c_2^2 f^4 f' - 4\beta c_1 c_2 f^3 f'^2 + 2c_1^2 f^2 f'^3 + 8\gamma f^2 f'^3 - 4c_1 T_r f^2 f'^3 + 32\nu f'^5 + 4c_1 c_2 \beta f^4 f'' - 3c_1^2 f^3 f' f''$$
$$+ 4c_1 f^3 T_r f' f'' + c_1^2 f^4 f''' = 0 \tag{34}$$

To get the MS of Equation (34), we use anstaz [48]:

$$f = b_0 \cosh(a_1 \xi + a_2) + b_1 \cos(a_3 \xi + a_4) + b_2 \cosh(a_5 \xi + a_6), \tag{35}$$

where a_1, a_2, a_3, a_4, a_5 and a_6 are any specific constants. Substituting Equation (35) into Equation (34) with Mathematica and letting the coefficients of hyperbolic and trigonometric functions to zero:

Set I. When:

$$a_1 = a_1, a_2 = a_2, a_3 = \frac{-1}{2} a_5, a_4 = a_4, a_5 = a_5, b_0 = 0, b_1 = b_1, c_1 = c_1. \tag{36}$$

Using the above values, we have:

$$\Delta_9 = \frac{2e^{i(-c_2 t + k_2 z)} \left(\frac{1}{2} a_5 b_1 \cos\left(a_4 - \frac{1}{2} a_5(-c_1 t + k_1 z)\right) \sin\left(a_4 - \frac{1}{2} a_5(-c_1 t + k_1 z)\right) + \Omega_5 \right)}{b_1 \cos\left(a_4 - \frac{1}{2} a_5(-c_1 t + k_1 z)\right) + b_2 \cosh(a_6 + a_5(-c_1 t + k_1 z))}, \tag{37}$$

where $\Omega_5 = a_5 b_2 \cosh(a_6 + a_5(-c_1 t + k_1 z)) \sinh(a_6 + a_5(-c_1 t + k_1 z))$.

11. Homoclinic Breather (HB)

In this approach we assume f the form [48]:

$$f = e^{-p(a_2 + a_1 \xi)} + b_1 e^{p(a_4 + a_3 \xi)} + b_0 \cos(p_1(a_6 + a_5 \xi)), \tag{38}$$

where $a_i's$ denotes any particular constants. Inserting Equation (38) into Equation (34) and collecting coefficients of exponential and trigonometric functions to be zero yields:

Set I. When:

$$a_1 = \frac{1}{2} a_5, a_2 = a_2, a_3 = a_3, c_1 = \frac{-2a_5^2 \nu p^2}{T_r}, b_1 = b_1, a_5 = a_5. \tag{39}$$

Via the above values we obtain:

$$\Delta_{10} = \frac{2 \left(\frac{-1}{2} a_5 b_1 p e^{p\left(a_4 - \frac{1}{2} a_4 \left(k_1 z + \frac{2a_5^2 p^2 t \nu}{T_r}\right)\right)} - \frac{1}{2} a_5 p e^{-p\left(a_2 - \frac{1}{2} a_5 \left(k_1 z + \frac{2a_5^2 p^2 t \nu}{T_r}\right)\right)} \right) e^{i(-c_2 t + k_2 z)}}{b_1 e^{p\left(a_4 - \frac{1}{2} a_4 \left(k_1 z + \frac{2a_5^2 p^2 t \nu}{T_r}\right)\right)} + e^{-p\left(a_2 - \frac{1}{2} a_5 \left(k_1 z + \frac{2a_5^2 p^2 t \nu}{T_r}\right)\right)}}. \tag{40}$$

12. M-Shaped Rational Solitons

For these solutions, we consider the form [48,53]:

$$f = (d_1 \xi + d_2)^2 + (d_3 \xi + d_4)^2 + d_5, \tag{41}$$

where $d_i (1 \leq i \leq 5)$, are any parameters. Put f into Equation (34) and solving coefficients of ξ to get subsequent result on parameters:

Set I. Whenever $d_5 = d_2 = 0$:

$$d_1 = id_3, d_3 = d_3, d_4 = \frac{c_1^2 d_3 \sqrt{c_1^4 d_3^2 + 24\beta c_1 c_2 \gamma}}{6\beta c_1 c_2}, c_1 = c_1, c_2 = c_2. \quad (42)$$

Using the above values, we obtain:

$$\Delta_{11} = \frac{2e^{i(-c_2 t + k_2 z)}\left(-2d_3^2(-c_1 t + k_1 z) + 2d_3\left(d_3(-c_1 t + k_1 z) + \frac{c_1^2 d_3 \sqrt{c_1^4 d_3^2 + 24\beta c_1 c_2 \gamma}}{6\beta c_1 c_2}\right)\right)}{-d_3^2(-c_1 t + k_1 z)^2 + \left(d_3(-c_1 t + k_1 z) + \frac{c_1^2 d_3 \sqrt{c_1^4 d_3^2 + 24\beta c_1 c_2 \gamma}}{6\beta c_1 c_2}\right)^2}. \quad (43)$$

13. Interactional Solutions with Double Exponential Form

We use the following hypothesis [48]:

$$f = b_1 e^{-a_1 \xi + a_2} + b_2 e^{a_3 \xi + a_4}. \quad (44)$$

where a_1, a_2, a_3 and a_4 are some constants. Inserting Equation (44) into Equation (34) and solving coefficients of exponential functions, a system of equations is obtained. By solving it:

Set I.

$$a_1 = (2 - \sqrt{3})a_3, a_2 = a_2, c_1 = \frac{8 a_3^2 \nu \left(7 - 4\sqrt{3}\right)}{T_r}, a_3 = a_3, a_4 = a_4. \quad (45)$$

Using the above values we have:

$$\Delta_{12} = \frac{2\left(a_3 b_2 e^{a_4 + a_3\left(k_1 z - \frac{8(7-4\sqrt{3}) a_3^2 t \nu}{T_r}\right)} + (2 - \sqrt{3}) a_3 b_1 e^{a_2 + (2-\sqrt{3}) a_3 \left(k_1 z - \frac{8(7-4\sqrt{3}) a_3^2 t \nu}{T_r}\right)}\right) e^{i(-c_2 t + k_2 z)}}{b_2 e^{a_4 + a_3\left(k_1 z - \frac{8(7-4\sqrt{3}) a_3^2 t \nu}{T_r}\right)} + b_1 e^{a_2 + (2-\sqrt{3}) a_3 \left(k_1 z - \frac{8(7-4\sqrt{3}) a_3^2 t \nu}{T_r}\right)}}. \quad (46)$$

14. Kink Cross-Rational (KCR) Solutions

For KCR solutions, we consider f as [54,55]:

$$f = g_0 + e^{-(a_1 \xi + a_2)} + k_1 e^{a_1 \xi + a_2} + (b_1 \xi + b_2)^2 + (b_3 \xi + b_4)^2, \quad (47)$$

where a_i and b_i are some constants. Inserting Equation (47) into Equation (34) and solving coefficients of exponential functions:

Set I.

$$a_1 = \sqrt{\frac{-3}{32\mu}} c_1, b_1 = b_1, b_2 = b_2, k_1 = 0, a_2 = a_2, \nu = \frac{2}{5}\mu, T_r = \frac{3\sqrt{\frac{-3}{32\mu}} c_1^2 + 8\beta c_2}{4\sqrt{\frac{-3}{32\mu}} c_1}, b_3 = b_3, b_4 = b_4. \quad (48)$$

Using the above values we have:

$$\Delta_{13} = \frac{2e^{i(-c_2 t + k_2 z)}\left(-2b_1(b_2 - b_1 c_2 t) + 2b_3(b_4 - b_3 c_2 t) - \frac{1}{4}\sqrt{-\frac{3}{2\mu}} c_2 e^{-a_2 + \frac{1}{4}\sqrt{-\frac{3}{2\mu}} c_2^2 t}\right)}{e^{-a_2 + \frac{1}{4}\sqrt{-\frac{3}{2\mu}} c_2^2 t} + g_0 + (b_2 - b_1 c_2 t)^2 + (b_4 - b_3 c_2 t)^2}. \quad (49)$$

15. Periodic Cross-Rational (PCR) Solutions

We use the following hypothesis [54,55]:

$$f = g_0 + (a_1 \xi + a_2)^2 + (a_3 \xi + a_4)^2 + k_1 \cos(b_1 \xi + b_2) + k_2 \cosh(b_3 \xi + b_4), \quad (50)$$

where a_i and b_i are some constants. Inserting Equation (50) into Equation (34) and solving coefficients of exponential, trigonometric and hyperbolic functions:

Set I.
$$a_1 = a_1, b_3 = \frac{-4\gamma}{3k_2c_1^2}, c_2 = 0, T_r = \frac{3}{4}c_1, b_1 = 0, b_4 = b_4. \tag{51}$$

Using the above values we have:

$$\Delta_{14} = \frac{2e^{i(k_2z)}\left(2a_1(a_2 + a_1(-c_1t+k_1z))^2 + 2a_3(a_4 + a_3(-c_1t+k_1z))^2 - \frac{4\gamma \sinh\left(b_4 - \frac{4(-c_1t+k_1z)\gamma}{3c_1^2k_2}\right)}{3c_1^2}\right)}{g_0 + (a_2 + a_1(-c_1t+k_1z))^2 + (a_4 + a_3(-c_1t+k_1z))^2 + k_2\cosh\left(b_4 - \frac{4(-c_1t+k_1z)\gamma}{3c_1^2k_2}\right)}. \tag{52}$$

16. Result and Discussions

A lot of work has been done on the proposed model: Akhmediev et al. found singularities via a simple approach [56], Soto Crespo et al. studied pulse solutions for the case of normal group-velocity dispersion [57], Yan et al. found stable transmission of solitons for the concerned model via the asymmetric method [58], Biswas et al. worked on Dromion-like structures for the variable-coefficients CQGL-equation by using the asymmetric method [59], Gurevich et al. investigated soliton explosions for the CQGL-equation via explosion modes [60], Uzunov et al. studied pulsating solutions for the CQGL-equation by using the variation method and the method of moments [61], Nikolov et al. interpreted the influence of the higher-order effects on the solutions for the concerned model [62], Mihalache et al. analyzed the coaxial vortex solitons for the CQGL-Equation [63], Fang et al. worked on soliton dynamics [64], Djoko et al. investigated the effects of the septic nonlinearity [65], Mou et al. studied discrete localized excitations [66] and Liu et al. analyzed harmonic and damped motions of dissipative solitons for the proposed model [67]. However, in this work, we have applied the appropriate transformations method to obtain the stated solutions for the governing model.

This article contains five classes of breather solutions (i.e., MB, KBM, GB, AB and homoclinic breather solutions), as well as lump, lump one stripe, lump two stripe and rogue wave solutions. Furthermore, a detailed analysis of SRW solution is made. Multiwave, M-shaped and interactional solutions are computed for ensuing model. These type of solutions, utilized in diverse fields of sciences, i.e., optics, engineering, physics and biology etc. [11–21]. A breather is a nonlinear localized wave and is a periodic solution of discrete lattice equations. Our newly attained results show a discrepancy of their shapes by appropriate choices of parameters. Now, we can definitely understand the geometric structure from Figure 1, which shows the lump profiles with one bright and dark soliton of the solution Δ_1 in Equation (7) via distinct parameters $\omega = 1$. The bright and dark soliton behavior of three-dimensional profiles steadily increases the value of (i) $a_1 = 5$, (ii) $a_1 = 10$ and (iii) $a_1 = -3$. Figure 2 shows the contour shapes for Figure 1 successively. The lump one stripe profiles of the solution Δ_2 in Equation (10) are interpreted via distinct values of $\omega = 5, k_1 = 2, \rho = 4, \gamma = -1, p = 2, q = -1, \nu = 1$ and $b_0 = 3$. Three-dimensional profiles are shown in Figure 3 at (i) $a_1 = 5$, (ii) $a_1 = 10$ and (iii) $a_1 = -2$. Figure 4 shows the contour shapes for Figure 3 successively. Similarly, Figure 5 shows the lump two stripe graphs of the solution Δ_3 in Equation (13) for the distinct values of $\omega = 5, k_1 = 2, \rho = 4, \gamma = -1, k_2 = 1, k_3 = 1, k_4 = 2$ and $b_0 = 3$, with three-dimensional profiles at (i) $a_0 = 5$, (ii) $a_0 = 10$ and (iii) $a_0 = -2$. Figure 6 builds contour profiles for Figure 5 successively. The MB graphs of the solution Δ_4 in Equation (16) are interpreted via distinct values of $\omega = 5, p_1 = 2, p_2 = 3, \alpha_1 = 1, \alpha_2 = 2.5, \lambda_1 = 1, \lambda_2 = 2, \beta_2 = 3, \rho = 4$ and $\gamma_2 = 1$. Three-dimensional profiles at (i) $a_0 = 5$, (ii) $a_0 = 10$ and (iii) $a_0 = -1$ are shown in Figure 7. Figure 8 shows the contour profiles for Figure 7. In the same way, Figure 9 presents the KMB graphs of solution Δ_5 in Equation (19) through values of $a_1 = 2, a_3 = 1, a_4 = 3, \omega = 5, p_1 = 2, p_2 = 3, b_1 = 1, b_2 = 2.5, b_3 = 1, b_4 = 2$ and $\rho = 4$, with three-dimensional profiles at (i) $a_2 = 5$,

(ii) $a_2 = 20$ and (iii) $a_2 = -1$. Figure 10 shows the contour profiles for Figure 9. The GB profiles of the solution Δ_6 in Equation (24) are formed through values of $\kappa = 5, b = 1$ and $\rho = 4$. Three-dimensional graphs at (i) $\sigma = 0.2$, (ii) $\sigma = 0.8$ and (iii) $\sigma = -0.1$ are shown in Figure 11. Similarly, Figure 12 shows the contour profiles for Figure 11. The AB profiles of the solution Δ_7 in Equation (27) are formed through values of $a = 5, b = 1, c = 3, p_0 = 4$ and $m = 5$. Three-dimensional graphs at (i) $\beta = 5$, (ii) $\beta = 10$ and (iii) $\beta = -3$ are shown in Figure 13, while Figure 14 shows the contour graphs for Figure 13. The SRW profiles of the solution Δ_8 in Equation (30) are constructed for values of $\epsilon = 0.5, b = 1, c = 3, \gamma = 0.1$, $\nu = 10, \mu = 2$ and $\kappa = 2$. Three-dimensional graphs at (i) $\delta = -5$, (ii) $\delta = 10$ and (iii) $\delta = 20$ are shown in Figure 14. Figure 15 shows the contour graphs for Figure 14. Similarly, MS graphs of solution Δ_9 in Equation (37) are formed with $a_6 = 0.2, c_1 = 1, k_1 = 3, a_4 = 0.1$, $b_1 = 10, b_2 = 2, c_2 = 2$ and $k_2 = 3$. Three-dimensional graphs at (i) $a_5 = -5$, (ii) $a_5 = 3$ and (iii) $a_5 = 7$ are shown in Figure 15. Figure 16 shows the contour shapes for Figure 15. The HB profiles of solution Δ_{11} in Equation (43) are constructed for values of $c_1 = 2, c_2 = 1$, $k_1 = 3, k_2 = 0.1, \gamma = 1$ and $\beta = 5$. Three-dimensional graphs at (i) $d_3 = -5$, (ii) $d_3 = 3$ and (iii) $d_3 = 15$ are shown in Figure 17. Figure 18 shows the contour shapes for Figure 17, while the MS profiles of the solution Δ_{11} in Equation (40) are constructed for values of $b_1 = 0.5, p = 1, a_4 = 3, a_2 = 2, k_1 = 0.1, \nu = 1$ and $T_r = 2$. Three-dimensional graphs at (i) $a_5 = -5$, (ii) $a_5 = 3$ and (iii) $a_5 = 10$ are shown in Figure 19. Figure 20 shows the contour shapes for Figure 19. When the value of a_5 steadily increases, we can see that the waves come closer to interact with each other. In the same manner, Figure 21 presents the soliton profiles of the solution Δ_{12} in Equation (46) for values of $a_4 = 2, b_2 = 1, b_1 = 3, a_2 = 0.1$, $T_r = 1, c_2 = 5, k_2 = 2$ and $\nu = 3$, with three-dimensional graphs at (i) $a_3 = -5$, (ii) $a_3 = 0.1$ and (iii) $a_5 = 4$. When the value of k_2 steadily increases, we can see from the behavior of the M-shaped wave that the waves come closer to interact with each other. Similarly, Figure 22 shows the contour shapes for Figure 21 successively. The KCR profiles of the solution Δ_{13} in Equation (49) are formed for values of $b_2 = 1, b_1 = 3, a_2 = 0.1, \mu = 2, g_0 = 3$, $b_3 = 2, b_4 = 5, c_2 = 4$ and $k_2 = 2$. Three-dimensional graphs at (i) $a_2 = -5$, (ii) $a_2 = 1$ and (iii) $b_2 = 40$ are shown in Figure 23. Figure 24 shows the contour shapes for Figure 23 successively. The PCR graphs of the solution Δ_{14} in Equation (52) are formed for particular values of $b_2 = 1, a_4 = 2, a_2 = -3, \mu = 2, g_0 = 7, b_2 = 1, c_1 = 3, k_1 = 0.1, c_2 = 6, \gamma = 2$ and $k_2 = 1$. Three-dimensional graphs at (i) $a_1 = -4$, (ii) $a_1 = 0$ and (iii) $a_1 = 30$ are shown in Figure 25. Finally, Figures 26–28 shows the contour shapes for Figure 25 successively.

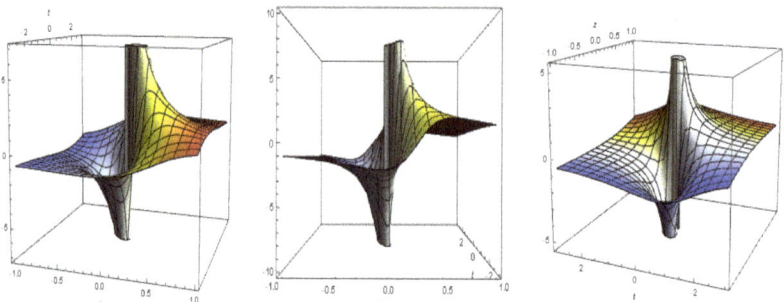

Figure 1. The lump profiles of the solution Δ_1 in Equation (7) are presented via distinct parameters $\omega = 1$. Three-dimensional profiles at (i) $a_1 = 5$, (ii) $a_1 = 10$ and (iii) $a_1 = -3$.

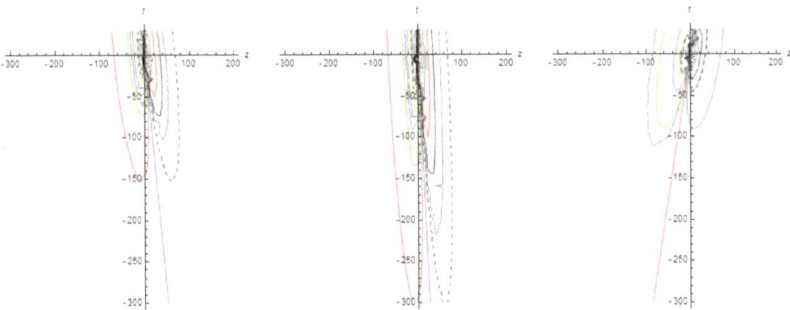

Figure 2. Contours graphs for Figure 1.

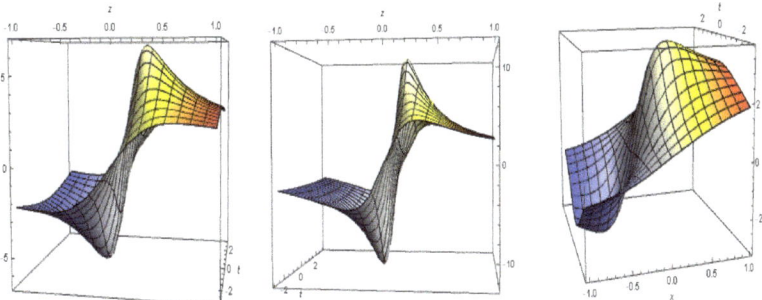

Figure 3. The lump one stripe profiles of the solution Δ_2 in Equation (10) are interpreted via distinct values of $\omega = 5, k_1 = 2, \rho = 4, \gamma = -1, p = 2, q = -1, \nu = 1, b_0 = 3$. Three-dimensional profiles are shown in (i) $a_1 = 5$, (ii) $a_1 = 10$ and (iii) $a_1 = -2$.

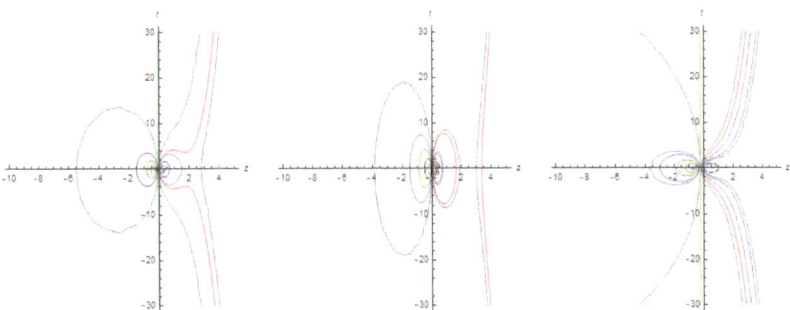

Figure 4. Contour displays for Figure 3.

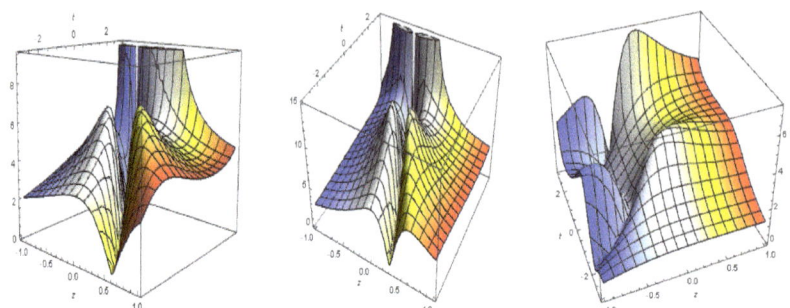

Figure 5. The lump two stripe graphs of the solution Δ_3 in Equation (13) are interpreted via distinct values of $\omega = 5, k_1 = 2, \rho = 4, \gamma = -1, k_2 = 1, k_3 = 1, k_4 = 2, b_0 = 3$. Three-dimensional profiles at (i) $a_0 = 5$, (ii) $a_0 = 10$ and (iii) $a_0 = -2$.

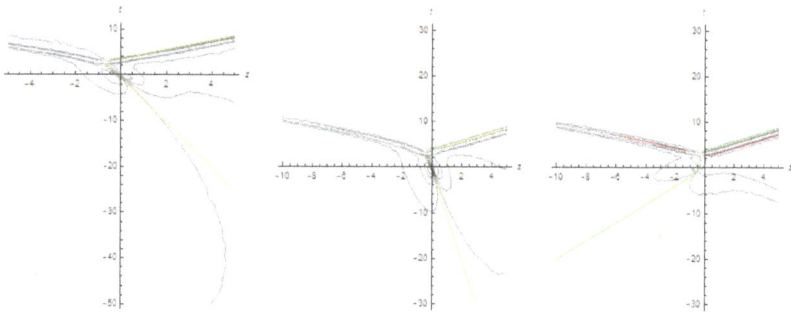

Figure 6. Contour graphs for Figure 5.

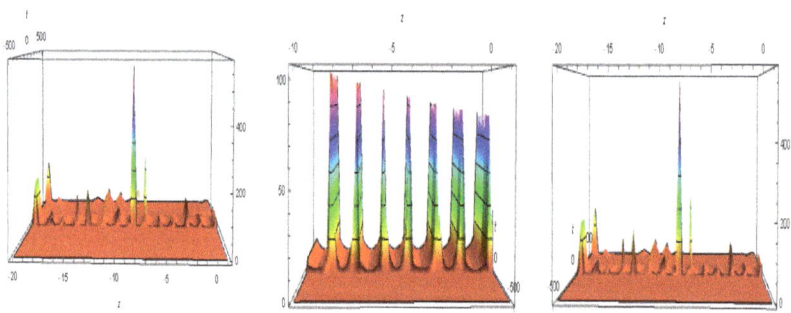

Figure 7. The MB graphs of the solution Δ_4 in Equation (16) are interpreted via distinct values of $\omega = 5, p_1 = 2, p_2 = 3, \alpha_1 = 1, \alpha_2 = 2.5, \lambda_1 = 1, \lambda_2 = 2, \beta_2 = 3, \rho = 4, \gamma_2 = 1$. Three-dimensional profiles at (i) $a_0 = 5$, (ii) $a_0 = 10$ and (iii) $a_0 = -1$.

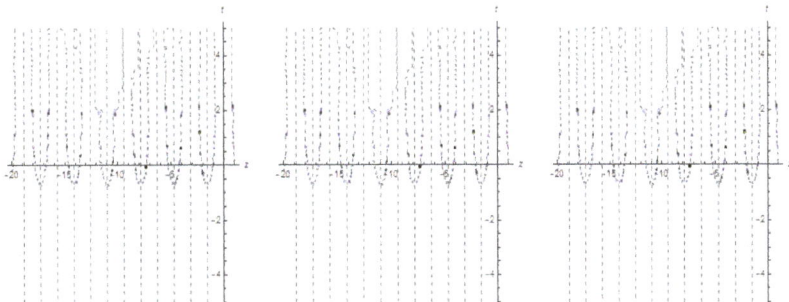

Figure 8. Contour graphs for Figure 7.

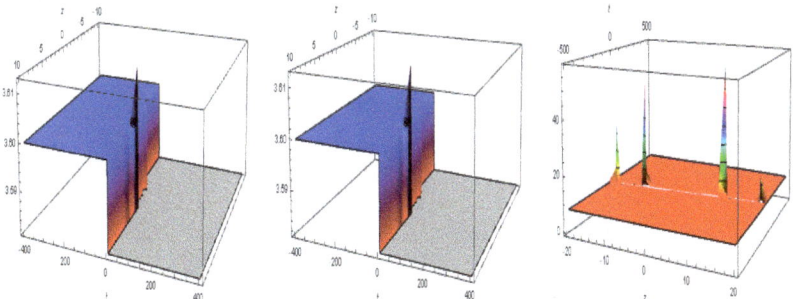

Figure 9. The KMB graphs of the solution Δ_5 in Equation (19) are interpreted through values of $a_1 = 2$, $a_3 = 1$, $a_4 = 3$, $\omega = 5$, $p_1 = 2$, $p_2 = 3$, $b_1 = 1$, $b_2 = 2.5$, $b_3 = 1$, $b_4 = 2$ and $\rho = 4$. Three-dimensional profiles at (i) $a_2 = 5$, (ii) $a_2 = 20$ and (iii) $a_2 = -1$.

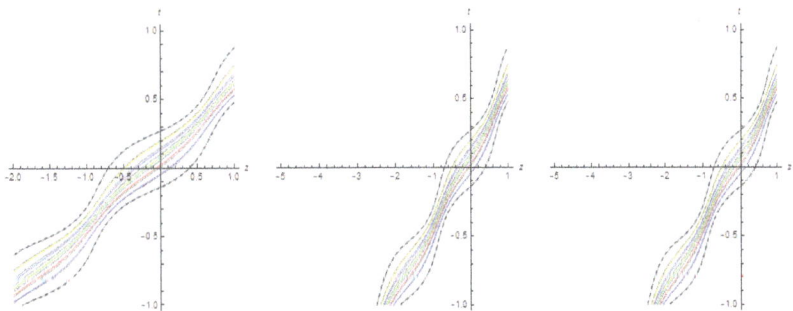

Figure 10. Contour graphs for Figure 9.

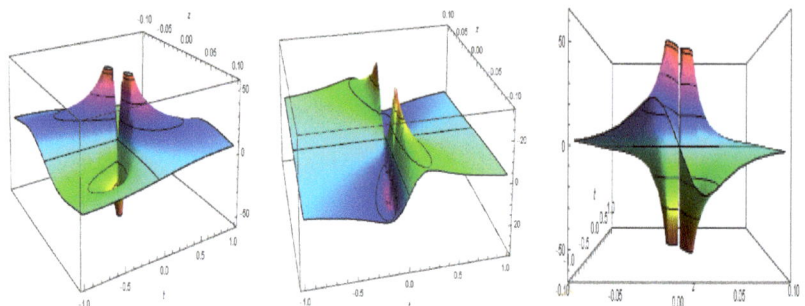

Figure 11. The GB profiles of the solution Δ_6 in Equation (24) are made through values of $\kappa = 5$, $b = 1$ and $\rho = 4$. Three-dimensional graphs at (i) $\sigma = 0.2$, (ii) $\sigma = 0.8$ and (iii) $\sigma = -0.1$.

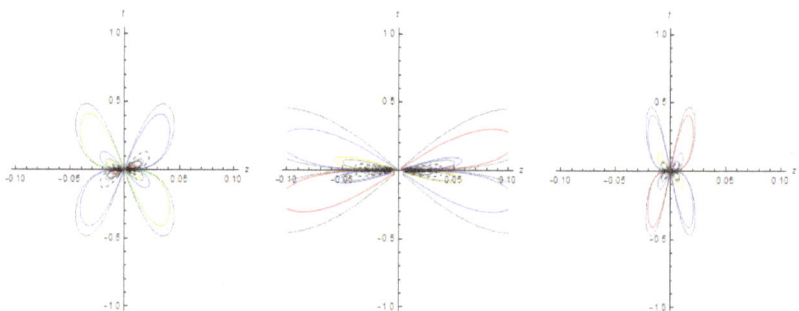

Figure 12. Contour graphs for Figure 11.

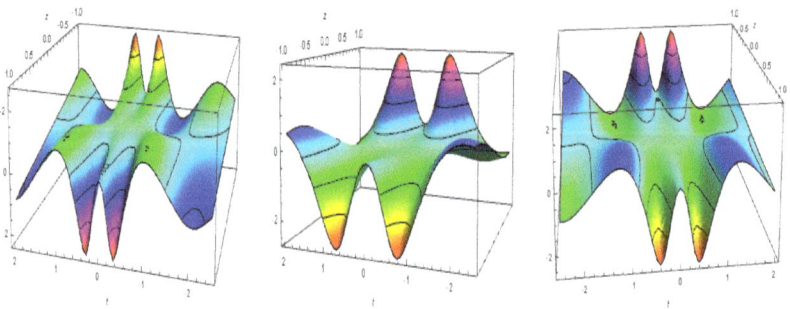

Figure 13. The AB profiles of the solution Δ_7 in Equation (27) are made through values of $a = 5$, $b = 1$, $c = 3$, $p_0 = 4$ and $m = 5$. Three-dimensional graphs at (i) $\beta = 5$, (ii) $\beta = 10$ and (iii) $\beta = -3$.

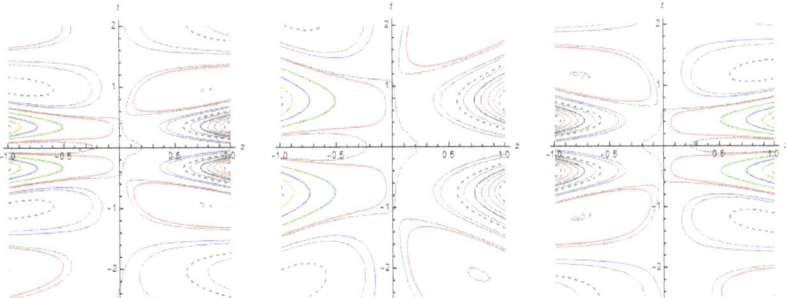

Figure 14. Contour slots for Figure 13.

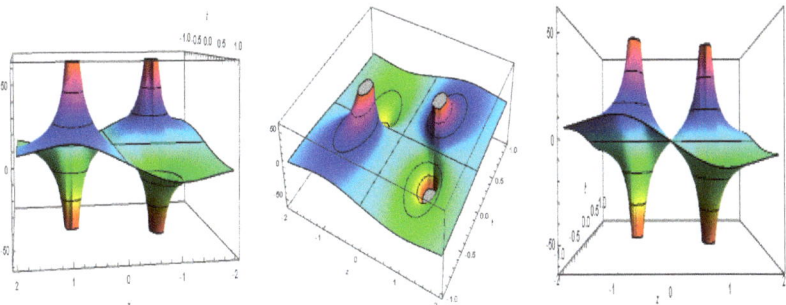

Figure 15. The SRW profiles of the solution Δ_8 in Equation (30) are made for values of $\epsilon = 0.5$, $b = 1$, $c = 3$, $\gamma = 0.1$, $\nu = 10$, $\mu = 2$ and $\kappa = 2$. Three-dimensional graphs at (i) $\delta = -5$, (ii) $\delta = 10$ and (iii) $\delta = 20$.

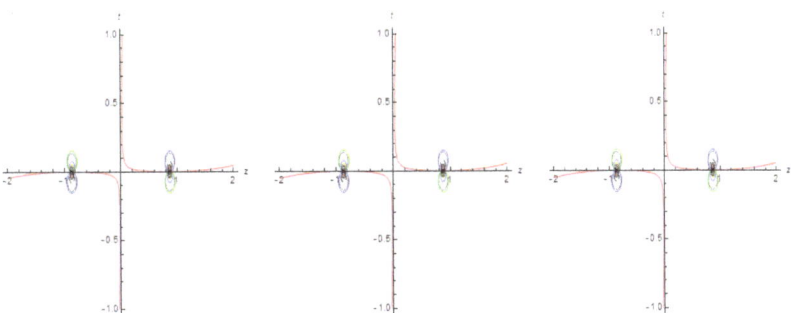

Figure 16. Contour slots for Figure 15.

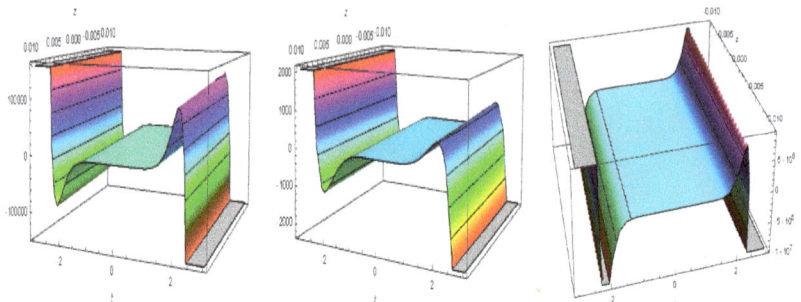

Figure 17. The MS graphs of the solution Δ_9 in Equation (37) are made for values of $a_6 = 0.2, c_1 = 1, k_1 = 3, a_4 = 0.1, b_1 = 10, b_2 = 2, c_2 = 2, k_2 = 3$. Three-dimensional graphs at (i) $a_5 = -5$, (ii) $a_5 = 3$ and (iii) $a_5 = 7$.

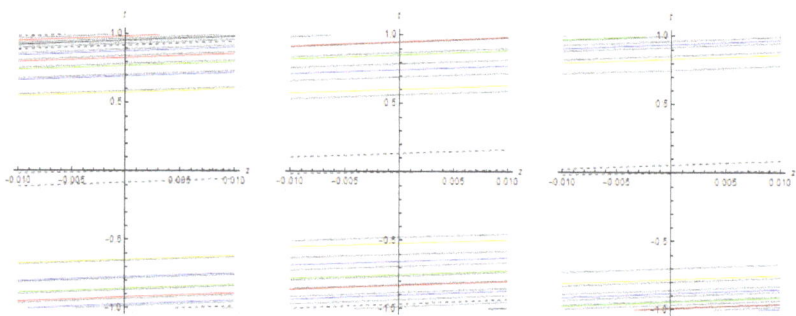

Figure 18. Contour slots for Figure 17.

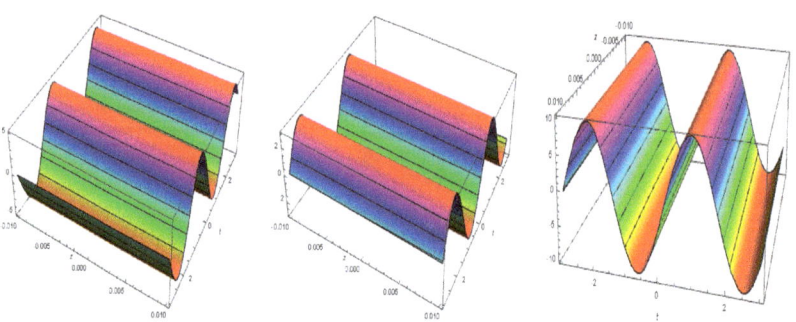

Figure 19. The HB profiles of the solution Δ_{11} in Equation (43) are constructed for values of $c_1 = 2, c_2 = 1, k_1 = 3, k_2 = 0.1, \gamma = 1$ and $\beta = 5$. Three-dimensional graphs at (i) $d_3 = -5$, (ii) $d_3 = 3$ and (iii) $d_3 = 15$.

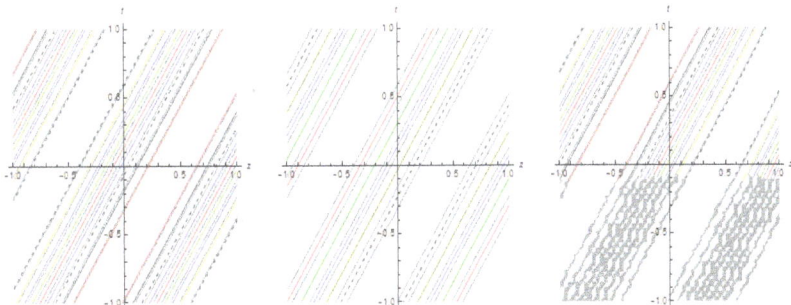

Figure 20. Contour slots for Figure 19.

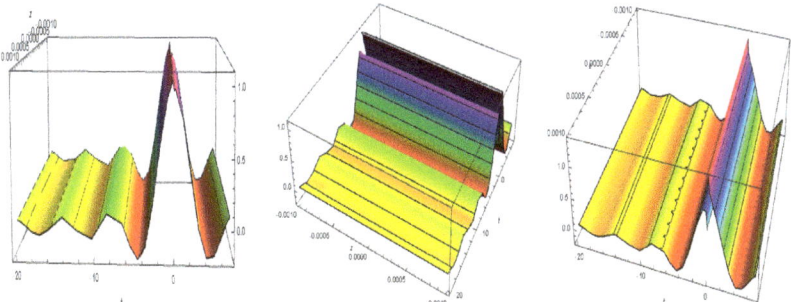

Figure 21. The MS profiles of the solution Δ_{11} in Equation (40) are constructed for values of $b_1 = 0.5$, $p = 1, a_4 = 3, a_2 = 2, k_1 = 0.1, \nu = 1$ and $T_r = 2$. Three-dimensional graphs at (i) $a_5 = -5$, (ii) $a_5 = 3$ and (iii) $a_5 = 10$.

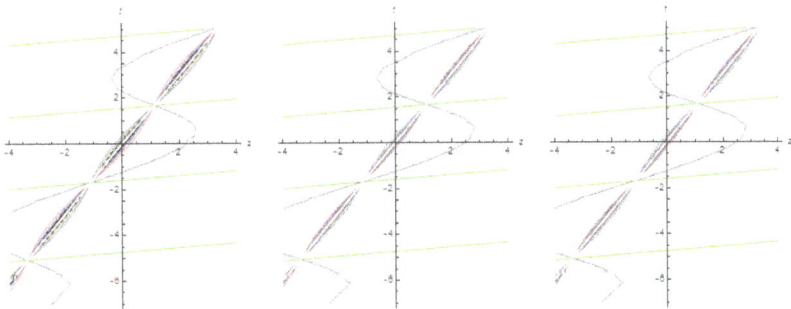

Figure 22. Contour slots for Figure 21.

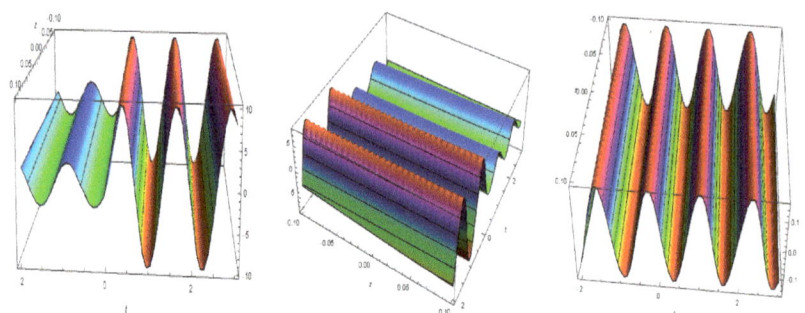

Figure 23. The soliton profiles of the solution Δ_{12} in Equation (46) are made for values of $a_4 = 2$, $b_2 = 1$, $b_1 = 3$, $a_2 = 0.1$, $T_r = 1$, $c_2 = 5$, $k_2 = 2$ and $v = 3$. Three-dimensional graphs at (i) $a_3 = -5$, (ii) $a_3 = 0.1$ and (iii) $a_5 = 4$.

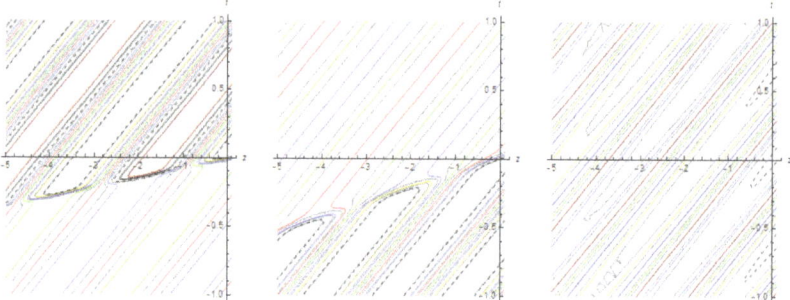

Figure 24. Contour profiles for Figure 23.

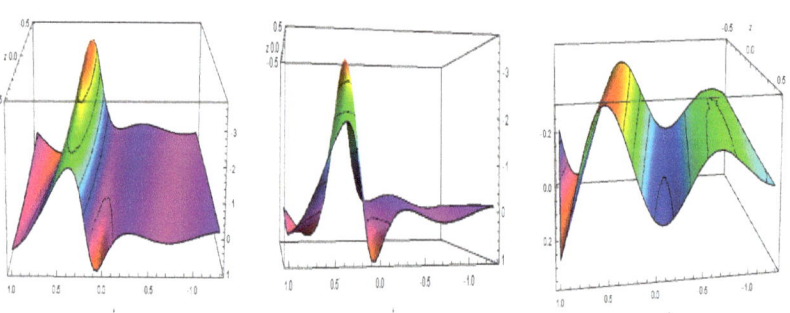

Figure 25. The KCR profiles of the solution Δ_{13} in Equation (49) are formed for values of $b_2 = 1$, $b_1 = 3$, $a_2 = 0.1$, $\mu = 2$, $g_0 = 3$, $b_3 = 2$, $b_4 = 5$, $c_2 = 4$ and $k_2 = 2$. Three-dimensional graphs at (i) $a_2 = -5$, (ii) $a_2 = 1$ and (iii) $b_2 = 40$.

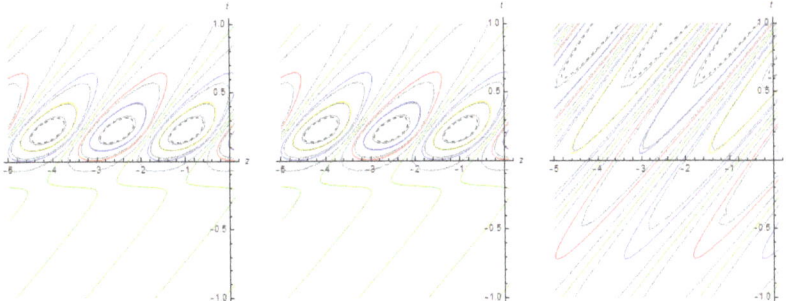

Figure 26. Contour profiles for Figure 25.

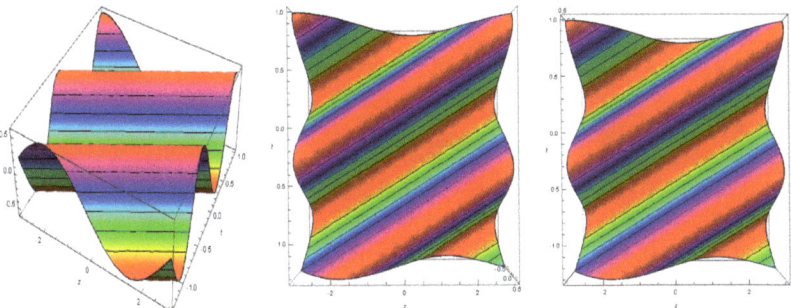

Figure 27. The PCR graphs of the solution Δ_{14} in Equation (52) are formed for particular values of $b_2 = 1$, $a_4 = 2$, $a_2 = -3$, $\mu = 2$, $g_0 = 7$, $b_2 = 1$, $c_1 = 3$, $k_1 = 0.1$, $c_2 = 6$ and $\gamma = 2$, $k_2 = 1$. Three-dimensional graphs at (i) $a_1 = -4$, (ii) $a_1 = 0$ and (iii) $a_1 = 30$.

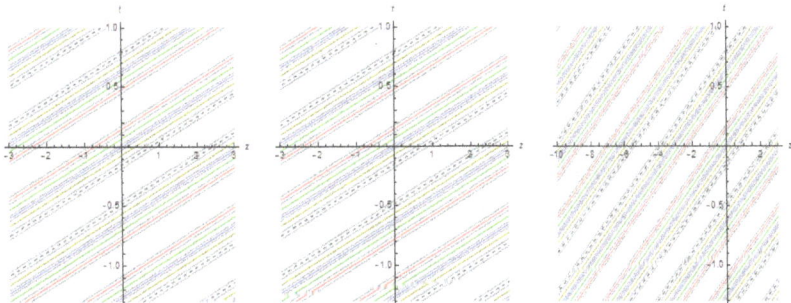

Figure 28. Shows contour shapes for Figure 27.

17. Concluding Remarks

We have considered the CQGL-equation under the influence of intrapulse Raman scattering (IRS) and constructed distinct localized wave solutions by employing test functions with the aid of an appropriate transformations method. Five classes of breather solutions (i.e., Ma, Kuznetsov-Ma, GB, AB, homoclinic breather solutions), as well as lump, lump one stripe, lump two stripe and rogue wave solutions were successfully evaluated. Furthermore, a detailed analysis of SRW solution was performed. Multiwave, M-shaped, interactional solutions, KCR solutions and PCR solutions are computed for the ensuing model. Interaction behaviors between multiple-lump waves and soliton were also discussed. Multiple-lump wave evolution with time was also observed. We graphically presented many valuable results obtained here. The conditions imposed on the parameters have been explicitly demonstrated to guarantee that they were well defined and that the solutions were localized. To our knowledge, the results are new for the governing equation. These results may be useful for the experimental realization of undistorted transmission of optical waves in optical fibers and further understanding of their optical transmission properties. Finally, we hope that the exact nature of these solitary waves interpreted here may be profitably exploited in designing the optimal Raman fiber laser experiments.

Author Contributions: Conceptualization, A.R.S. and S.T.R.R.; methodology, A.R.S.; software, S.T.R.R.; validation, H.Z., S.T.R.R.; formal analysis, S.T.R.R.; investigation, A.R.S.; writing—original draft preparation, S.T.R.R.; writing—review and editing, A.R.S.; visualization, S.T.R.R.; supervision, A.R.S.; project administration, H.Z.; funding acquisition, H.Z. All authors have read and agreed to the published version of the manuscript.

Funding: Deputyship for Research and Innovation, Ministry of Education in Saudi Arabia for funding this research work the project number (141/442).

Institutional Review Board Statement: Not applicable.

Informed Consent Statement: Not applicable.

Data Availability Statement: Not applicable.

Acknowledgments: The authors extend their appreciation to the Deputyship for Research and Innovation, Ministry of Education in Saudi Arabia for funding this research work the project number (141/442). Furthermore, the authors would like to extend their appreciation to Taibah University for its supervision support.

Conflicts of Interest: The authors declare no conflict of interest.

References

1. Kumar, S.; Kumar, D.; Kharbanda, H. Lie symmetry analysis, abundant exact solutions and dynamics of multisolitons to the (2 + 1)-dimensional KP-BBM equation. *Pramana* **2021**, *95*, 33. [CrossRef]
2. Kumar, S.; Kumar, D. Lie symmetry analysis and dynamical structures of soliton solutions for the (2 + 1)-dimensional modified CBS equation. *Int. J. Mod. Phys. B* **2020**, *34*, 2050221. [CrossRef]
3. Kumar, S.; Kumar, A. Lie symmetry reductions and group invariant solutions of (2 + 1)-dimensional modified Veronese web equation. *Nonlinear Dyn.* **2019**, *98*, 1891–1903. [CrossRef]
4. Kumar, S.; Niwas, M.; ; Wazwaz, A.M. Lie symmetry analysis, exact analytical solutions and dynamics of solitons for (2 + 1)-dimensional NNV equations. *Phys. Scr.* **2020**, *95*, 095204. [CrossRef]
5. Kumar, S.; Rani, S. Lie symmetry reductions and dynamics of soliton solutions of (2 + 1)-dimensional Pavlov equation. *Pramana* **2020**, *94*, 116. [CrossRef]
6. Kudryashov, N.A. The generalized Duffing oscillator. *Commun. Nonlinear Sci. Numer. Simul.* **2021**, *93*, 105526. [CrossRef]
7. Kudryashov, N.A. Model of propagation pulses in an optical fiber with a new law of refractive indices. *Optik* **2021**, *248*, 168160. [CrossRef]
8. Kudryashov, N.A. Solitary waves of the non-local Schrödinger equation with arbitrary refractive index. *Optik* **2021**, *231*, 166443. [CrossRef]
9. Kudryashov, N.A. Almost general solution of the reduced higher-order nonlinear Schrödinger equation. *Optik* **2021**, *230*, 166347. [CrossRef]
10. Kudryashov, N.A. Periodic and solitary waves in optical fiber Bragg gratings with dispersive reflectivity. *Chin. J. Phys.* **2020**, *66*, 401–405. [CrossRef]
11. Younas, U.; Younis, M.; Seadawy, A.R.; Rizvi, S.T.R.; Althobaiti, S.; Sayed, S. Diverse exact solutions for modified nonlinear Schrödinger equation with conformable fractional derivative. *Results Phys.* **2021**, *20*, 103766. [CrossRef]
12. Akram, U.; Seadawy, A.R.; Rizvi, S.T.R.; Younis, M.; Althobaiti, S.; Sayed, S. Traveling wave solutions for the fractional Wazwaz–Benjamin–Bona–Mahony model in arising shallow water waves. *Results Phys.* **2021**, *20*, 103725. [CrossRef]
13. Seadawy, A.R.; Bilal, M.; Younis, M.; Rizvi, S.T.R.; Althobaiti, S.; Makhlouf, M.M. Analytical mathematical approaches for the double-chain model of DNA by a novel computational technique. *Chaos Solitons Fractals* **2021**, *144*, 110669. [CrossRef]
14. Seadawy, A.R.; Rehman, S.U.; Younis, M.; Rizvi, S.T.R.; Althobaiti, S.; Makhlouf, M.M. Modulation instability analysis and longitudinal wave propagation in an elastic cylindrical rod modelled with Pochhammer-Chree equation. *Phys. Scr.* **2021**, *96*, 045202. [CrossRef]
15. Seadawy, A.R.; Rizvi, S.T.R.; Ahmad, S.; Younis, M.; Baleanu, D. Lump, lump-one stripe, multiwave and breather solutions for the Hunter–Saxton equation. *Open Phys.* **2021**, *19*, 1–10. [CrossRef]

16. Bilal, M.; Seadawy, A.R.; Younis, M.; Rizvi, S.T.R.; El-Rashidy, K.; Mahmoud, S.F. Analytical wave structures in plasma physics modelled by Gilson-Pickering equation by two integration norms. *Results Phys.* **2021**, *23*, 103959. [CrossRef]
17. Rizvi, S.T.R.; Seadawy, A.R.; Younis, M.; Ali, I.; Althobaiti, S.; Mahmoud, S.F. Soliton solutions, Painleve analysis and conservation laws for a nonlinear evolution equation. *Results Phys.* **2021**, *23*, 103999. [CrossRef]
18. Rizvi, S.T.R.; Seadawy, A.R.; Younis, M.; Iqbal, S.; Althobaiti, S.; El-Shehawi, A.M. Various optical soliton for a weak fractional nonlinear Schrödinger equation with parabolic law. *Results Phys.* **2021**, *23*, 103998. [CrossRef]
19. Seadawy, A.R.; Rizvi, S.T.; Ali, I.; Younis, M.; Ali, K.; Makhlouf, M.M.; Althobaiti, A. Conservation laws, optical molecules, modulation instability and Painlevé analysis for the Chen–Lee–Liu model. *Opt. Quantum Electron.* **2021**, *53*, 172. [CrossRef]
20. Tariq, K.U.; Zainab, H.; Seadawy, A.R.; Younis, M.; Rizvi, S.T.R.; Abd Allah, A.M. On some novel optical wave solutions to the paraxial M-fractional nonlinear Schrödinger dynamical equation. *Opt. Quantum Electron.* **2021**, *53*, 219. [CrossRef]
21. Ahmed, S.; Ashraf, R.; Seadawy, A.R.; Rizvi, S.T.R.; Younis, M.; Althobaiti, A.; El-Shehawi, A.M. Lump, multi-wave, kinky breathers, interactional solutions and stability analysis for general $(2+1)$-rth dispersionless Dym equation. *Results Phys.* **2021**, *25*, 104160. [CrossRef]
22. Maan, N.; Goyal, A.; Raju, T.S.; Kumar, C.N. Chirped Lambert W-kink solitons of the complex cubic-quintic Ginzburg-Landau equation with intrapulse Raman scattering. *Phys. Lett. A* **2020**, *384*, 126675.
23. Kumar, S.; Kumar, D.; Kumar, A. Lie symmetry analysis for obtaining the abundant exact solutions, optimal system and dynamics of solitons for a higher-dimensional Fokas equation. *Chaos Solitons Fractals* **2021**, *142*, 110507. [CrossRef]
24. Gao, X.Y.; Guo, Y.J.; Shan, W.R.; Yuan, Y.Q.; Zhang, C.R.; Chen, S.S. Magneto-optical/ferromagnetic-material computation: Bäcklund transformations, bilinear forms and N solitons for a generalized $(3+1)$-dimensional variable-coefficient modified Kadomtsev–Petviashvili system. *Appl. Math. Lett.* **2021**, *111*, 106627. [CrossRef]
25. Li, P.; Li, R.; Dai, C. Existence, symmetry breaking bifurcation and stability of two-dimensional optical solitons supported by fractional diffraction. *Opt. Express* **2021**, *29*, 3193–3210. [CrossRef]
26. Xu, G.; Nielsen, A.U.; Garbin, B.; Hill, L.; Oppo, G.L.; Fatome, J.; Erkintalo, M. Spontaneous symmetry breaking of dissipative optical solitons in a two-component Kerr resonator. *Nat. Commun.* **2021**, *12*, 4023. [CrossRef] [PubMed]
27. Kaur, L.; Wazwaz, A.M. Einstein's vacuum field equation: Painlevé analysis and Lie symmetries. *Waves Random Complex Media* **2021**, *31*, 199–206. [CrossRef]
28. Noeiaghdam, S.; Sidorov, D.; Wazwaz, A.M.; Sidorov, N.; Sizikov, V. The Numerical Validation of the Adomian Decomposition Method for Solving Volterra Integral Equation with Discontinuous Kernels Using the CESTAC Method. *Mathematics* **2021**, *9*, 260. [CrossRef]
29. Seadawy, A.R.; Ahmed, H.M.; Rabie, W.B.; Biswas, A. Chirp-free optical solitons in fiber Bragg gratings with dispersive reflectivity having polynomial law of nonlinearity. *Optik* **2021**, *225*, 165681. [CrossRef]
30. He, J.H. Variational principle and periodic solution of the Kundu-Mukherjee-Naskar equation. *Results Phys.* **2020**, *17*, 103031. [CrossRef]
31. Wazwaz, A.M. The Hirota bilinear method and the tanh–coth method for multiple-soliton solutions of the Sawada–Kotera–Kadomtsev–Petviashvili equation. *Appl. Math. Comput.* **2008**, *200*, 160–166.
32. Seadawy, A.R.; Cheemaa, N. Applications of extended modified auxiliary equation mapping method for high-order dispersive extended nonlinear Schrödinger equation in nonlinear optics. *Mod. Phys. Lett. B* **2019**, *33*, 1950203. [CrossRef]
33. Farah, N.; Seadawy, A.R.; Ahmad, S.; Rizvi, S.T.R.; Younis, M. Interaction properties of soliton molecules and Painleve analysis for nano bioelectronics transmission model. *Opt. Quantum Electron.* **2020**, *52*, 329. [CrossRef]
34. Gaber, A.A.; Aljohani, A.F.; Ebaid, A.; Machado, J.T. The generalized Kudryashov method for nonlinear space–time fractional partial differential equations of Burgers type. *Nonlinear Dyn.* **2019**, *95*, 361–368 [CrossRef]
35. Rizvi, S.T.R.; Ali, K.; Ahmad, M. Optical solitons for Biswas–Milovic equation by new extended auxiliary equation method. *Optik* **2020**, *204*, 164181. [CrossRef]
36. Ghaffar, A.; Ali, A.; Ahmed, S.; Akram, S.; Baleanu, D.; Nisar, K.S. A novel analytical technique to obtain the solitary solutions for nonlinear evolution equation of fractional order. *Adv. Differ. Equ.* **2020**, *2020*, 308. [CrossRef]
37. Bashir, A.; Seadawy, A.R.; Rizvi, S.T.R.; Younis, M.; Ali, I.; Abd Allah, A.M. Application of scaling invariance approach, P-test and soliton solutions for couple of dynamical models. *Results Phys.* **2021**, *25*, 104227. [CrossRef]
38. Seadawy, A.R.; Bilal, M.; Younis, M.; Rizvi, S.T.R.; Makhlouf, M.M.; Althobaiti, S. Optical solitons to birefringent fibers for coupled Radhakrishnan–Kundu–Lakshmanan model without four-wave mixing. *Opt. Quantum Electron.* **2021**, *53*, 324. [CrossRef]
39. Yusuf, A.; Inc, M.; Aliyu, A.I.; Baleanu, D. Efficiency of the new fractional derivative with nonsingular Mittag–Leffler kernel to some nonlinear partial differential equations. *Chaos Solitons Fractals* **2018**, *116*, 220–226. [CrossRef]
40. Merabti, A.; Triki, H.; Azzouzi, F.; Zhou, Q.; Biswas, A.; Liu, W.; Abdessetar, E.A. Propagation properties of chirped optical similaritons with dual-power law nonlinearity. *Chaos Solitons Fractals* **2020**, *140*, 110158.
41. Celik, N.; Seadawy, A.R.; Ozkan, Y.S.; Yaşar, E. A model of solitary waves in a nonlinear elastic circular rod: Abundant different type exact solutions and conservation laws. *Chaos Solitons Fractals* **2021**, *143*, 110486. [CrossRef]
42. Rizvi, S.T.R.; Seadawy, A.R.; Ahmed, S.; Younis, M.; Ali, K. Lump, rogue wave, multi-waves and Homoclinic breather solutions for $(2+1)$-Modified Veronese Web equation. *Int. J. Mod. Phys. B* **2021**, *35*, 2150055. [CrossRef]
43. Zhou, Y.; Manukure, S.; Ma, W.X. Lump and lump-soliton solutions to the Hirota Satsuma equation. *Commun. Nonlinear Sci. Numer. Simul.* **2019**, *68*, 56–62. [CrossRef]

44. Wang, H. Lump and interaction solutions to the (2 + 1)-dimensional Burgers equation. *Appl. Math. Lett.* **2018**, *85*, 27–34. [CrossRef]
45. Wu, P.; ; Zhang, Y.; Muhammad, I.; Yin, Q. Lump, periodic lump and interaction lump stripe solutions to the (2 + 1)-dimensional B-type Kadomtsev–Petviashvili equation. *Mod. Phys. Lett. B* **2018**, *32*, 1850106. [CrossRef]
46. Li, B.Q.; Ma, Y.L. multiple-lump waves for a (3 + 1)-dimensional Boiti–Leon–Manna–Pempinelli equation arising from incompressible fluid. *Comput. Math. Appl.* **2018**, *76*, 204–214. [CrossRef]
47. Yu, M.; Jang, J.K.; Okawachi, Y.; Griffith, A.G.; Luke, K.; Miller, S.A.; Gaeta, A.L. Breather soliton dynamics in microresonators. *Nat. Commun.* **2017**, *8*, 14569. [CrossRef] [PubMed]
48. Ahmed, I.; Seadawy, A.R.; Lu, D. Kinky breathers, W-shaped and multi-peak solitons interaction in (2 + 1)-dimensional nonlinear Schrödinger equation with Kerr law of nonlinearity. *Eur. Phys. J. Plus* **2019**, *134*, 120. [CrossRef]
49. Liu, Y.; Li, B.; Wazwaz, A.M. Novel high-order breathers and rogue waves in the Boussinesq equation via determinants. *Int. J. Mod. Phys. B* **2020**, *43*, 3701–3715. [CrossRef]
50. Lu, X.; Chen, S.J. Interaction solutions to nonlinear partial differential equations via Hirota bilinear forms: One-lump-multi-stripe and one-lump-multi-soliton types. *Nonlinear Dyn.* **2021**, *103*, 947–977. [CrossRef]
51. Singh, S.; Sakkaravarthi, K.; Murugesan, K.; Sakthivel, R. Benjamin-Ono equation: Rogue waves, generalized breathers, soliton bending, fission, and fusion. *Eur. Phys. J. Plus* **2020**, *135*, 823. [CrossRef]
52. Dudley, J.M.; Genty, G.; Dias, F.; Kibler, B.; Akhmediev, N. Modulation instability, Akhmediev Breathers and continuous wave supercontinuum generation. *Opt. Express* **2009**, *17*, 21497–21508. [CrossRef]
53. Ahmed, I.; Seadawy, A.R.; Lu, D. M-shaped rational solitons and their interaction with kink waves in the Fokas–Lenells equation. *Phys. Scr.* **2019**, *94*, 055205. [CrossRef]
54. Seadawy, A.R.; Rizvi, S.T.; Ashraf, M.A.; Younis, M.; Hanif, M. Rational solutions and their interactions with kink and periodic waves for a nonlinear dynamical phenomenon. *Int. J. Mod. Phys. B* **2021**, *35*, 2150236. [CrossRef]
55. Manafian, J.; Mohammadi Ivatloo, B.; Abapour, M. Breather wave, periodic, and cross-kink solutions to the generalized Bogoyavlensky-Konopelchenko equation. *Math. Methods Appl. Sci.* **2020**, *43*, 1753–1774. [CrossRef]
56. Akhmediev, N.N.; Afanasjev, V.V.; Soto-Crespo, J.M. Singularities and special soliton solutions of the cubic-quintic complex Ginzburg-Landau equation. *Phys. Rev. E* **1996**, *53*, 1190. [CrossRef]
57. Soto-Crespo, J.M.; Akhmediev, N.N.; Afanasjev, V.V.; Wabnitz, S. Pulse solutions of the cubic-quintic complex Ginzburg-Landau equation in the case of normal dispersion. *Phys. Rev. E* **1997**, *55*, 4783. [CrossRef]
58. Yan, Y.; Liu, W. Stable transmission of solitons in the complex cubic–quintic Ginzburg–Landau equation with nonlinear gain and higher-order effects. *Appl. Math. Lett.* **2019**, *98*, 171–176. [CrossRef]
59. Yan, Y.; Liu, W.; Zhou, Q.; Biswas, A. Dromion-like structures and periodic wave solutions for variable-coefficients complex cubic–quintic Ginzburg–Landau equation influenced by higher-order effects and nonlinear gain. *Nonlinear Dyn.* **2020**, *99*, 1313–1319. [CrossRef]
60. Gurevich, S.V.; Schelte, C.; Javaloyes, J. Impact of high-order effects on soliton explosions in the complex cubic-quintic Ginzburg Landau equation. *Phys. Rev. A* **2019**, *99*, 061803. [CrossRef]
61. Uzunov, I.M.; Georgiev, Z.D.; Arabadzhiev, T.N. Transitions of stationary to pulsating solutions in the complex cubic-quintic Ginzburg-Landau equation under the influence of nonlinear gain and higher-order effects. *Phys. Rev. E* **2018**, *97*, 052215. [CrossRef] [PubMed]
62. Uzunov, I.M.; Nikolov, S.G. Influence of the higher-order effects on the solutions of the complex cubic-quintic Ginzburg–Landau equation. *J. Mod. Opt.* **2020**, *67*, 606–618. [CrossRef]
63. Mihalache, D.; Mazilu, D.; Lederer, F.; Leblond, H.; Malomed, B.A. Collisions between coaxial vortex solitons in the three-dimensional cubic-quintic complex Ginzburg-Landau equation. *Phys. Rev. A* **2008**, *77*, 033817. [CrossRef]
64. Fang, J.J.; Mou, D.S.; Wang, Y.Y.; Zhang, H.C.; Dai, C.Q.; Chen, Y.X. Soliton dynamics based on exact solutions of conformable fractional discrete complex cubic Ginzburg–Landau equation. *Results Phys.* **2021**, *20*, 103710. [CrossRef]
65. Djoko, M.; Tabi, C.B.; Kofane, T.C. Effects of the septic nonlinearity and the initial value of the radius of orbital angular momentum beams on data transmission in optical fibers using the cubic-quintic-septic complex Ginzburg–Landau equation in presence of higher-order dispersions. *Chaos Solitons Fractals* **2021**, *147*, 110957. [CrossRef]
66. Mou, D.S.; Fang, J.J.; Fan, Y. Discrete localized excitations for discrete conformable fractional cubic–quintic Ginzburg–Landau model possessing the non-local quintic term. *Optik* **2021**, *244*, 167554. [CrossRef]
67. Liu, B.; Bo, W.; Liu, J.; Liu, J.; Shi, J.L.; Yuan, J.; Wu, Q. Simple harmonic and damped motions of dissipative solitons in two-dimensional complex Ginzburg-Landau equation supported by an external V-shaped potential. *Chaos Solitons Fractals* **2021**, *150*, 111126. [CrossRef]

Article

Bifurcation Theory, Lie Group-Invariant Solutions of Subalgebras and Conservation Laws of a Generalized (2+1)-Dimensional BK Equation Type II in Plasma Physics and Fluid Mechanics

Oke Davies Adeyemo [1], Lijun Zhang [1,2] and Chaudry Masood Khalique [1,*]

[1] Department of Mathematical Sciences, International Institute for Symmetry Analysis and Mathematical Modelling, Mafikeng Campus, North-West University, Private Bag X 2046, Mmabatho 2735, South Africa; adeyemodaviz@gmail.com (O.D.A.); li-jun0608@163.com (L.Z.)
[2] College of Mathematics and Systems Science, Shandong University of Science and Technology, Qingdao 266590, China
[*] Correspondence: masood.khalique@nwu.ac.za

Citation: Adeyemo, O.D.; Zhang, L.; Khalique, C.M. Bifurcation Theory, Lie Group-Invariant Solutions of Subalgebras and Conservation Laws of a Generalized (2+1)-Dimensional BK Equation Type II in Plasma Physics and Fluid Mechanics. *Mathematics* **2022**, *10*, 2391. https://doi.org/10.3390/math10142391

Academic Editor: Nikolai A. Kudryashov

Received: 21 May 2022
Accepted: 29 June 2022
Published: 7 July 2022

Publisher's Note: MDPI stays neutral with regard to jurisdictional claims in published maps and institutional affiliations.

Copyright: © 2022 by the authors. Licensee MDPI, Basel, Switzerland. This article is an open access article distributed under the terms and conditions of the Creative Commons Attribution (CC BY) license (https:// creativecommons.org/licenses/by/ 4.0/).

Abstract: The nonlinear phenomena in numbers are modelled in a wide range of fields such as chemical physics, ocean physics, optical fibres, plasma physics, fluid dynamics, solid-state physics, biological physics and marine engineering. This research article systematically investigates a (2+1)-dimensional generalized Bogoyavlensky–Konopelchenko equation. We achieve a five-dimensional Lie algebra of the equation through Lie group analysis. This, in turn, affords us the opportunity to compute an optimal system of fourteen-dimensional Lie subalgebras related to the underlying equation. As a consequence, the various subalgebras are engaged in performing symmetry reductions of the equation leading to many solvable nonlinear ordinary differential equations. Thus, we secure different types of solitary wave solutions including periodic (Weierstrass and elliptic integral), topological kink and anti-kink, complex, trigonometry and hyperbolic functions. Moreover, we utilize the bifurcation theory of dynamical systems to obtain diverse nontrivial travelling wave solutions consisting of both bounded as well as unbounded solution-types to the equation under consideration. Consequently, we generate solutions that are algebraic, periodic, constant and trigonometric in nature. The various results gained in the study are further analyzed through numerical simulation. Finally, we achieve conservation laws of the equation under study by engaging the standard multiplier method with the inclusion of the homotopy integral formula related to the obtained multipliers. In addition, more conserved currents of the equation are secured through Noether's theorem.

Keywords: a (2+1)-dimensional generalized Bogoyavlensky–Konopelchenko equation; Lie point symmetries; optimal system of Lie subalgebras; bifurcation theory; exact solitary wave solutions; conservation laws

MSC: 35B06; 35L65; 37J15

1. Introduction

Fluid mechanics is a branch of physics concerning the mechanics of fluids such as liquids, gases, and plasmas and the forces on them. Applications of fluid mechanics are found in a wide range of disciplines which include civil, chemical, mechanical as well as biomedical engineering, geophysics, oceanography, astrophysics, biology and meteorology [1–5]. Nonlinear partial differential equations (NLPDE) in the fields of mathematics and physics play numerous important roles in theoretical sciences. They are the most fundamental models essential for studying nonlinear phenomena. Such phenomena occur in oceanography, the aerospace industry, meteorology, nonlinear mechanics, biology, population ecology, plasma physics and fluid mechanics, to mention a few. In [1] the authors studied a generalized advection–diffusion equation which is a nonlinear partial differential equation in fluid mechanics, characterizing the motion of a buoyancy propelled plume in a bent-on absorptive medium. Moreover, in [2], a generalized Korteweg–de Vries–Zakharov–Kuznetsov equation was studied. This equation delineates mixtures of warm adiabatic fluid, hot isothermal as well as cold immobile background species applicable in fluid dynamics. Furthermore, the authors of [3] considered an NLPDE where they explored the important inclined magneto-hydrodynamic flow of an upper-convected Maxwell liquid through a leaky stretched plate. In addition, the heat transfer phenomenon was studied with the heat generation and absorption effect. Plasmas considered as 'the most abundant form of ordinary matter in the universe' have been observed to be associated with stars which extend to the rarefied intracluster medium and possibly the intergalactic regions [4]. For instance, the authors of [4], for various types of the cosmic dusty plasmas, considered an observationally/experimentally-supported (3+1)-dimensional generalized variable-coefficient Kadomtsev–Petviashvili (KP)-Burgers-type equation. This equation could depict the dust–magneto–acoustic, dust–acoustic, magneto–acoustic, positron–acoustic, ion–acoustic, ion, electron–acoustic, quantum–dust–ion–acoustic or dust–ion–acoustic waves in one of the cosmic/laboratory dusty plasmas. The reader can access more examples in [5–12].

Observation has shown that nonlinear partial differential equations appear to model diverse physical systems, such as found in water wave theory, condensed matters, nonlinear mechanics, the aerospace industry, plasma physics, nonlinear optics lattice dynamics and so on [13–19]. In order to really understand these physical phenomena, it is of immense importance to secure results for differential equations (DEs) that control these aforementioned phenomena. Moreover, the research on nonlinear travelling waves (periodic, solitary, kink together with anti-kink), as well as the integrability of diverse significant nonlinear partial differential equations in the likes of the KdV equation [20], sine-Gordon equation [21] and nonlinear Schrödinger equation [22] possess vast practical values. All these involved exact solutions afford us the opportunity of being given information that aids sound understanding of the mechanism involved in the complicated physical phenomena, as well as dynamical procedures that are modelled via these nonlinear evolution equations [23].

However, no general and systematic theory was available to be applied to NLPDEs so that their closed-form solutions can be obtained. Nonetheless, in recent times mathematicians and physicists have evolved effective techniques to achieve viable analytical solutions to NLPDEs, such as inverse scattering transform [13], Bäcklund transformation [24], F-expansion technique [25], extended simplest equation approach [26], Lie symmetry analysis [27–31], the $\left(\frac{G'}{G}\right)$—expansion technique [32], Darboux transformation [33], sine-Gordon equation expansion technique [34] as well as the Kudryashov approach [35], modified extended direct algebraic approach [36,37], the sine-cosine method [11], Hirota's bilinear technique [38], the exp-function expansion technique [12], and the auxiliary ordinary differential equation approach [10]; the list continues.

Furthermore, in recent years, the bifurcation technique [39] among other techniques has been used for obtaining both bounded and unbounded solutions of NLPDE. This technique allows for the extensive study of the dynamical performance of the analytic travelling wave solutions as well as their phase portrait analysis via the engagement of the theory of dynamical systems. In [40] Jiang et al. investigated the dynamical behaviour of points of equilibrium together with the bifurcations of phase portraits involved in the travelling wave results for the CH-γ equation. In addition, Saha [41] also exhibited the existence of smooth alongside non-smooth travelling wave solutions of generalized KP-MEW equations by the exploitation of the bifurcation theory of planar dynamical system. Das et al. [42,43] equally examined the existence together with stability analysis of the dispersive solution of the KP-BBM as well as KP equations with the prevalence of dispersion consequence.

A two-dimensional generalization of the well-recognized Korteweg–de Vries equation yields the Bogoyavlensky–Konopelchenko equation [44]:

$$p_t + \alpha p_{xxx} + \beta p_{xxy} + 6\alpha p p_x + 4\beta p p_y + 4\beta p_x \partial_x^{-1} p_y = 0, \quad (1)$$

with constant coefficients α and β, where $\partial_x^{-1} = \int dx$. Inserting $\partial_x^{-1} p = u$ into Equation (1), one attains the equivalent structure of (1) as [45]:

$$u_{tx} + 6\alpha u_x u_{xx} + 4\beta u_x u_{xy} + 4\beta u_y u_{xx} + \alpha u_{xxxx} + \beta u_{xxxy} = 0. \quad (2)$$

In [45] with $u_y = v_x$ in (2), the authors integrated the result once to obtain a system of NLPDE. Further, they utilized the Lie group theoretic approach to obtain solutions to the system of equations. Added to that is the fact that they engaged the method to secure conservation laws of the equations. Besides, the authors employed a new concept of nonlinear self-adjointness of differential equations in conjunction with formal Lagrangian for constructing nonlocal conservation laws of the system. In [46], Triki et al. investigated the Bogoyavlensky–Konopelchenko Equation (2) and secured some shock wave solutions to the equation. In addition, various applications of (2) were highlighted in [45,46]. This established version describes an interconnection of a long wave propagation directed towards the x-axis together with a Riemann wave propagation directed towards the y-axis [47]. Some authors examined (2) with 4β replaced by 3β and secured the solution of the resultant model. For instance, a Darboux transformation as well as some travelling wave solutions were given in [48] for Equation (2). We note that the replacement earlier mentioned presents Equation (2) as a special case of the KdV model in [49]. In addition to that, a few particular properties of the equation have also been explored.

Chen et al. [50] contemplated the NLPDE called (2+1)-dimensional generalized Bogoyavlensky–Konopelchenko equation stated as:

$$v_{tx} + \alpha(6v_x v_{xx} + v_{xxxx}) + \beta(v_{xxxy} + 3v_x v_{xy} + 3v_{xx} v_y) + \gamma_1 v_{xx} + \gamma_2 v_{xy} + \gamma_3 v_{yy} = 0, \quad (3)$$

which exists in plasma physics and fluid mechanics with α, β, γ_1, γ_2, γ_3, nonzero real valued constants and $v = v(t, x, y)$. The authors got the Lump-type solutions together with lump solutions of (3) with the employment of symbolic computation given in Hirota bilinear form [51] as:

$$(D_t D_x + \alpha D_x^4 + \beta D_x^3 D_y + \sigma D_x D_y + \gamma D_x^2 + \nu D_y^2) f \cdot f = 0,$$

achieved under the transformations:

$$u = 12\alpha \beta^{-1} (\ln f)_{xx}, \quad v = 12\alpha \beta^{-1} (\ln f)_x,$$

with nonzero real constants σ, γ and ν, where f is an analytic function depending on x, y and t, D_x, D_y and D_t are regarded as the bilinear derivative operators given by [38,51], which they used in constructing new closed-form and explicit solutions that include two-wave alongside polynomial solutions for the equation. In addition, the lump-type solution found comprises eleven parameters together with six independent parameters (arbitrary), as well as non-zero conditions. Not only that, lump solutions were achieved by considering a particular class of parameters, the motion track of which is also theoretically and graphically delineated. In the same vein, lower-order lump solution of (3) has been presented [52]. The authors of [53] confirmed in their work the existence of diverse wave structures for (3) delineating nonlinear waves in applied sciences. In this regard, on the basis of Hirota's bilinear structure and diverse test schemes, various kinds of exact solutions, comprising breather-wave, double soliton, rational, cross-kink, mixed-type, as well as interaction solutions to the equation, were formally extracted.

Moreover, in [54], the authors considered a version of (3) in the form:

$$u_{tx} + k_1 u_{xxxx} + k_2 u_{xxxy} + \frac{2k_1 k_3}{k_2} u_x u_{xx} + k_3 u_x u_{xy} + k_3 u_{xx} u_y + \gamma_1 u_{xx} + \gamma_2 u_{xy} + \gamma_3 u_{yy} = 0,$$

with real function $u = u(x,y,t)$ with scaled time variable t as well as scaled space variables x,y and real constants $k_1, k_2, k_3, \gamma_1, \gamma_2, \gamma_3$. They went ahead to examine the equation which applies in fluid mechanics and plasma physics by utilizing the Lie symmetry technique to obtain symmetries of the equation. Besides, the $\left(\frac{G'}{G}\right)$-expansion technique, polynomial expansion as well as power series expansion methods were adopted to achieve some solutions of the equation by the authors.

In this article, we investigate the (2+1)-dimensional generalized Bogoyavlensky–Konopelchenko equation ((2+1)-D genBKe), a version of (3) structured as:

$$\Delta \equiv u_{tx} + \alpha(6u_x u_{xx} + u_{xxxx}) + \beta u_{xxxy} + 3(\rho u_x u_{xy} + \delta u_{xx} u_y) + \gamma u_{xx} + \sigma u_{xy} + \nu u_{yy} = 0, \qquad (4)$$

applicable in plasma physics and fluid mechanics with $\alpha, \beta, \sigma, \gamma, \nu, \rho$ and δ as nonzero real valued constants. In the study, we carry out explicit solutions of the (2+1)-D genBKe (4) to achieve its abundant closed-form and travelling wave solutions. Thus, we catalogue the article in the subsequent format. Section 2, presents the Lie group analysis of Equation (4) where the obtained generators are adopted in computing its optimal system of Lie subalgebras. In addition, each Lie subalgebra is explored to reduce (4) and obtain solutions of the underlying equation. In Section 3, we adopt the bifurcation theory of the dynamical system to secure some nontrivial travelling wave solutions of the under-study equation. Numerical simulations of the secured solutions are conducted for further analysis and discussion in Section 4. Furthermore, Section 5 furnishes the conservation laws of (2+1)-D genBKe to be constructed via the standard multiplier technique with the use of the homotopy formula. In addition, we engage Noether's theorem to gain more conserved vectors of (4) with $\rho = 2\delta$. Shortly after, we present the concluding remarks.

2. Lie Symmetry Analysis

This section first presents the algorithm for the computation of the Lie point symmetries of (2+1)-D genBKe (4) together with its differential generators. Thereafter, we engage them to calculate the optimal system of Lie subalgebras and utilize them to generate exact solutions for (4).

2.1. Lie Point Symmetries

Here in this subsection, we contemplate the one-parameter Lie group of infinitesimal transformations

$$\begin{aligned}
\tilde{t} &\longrightarrow t + \varepsilon \xi^1(t,x,y,u) + O(\varepsilon^2), \\
\tilde{x} &\longrightarrow x + \varepsilon \xi^2(t,x,y,u) + O(\varepsilon^2), \\
\tilde{y} &\longrightarrow y + \varepsilon \xi^3(t,x,y,u) + O(\varepsilon^2), \\
\tilde{u} &\longrightarrow u + \varepsilon \eta(t,x,y,u) + O(\varepsilon^2),
\end{aligned}$$

with ε standing for the parameter of the group alongside $\xi^1, \xi^2, \xi^3, \eta$ serving as the infinitesimals of the transformations depending on t, x, y, and u. Thus utilizing ε (one-parameter), Lie group of infinitesimal transformation in compliance with invariant conditions [55,56], solution space (t,x,y,u) of (2+1)-D genBKe (4) stays invariant and can also transform into another space $(\tilde{t}, \tilde{x}, \tilde{y}, \tilde{u})$.

In accordance with the technique for deciding the infinitesimal generators of nonlinear differential equations (NLDE), we shall secure the infinitesimal generator of (4). Symmetry group of (2+1)-D genBKe (4) will be found by exploring vector field:

$$\mathcal{X} = \xi^1(t,x,y,u)\frac{\partial}{\partial t} + \xi^2(t,x,y,u)\frac{\partial}{\partial x} + \xi^3(t,x,y,u)\frac{\partial}{\partial y} + \eta(t,x,y,u)\frac{\partial}{\partial u}, \quad (5)$$

where $\xi^i, i = 1, 2, 3$ such that ξ's and η are functions depending on t, x, y alongside u. We recall that (5) is a symmetry of (2+1)-D genBKe (4) if invariance condition,

$$pr^{(4)}\mathcal{X}\Delta|_{\Delta=0} = 0, \quad (6)$$

holds. Here $pr^{(4)}\mathcal{X}$ denotes the fourth prolongation of $(\mathcal{X})$ [29] defined by:

$$pr^{(4)}\mathcal{X} = \mathcal{X} + \zeta^t\partial_{u_t} + \zeta^x\partial_{u_x} + \zeta^y\partial_{u_y} + \zeta^{tx}\partial_{u_{tx}} + \zeta^{xx}\partial_{u_{xx}} + \zeta^{xy}\partial_{u_{xy}} + \zeta^{yy}\partial_{u_{yy}}$$
$$+ \zeta^{xxxx}\partial_{u_{xxxx}} + \zeta^{xxxy}\partial_{u_{xxxy}},$$

with the $\zeta^t, \zeta^x, \zeta^y, \zeta^{tx}, \zeta^{xx}, \zeta^{xy}, \zeta^{yy}, \zeta^{xxxx}$ and ζ^{xxxy}, given as:

$$\zeta^t = D_t(\eta) - u_t D_t(\xi^1) - u_x D_t(\xi^2) - u_y D_t(\xi^3),$$
$$\zeta^x = D_x(\eta) - u_t D_x(\xi^1) - u_x D_x(\xi^2) - u_y D_x(\xi^3),$$
$$\zeta^y = D_y(\eta) - u_t D_y(\xi^1) - u_x D_y(\xi^2) - u_y D_y(\xi^3),$$
$$\zeta^{tx} = D_x(\zeta^t) - u_{tt} D_x(\xi^1) - u_{tx} D_x(\xi^2) - u_{ty} D_x(\xi^3),$$
$$\zeta^{xx} = D_x(\zeta^x) - u_{tx} D_x(\xi^1) - u_{xx} D_x(\xi^2) - u_{xy} D_x(\xi^3),$$
$$\zeta^{xy} = D_x(\zeta^y) - u_{ty} D_x(\xi^1) - u_{yx} D_x(\xi^2) - u_{yy} D_x(\xi^3),$$
$$\zeta^{yy} = D_y(\zeta^y) - u_{ty} D_y(\xi^1) - u_{xy} D_y(\xi^2) - u_{yy} D_y(\xi^3),$$
$$\zeta^{xxxx} = D_x(\zeta^{xxx}) - u_{xxxt} D_x(\xi^1) - u_{xxxx} D_x(\xi^2) - u_{xxxy} D_x(\xi^3),$$
$$\zeta^{xxxy} = D_x(\zeta^{xxy}) - u_{xxyt} D_x(\xi^1) - u_{xxxy} D_x(\xi^2) - u_{xxyy} D_x(\xi^3), \quad (7)$$

and the total derivatives D_t, D_x as well as D_y defined as:

$$D_t = \partial_t + u_t \partial_u + u_{tt} \partial_{u_t} + u_{tx} \partial_{u_x} + \cdots,$$
$$D_x = \partial_x + u_x \partial_u + u_{xx} \partial_{u_x} + u_{tx} \partial_{u_t} + \cdots,$$
$$D_y = \partial_y + u_y \partial_u + u_{yy} \partial_{u_y} + u_{yt} \partial_{u_t} + \cdots.$$

Writing out the expanded form of determining Equation (6) and splitting it over the various derivatives of u, we get twenty-two overdetermined systems of linear partial differential equations:

$$\xi_u^2 = 0, \; \xi_u^3 = 0, \; \xi_u^1 = 0, \; \eta_{uu} = 0, \; \xi_y^1 = 0, \; \xi_x^1 = 0, \; \xi_x^3 = 0, \; \eta_{xu} = 0,$$
$$\eta_{yu} - \xi_{xy}^2 = 0, \; \eta_{yu} - 3\xi_{xy}^2 = 0, \; \eta_u + \xi_x^2 = 0, \; \xi_y^3 - 3\xi_x^2 = 0,$$
$$\eta_u + \xi_x^2 = 0, \; \alpha\xi_x^2 + \beta\xi_y^2 - \alpha\xi_y^3 = 0, \; 2\alpha\eta_u - \delta\xi_y^2 - \rho\xi_y^2 + 2\alpha\xi_y^3 = 0, \; \xi_{xx}^2 = 0,$$
$$\eta_{tu} + 6\alpha\eta_{xx} + 3\rho\eta_{xy} + \sigma\eta_{yu} - \xi_{tx}^2 - \sigma\xi_{xy}^2 - \nu\xi_{yy}^2 + 4\alpha\eta_{xxxu} + 3\beta\eta_{xxyu} = 0,$$
$$6\alpha\eta_x + 3\delta\eta_y - \xi_t^2 + \gamma\xi_x^2 - \sigma\xi_y^2 + \gamma\xi_y^3 + 6\alpha\eta_{xxu} + 3\beta\eta_{xyu} = 0,$$
$$2\xi_x^2 - \xi_t^1 + \xi_y^3 = 0, \; 3\delta\eta_{xx} + 2\nu\eta_{yu} - \nu\xi_{yy}^3 + \beta\eta_{xxxu} = 0,$$
$$\eta_{tx} + \gamma\eta_{xx} + \sigma\eta_{xy} + \nu\eta_{yy} + \alpha\eta_{xxxx} + \beta\eta_{xxxy} = 0,$$
$$3\rho\eta_x + 2\sigma\xi_x^2 - 2\nu\xi_y^2 - \xi_t^3 + 3\beta\eta_{xxu} = 0.$$

Solving the system of linear PDEs via symbolic software MathLie, one procures ξ^1, ξ^2, ξ^3 and η given as:

$$\xi^1 = c_1, \quad \xi^2 = f_1(t), \quad \xi^3 = c_2 + c_3 t, \quad \eta = \frac{1}{3\delta\rho}\{\delta c_3 x - 2\alpha c_3 y + 3\delta\rho f_2(t) + \rho y f_1'(t)\}.$$

If we define arbitrary functions $f_1(t)$ and $f_2(t)$ as $f_1(t) = c_4$ and $f_2(t) = c_5$, where c_4 and c_5 are arbitrary constants, thus with the aid of (5), the solution purveys vectors:

$$\mathcal{X}_1 = \frac{\partial}{\partial x}, \quad \mathcal{X}_2 = \frac{\partial}{\partial y}, \quad \mathcal{X}_3 = \frac{\partial}{\partial t}, \quad \mathcal{X}_4 = \frac{\partial}{\partial u}, \quad \mathcal{X}_5 = t\frac{\partial}{\partial y} + \left(\frac{x}{3\rho} - \frac{2\alpha}{3\delta\rho}y\right)\frac{\partial}{\partial u}. \tag{8}$$

Theorem 1. *(2+1)-D genBK Equation (4) admits a five dimensional Lie algebra L_5 spanned by the vectors $\mathcal{X}_1, \ldots, \mathcal{X}_5$.*

The associated group transformations for $\mathcal{X}_1, \ldots, \mathcal{X}_5$ are

$$\begin{aligned}
G_1: & \quad (\tilde{t}, \tilde{x}, \tilde{y}, \tilde{u}) \longrightarrow (t, x + \varepsilon_1, y, u), \\
G_2: & \quad (\tilde{t}, \tilde{x}, \tilde{y}, \tilde{u}) \longrightarrow (t, x, y + \varepsilon_2, u), \\
G_3: & \quad (\tilde{t}, \tilde{x}, \tilde{y}, \tilde{u}) \longrightarrow (t + \varepsilon_3, x, y, u), \\
G_4: & \quad (\tilde{t}, \tilde{x}, \tilde{y}, \tilde{u}) \longrightarrow (t, x, y, u + \varepsilon_4), \\
G_5: & \quad (\tilde{t}, \tilde{x}, \tilde{y}, \tilde{u}) \longrightarrow \left(t, x, y + \varepsilon_5 t, u + \frac{\varepsilon_5}{3\rho} - \frac{2\alpha\varepsilon_5}{3\delta\rho}y - \frac{\alpha\varepsilon_5^2}{3\delta\rho}t\right),
\end{aligned}$$

with $\varepsilon_1, \ldots, \varepsilon_5$ representing real numbers. We realize that G_1 portrays the x-translation, G_2 the y-translation and G_3 the t-translation.

Theorem 2. *If $u = f(t, x, y)$ is a solution of the (2+1)-D genBKe (4), then so are the functions presented as:*

$$\begin{aligned}
G_1(\varepsilon_1): & \quad u(t, x, y) = f(t, x - \varepsilon_1, y), \\
G_2(\varepsilon_2): & \quad u(t, x, y) = f(t, x, y - \varepsilon_2), \\
G_3(\varepsilon_3): & \quad u(t, x, y) = f(t - \varepsilon_3, x, y), \\
G_4(\varepsilon_4): & \quad u(t, x, y) = f(t, x, y) + \varepsilon_4, \\
G_5(\varepsilon_5): & \quad u(t, x, y) = f(t, x, y - \varepsilon_5 t) - \frac{\varepsilon_5}{3\rho} + \frac{2\alpha\varepsilon_5}{3\delta\rho}y + \frac{\alpha\varepsilon_5^2}{3\delta\rho}t.
\end{aligned}$$

2.2. Optimal System of One-Dimensional Subalgebras

It is revealed that it is unfeasible to list all possible group-invariant solutions. As a result, the situation necessitates an effective, systematic and efficient means of classifying these solutions. The moment this is achieved, the optimal system of group-invariant solutions is then formed. Ibragimov et al. [57] invoke a robust approach that depends on the commutator table in achieving the one-dimensional subalgebras optimal system. In consequence, we give the commutator table (table of Lie brackets) of (4) associated with (8) in Table 1, that is

Table 1. Lie brackets.

$[\mathcal{X}_i, \mathcal{X}_j]$	$\mathcal{X}_1$	$\mathcal{X}_2$	$\mathcal{X}_3$	$\mathcal{X}_4$	$\mathcal{X}_5$
$\mathcal{X}_1$	0	0	0	0	$\delta \mathcal{X}_4$
$\mathcal{X}_2$	0	0	0	0	$-2\alpha \mathcal{X}_4$
$\mathcal{X}_3$	0	0	0	0	$3\delta\rho \mathcal{X}_2$
$\mathcal{X}_4$	0	0	0	0	0
$\mathcal{X}_5$	$-\delta \mathcal{X}_4$	$2\alpha \mathcal{X}_4$	$-3\delta\rho \mathcal{X}_2$	0	0

We state here that apparently $\{\mathcal{X}_1, \mathcal{X}_2, \mathcal{X}_3, \mathcal{X}_4, \mathcal{X}_5\}$ is closed under the Lie bracket. Besides, we express an arbitrary operator $\mathcal{X} \in L_5$ as:

$$\mathcal{X} = l^1 \mathcal{X}_1 + l^2 \mathcal{X}_2 + l^3 \mathcal{X}_3 + l^4 \mathcal{X}_4 + l^5 \mathcal{X}_5. \quad (9)$$

In a bid to secure the linear transformations related to vector $l = (l^1, l^2, l^3, l^4, l^5)$, we have the generator defined as:

$$E_i = c_{ij}^k l^j \frac{\partial}{\partial l^k}, \ i = 1, 2, 3, 4, 5, \quad (10)$$

with c_{ij}^k given for the relation $[\mathcal{X}_i, \mathcal{X}_j] = c_{ij}^k \mathcal{X}_k$. On taking cognizance of Equation (10) alongside Table 1, generators E_1, E_2, E_3, E_4, E_5 are presented as:

$$E_1 = \delta l^5 \frac{\partial}{\partial l^4}, \ E_2 = -2\alpha l^5 \frac{\partial}{\partial l^4}, \ E_3 = 3\delta \rho l^5 \frac{\partial}{\partial l^2}, \ E_4 = 0,$$

$$E_5 = 2\alpha l^2 \frac{\partial}{\partial l^4} - \delta l^1 \frac{\partial}{\partial l^4} - 3\delta \rho l^3 \frac{\partial}{\partial l^2}.$$

In association with E_1, E_2, E_3, E_4 and E_5, we give the Lie equations possessing parameters a_1, a_2, a_3, a_4 and a_5 having the initial criteria $\tilde{l}|_{a_i=0} = l, i = 1, \ldots 5$, as

$$\frac{d\tilde{l}^1}{da_1} = 0, \ \frac{d\tilde{l}^2}{da_1} = 0, \ \frac{d\tilde{l}^3}{da_1} = 0, \ \frac{d\tilde{l}^4}{da_1} = \delta \tilde{l}^5, \ \frac{d\tilde{l}^5}{da_1} = 0,$$

$$\frac{d\tilde{l}^1}{da_2} = 0, \ \frac{d\tilde{l}^2}{da_2} = 0, \ \frac{d\tilde{l}^3}{da_2} = 0, \ \frac{d\tilde{l}^4}{da_2} = -2\alpha \tilde{l}^5, \ \frac{d\tilde{l}^5}{da_2} = 0,$$

$$\frac{d\tilde{l}^1}{da_3} = 0, \ \frac{d\tilde{l}^2}{da_3} = 3\delta \rho \tilde{l}^5, \ \frac{d\tilde{l}^3}{da_3} = 0, \ \frac{d\tilde{l}^4}{da_3} = 0, \ \frac{d\tilde{l}^5}{da_3} = 0,$$

$$\frac{d\tilde{l}^1}{da_4} = 0, \ \frac{d\tilde{l}^2}{da_4} = 0, \ \frac{d\tilde{l}^3}{da_4} = 0, \ \frac{d\tilde{l}^4}{da_4} = 0, \ \frac{d\tilde{l}^5}{da_4} = 0,$$

$$\frac{d\tilde{l}^1}{da_5} = 0, \ \frac{d\tilde{l}^2}{da_5} = -3\delta \rho \tilde{l}^3, \ \frac{d\tilde{l}^3}{da_5} = 0, \ \frac{d\tilde{l}^4}{da_5} = -\delta \tilde{l}^1 + 2\alpha \tilde{l}^2, \ \frac{d\tilde{l}^5}{da_5} = 0. \quad (11)$$

Consequently, we give the transformations involved in the solution of Equations (11) as

$T_1 : \tilde{l}^1 = l^1, \ \tilde{l}^2 = l^2, \ \tilde{l}^3 = l^3, \ \tilde{l}^4 = l^4 + \delta a_1 l^5, \ \tilde{l}^5 = l^5,$

$T_2 : \tilde{l}^1 = l^1, \ \tilde{l}^2 = l^2, \ \tilde{l}^3 = l^3, \ \tilde{l}^4 = l^4 - 2\alpha a_2 l^5, \ \tilde{l}^5 = l^5,$

$T_3 : \tilde{l}^1 = l^1, \ \tilde{l}^2 = l^2 + 3\delta \rho a_3 l^5, \ \tilde{l}^3 = l^3, \ \tilde{l}^4 = l^4, \ \tilde{l}^5 = l^5,$

$T_4 : \tilde{l}^1 = l^1, \ \tilde{l}^2 = l^2, \ \tilde{l}^3 = l^3, \ \tilde{l}^4 = l^4, \ \tilde{l}^5 = l^5,$

$T_5 : \tilde{l}^1 = l^1, \ \tilde{l}^2 = l^2 - 3\delta \rho a_5 l^3, \ \tilde{l}^3 = l^3, \ \tilde{l}^4 = l^4 - 3\alpha \delta \rho a_5^2 l^3 + 2\alpha a_5 l^2 - \delta a_5 l^1, \ \tilde{l}^5 = l^5.$

Optimal Classification

We observe the fact that the transformations $T_i, i = 1, \ldots, 5$ actually map vector $\mathcal{X} \in L_5$ presented by (9) to vector $\tilde{\mathcal{X}} \in L_5$ expressed via the relation:

$$\tilde{\mathcal{X}} = \tilde{l}^1 \mathcal{X}_1 + \tilde{l}^2 \mathcal{X}_2 + \tilde{l}^3 \mathcal{X}_3 + \tilde{l}^4 \mathcal{X}_4 + \tilde{l}^5 \mathcal{X}_5.$$

The technique involved in the construction of optimal system in this process demands the simplification of general vector structured as:

$$l = (l^1, l^2, l^3, l^4, l^5), \quad (12)$$

by engaging transformations T_1, T_2, T_3, T_4, T_5. We are captivated to seek for simplest representative of each class of alike vectors of (12) by inserting these representatives in (9) and so, we gain one-dimensional subalgebras optimal system of (2+1)-D genBKe (4). Thus, we structured the classifications into two different cases.

Case 1. $l^5 \neq 0$

1.1. $l^1 = 0$,

We contemplate transformation T_3 by taking $a_3 = \frac{-l^2}{3\delta\rho l^5}$, we can then make $\tilde{l}^2 = 0$. Thus vector (12) reduces to the structure:

$$l = (0, 0, l^3, l^4, l^5). \tag{13}$$

Moreover, if we take $a_1 = \frac{-l^4}{\delta l^5}$ from T^1 which makes $\tilde{l}^4 = 0$, then we further reduce vector (13) to:

$$l = (0, 0, l^3, 0, l^5). \tag{14}$$

Evidently, since (14) cannot be further reduced, without loss of generality, we assume that $l^3 = 1$ and $l^5 = \pm 1$. Therefore, we have the optimal representative:

$$\mathcal{X}_3 \pm \mathcal{X}_5. \tag{15}$$

Next, we contemplate the case of $l^3 \neq 0$ and first consider the resultant subalgebra when $l^2 \neq 0$.

1.1.1. $l^3 \neq 0$,

1.1.1.1. $l^2 \neq 0$,

By taking $a_2 = \frac{l^4}{2\alpha l^5}$ from transformation T_1, we can make $\tilde{l}^4 = 0$. Now, since $l^1 = 0$ and $l^2 = l^3 = l^5 \neq 0$, then vector (12) becomes:

$$l = (0, l^2, l^3, 0, l^5).$$

If we suppose that $l^2 = 1$ and $l^3 = l^5 = \pm 1$, then we have the representative

$$\mathcal{X}_2 \pm \mathcal{X}_3 \pm \mathcal{X}_5. \tag{16}$$

Remark 1. *We notice here that for the case of $l^2 = 0$, we achieve an optimal representative earlier obtained and consequently contribute no additional subalgebra to the optimal system.*

1.1.2. $l^3 = 0$.

We take, in this case, $a_3 = \frac{-l^2}{3\delta\rho l^5}$ from T_3, so that we make $\tilde{l}^2 = 0$. In addition, by considering $a_5 = \frac{-l^4}{2\alpha l^2 - \delta l^2}$ in T_5, thereby making $\tilde{l}^4 = 0$, we secure vector:

$$l = (0, 0, 0, 0, l^5)$$

and so we have the optimal representative:

$$\mathcal{X}_5. \tag{17}$$

1.1.2.1. $l^4 \neq 0$.

By taking $a_5 = \frac{l^2}{3\delta\rho l^3}$ from T_5, we have the reduced form of vector (12) as

$$l = (0, 0, 0, l^4, l^5),$$

which can not be simplified further and so we gain the representative:

$$\mathcal{X}_4 \pm \mathcal{X}_5. \tag{18}$$

Now, we contemplate some subcases when $l^1 \neq 0$ with a view to obtaining all possible optimal representatives.

1.2. $l^1 \neq 0$,
1.2.1. $l^4 = 0$,
1.2.1.1. $l^3 \neq 0$,

By making $a_3 = \frac{-l^2}{3\delta\rho l^5}$ in transformation T_3 which occasions the possibility of making $\bar{l}^2 = 0$, we have the vector:

$$l = (l^1, 0, l^3, 0, l^5),$$

which we can not further streamline and so we gain the optimal representative:

$$\mathcal{X}_1 \pm \mathcal{X}_3 \pm \mathcal{X}_5. \tag{19}$$

1.2.1.2. $l^3 = 0$.

By taking in transformation T_5, $a_5 = \frac{-l^4}{2\alpha l^2 - \delta l^2}$ and $a_5 = \frac{l^2}{3\delta\rho l^3}$, we have the vector:

$$l = (0, 0, 0, l^4, l^5),$$

which can not be simplified further and so we gain the representative:

$$\mathcal{X}_1 \pm \mathcal{X}_5. \tag{20}$$

Next, we consider the case of $l^4 \neq 0$ and then take into account the resultant subalgebra when $l^3 = 0$.

1.2.2. $l^4 \neq 0$,
1.2.2.1. $l^3 = 0$,

By taking $a_3 = \frac{-l^2}{3\delta\rho l^5}$ in transformation T_3, we make $\bar{l}^2 = 0$ and so we have vector:

$$l = (l^1, 0, 0, l^4, l^5),$$

which gives rise to the optimal representative:

$$\mathcal{X}_1 \pm \mathcal{X}_4 \pm \mathcal{X}_5. \tag{21}$$

We reveal here that remark (1) absolutely applies to the case of $l^4 = 0$ and $l^3 \neq 0$.

Case 2. $l^5 = 0$.

In this second part of the process, we contemplate the structure of vector (12) as:

$$l = (l^1, l^2, l^3, l^4, 0). \tag{22}$$

Finally, we consider the case of $l^4 \neq 0$ and then take into account the optimal representatives when $l^1 = 0$.

2.1. $l^4 \neq 0$,
2.1.1. $l^1 = 0$.

By contemplating the parameter $a_5 = \frac{l^2}{3\delta\rho l^3}$ in transformation T_5, one can definitely make $\bar{l}^2 = 0$ and so, we have the reduced form of vector (22) to be given as:

$$l = (0, 0, l^3, l^4, 0),$$

which consequently yields the optimal representative:

$$\mathcal{X}_3 \pm \mathcal{X}_4. \tag{23}$$

2.1.2. $l^1 \neq 0$.

Conversely, if we consider $l^1 \neq 0$ with $l^3 = 0$, using T_3 where $a_3 = \frac{-l^2}{3\delta\rho l^5}$, occasions vector (22) giving us:

$$l = (l^1, 0, 0, l^4, 0)$$

and so we gain the subalgebra

$$\mathcal{X}_1 \pm \mathcal{X}_4. \tag{24}$$

2.2. $l^4 = 0$.

By taking $l^2 \neq 0$ and also considering the converse ($l^2 = 0$) with the use of T_5 where $a_5 = \frac{l^2}{3\delta\rho l^3}$, we gain the respective subalgebras:

$$\mathcal{X}_1 \pm \mathcal{X}_2 \pm \mathcal{X}_3, \ \mathcal{X}_1 \pm \mathcal{X}_3. \tag{25}$$

2.2.1. $l^3 = 0$,

If we take the parameter $a_5 = \frac{l^2}{3\delta\rho l^3}$ in transformation T_5, that is $\bar{l}^2 = 0$, one gets:

$$\mathcal{X}_1. \tag{26}$$

Finally, if we take $l^1 = 0$ with $l^2 \neq 0$ and in addition contemplate a case of $l^3 \neq 0$ with $l^1 = 0$, we get in the respective situations:

$$\mathcal{X}_2, \ \mathcal{X}_3. \tag{27}$$

Conclusively, by gathering the operators secured (that is, (15)–(21), (23)–(25) and (27)), we arrive at a theorem, which is:

Theorem 3. *The subsequent operators provide an optimal system of one-dimensional subalgebras of the Lie algebra which is spanned by vectors $\mathcal{X}_1, \mathcal{X}_2, \mathcal{X}_3, \mathcal{X}_4, \mathcal{X}_5$ of (2+1)-D genBKe (4):*

$\mathcal{X}_1, \mathcal{X}_2, \mathcal{X}_3, \mathcal{X}_5, \mathcal{X}_3 \pm \mathcal{X}_5, \mathcal{X}_4 \pm \mathcal{X}_5, \mathcal{X}_1 \pm \mathcal{X}_5, \mathcal{X}_3 \pm \mathcal{X}_4, \mathcal{X}_1 \pm \mathcal{X}_3, \mathcal{X}_1 \pm \mathcal{X}_4, \mathcal{X}_2 \pm \mathcal{X}_3 \pm \mathcal{X}_5, \mathcal{X}_1 \pm \mathcal{X}_3 \pm \mathcal{X}_5, \mathcal{X}_1 \pm \mathcal{X}_4 \pm \mathcal{X}_5, \mathcal{X}_1 \pm \mathcal{X}_2 \pm \mathcal{X}_3.$

2.3. Group-Invariants and Some Exact Solutions

This subsection presents group-invariant solutions of (2+1)-D genBKe (4) by exploring results presented in Theorem 3. Thus, furnishing some exact solutions of (4). Therefore, we utilize the Lagrangian system given as [27,29]:

$$\frac{dt}{\xi^1(t,x,y,u)} = \frac{dx}{\xi^2(t,x,y,u)} = \frac{dy}{\xi^3(t,x,y,u)} = \frac{du}{\eta(t,x,y,u)},$$

to secure the group-invariant solutions related to the vector fields.

2.3.1. Optimal Subalgebra $\mathcal{X}_1$

The characteristic equation corresponding to optimal subalgebra $\mathcal{X}_1 = \partial/\partial x$ is

$$\frac{dt}{0} = \frac{dx}{1} = \frac{dy}{0} = \frac{du}{0}. \tag{28}$$

On solving system (28), one gains invariants alongside their group-invariant as:

$$T = t, \ Y = y, \text{ where } u(t,x,y) = G(T,Y). \tag{29}$$

Therefore, by using the functions and variables from (29) in (4), we obtain:

$$G_{YY} = 0,$$

which gives a solution in terms of T and Y but by back-substitution, we have

$$u(t,x,y) = f_1(t)y + f_2(t). \tag{30}$$

Arbitrary functions f_1 and f_2 are depending on t in (30), a solution of (4).

2.3.2. Optimal Subalgebra $\mathcal{X}_2$

The group-invariant associated with optimal subalgebra $\mathcal{X}_2 = \partial/\partial y$ is calculated as:

$$u(t,x,y) = G(T,X), \text{ with } T = t, \ X = x. \tag{31}$$

On utilizing the obtained group-invariant, (2+1)-D genBKe (4) is transformed to:

$$G_{TX} + 6\alpha G_X G_{XX} + \alpha G_{XXXX} + \gamma G_{XX} = 0. \tag{32}$$

As a consequence, we gain a logarithmic-hyperbolic function solution in this regard as:

$$G(T,X) = 2A_2 \tanh(A_1 T + A_2 X + A_0) + A_2 \ln\left\{\frac{\tanh(A_1 T + A_2 X + A_0) - 1}{\tanh(A_1 T + A_2 X + A_0) + 1}\right\}$$
$$+ \frac{4}{3}A_2^2 X - \frac{\gamma}{6\alpha}X - \frac{A_1}{6\alpha A_2}X + \int f(T)dT,$$

where A_0, A_1 as well as A_2 are arbitrary constants. Therefore, on retrograding to the basic variables, one achieves a solution of (2+1)-D genBKe (4) in this case as:

$$u(t,x,y) = 2A_2 \tanh(A_1 t + A_2 x + A_0) + A_2 \ln\left\{\frac{\tanh(A_1 t + A_2 x + A_0) - 1}{\tanh(A_1 t + A_2 x + A_0) + 1}\right\}$$
$$+ \frac{4}{3}A_2^2 x - \frac{\gamma}{6\alpha}x - \frac{A_1}{6\alpha A_2}x + \int f(t)dt. \tag{33}$$

Further investigation of PDE (32) reveals that it has four Lie point symmetries,

$$R_1 = \frac{\partial}{\partial T} + F_1(T)\frac{\partial}{\partial G}, \ R_1 = \frac{\partial}{\partial X} + F_2(T)\frac{\partial}{\partial G}, \ R_3 = T\frac{\partial}{\partial X} + \left(\frac{1}{6\alpha}X + F_3(T)\right)\frac{\partial}{\partial G},$$
$$R_4 = T\frac{\partial}{\partial T} + \frac{1}{3}X\frac{\partial}{\partial X} + \left(F_4(T) - \frac{\gamma}{9\alpha}X - \frac{1}{3}G\right)\frac{\partial}{\partial G}.$$

We contemplate some special cases of the generators obtained. Letting $F_1(T) = 1$, we have solution of R_1 as $G(T,X) = T + \phi(r), r = X$, that further reduces (4) to:

$$\gamma\phi''(r) + 6\alpha\phi'(r)\phi''(r) + \alpha\phi''''(r) = 0,$$

whose result furnishes a trigonometric function solution of (2+1)-D genBKe (4) as:

$$u(t,x,y) = t - \sqrt{\frac{\gamma}{\alpha}} \tan\left[\sqrt{\frac{\gamma}{4\alpha}}(x \pm \sqrt{\alpha}C_0)\right] + C_1. \tag{34}$$

C_0 and C_1 are integration constants. Moreover, taking $F_2(T) = 1$, we have $G(T,X) = X + \phi(r), r = T$, which gives a trivial solution. Besides, for $F_1(T) = F_2(T) = 0$, we consider a linear combination $Q = c_0 R_1 + c_1 R_2$ whose solution is $G(T,X) = \phi(r), r = c_0 X - c_1 T$. Utilizing the gained outcome, we reduce Equation (4) to:

$$\gamma c_0 \phi''(r) - c_1 \phi''(r) + 6\alpha c_0^2 \phi'(r)\phi''(r) + \alpha c_0^3 \phi''''(r) = 0. \tag{35}$$

On solving nonlinear ordinary differential equation (NODE) (35), we secure:

$$u(t,x,y) = C_1 \mp \sqrt{\frac{c_1 - \gamma c_0}{\alpha c_0}} \tanh\left[\frac{1}{2c_0^{3/2}}\sqrt{\frac{c_1 - \gamma c_0}{\alpha}}\left(c_0^{3/2}\sqrt{\alpha}C_0 \mp (c_0 x - c_1 t)\right)\right], \tag{36}$$

which is an hyperbolic solution of (4) with C_0 and C_1, integration constants. In addition, taking $F_3(T) = 0$, we have outcome $G(T,X) = X^2/12\alpha T + \phi(r), r = T$, which gives no solution of interest. Besides, for $F_4(T) = 0$, we have the result $G(T,X) = T^{-1/3}\phi(r) - \gamma X/6\alpha$, $r = XT^{-1/3}$ which eventually transforms (4) to:

$$18\alpha\phi'(r)\phi''(r) + 3\alpha\phi''''(r) - r\phi''(r) - 2\phi'(r) = 0.$$

2.3.3. Optimal Subalgebra $\mathcal{X}_3$

Lie optimal subalgebra $\mathcal{X}_3 = \partial/\partial t$ reduces (2+1)-D genBKe (4) to the PDE

$$\sigma G_{XY} + \gamma G_{XX} + \nu G_{YY} + 6\alpha G_X G_{XX} + 3\rho G_X G_{XY} + 3\delta G_Y G_{XX} + \alpha G_{XXXX} + \beta G_{XXXY} = 0 \tag{37}$$

through the group-invariant alongside its invariants calculated and presented as

$$u(t,x,y) = G(X,Y), \quad \text{whereas} \quad X = x, \ Y = y.$$

Consequently, we secure a solution of (37) with respect to X and Y but by back-substitution, we find a steady-state hyperbolic solution of (4) in this regard as:

$$u(t,x,y) = \left[\left(\Omega_0\rho + \Omega_0\delta + 4\alpha\nu - \delta\sigma - \rho\sigma - 4A_1^2\beta\delta - 4A_1^2\beta\rho\right)\cosh\left(\frac{\Omega_1}{2\nu}\right)\right]^{-1}$$

$$\times \left\{4\Omega_0 A_1\beta\sinh\left(\frac{\Omega_1}{2\nu}\right) - 16A_1^3\beta^2\sinh\left(\frac{\Omega_1}{2\nu}\right) - 4A_1^2 A_2\beta\delta\cosh\left(\frac{\Omega_1}{2\nu}\right)\right.$$

$$- 4A_1^2 A_2\beta\rho\cosh\left(\frac{\Omega_1}{2\nu}\right) + 8A_1\alpha\nu\sinh\left(\frac{\Omega_1}{2\nu}\right) - 4A_1\beta\sigma\sinh\left(\frac{\Omega_1}{2\nu}\right)$$

$$+ \Omega_0 A_2\delta\cosh\left(\frac{\Omega_1}{2\nu}\right) + \Omega_0 A_2\rho\cosh\left(\frac{\Omega_1}{2\nu}\right) + 4A_2\alpha\nu\cosh\left(\frac{\Omega_1}{2\nu}\right)$$

$$\left. - A_2\delta\sigma\cosh\left(\frac{\Omega_1}{2\nu}\right) - A_2\rho\sigma\cosh\left(\frac{\Omega_1}{2\nu}\right)\right\}, \tag{38}$$

where $\Omega_0 = \sqrt{16A_1^4\beta^2 - 16\alpha\nu A_1^2 + 8\sigma\beta A_1^2 - 4\gamma\nu + \sigma^2}$, $\Omega_1 = \Omega_0 A_1 y - 4A_1^3\beta y + 2A_1\nu x - A_1\sigma y + 2A_0\nu$, where A_0 and A_1 are arbitrary constants of solution. On performing the Lie symmetry analysis on (37), we obtain translation symmetries

$$R_1 = \frac{\partial}{\partial X}, \quad R_2 = \frac{\partial}{\partial Y}, \quad R_3 = \frac{\partial}{\partial G}.$$

We contemplate the linear combination of the three generators as $Q = c_0\partial/\partial X + c_1\partial/\partial Y + c_2\partial/\partial G$. Therefore, Q furnishes the solution $G(X,Y) = c_2/c_0 X + \phi(r)$, where $r = Y - c_1/c_0 X$. Engaging the function and its variables, we reduce (4) to:

$$\alpha c_1^4\phi^{(4)}(r) - \beta c_1^3 c_0\phi^{(4)}(r) + 6\alpha c_1^2 c_2 c_0\phi''(r) + \gamma c_1^2 c_0^2\phi''(r) + c_0^4\nu\phi''(r) - 3c_1 c_2 c_0^2\rho\phi''(r)$$
$$- c_1 c_0^3\sigma\phi''(r) - 6\alpha c_1^3 c_0\phi'(r)\phi''(r) + 3c_1^2 c_0^2\delta\phi'(r)\phi''(r) + 3c_1^2 c_0^2\rho\phi'(r)\phi''(r) = 0. \tag{39}$$

On solving the fourth-order NODE (39), we achieve the trigonometric function:

$$u(t,x,y) = \pm\frac{1}{\sqrt{c_0\Delta_0 c_1^2(2\alpha c_1 - c_0(\delta + \rho))}}\left\{-2\Delta_0 i\sqrt{\Delta_1}\tan\left[\frac{\sqrt{\Delta_0}}{2\Delta_1}\left(\alpha c_1^4 A_1\right.\right.\right.$$

$$\left.\left.\left. - \beta c_0 c_1^3 A_1 \mp i(c_0 y - c_1 x)\sqrt{\frac{\Delta_1}{c_0}}\right)\right]\right\} + \frac{c_2}{c_0}x + A_2, \tag{40}$$

where $\Delta_0 = \sigma c_0^2 c_1 - \nu c_0^3 - 6\alpha c_1^2 c_2 + c_0 c_1 (3\rho c_2 - \gamma c_1)$, $\Delta_1 = c_1^3(\alpha c_1 - \beta c_0)$ with constant of integrations A_1 and A_2. We observe that the obtained result presented in (40) is a steady-state complex trigonometric function solution of (4).

2.3.4. Optimal Subalgebra $\mathcal{X}_3 + a\mathcal{X}_5$, $a \in \{-1, 1\}$

The group-invariant related to subalgebra $\mathcal{X}_3 + a\mathcal{X}_5$ is calculated and presented as:

$$u(t,x,y) = G(X,Y) + \frac{2a^2\alpha}{9\delta\rho}t^3 + \frac{a}{3\rho}x - \frac{2a\alpha}{3\delta\rho}y, \text{ where } X = x, \ Y = y - \frac{1}{2}at^2. \quad (41)$$

Invoking the function given in (41) along with the variables, we transform (4) to:

$$aG_{XY} + \sigma G_{XY} + \gamma G_{XX} + \nu G_{YY} - atG_{XY} + 3\rho G_X G_{XY} + 6\alpha G_X G_{XX}$$
$$+ 3\delta G_Y G_{XX} + \alpha G_{XXXX} + \beta G_{XXXY} = 0. \quad (42)$$

On applying the Lie theoretic approach on (42), we achieve three generators:

$$R_1 = \frac{\partial}{\partial X}, \ R_2 = \frac{\partial}{\partial Y}, \ R_3 = \frac{\partial}{\partial G}.$$

Now, the similarity solution of $R_1 = \partial/\partial X$ purveys $G(X,Y) = \phi(r)$, with $r = Y$. Thus using the function reduces (4) to differential equation $\phi''(r) = 0$ whose solution is:

$$\phi(r) = A_0 r + A_1,$$

where A_0 and A_1 are integration constants. On retrograding to the basic variables,

$$u(t,x,y) = \frac{2a^2\alpha}{9\delta\rho}t^3 + \frac{a}{3\rho}x - \frac{2a\alpha}{3\delta\rho}y + A_0\left(y - \frac{1}{2}at^2\right) + A_1. \quad (43)$$

Next, we gain the solution related to generator R_2 as $G(X,Y) = \phi(r)$, with $r = X$. In consequence, we reduce Equation (4) to a fourth-order NODE expressed as:

$$\gamma \phi''(r) + 6\alpha \phi'(r)\phi''(r) + \alpha \phi''''(r) = 0.$$

Thus, on solving the NODE and reverting to the fundamental variables, one obtains:

$$u(t,x,y) = \frac{2a^2\alpha}{9\delta\rho}t^3 + \frac{a}{3\rho}x - \frac{2a\alpha}{3\delta\rho}y - \sqrt{\frac{\gamma}{\alpha}}\tan\left[\sqrt{\frac{\gamma}{4\alpha}}(x \pm \sqrt{\alpha}A_1)\right] + A_2, \quad (44)$$

with A_1 and A_2, integration constants. On contemplating the combination of R_1 and R_2 as $Q = c_0 R_1 + c_1 R_2$. In consequence, Q furnishes the solution $G(X,Y) = \phi(r)$, where $r = Y - c_1/c_0 X$. Imploring the function and its variables transforms (4) to:

$$ac_1 c_0^3 t \phi''(r) - ac_1 c_0^3 \phi''(r) + \alpha c_1^4 \phi^{(4)}(r) - \beta c_1^3 c_0 \phi^{(4)}(r) + \gamma c_1^2 c_0^2 \phi''(r) + c_0^4 \nu \phi''(r)$$
$$- c_1 c_0^3 \sigma \phi''(r) - 6\alpha c_1^3 c_0 \phi'(r)\phi''(r) + 3c_1^2 c_0^2 \delta \phi'(r)\phi''(r) + 3c_1^2 c_0^2 \rho \phi'(r)\phi''(r) = 0. \quad (45)$$

On solving NODE (45), we secure a complex tan-hyperbolic solution of (4) as:

$$u(t,x,y) = \frac{2a^2\alpha}{9\delta\rho}t^3 + \frac{a}{3\rho}x - \frac{2a\alpha}{3\delta\rho}y \pm \frac{2i\Omega_1}{c_1^2(2\alpha c_1 - c_0(\delta + \rho))}\tanh\left\{\frac{\Omega_2}{2c_1^3(\alpha c_1 - \beta c_0)}\right.$$
$$\left. \times \left[\alpha c_1^4 A_1 - \beta c_0 c_1^3 A_1 \mp i\sqrt{c_0(c_1^3(\alpha c_1 - \beta c_0))}\left(y - \frac{a}{2}t^2 - \frac{c_1}{c_0}x\right)\right]\right\} + A_2, \quad (46)$$

where $\Omega_1 = \sqrt{c_1^3(\alpha c_1 - \beta c_0)(vc_0^2 + \gamma c_1^2 + c_0c_1(a(t-1) - \sigma))}$, A_1 together with A_2 constant of integration and $\Omega_2 = \sqrt{c_0(vc_0^2 + \gamma c_1^2 + c_0c_1(a(t-1) - \sigma))}$. Furthermore, we contemplate the combinations of all the symmetries as $Q = c_0R_1 + c_1R_2 + c_2R_3$. Hence, Q produces the solution $G(X, Y) = c_2/c_0 X + \phi(r)$, where $r = Y - c_1/c_0 X$. On utilizing function $G(X, Y)$ as well as its variables, we reduce (4) to NODE

$$ac_1c_0^3 t\phi''(r) - ac_1c_0^3\phi''(r) + \alpha c_1^4\phi^{(4)}(r) - \beta c_1^3 c_0\phi^{(4)}(r) + 6\alpha c_1^2 c_2 c_0\phi''(r) + \gamma c_1^2 c_0^2 \phi''(r)$$
$$+ c_0^4 v \phi''(r) - 3c_1c_2c_0^2\rho\phi''(r) - c_1c_0^3\sigma\phi''(r) - 6\alpha c_1^3 c_0\phi'(r)\phi''(r) + 3c_1^2c_0^2\delta\phi'(r)\phi''(r)$$
$$+ 3c_1^2c_0^2\rho\phi'(r)\phi''(r) = 0. \tag{47}$$

The solution of (47) gives us complex trigonometric function satisfying (4) as:

$$u(t, x, y) = \frac{2a^2\alpha}{9\delta\rho}t^3 + \frac{a}{3\rho}x - \frac{2a\alpha}{3\delta\rho}y + \frac{c_2}{c_0}x \pm \frac{2\Omega_3 i\sqrt{c_1^3(\alpha c_1 - \beta c_0)}}{\sqrt{-c_0\Omega_3 c_1^2(2\alpha c_1 - c_0(\rho + \delta))}}$$
$$\times \tan\left\{\frac{\sqrt{-\Omega_3}}{2c_1^3(\alpha c_1 - \beta c_0)}\left[\beta c_0 c_1^3 A_1 - \alpha c_1^4 A_1 \mp \sqrt{c_0 c_1^3(\alpha c_1 - \beta c_0)}\right.\right.$$
$$\left.\left.\times \left(y - \frac{a}{2}t^2 - \frac{c_1}{c_0}x\right)\right]\right\} + A_2, \tag{48}$$

where $\Omega_3 = vc_0^3 + c_0c_1^2(a(t-1) - \sigma) + 6\alpha c_1^2 c_2 + c_0c_1(\gamma c_1 - 3\rho c_2)$ with A_1 and A_2 representing the integration constants of the solution.

2.3.5. Optimal Subalgebra $\mathcal{X}_2 + a\mathcal{X}_3 + b\mathcal{X}_5$, $a, b \in \{-1, 1\}$

We reduce (4) via $\mathcal{X}_2 + a\mathcal{X}_3 + b\mathcal{X}_5$ to a NLPDE with dependent variables X, Y as:

$$3a\gamma\rho G_{XX} + 3a\sigma\rho G_{XY} + 3av\rho G_{YY} - 3\rho G_{XY} + 9a\rho^2 G_X G_{XY} + 18a\alpha\rho G_X G_{XX}$$
$$+ 9a\delta\rho G_Y G_{XX} + 3a\alpha\rho G_{XXXX} + 3a\beta\rho G_{XXXY} + b = 0, \tag{49}$$

by utilizing the invariants with their group-invariant expressed via the function

$$X = x, \quad Y = \frac{1}{2a}\left(2ay - bt^2 - 2t\right), \text{ where we calculated the group-invariant as}$$
$$u(t, x, y) = G(X, Y) + \frac{2b^2\alpha}{9a^2\delta\rho}t^3 + \frac{b\alpha}{3a^2\delta\rho}t^2 + \left(\frac{b}{3a\rho}x - \frac{2b\alpha}{3a\delta\rho}y\right)t. \tag{50}$$

On applying Lie symmetry algorithm to Equation (49), we achieve three generators

$$R_1 = \frac{\partial}{\partial X}, \quad R_2 = \frac{\partial}{\partial Y}, \quad R_3 = \frac{\partial}{\partial G}.$$

Similarity solution to $R_1 = \partial/\partial X$ yields $G(X, Y) = \phi(r)$, where $r = Y$. Therefore using the function reduces (4) to the linear ordinary differential equation (LODE)

$$3a\rho v \phi''(r) + b = 0.$$

The solution to the LODE is $\phi(r) = -br^2/6av\rho + A_1r + A_2$, where A_1 and A_2 are integration constants. Hence, solution to (2+1)-D genBKe (4) in this regard is:

$$u(t, x, y) = \frac{2b^2\alpha}{9a^2\delta\rho}t^3 + \frac{b\alpha}{3a^2\delta\rho}t^2 + \left(\frac{b}{3a\rho}x - \frac{2b\alpha}{3a\delta\rho}y\right)t - \frac{b}{24a^3v\rho}\left(2ay - bt^2 - 2t\right)^2$$
$$+ \frac{A_1}{2a}\left(2ay - bt^2 - 2t\right) + A_2. \tag{51}$$

In the same vein, generator R_2 furnishes $G(X, Y) = \phi(r), r = X$, so (4) becomes:

$$3a\alpha\rho\phi''''(r) + 3a\gamma\rho\phi''(r) + 18a\alpha\rho\phi'(r)\phi''(r) + b = 0. \tag{52}$$

No solution of (52) can be secured. However, considering a special case of the equation with $b = 0$, one achieves a trigonometric solution of (4) in this regard as

$$u(t, x, y) = \frac{2b^2\alpha}{9a^2\delta\rho}t^3 + \frac{b\alpha}{3a^2\delta\rho}t^2 + \left(\frac{b}{3a\rho}x - \frac{2b\alpha}{3a\delta\rho}y\right)t$$
$$- \sqrt{\frac{\gamma}{\alpha}} \tan\left(\sqrt{\frac{\gamma}{4\alpha}}(x \mp \sqrt{\alpha}A_1)\right) + A_2, \tag{53}$$

which is actually an algebraic-trigonometric solution of (2+1)-D genBKe (4). Further, imploring generators R_1 and R_2, we obtain solution function $G(X, Y) = \phi(r), r = Y - c_1/c_0 X$. On applying the function in Equation (4) changes it to NODE

$$3a\alpha c_1^4 \rho \phi^{(4)}(r) - 3a\beta c_1^3 c_0 \rho \phi^{(4)}(r) + 3a\gamma c_1^2 c_0^2 \rho \phi''(r) + 3ac_0^4 \nu \rho \phi''(r) - 3ac_1 c_0^3 \rho \sigma \phi''(r)$$
$$- 18a\alpha c_1^3 c_0 \rho \phi'(r)\phi''(r) + 9ac_1^2 c_0^2 \delta \rho \phi'(r)\phi''(r) + 9ac_1^2 c_0^2 \rho^2 \phi'(r) \phi''(r) + bc_0^4$$
$$+ 3c_1 c_0^3 \rho \phi''(r) = 0. \tag{54}$$

We let $b = 0$ to gain an elliptic solution of (54) and give it a simple representation:

$$\alpha_0 \phi''(r) + \alpha_1 \phi'(r) \phi''(r) + \alpha_2 \phi^{(4)}(r) = 0 \tag{55}$$

where $\alpha_0 = 3a\gamma c_1^2 c_0^2 \rho + 3ac_0^4 \nu \rho - 3ac_1 c_0^3 \rho \sigma + 3c_1 c_0^3 \rho$, $\alpha_1 = -18a\alpha c_0 c_1^3 \rho + 9ac_0^2 c_1^2 \delta \rho + 9ac_0^2 c_1^2 \rho^2$, $\alpha_2 = 3a\alpha c_1^4 \rho - 3a\beta c_0 c_1^3 \rho$. Integrating (55) twice with $\phi'(r) = \Theta(r)$ gives

$$\Theta'(r)^2 = -\frac{\alpha_1}{3\alpha_2}\Theta(r)^3 - \frac{\alpha_0}{\alpha_2}\Theta(r)^2 - \frac{2A_0}{\alpha_2}\Theta(r) - \frac{2A_1}{\alpha_2}, \tag{56}$$

where A_0 and A_1 are integration constants. We engage the transformation,

$$\Theta(r) = -\frac{12\alpha_2}{\alpha_1}\wp(r) - \frac{\alpha_0}{\alpha_1}. \tag{57}$$

Thus, we reckon Equation (56) as NODE with Weierstrass elliptic function [58,59]

$$\wp'(r)^2 - 4\wp(r)^3 + g_1 \wp(r) + g_2 = 0, \tag{58}$$

with the involved Weierstrass elliptic invariants g_1 and g_2 expressed as:

$$g_1 = \frac{1}{12\alpha_2^2}\left(\alpha_0^2 - 2\alpha_1 A_0\right), \text{ and } g_2 = \frac{1}{216\alpha_2^3}\left\{\alpha_0^3 + 3\alpha_1(\alpha_1 A_1 - \alpha_0 A_0)\right\}. \tag{59}$$

Contemplating (57) alongside (58) and reverting to the basic variables yields:

$$u(t, x, y) = \frac{2b^2\alpha}{9a^2\delta\rho}t^3 + \frac{b\alpha}{3a^2\delta\rho}t^2 + \left(\frac{b}{3a\rho}x - \frac{2b\alpha}{3a\delta\rho}y\right)t - \frac{\alpha_0}{2a\alpha_1}\left(2ay - bt^2 - 2t\right)$$
$$+ \frac{\alpha_0 c_1}{\alpha_1 c_0}x + \frac{12\alpha_2}{\alpha_1}\zeta\left\{\frac{1}{2a}\left(2ay - bt^2 - 2t\right) - \frac{c_1}{c_0}x; \frac{1}{12\alpha_2^2}\left(\alpha_0^2 - 2\alpha_1 A_0\right),\right.$$
$$\left.\frac{1}{216\alpha_2^3}\left\{\alpha_0^3 + 3\alpha_1(\alpha_1 A_1 - \alpha_0 A_0)\right\}\right\}. \tag{60}$$

Next, we consider the combination of obtained symmetries as $Q = c_0 \partial/\partial X + c_1 \partial/\partial Y + c_2 \partial/\partial G$. Consequently, Q gives the function $G(X,Y) = c_2/c_0 X + \phi(r)$, where $r = Y - c_1/c_0 X$. Invoking the function and its variables, we reduce (4) to:

$$3a\alpha c_1^4 \rho \phi^{(4)}(r) - 3a\beta c_1^3 c_0 \rho \phi^{(4)}(r) + 18a\alpha c_1^2 c_2 c_0 \rho \phi''(r) + 3a\gamma c_1^2 c_0^2 \rho \phi''(r) + 3ac_0^4 \nu \rho \phi''(r)$$
$$- 9ac_1 c_2 c_0^2 \rho^2 \phi''(r) - 3ac_1 c_0^3 \rho \sigma \phi''(r) - 18a\alpha c_1^3 c_0 \rho \phi'(r)\phi''(r) + 9ac_1^2 c_0^2 \delta \rho \phi'(r)\phi''(r)$$
$$+ 9ac_1^2 c_0^2 \rho^2 \phi'(r)\phi''(r) + bc_0^4 + 3c_1 c_0^3 \rho \phi'''(r) = 0. \qquad (61)$$

Just as earlier demonstrated, we present simplified structure of (61) with $b = 0$ as:

$$\alpha_5 \phi^{(4)}(r) + 6\alpha_4 \phi'(r)\phi''(r) - \alpha_3 \phi''(r) = 0, \qquad (62)$$

where $\alpha_3 = 9ac_1 c_2 c_0^2 \rho^2 + 3ac_1 c_0^3 \rho \sigma - 18a\alpha c_1^2 c_2 c_0 \rho - 3a\gamma c_1^2 c_0^2 \rho - 3c_1 c_0^3 \rho - 3ac_0^4 \nu \rho$, $\alpha_4 = -3a\alpha c_1^3 c_0 \rho + 3/2 ac_1^2 c_0^2 \delta \rho + 3/2 ac_1^2 c_0^2 \rho^2$, $\alpha_5 = 3a\alpha c_1^4 \rho - 3a\beta c_1^3 c_0 \rho$. On Integrating (62)

$$\alpha_5 \phi'''(r) + 3\alpha_4 \phi'(r)^2 - \alpha_3 \phi'(r) + K_0 = 0, \qquad (63)$$

with integration constant K_0. On engaging the representations expressed as:

$$\phi'(r) = \frac{\alpha_5}{\alpha_4} \Theta(r), \quad \lambda = \frac{\alpha_3}{\alpha_5}, \quad K_1 = \frac{K_0 \alpha_4}{\alpha_5^2}, \qquad (64)$$

Equation (63) then becomes the second order nonlinear differential equation:

$$\Theta''(r) + 3\Theta(r)^2 - \lambda \Theta(r) + K_1 = 0 \qquad (65)$$

Equation (65) multiplied by $\Theta'(r)$ and integrating the outcome furnishes,

$$\Theta'(r)^2 = -(2\Theta(r)^3 - \lambda \Theta(r)^2 + 2K_1 \Theta(r) + 2K_2),$$

with integration constant K_2. Suppose that the algebraic equation $\Theta(r)^3 - \frac{1}{2}\lambda\Theta(r)^2 + K_1 \Theta(r) + K_2 = 0$ possesses roots $\vartheta_1, \vartheta_2, \vartheta_3$ with the property $\vartheta_1 > \vartheta_2 > \vartheta_3$, then

$$\Theta'(r)^2 = -2(\Theta(r) - \vartheta_1)(\Theta(r) - \vartheta_2)(\Theta(r) - \vartheta_3). \qquad (66)$$

Equation (66) possess a highly famous solution expressed with regards to Jacobi elliptic function (cn) [58,60] which we present in the structure,

$$\Theta(r) = \vartheta_2 + (\vartheta_1 - \vartheta_2)\,\mathrm{cn}^2\left(\sqrt{\frac{\vartheta_1 - \vartheta_3}{2}} r \Big| \Delta^2 \right), \quad \text{where } \Delta^2 = \frac{\vartheta_1 - \vartheta_2}{\vartheta_1 - \vartheta_3}. \qquad (67)$$

Reckoning (67) as well as (64) and retrograding to the basic variables gives:

$$u(t,x,y) = \frac{2b^2 \alpha}{9a^2 \delta \rho} t^3 + \frac{b\alpha}{3a^2 \delta \rho} t^2 + \left(\frac{b}{3a\rho} - \frac{2b\alpha}{3a\delta\rho} y\right) t + \frac{\alpha_5}{\alpha_4} \left\{ \frac{r(\vartheta_2 + \vartheta_1(\Delta^2 - 1))}{\Delta^2} \right.$$
$$\left. + \frac{\sqrt{2}(\vartheta_1 - \vartheta_2)\,\mathrm{dn}\left(\sqrt{\frac{\vartheta_1-\vartheta_3}{2}}r\Big|\Delta^2\right) E\left[\mathrm{am}\left(\sqrt{\frac{\vartheta_1-\vartheta_3}{2}}r\Big|\Delta^2\right)\Big|\Delta^2\right]}{\sqrt{\vartheta_1 - \vartheta_3}\Delta^2 \sqrt{\mathrm{dn}\left(\sqrt{\frac{\vartheta_1-\vartheta_3}{2}}r\Big|\Delta^2\right)^2}} \right\} + \frac{c_2}{c_0} x, \qquad (68)$$

with E representing elliptic integral of the second kind while 'am' and 'dn' are respectively amplitude and delta elliptic functions. Besides, we notice that in relation (67) and (68) some limits of Jacobi elliptic functions cn and dn exist which give rise to some other functions such as hyperbolic and trigonometric. For instance, $\lim_{\Delta^2 \to 0} \mathrm{cn}\left(r\big|\Delta^2\right) = \cos(r)$,

$\lim_{\Delta^2 \to 0} \mathrm{dn}\left(r|\Delta^2\right) = 1$, $\lim_{\Delta^2 \to 1} \mathrm{cn}\left(r|\Delta^2\right) = \mathrm{sech}(r)$ and $\lim_{\Delta^2 \to 1} \mathrm{dn}\left(r|\Delta^2\right) = \mathrm{sech}(r)$, whereas $r = 1/2a(2ay - bt^2 - 2t) - c_1/c_0 x$.

2.3.6. Optimal Subalgebra $\mathcal{X}_1 + a\mathcal{X}_3 + b\mathcal{X}_5$, $a, b \in \{-1, 1\}$

Lie optimal subalgebra $\mathcal{X}_1 + a\mathcal{X}_3 + b\mathcal{X}_5$ produces similarity transformation variables,

$$X = \frac{1}{a}(ax - t),\ Y = \frac{1}{2a}\left(2ay - bt^2\right),\ \text{whereas the group-invariant is secured as}$$

$$u(t, x, y) = G(X, Y) + \frac{2b^2 \alpha}{9a^2 \delta \rho} t^3 - \frac{b}{6a^2 \rho} t^2 + \left(\frac{b}{3a\rho} x - \frac{2b\alpha}{3a\delta\rho} y\right) t.$$

Engaging the found similarity variables reduces (2+1)-D genBKe (4) to an NLPDE

$$3a\gamma\rho G_{XX} + 3a\sigma\rho G_{XY} + 3a\nu\rho G_{YY} - 3\rho G_{XX} + 9a\rho^2 G_X G_{XY} + 18a\alpha\rho G_X G_{XX} + 9a\delta\rho G_Y G_{XX} + 3a\alpha\rho G_{XXXX} + 3a\beta\rho G_{XXXY} + b = 0, \quad (69)$$

The Lie theoretic approach used in studying Equation (69) yields its symmetries as:

$$R_1 = \frac{\partial}{\partial X},\ R_2 = \frac{\partial}{\partial Y},\ R_3 = \frac{\partial}{\partial G}.$$

On following the usual process solution to $R_1 = \partial/\partial X$ secures $G(X, Y) = \phi(r)$, with $r = Y$. Subsequently utilizing the function obtained reduces (4) to the LODE,

$$3a\rho\nu\phi''(r) + b = 0. \quad (70)$$

On solving the linear ordinary differential Equation (70), we obtain a solution of (4) as:

$$u(t, x, y) = \frac{A_0}{2a}\left(2ay - bt^2\right) + \frac{2b^2\alpha}{9a^2\delta\rho} t^3 - \frac{b}{6a^2\rho} t^2 + \left(\frac{b}{3a\rho} x - \frac{2b\alpha}{3a\delta\rho} y\right) t$$
$$- \frac{b}{24a^3\nu\rho}\left(2ay - bt^2 - 2t\right)^2 + A_1, \quad (71)$$

with integration constants A_0 and A_1. In addition R_2 gives the solution $G(X, Y) = \phi(r)$, with $r = X$. On engaging the function secured, we reduce (4) to the LODE,

$$3a\alpha\rho\phi''''(r) + 3a\gamma\rho\phi''(r) + 18a\alpha\rho\phi'(r)\phi''(r) - 3\rho\phi''(r) + b = 0.$$

In a bid to secure a solution of (4) in this instance, we let $b = 0$ and, as a consequence:

$$u(t, x, y) = \frac{2\alpha b^2 t^3}{9a^2\delta\rho} - \frac{bt^2}{6a^2\rho} + \frac{bx}{3a\rho} - \frac{2\alpha by}{3a\delta\rho} - \frac{(a\gamma - 1)\sqrt{a\alpha(1 - a\gamma)}}{a\alpha(1 - a\gamma)}$$
$$\times \tanh\left[\frac{1}{2}\sqrt{\frac{1 - a\gamma}{a\alpha}}\left(\frac{ax - t}{a} \pm \sqrt{a\alpha}C_1\right)\right] + C_2, \quad (72)$$

which is an algebraic–hyperbolic solution of (2+1)-D genBKe (4) with integration constants C_1 and C_2. On following the usual procedure, R_1 and R_2 linearly combined yields the solution $G(X, Y) = \phi(r)$, $r = c_0 Y - c_1 X$ and these transform (4) to:

$$3a\alpha c_1^4 \rho\phi^{(4)}(r) - 3a\beta c_0 c_1^3 \rho\phi^{(4)}(r) + 3a\gamma c_1^2 \rho\phi''(r) + 3ac_0^2 \nu\rho\phi''(r) - 3ac_0 c_1\rho\sigma\phi''(r) + b$$
$$- 18a\alpha c_1^3 \rho\phi'(r)\phi''(r) + 9ac_0 c_1^2 \delta\rho\phi'(r)\phi''(r) + 9ac_0 c_1^2 \rho^2 \phi'(r)\phi''(r) - 3c_1^2 \rho\phi''(r) = 0. \quad (73)$$

Now, having observed that no solution of (73) can be secured in its current state, we take a special case $b = 0$ of the equation. We present in an easier way (73) as:

$$\beta_2 \phi^{(4)}(r) - \beta_1 \phi'(r) \phi''(r) - \beta_0 \phi''(r) = 0, \tag{74}$$

where $\beta_0 = 3ac_1c_0\rho\sigma + 3c_1^2\rho - 3a\gamma c_1^2\rho - 3ac_0^2\nu\rho - 9ac_0c_1^2\delta\rho - 9ac_0c_1^2\rho^2$, $\beta_2 = 3a\alpha c_1^4\rho - 3a\beta c_0c_1^3\rho$. We let $\phi'(r) = \Theta(r)$ in (74) and integrating the equation gives

$$2\beta_2 \Theta''(r) - \beta_1 \Theta(r)^2 - 2\beta_0 \Theta(r) = 2C_0, \tag{75}$$

where C_0 is the integration constant. On taking the multiplication of (75) and $\Theta'(r)$ and subsequently integrating the resulting NODE, one then achieves:

$$\Theta'(r)^2 = \frac{\beta_1}{3\beta_2} \Theta(r)^3 + \frac{\beta_0}{\beta_2} \Theta(r)^2 + \frac{2C_0}{\beta_2} \Theta(r) + \frac{2C_1}{\beta_2}, \tag{76}$$

with integration constant C_1. We get a Weierstrass elliptic solution [61] of (4) via:

$$\Theta(r) = W(r) - \frac{\beta_0}{\beta_1}, \tag{77}$$

which is the transformation needed in this regard to reduce (76) to elliptic function,

$$W_\xi^2 = 4W^3 - g_2 W - g_3, \text{ where } \xi = \sqrt{\frac{\beta_1}{12\beta_2}} r. \tag{78}$$

That is, a Weierstrass elliptic function with elliptic invariants g_1 and g_2 secured as:

$$g_1 = \frac{24C_0}{\beta_1} - \frac{12\beta_0^2}{\beta_1^2}, \text{ and } g_2 = \frac{8\beta_0^3}{\beta_1^3} - \frac{24\beta_0 C_0}{\beta_1^2} + \frac{24C_1}{\beta_1}. \tag{79}$$

On reckoning (77), we possess the solution of (76) with regards to $\Theta(r)$ as:

$$\Theta(r) = \wp\left(\sqrt{\frac{\beta_1}{12\beta_2}}(r - r_0); \frac{24C_0}{\beta_1} - \frac{12\beta_0^2}{\beta_1^2}, \frac{8\beta_0^3}{\beta_1^3} - \frac{24C_0\beta_0}{\beta_1^2} + \frac{24C_1}{\beta_1}\right) - \frac{\beta_0}{\beta_1}.$$

On reverting to the basic variables, one achieves the solution of Equation (4) as:

$$u(t,x,y) = \frac{2\alpha b^2 t^3}{9a^2 \delta \rho} - \frac{bt^2}{6a^2 \rho} + \left(\frac{bx}{3a\rho} - \frac{2\alpha by}{3a\delta\rho}\right)t - 2\sqrt{\frac{3\beta_2}{\beta_1}} \zeta \left\{\frac{1}{2}\sqrt{\frac{\beta_1}{3\beta_2}}\right.$$

$$\times \left[\frac{c_0}{2a}(2ay - bt^2) - \frac{c_1}{a}(ax - t)\right] - r_0; \frac{24C_0}{\beta_1} - \frac{12\beta_0^2}{\beta_1^2}, \frac{8\beta_0^3}{\beta_1^3} - \frac{24C_0\beta_0}{\beta_1^2}$$

$$\left. + \frac{24C_1}{\beta_1}\right\} - \frac{\beta_0}{\beta_1}\left[\frac{c_0}{2a}(2ay - bt^2) - \frac{c_1}{a}(ax - t)\right] - r_0, \tag{80}$$

which is a Weierstrass elliptic solution of (4) where r_0 is an arbitrary constant. Next, we contemplate the combination of the three found symmetries as performed earlier, and secure $G(X,Y) = c_2 X + c_0 \phi(r)$, with $r = c_0 Y - c_1 X$ which transform (4) to:

$$3a\alpha c_0 c_1^4 \rho \phi^{(4)}(r) - 3a\beta c_0^2 c_1^3 \rho \phi^{(4)}(r) + 18a\alpha c_0 c_2 c_1^2 \rho \phi''(r) + 3a\gamma c_0 c_1^2 \rho \phi''(r) + b$$
$$- 9ac_0^2 c_2 c_1 \rho^2 \phi''(r) - 3ac_0^2 c_1 \rho\sigma \phi''(r) - 18a\alpha c_1^3 \rho \phi'(r)\phi''(r) + 9ac_0^3 c_1^2 \delta\rho \phi'(r) \phi''(r)$$
$$+ 9ac_0^3 c_1^2 \rho^2 \phi'(r) \phi''(r) - 3c_0 c_1^2 \rho \phi''(r) + 3ac_0^3 \nu \rho \phi''(r) = 0.$$

In order to gain more general solution of (4) in this regard, we let $b = 0$ and so:

$$\beta_3 \phi^{(4)}(r) + 12\beta_4 \phi'(r)\phi''(r) - \beta_5 \phi''(r) = 0, \quad (81)$$

where $\beta_3 = 3a\alpha c_0 c_1^4 \rho - 3a\beta c_0^2 c_1^3 \rho$, $\beta_4 = 3/4ac_0^3 c_1^2 \delta \rho + 3/4ac_0^3 c_1^2 \rho^2 - 3/2a\alpha c_0^2 c_1^3 \rho$, $\beta_5 = 9ac_0^2 c_2 c_1 \rho^2 - 18a\alpha c_0 c_2 c_1^2 \rho - 3a\gamma c_0 c_1^2 \rho + 3ac_0^2 c_1 \rho\sigma + 3c_0 c_1^2 \rho - 3ac_0^3 \nu \rho$. On the integration of Equation (81) and invoking the representation $\phi'(r) = \beta_3/2\beta_4 \, \Theta(r)$, we obtain:

$$\Theta''(r) + 3\Theta(r)^2 - \omega\Theta(r) + A_1 = 0, \quad (82)$$

where $\omega = \beta_5/\beta_3$ with $A_1 = 2\beta_4 A_0/\beta_3^2$, A_0 and A_1 being integration constants. Next, we multiply (82) by $\Theta'(r)$ and integrate the result with regards to r and secure

$$\Theta'(r)^2 + 2\Theta(r)^3 - \omega\Theta(r)^2 + 2A_1\Theta(r) + 2A_2 = 0. \quad (83)$$

Thus, (83) occasions a well notable Jacobi elliptic cosine function solution [61] with cubic polynomial roots $\theta_3 < \theta_2 < \theta_1$ and besides, parameter $0 \leq \Omega_0^2 \leq 1$. In consequence, we recover $u(t, x, y)$, the solution of Equation (4) in this instance as:

$$u(t, x, y) = \frac{2\alpha b^2 t^3}{9a^2 \delta \rho} + \frac{bx}{3a\rho}t - \frac{bt^2}{6a^2 \rho} - \frac{2\alpha by}{3a\delta \rho}t + \frac{c_2}{a}(ax - t) + \theta_2 r$$

$$+ \frac{c_0 \beta_3}{2\beta_4} \left\{ \frac{\sqrt{2}(\theta_1 - \theta_2) \operatorname{sn}\left(\sqrt{\frac{\theta_1 - \theta_3}{2}} r \big| \Omega_0^2\right) \cos^{-1}\left[\operatorname{dn}\left(\sqrt{\frac{\theta_1 - \theta_3}{2}} r \big| \Omega_0^2\right) \big| \Omega_0^2\right]}{\sqrt{\theta_1 - \theta_3}\sqrt{1 - \operatorname{dn}\left(\sqrt{\frac{\theta_1 - \theta_3}{2}} r \big| \Omega_0^2\right)^2}} \right\}, \quad (84)$$

where $\Omega_0^2 = (\theta_1 - \theta_2)/(\theta_1 - \theta_3)$ and $r = c_0/2a(2ay - bt^2) - c_1/a(ax - t)$. Moreover, the Jacobi sine elliptic function sn possesses the property that as $\Omega_0^2 \to 0$, we have $\operatorname{sn}(r) \to \sin(r)$ and as $\Omega_0^2 \to 1$, we also obtain $\operatorname{sn}(r) \to \tanh(r)$.

2.3.7. Optimal Subalgebra $\mathcal{X}_1 + a\mathcal{X}_2 + b\mathcal{X}_3$, $a, b \in \{-1, 1\}$

The Lagrangian system related to $\mathcal{X}_1 + a\mathcal{X}_2 + b\mathcal{X}_3$ solves to give group-invariant

$$u(t, x, y) = G(X, Y), \text{ where } X = x - t/b, \ Y = y - at/b. \quad (85)$$

On using the function alongside other expressions from (85) in (4), we have:

$$b\gamma G_{XX} + b\sigma G_{XY} + b\nu G_{YY} - aG_{XY} - G_{XX} + 3b\rho G_X G_{XY} + 6b\alpha G_X G_{XX}$$
$$+ 3b\delta G_Y G_{XX} + b\alpha G_{XXXX} + b\beta G_{XXXY} = 0. \quad (86)$$

As a consequence, we secure the solution of (86) with respect to X and Y but reverting to the fundamental variables gives a solution of (2+1)-D genBKe (4) as:

$$u(t, x, y) = \frac{-4i(\beta\Omega_0 + \alpha\beta + b(2\alpha\nu - \beta\sigma - 4\beta^2 A_1^2))}{\Omega_0(\delta + \rho) + \Omega_1} \left\{ A_1 \operatorname{sech}\left[\frac{1}{2b^2\nu}\left(a^2 A_1 t\right.\right.\right.$$

$$+ \Omega_0 A_1(at - by) + b^2(A_1(\sigma + 4\beta A_1^2)y - \nu(2A_0 + 2A_1 x)) - bA_1(ay$$

$$\left.\left.\left. + t(a(\sigma + 4\beta A_1^2) - 2\nu))\right)\right]\right\} \left\{ A_2(\Omega_0(\delta + \rho) + a(\delta + \rho) + b(4\alpha\nu - \delta\sigma\right.$$

$$\left. - \rho\sigma - 4\beta A_1^2(\delta + \rho))) + \operatorname{sech}\left[\frac{1}{2b^2\nu}\left(a^2 A_1 t + \Omega_0 A_1(at - by)\right.\right.\right.$$

$$\left.\left.\left. + b^2\left[4A_1 y\left(\frac{1}{4}\sigma + \beta A_1^2\right) - \nu(2A_1 x + i\pi + 2A_0)\right] - 4A_1 b\left[\frac{1}{4}ay\right.\right.\right.$$

$$+ t\left[a\left(\beta A_1^2 + \frac{1}{4}\sigma\right) - \frac{1}{2}\nu\right]\right)\right]\bigg\}^{-1}, \tag{87}$$

where $\Omega_0 = \sqrt{\nu(4b - 4b^2\gamma - 16\alpha b^2 A_1^2) + (a - b\sigma - 4b\beta A_1^2)}$, $\Omega_1 = a(\delta + \rho) + b(4\alpha\nu - \delta\sigma - \rho\sigma - 4\beta(\delta + \rho)A_1^2)$ with constants A_0 and A_1 arbitrary. Function (87) is a complex bright soliton solution of (4). Furthermore, investigation revealed that Equation (86) possesses three Lie point symmetries which are given as

$$R_1 = \frac{\partial}{\partial X}, \quad R_2 = \frac{\partial}{\partial Y}, \quad R_3 = \frac{\partial}{\partial G}.$$

Linearly combining the symmetries furnishes the function $G(X, Y) = c_2 X + c_0 \phi(r)$, with $r = c_0 Y - c_1 X$. Thus, on engaging the function, we further reduce (4) to:

$$b\beta c_0 c_1^3 \phi^{(4)}(r) - ac_0 c_1 \phi''(r) - \alpha bc_1^4 \phi^{(4)}(r) - 6\alpha bc_2 c_1^2 \phi''(r) - b\gamma c_1^2 \phi''(r) - bc_0^2 \nu \phi''(r)$$
$$+ 3bc_0 c_2 c_1 \rho \phi''(r) + bc_0 c_1 \sigma \phi''(r) + 6\alpha bc_0 c_1^3 \phi'(r)\phi''(r) - 3bc_0^2 c_1^2 \delta \phi'(r)\phi''(r)$$
$$- 3bc_0^2 c_1^2 \rho \phi'(r)\phi''(r) + c_1^2 \phi''(r) = 0. \tag{88}$$

Therefore, we present Equation (88) in a lesser structure as:

$$\alpha_1 \phi''(r) - \alpha_2 \phi'(r) \phi''(r) + \alpha_3 \phi^{(4)}(r) = 0, \tag{89}$$

$\alpha_1 = -ac_0 c_1 + c_1^2 - 6\alpha bc_2 c_1^2 - b\gamma c_1^2 - bc_0^2 \nu + 3bc_0 c_2 c_1 \rho + bc_0 c_1 \sigma$, $\alpha_2 = 3bc_0^2 c_1^2 \delta + 3bc_0^2 c_1^2 \rho - 6\alpha bc_0 c_1^3$, $\alpha_3 = b\beta c_0 c_1^3 - \alpha bc_1^4$. We set $\phi'(r) = \Theta(r)$ in (89) and by integrating the resulting NODE repeatedly two times, we secure a first order NODE presented as:

$$\Theta'(r)^2 = \frac{\alpha_2}{3\alpha_3}\Theta(r)^3 - \frac{\alpha_1}{\alpha_3}\Theta(r)^2 - \frac{2C_0}{\alpha_3}\Theta(r) - \frac{2C_1}{\alpha_3},$$

with constants of integration C_0 and C_1. On contemplating the cubic polynomial $\frac{\alpha_2}{3\alpha_3}\Theta(r)^3 - \frac{\alpha_1}{\alpha_3}\Theta(r)^2 - \frac{2C_0}{\alpha_3}\Theta(r) - \frac{2C_1}{\alpha_3} = 0$, whose real roots are $a_2 < a_1 < a_0$, we have

$$\Theta_r^2 = \frac{\alpha_2}{3\alpha_3}(\Theta - a_0)(\Theta - a_1)(\Theta - a_2),$$

with real roots a_0, a_1 as well as a_2 satisfying algebraic relations expressed as:

$$a_0 a_1 + a_0 a_2 + a_1 a_2 = -\frac{2C_0}{\alpha_3}, \quad a_0 a_1 a_2 = -\frac{2C_1}{\alpha_3}, \quad a_0 + a_1 + a_2 = -\frac{\alpha_1}{\alpha_3}.$$

According to [62], we express a primitive solution of (4) via the elliptic function,

$$u(t, x, y) = c_2 x - \frac{c_2}{b}t + c_0\bigg\{\sqrt{\frac{12\alpha_3(a_0 - a_1)^2}{\alpha_2(a_0 - a_2)\Delta_0^8}}\bigg\{\text{EllipticE}\left[\text{sn}\left(\frac{\alpha_2(a_0 - a_2)}{12\alpha_3}(r - r_0),\right.\right.$$
$$\Delta_0^2\bigg), \Delta_0^2\bigg]\bigg\} + \left[a_1 - (a_0 - a_1)\frac{1 - \Delta_0^4}{\Delta_0^4}\right](r - r_0) + C_2\bigg\}, \tag{90}$$

with $r = c_0(y - at/b) - c_1(x - t/b)$, r_0 and C_2 arbitrary constants. Besides, parameter Δ_0^2 and incomplete elliptic integral EllipticE$[m; z]$ are accordingly expressed as:

$$\Delta_0^2 = \frac{a_0 - a_1}{a_0 - a_2} \quad \text{and} \quad \text{EllipticE}[m; z] = \int_0^m \sqrt{\frac{1 - z^2 w^2}{1 - w^2}} dw.$$

3. Travelling Wave Solutions

We examine the travelling wave solutions of the (2+1)-D genBKe (4). Generally speaking, travelling wave solutions of a partial differential equation emanates as special group-invariant solutions wherein the considered group is translational with respect to space of independent variables.

Here in this study, we engage linear combination of the translation operators $\mathcal{X}_1$, $\mathcal{X}_2$ and $\mathcal{X}_3$, namely $\mathcal{X} = \rho\mathcal{X}_1 + \varepsilon\mathcal{X}_2 + \mu\mathcal{X}_3$ with constant values σ and ε. Following the usual Lie symmetry procedure, we utilize $\mathcal{X}$ to reduce (4) to fourth-order NODE,

$$A\psi''(z) - B\psi'(z)\psi''(z) + C\psi''''(z) = 0, \quad (91)$$

via the travelling wave $z = px + qy + rt$ where $p = \varepsilon$, $q = \mu c - \rho$, $r = -\varepsilon c$ and so $A = p(r + \sigma q + \gamma p) + v q^2$, $B = -6p^2(\alpha p + \beta q)$ and $C = p^3(\alpha p + \beta q)$.

Integrating (91) just once supplies a third-order ODE,

$$A\psi' - \frac{1}{2}B\psi'^2 + C\psi''' + C_1 = 0, \quad (92)$$

where C_1 is regarded as an integration constant. Multiplying Equation (92) by ψ'', integrating once as well as simplifying the resulting equation, we have the second-order nonlinear ODE

$$\frac{1}{2}A(\psi')^2 - \frac{1}{6}B(\psi')^3 + \frac{1}{2}C(\psi'')^2 + C_1\psi' + C_2 = 0, \quad (93)$$

where C_2 is an integration constant. Equation (93) can be rewritten as

$$(\psi'')^2 = \frac{B}{3C}(\psi')^3 - \frac{A}{C}(\psi')^2 - \frac{2C_1}{C}\psi' - \frac{2C_2}{C}. \quad (94)$$

Suppose $\Psi = \psi'$, Equation (94) becomes:

$$\Psi'^2 = \frac{B}{3C}\Psi^3 - \frac{A}{C}\Psi^2 - \frac{2C_1}{C}\Psi - \frac{2C_2}{C}. \quad (95)$$

3.1. Bifurcation and Explicit Solutions

Here we use the bifurcation theory method [39,63,64] of dynamical systems to obtain some nontrivial solutions of (95), which is the reduced form of (91).

Suppose from Equation (95) we say:

$$P_3(\Psi) = \frac{B}{3C}\Psi^3 - \frac{A}{C}\Psi^2 - \frac{2C_1}{C}\Psi - \frac{2C_2}{C}. \quad (96)$$

We can deduce from Equation (94) that:

$$\frac{d^2\Psi}{dz^2} = \frac{B}{2C}\Psi^2 - \frac{A}{C}\Psi - \frac{C_1}{C}. \quad (97)$$

Let $\Psi' = w$, then (95) is equivalent to planar dynamical system,

$$\frac{d\Psi}{dz} = w, \quad \frac{dw}{d\Psi} = \frac{B}{2C}\Psi^2 - \frac{A}{C}\Psi - \frac{C_1}{C}, \quad (98)$$

which invariably possesses the first integral $H(\Psi, w)$ calculated as:

$$H(\Psi, w) = \frac{w^2}{2} - \frac{B}{6C}\Psi^3 + \frac{A}{2C}\Psi^2 + \frac{C_1}{C}\Psi = h, \quad (99)$$

where h is the constant of integration and function $H(\Psi, w)$ is Hamiltonian.

It is obvious to see that Hamiltonian $H(\Psi, w) = h = -\frac{C_2}{C}$ corresponds to Equation (96). As a result, we observe that the dynamical system behaviors of ordinary differential

Equation (95) from the orbits of the above system (98) relates to $H(\Psi,w) = -\frac{C_2}{C}$. Apparently, phase orbits given via the vector field relative to system (98) decides all the results that can be gained for (96).

An investigation of bifurcation of the planar dynamical system (98) secures diverse kinds of solutions of (96) contemplated under various coefficient conditions. Thus, the dynamical character and closed-form solutions of ODE (96) are generated.

We first study the equilibrium points of the system (98) to attain the dynamical action of the system. Evidently, the roots of $P_3'(\Psi) = 0$ are regarded as the abscissas of the points of equilibrium included in the system (98). Moreover, we suppose that Ψ_e is one of the roots of $P_3'(\Psi) = 0$, meaning that, $(\Psi_e, 0)$ stands as an equilibrium point of system (98). By the reason of theory of planar dynamical systems [63,64], the matrix needs to be studied.

$$Df(\Psi_0, 0) = \begin{bmatrix} 0 & 1 \\ P_3''(\Psi_e) & 0 \end{bmatrix}$$

where

$$P_3''(\Psi_e) = \frac{2B}{C}\Psi - \frac{2A}{C}$$

of the linearized system of (98) exists at a point $(\Psi_e, 0)$. The point of equilibrium $(\Psi, 0)$ is a center which has a punctured neighborhood wherein any solution procured is taken as a periodic orbit; if $det(Df(\Psi_e, 0)) = -P_3''(\Psi_e) > 0$. It is said to be a saddle point if $det(Df(\Psi_e, 0)) = -P_3''(\Psi_e) < 0$. Nevertheless, we call it a cusp point if $det(Df(\Psi_e, 0)) = -P_3''(\Psi_e) = 0$. It is needed to equally investigate boundary curves related to the centers as well as the orbits that serve as a connector between the saddle points or cusp points which the Hamiltonian $H(\Psi, w) = h$ determines in order to obtain the phase portraits other than the equilibriums. Evidently, system (98) possesses neither equilibrium point nor a cusp when $\frac{A^2+2BC_1}{C^2} \leq 0$, hence system (98) has no trivial nontrivial bounded solutions. Nonetheless, (98) has two equilibrium points when $\frac{A^2+2BC_1}{C^2} > 0$. Let

$$\Psi_e^\pm = \frac{1}{B}\left(A \pm \sqrt{A^2 + 2BC_1}\right)$$

$$H(\Psi_e^\pm, 0) = h_\pm = \frac{1}{3B^2C}\left((A^2 + 2BC_1)[A \pm \sqrt{A^2 + 2BC_1}] + ABC_1\right),$$

then $(\Psi_e^+, 0)$ is a saddle point, $(\Psi_e^-, 0)$ is also a center and $h_+ > h_-$.

When we have $h_+ > h > h_-$, Hamiltonian $H(\Psi, w) = h$ defines a family of periodic orbits present around the center given as $(u_e^-, 0)$ which is confined by the boundary curves defined by function $H(\Psi, w) = h_+$. Notwithstanding, $H(\Psi, w) = h_+$ explains a homoclinic orbit that passes through the saddle point $(\Psi_e^+, 0)$.

We now consider some cases of (96) and obtain the following solutions.

Case (1.) Equation (96) possesses a bounded solution which approaches Ψ_e^+ as z goes to infinity:

$$\Psi(z) = \frac{1}{B}\left\{(A + \sqrt{A^2 + 2BC_1}) - 3\sqrt{A^2 + 2BC_1}\,\text{sech}^2\left[\frac{1}{2}\sqrt[4]{\left(\frac{A^2 + 2BC_1}{C^2}\right)}(z - z_0)\right]\right\}, \quad (100)$$

where z_0 is an arbitrary constant. Integrating (100) and returning to the original variables secures a nontrivial solitary wave solution of (4) in this regard as:

$$u(t, x, y) = \frac{1}{B}\left\{\left(\sqrt{A^2 + 2BC_1} + A\right)z - z_0 - \frac{6\sqrt{A^2 + 2BC_1}}{\sqrt[4]{\frac{A^2+2BC_1}{C^2}}}\right.$$

$$\left. \times \tanh\left(\frac{1}{2}\sqrt[4]{\frac{A^2 + 2BC_1}{C^2}}z - z_0\right)\right\}, \quad (101)$$

with $z = px + qy + rt$ and z_0 arbitrary constant. We also have a constant solution

$$\Psi(z) = \frac{1}{B}\left(A + \sqrt{A^2 + 2BC_1}\right)$$

as well as an unbounded solution:

$$\Psi(z) = \frac{1}{B}\left\{(A + \sqrt{A^2 + 2BC_1}) + 3\sqrt{A^2 + 2BC_1}\,\text{csch}^2\left[\frac{1}{2}\sqrt[4]{\left(\frac{A^2 + 2BC_1}{C^2}\right)}(z - z_0)\right]\right\}. \quad (102)$$

Integrating (102) and retrograding to the original variables, we secure an unbounded solution of (2+1)-dimensional gBK (4) as:

$$u(t, x, y) = \frac{1}{B}\left\{\left(\sqrt{A^2 + 2BC_1} + A\right)z - z_0 - \frac{6\sqrt{A^2 + 2BC_1}}{\sqrt[4]{\frac{A^2 + 2BC_1}{C^2}}}\right.$$

$$\left. \times \coth\left(\frac{1}{2}\sqrt[4]{\frac{A^2 + 2BC_1}{C^2}}z - z_0\right)\right\}, \quad (103)$$

where $z = px + qy + rt$ and z_0 is an arbitrary constant.

Case (2.) Since $\frac{B}{3C} > 0$, then for any arbitrary real constant

$$\Phi \in \left(\frac{\left(A - 2\sqrt{A^2+2BC_1}\right)}{B}, \frac{\left(A - \sqrt{A^2+2BC_1}\right)}{B}\right),$$

$$\Psi(z) = \Phi - \frac{1}{2}\left(3\Phi - \frac{3A}{B} + \sqrt{-3\Phi^2 + \frac{6A}{B}\Phi + \frac{9A^2}{B^2} + \frac{24C_1}{B}}\right)\text{sn}^2(\Omega_+(z - z_0), k_+), \quad (104)$$

where

$$\Omega_+ = \frac{\sqrt{2}}{4}\sqrt{-\frac{B}{C}\Phi + \frac{A}{C} + \frac{B}{3C}\sqrt{-3\Phi^2 + \frac{6A}{B}\Phi + \frac{9A^2}{B^2} + \frac{24C_1}{B}}} \quad \text{and}$$

$$k_+ = \frac{2\sqrt{3\Phi^2 - \frac{6A}{B}\Phi - \frac{6C_1}{B}}}{-3\Phi + \frac{3A}{B} + \sqrt{-3\Phi^2 + \frac{6A}{B}\Phi + \frac{9A^2}{B^2} + \frac{24C_1}{B}}}.$$

The integration of (104) secures a bounded nontrivial solution of (4) as:

$$u(t, x, y) = kz + P_0 \left\{\sqrt{6(3A - BP_1)}\left(Q + \frac{E[\text{am}(R)|R_1]\left[\text{sn}^2(S|S_1) - S_2\right]}{\text{dn}(Q_1|Q_2)\sqrt{1 - \frac{2\sqrt{3}Q_0\,\text{sn}^2(R)}{P_1 - \frac{3A}{B}}}}\right)\right\}$$

$$P_0 = \frac{1}{B\sqrt{\frac{3A - 3Bk + \sqrt{3B}\sqrt{\frac{3A^2 + 2BkA - B^2k^2 + 8BC_1}{B^2}}}{C}}}, \quad P_1 = 3k + \sqrt{\frac{9A^2 + 6BkA - 3B^2k^2 + 24BC_1}{B^2}}$$

$$Q = \frac{z\sqrt{\frac{3A + B\left(\sqrt{\frac{9A^2 + 6BkA - 3B^2k^2 + 24BC_1}{B^2}} - 3k\right)}{C}}\left(-\frac{3A}{B} - 3k + \sqrt{\frac{9A^2 + 6BkA - 3B^2k^2 + 24BC_1}{B^2}}\right)}{12\sqrt{2}\sqrt{\frac{k(Bk - 2A) - 2C_1}{B}}},$$

$$R = \dfrac{z\sqrt{\dfrac{3A+B\left(\sqrt{\dfrac{9A^2+6BkA-3B^2k^2+24BC_1}{B^2}}-3k\right)}{C}}}{2\sqrt{6}}\Bigg|\dfrac{2\sqrt{3}Q_0}{-\dfrac{3A}{B}-3k+\sqrt{\dfrac{9A^2+6BkA-3B^2k^2+24BC_1}{B^2}}},$$

$$S = \dfrac{z\sqrt{\dfrac{3A+B\left(\sqrt{\dfrac{9A^2+6BkA-3B^2k^2+24BC_1}{B^2}}-3k\right)}{C}}}{2\sqrt{6}}, \quad R_1 = \dfrac{2\sqrt{3}\sqrt{\dfrac{k(Bk-2A)-2C_1}{B}}}{-\dfrac{3A}{B}-3k+\sqrt{\dfrac{9A^2+6BkA-3B^2k^2+24BC_1}{B^2}}},$$

$$S_1 = \dfrac{2\sqrt{3}\sqrt{\dfrac{k(Bk-2A)-2C_1}{B}}}{-\dfrac{3A}{B}-3k+\sqrt{\dfrac{9A^2+6BkA-3B^2k^2+24BC_1}{B^2}}}, \quad Q_1 = \dfrac{z\sqrt{\dfrac{3A+B\left(\sqrt{\dfrac{9A^2+6BkA-3B^2k^2+24BC_1}{B^2}}-3k\right)}{C}}}{2\sqrt{6}},$$

$$S_2 = \dfrac{-\dfrac{3A}{B}-3k+\sqrt{\dfrac{9A^2+6BkA-3B^2k^2+24BC_1}{B^2}}}{2\sqrt{3}\sqrt{\dfrac{k(Bk-2A)-2C_1}{B}}}, \quad Q_2 = \dfrac{2\sqrt{3}\sqrt{\dfrac{k(Bk-2A)-2C_1}{B}}}{-\dfrac{3A}{B}-3k+\sqrt{\dfrac{9A^2+6BkA-3B^2k^2+24BC_1}{B^2}}},$$

where $E[\text{am}(R|R_1)]$ is an elliptic integral of the second kind $\text{sn}(S|S_1)$, $\text{am}(R|R_1)$ and $\text{dn}(Q_1|Q_2)$ denotes accordingly elliptic sine, amplitude as well as delta functions. In addition to that, variable $z = px + qy + rt$ with arbitrary constant z_0 is taken as zero.

Case (3.) Equation (96) possesses no nontrivial bounded solutions. However, at the instance when $\dfrac{-2C_2}{C} = 2h_-$, we have an unbounded solution that is expressed as

$$\Psi(z) = \dfrac{1}{B}\left\{(A - \sqrt{A^2 + 2BC_1}) + 3\sqrt{A^2 + 2BC_1}\,\sec^2\left[\dfrac{1}{2}\sqrt[4]{\left(\dfrac{A^2 + 2BC_1}{C^2}\right)}(z - z_0)\right]\right\} \quad (105)$$

and a constant solution also given in this case as:

$$\Psi(z) = \dfrac{1}{B}\left(A - \sqrt{A^2 + 2BC_1}\right).$$

Integrating (105) with regards to variable $z - z_0$, one achieves:

$$u(t, x, y) = \dfrac{1}{B}\left\{V_0 \tan\left(\dfrac{1}{2}(z - z_0)\sqrt[4]{\dfrac{A^2 + 2BC_1}{C^2}}\right) + (z - z_0)\left(A - \sqrt{A^2 + 2BC_1}\right)\right\}, \quad (106)$$

where we have $V_0 = \dfrac{6\sqrt{A^2+2BC_1}}{\sqrt[4]{\dfrac{A^2+2BC_1}{C^2}}}$, $z = px + qy + rt$ and z_0 as an arbitrary constant.

We note from the dynamical system earlier stated that we can deduce the fact that:

$$\dfrac{dw}{d\Psi} = B_0 \Psi^2 + B_1 \Psi + B_2, \quad (107)$$

where $B_0 = \dfrac{B}{2C}$, $B_1 = -\dfrac{A}{C}$ and $B_2 = -\dfrac{C_1}{C}$. In clear terms, we can suggest that phase orbits given by the vector fields of dynamical system (98) determined the collection of all the solutions of (97). Thus, we state here that bounded solutions of (97) relates to the bounded phase orbits that system (98) has which will have to be investigated. Along the orbit connected with $H(\Psi, w) = h$, we have:

$$\left(\dfrac{d\Psi}{dz}\right)^2 = \dfrac{2B_0}{3}\Psi^3 + B_1 \Psi^2 + 2B_2 \Psi + 2h. \quad (108)$$

As a consequence, the general formula associated with the solutions of (97) can as well be given viz;

$$\int_0^\Psi \frac{d\Psi}{\sqrt{(2B_0\Psi^3/3) + B_1\Psi^2 + 2B_2\Psi + 2h}} = \pm \int_{z_0}^z dz. \tag{109}$$

Nonetheless, it may be laborious to know the properties as well as the shapes of (109) that are actually decided by the parameters B_0, B_1, B_2 and h. Obviously, the abscissas possessed by equilibrium points of dynamical system (98) are zeros of $B_0\Psi^2 + B_1\Psi + B_2 = 0$. Clearly, the system (98) has no bounded orbits when $B_1^2 - 4B_0B_2 < 0$. We suppose that $B_1^2 - 4B_0B_2 > 0$ in order for us to examine the bounded orbits owned by system (98). We designate $\Psi_\pm = (-B_1 \pm \sqrt{B_1^2 - 4B_0B_2})/2B_0$, and as such we have $E_+(\Psi_+, 0)$ alongside $E_-(\Psi_-, 0)$ which represent two equilibrium points of system (98). As expounded by the theory of planar dynamical system, we realize that E_- is a center and also E_+ is a saddle point. We indicate here that $h_\pm = H(\Psi_\pm, 0)$, and, by doing a careful computation, we achieve:

$$h_\pm = \frac{1}{12B_0^2}\left\{\left(B_1^2 - 4B_0B_2\right)\left[-B_1 \pm \sqrt{B_1^2 - 4B_0B_2}\right] + 2B_0B_1B_2\right\}. \tag{110}$$

Evidently, $h_- < h < h_+$ and we have it that $H(\Psi, w) = h_+$ correlates to homoclinic orbits. Moreover, $H(\Psi, w) = h_-$ relates to the center E_- and then $H(\Psi, w) = h$, where $h_+ < h < h_-$ is related to a class of closed orbits that surround center E_- which are encompassed by a homoclinic orbit. Meaning that (109) defines bounded solutions if and only if the condition given as $h_+ \le h < h_-$ holds. Precisely, (109) explains a family of periodic solutions whenever $h_+ < h < h_-$.

When $h = h_+$, Equation (109) explains a bounded solution that tends towards Ψ_+ as z goes to infinity. In fact,

$$\frac{2B_0}{3}\Psi^3 + B_1\Psi^2 + 2B_2\Psi + 2h_+ = \frac{2B_0}{3}(\Psi - \Psi_+)^2(\Psi - \Psi_0),$$

with $\Psi_0 = -(B_1 + 2\sqrt{B_1^2 - 4B_0B_2})/2B_0$. In consequence (109) can be reduced to:

$$\int_{\Psi_0}^\Psi \frac{d\Psi}{(\Psi - \Psi_+)\sqrt{B_0(\Psi - \Psi_0)}} = \sqrt{\frac{2}{3}}(z - z_0),$$

from which we can get the exact solution in the structure of a secant hyperbolic

$$\Psi = \Psi_+ - (\Psi_+ - \Psi_0)\operatorname{sech}^2\left(\sqrt{\frac{B_0(\Psi_+ - \Psi_0)}{6}}(z - z_0)\right), \tag{111}$$

where $z = px + qy + rt$ and z_0 is an arbitrary constant. By further simplification, Equation (111) becomes:

$$\Psi = \Psi_+ - \frac{3\sqrt{B_1^2 - 4B_0B_2}}{2B_0}\operatorname{sech}^2\left[\frac{1}{2}\left[B_1^2 - 4B_0B_2\right]^{1/4}(z - z_0)\right], \tag{112}$$

and this is regarded as an exact bounded solution of (97).

Therefore, we consider the lemma stated as follows.

Lemma 1. *The general second-order ODE (97) has bounded solutions if and only if $B_1^2 - 4B_0B_2 > 0$. The bounded solutions can be expressed as (109) in an implicit form. In fact, provided $h_- < h < h_+$, (109) defines a family of bounded periodic solutions and $h = h_+$ defines a bounded solution which approaches Ψ_+ as z goes to infinity and can be expressed explicitly as (112), where $\Psi_+ = (-B_1 + \sqrt{B_1^2 - 4B_0B_2})/2B_0$ and $h_\pm$ is defined by (110).*

Bounded Travelling Wave Solutions to the Generalized (2+1)-Dimensional Bogoyavlensky–Konopelchenko Equation

According to analysis and results in the above subsection, it is evident that (97) possesses only two kinds of bounded solutions, amidst of which one is found out to be a family of periodic solutions whereas another is discovered to be a family of solutions which approaches a fixed number as z tends to infinity. It is noteworthy to assert here that what we are targeting is to study the bounded travelling wave solutions associated with (2+1)-D genBKe (4) which are determined via $\Psi = d\psi/dz$, and Ψ satisfies (97). So we have to investigate how we can get the bounded solution of (97).

Visibly, $\psi(z) = \int_{z_0}^{z} \Psi(z) dz$ whereas $\Psi(z)$ can implicitly be expressed as stated in (109). By virtue of the geometry meaning of the integral as well as the properties of the solutions of (97), we get the travelling wave solutions to the (2+1)-D genBKe (4). In order to achieve the bounded solutions needed, we choose the integral constant C_1 to be zero that implies $B_2 = 0$ in (112) and as such

$$\psi(z) = C_1 - \frac{3\sqrt{|B_1|}}{B_0} \tanh\left[\frac{\sqrt{|B_1|}}{2}(z - z_0)\right];$$

which means

$$\psi(z) = C_1 + \frac{16p}{3}\sqrt{\left|\frac{(r + \sigma q + \gamma p)}{p^2(\alpha p + \beta q)}\right|} \tanh\left[\frac{1}{2}\sqrt{\left|\frac{(r + \sigma q + \gamma p)}{p^2(\alpha p + \beta q)}\right|}(z - z_0)\right],$$

that is, the family of analytic bounded kink traveling wave solutions to the (2+1)-D gen-BKe (4), with $z = px + qy + rt$ and z_0 alongside C_1 regarded as arbitrary constants.

Nonetheless, we may not be able to achieve bounded solutions from the family of periodic solutions of (97). We can easily see that if $\Psi(z)$ is a periodic solutions of (97), in the same vein, $\psi(z) = \int_{z_0}^{z} \Psi(z) dz$ is bounded if and only if $\int_{0}^{T} \Psi(z) dz = 0$, where T represents the period of the function $\Psi(z)$. Recall that the period of the function $\Psi(z)$ which is given by (109) with $h_- < h < h_+$ is dependent continuously on the parameters, B_0, B_1, B_2 and h. So $\int_{0}^{T} \Psi(z) dz$ continuously depends on the parameters, B_0, B_1, B_2 and h as well. Suppose we have it that $V(B_0, B_1, B_2, h) = \int_{0}^{T} \Psi(z) dz$; as a consequence, $V(B_0, B_1, B_2, h)$ is defined as a continuous function of B_0, B_1, B_2 and h. The prove to showcase the existence of the root of $V(B_0, B_1, B_2, h) = 0$ to furnish us with the idea of the existence of the bounded periodic travelling wave solutions to (2+1)-D genBKe (4) is given in [65].

Theorem 4. *The generalized (2+1)-dimensional Bogoyavlensky–Konopelchenko equation possesses two types of bounded travelling wave solutions given as:*

(1) *The generalized (2+1)-dimensional Bogoyavlensky–Konopelchenko equation has a family of analytic bounded kink travelling wave solutions:*

$$u(t, x, y) = C_1 + \frac{16p}{3}\sqrt{\left|\frac{(r + \sigma q + \gamma p)}{p^2(\alpha p + \beta q)}\right|} \tanh\left[\frac{1}{2}\sqrt{\left|\frac{(r + \sigma q + \gamma p)}{p^2(\alpha p + \beta q)}\right|}(px + qy + rt - z_0)\right], \quad (113)$$

where z_0 and C_1 are two arbitrary constants;

(2) *The generalized (2+1)-dimensional Bogoyavlensky–Konopelchenko equation possesses at least two families of bounded periodic travelling wave solutions which are determined implicitly by (109) and*

$$u(z) = \int_{z_0}^{z} \Psi(z) dz,$$

where $z = px + qy + rt$ and z_0 is an arbitrary constant.

4. Dynamical Wave Behaviour and Analysis of Solutions

The physical phenomena of those secured closed-form solutions can be captured more clearly via graphical evaluation. The obtained solutions of the (2+1)-D genBKe equation comprises kink and anti-kink waves, periodic solitons waves, multi-soliton waves, singular solitons, as well as mixed dark–bright waves of different dynamical structures. Those secure solutions contain several sets of arbitrary constants and functions, which consequently exhibit diverse dynamical structures of multiple solitons through their numerical simulations. We present the structure of the dynamical behaviour of the waves in 3D, 2D and density plots with the aid of Maple software. The singular periodic wave structure in Figure 1 depicts the dynamics of solitary wave solution (34) where we utilize the parameters values $\gamma = 100$, $\alpha = 1$, $C_0 = 1$, C_1 with variables $y = 0$ and $-1 \leq t, x \leq 1$. Figure 2 represents topological kink soliton solution (36) in 3D, 2D and density plots where we engage values $\gamma = 1$, $\alpha = 4$, $C_0 = 1$, $C_1 = 10$, $c_0 = 1$, $c_1 = 100$ where $y = 0$, $-10 \leq t \leq 10$ and $-4 \leq x \leq 4$. Now, for (30), we contemplate a few different choices of arbitrary functions $f_1(t)$ and $f_2(t)$ and for the fact that the solution contains variable y, we consider another function of y as $g(y)$. Therefore, since the solution is a function of t and y, we first consider $f(t) = 3\,\text{sech}^4(t)$, $f(t) = (f_1(t), f_2(t))$ and $g(y) = \cos(y) - \sin(y)$, using Maple software, we further illustrate the solution in Figure 3 with the range $-\pi \leq t \leq \pi$ and $-2\pi \leq y \leq 3\pi$ where we have $x = 0$. Hence, the numerical simulation reveals a doubly-periodic interaction between two-solitons with different amplitudes. Further, we choose $f(t) = 3\,\text{sech}^4(t)$ and $g(y) = -(2\tanh(y) + \cos(y))$ in Figure 4 where we have variables $x = 0$ as well as t and y in the range $-\pi \leq t \leq \pi$ and $-2\pi \leq y \leq 3\pi$. This then exhibits periodic interaction between solitons at varying amplitude and frequency along yt-axis. Moreover, on selecting $f(t) = 3\,\text{sech}(t)$ and $g(y) = -(2\tanh^2(y) + \sin(y))$, we plot Figure 5 where $-\pi \leq t \leq \pi$, $-2\pi \leq y \leq 3\pi$ and $x = 0$. This occasions periodic interaction between solitons travelling at different amplitude but moving in the same direction. In Figure 6 we choose $f(t) = 3\,\text{sech}(t) - \text{Si}(t)$ and $g(y) = -\sin(y)$ along with $-3\pi \leq t \leq 3\pi$ and $-2\pi \leq y \leq 4\pi$. We can see in the figure three soliton interactions. These include a kink with t-axis periodic and y-axis periodic, which is clearly revealed in the propagation of the amplitude. Meanwhile, selection of $f(t) = 3\,\text{sech}(t)$ and $g(y) = -(2\,\text{cn}(t, y) + \sin(y))$ with $x = 0$, $-3\pi \leq t \leq \pi$ and $-2\pi \leq y \leq 3\pi$ furnishes doubly-periodic and 1-soliton interactions as portrayed in Figure 7. The interaction depicts an upsurge of wave propagating at varying amplitude, travelling at different velocity and time intervals. Moreover, we can see in Figure 8 a periodic interaction existing between two-solitons with opposite amplitude and propagating at a uniform frequency. This is achieved by allocating $f(t) = 3\,\text{sech}(t)$ and $g(y) = -3t\cos(y)$ where $x = 0$, $-\pi \leq t \leq \pi$ and $-2\pi \leq y \leq 6\pi$. Besides, Figure 9 exhibits wave dynamical behaviour surfacing from a collision between a kink and a soliton solution purveyed by assigning $f(t) = 4\,\text{sech}(t)$ and $g(y) = t\tanh(y)$ with $x = 0$, $-\pi \leq t \leq \pi$ and $-\pi \leq y \leq 4\pi$. Finally on wave interactions, we assign functions $f(t) = 40\,\text{sech}(t)$ and $g(y) = 20t\,\text{sech}^2(y)$ in Figure 10 where $x = 0$, $-\pi \leq t \leq \pi$ and $-\pi \leq y \leq 4\pi$. The resultant effect of the soliton collisions gives a two-soliton wave propagating with opposite amplitude along yt-axis.

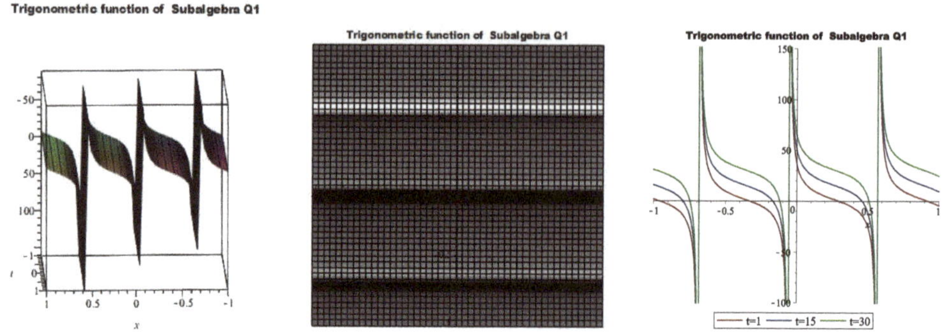

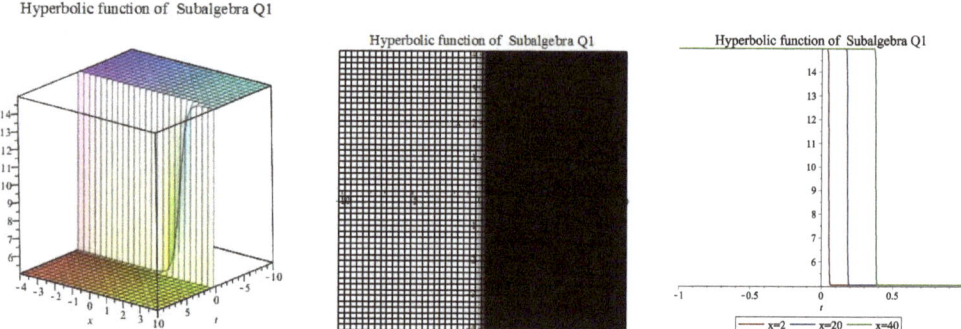

Figure 1. Solitary wave depiction of singular periodic solution (34) at $y = 0$.

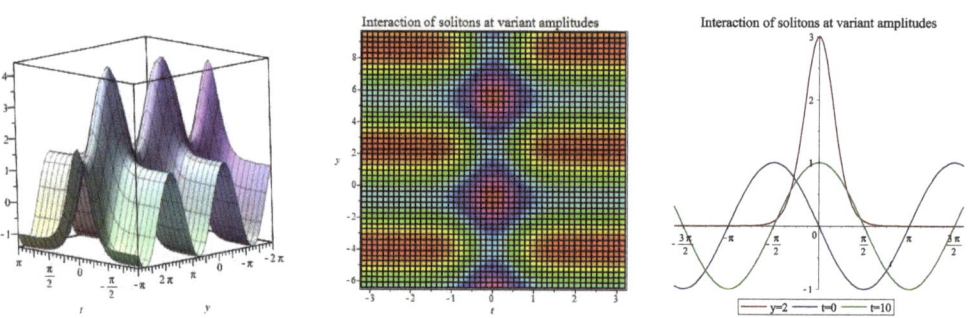

Figure 2. Solitary wave depiction of topological anti-kink soliton (36) at $y = 0$.

Figure 3. Wave depiction of soliton interaction with variant amplitudes at $x = 0$.

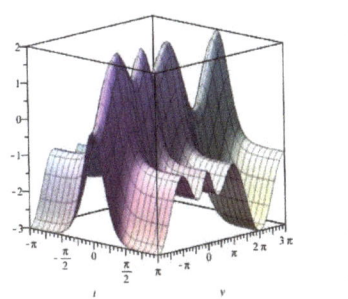
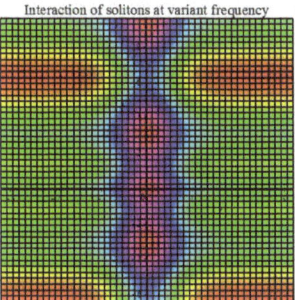
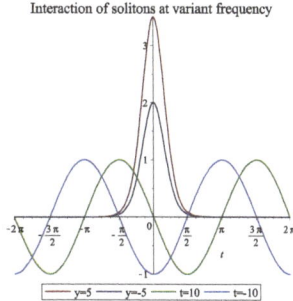

Figure 4. Wave profile depiction of soliton interaction with different amplitudes, frequency and also propagating along the same direction when variable $x = 0$.

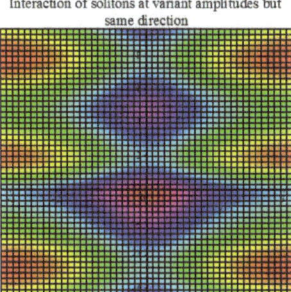
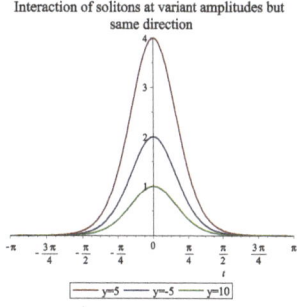

Figure 5. Wave profile depiction of soliton interaction with varying amplitudes but acting and propagating along the same direction where we have variable $x = 0$.

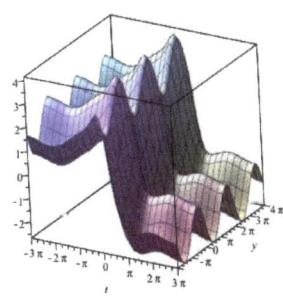
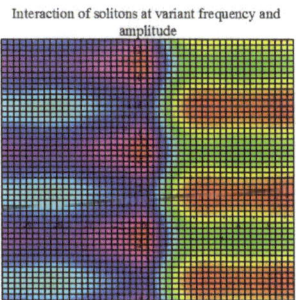
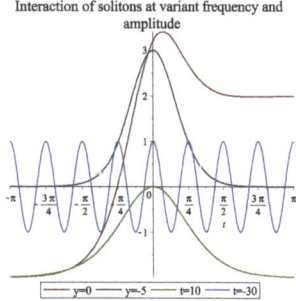

Figure 6. Wave profile depiction of soliton interaction with variant amplitudes and frequency with the wave propagation taking place at different level when $x = 0$.

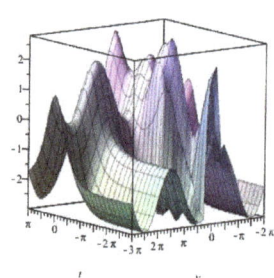 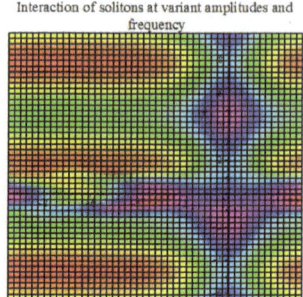 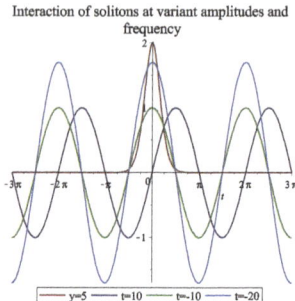

Figure 7. Wave profile depiction of soliton interaction with varying amplitudes, frequency and also propagating at different time intervals when variable $x = 0$.

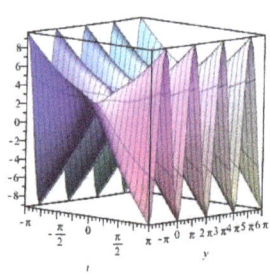 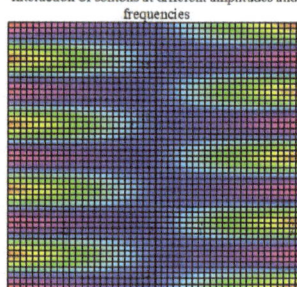 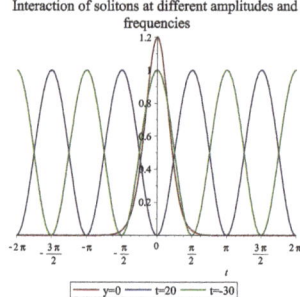

Figure 8. Wave profile depiction of soliton interaction with variant amplitudes and frequency with the propagation in the opposite directions when we have variable $x = 0$.

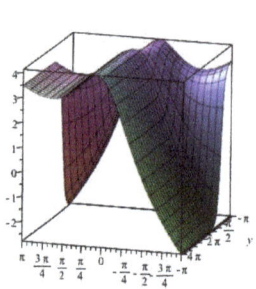 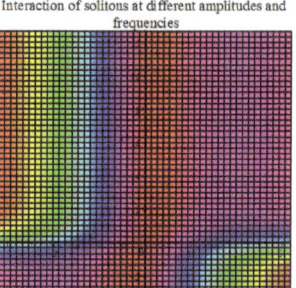 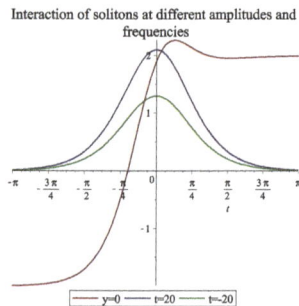

Figure 9. Wave depiction of soliton interaction at different amplitude with $x = 0$.

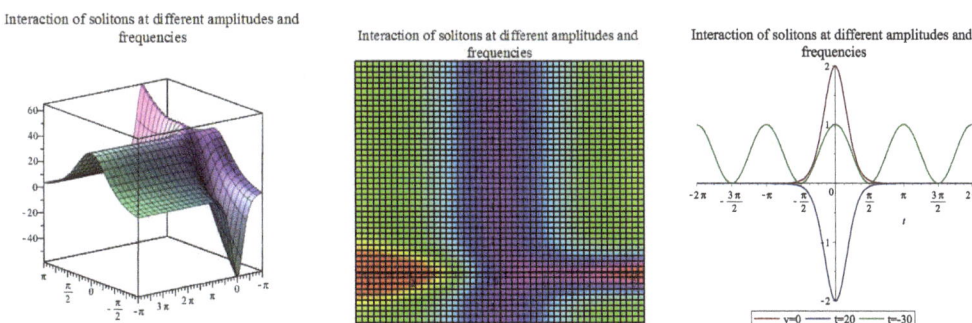

Figure 10. Wave profile depiction of soliton interaction at varying amplitude and propagating at a constant velocity and also moving in different directions when $x = 0$.

Next, the kink solution (72) is depicted with Figure 11 with dissimilar constant values $a = 1, b = 1, C_1 = 1, C_2 = 2, \alpha = 2, \delta = 1, \gamma = -1, \rho = 1$ at $y = 1$ and $-10 \leq t, x \leq 10$. The various dynamical behaviour of periodic solution (84) is exhibited in Figures 12–14 using parameter values $a = -1, b = -1, c_0 = 1, c_1 = 1, c_2 = -1, \alpha = 1, \beta_3 = 1, \beta_4 = 1, \delta = 1, \rho = 1, \theta_1 = 9, \theta_2 = 1, \theta_3 = -1, \Omega_0^2 = 0.09$ at $t = 2$ and $-2 \leq x, y \leq 2, a = -1, b = -1, c_0 = 1, c_1 = 1, c_2 = -1, \alpha = 1, \beta_3 = 1, \beta_4 = 1, \delta = 1, \rho = 1, \theta_1 = 9, \theta_2 = 1, \theta_3 = -1, \Omega_0^2 = 0.09$ at $t = 5$ and $-2 \leq x, y \leq 2$ as well as $a = -1, b = -1, c_0 = 1, c_1 = 1, c_2 = -1, \alpha = 1, \beta_3 = 1, \beta_4 = 1, \delta = 1, \rho = 1, \theta_1 = 9, \theta_2 = 1, \theta_3 = -1, \Omega_0^2 = 0.09$ at $t = 2$ and $-2 \leq x, y \leq 2$ accordingly. Moreover, the motion character of solution are further depicted in Figures 15 and 16 respectively via values $a = -1, b = -1, c_0 = 1, c_1 = 1, c_2 = -1, \alpha = 1, \beta_3 = 1, \beta_4 = 1, \delta = 1, \rho = 1, \theta_1 = 40, \theta_2 = 2, \theta_3 = -5, \Omega_0^2 = 0.26$ at $t = 2$ and $-2 \leq x, y \leq 2$ alongside $a = -1, b = -1, c_0 = 1, c_1 = 1, c_2 = -1, \alpha = 1, \beta_3 = 1, \beta_4 = 1, \delta = 1, \rho = 1, \theta_1 = 50, \theta_2 = 5, \theta_3 = -5, \Omega_0^2 = 0.26$ at $t = 3$ and $-2 \leq x, y \leq 2$. The Weierstrass elliptic function solution (60) is represented graphically in Figure 17 with unalike parametric values $a = 1, b = 1, c_0 = 1, c_1 = 2, \alpha = 2, \alpha_0 = 1, \alpha_1 = 1, \alpha_2 = 2, \delta = 1, \rho = 1, A_0 = 1, A_1 = 2$ where $y = 1$ and $-10 \leq x, y \leq 10$. This wave depiction reveals a multi-soliton wave structure which is a significant wave in nonlinear science and engineering.

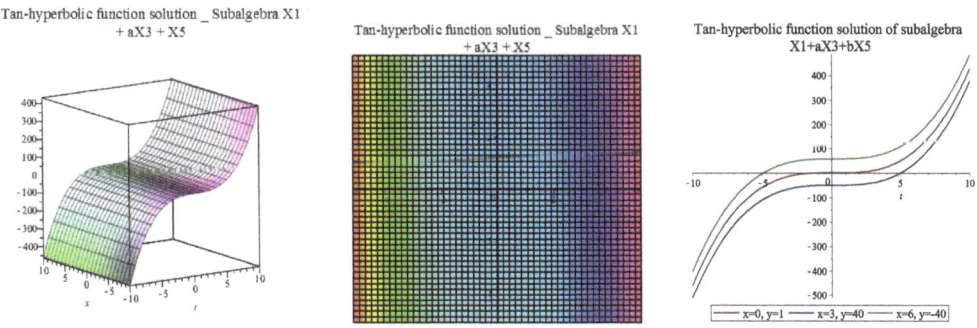

Figure 11. Solitary wave depiction of hyperbolic function solution (72) at $y = 1$.

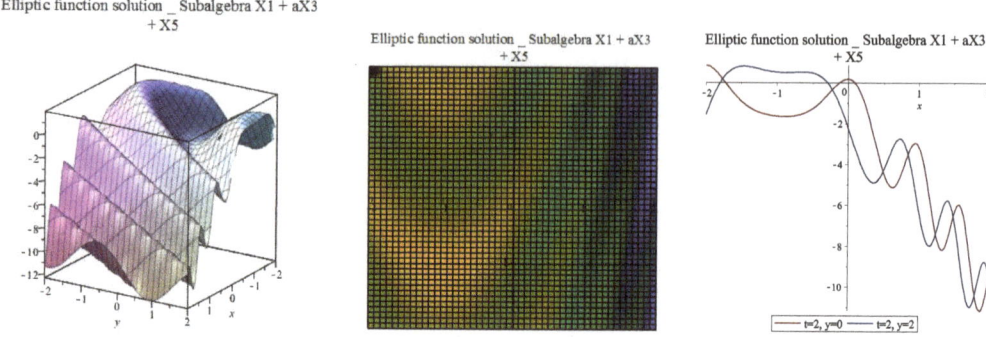

Figure 12. Solitary wave profile depiction of elliptic solution (84) at $t = 2$.

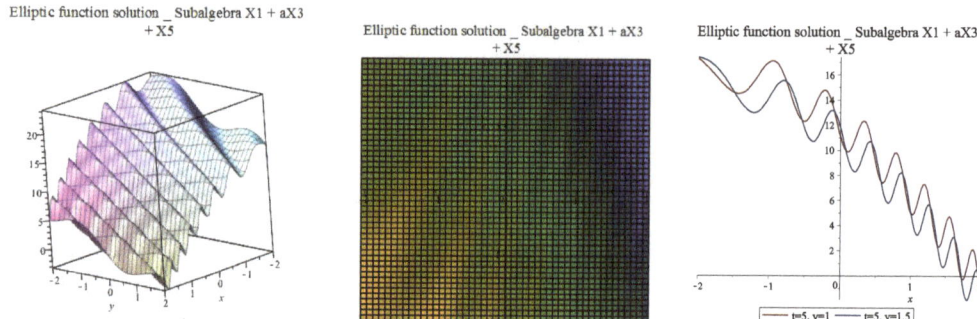

Figure 13. Solitary wave profile depiction of elliptic solution (84) at $t = 5$.

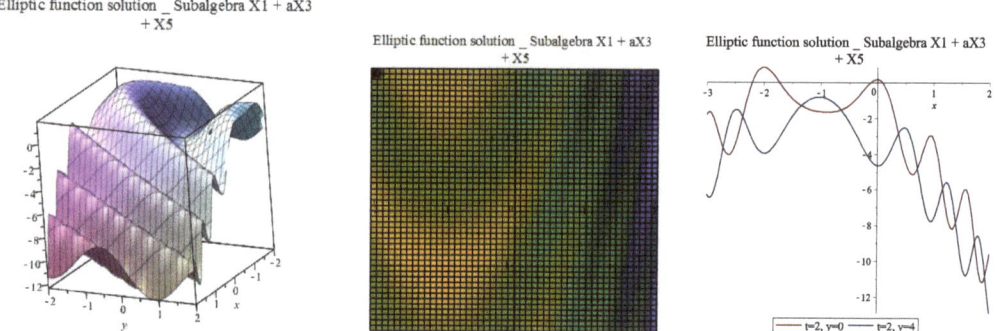

Figure 14. Solitary wave profile depiction of elliptic solution (84) at $t = 2$.

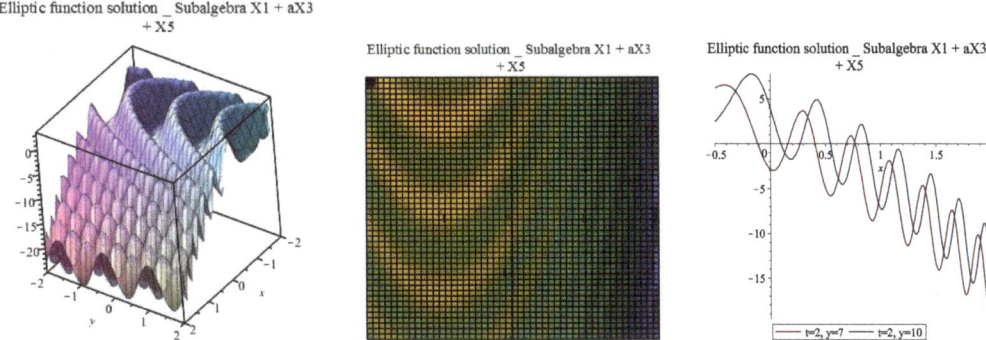

Figure 15. Solitary wave profile depiction of elliptic solution (84) at $t = 2$.

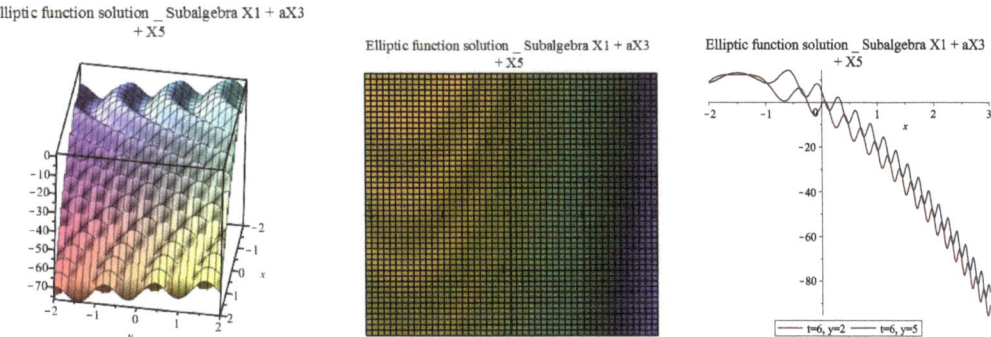

Figure 16. Solitary wave profile depiction of elliptic solution (84) at $t = 3$.

Further, we depict the elliptic integral solution (68) in Figures 18–21. This is achieved by invoking dissimilar constant values $a = -1$, $b = -1$, $c_0 = 1$, $c_2 = -1$, $\alpha = 2$, $\alpha_4 = 1$, $\alpha_5 = 1$, $\delta = 1$, $\rho = 1$, $\vartheta_1 = 3$, $\vartheta_2 = 2$, $\vartheta_3 = 1$, $\Delta^2 = 0.09$ at $t = 2$ and $-1 \leq x, y \leq 1$, $a = -1$, $b = -1$, $c_0 = 1$, $c_2 = 1$, $\alpha = 2$, $\alpha_4 = 1$, $\alpha_5 = 5$, $\delta = 1$, $\rho = 1$, $\vartheta_1 = 3$, $\vartheta_2 = 2$, $\vartheta_3 = 1$, $\Delta^2 = 0.09$ when $t = 1$ and $-1 \leq x, y \leq 1$, $a = 1$, $b = -1$, $c_0 = 1$, $c_2 = 1$, $\alpha = 2$, $\alpha_4 = 1$, $\alpha_5 = 5$, $\delta = 1$, $\rho = 1$, $\vartheta_1 = 3$, $\vartheta_2 = 2$, $\vartheta_3 = 1$, $\Delta^2 = 0.09$ at $t = 1$ and $-1 \leq x, y \leq 1$ as well as $a = 1$, $b = 1$, $c_0 = 1$, $c_2 = 0$, $\alpha = 1$, $\alpha_4 = 1$, $\alpha_5 = 1$, $\delta = 1$, $\rho = 1$, $\vartheta_1 = 3$, $\vartheta_2 = 2$, $\vartheta_3 = 1$, $\Delta^2 = 0.08$ at $t = 0$ and $-1 \leq x, y \leq 1$ respectively. We notice that the dynamical wave behaviour of elliptic integral solution (68) reveals a mixed dark and bright soliton wave profile which is akin to hyperbolic secant and hyperbolic tangent functions. It is known that the elliptic solution disintegrates to elementary hyperbolic functions by taking some special limits. These functions comprise secant hyperbolic and tangent hyperbolic. It will be recalled that these two constitute bell and anti-bell shapes respectively. As a consequence, this asserted relationship and the interconnections between elliptic solutions and the involved functions are conspicuously revealed in Figures 18–21.

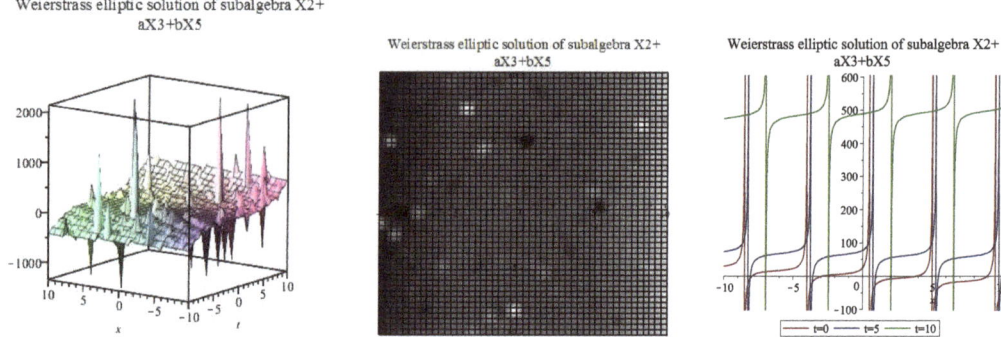

Figure 17. Solitary wave depiction of Weierstrass elliptic solution (60) at $y = 1$.

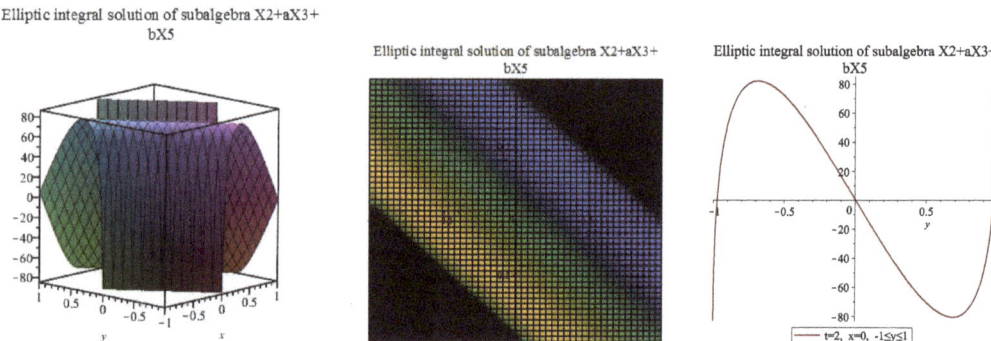

Figure 18. Solitary wave depiction of elliptic integral solution (68) at $t = 2$.

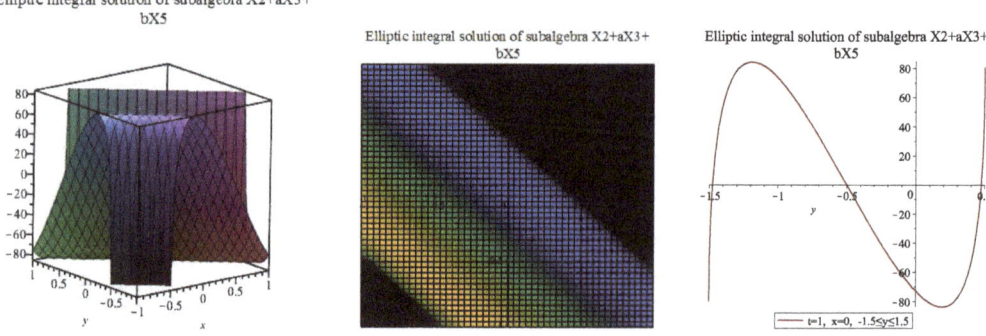

Figure 19. Solitary wave depiction of elliptic integral solution (68) at $t = 1$.

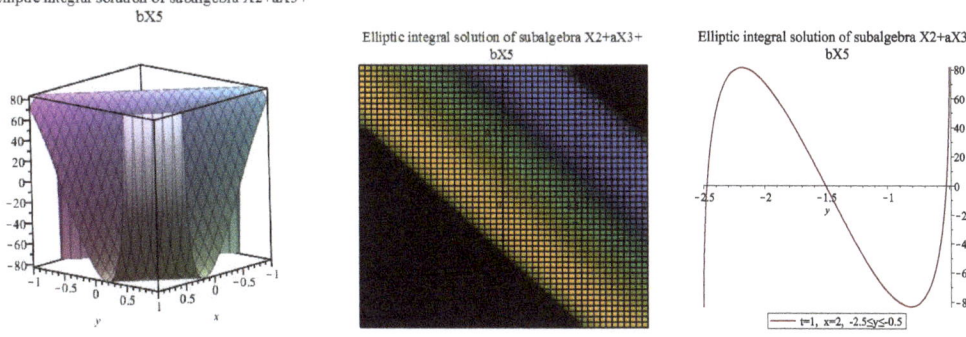

Figure 20. Solitary wave depiction of elliptic integral solution (68) at $t = 1$.

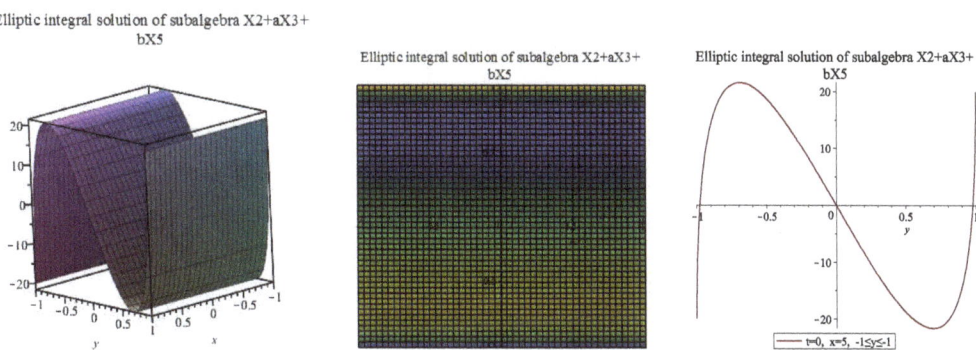

Figure 21. Solitary wave depiction of elliptic integral solution (68) at $t = 0$.

The various nontrivial solitary wave solutions obtained from bifurcation analysis of (2+1)-D genBKe (4) in this study, to actually view their dynamical character, numerical simulation of the involved parameters are performed using Mathematica 11.3. Therefore, we reveal the nontrivial bounded solution (101) via 3D, 2D and density plots in Figure 22 with varying parameter values $r = 0.2$, $p = 0.1$, $q = 0.3$, $A = 0.05$, $B = 5$, $C = 1.02$, $C_1 = 8$ with $t = 0.4$ and $-6 \leq x, y \leq 6$. The solution (103) is portrayed in Figure 23 using unalike values $r = 0.2$, $p = 0.1$, $q = 0.3$, $A = 0.05$, $B = 7$, $C = 1.05$, $C_1 = 9$ with $t = 0.7$ and $-8 \leq x, y \leq 8$. Moreover, unbounded solution (106) is represented in Figure 24 through 3D, 2D as well as the density plot with constant values $r = 0.2$, $p = 0.1$, $q = 0.3$, $A = 0.5$, $B = 5$, $C = 1$, $C_1 = 4$ with $t = 0.2$ and $-10 \leq x, y \leq 10$. We further exhibit the travelling wave solution (113) in Figures 25–28 using dissimilar values of parameters respectively given as: $r = 0.5$, $p = 1$, $q = 1$, $\alpha = 5$, $\beta = 200$, $\sigma = 90$, $\gamma = 100$, $C_1 = 4$ with $t = -2$ and $-10 \leq x, y \leq 10$; $r = 0.1$, $p = 1$, $q = 1$, $\alpha = -50$, $\beta = 200$, $\sigma = 90$, $\gamma = 100$, $C_1 = 0$ with $x = -3$ and $-10 \leq t, y \leq 10$; $r = 0.1$, $p = 1$, $q = 1$, $\alpha = -50$, $\beta = 200$, $\sigma = 90$, $\gamma = 100$, $C_1 = 0$ with $x = 3$ and $-10 \leq t, y \leq 10$; $r = 0.1$, $p = 1$, $q = 1$, $\alpha = -50$, $\beta = 200$, $\sigma = 90$, $\gamma = 100$, $C_1 = 0$ with $y = 5$ and $-10 \leq t, x \leq 10$.

Significant observations

Figure 17 portrays a localized wave structure of multi-solitons of Equation (4). The dynamical structure appears due to the balance between nonlinearity and the dispersion term. Figures 18–21 depicts the coexistence between bright and dark solitons with various wave structures. It is eminent that bright soliton profiles are identified with hyperbolic secant functions. The bright soliton solution usually assumes a bell-shaped figure and also propagates in an undistorted manner without any variation in shape for arbitrarily long distances. Nevertheless, dark soliton solutions which usually exhibit anti-bell wave structures, configured also as topological optical solitons, are characterized by hyperbolic tangent functions.

Moreover, important to note is the fact that Equation (56) which can be seen in various cases of symmetry reductions via optimal subalgebras in this study is reminiscent of the ordinary differential equation (ODE) achieved in the quintessential work conducted by Korteweg along with De Vries in [18]. In addition to that, this ODE is interconnected with long waves which propagate along a rectangular canal. Moreover, ODE (56) delineates stationary waves and by imposing some certain constraints for example having the fluid undisturbed at infinity, Korteweg and De Vries secured negative and positive solitary waves alongside cnoidal wave solutions [18,66].

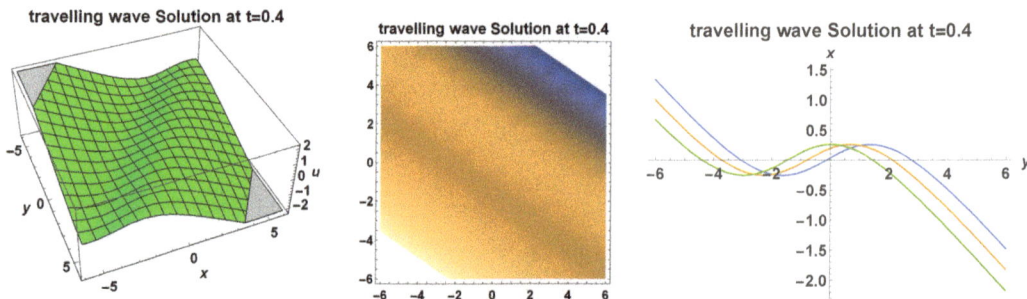

Figure 22. Wave profile depiction of nontrivial bounded solution (101) at $t = 0.4$.

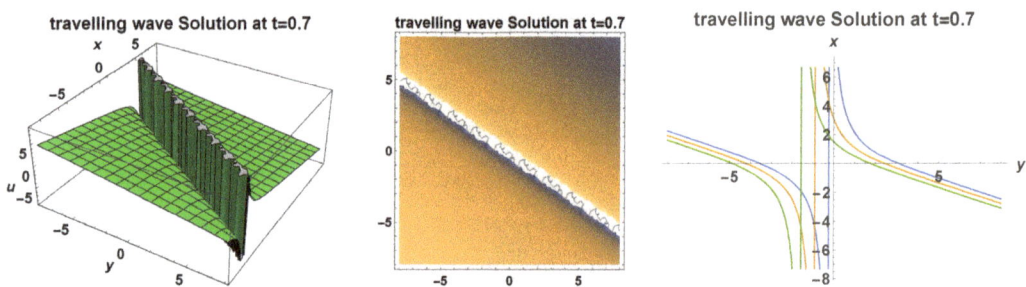

Figure 23. Wave profile depiction of nontrivial unbounded solution (103) at $t = 0.7$.

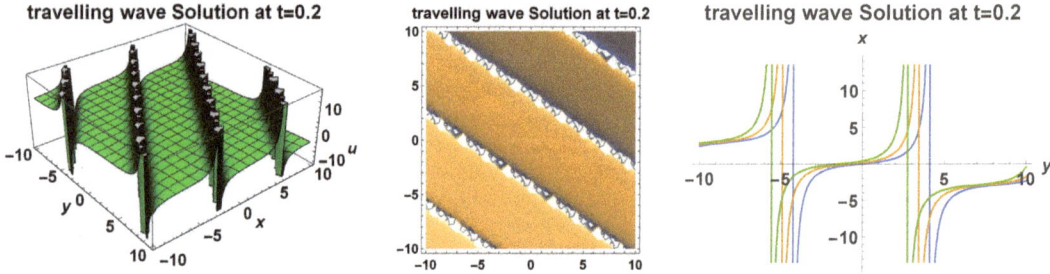

Figure 24. Wave profile depiction of nontrivial unbounded solution (106) at $t = 0.2$.

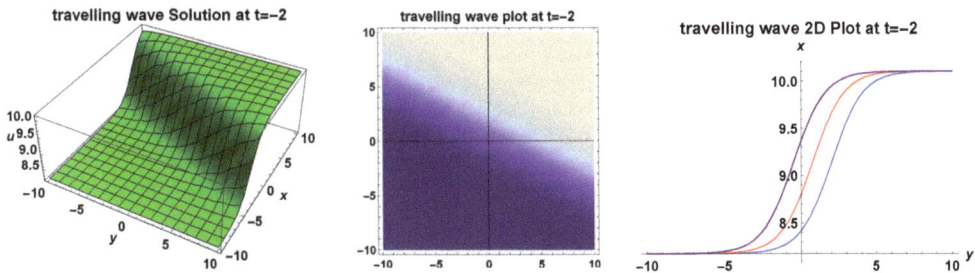

Figure 25. Tavelling wave profile depiction of nontrivial solution (113) at $t = -2$.

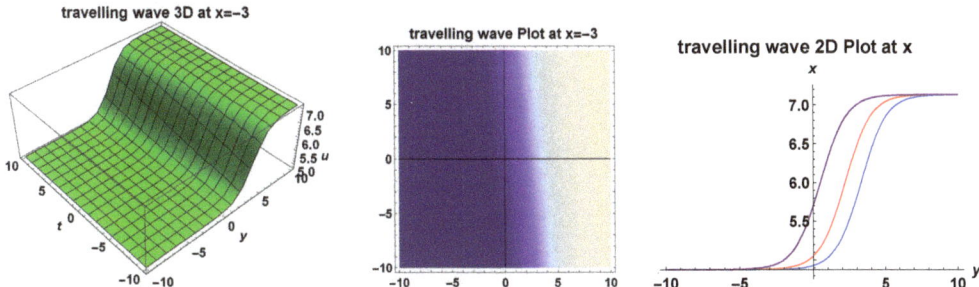

Figure 26. Tavelling wave profile depiction of nontrivial solution (113) at $x = -3$.

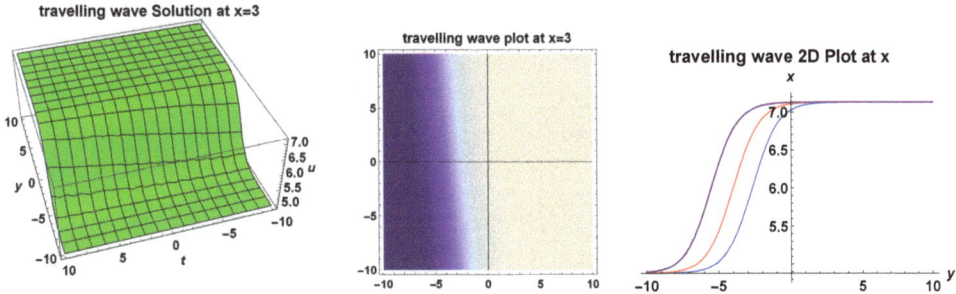

Figure 27. Tavelling wave profile depiction of nontrivial solution (113) at $x = 3$.

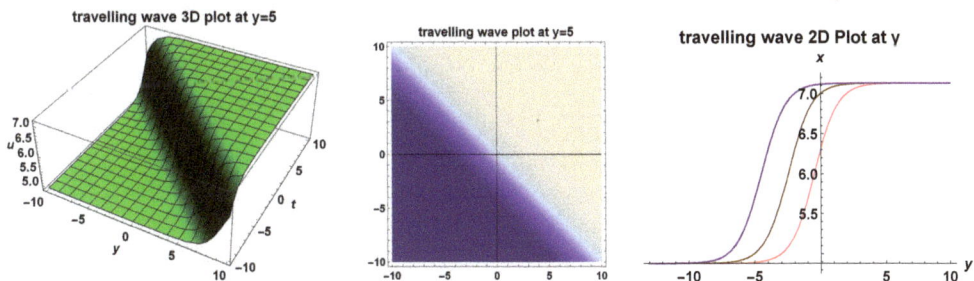

Figure 28. Tavelling wave profile depiction of nontrivial solution (113) at $y = 5$.

5. Conservation Laws

This section reveals the constructed conservation laws for (2+1)-D genBKe (4) by the engagement of the multipier method [67] along with the well-known Noether's theorem [68].

5.1. Conserved Vectors via Homotopy Formula

It is germane to state that the multiplier technique is advantageous in the sense that it works for any PDE either with or without variational principle [6,28,67]. In other words, the multiplier method does not require the availability of variational principle before the conserved vectors of a given PDE is obtained. To derive the conserved vectors of (2+1)-D genBKe (4), we first determine the second-order multipliers via the criteria,

$$\frac{\delta}{\delta u}(\Lambda\Delta) = 0, \tag{114}$$

with $\Lambda = \Lambda(t,x,y,u,u_t,u_x,u_y,u_{xx},u_{xy})$ and the Euler operator $\delta/\delta u$ expressed as:

$$\frac{\delta}{\delta u} = \frac{\partial}{\partial u} - D_t\frac{\partial}{\partial u_t} - D_x\frac{\partial}{\partial u_x} - D_y\frac{\partial}{\partial u_y} + D_tD_x\frac{\partial}{\partial u_{tx}} + D_xD_y\frac{\partial}{\partial u_{xy}} + D_x^2\frac{\partial}{\partial u_{xx}} + D_y^2\frac{\partial}{\partial u_{yy}} + D_x^4\frac{\partial}{\partial u_{xxxx}} + D_x^3D_y\frac{\partial}{\partial u_{xxxy}}.$$

On expanding Equation (114) and using the standard Lie theory algorithm, one achieves:

$$\Lambda_{yy} = 0, \ \Lambda_{yu_x} = 0, \ \Lambda_{u_xu_x} = 0, \ \Lambda_x = 0, \ \Lambda_u = 0, \ \Lambda_{u_t} = 0,$$
$$\Lambda_{u_y} = 0, \ \Lambda_{u_{xx}} = 0, \ \Lambda_{u_{xy}} = 0,$$

which can be solved without much tedious process thereby giving the value of Λ as

$$\Lambda(t,x,y,u,u_t,u_x,u_y,u_{xx},u_{xy}) = f_1'(t)y - 3(\rho-\delta)u_x f_1(t) + C_1 u_x + f_2(t), \tag{115}$$

with arbitrary functions $f_1(t)$ and $f_2(t)$ dependent on t. Meanwhile, the homotopy integral formula [69] for the multiplier can be expressed as:

$$T = \int_0^1 \left\{ u\left(\left(\frac{\partial\Lambda\Delta}{\partial u_t}\right)\Big|_{u=u_{(\lambda)}} - D_x\left(\frac{\partial\Lambda\Delta}{\partial u_{tx}}\right)\Big|_{u=u_{(\lambda)}}\right)\right\}d\lambda,$$

$$X = \int_0^1 \Big\{ u\left(\left(\frac{\partial\Lambda\Delta}{\partial u_x}\right)\Big|_{u=u_{(\lambda)}} - D_x\left(\frac{\partial\Lambda\Delta}{\partial u_{xx}}\right)\Big|_{u=u_{(\lambda)}} + D_x^2\left(\frac{\partial\Lambda\Delta}{\partial u_{xxx}}\right)\Big|_{u=u_{(\lambda)}}\right.$$
$$-D_x^3\left(\frac{\partial\Lambda\Delta}{\partial u_{xxxx}}\right)\Big|_{u=u_{(\lambda)}}\right) + u_t\left(\frac{\partial\Lambda\Delta}{\partial u_{tx}}\right)\Big|_{u=u_{(\lambda)}} - u_y\left(D_x\left(\frac{\partial\Lambda\Delta}{\partial u_{xy}}\right)\Big|_{u=u_{(\lambda)}}\right)$$
$$-D_x^2\left(\frac{\partial\Lambda\Delta}{\partial u_{xxy}}\right)\Big|_{u=u_{(\lambda)}}\right) + u_x\left(\left(\frac{\partial\Lambda\Delta}{\partial u_{xx}}\right)\Big|_{u=u_{(\lambda)}} - D_x\left(\frac{\partial\Lambda\Delta}{\partial u_{xxx}}\right)\Big|_{u=u_{(\lambda)}}\right)$$
$$+u_{xy}\left(\left(\frac{\partial\Lambda\Delta}{\partial u_{xy}}\right)\Big|_{u=u_{(\lambda)}} - D_x\left(\frac{\partial\Lambda\Delta}{\partial u_{xxy}}\right)\Big|_{u=u_{(\lambda)}}\right) + u_{xx}\left(\left(\frac{\partial\Lambda\Delta}{\partial u_{xxx}}\right)\Big|_{u=u_{(\lambda)}}\right) \quad (116)$$
$$+u_{xxx}\left(\left(\frac{\partial\Lambda\Delta}{\partial u_{xxxx}}\right)\Big|_{u=u_{(\lambda)}}\right) + u_{xy}\left(-D_x\left(\frac{\partial\Lambda\Delta}{\partial u_{xxy}}\right)\Big|_{u=u_{(\lambda)}}\right)$$
$$+u_{xxy}\left(\left(\frac{\partial\Lambda\Delta}{\partial u_{xxy}}\right)\Big|_{u=u_{(\lambda)}}\right)\Big\}d\lambda,$$

$$Y = \int_0^1 \Big[u\left\{\left(\frac{\partial\Lambda\Delta}{\partial u_y}\right)\Big|_{u=u_{(\lambda)}} - D_y\left(\frac{\partial\Lambda\Delta}{\partial u_{yy}}\right)\Big|_{u=u_{(\lambda)}} - D_x\left(\frac{\partial\Lambda\Delta}{\partial u_{xy}}\right)\Big|_{u=u_{(\lambda)}}\right.$$
$$-D_x^3\left(\frac{\partial\Lambda\Delta}{\partial u_{xxxy}}\right)\Big|_{u=u_{(\lambda)}}\Big\} + u_y\left(\frac{\partial\Lambda\Delta}{\partial u_{yy}}\right)\Big|_{u=u_{(\lambda)}} + u_x\left(\frac{\partial\Lambda\Delta}{\partial u_{xy}}\right)\Big|_{u=u_{(\lambda)}}$$
$$+u_{xxx}\left(\frac{\partial\Lambda\Delta}{\partial u_{xxxy}}\right)\Big|_{u=u_{(\lambda)}}\Big]d\lambda.$$

As a consequence, the three multipliers $\Lambda_1 = u_x$, $\Lambda_2 = f_1'(t)y - 3(\rho - \delta)u_x f_1(t)$ and $\Lambda_3 = f_2(t)$ from (115) secures the conservation laws, accordingly as:

$$T_1 = \frac{1}{4}u_x^2 - \frac{1}{4}uu_{xx},$$

$$X_1 = \frac{1}{8}\beta uu_{xxxy} + \frac{1}{4}\sigma uu_{xy} + \frac{1}{2}vuu_{yy} + \alpha u_x u_{xxx} + \frac{5}{8}\beta u_x u_{xxy} + \frac{1}{4}\sigma u_x u_y$$
$$- \frac{3}{8}\beta u_{xx}u_{xy} + \frac{1}{8}\beta u_{xxx}u_y + \delta u_x^2 u_y + \frac{1}{2}\rho u_x^2 u_y + \frac{1}{2}\gamma u_x^2 + \frac{1}{4}u_t u_x$$
$$- \frac{1}{2}\alpha u_{xx}^2 + \frac{1}{4}uu_{tx} + 2\alpha u_x^3 + \rho uu_x u_{xy} - \delta uu_x u_{xy},$$

$$Y_1 = \delta uu_x u_{xx} - \rho uu_x u_{xx} + \frac{1}{2}\rho u_x^3 + \frac{1}{4}\sigma u_x^2 - \frac{1}{8}\beta u_{xx}^2 - \frac{1}{4}\sigma uu_{xx} + \frac{1}{2}vu_x u_y$$
$$+ \frac{1}{4}\beta u_x u_{xxx} - \frac{1}{8}\beta uu_{xxxx} - \frac{1}{2}vuu_{xy};$$

$$T_2 = \frac{3}{4}\rho uu_{xx}f_1(t) - \frac{3}{4}\delta f_1(t)uu_{xx} + \frac{3}{4}\delta u_x^2 f_1(t) - \frac{3}{4}\rho u_x^2 f_1(t) + \frac{1}{2}yu_x f_1'(t),$$

$$X_2 = \frac{3}{4}\delta u_t u_x f_1(t) - \frac{3}{4}\rho u_t u_x f_1(t) + 3\alpha u_x^2 y f_1'(t) + \frac{3}{2}\gamma \delta u_x^2 f_1(t) + \gamma y u_x f_1'(t)$$
$$+ \alpha y u_{xxx} f_1'(t) + \frac{3}{4}\beta y u_{xxy} f_1'(t) + \frac{1}{2}\sigma y u_y f_1'(t) + 6\alpha \delta u_x^3 f_1(t) - 6\alpha \rho u_x^3 f_1(t)$$
$$+ 3\delta^2 u_x^2 u_y f_1(t) - \frac{3}{2}\rho^2 u_x^2 u_y f_1(t) + \frac{3}{4}\delta uu_{tx}f_1(t) - \frac{3}{4}\rho uu_{tx}f_1(t) + \frac{3}{2}\alpha \rho u_{xx}^2 f_1(t)$$
$$- \frac{3}{4}\delta uu_x f_1'(t) - \frac{3}{2}\gamma \rho u_x^2 f_1(t) - \frac{3}{2}\alpha \delta u_{xx}^2 f_1(t) - \frac{3}{4}\rho \sigma u_x u_y f_1(t) - 3\rho^2 uu_x u_{xy} f_1(t)$$
$$- \frac{3}{2}\delta \rho u_x^2 u_y f_1(t) - \frac{15}{8}\beta \rho f_1(t)u_x u_{xxy} + \frac{3}{4}\delta \sigma u_x u_y f_1(t) - 3\delta^2 uu_x u_{xy} f_1(t)$$
$$- \frac{3}{4}\rho \sigma uu_{xy} f_1(t) + \frac{3}{4}\delta \sigma uu_{xy} f_1(t) - \frac{3}{8}\beta \rho uu_{xxxy} f_1(t) + \frac{3}{8}\beta \delta uu_{xxxy} f_1(t)$$
$$+ \frac{3}{4}\rho yu_x u_y f_1'(t) + 6\delta \rho uu_x u_{xy} f_1(t) - \frac{1}{4}\beta u_{xx} f_1'(t) - \frac{1}{2}u_y f_1''(t) - \frac{1}{2}\sigma u f_1'(t)$$
$$+ \frac{1}{2}yu_t f_1'(t) - \frac{3}{2}vpuu_{yy} f_1(t) + 3\alpha \delta u_x u_{xxx} f_1(t) - 3\alpha \rho u_x u_{xxx} f_1(t)$$
$$+ \frac{15}{8}\beta \delta u_x u_{xxy} f_1(t) + \frac{3}{2}\delta v f_1(t)uu_{yy} - \frac{3}{2}\delta yuu_{xy} f_1'(t) + \frac{3}{4}\rho yuu_{xy} f_1'(t)$$
$$+ \frac{3}{2}\delta yu_x u_y f_1'(t) - \frac{9}{8}\beta \delta u_{xx} u_{xy} f_1(t) + \frac{9}{8}\beta \rho u_{xx} u_{xy} f_1(t) + \frac{3}{8}\beta \delta u_{xxx} u_y f_1(t)$$
$$- \frac{3}{8}\beta \rho u_{xxx} u_y f_1(t),$$

$$Y_2 = \frac{3}{2}v\rho uu_{xy}f_1(t) - \frac{3}{2}\delta vuu_{xy}f_1(t) + \frac{3}{8}\beta \rho uu_{xxxx}f_1(t) + \frac{3}{4}\rho \sigma uu_{xx}f_1(t)$$
$$- \frac{3}{8}\beta \delta uu_{xxxx}f_1(t) - \frac{3}{4}\delta \sigma uu_{xx}f_1(t) + \frac{3}{2}\delta yu_{xx}f_1'(t) - \frac{3}{4}\rho yuu_{xx}f_1'(t)$$
$$+ 3\rho^2 uu_x u_{xx}f_1(t) - \frac{3}{2}v\rho u_x u_y f_1(t) + 3\delta^2 uu_x u_{xx}f_1(t) - 6\delta \rho uu_x u_{xx}f_1(t)$$
$$+ \frac{3}{4}\beta \delta u_x u_{xxx}f_1(t) - \frac{3}{4}\beta \rho u_x u_{xxx}f_1(t) + \frac{3}{2}\delta v u_x u_y f_1(t) + \frac{3}{2}\delta \rho u_x^3 f_1(t)$$
$$+ \frac{3}{4}\rho yu_x^2 f_1'(t) + \frac{3}{4}\delta \sigma u_x^2 f_1(t) - \frac{3}{4}\rho \sigma u_x^2 f_1(t) - \frac{3}{8}\beta \delta u_{xx}^2 f_1(t) + \frac{3}{8}\beta \rho u_{xx}^2 f_1(t)$$
$$+ \frac{1}{2}\sigma yu_x f_1'(t) + \frac{1}{4}\beta yu_{xxx}f_1'(t) + vyu_y f_1'(t) - \frac{3}{2}\rho^2 u_x^3 f_1(t) - vu f_1'(t);$$

$$T_3 = \frac{1}{2}u_x f_2(t),$$

$$X_3 = \frac{3}{4}\beta u_{xxy}f_2(t) + 3\alpha u_x^2 f_2(t) + \gamma u_x f_2(t) + \frac{1}{2}\sigma u_y f_2(t) + \alpha u_{xxx}f_2(t)$$

$$- \frac{3}{2}\delta u u_{xy} f_2(t) + \frac{3}{4}\rho u u_{xy} f_2(t) + \frac{3}{2}\delta u_x u_y f_2(t) + \frac{3}{4}\rho u_x u_y f_2(t) + \frac{1}{2}u_t f_2(t)$$
$$- \frac{1}{2}u f_2'(t),$$

$$Y_3 = \frac{1}{2}\sigma u_x f_2(t) + \frac{1}{4}\beta u_{xxx} f_2(t) + v u_y f_2(t) + \frac{3}{2}\delta u u_{xx} f_2(t) - \frac{3}{4}\rho u u_{xx} f_2(t)$$
$$+ \frac{3}{4}\rho u_x^2 f_2(t).$$

5.2. Conserved Vectors via Noether Theorem

This subsection furnishes the Noether theorem [68,69] to achieve the conserved currents of the (2+1)-D genBKe (4) with $\rho = 2\delta$. Consequently, Equation (4) admits a Lagrangian Lagrangian ($\mathcal{L}$) whose equivalent minimal differential order is given as:

$$\mathcal{L} = \frac{1}{2}\beta u_{xx} u_{xy} - \frac{1}{2}u_t u_x - \alpha u_x^3 + \frac{1}{2}\alpha u_{xx}^2 - \frac{1}{2}\gamma u_x^2 - \frac{3}{2}\delta u_x^2 u_y - \frac{1}{2}\sigma u_x u_y - \frac{1}{2}v u_y^2, \quad (117)$$

which can easily be ascertained by inspection. Thus we arrive at a Lemma:

Lemma 2. *The (2+1)-D genBKe (4) forms the Euler–Lagrange equation with the functional*

$$J(v) = \int_0^\infty \int_0^\infty \int_0^\infty \mathcal{L}(t, x, y, u_t, u_x, u_y, u_{xx}, u_{xy}) dt dx dy,$$

where the conforming function of Lagrange $\mathcal{L}$ is as given in (117).

We achieve variational symmetry $\mathcal{P}$ by employing symmetry invariance condition expressed as:

$$pr^{(2)}\mathcal{P}\mathcal{L} + \mathcal{L}[D_t(\xi^1) + D_x(\xi^2) + D_y(\xi^3)] = D_t(B^t) + D_x(B^x) + D_y(B^y), \quad (118)$$

with the gauge functions B^t, B^x and B^y depending on (t, x, y, u). In addition, the second prolongation $pr^{(2)}\mathcal{P}$ of $\mathcal{P}$ can be recovered by the relation:

$$pr^{(2)}\mathcal{P} = \mathcal{P} + \zeta^t \frac{\partial}{\partial u_t} + \zeta^x \frac{\partial}{\partial u_x} + \zeta^y \frac{\partial}{\partial u_y} + \zeta^{xx} \frac{\partial}{\partial u_{xx}} + \zeta^{xy} \frac{\partial}{\partial u_{xy}},$$

with the variable coefficients as defined in (7) and $\mathcal{P} = \xi^1 \partial/\partial x + \xi^2 \partial/\partial y + \xi^3 \partial/\partial t + \eta \partial/\partial u$. Separating the monomials from the expansion of (118) secures the presented system of linear partial differential equations. They are:

$\zeta_x^1 = 0,\ B_u^t + 2\zeta_u^1 = 0,\ \zeta_u^1 + B_u^t = 0,\ \zeta_t^1 + \zeta_y^3 - B_t^t + 2\eta_u - 3\zeta_x^2 = 0,$

$\zeta_u^1 = 0,\ \zeta_x^2 = 0,\ \eta_x = 0,\ \zeta_u^2 = 0,\ \zeta_u^3 = 0,\ \zeta_{uu}^1 = 0,\ \zeta_{uu}^2 = 0,\ \zeta_u^1 + B_u^t = 0,$

$\eta_{uu} - 2\zeta_{xu}^2 = 0,\ 2\eta_{xu} - \zeta_{xx}^2 = 0,\ \zeta_u^1 = 0,\ \zeta_x^1 = 0,\ \zeta_u^3 = 0,\ \zeta_x^3 = 0,\ \zeta_x^3 = 0,$

$\zeta_{xu}^1 = 0,\ B_u^t + \zeta_u^1 = 0,\ \zeta_{xu}^1 = 0,\ \zeta_{xx}^1 = 0,\ \zeta_{uu}^3 = 0,\ \zeta_{xu}^3 = 0,\ \zeta_{xu}^3 = 0,\ \zeta_{xx}^3 = 0,$

$\eta_{xx} = 0,\ B_u^t + 2\zeta_u^1 = 0,\ \zeta_u^3 = 0,\ \zeta_u^1 + B_u^t = 0,\ 4\alpha\zeta_u^3 + 5\beta\zeta_u^2 = 0,\ 2\alpha\zeta_u^3 + 3\delta\zeta_u^2 = 0,$

$4\alpha\zeta_{xu}^1 + \beta\zeta_{yu}^1 = 0,\ 2\alpha\zeta_{uu}^3 + \beta\zeta_{uu}^2 = 0,\ 2\alpha\eta_{xx} + \beta\eta_{xy} = 0,\ \beta\zeta_{xy}^1 + 2\alpha\zeta_{xx}^1 = 0,$

$B_x^x + B_y^y = 0,\ 2\alpha\eta_{uu} - \beta\zeta_{uy}^2 - 4\alpha\zeta_{xu}^2 = 0,\ 2\beta\eta_{xu} - 2\beta\zeta_{xy}^3 - 2\alpha\zeta_{xx}^3 = 0,$

$6\delta\zeta_x^3 + \sigma\zeta_u^3 + v\zeta_u^2 = 0,\ \sigma\zeta_x^1 + 2v\zeta_y^1 + \zeta_x^3 = 0,\ \sigma\eta_x + 2v\eta_y + 2B_u^y = 0,$

$\beta\eta_{uu} - 4\alpha\zeta_{xu}^3 - \beta\zeta_{uy}^3 - \beta\zeta_{xu}^2 = 0,\ \beta\eta_{uy} - \beta\zeta_{xy}^2 + 4\alpha\eta_{xu} - 2\alpha\zeta_{xx}^2 = 0,$

$\sigma\zeta_u^1 + 6\delta\zeta_x^1 + \sigma B_u^t + \zeta_u^3 = 0,\ \eta_t + 2\gamma\eta_x + \sigma\eta_y + 2B_u^x = 0,$

$6\alpha\zeta_x^1 + 3\delta\zeta_y^1 + \gamma\zeta_u^1 + \gamma B_u^t + \zeta_u^2 = 0,\ B_t^t - \zeta_y^3 + 2\gamma\zeta_x^1 + \sigma\zeta_y^1 - 2\eta_u = 0,$

$\zeta_t^2 - \gamma\zeta_t^1 - \gamma\zeta_y^3 + \gamma B_t^t - 2\gamma\eta_u + \gamma\zeta_x^2 + \sigma\zeta_y^2 - 6\alpha\eta_x - 3\delta\eta_y = 0$

$$\gamma \xi_u^2 - 2\alpha \xi_t^1 - 2\alpha \xi_y^3 + 2\alpha B_t^t - 6\alpha \eta_u + 4\alpha \xi_x^2 + 3\delta \xi_y^2 = 0,$$
$$6\alpha \xi_x^3 - 9\delta \eta_u + 3\delta \xi_x^2 + \gamma \xi_u^3 + \sigma \xi_u^2 + 3\delta B_t^t - 3\delta \xi_t^1 = 0,$$
$$2\gamma \xi_x^3 - 6\delta \eta_x - 2\sigma \eta_u + 2\nu \xi_y^2 - \sigma \xi_t^1 + \sigma B_t^t + \xi_t^3 = 0,$$
$$2\beta \eta_u - 3\beta \xi_x^2 - 4\alpha \xi_x^3 + \beta \xi_t^1 + \beta \xi_y^3 - \beta B_t^t = 0,$$
$$\sigma \xi_x^3 - \nu \xi_x^2 + \nu B_t^t - \nu \xi_t^1 - 2\nu \eta_u + \nu \xi_y^3 = 0.$$

We achieve the solution of the system with regards to ξ^1, ξ^2, ξ^3 and η as

$$\xi^1 = c_1 t + c_2, \quad \xi^3 = \frac{2}{3} c_1 y - \frac{4\alpha \nu}{9\delta} c_1 t + \frac{1}{3} c_1 \sigma t + c_3, \quad B^t = \frac{2}{3} c_1 t + F_3(x, y),$$

$$\xi^2 = \frac{1}{3} c_1 x + \frac{2\alpha}{9\delta} c_1 y + F_1(t), \quad \eta = -\frac{1}{27\delta^2} \{(-2\sigma\alpha c_1 + 6\gamma c_1 \delta - 9\delta F_1'(t))y\} + F_2(t),$$

$$B^x = \frac{1}{54\delta^2} \{(6\gamma c_1 \delta \sigma - 2c_1 \alpha \sigma^2 - 9\delta \sigma F_1'(t) - 9\delta y F_1''(t) - 27\delta^2 F_2'(t))u\} + G(t, x, y),$$

$$B^y = \frac{1}{27\delta^2} \{\nu(6\gamma c_1 \delta - 2\sigma\alpha c_1 - 9\delta F_1'(t))u\} - \int G_x(t, x, y) dy + F_4(t, x).$$

Functions $F_1(t)$, $F_2(t)$, $F_3(x, y)$, $F_4(x, t)$, and $G(t, x, y)$ in the solution are arbitrary so are constants c_1, c_2 and c_3. Thus, we have the five Noether symmetries together with their respective gauge functions as:

$$\mathcal{P}_1 = \frac{\partial}{\partial t}, \quad B^t = 0, \quad B^x = 0, \quad B^y = 0,$$

$$\mathcal{P}_2 = \frac{\partial}{\partial y}, \quad B^t = 0, \quad B^x = 0, \quad B^y = 0,$$

$$\mathcal{P}_3 = t\frac{\partial}{\partial t} + \left(\frac{1}{3}x + \frac{2\alpha}{9\delta}y\right)\frac{\partial}{\partial x} + \left(\frac{2}{3}y - \frac{4\alpha\nu}{9\delta}t + \frac{1}{3}\sigma t\right)\frac{\partial}{\partial y} - \frac{1}{27\delta^2}(6\gamma\delta - 2\sigma\alpha)\frac{\partial}{\partial u},$$

$$B^t = \frac{2}{3}t, \quad B^x = \frac{\sigma}{54\delta^2}(6\gamma\delta - 2\alpha\sigma)u, \quad B^y = \frac{\nu}{27\delta^2}(6\gamma\delta - 2\alpha\sigma)u,$$

$$\mathcal{P}_{F_1} = F_1(t)\frac{\partial}{\partial x} + \frac{1}{3\delta}yF_1'(t)\frac{\partial}{\partial u}, \quad B^t = 0, \quad B^x = -\left(\frac{9\sigma}{54\delta}F_1'(t) + \frac{9}{54\delta}yF_1''(t)\right)u,$$

$$B^y = -\frac{\nu}{3\delta}F_1'(t)u,$$

$$\mathcal{P}_{F_2} = F_2(t)\frac{\partial}{\partial u}, \quad B^t = 0, \quad B^x = -\frac{1}{2}F_2'(t)u, \quad B^y = 0.$$

We invoke the relation [70]:

$$T^k = \mathcal{L}\tau^k + (\xi^\alpha - \psi_{x^j}^\alpha \tau^j)\left(\frac{\partial \mathcal{L}}{\partial \psi_{x^k}^\alpha} - \sum_{l=1}^{k} D_{x^l}\left(\frac{\partial \mathcal{L}}{\partial \psi_{x^l x^k}^\alpha}\right)\right) + \sum_{l=k}^{n}(\eta_l^\alpha - \psi_{x^l x^j}^\alpha \tau^j)\frac{\partial \mathcal{L}}{\partial \psi_{x^k x^l}^\alpha},$$

to secure the conserved vectors for the six Noether symmetries respectively as:

$$T_1^t = \frac{1}{2}\alpha u_{xx}^2 - \alpha u_x^3 - \frac{1}{2}\gamma u_x^2 + \frac{1}{2}\beta u_{xx} u_{xy} - \frac{3}{2}\delta u_x^2 u_y - \frac{1}{2}\sigma u_x u_y - \frac{1}{2}\nu u_y^2,$$

$$T_1^x = 3\alpha u_t u_x^2 + \alpha u_t u_{xxx} - \alpha u_{xx} u_{tx} + \gamma u_t u_x + \frac{3}{4}\beta u_t u_{xxy} - \frac{1}{4}\beta u_{xx} u_{ty}$$
$$- \frac{1}{2}\beta u_{tx} u_{xy} + 3\delta u_t u_x u_y + \frac{1}{2}\sigma u_t u_y + \frac{1}{2}u_t^2,$$

$$T_1^y = \frac{1}{4}\beta u_t u_{xxx} - \frac{1}{4}\beta u_{xx} u_{tx} + \frac{3}{2}\delta u_t u_x^2 + \frac{1}{2}\sigma u_t u_x + \nu u_t u_y;$$

$$T_2^t = \frac{1}{2}u_x u_y,$$

$$T_2^x = \frac{1}{2}u_t u_y + 3\alpha u_x^2 u_y + \alpha u_{xxx} u_y - \alpha u_{xx} u_{xy} + \frac{3}{4}\beta u_y u_{xxy} - \frac{1}{2}\beta u_{xy}^2$$
$$- \frac{1}{4}\beta u_{xx} u_{yy} + \gamma u_x u_y + 3\delta u_x u_y^2 + \frac{1}{2}\sigma u_y^2,$$
$$T_2^y = \frac{1}{2}\alpha u_{xx}^2 - \frac{1}{2}u_t u_x - \alpha u_x^3 - \frac{1}{2}\gamma u_x^2 + \frac{1}{4}\beta u_{xx} u_{xy} + \frac{1}{4}\beta u_{xxx} u_y + \frac{1}{2}\nu u_y^2;$$

$$T_3^t = \frac{1}{6}xu_x^2 - t\alpha u_x^3 - \frac{1}{2}\gamma t u_x^2 - \frac{3}{2}\delta t u_y u_x^2 + \frac{1}{9\delta}\alpha y u_x^2 - \frac{1}{27\delta^2}\alpha \sigma y u_x$$
$$+ \frac{1}{3}y u_y u_x - \frac{2}{9\delta}\alpha v t u_y u_x - \frac{1}{3}t\sigma u_y u_x + \frac{1}{9\delta}y\gamma u_x - \frac{1}{2}v t u_y^2$$
$$+ \frac{1}{2}\alpha t u_{xx}^2 + \frac{1}{2}\beta t u_{xy} u_{xx},$$

$$T_3^x = \frac{2}{3}x\alpha u_x^3 + \frac{4}{9\delta}\alpha^2 y u_x^3 + \frac{1}{6}\gamma x u_x^2 - \frac{2}{9\delta^2}\alpha^2 \sigma y u_x^2 + \frac{7}{3}\alpha y u_y u_x^2 + \frac{1}{2}\delta x u_y u_x^2$$
$$- \frac{4}{3\delta}\alpha^2 v t u_y u_x^2 + \alpha\sigma t u_y u_x^2 + 3\alpha t u_t u_x^2 + \frac{7}{9\delta}\alpha\gamma y u_x^2 + 2\delta y u_y^2 u_x$$
$$- \frac{4}{3}\alpha v t u_y^2 u_x + \delta\sigma t u_y^2 u_x - \frac{2}{27\delta^2}\alpha\gamma\sigma y u_x + \frac{4}{3}\gamma y u_y u_x - \frac{4}{9\delta}\alpha\gamma v t u_y u_x$$
$$+ \frac{1}{3}\gamma\sigma t u_y u_x - \frac{2}{9\delta}\alpha\sigma y u_y u_x - \frac{1}{6}\beta u_{xy} u_x - \frac{1}{3}\alpha u_{xx} u_x - \frac{1}{18\delta}\alpha\beta u_{xx} u_x$$
$$+ \frac{1}{4}\beta x u_{xxy} u_x + \frac{1}{6\delta}\alpha\beta y u_{xxy} u_x + \frac{1}{3}x\alpha u_{xxx} u_x + \frac{2}{9\delta}\alpha^2 y u_{xxx} u_x$$
$$+ \gamma t u_t u_x + 3\delta t u_y u_t u_x + \frac{2}{9\delta}\gamma^2 y u_x + \frac{1}{6}\sigma^2 t u_y^2 - \frac{1}{6}v x u_y^2 - \frac{1}{9\delta}\alpha v y u_y^2$$
$$+ \frac{1}{3}\sigma y u_y^2 - \frac{2}{9\delta}\alpha v\sigma t u_y^2 - \frac{1}{3}\beta y u_{xy}^2 + \frac{2}{9\delta}\alpha\beta v t u_{xy}^2 - \frac{1}{6}\beta\sigma t u_{xy}^2 - \frac{1}{6}\alpha x u_{xx}^2$$
$$- \frac{1}{9\delta}\alpha^2 y u_{xx}^2 - \frac{1}{27\delta^2}\alpha\sigma^2 y u_y + \frac{1}{9\delta}\gamma\sigma y u_y + \frac{1}{54\delta^2}\alpha\beta\sigma u_{xx} - \frac{1}{6}\beta u_y u_{xx}$$
$$- \frac{1}{6}y\beta u_{yy} u_{xx} + \frac{1}{9\delta}\alpha\beta v t u_{yy} u_{xx} - \frac{1}{12}\beta\sigma t u_{yy} u_{xx} + \frac{1}{2}t u_t^2 - \frac{2}{3}\alpha y u_{xy} u_{xx}$$
$$- \frac{1}{12}\beta x u_{xy} u_{xx} + \frac{4}{9\delta}\alpha^2 v t u_{xy} u_{xx} - \frac{1}{3}\alpha\sigma t u_{xy} u_{xx} - \frac{1}{18\delta}\alpha\beta y u_{xy} u_{xx}$$
$$- \frac{1}{18\delta}\beta\gamma u_{xx} - \frac{1}{18\delta^2}\alpha\beta\sigma y u_{xxy} + \frac{1}{2}\beta y u_y u_{xxy} - \frac{1}{3\delta}\alpha\beta v t u_y u_{xxy}$$
$$+ \frac{1}{4}\beta\sigma t u_y u_{xxy} + \frac{1}{6\delta}\beta\gamma y u_{xxy} - \frac{2}{27\delta^2}\alpha^2 \sigma y u_{xxx} + \frac{2}{3}\alpha y u_y u_{xxx}$$
$$- \frac{4}{9\delta}\alpha^2 v t u_y u_{xxx} + \frac{1}{3}\alpha\sigma t u_y u_{xxx} + \frac{2}{9\delta}\alpha\gamma y u_{xxx} - \frac{1}{27\delta^2}\alpha\sigma y u_t + \frac{1}{3}y u_y u_t$$
$$- \frac{2}{9\delta}\alpha v t u_y u_t + \frac{2}{3}\sigma t u_y u_t + \frac{3}{4}\beta t u_{xxy} u_t + \alpha t u_{xxx} u_t + \frac{1}{9\delta}\gamma y u_t - \frac{1}{4}\beta t u_{xx} u_{ty}$$
$$- \frac{1}{2}\beta t u_{xy} u_{tx} - \alpha t u_{xx} u_{tx} - \frac{1}{9\delta}\gamma\sigma u + \frac{1}{27\delta^2}\alpha\sigma^2 u,$$

$$T_3^y = \frac{1}{2}\delta x u_x^3 - \frac{1}{3}\alpha y u_x^3 + \frac{4}{9\delta}\alpha^2 v t u_x^3 - \frac{1}{3}\alpha\sigma t u_x^3 + \frac{2}{9\delta}\alpha\gamma v t u_x^2 + \frac{1}{6}\sigma x u_x^2$$
$$- \frac{1}{6}\gamma\sigma t u_x^2 + \frac{3}{2}\delta t u_t u_x^2 - \frac{1}{27\delta^2}\alpha\sigma^2 y u_x + \frac{1}{9\delta}\gamma\sigma y u_x + \frac{1}{3}v x u_y u_x$$
$$+ \frac{2}{9\delta}\alpha v y u_y u_x - \frac{1}{12}\beta u_{xx} u_x + \frac{1}{12}\beta x u_{xxx} u_x + \frac{1}{18\delta}\alpha\beta y u_{xxx} u_x$$
$$- \frac{1}{3}y u_t u_x + \frac{2}{9\delta}\alpha v t u_t u_x + \frac{1}{3}\sigma t u_t u_x - \frac{2}{9\delta}\alpha v^2 t u_y^2 + \frac{1}{3}v y u_y^2 + \frac{1}{6}v\sigma t u_y^2$$
$$+ \frac{1}{3}\alpha y u_{xx}^2 - \frac{1}{12}\beta x u_{xx}^2 - \frac{2}{9\delta}\alpha^2 v t u_{xx}^2 + \frac{1}{6}\alpha\sigma t u_{xx}^2 - \frac{1}{18\delta}\alpha\beta y u_{xx}^2$$
$$+ \frac{2}{9\delta}\gamma v y u_y - \frac{2}{27\delta^2}\alpha v\sigma y u_y + \frac{1}{6}\beta y u_{xy} u_{xx} - \frac{1}{9\delta}\alpha\beta v t u_{xy} u_{xx}$$

$$+ \frac{1}{12}\beta\sigma t u_{xy} u_{xx} - \frac{1}{54\delta^2}\alpha\beta\sigma y u_{xxx} + \frac{1}{6}\beta y u_y u_{xxx} - \frac{1}{9\delta}\alpha\beta v t u_y u_{xxx}$$
$$+ \frac{1}{12}\beta\sigma t u_y u_{xxx} + \frac{1}{18\delta}\beta\gamma y u_{xxx} + v t u_y u_t + \frac{1}{4}\beta t u_{xxx} u_t$$
$$- \frac{1}{4}\beta t u_{xx} u_{tx} - \frac{2}{9\delta}\gamma v u + \frac{2}{27\delta^2}\alpha v \sigma u;$$

$$T^t_{F_1} = \frac{1}{2}u_x^2 F_1(t) - \frac{1}{6\delta}y u_x F_1'(t),$$

$$T^x_{F_1} = 2\alpha u_x^3 F_1(t) + \alpha u_{xxx} u_x F_1(t) - \frac{1}{2}\alpha u_{xx}^2 F_1(t) + \frac{1}{2}\gamma u_x^2 F_1(t)$$
$$+ \frac{3}{4}\beta u_x u_{xxy} F_1(t) - \frac{1}{4}\beta u_{xx} u_{xy} F_1(t) + \frac{3}{2}\delta u_x^2 u_y F_1(t) - \frac{1}{6\delta}y u_t F_1'(t)$$
$$- \frac{1}{2}v u_y^2 F_1(t) + \frac{1}{12\delta}\beta u_{xx} F_1'(t) - \frac{1}{\delta}\alpha y u_x^2 F_1'(t) - \frac{1}{3\delta}\alpha y u_{xxx} F_1'(t)$$
$$- \frac{1}{4\delta}\beta y u_{xxy} F_1'(t) - \frac{1}{3\delta}\gamma y u_x F_1'(t) - y u_x u_y F_1'(t) - \frac{1}{6\delta}\sigma y u_y F_1'(t)$$
$$+ \frac{1}{6\delta}\sigma u F_1'(t) + \frac{1}{6\delta}y u F_1''(t),$$

$$T^y_{F_1} = \frac{1}{4}\beta u_{xxx} u_x F_1(t) - \frac{1}{4}\beta u_{xx}^2 F_1(t) + \frac{3}{2}\delta u_x^3 F_1(t) + \frac{1}{2}\sigma u_x^2 F_1(t)$$
$$+ v u_x u_y F_1(t) - \frac{1}{12\delta}\beta y u_{xxx} F_1'(t) - \frac{1}{6\delta}\sigma y u_x F_1'(t) - \frac{1}{2}y u_x^2 F_1'(t)$$
$$- \frac{1}{3\delta}v y u_y F_1'(t) + \frac{1}{3\delta}v u F_1'(t);$$

$$T^t_{F_2} = -\frac{1}{2}u_x F_2(t),$$

$$T^x_{F_2} = -3\alpha u_x^2 F_2(t) - \alpha u_{xxx} F_2(t) - \gamma u_x F_2(t) - \frac{3}{4}\beta u_{xxy} F_2(t) - 3\delta u_x u_y F_2(t)$$
$$- \frac{1}{2}\sigma u_y F_2(t) - \frac{1}{2}u_t F_2(t) + \frac{1}{2}u F_2'(t),$$

$$T^y_{F_2} = -\frac{1}{4}\beta u_{xxx} F_2(t) - \frac{3}{2}\delta u_x^2 F_2(t) - \frac{1}{2}\sigma u_x F_2(t) - v u_y F_2(t).$$

6. Particular Notes on the Conservation Laws

In the latter part of our investigation in this study, local conservation laws, which have an important place in the use of linearization techniques, numerical schemes as well as stability analysis of solutions were achieved. It is well understood that conservation laws are the key ingredients in a bid to deduce the physical aspects of the underlying model. Some well known conserved quantities in physics are the conservation of mass (or matter), energy (power), momentum (linear or angular) as well as Hamiltonian. For instance, the conservation of energy is a consequence of the time invariance of physical systems. In this regard, added to the fact already known that the prevalence of functions in the conserved quantities reveals that the model under consideration has a limitless number of conservation laws, T^1, X^1 and Y^1 correspond to conservation of momentum.

7. Conclusions

This paper presents a study carried out on the (2+1)-dimensional generalized Bogoyavlensky–Konopelchenko Equation (4). Lie group analysis is invoked to obtain solutions to the equation via the corresponding optimal system of Lie subalgebras in one dimension where various members of the system are engaged to perform the reductions of (4). As a result of the action, diverse solitary wave solutions were achieved and these include elliptic integrals, trigonometric, Weierstrass, complex, topological kink and anti-kink functions. Moreover, on adopting the bifurcation theory of dynamical systems, we obtained nontrivial bounded and unbounded travelling wave solutions of (4) comprising algebraic, rational, periodic, hyperbolic as well as trigonometric functions. Numerical simulations of the various results gained are performed, analyzed and discussed. Further to that, we derived conservation laws of the equation by engaging the multiplier technique and Noether's theorem where we secured various local conserved vectors. In addition to the diverse advantages and merits of the achieved solutions in this study in various fields of science and engineering, the conservation laws investigated are also of importance. In classical physics, we have these laws consisting of the conservation of energy, and linear as well as angular momentum. Conserved quantities are crucial to our comprehension of the physical world which are seen to be basic laws of nature. Thus, they possess a wide range of applications in physics, and in other diverse fields of study, for instance, chemistry and engineering to mention a few. Some of these applications have been given earlier. Therefore, our results can be utilized for experimental and applied purposes for further studies in various areas of research in science, technology and engineering.

Author Contributions: Conceptualization, O.D.A. and L.Z.; methodology, O.D.A. and L.Z.; software, O.D.A.; validation, O.D.A., L.Z. and C.M.K.; writing—original draft preparation, O.D.A.; writing—review and editing, O.D.A. and C.M.K. All authors have agreed to the published version of the manuscript.

Funding: This research received no external funding.

Acknowledgments: O. D. Adeyemo thanks Shandong University of Science and Technology, People's Republic of China for the three months financial support given during his visit. It shall not be forgotten.

Conflicts of Interest: The authors declare no conflict of interest.

Abbreviations

ODEs	Ordinary Differential equations
LODEs	Linear Ordinary Differential equations
NODEs	Nonlinear Ordinary Differential equations
PDEs	Partial differential equations
NLDEs	Nonlinear differential equations
NLPDEs	Nonlinear partial differential equations
LIPDEs	Linear partial differential equations
KdV	Kortweg-de Vries
KP	Kadomtsev–Petviashvili
KP-MEW	Kadomtsev–Petviashvili-Modified Equal Width equation
KP-BBM	Kadomtsov-Petviashivilli-Benjamin-Bona-Mahony
(2+1)-D genBKe	(2+1)-dimensional generalized Bogoyavlensky–Konopelchenko equation
2D	Two-dimensional
3D	Three-dimensional

References

1. Adeyemo, O.D.; Motsepa, T.; Khalique, C.M. A study of the generalized nonlinear advection-diffusion equation arising in engineering sciences. *Alex. Eng. J.* **2022**, *61*, 185–194. [CrossRef]
2. Khalique, C.M.; Adeyemo, O.D. A study of (3+1)-dimensional generalized Korteweg–de Vries–Zakharov–Kuznetsov equation via Lie symmetry approach. *Results Phys.* **2020**, *18*, 103197. [CrossRef]
3. Shafiq, A.; Khalique, C.M. Lie group analysis of upper convected Maxwell fluid flow along stretching surface. *Alex. Eng. J.* **2020**, *59*, 2533–2541. [CrossRef]
4. Gao, X.Y.; Guo, Y.J.; Shan, W.R. Cosmic dusty plasmas via a (3+1)-dimensional generalized variable-coefficient Kadomtsev-Petviashvili-Burgers-type equation: Auto-Bäcklund transformations, solitons and similarity reductions plus observational/experimental supports. *Waves Random Complex Media* **2021**, 1–21. [CrossRef]

5. Khalique, C.M.; Adeyemo, O.D. Langrangian formulation and solitary wave solutions of a generalized Zakharov-Kuznetsov equation with dual power-law nonlinearity in physical sciences and engineering. *J. Ocean Eng. Sci.* **2021**. [CrossRef]
6. Khalique, C.M.; Adeyemo, O.D. Closed-form solutions and conserved vectors of a generalized (3+1)-dimensional breaking soliton equation of engineering and nonlinear science. *Mathematics* **2020**, *8*, 1692. [CrossRef]
7. Adeyemo, O.D. Applications of cnoidal and snoidal wave solutions via an optimal system of subalgebras for a generalized extended (2+1)-D quantum Zakharov-Kuznetsov equation with power-law nonlinearity in oceanography and ocean engineering. *J. Ocean Eng. Sci.* **2022**, in press. [CrossRef]
8. Adeyemo, O.D.; Khalique, C.M. Dynamics of soliton waves of group-invariant solutions through optimal system of an extended KP-like equation in higher dimensions with applications in medical sciences and mathematical physics. *J. Geom. Phys.* **2022**, *177*, 104502. [CrossRef]
9. Adeyemo, O.D.; Khalique, C.M. Dynamical soliton wave structures of one-dimensional Lie subalgebras via group-invariant solutions of a higher-dimensional soliton equation in ocean physics and mechatronics engineering. *Commun. Appl. Math. Comput.* **2022**, in press.
10. Jiong, S. Auxiliary equation method for solving nonlinear partial differential equations. *Phys. Lett. A* **2003**, *309*, 387–396.
11. Wazwaz, A.M. The tanh and sine-cosine method for compact and noncompact solutions of nonlinear Klein Gordon equation. *Appl. Math. Comput.* **2005**, *167*, 1179–1195. [CrossRef]
12. He, J.H.; Wu, X.H. Exp-function method for nonlinear wave equations. *Chaos Soliton Fract.* **2006**, *30*, 70. [CrossRef]
13. Ablowitz, M.J.; Clarkson, P.A. *Solitons, Nonlinear Evolution Equations and Inverse Scattering*; Cambridge University Press: Cambridge, UK, 1991.
14. Adomian, G. *Solving Frontier Problems of Physics: The Decomposition Method*; Kluwer Academic Publishers: Dordrecht, The Netherlands, 1994.
15. Agrawal, G.P. *Nonlinear Fiber Optics*; Academic Press: New York, NY, USA, 1995.
16. Shukla, P.K.; Mamun, A.A. *Introduction to Dusty Plasma Physics*; Institute of Physics Publishing: Bristol, UK, 2002.
17. Kochanov, M.B.; Kudryashov, N.A.; Sinel'shchikov, D.I. Non-linear waves on shallow water under an ice cover, higher order expansions. *J. Appl. Math. Mech.* **2013**, *77*, 25–32. [CrossRef]
18. Korteweg, D.J.; Vries, G.D. On the change of form of long waves advancing in a rectangular canal, and on a new type of long stationary waves. *Lond. Edinb. Dubl. Phil. Mag.* **1895**, *39*, 422–443. [CrossRef]
19. El-Tantawy, S.A.; Moslem, W.M. Nonlinear structures of the Korteweg-de Vries and modified Korteweg-de Vries equations in non-Maxwellian electron-positron-ion plasma: Solitons collision and rogue waves. *Phys. Plasmas* **2014**, *21*, 052112. [CrossRef]
20. Gardner, C.S.; Greene, J.M.; Kruskal, M.D.; Miura, R.M. Method for solving the Korteweg-de Vries equation. *Phys. Rev. Lett.* **1967**, *19*, 1095–1097. [CrossRef]
21. Yu, J.; Lou, S.Y. Deformation and (3+1)-dimensional integrable model. *Sci. China Ser. A* **2000**, *43*, 655–660. [CrossRef]
22. Lou, S.Y. Searching for higher dimensional integrable models from lower ones via Painlevé analysis. *Phys. Lett.* **1998**, *80*, 5027–5031 [CrossRef]
23. El-Wakii, S.A.; Abdou, M.A.; Elhanbaly, A. New solitons and periodic wave solutions for nonlinear evolution equations. *Phys. Lett. A* **2006**, *353*, 40–47. [CrossRef]
24. Gu, C.H. *Soliton Theory and Its Application*; Zhejiang Science and Technology Press: Hangzhou, China, 1990.
25. Zhou, Y.; Wang, M.; Wang, Y. Periodic wave solutions to a coupled KdV equations with variable coefficients. *Phys. Lett. A* **2003**, *308*, 31–36. [CrossRef]
26. Kudryashov, N.A.; Loguinova, N.B. Extended simplest equation method for nonlinear differential equations. *Appl. Math. Comput.* **2008**, *205*, 396–402. [CrossRef]
27. Ovsiannikov, L.V. *Group Analysis of Differential Equations*; Academic Press: New York, NY, USA, 1982.
28. Bluman, G.W.; Kumei, S. *Symmetries and Differential Equations*; Springer: New York, NY, USA, 1989.
29. Olver, P.J. *Applications of Lie Groups to Differential Equations, Graduate Texts in Mathematics*, 2nd ed.; Springer: Berlin, Germany, 1993; Volume 107.
30. Ibragimov, N.H. *CRC Handbook of Lie Group Analysis of Differential Equations*; CRC Press: Boca Raton, FL, USA, 1994; Volume 1.
31. Ibragimov, N.H. *Elementary Lie Group Analysis and Ordinary Differential Equations*; John Wiley & Sons: Chichester, NY, USA, 1999.
32. Wang, M.; Li, X.; Zhang, J. The $(G'/G)-$ expansion method and travelling wave solutions for linear evolution equations in mathematical physics. *Phys. Lett. A* **2005**, *24*, 1257–1268.
33. Matveev, V.B.; Salle, M.A. *Darboux Transformations and Solitons*; Springer: New York, NY, USA, 1991.
34. Chen, Y.; Yan, Z. New exact solutions of (2+1)–dimensional Gardner equation via the new sine-Gordon equation expansion method. *Chaos Solitons Fract.* **2005**, *26*, 399–406. [CrossRef]
35. Kudryashov, N.A. Simplest equation method to look for exact solutions of nonlinear differential equations. *Chaos Solitons Fract.* **2005**, *24*, 1217–1231. [CrossRef]
36. Hossain, A.K.M.K.S.; Akbar, M.A. Traveling wave solutions of nonlinear evolution equations via modified simple equation method. *Int. J. Appl. Math. Theor. Phys.* **2017**, *3*, 20–25. [CrossRef]
37. Seadawy, A.R. Fractional solitary wave solutions of the nonlinear higher-order extended KdV equation in a stratified shear flow: Part I. *Comput. Math. Appl.* **2015**, *70*, 345–352. [CrossRef]
38. Hirota, R. *The Direct Method in Soliton Theory*; Cambridge University Press: Cambridge, UK, 2004.

39. Zhang, L.; Khalique, C.M. Classification and bifurcation of a class of second-order ODEs and its application to nonlinear PDEs. *Discret. Contin. Dyn. Syst. Ser. S* **2018**, *11*, 777–790. [CrossRef]
40. Jiang, B.; Liu, Y.; Zhang, J. Bifurcations and some new travelling wave solutions for the CH-γ equation. *App. Math. Comput.* **2014**, *228*, 220–233. [CrossRef]
41. Saha, A. Bifurcation of travelling wave solutions for the generalized KP-MEW eequations. *Commun. Nonlinear Sci. Numer. Simul.* **2012**, *17*, 3539–3551. [CrossRef]
42. Ganguly, A.; Das, A. Explicit solutions and stability analysis of the (2+1)-dimensional KP-BBM equation with dispersion effect. *Commun. Nonlinear Sci. Numer. Simul.* **2015**, *25*, 102–117. [CrossRef]
43. Das, A.; Ganguly, A. Existence and stability of dispersive solutions to the Kadomtsev–Petviashvili equation in the presence of dispersion effect. *Commun. Nonlinear Sci. Numer. Simul.* **2017**, *48*, 326–339. [CrossRef]
44. Xin, X.; Liu, X.; Zhang, L. Explicit solutions of the Bogoyavlensky-Konoplechenko equation. *Appl. Math. Comput.* **2010**, *215*, 3669–3673. [CrossRef]
45. Ray, S.S. On conservation laws by Lie symmetry analysis for (2+1)-dimensional Bogoyavlensky–Konopelchenko equation in wave propagation. *Comput. Math. Appl.* **2017**, *74*, 1158–1165. [CrossRef]
46. Triki, H.; Jovanoski, Z.; Biswa, A. Shock wave solutions to the Bogoyavlensky–Konopelchenko equation. *Indian J. Phys.* **2014**, *88*, 71–74. [CrossRef]
47. Konopelchenko, B.G. *Solitons in Multidimensions-Inverse Spectral Transfrom Method*; World Scientific: River Edge, NJ, USA, 1993.
48. Prabhakar, M.V.; Bhate, H. Exact solutions of the Bogoyavlensky-Konoplechenco equation. *Lett. Math. Phys.* **2003**, *64*, 1–6. [CrossRef]
49. Bogoyavlenski, O.I. Overturning solitons in new two-dimensional integrable equations. *Math. USSR-Izv.* **1990**, *34*, 245–259. [CrossRef]
50. Chen, S.T.; Ma, W.X. Exact solutions to a generalized Bogoyavlensky–Konopelchenko equation via maple symbolic computations. *Complexity* **2019**, *2019*, 8787460. [CrossRef]
51. Li, Q.; Chaolu, T.; Wang, Y. Lump-type solutions and lump solutions for the (2+1)-dimensional generalized Bogoyavlensky–Konopelchenko equation. *Comp. Math. Appl.* **2019**, *77*, 2077–2085. [CrossRef]
52. Chen, S.T.; Ma, W.X. Lump solution to a generalized Bogoyavlensky–Konopelchenko equation. *Front. Math. China* **2018**, *13*, 525–534. [CrossRef]
53. Pouyanmehr, R.; Hosseini, K.; Ansari, R. Different wave structures to the (2+1)-dimensional generalized Bogoyavlensky–Konopelchenko equation. *Int. J. Appl. Comput. Math.* **2019**, *5*, 1–12. [CrossRef]
54. Liu, F.Y.; Gao, Y.T.; Yu, X.; Li, L.Q.; Ding, C.C. Lie group analysis and analytic solutions for a (2+1)-dimensional generalized Bogoyavlensky–Konopelchenko equation in fluid mechanics and plasma physics. *Eur. Phys. J. Plus* **2021**, *136*, 1–14. [CrossRef]
55. Bluman, G.W.; Cole, J.D. *Similarity Methods for Differential Equations*; Springer: New York, NY, USA, 1974.
56. Olver, P.J. *Application of Lie Groups to Differential Equations*; Springer: New York, NY, USA, 1993.
57. Grigoriev, Y.N.; Kovalev, V.F.; Meleshko, S.V.; Ibragimov, N.H. *Symmetries of Integro-Differential Equations: With Applications in Mechanics and Plasma Physics*; Springer: New York, NY, USA, 2010.
58. Gradshteyn, I.S.; Ryzhik, I.M. *Table of Integrals, Series, and Products*, 7th ed.; Academic Press: New York, NY, USA, 2007.
59. Akhiezer, N.I. *Elements of The Theory of Elliptic Functions*; American Mathematical Society: Providence, RI, USA, 1990.
60. Kudryashov, N.A. *Analytical Theory of Nonlinear Differential Equations*; Igevsk Institute of Computer Investigations: Moskow, Russia, 2004.
61. Kudryashov, N.A. First integrals and general solution of the Fokas-Lenells equation. *Optik* **2019**, *195*, 163135. [CrossRef]
62. Billingham, J.; King, A.C. *Wave Motion*; Cambridge University Press: Cambridge, UK, 2000.
63. Chow, S.N.; Hale, J.K. *Method of Bifurcation Theory*; Springer: New York, NY, USA, 1981.
64. Guckenheimer, J.; Holmes, P. *Dynamical Systems and Bifurcations of Vector Fields*; Springer: New York, NY, USA, 1983.
65. Zhang, L.; Khalique, C.M. Traveling wave solutions and infinite-dimensional linear spaces of multiwave solutions to Jimbo-Miwa equation. *Abstr. Appl. Anal.* **2014**, *2014*, 963852. [CrossRef]
66. Drazin, P.G.; Johnson, R.S. *Solitons: An Introduction*; Cambridge University Press: Cambridge, UK, 1989.
67. Anco, S.C.; Bluman, G.W. Direct construction method for conservation laws of partial differential equations. Part I: Examples of conservation law classifications. *Eur. J. Appl. Math.* **2002**, *13*, 545–566. [CrossRef]
68. Noether, E. Invariante variationsprobleme. *Nachrichten Ges. Wiss. Göttingen Math.-Phys. Kl.* **1918**, *2*, 235–257.
69. Anco, S.C. Generalization of Noethers Theorem in modern Form to Nonvariational Partial Differential Equations. In *Recent Progress and Modern Challenges in Applied Mathematics, Modeling and Computational Science*; Melnik, R., Makarov, R., Beglair, J., Eds.; Fields Institute Communications; Springer: New York, NY, USA, 2017; Volume 79.
70. Sarlet, W. Comment on 'conservation laws of higher order nonlinear PDEs and the variational conservation laws in the class with mixed derivatives'. *J. Phys. A Math. Theor.* **2010**, *43*, 458001. [CrossRef]

Article

Highly Dispersive Optical Solitons in Fiber Bragg Gratings with Kerr Law of Nonlinear Refractive Index

Elsayed M. E. Zayed [1], Mohamed E. M. Alngar [2], Reham M. A. Shohib [3], Anjan Biswas [4,5,6,7,8], Yakup Yıldırım [9], Salam Khan [10], Luminita Moraru [11,*], Simona Moldovanu [12] and Catalina Iticescu [11]

1. Mathematics Department, Faculty of Science, Zagazig University, Zagazig 44519, Egypt
2. Basic Science Department, Faculty of Computers and Artificial Intelligence, Modern University for Technology & Information, Cairo 11585, Egypt
3. Basic Science Department, Higher Institute of Foreign Trade & Management Sciences, New Cairo Academy, Cairo 11765, Egypt
4. Department of Mathematics and Physics, Grambling State University, Grambling, LA 71245, USA
5. Mathematical Modeling and Applied Computation (MMAC) Research Group, Department of Mathematics, King Abdulaziz University, Jeddah 21589, Saudi Arabia
6. Department of Applied Mathematics, National Research Nuclear University, 31 Kashirskoe Hwy, 115409 Moscow, Russia
7. Department of Applied Sciences, Cross–Border Faculty, Dunarea de Jos University of Galati, 111 Domneasca Street, 800201 Galati, Romania
8. Department of Mathematics and Applied Mathematics, Sefako Makgatho Health Sciences University, Medunsa 0204, South Africa
9. Department of Computer Engineering, Biruni University, Isanbul 34010, Turkey
10. Department of Physics, Chemistry and Mathematics, Alabama A & M University, Normal, AL 35762, USA
11. Department of Chemistry, Physics and Environment, Faculty of Sciences and Environment, Dunarea de Jos University of Galati, 47 Domneasca Street, 800008 Galati, Romania
12. Department of Computer Science and Information Technology, Faculty of Automation, Computers, Electrical Engineering and Electronics, Dunarea de Jos University of Galati, 47 Domneasca Street, 800008 Galati, Romania
* Correspondence: luminita.moraru@ugal.ro

Abstract: This paper obtains highly dispersive optical solitons in fiber Bragg gratings with the Kerr law of a nonlinear refractive index. The generalized Kudryashov's approach as well as its newer version makes this retrieval possible. A full spectrum of solitons is thus recovered.

Keywords: Kudryashov; Bragg gratings; solitons

MSC: 78A60

1. Introduction

One of the newly developed concepts in nonlinear optics, applicable to a variety of optoelectronic devices, is highly dispersive (HD) solitons. This emerges out of dire necessity when chromatic dispersion (CD) runs low. Thus, to replenish this low count, additional dispersion terms are taken into consideration. These are sixth-order dispersion (6OD); fifth-order dispersion (5OD); fourth-order dispersion (4OD); third-order dispersion (3OD); and inter–modal dispersion (IMD). The effect of soliton radiation, with such higher order dispersion terms to offset the low count of CD, is neglected to keep the model simple. Other means to compensate for the low count of CD is to introduce Bragg gratings in the fiber structure so that the dispersive reflectivity that it produces additionally replenishes this low count [1–32]. The current paper is the first of its kind to include both effects to offset this low CD. Such a model would also lead to soliton solutions.

The model would, therefore, be handled with the Kerr law of nonlinearity. The method of integrability would be two-fold and both due to Kudryashov. The first approach is the generalized Kudryashov's approach, followed by the lately developed enhanced

Kudryashov's scheme [9–16]. These two approaches can collectively yield a full spectrum of solitons, which are recovered and enumerated in the present paper. The parametric restrictions, also known as certain conditions, are extracted for the solitons to exist. The remaining details are presented in the rest of the paper via the unique integration tools that are discussed.

Governing Model

The perturbed HD nonlinear Schrödinger's equation is firstly introduced as below:

$$i\varphi_t + ia_1\varphi_x + a_2\varphi_{xx} + ia_3\varphi_{xxx} + a_4\varphi_{xxxx} + ia_5\varphi_{xxxxx} + a_6\varphi_{xxxxxx} + b|\varphi|^2\varphi \\ = i\left[\lambda(|\varphi|^2\varphi)_x + \mu(|\varphi|^2)_x\varphi + \theta|\varphi|^2\varphi_x\right], \quad (1)$$

such that θ, μ, λ, b and a_l, ($l = 1$–6) depict real-valued constant parameters, whereas $\varphi(x,t)$ purports a complex-valued function. Setting $\lambda = \mu = \theta = 0$ extracts the governing equation [16]. a_1 comes from the IMD, a_2 implies to the CD, a_3 is related to the 3OD, a_4 stems from the 4OD, a_5 purports the 5OD and a_6 stands for the 6OD. The first term arises from the temporal evolution, where $i = \sqrt{-1}$. μ and θ yield the nonlinear dispersions, b arises from Kerr law nonlinearity, λ comes from the self-steepening (SS) and $\varphi = \varphi(x,t)$ purports the soliton wave.

For the first time in fiber Bragg gratings, the strategic governing model derived from (1) reads as

$$iU_t + ia_{11}V_x + a_{12}V_{xx} + ia_{13}V_{xxx} + a_{14}V_{xxxx} + ia_{15}V_{xxxxx} + a_{16}V_{xxxxxx} \\ + (b_{11}|U|^2 + b_{12}|V|^2)U + i\alpha_1 U_x + \beta_1 V + \sigma_1 U^*V^2 \\ = i\left[\lambda_1(|U|^2 U)_x + \mu_1(|U|^2)_x U + \theta_1 |U|^2 U_x\right], \quad (2)$$

and

$$iV_t + ia_{21}U_x + a_{22}U_{xx} + ia_{23}U_{xxx} + a_{24}U_{xxxx} + ia_{25}U_{xxxxx} + a_{26}U_{xxxxxx} \\ + (b_{21}|V|^2 + b_{22}|U|^2)V + i\alpha_2 V_x + \beta_2 U + \sigma_2 V^*U^2 \\ = i\left[\lambda_2(|V|^2 V)_x + \mu_2(|V|^2)_x V + \theta_2 |V|^2 V_x\right], \quad (3)$$

such that σ_j, λ_j, μ_j, α_j, β_j, θ_j, b_{j1}, b_{j2} and a_{jl}, ($1 \leq l \leq 6, j = 1, 2$) depict real-valued constant parameters, whereas $V(x,t)$ and $U(x,t)$ purport complex-valued functions. a_{j1} and α_j come from the IMD, a_{j2} imply the CD, a_{j3} are related to the 3OD, a_{j4} stem from the 4OD, a_{j5} purport the 5OD and a_{j6} stand for the 6OD. The first terms arise from the temporal evolution, where $i = \sqrt{-1}$. μ_j and θ_j yield the nonlinear dispersions, σ_j denote the four-wave mixing, b_{j1} arise from the self-phase modulation, β_j signify the detuning parameters, b_{j2} denote the cross-phase modulation, λ_j signify the SS, whilst $V(x,t)$ and $U(x,t)$ purport the soliton waves.

2. Mathematical Analysis

The governing model admits the analytical solutions

$$U(x,t) = g_1(\xi) \exp[i\Omega(x,t)],$$
$$V(x,t) = g_2(\xi) \exp[i\Omega(x,t)], \quad (4)$$

such that

$$\Omega(x,t) = -\kappa x + \omega t + \theta_0, \quad \xi = x - vt. \quad (5)$$

Here, $g_j(\xi)$ and $\Omega(x,t)$ signify real-valued functions, whereas v, k, ω and θ_0 purport real-valued constants. For the soliton wave, $\Omega(x,t)$ depicts the phase component, ξ depicts the wave variable, θ_0 arises from the phase constant, v stems from the velocity, ω denotes the wave number, $g_j(\xi)$ come from the amplitude components and κ depicts the frequency.

Placing (4) and (5) into (2) and (3) extracts the strategic equations

$$a_{16}g_2^{(6)} + (a_{14} - 5a_{15}\kappa - 15a_{16}\kappa^2)g_2^{(4)}$$
$$+ (a_{12} + 3a_{13}\kappa - 6a_{14}\kappa^2 - 10a_{15}\kappa^3 + 15a_{16}\kappa^4)g_2''$$
$$+ (\alpha_1 k - \omega)g_1 + (\beta_1 - a_{12}\kappa^2 + a_{11}\kappa + a_{14}\kappa^4 - a_{13}\kappa^3 - a_{16}\kappa^6 + a_{15}\kappa^5)g_2 \quad (6)$$
$$+ [b_{11} - \kappa(\lambda_1 + \theta_1)]g_1^3 + (b_{12} + \sigma_1)g_1 g_2^2 = 0,$$

$$a_{26}g_1^{(6)} + (a_{24} - 5a_{25}\kappa - 15a_{26}\kappa^2)g_1^{(4)}$$
$$+ (a_{22} + 3a_{23}\kappa - 6a_{24}\kappa^2 - 10a_{25}\kappa^3 + 15a_{26}\kappa^4)g_1''$$
$$+ (\alpha_2 k - \omega)g_2 + (a_{21}\kappa + \beta_2 - a_{23}\kappa^3 - a_{22}\kappa^2 + a_{25}\kappa^5 + a_{24}\kappa^4 - a_{26}\kappa^6)g_1 \quad (7)$$
$$+ [b_{21} - \kappa(\lambda_2 + \theta_2)]g_2^3 + (b_{22} + \sigma_2)g_1^2 g_2 = 0,$$

$$(a_{15} - 6a_{16}\kappa)g_2^{(5)} + (a_{13} - 4a_{14}\kappa - 10a_{15}\kappa^2 + 20a_{16}\kappa^3)g_2'''$$
$$- [3\lambda_1 + 2\mu_1 + \theta_1]g_1^2 g_1' + (\alpha_1 - v)g_1' \quad (8)$$
$$+ (a_{11} - 2a_{12}\kappa - 3a_{13}\kappa^2 + 4a_{14}\kappa^3 + 5a_{15}\kappa^4 - 6a_{16}\kappa^5)g_2' = 0,$$

$$(a_{25} - 6a_{26}\kappa)g_1^{(5)} + (a_{23} - 4a_{24}\kappa - 10a_{25}\kappa^2 + 20a_{26}\kappa^3)g_1'''$$
$$- [3\lambda_2 + 2\mu_2 + \theta_2]g_2^2 g_2' + (\alpha_2 - v)g_2' \quad (9)$$
$$+ (a_{21} - 2a_{22}\kappa - 3a_{23}\kappa^2 + 4a_{24}\kappa^3 + 5a_{25}\kappa^4 - 6a_{26}\kappa^5)g_1' = 0.$$

Set

$$g_2(\xi) = \Pi g_1(\xi), \quad \Pi \neq 0, \quad \Pi \neq 1, \quad (10)$$

where Π depicts real-valued constant parameters. Hence, Equations (6)–(9) appear as

$$a_{16}\Pi g_1^{(6)} + (a_{14} - 5a_{15}\kappa - 15a_{16}\kappa^2)\Pi g_1^{(4)}$$
$$+ (a_{12} + 3a_{13}\kappa - 6a_{14}\kappa^2 - 10a_{15}\kappa^3 + 15a_{16}\kappa^4)\Pi g_1''$$
$$+ [\alpha_1 k - \omega + (\beta_1 - a_{12}\kappa^2 + a_{11}\kappa + a_{14}\kappa^4 - a_{13}\kappa^3 - a_{16}\kappa^6 + a_{15}\kappa^5)\Pi]g_1 \quad (11)$$
$$+ [b_{11} - \kappa(\lambda_1 + \theta_1) + (b_{12} + \sigma_1)\Pi^2]g_1^3 = 0,$$

$$a_{26}g_1^{(6)} + (a_{24} - 5a_{25}\kappa - 15a_{26}\kappa^2)g_1^{(4)}$$
$$+ (a_{22} + 3a_{23}\kappa - 6a_{24}\kappa^2 - 10a_{25}\kappa^3 + 15a_{26}\kappa^4)g_1''$$
$$+ [(\alpha_2 k - \omega)\Pi + a_{21}\kappa + \beta_2 - a_{23}\kappa^3 - a_{22}\kappa^2 + a_{25}\kappa^5 + a_{24}\kappa^4 - a_{26}\kappa^6]g_1 \quad (12)$$
$$+ [b_{22} + \sigma_2 + b_{21}\Pi^2 - \kappa(\lambda_2 + \theta_2)\Pi^2]\Pi g_1^3 = 0,$$

$$(a_{15} - 6a_{16}\kappa)\Pi g_1^{(5)} + (a_{13} - 4a_{14}\kappa - 10a_{15}\kappa^2 + 20a_{16}\kappa^3)\Pi g_1'''$$
$$- [3\lambda_1 + 2\mu_1 + \theta_1]g_1^2 g_1' \quad (13)$$
$$+ [\alpha_1 - v + (a_{11} - 2a_{12}\kappa - 3a_{13}\kappa^2 + 4a_{14}\kappa^3 + 5a_{15}\kappa^4 - 6a_{16}\kappa^5)\Pi]g_1' = 0,$$

$$(a_{25} - 6a_{26}\kappa)g_1^{(5)} + (a_{23} - 4a_{24}\kappa - 10a_{25}\kappa^2 + 20a_{26}\kappa^3)g_1'''$$
$$- [3\lambda_2 + 2\mu_2 + \theta_2]\Pi^3 g_1^2 g_1' \quad (14)$$
$$+ [(\alpha_2 - v)\Pi + a_{21} - 2a_{22}\kappa - 3a_{23}\kappa^2 + 4a_{24}\kappa^3 + 5a_{25}\kappa^4 - 6a_{26}\kappa^5]g_1' = 0.$$

Equations (13) and (14) yield the certain restrictions

$$\kappa = \frac{a_{j5}}{6a_{j6}}, \quad (15)$$

$$a_{j3} - 4a_{j4}\kappa - 10a_{j5}\kappa^2 + 20a_{j6}\kappa^3 = 0, \quad (16)$$

$$3\lambda_j + 2\mu_j + \theta_j = 0, \quad (17)$$

$$v = -\alpha_1 + (a_{11} - 2a_{12}\kappa - 3a_{13}\kappa^2 + 4a_{14}\kappa^3 + 5a_{15}\kappa^4 - 6a_{16}\kappa^5)\Pi,$$
$$v = -\alpha_2 + \frac{1}{\Pi}(a_{21} - 2a_{22}\kappa - 3a_{23}\kappa^2 + 4a_{24}\kappa^3 + 5a_{25}\kappa^4 - 6a_{26}\kappa^5), \quad (18)$$

while Equation (18) extracts the constraint relation

$$\alpha_2 = \frac{\alpha_1\Pi + (a_{21} - 2a_{22}\kappa - 3a_{23}\kappa^2 + 4a_{24}\kappa^3 + 5a_{25}\kappa^4 - 6a_{26}\kappa^5) - (a_{11} - 2a_{12}\kappa - 3a_{13}\kappa^2 + 4a_{14}\kappa^3 + 5a_{15}\kappa^4 - 6a_{16}\kappa^5)\Pi^2}{\Pi}. \quad (19)$$

Moreover, Equations (11) and (12) admit the strategic constraints

$$\begin{aligned}\frac{a_{16}\Pi}{a_{26}} &= \frac{(a_{14}-5a_{15}\kappa-15a_{16}\kappa^2)\Pi}{a_{24}-5a_{25}\kappa-15a_{26}\kappa^2} \\ &= \frac{(a_{12}+3a_{13}\kappa-6a_{14}\kappa^2-10a_{15}\kappa^3+15a_{16}\kappa^4)\Pi}{a_{22}+3a_{23}\kappa-6a_{24}\kappa^2-10a_{25}\kappa^3+15a_{26}\kappa^4} \\ &= \frac{\alpha_1 k-\omega+(\beta_1+a_{11}\kappa-a_{12}\kappa^2-a_{13}\kappa^3+a_{14}\kappa^4+a_{15}\kappa^5-a_{16}\kappa^6)\Pi}{(\alpha_2 k-\omega)\Pi+\beta_2+a_{21}\kappa-a_{22}\kappa^2-a_{23}\kappa^3+a_{24}\kappa^4+a_{25}\kappa^5-a_{26}\kappa^6} \\ &= \frac{b_{11}-\kappa(\lambda_1+\theta_1)+(b_{12}+\sigma_1)\Pi^2}{[b_{22}+\sigma_2+b_{21}\Pi^2-\kappa(\lambda_2+\theta_2)\Pi^2]\Pi},\end{aligned} \qquad (20)$$

and the certain parametric restrictions

$$\omega = \frac{\Pi\left[\begin{array}{c}17\kappa^2(a_{26}a_{12}-a_{16}a_{22})-11\kappa^3(a_{16}a_{23}-a_{26}a_{13}) \\ +20a_{16}(\Pi\alpha_2 k+\beta_2+a_{21}\kappa)-20a_{26}(\beta_1+\kappa a_{11})\end{array}\right]-20a_{26}\alpha_1 k}{20(a_{16}\Pi^2-a_{26})},$$

$$a_{24} = \frac{a_{16}a_{22}+3a_{16}a_{23}\kappa-a_{26}a_{12}-3a_{26}a_{13}\kappa+8a_{26}a_{14}\kappa^2}{8a_{16}\kappa^2},$$

$$a_{25} = \frac{40a_{26}a_{15}\kappa^3+a_{16}a_{22}+3a_{16}a_{23}\kappa-a_{26}a_{12}-3a_{26}a_{13}\kappa}{40a_{16}\kappa^3},$$

$$b_{22} = \frac{a_{26}b_{11}-a_{26}\kappa\lambda_1-a_{26}\kappa\theta_1+(a_{16}\kappa\lambda_2-a_{16}b_{21}+a_{16}\kappa\theta_2)\Pi^4+(a_{26}b_{12}+a_{26}\sigma_1-a_{16}\sigma_2)\Pi^2}{a_{16}\Pi^2}. \qquad (21)$$

Equation (11) is also extracted as

$$g_1^{(6)}+\Omega_4 g_1^{(4)}+\Omega_2 g_1''+\Omega_1 g_1+\Omega_3 g_1^3 = 0, \qquad (22)$$

where

$$\begin{aligned}\Omega_4 &= \frac{a_{14}-5a_{15}\kappa-15a_{16}\kappa^2}{a_{16}}, \\ \Omega_2 &= \frac{a_{12}+3a_{13}\kappa-6a_{14}\kappa^2-10a_{15}\kappa^3+15a_{16}\kappa^4}{a_{16}}, \\ \Omega_1 &= -\frac{\alpha_1 k-\omega+(\beta_1-a_{12}\kappa^2+a_{11}\kappa+a_{14}\kappa^4-a_{13}\kappa^3-a_{16}\kappa^6+a_{15}\kappa^5)\Pi}{a_{16}\Pi}, \\ \Omega_3 &= \frac{b_{11}-\kappa(\lambda_1+\theta_1)+(b_{12}+\sigma_1)\Pi^2}{a_{16}\Pi}.\end{aligned} \qquad (23)$$

From the standpoint of electromagnetic theory, Equations (1)–(3) are a far cry from the basic alphabets of electromagnetic theory, namely Maxwell's equation. It is well known that Maxwell's equation led to the derivation of the nonlinear Schrodinger's equation (NLSE) with the Kerr law of nonlinear refractive index by the aid of multiple scales. This is alternatively known as the cubic Schrodinger's equation. It is interesting to point out here that NLSE is a special case of the Schrodinger's equation that appears in Quantum Mechanics when the potential function is the intensity of light. This so happens since the refractive index of light is intensity dependent. Thus, there exists a close proximity between Schrodinger's equation in Quantum Mechanics and NLSE in Quantum Optics. The extended or perturbed version of NLSE is also derived from Maxwell's equation with the inclusion of higher order perturbation terms. These are typically some of the Hamiltonian type of perturbation terms that would include self-steepening effect, self-frequency shift, inter-modal dispersion, detuning effect, and others.

Later, it was realized that the CD alone turns out to be insufficient to maintain the much-needed delicate balance between CD and self-phase modulation (SPM) because of its depletion with trans-continental and trans-oceanic distance soliton transmission through optical fibers. This would lead to a catastrophic pulse collapse. Thus, to circumvent this situation, the concept of HD solitons was conceived a couple of years ago where the low count of CD would be supplemented with higher order dispersion terms. Another engineering marvel that was proposed a couple of decades ago is the introduction of the gratings structure by Bragg, which would lead to the arrest of the pulse collapse and introduce dispersive reflectivity which would maintain the necessary balance between CD and SPM. The current paper is a combination of both, namely introducing HD solitons as well as Bragg grating's structure to ensure the uninterrupted long-distance transmission of solitons. Thus, Equations (2) and (3) can be derived from (1), just as the coupled equation for birefringent fibers are derived from the scalar version of the NLSE. Here, in (2) and (3), the variables U and V represent the forward and backward propagating waves in the cubic nonlinear core.

In this paper, the higher order dispersion terms as well as the nonlinear dispersion due to θ_j (j = 1, 2) are all taken to be strong dispersion. This would only slow down the soliton of the soliton and would introduce some constraints or connectivity between these dispersions and other Hamiltonian perturbation parameters. These are reflected in relations (15)–(17) and the velocity slowdown is reflected in (18) along the two core components. However, the integrability of model (2) and (3) would not be affected. Evidently, these dispersion terms would introduce a considerable amount of soliton radiation. This effect is discarded in the current paper since the study of soliton radiation falls in the continuous regime and can be handled as a separate project with the usage of the variational principle or the method of moments, or even by the theory of unfoldings. Finally, if the dispersive effect was taken to be weak, it would lead to the emergence of quasi-monochromatic solitons that can be recovered only with the usage of multiple scales [21]. However, again, this is outside the scope of the current work.

While the governing equation with Hamiltonian perturbation terms is integrable with the application of the inverse scattering transform which would have additionally revealed soliton radiation effects analytically, this paper focuses on the retrieval of bound state solitons only by the aid of the generalized Kudryashov's approach and the enhanced Kudryashov's method. The details of the retrieval of solitons using these two algorithms are presented in the subsequent sections.

3. Generalized Kudryashov's Method

The integration technique satisfies the analytical solution

$$g_1(\xi) = \frac{\sum_{k=0}^{N} A_k F^k(\xi)}{\sum_{h=0}^{M} B_h F^h(\xi)}, \quad A_N \neq 0, \ B_M \neq 0, \tag{24}$$

such that $F(\xi)$ admits the ancillary equation

$$F'(\xi) = F(\xi)[F(\xi) - 1] \ln H, \quad 0 < H \neq 1, \tag{25}$$

and the explicit solutions

$$F(\xi) = \frac{1}{1 + \varepsilon \exp_H(\xi)}, \tag{26}$$

$$F(\xi) = \frac{1}{1 + \varepsilon[\cosh(\xi \ln H) + \sinh(\xi \ln H)]}. \tag{27}$$

Here, $\varepsilon = \pm 1$, $\exp_H(\xi) = H^{(\xi)}$, A_k ($k = 1 - N$) and B_h ($h = 1 - M$) denote constants, whereas N and M arise from the balance principle.

Setting $\varepsilon = 1$, Equation (27) evolves as the dark soliton

$$F(\xi) = \frac{1}{2}\left[1 - \tanh\left(\frac{1}{2}\xi \ln H\right)\right], \tag{28}$$

whilst setting $\varepsilon = -1$, Equation (27) yields the singular soliton

$$F(\xi) = \frac{1}{2}\left[1 - \coth\left(\frac{1}{2}\xi \ln H\right)\right]. \tag{29}$$

Balancing g_1^3 with $g_1^{(6)}$ extracts the restriction

$$N - M + 6 = 3(N - M) \Longrightarrow N = 3 + M. \tag{30}$$

When $M = 1$, Equation (24) reads as

$$g_1(\xi) = \frac{A_4 F^4(\xi) + A_3 F^3(\xi) + A_2 F^2(\xi) + A_1 F(\xi) + A_0}{B_1 F(\xi) + B_0}, \quad A_4 \neq 0, \quad B_1 \neq 0. \tag{31}$$

Placing (31) with the usage of (25) into (22) leaves us the results

$$A_4 = 24 B_1 \sqrt{-\tfrac{35}{\Omega_3}} \ln^3 H, \quad A_3 = 0, \quad A_2 = -54 B_1 \sqrt{-\tfrac{35}{\Omega_3}} \ln^3 H,$$

$$A_1 = 6 B_1 \sqrt{-\tfrac{35}{\Omega_3}} \ln^3 H, \quad A_0 = 9 B_1 \sqrt{-\tfrac{35}{\Omega_3}} \ln^3 H, \quad B_1 = B_1, \quad B_0 = \tfrac{3}{2} B_1, \tag{32}$$

$$\Omega_4 = -83 \ln^2 H, \quad \Omega_2 = 946 \ln^4 H, \quad \Omega_1 = 1260 \ln^6 H, \quad \Omega_3 < 0. \tag{33}$$

Inserting (32) together with (27)–(29) into (31) acquires the explicit solutions:

(I) The combo bright-singular soliton solutions:

$$U(x,t) = \pm 9 \sqrt{-\tfrac{35}{\Omega_3} \left(\ln^3 H \right)} \left[1 + \frac{4 - 6 \left\{ \begin{array}{l} 1 + \varepsilon \sinh[(x - vt) \ln H] \\ + \varepsilon \cosh[(x - vt) \ln H] \end{array} \right\}}{\left\{ \begin{array}{l} 1 + \varepsilon \sinh[(x - vt) \ln H] \\ + \varepsilon \cosh[(x - vt) \ln H] \end{array} \right\}^3} \right] \tag{34}$$
$$\times \exp[i(-\kappa x + \omega t + \theta_0)],$$

$$V(x,t) = \pm 9 \Pi \sqrt{-\tfrac{35}{\Omega_3} \left(\ln^3 H \right)} \left[1 + \frac{4 - 6 \left\{ \begin{array}{l} 1 + \varepsilon \sinh[(x - vt) \ln H] \\ + \varepsilon \cosh[(x - vt) \ln H] \end{array} \right\}}{\left\{ \begin{array}{l} 1 + \varepsilon \sinh[(x - vt) \ln H] \\ + \varepsilon \cosh[(x - vt) \ln H] \end{array} \right\}^3} \right] \tag{35}$$
$$\times \exp[i(-\kappa x + \omega t + \theta_0)].$$

(II) The singular soliton solutions:

$$U(x,t) = \pm 3 \sqrt{-\tfrac{35}{\Omega_3} \left(\ln^3 H \right)} \left\{ \coth^2 \left[\tfrac{1}{2} (x - vt) \ln H \right] - 3 \right\} \coth \left[\tfrac{1}{2} (x - vt) \ln H \right] \tag{36}$$
$$\times \exp[i(-\kappa x + \omega t + \theta_0)],$$

$$V(x,t) = \pm 3 \Pi \sqrt{-\tfrac{35}{\Omega_3} \left(\ln^3 H \right)} \left\{ \coth^2 \left[\tfrac{1}{2} (x - vt) \ln H \right] - 3 \right\} \coth \left[\tfrac{1}{2} (x - vt) \ln H \right] \tag{37}$$
$$\times \exp[i(-\kappa x + \omega t + \theta_0)].$$

(III) The dark soliton solutions:

$$U(x,t) = \pm 3 \sqrt{-\tfrac{35}{\Omega_3} \left(\ln^3 H \right)} \left\{ \tanh^2 \left[\tfrac{1}{2} (x - vt) \ln H \right] - 3 \right\} \tanh \left[\tfrac{1}{2} (x - vt) \ln H \right] \tag{38}$$
$$\times \exp[i(-\kappa x + \omega t + \theta_0)],$$

$$V(x,t) = \pm 3 \Pi \sqrt{-\tfrac{35}{\Omega_3} \left(\ln^3 H \right)} \left\{ \tanh^2 \left[\tfrac{1}{2} (x - vt) \ln H \right] - 3 \right\} \tanh \left[\tfrac{1}{2} (x - vt) \ln H \right] \tag{39}$$
$$\times \exp[i(-\kappa x + \omega t + \theta_0)].$$

4. Enhanced Kudryashov's Method

The integration algorithm admits the explicit solution

$$g_1(\xi) = \sum_{j=0}^{N} K_j Z^j(\xi), \quad K_N \neq 0, \tag{40}$$

such that $Z(\xi)$ holds the ancillary equation

$$Z'^2(\xi) = Z^2(\xi) \left[1 - \pi Z^{2s}(\xi) \right] \ln^2 H, \quad 0 < H \neq 1, \tag{41}$$

and the analytical solution

$$Z(\xi) = \left[\frac{4\eta}{(4\eta^2 - \pi)\sinh(s\xi \ln H) + (4\eta^2 + \pi)\cosh(s\xi \ln H)} \right]^{\frac{1}{s}}. \quad (42)$$

Here π, K_j ($j = 0 - N$), s and η depict real-valued constant parameters. Balancing g_1^3 and $g_1^{(6)}$ in (22) secures the certain restriction

$$3N = N + 6s \Longrightarrow N = 3s. \quad (43)$$

Case 1: When $s = 1$, Equation (40) evolves as

$$g_1(\xi) = K_3 Z^3(\xi) + K_2 Z^2(\xi) + K_1 Z(\xi) + K_0, \quad K_3 \neq 0. \quad (44)$$

Inserting (44) with the help of (41) into (22) leaves us the results:
Result 1:

$$K_3 = -24\pi \sqrt{\frac{35\pi}{\Omega_3}} \ln^3 H, \quad K_2 = 0, \quad K_1 = \frac{288}{17} \sqrt{\frac{35\pi}{\Omega_3}} \ln^3 H, \quad K_0 = 0, \quad (45)$$

$$\Omega_4 = \frac{581}{17} \ln^2 H, \quad \Omega_2 = \frac{92659}{289} \ln^4 H, \quad \Omega_1 = -\frac{102825}{289} \ln^6 H, \quad \pi\Omega_3 > 0. \quad (46)$$

Plugging (45) with the usage of (42) into (44) formulates the combo solitons

$$U(x,t) = \pm 24 \sqrt{\frac{35\pi}{\Omega_3}} \left(\ln^3 H \right) \left(\frac{4\eta}{(4\eta^2 - \pi)\sinh[(x-vt)\ln H] + (4\eta^2 + \pi)\cosh[(x-vt)\ln H]} \right) \quad (47)$$

$$\times \left\{ \frac{12}{17} - \pi \left(\frac{4\eta}{(4\eta^2 - \pi)\sinh[(x-vt)\ln H] + (4\eta^2 + \pi)\cosh[(x-vt)\ln H]} \right)^2 \right\} \times \exp[i(-\kappa x + \omega t + \theta_0)],$$

$$V(x,t) = \pm 24\Pi \sqrt{\frac{35\pi}{\Omega_3}} \left(\ln^3 H \right) \left(\frac{4\eta}{(4\eta^2 - \pi)\sinh[(x-vt)\ln H] + (4\eta^2 + \pi)\cosh[(x-vt)\ln H]} \right) \quad (48)$$

$$\times \left\{ \frac{12}{17} - \pi \left(\frac{4\eta}{(4\eta^2 - \pi)\sinh[(x-vt)\ln H] + (4\eta^2 + \pi)\cosh[(x-vt)\ln H]} \right)^2 \right\} \times \exp[i(-\kappa x + \omega t + \theta_0)].$$

When $\Omega_3 > 0$ and $\pi = 4\eta^2$, the bright solitons evolve as

$$U(x,t) = \pm \frac{24}{17} \sqrt{\frac{35}{\Omega_3}} \left(\ln^3 H \right) \{12 - 17 \operatorname{sech}^2[(x-vt)\ln H]\} \quad (49)$$
$$\times \operatorname{sech}[(x-vt)\ln H] \exp[i(-\kappa x + \omega t + \theta_0)],$$

$$V(x,t) = \pm \frac{24}{17} \Pi \sqrt{\frac{35}{\Omega_3}} \left(\ln^3 H \right) \{12 - 17 \operatorname{sech}^2[(x-vt)\ln H]\} \quad (50)$$
$$\times \operatorname{sech}[(x-vt)\ln H] \exp[i(-\kappa x + \omega t + \theta_0)],$$

where as setting $\Omega_3 < 0$ and $\pi = -4\eta^2$ secures the singular solitons

$$U(x,t) = \pm \frac{24}{17} \sqrt{-\frac{35}{\Omega_3}} \left(\ln^3 H \right) \{12 + 17 \operatorname{csch}^2[(x-vt)\ln H]\} \quad (51)$$
$$\times \operatorname{csch}[(x-vt)\ln H] \exp[i(-\kappa x + \omega t + \theta_0)],$$

$$V(x,t) = \pm \frac{24}{17} \Pi \sqrt{-\frac{35}{\Omega_3}} \left(\ln^3 H \right) \{12 + 17 \operatorname{csch}^2[(x-vt)\ln H]\} \quad (52)$$
$$\times \operatorname{csch}[(x-vt)\ln H] \exp[i(-\kappa x + \omega t + \theta_0)].$$

Result 2:

$$K_3 = 24\pi \sqrt{\frac{35\pi}{\Omega_3}} \ln^3 H, \quad K_2 = 0, \quad K_1 = 0, \quad K_0 = 0, \quad (53)$$

$$\Omega_4 = -83\ln^2 H, \quad \Omega_2 = 1891\ln^4 H, \quad \Omega_1 = -11025\ln^6 H, \quad \pi\Omega_3 > 0. \tag{54}$$

Placing (53) with the help of (42) into (44) formulates the combo solitons

$$U(x,t) = \pm 24\pi\sqrt{\tfrac{35\pi}{\Omega_3}}\left(\frac{4\eta\ln H}{(4\eta^2-\pi)\sinh[(x-vt)\ln H]+(4\eta^2+\pi)\cosh[(x-vt)\ln H]}\right)^3 \\ \times \exp[i(-\kappa x+\omega t+\theta_0)], \tag{55}$$

$$V(x,t) = \pm 24\Pi\pi\sqrt{\tfrac{35\pi}{\Omega_3}}\left(\frac{4\eta\ln H}{(4\eta^2-\pi)\sinh[(x-vt)\ln H]+(4\eta^2+\pi)\cosh[(x-vt)\ln H]}\right)^3 \\ \times \exp[i(-\kappa x+\omega t+\theta_0)]. \tag{56}$$

When $\Omega_3 > 0$ and $\pi = 4\eta^2$, the bright solitons read as

$$U(x,t) = \pm 24\sqrt{\tfrac{35}{\Omega_3}}\left(\ln^3 H\right)\operatorname{sech}^3[(x-vt)\ln H]\exp[i(-\kappa x+\omega t+\theta_0)], \tag{57}$$

$$V(x,t) = \pm 24\Pi\sqrt{\tfrac{35}{\Omega_3}}\left(\ln^3 H\right)\operatorname{sech}^3[(x-vt)\ln H]\exp[i(-\kappa x+\omega t+\theta_0)], \tag{58}$$

whereas $\Omega_3 < 0$ and $\pi = -4\eta^2$ retrieves the singular solitons

$$U(x,t) = \pm 24\sqrt{-\tfrac{35}{\Omega_3}}\left(\ln^3 H\right)\operatorname{csch}^3[(x-vt)\ln H]\exp[i(-\kappa x+\omega t+\theta_0)], \tag{59}$$

$$V(x,t) = \pm 24\Pi\sqrt{-\tfrac{35}{\Omega_3}}\left(\ln^3 H\right)\operatorname{csch}^3[(x-vt)\ln H]\exp[i(-\kappa x+\omega t+\theta_0)]. \tag{60}$$

Case 2: When $s=2$, Equation (40) reads as

$$g_1(\xi) = K_6 Z^6(\xi) + K_5 Z^5(\xi) + K_4 Z^4(\xi) + K_3 Z^3(\xi) \\ + K_2 Z^2(\xi) + K_1 Z(\xi) + K_0, \quad K_6 \neq 0. \tag{61}$$

Plugging (61) with the help of (41) into (22) reveals the results:
Result 1:

$$K_6 = -\tfrac{192}{17}\pi\sqrt{\tfrac{10115\pi}{\Omega_3}}\ln^3 H, \quad K_5 = 0, \quad K_4 = 0, \quad K_3 = 0, \\ K_2 = \tfrac{2304}{289}\sqrt{\tfrac{10115\pi}{\Omega_3}}\ln^3 H, \quad K_1 = 0, \quad K_0 = 0, \tag{62}$$

$$\Omega_4 = \tfrac{2324}{17}\ln^2 H, \quad \Omega_2 = \tfrac{1482544}{289}\ln^4 H, \quad \Omega_1 = -\tfrac{6580800}{289}\ln^6 H, \quad \pi\Omega_3 > 0. \tag{63}$$

Inserting (62) with the usage of (42) into (61) extracts the combo solitons

$$U(x,t) = \pm 192\sqrt{\tfrac{35\pi}{\Omega_3}}\left(\ln^3 H\right)\left(\frac{4\eta}{(4\eta^2-\pi)\sinh[2(x-vt)\ln H]+(4\eta^2+\pi)\cosh[2(x-vt)\ln H]}\right) \\ \times\left\{\tfrac{12}{17}-\pi\left(\tfrac{4\eta}{(4\eta^2-\pi)\sinh[2(x-vt)\ln H]+(4\eta^2+\pi)\cosh[2(x-vt)\ln H]}\right)^2\right\}\times\exp[i(-\kappa x+\omega t+\theta_0)], \tag{64}$$

$$V(x,t) = \pm 192\Pi \sqrt{\frac{35\pi}{\Omega_3}} \left(\ln^3 H\right) \left(\frac{4\eta}{\begin{array}{c}(4\eta^2 - \pi)\sinh[2(x-vt)\ln H] \\ +(4\eta^2 + \pi)\cosh[2(x-vt)\ln H]\end{array}}\right) \tag{65}$$
$$\times \left\{\frac{12}{17} - \pi \left(\frac{4\eta}{(4\eta^2-\pi)\sinh[2(x-vt)\ln H]+(4\eta^2+\pi)\cosh[2(x-vt)\ln H]}\right)^2\right\}$$
$$\times \exp[i(-\kappa x + \omega t + \theta_0)].$$

When $\Omega_3 > 0$ and $\pi = 4\eta^2$ the bright solitons come out as

$$U(x,t) = \pm \frac{192}{17}\sqrt{\frac{35}{\Omega_3}}\left(\ln^3 H\right)\text{sech}[2(x-vt)\ln H]\{12 - 17\,\text{sech}^2[2(x-vt)\ln H]\} \tag{66}$$
$$\times \exp[i(-\kappa x + \omega t + \theta_0)],$$

$$V(x,t) = \pm \frac{192}{17}\Pi\sqrt{\frac{35}{\Omega_3}}\left(\ln^3 H\right)\text{sech}[2(x-vt)\ln H]\{12 - 17\,\text{sech}^2[2(x-vt)\ln H]\} \tag{67}$$
$$\times \exp[i(-\kappa x + \omega t + \theta_0)],$$

whilst setting $\Omega_3 < 0$ and $\pi = -4\eta^2$ acquires the singular solitons

$$U(x,t) = \pm \frac{24}{17}\sqrt{-\frac{35}{\Omega_3}}\left(\ln^3 H\right)\text{csch}[2(x-vt)\ln H]\{12 + 17\,\text{csch}^2[2(x-vt)\ln H]\} \tag{68}$$
$$\times \exp[i(-\kappa x + \omega t + \theta_0)],$$

$$V(x,t) = \pm \frac{24}{17}\Pi\sqrt{-\frac{35}{\Omega_3}}\left(\ln^3 H\right)\text{csch}[2(x-vt)\ln H]\{12 + 17\,\text{csch}^2[2(x-vt)\ln H]\} \tag{69}$$
$$\times \exp[i(-\kappa x + \omega t + \theta_0)].$$

<u>Result 2:</u>

$$K_6 = 192\pi\sqrt{\frac{35\pi}{\Omega_3}}\ln^3 H, \quad K_5 = 0, \quad K_4 = 0, \quad K_3 = 0, K_2 = 0, \quad K_1 = 0, \quad K_0 = 0, \tag{70}$$

$$\Omega_4 = -332\ln^2 H, \quad \Omega_2 = 30256\ln^4 H, \quad \Omega_1 = -705600\ln^6 H, \quad \pi\Omega_3 > 0. \tag{71}$$

Putting (70) with the usage of (42) into (61) secures the combo solitons

$$U(x,t) = \pm 192\pi\sqrt{\frac{35\pi}{\Omega_3}}\left(\frac{4\eta\ln H}{\begin{array}{c}(4\eta^2 - \pi)\sinh[2(x-vt)\ln H] \\ +(4\eta^2 + \pi)\cosh[2(x-vt)\ln H]\end{array}}\right)^3 \tag{72}$$
$$\times \exp[i(-\kappa x + \omega t + \theta_0)],$$

$$V(x,t) = \pm 192\Pi\pi\sqrt{\frac{35\pi}{\Omega_3}}\left(\frac{4\eta\ln H}{\begin{array}{c}(4\eta^2 - \pi)\sinh[2(x-vt)\ln H] \\ +(4\eta^2 + \pi)\cosh[2(x-vt)\ln H]\end{array}}\right)^3 \tag{73}$$
$$\times \exp[i(-\kappa x + \omega t + \theta_0)].$$

When $\Omega_3 > 0$ and $\pi = 4\eta^2$, the bright solitons shape up as

$$U(x,t) = \pm 192\sqrt{\frac{35}{\Omega_3}}\left(\ln^3 H\right)\text{sech}^3[2(x-vt)\ln H]\exp[i(-\kappa x + \omega t + \theta_0)], \tag{74}$$

$$V(x,t) = \pm 192\Pi\sqrt{\frac{35}{\Omega_3}}\left(\ln^3 H\right)\text{sech}^3[2(x-vt)\ln H]\exp[i(-\kappa x + \omega t + \theta_0)], \tag{75}$$

where as setting $\Omega_3 < 0$ and $\pi = -4\eta^2$ formulates the singular solitons

$$U(x,t) = \pm 192\sqrt{-\frac{35}{\Omega_3}\left(\ln^3 H\right)}\, \text{csch}^3[2(x-vt)\ln H]\exp[i(-\kappa x + \omega t + \theta_0)], \qquad (76)$$

$$V(x,t) = \pm 192\Pi\sqrt{-\frac{35}{\Omega_3}\left(\ln^3 H\right)}\, \text{csch}^3[2(x-vt)\ln H]\exp[i(-\kappa x + \omega t + \theta_0)]. \qquad (77)$$

5. Conclusions

The current work is the first of its kind to combine the two compensatory means to offset the low count of CD that is being implemented in optoelectronics for the first time. HD solitons were implemented together with a Bragg gratings structure to produce dispersive reflectivity that would work together to create performance enhancement. The effect of soliton radiation and slowdown of solitons due to the presence of higher order dispersions are neglected. The retrieval of solitons for the model has been successfully achieved by the two Kudryashov approaches. The enhanced Kudryashov's approach turned out to be especially useful for bright solitons, while the generalized Kudryashov's scheme failed to recover the much-needed bright solitons.

This successful retrieval of solitons paves the way for further developments in this newly formulated model. An immediate thought would be to obtain the conservation laws to the governing model that would give a plethora of physical insight into the governing model, which would follow up with additional features such as the quasi-monochromatic soliton dynamics and others. Later, this model would also be taken up with additional forms of self–phase modulation. We are awaiting the results that align with the latest findings [17–20] and expect to receive them soon.

Author Contributions: Conceptualization, E.M.E.Z. and M.E.M.A.; methodology, R.M.A.S. and S.K.; software, A.B. and C.I.; writing—original draft preparation, Y.Y.; writing—review and editing, L.M. and S.M. All authors have read and agreed to the published version of the manuscript.

Funding: This research received no external funding.

Institutional Review Board Statement: Not applicable.

Informed Consent Statement: Not applicable.

Data Availability Statement: All data generated or analyzed during this study are included in this manuscript.

Acknowledgments: The authors thank the anonymous referees whose comments helped to improve the paper.

Conflicts of Interest: The authors declare no conflict of interest.

References

1. Ahmed, T.; Atai, J. Bragg solitons in systems with separated nonuniform Bragg grating and nonlinearity. *Phys. Rev. E* **2017**, *96*, 032222. [CrossRef] [PubMed]
2. Ahmed, T.; Atai, J. Soliton–soliton dynamics in a dual-core system with separated nonlinearity and nonuniform Bragg grating. *Nonlinear Dyn.* **2019**, *97*, 1515–1523. [CrossRef]
3. Akter, A.; Islam, M.J.; Atai, J. Effect of dispersive reflectivity on the stability of gap solitons in dual–core Bragg gratings with cubic–quintic nonlinearity. In Proceedings of the 7th International Conference on Photonics, Optics and Laser Technology (Photoptics 2019), 19–23, Prague, Czech Republic, 25–27 February 2019.
4. Akter, A.; Islam, M.; Atai, J. Quiescent gap solitons in coupled nonuniform Bragg gratings with cubic–quintic nonlinearity. *Appl. Sci.* **2021**, *11*, 4833. [CrossRef]
5. Anam, N.; Ahmed, T.; Atai, J. Bragg grating solitons in a dual–core system with separated Bragg grating and cubic–quintic nonlinearity. In Proceedings of the 7th International Conference on Photonics, Optics and Laser Technology (Photoptics 2019), 24–28, Prague, Czech Republic, 25–27 February 2019.
6. Atai, J.; Malomed, B.A. Families of Bragg-grating solitons in a cubic–quintic medium. *Phys. Lett. A* **2001**, *284*, 247–252. [CrossRef]
7. Atai, J.; Malomed, B.A. Solitary waves in systems with separated Bragg grating and nonlinearity. *Phys. Rev. E* **2001**, *64*, 066617. [CrossRef]
8. Biswas, A.; Konar, S. *Introduction to Non-Kerr Law Optical Solitons*; CRC Press: Boca Raton, FL, USA, 2006.

9. Kan, K.V.; Kudryashov, N.A. Solitary waves for the sixth order nonlinear differential equation in optical fiber Bragg grating. *AIP Conf. Proc.* **2022**, *2425*, 340008.
10. Kan, K.V.; Kudryashov, N.A. Solitary waves described by a high-order system in optical fiber Bragg gratings with arbitrary refractive index. *Math. Methods Appl. Sci.* **2022**, *45*, 1072–1079. [CrossRef]
11. Kudryashov, N.A. Periodic and solitary waves in optical fiber Bragg gratings with dispersive reflectivity. *Chin. J. Phys.* **2020**, *66*, 401–405. [CrossRef]
12. Zayed, E.M.E.; Alngar, M.E.M.; Biswas, A.; Asma, M.; Ekici, M.; Alzahrani, A.K.; Belic, M.R. Optical soliton and conservation laws with generalized Kudryashov's law of refractive index. *Chaos Soliton Fract.* **2020**, *139*, 110284. [CrossRef]
13. Zayed, E.M.E.; Alngar, M.E.M. Optical soliton solutions for the generalized Kudryashov equation of propagation pulse in optical fiber with power nonlinearities by three integration algorithms. *Math. Methods Appl. Sci.* **2021**, *44*, 315–324. [CrossRef]
14. Zayed, E.M.E.; Alngar, M.E.M.; Biswas, A.; Kara, A.H.; Ekici, M.; Alzahrani, A.K.; Belic, M.R. Cubic–quartic optical solitons and conservation law with Kudryashov's sextic power law of refractive index. *Optik* **2021**, *227*, 166059. [CrossRef]
15. Zayed, E.M.E.; Alngar, M.E.M.; El–Horbaty, M.M.; Biswas, A.; Ekici, M.; Zhou, Q.; Khan, S.; Mallawi, F.; Belic, M.R. Highly dispersive optical solitons in the nonlinear Schrodinger's equation having polynomial law of the refractive index change. *Indian J. Phys.* **2021**, *95*, 109–119. [CrossRef]
16. Zayed, E.M.E.; Al–Nowehy, A.; Alngar, M.E.M.; Biswas, A.; Asma, M.; Ekici, M.; Alzahrani, A.K. Highly dispersive optical solitons in birefringent fibers with four nonlinear forms using Kudryashov's approach. *J. Opt.* **2021**, *50*, 120–131. [CrossRef]
17. Zhao, Y.; Lei, Y.B.; Xu, Y.X.; Xu, S.; Triki, H.; Biswas, A.; Zhou, Q. Vector spatiotemporal solitons and their memory features in cold Rydberg gases. *Chin. Phys. Lett.* **2022**, *39*, 034202. [CrossRef]
18. Zhou, Q.; Wang, T.; Biswas, A.; Liu, W. Nonlinear control of logic structure of all–optical logic devices using soliton interactions. *Nonlinear Dyn.* **2022**, *107*, 1215–1222. [CrossRef]
19. Zhou, Q.; Zhong, Y.; Triki, H.; Sun, Y.; Xu, S.; Liu, W.; Biswas, A. Chirped bright and kink solitons in nonlinear optical fibers with weak nonlocality and cubic-quintic-septic nonlinearity. *Chin. Phys. Lett.* **2022**, *39*, 044202. [CrossRef]
20. Zhou, Q. Influence of parameters of optical fibers on optical soliton interactions. *Chin. Phys. Lett.* **2022**, *39*, 010501. [CrossRef]
21. Biswas, A.; Topkara, E.; Johnson, S.; Zerrad, E.; Konar, S. Quasi—stationary optical solitons with non—Kerr law media with full nonlinearity. *J. Nonlinear Opt. Phys. Mater.* **2011**, *20*, 309–325. [CrossRef]
22. Islam, M.J.; Atai, J. Stability of moving Bragg solitons in a semilinear coupled system with cubic–quintic nonlinearity. *J. Mod. Opt.* **2021**, *68*, 365–373. [CrossRef]
23. Islam, M.; Atai, J. Stability of moving gap solitons in linearly coupled Bragg gratings with cubic–quintic nonlinearity. *Nonlinear Dyn.* **2018**, *91*, 2725–2733. [CrossRef]
24. Chowdhury, S.S.; Atai, J. Interaction dynamics of Bragg grating solitons in a semilinear dual-core system with dispersive reflectivity. *J. Mod. Opt.* **2016**, *63*, 2238–2245. [CrossRef]
25. Islam, M.J.; Atai, J. Stability of gap solitons in dual-core Bragg gratings with cubic-quintic nonlinearity. *Laser Phys. Lett.* **2014**, *12*, 015401. [CrossRef]
26. Dasanayaka, S.; Atai, J. Moving Bragg grating solitons in a cubic-quintic nonlinear medium with dispersive reflectivity. *Phys. Rev. E* **2013**, *88*, 022921. [CrossRef] [PubMed]
27. Dasanayaka, S.; Atai, J. Interactions of solitons in Bragg gratings with dispersive reflectivity in a cubic-quintic medium. *Phys. Rev. E* **2011**, *84*, 026613. [CrossRef] [PubMed]
28. Dasanayaka, S.; Atai, J. Stability of Bragg grating solitons in a cubic–quintic nonlinear medium with dispersive reflectivity. *Phys. Lett. A* **2010**, *375*, 225–229. [CrossRef]
29. Neill, D.R.; Atai, J.; Malomed, B.A. Dynamics and collisions of moving solitons in Bragg gratings with dispersive reflectivity. *J. Opt. A Pure Appl. Opt.* **2008**, *10*, 085105. [CrossRef]
30. Atai, J. Interaction of Bragg grating solitons in a cubic–quintic medium. *J. Opt. B Quantum Semiclassical Opt.* **2004**, *6*, S177. [CrossRef]
31. Cao, H.; Atai, J.; Zuo, J.; Yu, Y.; Gbadebo, A.; Xiong, B.; Hou, J.; Liang, P.; Gao, Y.; Shu, X. Simultaneous multichannel carrier-suppressed return-to-zero to non-return-to-zero format conversion using a fiber Bragg grating. *Appl. Opt.* **2015**, *54*, 6344–6350. [CrossRef]
32. Islam, J.; Atai, J. Stability of Bragg grating solitons in a semilinear dual-core system with cubic–quintic nonlinearity. *Nonlinear Dyn.* **2017**, *87*, 1693–1701. [CrossRef]

Article

On the Short Wave Instability of the Liquid/Gas Contact Surface in Porous Media

Vladimir A. Shargatov *, George G. Tsypkin, Sergey V. Gorkunov, Polina I. Kozhurina and Yulia A. Bogdanova

Ishlinsky Institute for Problems in Mechanics of the Russian Academy of Sciences, 119526 Moscow, Russia
* Correspondence: shargatov@mail.ru

Abstract: We consider a problem of hydrodynamic stability of the liquid displacement by gas in a porous medium in the case when a light gas is located above the liquid. The onset of instability and the evolution of the small shortwave perturbations are investigated. We show that when using the Darcy filtration law, the onset of instability may take place at an infinitely large wavenumber when the normal modes method is inapplicable. The results of numerical simulation of the nonlinear problem indicate that the anomalous growth of the amplitude of shortwave small perturbations persists, but the growth rate of amplitude decreases significantly compared to the results of linear analysis. An analysis of the stability of the gas/liquid interface is also carried out using a network model of a porous medium. It is shown that the results of surface evolution calculations obtained using the network model are in qualitative agreement with the results of the continual approach, but the continual model predicts a higher velocity of the interfacial surfaces in the capillaries. The growth rate of perturbations in the network model also increases with decreasing perturbation wavelength at a constant amplitude.

Keywords: porous media; stability; pore-scale network model; drainage

MSC: 35Q35; 35B35

1. Introduction

Stability of filtration flows with liquid/gas interfaces in rocks and soils has been studied both analytically and numerically in a large number of works. These problems are of great practical interest. Gas drainage is considered as an effective method to enhance oil recovery (see [1–4]). The efficiency of oil/water or oil/gas displacement depends on the stability of the interface between the oil-saturated region and the region containing displacement fluid (gas) [5]. An increase in the concentration of impurities and contamination of groundwater occurs when groundwater evaporates, as well as when the boundary between fresh water and solutions is unstable [6–9]. Another example where this instability plays a significant role is geothermic systems. In many cases, their existence can be explained by convective heat transfer to the surface of the Earth due to the instability of the interfaces between regions saturated with water, steam, and a steam–water mixture inside high-temperature rocks [10–15]. The problem of the stability of the water layer in the soil located above the air-saturated region was studied in [13,16] in relation to artificial underground structures. The occurrence of instability of the oil–gas interface during oil extraction from a field with a gas cap was investigated in [17].

These studies were provided by the use of the continual hydrodynamic approach. It was assumed that the filtration process is described by Darcy's law, and there is a narrow region that separates the gas and liquid region determined by some surface equation. It was shown in the linear approximation within the use of the normal mode method that for a given amplitude of the interface perturbation there is a certain range of parameters where the rate of growth of the amplitude increases indefinitely with decreasing wavelength [13–16].

This fact casts doubt on the applicability of the Darcy equation in the context of studying the onset of instability, as well as determining geometric characteristics of the finger-like structures of a liquid or gas. In [18] the stability of oil flow in a collector with a gas cap was studied under the assumption that oil motion obeys the Brinkman law. Within the normal mode analysis, it was established that the growth rate of short wave perturbations tends to zero with increasing wavenumber.

In recent times, pore-network modeling has been used increasingly to study water imbibition and drainage in porous media. Relative permeability studies conducted using the pore-scale network models have shown that the obtained results are in qualitative agreement with the data of laboratory measurements (e.g., see [19–25]. In [26], a network approach to the modeling of non-Newtonian rheology was used to understand some of the more detailed features of polymer flow in porous media. This approach provided a mathematical bridge between the behavior of the non-Newtonian fluid in a single capillary and the macroscopic behavior as deduced from the pressure drop–flow rate relation across the whole network model. In [27], the network approach was presented which simulates 2-phase oil/water displacement during water imbibition. In [28], a pore-network model of the shale matrix was developed and used to simulate CO_2 migration in organic-rich shale formations. The pore space is modeled as a set of pore bodies connected by pore throats. An imbibition efficiency calculation method was proposed in [29]. The acyclic pore model was improved and was used to study how the pore structure affects imbibition performance. An analytical analysis of the relationship between the pore-scale forces and the Darcy-scale pressure drops was presented in [30]. An extensive and detailed discussion of the application of network models can be found in [31–33].

In this work, we study the evolution of perturbations of the gas/oil contact surface with a decrease in pressure in an oil-saturated region and compare the results obtained within continual and network models of a porous media. When a liquid is displaced by a gas in a porous medium, the gas–liquid interface is linearly unstable within the continuum model using Darcy's law (see, for example, [17]). The rate of growth of interface perturbations increases indefinitely with decreasing wavelength at a constant amplitude of the perturbation. Below, we show that linear analysis is not applicable in this case, and we will use the numerical solution. The results of the numerical solution also show that the perturbation growth rate increases without limit with decreasing wavelength. In this case, the use of the continuum model is impossible without modification, which requires studies using direct numerical simulation on the pore scale. Therefore, we use simple network models to identify the physical mechanisms that can help achieve successful modeling of the interface motion. This paper is organized as follows: Section 2 contains the formulation of the problem within the framework of the continual model using Darcy's law. We show that the linear approximation is inapplicable for determining the growth rate of short-wave perturbations. In Section 3, we study the wavelength dependence of the growth rate of short-wave perturbations using a numerical approach in the framework of the continual model. In Section 4, a similar problem is studied within the network model of porous media. Section 5 contains a discussion of the obtained results and conclusion notes.

2. Formulation of the Problem

We consider the problem of oil extraction from the field with a gas cap. Assume that the gas cap is separated from the oil-saturated reservoir by a horizontal interface. When producing oil located under the gas zone, the pressure in the oil reservoir decreases, and the interface moves down. If the motion of the interface is unstable, gas breakdown may occur in the direction of the production well. In this case, regions saturated with immobile oil are formed. Thus, the study of the instability of filtration flows with a gas/liquid interface is an important issue when developing a field with a gas cap.

In recent years, gas gravity drainage technology has been widely used worldwide (see [1–4]). The flow diagram is shown in Figure 1 and is a simplification of the real-life example with the horizontal interlayer. Let a horizontal layer of a porous homogeneous medium be located over a high-permeability layer with constant pressure P_L. This layer models a horizontal production well or a hydraulic fracture. For the considered problem of the evolution of interface perturbations, the pressure may be assumed to be constant, since the permeability of this layer is several orders of magnitude higher than the permeability at $z > 0$. The problem is solved in Cartesian coordinates (x, y, z) with the axis z pointing upwards. In the low permeable layer at $0 < z < s(x,t)$ (Ω_f region) there is a liquid, and the region Ω_g ($z > s(x,t)$) is filled with gas with constant pressure P_g. Here, t is time and $s(x,t)$ is the z-coordinate of the interface. The horizontal coordinate x varies in the range $(-\infty, \infty)$.

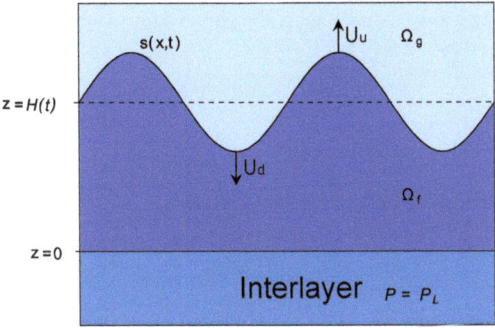

Figure 1. The computational domain used for the Darcy scale numerical simulation. Ω_f is the low-permeability liquid region, Ω_g the gas region. The highly permeable layer (the interlayer) is located at $z < 0$.

At the gas/liquid interface, pressure jumps so that the pressure drop equals to the capillary pressure

$$P_c(z) = P_{\Omega_f}(x, s(x,t)) - P_g. \qquad (1)$$

Here, the capillary pressure P_c is negative if the rock is wettable and positive otherwise. Similar to [17], we assume that capillary pressure depends on the vertical coordinate z.

In the region Ω_f, the continuity equation is valid, and we assume that Darcy's law is satisfied

$$\text{div } v_w = 0, \quad v_w = -\frac{k}{m\,\mu_w} \text{grad}\,(P - \rho_w g z). \qquad (2)$$

Here, v_w is the average pore velocity, m the ratio between the pores' area and the total cross-sectional area, k the permeability, μ_w the viscosity of the liquid, g the gravity, and ρ the density of the liquid. From Equation (2), it follows that the pressure inside the region Ω_f satisies the Laplace equation

$$\triangle P = 0. \qquad (3)$$

We neglect the evaporation of the liquid at the contact surface, so there is no mass flow through the gas/liquid interface. Therefore, the equation for the normal component of local velocity of the contact surface takes the form

$$V_n = -\frac{k}{m\,\mu_w}[\text{grad}\,(P - \rho_w g z)]_n. \qquad (4)$$

Similar equations have been used in [17].

Figure 1 presents the large-scale (Darcy scale) flow through porous media. The real gas/liquid interface is located in pores. If most of the moving interface are belonged to some narrow region between gas-dominated and liquid-dominated zones, this region may be approximated by the surface [14,15] as shown in Figure 1. This surface has a radius of curvature, but this radius is not used to calculate surface tension.

We write the problem equations and boundary conditions

$$
\begin{aligned}
(x,z) \in \Omega_f: &\quad \Delta P = 0, \\
z = 0: &\quad P = P_L, \\
z = s(x,t): &\quad P = P_g + P_c(z), \\
V_n = -\frac{k}{m\,\mu_w}[\text{grad}\,(P - \rho_w g z)]_n.
\end{aligned}
\tag{5}
$$

We introduce variable L with the dimension of length so that $L \geq s(x,0)$ and define dimensionless variables

$$\tau = \frac{tg\rho_w k}{\mu_w L m},\ \zeta = zL^{-1},\ \chi = xL^{-1},\ \bar{s} = sL^{-1},$$

$$p(\chi,\zeta,\tau) = P(x,z,t)(\rho_w g L)^{-1}.$$

We transform the relations (5) to the form

$$\frac{\partial^2}{\partial \zeta^2}p(\chi,\zeta,\tau) + \frac{\partial^2}{\partial \chi^2}p(\chi,\zeta,\tau) = 0, \tag{6}$$

$$p(\chi,0,\tau) = p_L, \tag{7}$$

$$p(\chi,\bar{s}(\chi,\tau),\tau) = p_c(\bar{s}(\chi,\tau)) + p_g, \tag{8}$$

$$\bar{V}_n = 1 - \frac{\partial}{\partial \zeta}p(\chi,\zeta,\tau)|_{\zeta=\bar{s}(\chi,\tau)}, \tag{9}$$

$$\bar{s}(\chi,0) = \bar{s}_0(\chi).$$

If the contact surface is flat and perpendicular to the axis ζ, then problem (6)–(9) has the solution independent of the coordinate χ

$$p_b(\zeta) = p_L + \frac{(p_g + p_c(h(\tau)) - p_L)\zeta}{h(\tau)}, \tag{10}$$

$$\frac{dh(\tau)}{d\tau} = \bar{V}_n = -1 - \frac{p_g + p_c(h(\tau)) - p_L}{h(\tau)}, \tag{11}$$

where $h(\tau)$ is the coordinate of the flat gas/liquid interface.

In [16,17], the evolution of the infinitesimal harmonic perturbations of the solution (10)–(11) was studied by the normal mode method, and expression is obtained for the growth rate of the amplitude of the perturbation of the interface $\hat{\eta}(\tau)$

$$\frac{d\hat{\eta}(\tau)}{d\tau} = \hat{\eta}(\tau)\frac{\alpha_d K}{\tanh(Kh(\tau))h(\tau)}, \tag{12}$$

where K is the wavenumber of perturbation, $\hat{\eta}(\tau)$ is its amplitude, and α_d is given by

$$\alpha_d = p_g + p_c(h(\tau)) - p_L - h(\tau)\,dp_c(\zeta)/d\zeta|_{\zeta=h(\tau)}. \tag{13}$$

If $\alpha_d > 0$, then the amplitude of perturbations increases. In the case $K \to 0$, we obtain

$$\frac{d\hat{\eta}(\tau)}{d\tau} \sim \hat{\eta}(\tau)\frac{\alpha_d}{h(\tau)}. \tag{14}$$

In the limit $K \to \infty$ we obtain

$$\frac{d\hat{\eta}(\tau)}{d\tau} \sim K\hat{\eta}(\tau)\frac{\alpha_d}{h(\tau)}. \tag{15}$$

The relationship (15) predicts an arbitrarily large growth rate with increasing K for any given amplitude. This result contradicts the physical essence of the process under consideration. This problem has been repeatedly pointed out in [13,17] and others.

The relation (15) is obtained under the assumption that

$$\left|\frac{d\bar{s}(\chi,\tau)}{d\chi}\right| \ll 1. \tag{16}$$

Since

$$\bar{s}(\chi,\tau) = h(\tau) + \hat{\eta}(\tau)e^{iK\chi}$$

and

$$\frac{d\bar{s}(\chi,\tau)}{d\chi} = iK\hat{\eta}(\tau)e^{iK\chi},$$

the condition (16) leads to

$$K\hat{\eta}(\tau) \ll 1. \tag{17}$$

From inequality (17) and relation (15), we then obtain that in the limit $K \to \infty$

$$\frac{d\hat{\eta}(\tau)}{d\tau} \ll \frac{\alpha_d}{h(\tau)}. \tag{18}$$

From expression (18), it follows that the growth rate of the amplitude is limited when condition (15) is valid. Inequality (18) is the condition for the applicability of the linear approximation. Thus, in the range of applicability of linear approximation, Darcy's law does not lead to unphysical values of the growth rate of the perturbation and the filtration rate.

Since the linear analysis of stability is inapplicable when the amplitude of the perturbations and wave length are of the same order of magnitude, we will study the evolution of the perturbation numerically.

3. The Rate of Change of the Amplitude of the Harmonic Disturbance in the Nonlinear Case

We consider the wavelength dependence of the rate of change of the amplitude of the harmonic perturbation without using the linear approximation. We will use the system of Equation (5) assuming that the capillary pressure is constant. In this case, in all relations used, the value P_g enters only in combination $P_g + P_c$. Hence, without loss of generality, we can set $P_c = 0$. In [16], it has been shown that gravity does not affect the evolution of perturbations, so in what follows we will consider the system of equations

$$\begin{aligned}
(x,z) \in \Omega_a: & \quad \Delta P = 0, \\
z = 0: & \quad P = P_L, \\
z = s(x,t): & \quad P = P_g, \\
V_n = -\kappa\,[\mathrm{grad}\,P]_n,
\end{aligned} \tag{19}$$

where $\kappa = k/(m\,\mu_w)$. Consider the evolution of the perturbations of the main flow. The main flow is described by the equations

$$P(z) = P_L + \frac{(P_g - P_L)z}{H(t)}, \tag{20}$$

$$\frac{dH(t)}{dt} = -\kappa\frac{P_g - P_L}{H(t)}, \tag{21}$$

Here, $H(t)$ is the coordinate of the flat gas/liquid interface.

In [34], a numerical–analytical method was proposed for evaluation of the filtration flow with gas/liquid interface under the assumption that the contact surface is infinitely thin, i.e., is a discontinuity. The Laplace Equation (3) for pressure is solved using the boundary element method. In a numerical calculation, the gas/liquid interface is a broken line composed of segments. The numerical method is described in detail in [34]. This method allows accurate and robust computation of the evolution of a multiply connected boundary of a water-saturated region in a porous media (see, e.g., [16,35–37]).

We set $\kappa = 1$, $H(t) = 1$, $P_L = 1$ and $P_g = 2$ and $A = 0.1$. Then, we set the coordinate of the perturbed gas/liquid interface according to the expression

$$s(x,0) = 1 + A\cos(Kx). \tag{22}$$

The pressure on the interface is assumed constant, so the liquid velocity is directed along the normal to this surface and is equal to the normal component of this surface's velocity. In the absence of perturbations, the flat interface would remain flat and move along the axis z with velocity $V_f = dH(t)/dt$. We denote by $U(x,t)$ the normal velocity of the interface in the reference frame moving along axis z with velocity V_f. For the velocity of the surface at the vertices of perturbations, we introduce notations U_u and U_d so that

$$U_u = U(0,t) - V_f, \quad U_d = -(U(\lambda/2,t) - V_f),$$

as shown in Figure 1.

Figures 2 and 3 show the normal velocity of various points of the contact surface $U(x,0)$ for the wave lengths $\lambda = 4$ and $\lambda = 0.04$. The results in Figure 2 were obtained for the amplitude value $A/\lambda = 0.025$, so that condition (17) is satisfied. In this case, the dependency of velocity on the coordinate x can be approximately described by the linear result $AK\sin(Kx)$. The growth rates of the amplitudes upwards U_u and downwards U_d differ insignificantly.

Figure 3 corresponds to $A/\lambda = 2.5$, so condition (17) is violated. In this case, the dependency of velocity on the coordinate x differ significantly from the dependency shown in Figure 2. The growth rate of the amplitude upwards U_u and downwards U_d differ by more than seven times, and the velocity of the surface $U(x)$ is close to zero outside the narrow regions in the vicinity of maximum and minimum points of the perturbation profile.

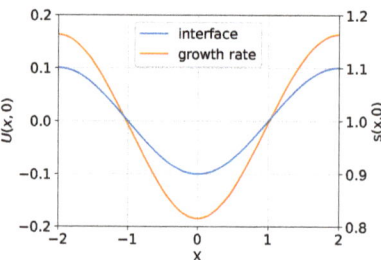

Figure 2. The interface (blue line) and growth rate (orange line) of the perturbations. Perturbation wave length is $\lambda = 4$, its amplitude is $A = 0.1$.

Figures 4 and 5 show the dependencies of the growth rate of perturbations amplitude U_d and U_u on the ratio A/λ. It can be seen from Figure 4 that for $A/\lambda < 0.1$ the calculated values of the amplitude growth rate upwards U_u and downwards U_d differ insignificantly and are in good agreement with the results obtained in the linear approximation. If $A/\lambda > 1$ (see Figure 5), the growth rate U_u is close to one. This means that the upper vertex of the perturbation profile stops, since the velocity of the interface V_f as a whole is equal to -1. The downwards growth rate U_d (blue line) increases linearly with A/λ, although significantly slower than linear analysis predicts (green line).

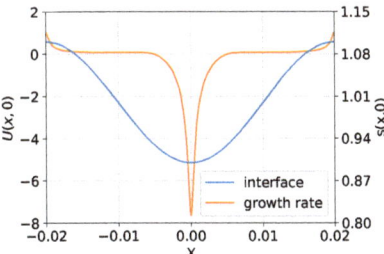

Figure 3. The interface (blue line) and growth rate (orange line) of the perturbations. Perturbation wave length is $\lambda = 0.04$, its amplitude is $A = 0.1$.

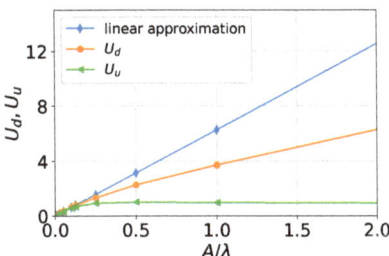

Figure 4. Dependence of U_d (orange line) and U_u (green line) on the ratio $A/\lambda \in (0,2)$. The blue line shows the linear approximation results.

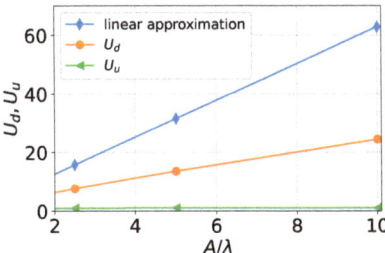

Figure 5. Dependence of U_d (orange line) and U_u (green line) on the ratio $A/\lambda \in (2,10)$. The blue line shows the linear approximation results.

From these results, it is clearly seen that the anomalous growth of short-wave perturbations is preserved in the nonlinear case.

If we introduce surface tension at the gas/liquid interface, then in the linear approximation, perturbations with a wavelength less than a certain threshold value decay, and the instability is not anomalous. In a porous medium at the pore scale, the gas / liquid interface cannot be represented as a smooth surface, since the movement occurs within individual capillaries. In this case, effective surface tension related to the curvature of the interfacial surface can only be introduced formally. Consider whether there is an unlimited increase in the growth rate of the perturbation amplitude with reduction of the wavelength, taking into account the microscopic features of the gas/liquid interface movement. To analyze the fundamental physical effects arising in this case, we will use the network model of porous media.

4. The Network Model of a Porous Medium

We represent a porous medium as a system of intersecting capillaries, as shown in Figure 6. Such a two-dimensional structure was proposed in [26] and used in [27] to calculate oil displacement by water. We assume that the gas–liquid interface in a pore throat is a simply connected surface. There is no the liquid behind the interface in a pore throat. All capillaries of the structure in each of the direction have the same length Δl. We assign indices (i, j) to each node so that its coordinate can be evaluated from relations $z_i = i\Delta l$ and $x_j = j\Delta l$. Assume that the velocity of the liquid depends on the length of the capillary, the pressure on its ends and a parameter κ. The latter is determined via the diameter and other properties of the capillary. There is a drop of pressure on the gas–liquid interface. This pressure drop equals the capillary pressure (see Equation (1)). If capillary pressure is constant, we may add the capillary pressure to the gas pressure Pa and ignore for the sake of simplicity.

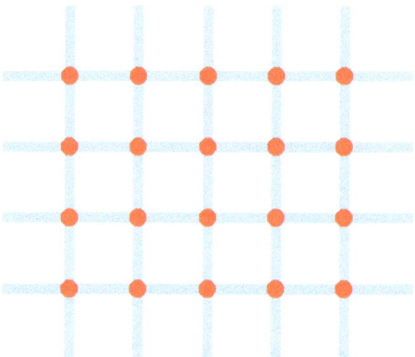

Figure 6. The network model of a porous medium.

We introduce the variable $C_{i,j}$ that equals one if the node is filled with liquid, and zero if it is filled with gas. In what follows, we will assume that each node filled with gas is connected to the gas cap by capillaries (also filled with gas). In this case, the pressure in each such node is P_g.

The velocity of the liquid in the vertical capillary connecting nodes (i, j) and $(i + 1, j)$ is given by the relation

$$v_{ij} = \begin{cases} \kappa \frac{P_{i,j}-P_{i+1,j}}{\Delta l}, & C_{i,j}=1,\ C_{i+1,j}=1, \\ \kappa \frac{P_{i,j}-P_g}{z_{sij}-z_i}, & C_{i,j}=1,\ C_{i+1,j}=0, \\ \kappa \frac{P_g-P_{i+1,j}}{z_{i+1}-z_{sij}}, & C_{i,j}=0,\ C_{i+1,j}=1, \end{cases} \qquad (23)$$

where z_{sij} is the z-coordinate of the gas/liquid interface inside the capillary connecting nodes (i, j) and $(i + 1, j)$.

Similarly, we calculate the velocity of the liquid in the horizontal capillary connecting nodes (i, j) and $(i, j + 1)$ with relations

$$u_{ij} = \begin{cases} \kappa \frac{P_{i,j}-P_{i,j+1}}{\Delta l}, & C_{i,j}=1,\ C_{i,j+1}=1, \\ \kappa \frac{P_{i,j}-P_g}{x_{sij}-x_j}, & C_{i,j}=1,\ C_{i,j+1}=0, \\ \kappa \frac{P_g-P_{i,j+1}}{x_{j+1}-x_{sij}}, & C_{i,j}=0,\ C_{i,j+1}=1. \end{cases} \qquad (24)$$

Here, x_{sij} is the x-coordinate of the gas/liquid interface inside the capillary connecting nodes (i, j) and $(i, j + 1)$.

We assume that the liquid does not accumulate inside the nodes. Hence, we obtain the conservation relation
$$u_{i,j} - u_{i,j-1} + v_{i,j} - v_{i-1,j} = 0. \tag{25}$$

Substituting the expressions for v and u (23), (24) into Equation (25) with $C_{i,j} = C_{i-1,j} = C_{i+1,j} = C_{i,j-1} = C_{i,j+1} = 1$ we obtain

$$\frac{P_{i-1,j} - 2P_{i,j} + P_{i+1,j}}{\Delta l} + \frac{P_{i,j-1} - 2P_{i,j} + P_{i,j+1}}{\Delta l} = 0. \tag{26}$$

The continuous analog of Equation (26) is

$$\Delta l \frac{\partial^2 P}{\partial z^2} + \Delta l \frac{\partial^2 P}{\partial x^2} = 0. \tag{27}$$

Equation (27) is equivalent to Equation (3), so the latter is approximated by Equation (26).

To determine the velocity of the gas/liquid interface, we need to calculate the liquid velocities in those capillaries that are not completely filled with liquid, as shown in Figure 7.

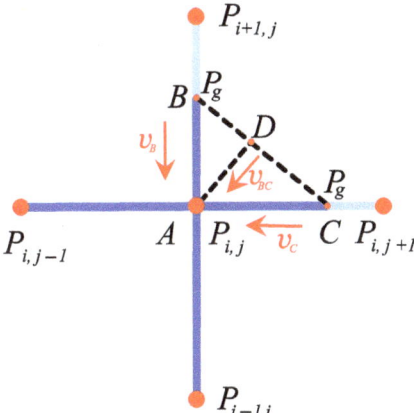

Figure 7. Diagram of the gas/liquid interface motion in capillaries.

Inside the capillary, connecting nodes (i, j) and $(i + 1, j)$, shown in Figure 7, liquid between points A and B have the velocity

$$v_B = \kappa \left(P_g - P_{i,j} \right) / \delta_{AB},$$

where δ_{AB} is the distance between points A and B. Similarly, the gas/liquid interface at the point C between nodes (i, j) and $(i, j + 1)$ has the velocity

$$v_C = \kappa \left(P_g - P_{i,j} \right) / \delta_{AC},$$

where δ_{AC} is the distance between points A and C.

If the stencil shown in Figure 7 is used to solve the continual model system (19) numerically, then the last equation of this system implies that the normal velocity of the interface (B, C) is determined by the expression

$$v_{BC} = \kappa \left(P_g - P_{i,j} \right) / \delta_{AD},$$

where

$$\delta_{AD} = \frac{\delta_{AB} \delta_{AC}}{\sqrt{\delta_{AB}^2 + \delta_{AC}^2}}.$$

The intersection point of the BC segment with the vertical capillary connecting nodes (i,j) and $(i+1,j)$ moves with velocity

$$\hat{v}_B = v_B \left(1 + \frac{\delta_{AB}^2}{\delta_{AC}^2}\right),$$

and the similar point on the horizontal capillary connecting nodes (i,j) and $(i,j+1)$ moves with velocity

$$\hat{v}_C = v_C \left(1 + \frac{\delta_{AC}^2}{\delta_{AB}^2}\right).$$

From these expressions, it follows that

$$\hat{v}_B > v_B, \; \hat{v}_C > v_C,$$

so the network model under consideration predicts a lower interface propagation velocity than the continual model does.

The exception is when the interface is parallel to the capillaries, as shown in Figure 8. In this case, both of the models give the same value of the interface velocity

$$v_{f1} = \kappa \, (P_g - P_L)/H.$$

However, significant differences between the network and continual models remain. Within the network model, the velocity of the liquid in vertical capillaries is v_{f1}, while in horizontal capillaries the liquid is at rest. The liquid inside horizontal capillaries is not displaced by gas when the contact surface moves, as shown in Figure 8. On the other hand, the continual model assumes complete liquid displacement.

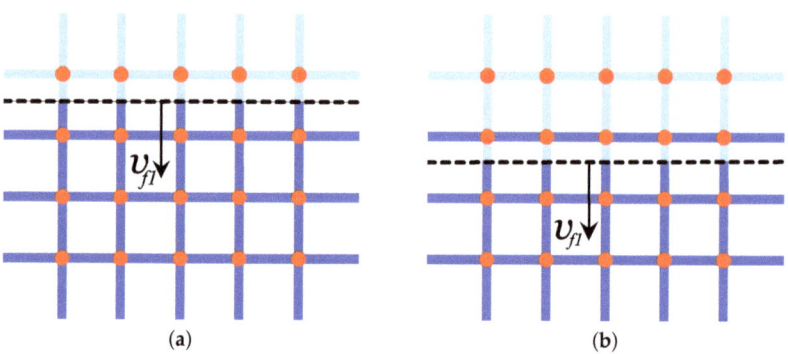

Figure 8. The network model and gas/liquid interface at $t = 0$ (**a**) and $t = \Delta l / v_{f1}$ (**b**).

If the flat contact surface is located relative to the capillaries, as shown in Figure 9, then the liquid velocity in any capillary is

$$v_{c2} = \kappa \frac{P_g - P_L}{\sqrt{2}H}.$$

The z-component of this velocity, i.e., normal velocity of the line segment connecting the interface points, is

$$v_{f2} = \kappa \frac{P_g - P_L}{2H}.$$

In this case, the liquid is displaced from all capillaries located above this line.

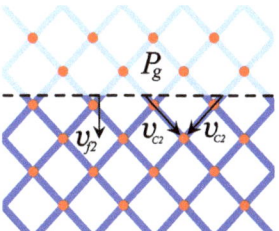

Figure 9. The network model and gas/liquid interface.

Thus, the considered capillary model exhibits strong anisotropy. The velocity of the flat contact surface can vary by a factor of two depending on the angle between the direction of interface propagation and the capillaries. The average mass flux in the direction of the z-axis is the same in both models. In this sense, the considered network model is isotropic. In the case shown in Figure 8, the contact surface has twice the velocity as in the case shown in Figure 9; however, in the first case, only half of the liquid is displaced.

When the shape of the gas/liquid interface is not flat, the problem reduces to the numerical solution of the system of the linear algebraic Equation (26). The number of equations in the system is equal to the number of nodes with unknown pressure.

This system has a sparse band matrix with five non-zero elements in each row, three of which are on and on either side of the main diagonal. We use the library SuperLU to solve this system of linear algebraic equations (SLAE) numerically.

We consider the case $\kappa = 1$, $h(\tau) = 1$, $P_c(\zeta) = 0$, $P_L = 1$ and $P_g = 2$. Within the linear approximation, the growth rate of the perturbation amplitude can be evaluated by the formula (14). In Figure 10, we show the results of calculating the amplitude growth rate depending on the ratio A/λ within the models mentioned above, as well as in linear approximation. The continual model predicts, as discussed above, lower velocity values.

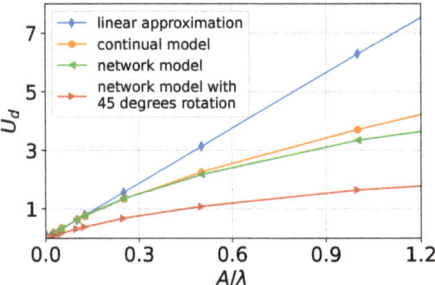

Figure 10. Growth rate calculation results: blue line—linear approximation; orange line—continual model; green line—network model; red line—network model with 45 degrees rotation.

We show that the network model has a discrete analogue of the anomalous shortwave instability. Consider the simplified network model shown in Figure 11. The network consists of one row of nodes with vertical coordinate $z = H$, and each node is connected with an interlayer by capillaries of length H. The pressure inside the interlayer is P_L. Inside the capillaries connected to nodes from above, the height of the liquid is h_1 for the first node and h_a for the others. The pressure at the gas/liquid interface is constant and equal to P_g. The total number of nodes is N.

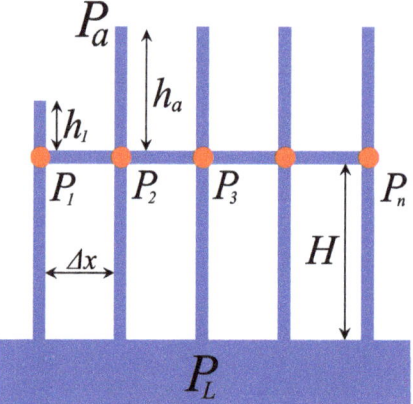

Figure 11. Simplified network model of a porous medium with one horizontal capillar layer. The parts of the channels filled with liquid are marked with a thick line.

For the first node, we have Equation (26) in the form

$$\frac{P_1 - P_g}{h_1} + \frac{P_1 - P_2}{\Delta x} + \frac{P_1 - P_L}{h} = 0. \tag{28}$$

For the N-th node we have

$$\frac{P_N - P_g}{h_a} + \frac{P_N - P_{N-1}}{\Delta x} + \frac{P_N - P_L}{h} = 0, \tag{29}$$

and for intermediate nodes with $1 < i < N$ Equation (26) gives

$$\frac{P_i - P_g}{h_a} + \frac{P_i - P_{i-1}}{\Delta x} + \frac{P_i - P_{i+1}}{\Delta x} + \frac{P_i - P_L}{h} = 0. \tag{30}$$

In the case of $N = 2$ from Equations (28) and (29) we obtain

$$U_1 = \kappa \frac{(P_L - P_g)(2 h_a + \Delta x)}{(h + 2 h_a + \Delta x) h_1 + h(h_a + \Delta x)}. \tag{31}$$

If $h_1 = h_a$ and $h_a \ll h$, from (31) we obtain

$$U_1 \approx \kappa \frac{P_L - P_g}{h}, \tag{32}$$

where U_1 is the absolute value of the velocity of the gas/liquid interface inside the upper capillary of the first node. In the case $h_1 \ll h_a$, $h_a \ll h$ and $h_a = \Delta x$, we have

$$U_1 \approx \frac{3}{2} \kappa \frac{P_L - P_g}{h}. \tag{33}$$

From (32) and (33), it follows that the liquid velocity inside the upper capillary of node 1 increases by 1.5 times with decreasing h_1 from Δx to 0 if the liquid height in neighboring nodes is constant and equal Δx. The relative change of the liquid height is small compared to h.

The shortwave perturbations occurs when $\Delta x \ll h_a$, $h_1 \ll h_a$, and $h_a \ll h$. In this case, if $N = 2$, we obtain

$$U_1 \approx 2\kappa \frac{P_L - P_g}{h}, \tag{34}$$

and the value U_1 in this limiting case increases indefinetly with an increase in the number of nodes N according to the expression

$$U_1 \approx N\kappa \frac{P_L - P_g}{h}. \tag{35}$$

Thus, the considered simplified network model with one row of nodes predicts an unbound increase in the growth rate of perturbations with decreasing wavelength.

The sophistication of the model by adding another row of nodes (see Figure 12) does not lead to a significant results change. For example, for the case shown in Figure 11 we obtain $U_1 = 2.407$, and $U_1 = 2.307$ for the case shown in Figure 12. This estimate is made for $N = 3$, $\Delta x = 0.001$, $h_a = 0.1$, and $h_1 = 0.1 h_a$. In the limiting case, when $\Delta x \ll h_a$, $h_1 \ll h_a$, and $h_a \ll h$, the result (35) stands.

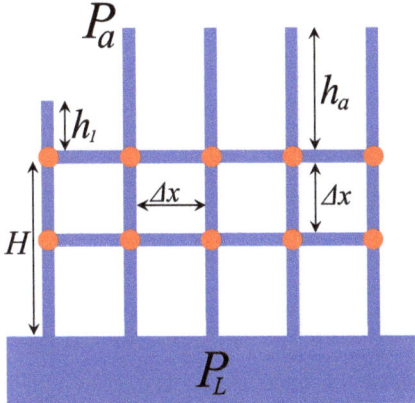

Figure 12. Simplified network model of a porous medium with two horizontal capillary layers. The parts of the channels filled with liquid are marked with a thick line.

If the perturbation curvature radius near the perturbation vertex is comparable to the capillary length Δl, then the height of the liquid column in neighboring vertical capillaries may vary significantly, as shown in Figure 13b. The fewer capillaries used in the network model, the greater this change. The results obtained above predict that the smaller the ratio of the heights of the liquid column in the right vertical capillary and the neighboring one, the greater the liquid velocity in the right capillary. In Figure 13a, the height of the liquid column in the right vertical capillary differs slightly from the height in the neighboring capillary. In Figure 13b, the height of the liquid column in the right capillary is several times less than in neighboring capillaries. As shown below, the calculations confirm that the interface velocities in the right capillary are significantly different for the cases shown in Figure 13a,b. We note that the positions of the perturbations differ only in the distance from the vertex to the nearest horizontal capillary filled with liquid.

In Figure 14, we show the dependence of the perturbation vertex growth rate U_d on the number of capillaries per perturbation wavelength. The results are presented for two positions of the vertex of the perturbation relative to the capillaries shown in Figure 13. When the number of capillaries exceeds 300, the difference in the velocity values turns out to be less than 10%, but when the number of capillaries is 40, the velocities differ by almost a factor of two.

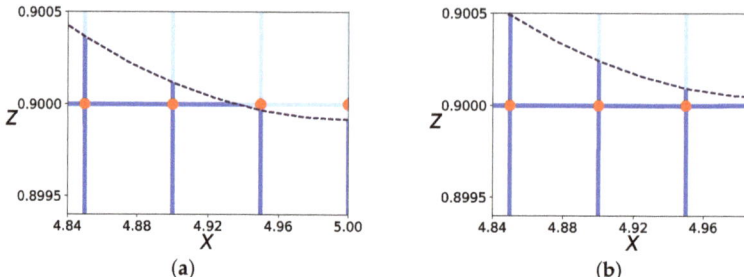

Figure 13. Two different examples of the location of the gas/liquid interface. The vertex of interface is located below (**a**) and above (**b**) the nearest horizontal capillary.

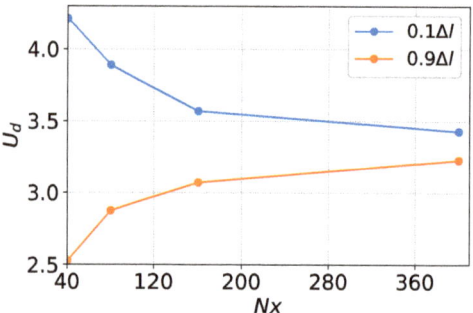

Figure 14. Amplitude growth rate at the lower point of perturbation at $x = \lambda/2$, depending on the number of vertical capillaries. The upper and lower lines correspond to the cases when the size of the part of the capillary occupied by the liquid is $0.1\Delta l$ (blue line) and $0.9\Delta l$ (orange line), respectively (see Figure 13a,b).

5. Discussion of Results and Conclusions

An analysis of the stability of the gas/liquid interface in a porous medium under the displacement of liquid by gas has been carried out. Within the continual model using the Darcy law, it has been shown that the linear analysis of stability by the normal modes method is not applicable in the case when the wave amplitude is small compared to the characteristic dimensions of the main flow but exceeds the perturbation wavelength. The onset of the shortwave instability of solutions of the continual model has been studied within the complete model, i.e., without resorting to linearization. Such a study has been carried out using the original numerical method developed by the authors. This method allows accurate and robust computation of the evolution of perturbations of the gas/liquid interface. It has been found that the rate of amplitude growth increases with decreasing wavelength. No signs of reaching the asymptotic value have been found up to the ratio of the amplitude to the wavelength equal to 10.

The network model has also been used to study the shortwave instability as a tool for improving the understanding of the physics and micromechanics of liquid flow in a porous medium in that part of the regularities that remain outside the scope of the continual model. A model with a regular topology and a coordination number of four has been used. It has been shown that although inside the region occupied by the liquid, the equations of the network model approximate the equations of the continual model well, the movement of interfacial surfaces in capillaries is not described by the continual model. The continual model predicts a higher velocity of the interfacial surface than the network one. In this case, the network model exhibits a significant anisotropy depending on the orientation when calculating the velocity of interfacial surfaces in capillaries. In the general case, the displacement of the liquid from the capillaries occurs incompletely, and the liquid remains in a part of the capillaries even under the assumption that the instability does not onset.

The performed calculations have shown that the velocity of the interfacial surfaces in the channels also increases with a decrease in the perturbation wavelength at a constant amplitude. Thus, the considered network model, like the continual model, does not allow predicting the width of the fastest growing finger-like structures observed in the experiment and should be improved. Such improvement, which primarily takes into account the processes occurring at the intersections of capillaries and the nonuniform distribution of the coordination number, is planned to be carried out at the next stage of the study.

Author Contributions: Conceptualization, V.A.S. and G.G.T.; funding acquisition, G.G.T.; investigation, V.A.S., S.V.G. and P.I.K.; methodology, V.A.S. and G.G.T.; project administration, G.G.T.; resources, V.A.S. and G.G.T.; software, V.A.S., S.V.G. and P.I.K.; validation, Y.A.B.; supervision, V.A.S.; visualization, P.I.K.; writing—original draft, V.A.S. and G.G.T.; writing—review and editing, V.A.S., G.G.T. and Y.A.B. All authors have read and agreed to the published version of the manuscript.

Funding: The work was carried out with support from the Russian Science Foundation under the grant no. 21-11-00126.

Institutional Review Board Statement: Not applicable.

Informed Consent Statement: Not applicable.

Data Availability Statement: Not applicable.

Acknowledgments: We are grateful to four anonymous reviewers for their thorough and helpful comments.

Conflicts of Interest: The authors declare no conflict of interest.

References

1. Rao, D.N.; Ayirala, S.C.; Kulkarni, M.M.; Sharma, A.P. Development of Gas Assisted Gravity Drainage (GAGD) Process for Improved Light Oil Recovery, SPE Improved Oil Recovery Conference, SPE-89357-MS, 2004. Available online: https://onepetro.org/SPEIOR/proceedings-pdf/04IOR/All-04IOR/SPE-89357-MS/2884931/spe-89357-ms.pdf (accessed on 17 April 2004). [CrossRef]
2. Yu, H.Y.; Wang, L.; Zhou, D.; Wang, F.; Li, S.; Li, J.; Chen, X.; Cao, A.Y.; Han, H. Experimental Study on Sweep Characteristics of Gas Gravity Drainage in the Interlayer Oil Reservoir. *Front. Energy Res.* **2021**, *9*, 760315. [CrossRef]
3. Lai, F.; Li, Z.; Yang, Z.; Li, H.; Guo, Z.Z. The study of components mass transfer mechanism and the rules of fluid phase alteration in the process of hydrocarbon gas drive. *J. Nat. Gas Sci. Eng.* **2014**, *21*, 411–416. [CrossRef]
4. Ren, S.; Liu, Y.; Zhang, L.; Cui, G.; Gong, Z.; Wang, Y.; Han, B. Gravity Assisted Gas Injection: Assessment Model and Experimental Study. *J. China Univ. Pet. (Ed. Nat. Sci.)* **2018**, *42*, 59–66.
5. Saffman, P.; Taylor, G. The penetration of a fluid into a porous medium or Hele-Shaw cell containing a more viscous liquid. *Proc. R. Soc.* **1958**, *A-245*, 312–329.
6. de Rooij, G. Modeling fingered flow of water in soils owing to wetting front instability: A review. *J. Hydrol.* **2000**, *231*, 277–294. [CrossRef]
7. Rose, D.; Konukcu, F.; Gowing, J.; Aust, J. Effect of watertable depth on evaporation and salt accumulation from saline groundwater. *Aust. J. Soil Res.* **2005**, *43*, 565–573. [CrossRef]
8. Shokri-Kuehni, S.; Raaijmakers, B.; Kurz, T.; Or, D.; Helmig, R.; Shokri, N. Water Table Depth and Soil Salinization: From Pore-Scale Processes to Field-Scale Responses. *Water Resour. Res.* **2020**, *56*, e2019WR026707. [CrossRef]
9. Il'ichev, A.; Tsypkin, G.; Pritchard, D.; Richardson, C. Instability of the salinity profile during the evaporation of saline groundwater. *J. Fluid Mech.* **2008**, *614*, 87–104. [CrossRef]
10. Schubert, G.; Straus, J. Gravitational stability of water over steam in vapor-dominated geothermal system. *J. Geoph. Res.* **1980**, *85*, 6505–6512. [CrossRef]
11. Ramesh, P.; Torrance, K. Stability of boiling in porous media. *Int. J. Heat Mass Transf.* **1990**, *33*, 1895–1908. [CrossRef]
12. Pestov, I. Stability of vapour–liquid counter flow in porous media. *J. Fluid Mech.* **1998**, *364*, 273–295. [CrossRef]
13. Tsypkin, G.; Il'ichev, A. Instabilities of uniform filtration flows with phase transition. *J. Exp. Theor. Phys.* **2008**, *107*, 699–711.
14. Khan, Z.; Pritchard, D. Liquid-vapour fronts in porous media: Multiplicity and stability of front positions. *Int. J. Heat Mass Transf.* **2013**, *61*, 1–17. [CrossRef]
15. Khan, Z.; Pritchard, D. Anomaly of spontaneous transition to instability of liquid-vapour front in a porous medium. *Int. J. Heat Mass Transf.* **2015**, *84*, 448–455. [CrossRef]

16. Shargatov, V.; Il'ichev, A.; Tsypkin, G. Dynamics and stability of moving fronts of water evaporation in a porous medium. *Int. J. Heat Mass Transf.* **2015**, *83*, 552–561. [CrossRef]
17. Tsypkin, G.G. Instability of a light fluid over a heavy one under the motion of their interface in a porous medium. *Fluid Dyn.* **2020**, *55*, 213–219. [CrossRef]
18. Tsypkin, G.G.; Shargatov, V.A. Linear stability of a filtration flow with gas–oil interface within the brinkman approach. *Fluid Dyn.* **2022**, *57*, 273–280. [CrossRef]
19. McDougall, S.; Sorbie, K. The impact of wettability on waterflooding: Pore-scale simulation. *SPE Reserv. Eng.* **1995**, *10*, 208–213. [CrossRef]
20. Blunt, M. Effects of Heterogeneity and Wetting on Relative Permeability Using Pore Level Modeling. *SPE J.* **1997**, *2*, 70–87. [CrossRef]
21. Blunt, M. Pore Level Modeling of the Effects of Wettability. *SPE J.* **1997**, *2*, 494–510. [CrossRef]
22. Valvatne, P.; Blunt, M. Predictive pore-scale modeling of two-phase flow in mixed wet media. *Water Resour. Res.* **2004**, *40*. [CrossRef]
23. Øren, P.; Stig Bakke, S.; Arntzen, O. Extending Predictive Capabilities to Network Models. *SPE J.* **1998**, *3*, 324–336.
24. Man, H.N.; Jing, X. Network modelling of wettability and pore geometry effects on electrical resistivity and capillary pressure. *J. Pet. Sci. Eng.* **1999**, *24*, 255–267. [CrossRef]
25. Ryazanov, A.; Dijke, M.I.J.; Sorbie, K.S. Two-Phase Pore-Network Modelling: Existence of Oil Layers During Water Invasion. *Transp. Porous Media* **2009**, *80*, 79–99. [CrossRef]
26. Sorbie, K.; Clifford, P.; Jones, E. The rheology of pseudoplastic fluids in porous media using network modeling. *J. Colloid Interface Sci.* **1989**, *130*, 508–534. [CrossRef]
27. Li, J.; McDougall, R.; Sorbie, K. Dynamic pore-scale network model (PNM) of water imbibition in porous media. *Adv. Water Resour.* **2017**, *107*, 191–211. [CrossRef]
28. Zhang, P.; Celia, M.; Bandilla, K.; Hu, L.; Meegoda, J.N. A Pore-Network Simulation Model of Dynamic CO_2 Migration in Organic-Rich Shale Formations. *Transp. Porous Media* **2020**, *133*, 479–496. [CrossRef]
29. Shen, A.; Zhang, C.; Liu, Y.; Wang, F.; Liang, S. Acyclic pore model and its applications in imbibition efficiency calculation. *J. Pet. Sci. Eng.* **2022**, *208*, 109586. [CrossRef]
30. Raeini, A.Q.; Blunt, M.J.; Bijeljic, B. Direct simulations of two-phase flow on micro-CT images of porous media and upscaling of pore-scale forces. *Adv. Water Resour.* **2014**, *74*, 116–126. [CrossRef]
31. Martins, A.; Laranjeira, P.; Braga, C.; Mata, T. Modeling of transport phenomena in porous media using network models. *Prog. Porous Media Res.* **2009**, *5*, 165–261.
32. Hoogland, F.; Lehmann, P.; Mokso, R.; Or, D. Drainage mechanisms in porous media: From piston-like invasion to formation of corner flow networks. *Water Resour. Res.* **2016**, *52*, 8413–8436. [CrossRef]
33. Wopara, O.F.; Iyuke, S. Review of studies on pore-network modeling of wettability effects on waterflood oil recovery. *J. Pet. Gas Eng.* **2018**, *9*, 11–22.
34. Shargatov, V.A. Dynamics and Stability of Air Bubbles in a Porous Medium. *Comput. Math. Math. Phys.* **2018**, *58*, 1172–1187. [CrossRef]
35. Tsypkin, G.G.; Shargatov, V.A. Influence of capillary pressure gradient on connectivity of flow through a porous medium. *Int. J. Heat Mass Transf.* **2018**, *127*, 1053–1063. [CrossRef]
36. Shargatov, V.A.; Gorkunov, S.V.; Il'ichev, A.T. Dynamics of front-like water evaporation phase transition interfaces. *Commun. Nonlinear Sci. Numer. Simul.* **2019**, *67*, 223–236. [CrossRef]
37. Shargatov, V.; Gorkunov, S.; Il'ichev, A. Stability of finite perturbations of the phase transition interface for one problem of water evaporation in a porous medium. *Appl. Math. Comput.* **2020**, *378*, 125208. [CrossRef]

Article

Optical Solitons of the Generalized Nonlinear Schrödinger Equation with Kerr Nonlinearity and Dispersion of Unrestricted Order

Nikolay A. Kudryashov [1,2]

[1] Department of Applied Mathematics, National Research Nuclear University MEPhI (Moscow Engineering Physics Institute), 31 Kashirskoe Shosse, 115409 Moscow, Russia; nakudryashov@mephi.ru
[2] National Research Center "Kurchatov Center", 1 Akademika Kurchatova Sq., 115409 Moscow, Russia

Abstract: The family of the generalized Schrödinger equations with Kerr nonlinearity of unrestricted order is considered. The solutions of equations are looked for using traveling wave reductions. The Painlevé test is applied for finding arbitrary constants in the expansion of the general solution into the Laurent series. It is shown that the equation does not pass the Painlevé test but has two arbitrary constants in local expansion. This fact allows us to look for solitary wave solutions for equations of unrestricted order. The main result of this paper is the theorem of existence of optical solitons for equations of unrestricted order that is proved by direct calculation. The optical solitons for partial differential equations of the twelfth order are given in detail.

Keywords: generalized nonlinear Schrödinger equation; Kerr nonlinearity; optical soliton; simplest equation method; dispersion of unrestricted order

MSC: 35A24; 35C05; 35C07; 35C08

1. Introduction

The investigation of the effect of high-order dispersion on the propagation of pulses in a nonlinear optical medium has been presented in several papers (see, for example, papers [1–17]). Usually, these studies were aimed at constructing optical solitons for specific high-order equations. The appearance of terms with a high order of dispersion in the generalized nonlinear Schrödinger equation is explained by taking into account the expansion of the mode propagation constant in a Taylor series around the carrier frequency [18–20]. The influence of terms with high-order derivatives is usually neglected, since the coefficients of these derivatives have smaller values compared to the coefficients for low-order derivatives. However, it is known that neglecting the influence of high-order derivatives in nonlinear mathematical models is often incorrect, since their influence appears at late times and long distances of wave propagation. In this connection, in the paper [12], a hypothesis about the form of an optical soliton for the generalized nonlinear Schrödinger equations with Kerr nonlinearity and an unrestricted order of dispersion was formulated.

In this paper, we consider the family of the generalized nonlinear Schrödinger equations in the form

$$i\,q_t + \sum_{j=1}^{n} \alpha_{2j}\, q_{2j,x} + i \sum_{j=2}^{n} \alpha_{2j-1}\, q_{2j-1,x} = \beta\, |q|^2\, q, \qquad (1)$$

$$n \in \mathbb{N}, \qquad q_{m,x} = \frac{\partial^m q}{\partial x^m}, \qquad m \in \mathbb{N},$$

where $i^2 = -1$, $q(x,t)$ is a complex function, and t and x are independent variables.

The following equations belong to the equations of family (1). We have the famous nonlinear Schrödinger equation at $n = 1$ [19]:

$$i\, q_t + \alpha_2\, q_{xx} = \beta\, |q|^2\, q. \tag{2}$$

Substituting $n = 2$ into (1) yields the partial differential equation of the fourth order [11]:

$$i\, q_t + \alpha_2\, q_{xx} + i\, \alpha_3\, q_{xxx} + \alpha_4\, q_{xxxx} = \beta\, |q|^2\, q. \tag{3}$$

The differential equation of the sixth order in the form [12]

$$i\, q_t + \alpha_2\, q_{xx} + i\, \alpha_3\, q_{xxx} + \alpha_4\, q_{xxxx} + i\, \alpha_5\, q_{xxxxx} + \alpha_6\, q_{xxxxxx} = \beta\, |q|^2\, q \tag{4}$$

is obtained by substituting $n = 3$ into (1), and so on.

At first glance, it seems that Equation (1) does not have any physical meaning and cannot have any physical applications. However, it should be kept in mind that the second term of the Taylor series expansion of the function $q(x, t)$ is used to take into account the effect of dispersion in the nonlinear Schrödinger equation [19]. Equation (1) is interesting in that it takes into account higher orders of dispersion when describing the propagation of a pulse in an optical medium.

The objective of this paper is to find the optical solitons of Equation (1) at all integer $n \in \mathbb{N}$ in analytical form.

The paper is organized as follows. In Section 2, we use the Painlevé test to investigate the integrability of Equation (1). Using traveling wave reduction, we obtain two arbitrary constants in the expansion of the general solution in the Laurent series. In Section 3, we prove the theorem of existence of optical solutions for the generalized nonlinear Schrödinger equation with the Kerr nonlinearity and dispersion of unrestricted order. We present the form of optical soliton for the equation with the unrestricted order of dispersion. In Section 4, we present the calculations of parameters of the equation and optical soliton of the generalized nonlinear Schrödinger equation of the twelfth order.

2. Application of the Painlevé Test to Equation (1)

We look for the optical solitons of Equation (1) in the form

$$q(x, t) = y(z)\, e^{i(kx + \omega t + \theta_0)}. \tag{5}$$

Substituting (5) into Equation (1), we obtain the imaginary part of Equation (1) in the linear form

$$\sum_{j=1}^{n} P_{2j-1}\, y_{2j-1,z} = 0 \tag{6}$$

and the real part of the nonlinear equation in the form

$$\sum_{j=1}^{n} P_{2j}\, y_{2j,z} - \beta\, y(z)^3 = 0, \tag{7}$$

where P_{2j} and P_{2j+1} are expressions depending on the coefficients α_{2j}, $(j = 1, \ldots, n)$ and α_{2j+1}, $(j = 0, \ldots, n-1)$.

In the next section, we demonstrate that the problem of finding optical solitons of Equation (1) is reduced to the solution of Equation (7). In this section, we apply the Painlevé test to understand the integrability of Equation (7).

It is well known that the Painlevé analysis is one of the powerful approaches for determining the integrability of nonlinear differential equations. It allows us to find the necessary conditions for the existence of a general solution of a differential equation. The application of the Painlevé test to the analysis of nonlinear differential equations consists, as a rule, of three consecutive steps. In the first step, an equation with leading terms corresponding to Equation (7) and the number of branches of the expansion in the Laurent series are found.

Taking into account Equation (7), we obtain the equation with the leading members in the form

$$\alpha_{2n} y_{2n,z} - \beta y^3 = 0. \tag{8}$$

Equation (8) is autonomous, and the first term in the expansion of the general solution of Equation (7) in the Laurent series is determined by substituting the expression

$$y(z) = d_0 z^p \tag{9}$$

into (8).

We obtain two branches of the expansion of the general solution of Equation (7):

$$p = -n, \quad d_0 = \pm \sqrt{\frac{\alpha_{2n}(3n-1)!}{\beta(n-1)!}}. \tag{10}$$

In the second step, we define the Fuchs indices that can determine the arbitrary coefficients of the expansion of the general solution into a Laurent series. With this aim, we substitute the solution in the form

$$y(z) = \pm \sqrt{\frac{\alpha_{2n}(3n-1)!}{\beta(n-1)!}} z^{-n} + d_j z^{j-n} \tag{11}$$

into Equation (8) and equate the coefficients of d_j to zero. As a result, we obtain the algebraic equation for the index j in the form

$$E = (n-j)(n-j+1)(n-j+2)\ldots(3n-2-j)(3n-j-1)- \tag{12}$$

$$3n(n+1)(n+2)\ldots(3n-2)(3n-1) = 0.$$

From Equation (12), the two following integer Fuchs indices follow in the form

$$j_1 = -1, \quad j_2 = 4n. \tag{13}$$

We cannot find the other Fuchs indices in the general case. We performed calculations for $n = 2, 3, 4, 5,$ and $n = 6$ and found that remaining Fuchs indices are complex numbers. As a result, we obtain that Equation (7) does not pass the Painlevé test.

We see that there is always one arbitrary constant z_0 in the expansion of the solution into the Laurent series because we can shift $z \to z - z_0$. However, in the third step, we have to check the coefficient at $j = 4n$ in the Laurent series expansion. Unfortunately, for this step of the Painlevé test, one can only check easily for the first several values of n.

For example, let us consider Equation (7) at $n = 3$. It takes the form

$$a_6 y_{zzzzzz} + a_4 y_{zzzz} + a_2 y_{zz} - a_0 y - \beta y^3 = 0, \tag{14}$$

where the coefficients $a_6, a_4, a_2,$ and a_0 depend on coefficients $\alpha_6, \alpha_4, \alpha_2, k,$ and w by formulas

$$a_6 = \alpha_6, \quad a_4 = \alpha_4 + 15 k^2 \alpha_6, \quad a_2 = \alpha_2 + 6 k^2 \alpha_4 + 75 k^4 \alpha_6,$$

$$\tag{15}$$

$$a_0 = w + k^2 \alpha_2 + 3 k^4 \alpha_4 + 35 k^6 \alpha_6.$$

The equation with leading members corresponding to Equation (14) can be written as

$$a_6 y_{zzzzzz} - \beta y^3 = 0. \tag{16}$$

Substituting

$$y = \frac{b_0}{z^p} \tag{17}$$

into Equation (14), we obtain two branches of the expansion of the general solution of Equation (14):

$$p = 3, \quad b_0 = \pm 24 \sqrt{\frac{35 a_6}{\beta}}. \tag{18}$$

Substituting the solution $y(z)$ in the form

$$y = \pm 24 \sqrt{\frac{35 a_6}{\beta}} z^{-3} + b_j z^{j-3} \tag{19}$$

again into Equation (16) and equating coefficients of a_j to zero, we find the following Fuchs indices

$$j_1 = -1, \quad j_2 = 12, \quad j_{3,4,5,6} = \frac{11}{2} \pm \frac{\sqrt{-67 \pm 4i\sqrt{1151}}}{2}. \tag{20}$$

We obtain that Equation (14) does not pass the Painlevé test and therefore is not integrable.

However, we need to check the arbitrary coefficient corresponding to the Fuchs index $j_2 = 12$. With this aim we use the Laurent series for the solution of Equation (14) with undetermined coefficients in the form

$$y(z) = \frac{b_0}{z^3} + \frac{b_1}{z^2} + \frac{b_2}{z} + b_3 + b_4 z + b_5 z^2 + b_6 z^3 + b_7 z^4 + b_8 z^5 +$$

$$b_9 z^6 + b_{10} z^7 + b_{11} z^8 + b_{12} z^9 + \ldots \tag{21}$$

Substituting series (21) into Equation (14), we obtain the following values of coefficients for the expansion of the solution in the Laurent series

$$b_0 = \pm 24 \sqrt{\frac{35 a_6}{\beta}}, \quad b_1 = 0, \quad b_2 = \frac{12 a_4 \sqrt{35 \beta a_6}}{83 \beta a_6}, \quad b_3 = 0, \tag{22}$$

$$b_4 = \frac{a_2 \sqrt{35 \beta a_6}}{210 \beta a_6} - \frac{1177 a_4^2 \sqrt{35 \beta a_6}}{1446690 \beta a_6^2}, \quad b_5 = 0, \tag{23}$$

$$b_6 = -\frac{a_0 \sqrt{35 \beta a_6}}{2520 \beta a_6} - \frac{11 a_2 a_4 \sqrt{35 \beta a_6}}{209160 \beta a_6^2} + \frac{967 a_4^3 \sqrt{35 \beta a_6}}{120075270 \beta a_6^3}, \quad b_7 = 0, \tag{24}$$

$$b_8 = \frac{\sqrt{35 \beta a_6} \, a_0 a_4}{418320 \beta a_6^2} - \frac{\sqrt{35 \beta a_6} \, a_2^2}{1058400 \beta a_6^2} + \frac{2857 \sqrt{35 \beta a_6} \, a_2 a_4^2}{3645658800 \beta a_6^3} -$$

$$\frac{4775989 \sqrt{35 \beta a_6} \, a_4^4}{50229886946400 \beta a_6^4}, \quad b_9 = 0, \tag{25}$$

$$b_{10} = \frac{\sqrt{35 \beta a_6} \, a_0 a_2}{23284800 \beta a_6^2} - \frac{337 \sqrt{35 \beta a_6} \, a_0 a_4^2}{13367415600 \beta a_6^3} + \frac{431 \sqrt{35 \beta a_6} a_2^2 a_4}{20292703200 \beta a_6^3} -$$

$$\frac{1524433 \sqrt{35 \beta a_6} \, a_2 a_4^3}{139796432344800 \beta a_6^4} + \frac{2194769053 \sqrt{35 \beta a_6} \, a_4^5}{19261152448466544400 \beta a_6^5}, \quad b_{11} = 0. \tag{26}$$

We also obtain that b_{12} is an arbitrary constant. As a result, we obtain the expansion in the Laurent series with two arbitrary constants, taking into account the arbitrariness of b_{12} and z_0 because we can change the variable $z \to z - z_0$. Therefore, Equation (7) is not integrable but this equation can have the special solution with two arbitrary constants. This fact tells us that the solution of Equation (7) can be found using the method of simplest equations [21].

3. Theorem of Existence for the Optical Soliton of Equation (1) with Unrestricted Dispersion

In this section, we prove that Equation (1) at any integer n has the solution in the form of bright optical soliton. We formulate this fact in the form of the following theorem.

Theorem 1. *The function of x and t in the form*

$$q(x,t) = \frac{2^{2n} A_n \mu^n e^{i(kx+\omega t - \theta_0)}}{\left(4\mu v e^{-\sqrt{\mu}(x-C_0 t - x_0)} + e^{\sqrt{\mu}(x-C_0 t - x_0)}\right)^n}, \qquad (27)$$

where A_n, μ, v, k, x_0, and θ_0 are arbitrary constants and value $2n$ gives the order of equation, is a bright soliton of Equation (1) at any integer $n \in \mathbb{N}$ and certain constraints on α_j ($j = 1, 2, \ldots n$), C_0, and ω.

Proof. The proof of this theorem is obtained using direct calculations.

For compatibility of the system of Equations (6) and (7) we first find the constraints on the coefficients α_{2j-1} ($j = n, n-1, \ldots, 2$) and C_0 from the linear Equation (6). In this case, any smooth function $y(z)$ is a solution of Equation (6). Therefore, the problem of finding the solution of Equation (1) is reduced to the solution of Equation (7).

We look for the solution of Equation (7) as follows [21–25]:

$$y(z) = A_n R(z)^n, \qquad (28)$$

where $R(z)$ is a solution of Equation [21]:

$$R_z^2 = \mu R^2 - v R^4. \qquad (29)$$

Differentiating (29) with respect to z, we obtain

$$R_{zz} = \mu R - 2v R^3. \qquad (30)$$

It is easy to see that all solutions of Equation (29) are also solutions of Equation (30). Taking into account the solution (28) and Equations (29) and (30), we obtain

$$y_{zz} = A_n n^2 \mu R^n - A_n v n(n+1) R^{n+2}, \qquad (31)$$

$$y_{zzzz} = A_n \mu^2 n^4 R^n - 2 A_n \mu v \left(n^4 + 3n^2 + 4n^2 + 2n\right) R^{n+2} + \\ A_n v^2 \left(n^4 + 6n^3 + 11n^2 + 6n\right) R^{n+4}. \qquad (32)$$

By induction we obtain the equality

$$y_{2n,z} = A_n F_n \mu^n R^n + \ldots + A_n v^n G_n R^{3n}, \quad y_{2n,z} = \frac{d^{2n} y}{dz^{2n}}, \qquad (33)$$

where F_n and G_n are polynomials in n.

One can also note that

$$y^3 = A_n^3 R(z)^{3n}. \qquad (34)$$

Taking into account (33) and (34), we can find the coefficient from Equation (7) in the form

$$a_{2n} = (-1)^n \frac{A_n^2 \beta}{G_n \nu^n}. \tag{35}$$

Then, using the value a_{2n}, we can find the coefficients a_{2j} $(j = n-1, n-2, \ldots, 1)$ and ω.

The solution of Equation (29) takes the form [21–25]

$$R(z) = \pm \frac{4\mu}{4\mu\nu e^{-\sqrt{\mu}(z-z_1)} + e^{\sqrt{\mu}(z-z_0)}}. \tag{36}$$

Substituting (36) into (28), we obtain the function (27) that is a solution of Equation (1) with constraints on the parameters of the equation. Thus, there is always solution (27) of Equation (1). □

We have to note that solution (27) of Equation (1) in the case of an unrestricted order is new. However, earlier, in papers [11,12,26], solutions were found at $n=1$, $n=2$, and $n=3$. These solutions coincide with solutions obtained by formulas (27) at $n=1$, $n=2$, and $n=3$. The approach of this section can also be used to study fractional differential equations considered in papers [27–29].

4. Optical Solitons of the Twelfth-Order Equation (1)

Let us demonstrate the application of the method for construction of solution (27) of the twelfth-order Equation (1). Assuming $n=6$ in Equation (1), we obtain the equation in the form

$$i\,q_t + \alpha_2\,q_{2,x} + i\,\alpha_3\,q_{3,x} + \alpha_4\,q_{4,x} + i\,\alpha_5\,q_{5,x} + \alpha_6\,q_{6,x} + i\,\alpha_7\,q_{7,x} + \\ \alpha_8\,q_{8,x} + i\,\alpha_9\,q_{9,x} + \alpha_{10}\,q_{10,x} + i\,\alpha_{11}\,q_{11,x} + \alpha_{12}\,q_{12,x} = \beta\,|q|^2\,q. \tag{37}$$

Substituting solution (5) into Equation (37) and equating the imaginary and real parts to zero, we obtain the system of Equations (6) and (7). The equation for the imaginary part takes the form

$$(12\,\alpha_{12}\,k + \alpha_{11})\,y_{11,z} + \left(10\,\alpha_{10}\,k - 220\,\alpha_{12}k^3 - 55\,\alpha_{11}\,k^2 + \alpha_9\right)y_{9,z} + \\ \left(792\,\alpha_{12}\,k^5 + 330\,\alpha_{11}\,k^4 - 120\,\alpha_{10}\,k^3 - 36\,\alpha_9\,k^2 + 8\,\alpha_8\,k + \alpha_7\right)y_{7,z} + \\ \left(252\,\alpha_{10}\,k^5 - 792\,\alpha_{12}\,k^7 - 462\alpha_{11}k^6 + 126\alpha_9\,k^4 - 56\,\alpha_8,k^3 - 21\,\alpha_7\,k^2 + \\ 6\,\alpha_6\,k + \alpha_5\right)y_{5,z} + \left(220\,\alpha_{12}\,k^9 + 165\,\alpha_{11}\,k^8 - 120\,\alpha_{10}\,k^7 - 84\,\alpha_9\,k^6 + \\ 56\,\alpha_8\,k^5 + 35\,\alpha_7\,k^4 - 20\,\alpha_6\,k^3 - 10\,\alpha_5\,k^2 + 4\,\alpha_4\,k + \alpha_3\right)y_{3,z} + \\ \left(10\,\alpha_{10}k^9 - 12\,\alpha_{12}\,k^{11} - 11\,\alpha_{11}\,k^{10} + 9\,\alpha_9\,k^8 - 8\,\alpha_8\,k^7 - 7\,\alpha_7\,k^6 + \\ 6\,\alpha_6\,k^5 + 5\,\alpha_5\,k^4 - 4\,\alpha_4\,k^3 - 3\,\alpha_3\,k^2 + 2\,\alpha_2\,k - C_0\right)y_z = 0 \tag{38}$$

The equation for the real part can be written as

$$\begin{aligned}
&\alpha_{12}y_{12,z} + \left(\alpha_{10} - 66\alpha_{12}k^2 - 11\alpha_{11}k\right)y_{10,z} + \left(495\alpha_{12}k^4 + 165\alpha_{11}k^3 - \right.\\
&\left.45\alpha_{10}k^2 - 9\alpha_9 k + \alpha_8\right)y_{8,z} + \left(210\alpha_{10}k^4 - 924\alpha_{12}k^6 - 462\alpha_{11}k^5 + \right.\\
&\left.84\alpha_9 k^3 - 28\alpha_8 k^2 - 7\alpha_7 k + \alpha_6\right)y_{6,z} + \left(\alpha_4 + 495\alpha_{12}k^8 + 330\alpha_{11}k^7 - \right.\\
&\left.210\alpha_{10}k^6 - 126\alpha_9 k^5 + 70\alpha_8 k^4 + 35\alpha_7 k^3 - 15\alpha_6 k^2 - 5\alpha_5 k\right)y_{4,z} + \\
&\left(45\alpha_{10}k^8 - 66\alpha_{12}k^{10} - 55\alpha_{11}k^9 + 36\alpha_9 k^7 - 28\alpha_8 k^6 - 21\alpha_7 k^5 + \right.\\
&\left.15\alpha_6 k^4 + 10\alpha_5 k^3 - 6\alpha_4 k^2 - 3\alpha_3 k + \alpha_2\right)y_{2,z} + \left(\alpha_{12}k^{12} + \alpha_{11}k^{11} - \right.\\
&\alpha_{10}k^{10} - \alpha_9 k^9 + \alpha_8 k^8 + \alpha_7 k^7 - \alpha_6 k^6 - \alpha_5 k^5 + \alpha_4 k^4 + \alpha_3 k^3 - \\
&\left.\alpha_2 k^2 - \omega\right)y - \beta y^3 = 0.
\end{aligned} \qquad (39)$$

From Equation (38) we obtain the constraints on the parameters of Equation (1) in the form

$$\alpha_{11} = -12\alpha_{12}k, \qquad (40)$$

$$\alpha_9 = -440\alpha_{12}k^3 - 10\alpha_{10}k, \qquad (41)$$

$$\alpha_7 = -12672\alpha_{12}k^5 - 240\alpha_{10}k^3 - 8\alpha_8 k, \qquad (42)$$

$$\alpha_5 = -215424\alpha_{12}k^7 - 4032\alpha_{10}k^5 - 112\alpha_8 k^3 - 6\alpha_6 k, \qquad (43)$$

$$\alpha_3 = -1745920\alpha_{12}k^9 - 32640\alpha_{10}k^7 - 896\alpha_8 k^5 - 40\alpha_6 k^3 - 4\alpha_4 k, \qquad (44)$$

$$\begin{aligned}C_0 = &\ 4245504\alpha_{12}k^{11} + 79360\alpha_{10}k^9 + 2176\alpha_8 k^7 + \\ & 96\alpha_6 k^5 + 8\alpha_4 k^3 + 2\alpha_2 k.\end{aligned} \qquad (45)$$

Equation (38) is satisfied for any smooth function $y(z)$ at conditions (40)–(45). We look for the solution of Equation (39) in the form

$$y(z) = A_6 R(z)^6, \qquad (46)$$

where $R(z)$ is the function (36). Substituting (36) into Equation (39) and taking into account the derivatives of $R(z)$ and conditions (40)–(45), we obtain the polynomial in $R(z)$ which has to be equal to zero. Equating the coefficients of this polynomial to zero, we find the additional constraints on the parameters of Equation (1) in the form

$$\alpha_{12} = \frac{A_6^2 \beta}{2964061900800\, \nu^6}, \qquad (47)$$

$$\alpha_{10} = -\frac{\beta\left(33k^2 + 398\mu\right)A_6^2}{1482030950400\, \nu^6}, \qquad (48)$$

$$\alpha_8 = \frac{A_6^2 \beta\left(165k^4 + 11940k^2\mu + 82256\mu^2\right)}{988020633600\, \nu^6}, \qquad (49)$$

$$\alpha_6 = -\frac{A_6^2 \beta\left(231k^6 + 41790k^4\mu + 1727376k^2\mu^2 + 9460432\mu^3\right)}{741015475200\, \nu^6}, \qquad (50)$$

$$\alpha_4 = \frac{A_6{}^2 \beta k^8}{5988003840\, v^6} + \frac{199\, k^6 \mu\, A_6{}^2 \beta}{3528645120\, v^6} + \frac{5141\, k^4 \mu^2 A_6{}^2 \beta}{882161280\, v^6} +$$

$$\frac{34781\, k^2 \mu^3 A_6{}^2 \beta}{181621440\, v^6} + \frac{2930269\, \mu^4 A_6{}^2 \beta}{2894591700\, v^6}, \tag{51}$$

$$\alpha_2 = -\frac{A_6{}^2 \beta k^{10}}{44910028800\, v^6} - \frac{199\, A_6{}^2 \beta k^8 \mu}{16467010560\, v^6} - \frac{5141\, A_6{}^2 \beta k^6 \mu^2}{2205403200\, v^6} -$$

$$\frac{34781\, A_6{}^2 \beta k^4 \mu^3}{181621440\, v^6} - \frac{2930269\, A_6{}^2 \beta k^2 \mu^4}{482431950\, v^6} - \frac{3131984\, \mu^5 A_6{}^2 \beta}{80405325\, v^6}, \tag{52}$$

$$\omega = \frac{A_6{}^2 \beta k^{12}}{269460172800\, v^6} + \frac{199\, A_6{}^2 \beta k^{10} \mu}{82335052800\, v^6} + \frac{5141\, A_6{}^2 \beta k^8 \mu^2}{8821612800\, v^6} +$$

$$\frac{34781\, A_6{}^2 \beta k^6 \mu^3}{544864320\, v^6} + \frac{2930269\, A_6{}^2 \beta k^4 \mu^4}{964863900\, v^6} + \frac{3131984\, A_6{}^2 \beta k^2 \mu^5}{80405325\, v^6} -$$

$$\frac{4096\, A_6{}^2 \beta \mu^6}{7293\, v^6}. \tag{53}$$

The solution of the generalized Schrödinger Equation (37) can be written as follows:

$$q(x,t) = \frac{4096\, A_6\, \mu^6\, e^{i(kx+\omega t+\theta_0)}}{\left(4\mu v\, e^{-\sqrt{\mu}(x-C_0 t - z_0)} + e^{\sqrt{\mu}(x - C_0 t - z_0)}\right)^6}. \tag{54}$$

One can note that A_6, μ, v, k, z_0, and θ_0 are arbitrary constants in solution (54). However, the parameters C_0 and ω are determined by formulas (45) and (53). The other parameters of Equation (37) are found taking into account formulas (40)–(44) and (47)–(52).

5. Conclusions

In this paper, we considered the generalized Schrödinger equation with Kerr nonlinearity and unrestricted order of dispersion. We applied the Painlevé test and showed that equations of this family are not integrable in the general case, and the Cauchy problem cannot be solved by the inverse scattering transform. However, we obtained that there are two arbitrary constants in the expansion of the general solution into the Laurent series and we showed there are special solutions of Equation (1). We looked for solutions of this equation using the traveling wave reduction. We proved the theorem claiming that all differential equations of this family have optical solitons in analytical form. We presented the detailed calculations for the nonlinear differential equations of the twelfth order.

Funding: This research was funded by Russian Science Foundation. Grant number 22-11-00141.

Data Availability Statement: Not applicable.

Acknowledgments: This research was supported by Russian Science Foundation Grant No. 22-11-00141 "Development of analytical and numerical methods for modeling waves in dispersive wave guides". The author is grateful to the anonymous reviewers for valuable remarks on the paper, contributing to its improvement. The author also declares that there are no conflicts of interest.

Conflicts of Interest: The authors declare no conflict of interest.

References

1. Biswas, A.; Ekici, M.; Dakova, A.; Khan, S.; Moshokoa, S.P.; Alshehri, H.M.; Belic, M.R. Highly dispersive optical soliton perturbation with Kudryashov's sextic-power law nonlinear refractive index by semi-inverse variation. *Results Phys.* **2021**, *27*, 104539. [CrossRef]
2. Biswas, A.; Sonmezoglu, A.; Ekici, M.; Alshomrani, A.S.; Belic, M.R. Highly dispersive singular optical solitons with Kerr law nonlinearity by Jacobi's elliptic ds function expansion. *Optik* **2019**, *192*, 162954. [CrossRef]
3. Biswas, A.; Ekici, M.; Sonmezoglu, A.; Belic, M.R. Highly dispersive optical solitons in absence of self-phase modulation by Jacobi's elliptic function expansion. *Optik* **2019**, *189*, 109–120. [CrossRef]

4. Elsherbeny, A.M.; El-Barkouky, R.; Seadawy, A.R.; Ahmed, H.M.; El-Hassani, R.M.I.; Arnous, A.H. Highly dispersive optical soliton perturbation of Kudryashov's arbitrary form having sextic-power law refractive index. *Int. J. Mod. Phys. B* **2021**, *35*, 2150247. [CrossRef]
5. Gonzalez-Gaxiola, O.; Biswas, A.; Alshomrani, A.S. Highly dispersive optical solitons having Kerr law of refractive index with Laplace-Adomian decomposition. *Rev. Mex. Fis.* **2020**, *66*, 291–296. [CrossRef]
6. Gonzalez-Gaxiola, O.; Biswas, A.; Asma, M.; Alzahrani, A.K. Highly dispersive optical solitons with non-local law of refractive index by Laplace-Adomian decomposition. *Opt. Quantum Electron.* **2021**, *53*, 55. [CrossRef]
7. Gonzalez-Gaxiola, O.; Biswas, A.; Alzahrani, A.K.; Belic, M.R. Highly dispersive optical solitons with a polynomial law of refractive index by Laplace-Adomian decomposition. *J. Comput. Electron.* **2021**, *20*, 1216–1223. [CrossRef]
8. Kohl, R.W.; Biswas, A.; Ekici, M.; Yildirim, Y.; Triki, H.; Alshomrani, A.S.; Belic, M.R. Highly dispersive optical soliton perturbation with quadratic-cubic refractive index by semi-inverse variational principle. *Optik* **2020**, *206*, 163621. [CrossRef]
9. Kohl, R.W.; Biswas, A.; Ekici, M.; Zhou, Q.; Khan, S.; Alshomrani, A.S.; Belic, M.R. Highly dispersive optical soliton perturbation with Kerr law by semi-inverse variational principle. *Optik* **2019**, *199*, 163226. [CrossRef]
10. Kudryashov, N.A. Implicit Solitary Waves for One of the Generalized Nonlinear Schrödinger Equations. *Mathematics* **2021**, *9*, 3024. [CrossRef]
11. Kudryashov, N.A. Highly Dispersive Optical Solitons of an Equation with Arbitrary Refractive Index. *Regul. Chaotic Dyn.* **2020**, *25*, 537–543. [CrossRef]
12. Kudryashov, N.A. Highly dispersive optical solitons of the generalized nonlinear eighth-order Schrodinger equation. *Optik* **2020**, *206*, 164335. [CrossRef]
13. Rabie, W.B.; Seadawy, A.R.; Ahmed, H.M. Highly dispersive Optical solitons to the generalized third-order nonlinear Schrödinger dynamical equation with applications. *Optik* **2021**, *241*, 167109. [CrossRef]
14. Wang, G.; Kara, A.H.; Biswas, A.; Guggilla, P.; Alzahrani, A.K.; Belic, M.R. Highly dispersive optical solitons in polarization-preserving fibers with Kerr law nonlinearity by Lie symmetry, Physics Letters. *Sect. A Gen. At. Solid State Phys.* **2022**, *421*, 127768.
15. Zayed, E.M.E.; Alngar, M.E.M.; El-Horbaty, M.M.; Biswas, A.; Ekici, M.; Zhou, Q.; Khan, S.; Mallawi, F.; Belic, M.R. Highly dispersive optical solitons in the nonlinear Schrödinger's equation having polynomial law of the refractive index change. *Indian J. Phys.* **2021**, *95*, 109–119. [CrossRef]
16. Zayed, E.M.E.; Al-Nowehy, A.-G.; Alngar, M.E.M.; Biswas, A.; Asma, M.; Ekici, M.; Alzahrani, A.K.; Belic, M.R. Highly dispersive optical solitons in birefringent fibers with four nonlinear forms using Kudryashov's approach. *J. Opt.* **2021**, *50*, 120–131. [CrossRef]
17. Zayed, E.M.E.; Gepreel, K.A.; El-Horbaty, M.; Biswas, A.; Yildirim, Y.; Alshehri, H.M. Highly dispersive optical solitons with complex ginzburg-landau equation having six nonlinear forms. *Mathematics* **2021**, *9*, 3270. [CrossRef]
18. Agrawal, G.P. *Nonlinear Fiber Optics*; Academic Press: Cambridge, MA, USA, 1989.
19. Kivshar, Y.S.; Agrawal, G.P. *Optical Solitons. From Fibers to Photonic Crystals*; Academic Press: Cambridge, MA, USA, 2003.
20. Kivshar, Y.S.; Malomed, B.A. Dynamics of solitons in nearly integrable systems. *Rev. Mod. Phys.* **1989**, *63*, 763–915. [CrossRef]
21. Kudryashov, N.A. Method for finding highly dispersive optical solitons of nonlinear differential equations. *Optik* **2020**, *206*, 163550. [CrossRef]
22. Arnous, A.H.; Biswas, A.; Yildirim, Y.; Zhou, Q.; Liu, W.J.; Alshomrani, A.S.; Alshehri, H.M. Cubic-quartic optical soliton perturbation with complex Ginzburg-Landau equation by the enhanced Kudryashov's method. *Chaos Solitons Fractals* **2022**, *155*, 11748. [CrossRef]
23. Ekici, M. Stationary optical solitons with Kudryashov's quintuple power law nonlinearity by extended Jacobi's elliptic function expansion. *J. Nonlinear Opt. Phys. Mater.* **2022**, *2022*, 2350008. [CrossRef]
24. Ozisik, M.; Secer, A.; Bayram, M.; Aydin, H. An encyclopedia of Kudryashov's integrability approaches applicable to optoelectronic devices. *Optik* **2022**, *265*, 169499. [CrossRef]
25. Sain, S.; Ghose-Choudhury, A.; Garai, S. Solitary wave solutions for the KdV-type equations in plasma: A new approach with the Kudryashov function. *Eur. Phys. J. Plus* **2021**, *136*, 226. [CrossRef]
26. Kudryashov, N.A. Highly dispersive solitary wave solutions of perturbed nonlinear Schrödinger equations. *Appl. Math. Comput.* **2020**, *371*, 124972. [CrossRef]
27. Hashemi, M.S.; Bahrami, F.; Najafi, R. Symmetrry analysis of steady—State fractional—Convection—Diffusion equation. *Optik* **2017**, *138*, 240–249. [CrossRef]
28. Xia, F.-L.; Jarad, F.; Hashemi, M.S.; Riaz, M.B. A reduction technique to solve the generalized nonlinear dispersive mK(m,n) equation with new local derivative. *Results Phys.* **2022**, *38*, 105512. [CrossRef]
29. Chu, Y.-M.; Inc, M.; Hashemi, M.S.; Eshaghi, S. Analytical treatment of regularized Prabhakar fractional differential equations by invariant subspaces. *Comput. Appl. Math.* **2022**, *41*, 271. [CrossRef]

Article

Mathematical Modeling of Gas Hydrates Dissociation in Porous Media with Water-Ice Phase Transformations Using Differential Constrains

Natalia Alekseeva [1,*], Viktoriia Podryga [2], Parvin Rahimly [2], Richard Coffin [1] and Ingo Pecher [1]

1 Department of Physical and Environmental Science, Texas A&M University—Corpus Christi, Corpus Christi, TX 78412, USA
2 Keldysh Institute of Applied Mathematics of Russian Academy of Sciences, 125047 Moscow, Russia
* Correspondence: nalekseeva@islander.tamucc.edu or alekseeva.nyu@gmail.com

Abstract: 2D numerical modeling algorithms of multi-component, multi-phase filtration processes of mass transfer in frost-susceptible rocks using nonlinear partial differential equations are a valuable tool for problems of subsurface hydrodynamics considering the presence of free gas, free water, gas hydrates, ice formation and phase transitions. In this work, a previously developed one-dimensional numerical modeling approach is modified and 2D algorithms are formulated through means of the support-operators method (SOM) and presented for the entire area of the process extension. The SOM is used to generalize the method of finite difference for spatially irregular grids case. The approach is useful for objects where a lithological heterogeneity of rocks has a big influence on formation and accumulation of gas hydrates and therefore it allows to achieve a sufficiently good spatial approximation for numerical modeling of objects related to gas hydrates dissociation in porous media. The modeling approach presented here consistently applies the method of physical process splitting which allows to split the system into dissipative equation and hyperbolic unit. The governing variables were determined in flow areas of the hydrate equilibrium zone by applying the Gibbs phase rule. The problem of interaction of a vertical fault and horizontal formation containing gas hydrates was investigated and test calculations were done for understanding of influence of thermal effect of the fault on the formation fluid dynamic.

Keywords: nonlinear partial differential equations; differential constraints; gas hydrates; multi-component fluid dynamic; permafrost formation

MSC: 00A71; 65N06; 76S05; 35M1

Citation: Alekseeva, N.; Podryga, V.; Rahimly, P.; Coffin, R.; Pecher, I. Modeling of Gas Hydrates Dissociation in Porous Media with Water-Ice Phase Transformations Using Differential Constrains. *Mathematics* **2022**, *10*, 3470. https://doi.org/10.3390/math10193470

Academic Editor: Nikolai A. Kudryashov

Received: 23 August 2022
Accepted: 21 September 2022
Published: 23 September 2022

Publisher's Note: MDPI stays neutral with regard to jurisdictional claims in published maps and institutional affiliations.

Copyright: © 2022 by the authors. Licensee MDPI, Basel, Switzerland. This article is an open access article distributed under the terms and conditions of the Creative Commons Attribution (CC BY) license (https://creativecommons.org/licenses/by/4.0/).

1. Introduction

Presently natural gas hydrates are studied extensively worldwide for reasons well beyond energy resources: besides the potential for becoming a novel fuel, methane hydrates present a potential hazard related [1,2] to methane emission during hydrate dissociation, particularly due to influence of climate changes. Part of the discovered and hypothetical occurrences are affiliated with permafrost regions and the Arctic Ocean shelves. In a large number of studies there are hypothesis formulated and detailly investigated about relationship between gas hydrates dissociation and multiple natural processes, including those with possible grave consequences, such as cratering onshore in northern regions and broad-scale gas fluxes through the ocean floor.

Capabilities of modeling of gas hydrates-related processes are still limited leading to a scientific debate on the effects of possible wide-spread gas hydrate dissociation. When applying the modeling to the gas hydrates processes in cryolithic zone of polar regions and shelves of the Arctic Ocean, it is necessary to consider one additional phase in the general scheme for calculations, which is the ice phase. The current study is devoted to mathematical modelling of gas hydrates dissociation in porous media allowing consideration of the presence of ice and the associated phase transitions. As the basis for the study the widely applied model of mass, energy and momentum balance equations is taken into account under the assumption of the thermodynamic equilibrium process behavior. Based on the balance equations, a unique method of physical processes splitting, established for 3-phase system and presented by the authors in their previous paper [3], is improved and applied for the "gas–water–gas hydrates–ice" 4-phase system. Furthermore, it is the first time when the characteristic properties for the splitted 4-phase system (i.e., upward/downward flow direction for saturation unit and ice phase concentration values) are analyzed . This study is dedicated to the newly-presented model of physical processes splitting for the 4-phase system and its results.

As the main method of analysis the physical processes splitting is used. This allows to split the system into dissipative equation and saturation unit, which is responsible for convection transfer of saturation parameters and primarily typified by hyperbolic features. The splitting approach allows to use implicit/explicit numerical solution schemes, which are applicable for phase transition problems, and avoid excessive time step refinement.

A gradual expansion of the method's capabilities is being conducted in the study by inclusion in the integrated algorithm increasing number of phases and components, which naturally appear in an array of scientific, technical and ecological problems.

In Section 2, in addition to the system "gas–water–gas hydrates", which was considered in previous works [4], there is a new icy phase included.

In Section 3, the saturation unit equations' properties are analyzed by method of characteristics.

In Section 4, based on the support-operators method (SOM) there were built difference schemes on nonregular grids of moderate-dimension, applied to the problems at hand, allowing to describe models with complex (heterogeneous) lithological structure and material properties by means of the support operators method [5,6].

In Section 5, the difference schemes, built in Section 4, are used for the models split by physical processes describing the "gas–water–gas hydrate–ice" system. In Section 6, there are test calculations are presented exemplified by the problem of interaction of vertical fault and horizontal seam containing gas hydrates.

Review of the Support-Operators Method (SOM), Mathematical Models and Software for Hydrates Formation

Calculations of gas hydrates phase transitions using different approaches were described in a large number of models considering generation, migration and accumulation of gas through the hydrate stability zone ([7–9]). Most models are based on regular grids which require high computational power and time to calculate the results. The support operators' method makes it possible to numerically simulate a number of problems of mathematical physics in complex inhomogeneous areas. The method was developed by Russian scientists and received worldwide recognition. In English literature, the terms "support operators' method", or SOM, and "mimetic finite difference method" are used. A detailed modern review is given in [5].

The application of this method makes it possible to carry out mathematical modeling of various problems of fluid filtration in the process of hydrocarbon production with a detailed account of the features of the geological and lithological structure of the reservoir, tectonic disturbances, allows to analyze both the dynamics of fluids on the scale of the entire field (and more broadly, the region), within the framework of one model, and local processing going on the area that is of most interest to the user.

The support operator method (SOM) is a generalization of the finite difference method to irregular grids. The great advantage of this method in comparison with others is its persistence, i.e., automatic fulfillment of the fluid mass conservation law incorporated into the main formulas of the method. This allows to avoid calculation errors in the form of the appearance of fictitious sources and sinks not related to the physics of the process, which arise on other methods.

The proposed method has been worked out in detail both in theoretical aspects (analysis of convergence, stability, accuracy estimates) and in practical ones. The developed software package supports both building of a computational grid—which is close in all details to the reservoir geometry—with the accuracy required by the user and at the same time with a relatively small number of nodes and carrying out calculations on it.

Application of the SOM to the problems of dissociation of gas hydrates in a porous media is described in [4] with references to earlier works. At present, the complex includes programs for calculating two-dimensional (areal or profile) joint filtration of liquid and gas on an irregular grid, as well as problems of dissociation of gas hydrates in a porous media.

The software package is open for expansion, i.e., to the inclusion of more complex models of hydro- and thermodynamics of reservoir fluids, theology of the reservoir matrix, etc. The proposed set of algorithms and programs can serve as a mathematical basis for predicting the behavior of reservoir fluids in the process of developing oil and gas fields, as well as gas hydrate deposits.

Currently, in addition to the support operator method [4], there are a number of computer systems for calculating fluid dynamics in the reservoir, taking into account gas hydrates, such as CMG STARS, STOMP-HYDT-KE [10], TOUGH+HYDRATE [11], developed by Lawrence Berkeley National Laboratory in the USA; MH21-HYDRES [12], created as part of the national hydration program in Japan with the support of a number of scientific and commercial organizations, RetrasoCodeBright (RCB) created in Norway [13], SuGaR-TCHM, developed in Germany [13], etc. They are based on the use of computer systems for solving ordinary problems of underground fluid dynamics with the inclusion of blocks corresponding to hydrate thermodynamics. These methods, developed earlier, continue to be modernized and supplemented with new blocks that allow us to study more complex problems, include additional phases and other elements of the physics of reservoir systems in the analysis of the deformation properties of reservoirs. New methods continue to emerge, for example [14]. The resulting developments are widely used in mathematical modeling of specific gas hydrate deposits and analysis of the results of laboratory experiments. Many of these software systems account for salt dissolved in water.

A review of several methods at the beginning of 2016 was carried out in [15], published in a special issue of the journal [16] dedicated to gas hydrates. This review reflects the state of mathematical modeling of hydrate fluid dynamics in the reservoir, as well as methods for calculating the kinetics of formation and dissociation of gas hydrates at the beginning of 2016. A modern review of some methods is contained in the work [17] devoted to international cooperation in the field of testing numerical methods for solving problems of underground hydrodynamics related to gas hydrates, in which a significant part of the groups involved in the development of the corresponding software takes part.

2. Physical Processes Splitting in Mathematical Model of the "Gas–Water–Gas Hydrates–Ice" System

For the hydrate equilibrium zone (HEZ) the initial conservation Equations (fluid mass balance equations for liquid (or ice) phase and gas in free and bounded state) in porous media can be expressed in the following divergence form (for water and gas accordingly):

$$\frac{\partial}{\partial t}\{m(S_v S_w \rho_{wi} + (1 - S_v)\rho_v \beta_w)\} + \mathrm{div}[\rho_w \mathbf{V}_w] + q_w = 0, \qquad (1)$$

$$\frac{\partial}{\partial t}\{m(S_v(1 - S_w)\rho_g + (1 - S_v)\rho_v(1 - \beta_w))\} + \mathrm{div}[\rho_g \mathbf{V}_g] + q_g = 0. \qquad (2)$$

Energy balance equation is written as following:

$$\frac{\partial}{\partial t}\{m[S_v(S_w\rho_{wi}\varepsilon_{wi}+(1-S_w)\rho_g\varepsilon_g)+(1-S_v)\rho_v\varepsilon_v]+(1-m)\rho_s\varepsilon_s\}$$
$$+\text{div}\{\rho_w\varepsilon_w\mathbf{V}_w+\rho_g\varepsilon_g\mathbf{V}_g+P(\mathbf{V}_w+\mathbf{V}_g)\}+\text{div}\,\mathbf{W}+q_s=0, \qquad (3)$$
$$\mathbf{W}=-(m(S_v(S_w\lambda_{wi}+(1-S_w)\lambda_g)+(1-S_v)\lambda_v)+(1-m)\lambda_s)\nabla T,$$

where indexes g, w, i, v, s are relating to gas, water, ice, hydrate, rock matrix of porous media, wi is relating to ice-water mixture; P—pressure, T—temperature, t—time, $m = m(\mathbf{r}, P)$—porosity, $\mathbf{r}$—position vector, S_w—water saturation (water and ice), β_w—mass fraction of water in hydrate, $S_g = 1 - S_w$—gas saturation, v—hydrate saturation, $S_v = 1 - v$—hydrate thawing, $\rho_l = \rho_l(P, T)$, $\lambda_l = \lambda_l(P, T)$, $\varepsilon_l = \varepsilon_l(P, T)$—densities, thermal conduction coefficients, internal energy of components ($l = g, w, v, s, i$), $\mathbf{V}_\alpha$ and q_α—filtration velocity and sources density of phase $\alpha = w, g$.

Let us introduce the following notation:

$C_i + C_w = 1$, C_i, C_w—solid ice and liquid water volume fractions;

$\rho_{wi} = C_w\rho_w + C_i\rho_i$—density of water-ice mixture;

$S_{vi} = S_v(1 - (1 - C_w)S_w)$—porous volume fraction ($m\delta V$) without solid inclusions hydrates and ice;

$S_{wi} = \dfrac{C_wS_w}{C_wS_w + (1 - S_w)}$—fraction of water in the system "liquid water–gas".

Consequently, solid part of porous volume ($m\delta V$) will be given by:

$$(1 - S_{vi}) = [(1 - S_v) + (1 - C_w)S_wS_v].$$

Thermodynamic parameters: $\lambda_{wi} = C_w\lambda_w + (1 - C_w)\lambda_i$—water–ice mixture thermal conductivity coefficient, $\varepsilon_{wi} = [C_w\rho_w\varepsilon_w + (1 - C_w)\rho_i\varepsilon_i]/\rho_{wi}$—water–ice mixture internal energy.

Capillary forces are neglected. It is assumed, that filtration velocities of liquid and gaseous phases in porous media satisfy the Darcy's Law:

$$\mathbf{V}_\alpha = -\frac{k_i \cdot k_{r\alpha i}}{\mu_\alpha}(\nabla P - \mathbf{g}\rho_\alpha), \quad \alpha = w, g, \qquad (4)$$

where $\mathbf{g}$—gravity acceleration vector, $k_i = k(\mathbf{r}, S_{vi}, P)$—recalculation of absolute permeability $k(\mathbf{r}, S_v, P)$ considering part of porous media with frozen water, $k_{r\alpha i} = k_{r\alpha}(S_{wi})$—recalculation of phase relative permeability $k_{r\alpha}(S_w)$, $\mu_\alpha = \mu_\alpha(P, T)$—viscosity of water and gas.

The system of Equations (1) and (2) at a fixed value of determinative thermodynamic variables is named saturation unit, meaning that these equations serve for determination of water saturation S_w and hydrate thawing S_v.

Dependence of the variables on pressure and temperature in the phase equilibrium zone comes down to dependence on pressure only on virtue phase equilibrium relationship, which in its concrete form does not influence the mathematical structure of the system of equations describing the process. There are a lot of studies devoted to analyzing these relationships. In the numerical calculations that were conducted for the present study, we used the model being developed in present paper, and the following relationship was used [18,19]:

$$T = T_{\text{dis}}(P) = A \ln P + B, \qquad (5)$$

where A and B—empirical constants.

Hydrate internal energy is being expressed through energies of the gas and water–ice mixture that the hydrate consists of as follows:

$$\beta_w i_{wi} + (1 - \beta_w)i_g = i_v + h_{tr}, \qquad (6)$$

where h_{tr}—internal latent heat of hydrate mass unit's phase transition.

Enthalpy:
$$i_l = \varepsilon_l + P/\rho_l, \tag{7}$$

where $\varepsilon_l(P, T)$—phase internal energy, index l denotes a phase ($\equiv g/w/wi/v$).

For the system of equations for thawed zone, where there are no hydrates, $S_v = 1$. In this case energy balance conservation Equations (1)–(3) take on the form of:

$$\frac{\partial}{\partial t}(mS_w\rho_{wi}) + \text{div}[\rho_w \mathbf{V}_w] + q_w = 0, \tag{8}$$

$$\frac{\partial}{\partial t}(m(1-S_w)\rho_g) + \text{div}[\rho_g \mathbf{V}_g] + q_g = 0, \tag{9}$$

$$\frac{\partial}{\partial t}\{m(S_w\rho_{wi}\varepsilon_{wi} + (1-S_w)\rho_g\varepsilon_g) + (1-m)\rho_w\varepsilon_w\} \\ + \text{div}\{\rho_w\varepsilon_w\mathbf{V}_w + \rho_g\varepsilon_g\mathbf{V}_g + P(\mathbf{V}_w + \mathbf{V}_g)\} + \text{div}\,\mathbf{W} + q_\varepsilon = 0, \tag{10}$$

where $\mathbf{W} = -(m(S_w\lambda_{wi} + (1-S_w)\lambda_g) + (1-m)\lambda_s)\nabla T$.

The system of Equations (1)–(5) completely describes filtration processes in porous media with solid rock matrix saturated with gas hydrates considering both its formation and dissociation in the hydrate equilibrium zone. Similarly, the system of Equations (8)–(10) describes filtration processes for the thawed zone with absence of gas hydrates.

The governing piezoconductive dissipative equation of the hydrates theory for determination of pressure P, similarly to [20], is derived as following:

$$m\delta_\varepsilon \left\{ S_v \left[S_w \frac{(\rho_{wi})_t}{\rho_{wi}} + (1-S_w)\frac{(\rho_g)_t}{\rho_g} \right] + (1-S_v)\frac{(\rho_v)_t}{\rho_v} + \frac{(m)_t}{m} \right\} \\ + \frac{\psi}{m\rho_v}\{m\{S_v[S_w\rho_{wi}(\varepsilon_{wi})_t + (1-S_w)\rho_g(\varepsilon_g)_t] + (1-S_v)\rho_v(\varepsilon_v)_t\}\} \tag{11} \\ + \frac{\psi}{m\rho_v}[(1-m)\rho_s\varepsilon_s]_t + \delta_\varepsilon \text{DIG} + \frac{\psi}{m\rho_v}\text{DIG}_\varepsilon = 0,$$

where

$$\text{DIG} = \frac{1}{\rho_{wi}}\text{div}(\rho_w\mathbf{V}_w) + \frac{1}{\rho_g}\text{div}(\rho_g\mathbf{V}_g) + \left(\frac{q_w}{\rho_{wi}} + \frac{q_g}{\rho_g}\right), \tag{12}$$

$$\text{DIG}_\varepsilon = \left[\text{div}(\rho_w\varepsilon_w\mathbf{V}_w) - \varepsilon_{wi}\,\text{div}(\rho_w\mathbf{V}_w)\right] + \left[\text{div}(\rho_g\varepsilon_g\mathbf{V}_g) - \varepsilon_g\,\text{div}(\rho_g\mathbf{V}_g)\right] \\ + \text{div}\left[P(\mathbf{V}_w + \mathbf{V}_g)\right] + \text{div}\,\mathbf{W} + (q_\varepsilon - \varepsilon_{wi}q_w - \varepsilon_g q_g) = (\varepsilon_w - \varepsilon_{wi})\,\text{div}(\rho_w\mathbf{V}_w) \tag{13} \\ + \rho_w\mathbf{V}_w\nabla\varepsilon_w + \rho_g\mathbf{V}_g\nabla\varepsilon_g + \text{div}\left[P(\mathbf{V}_w + \mathbf{V}_g)\right] + \text{div}\,\mathbf{W} + (q_\varepsilon - \varepsilon_{wi}q_w - \varepsilon_g q_g).$$

Here

$$\frac{\psi}{m\rho_v} = \left(\varphi - \frac{1}{\rho_v}\right) \geq 0, \quad \varphi = \frac{\beta_w}{\rho_{wi}} + \frac{(1-\beta_w)}{\rho_g} \tag{14}$$

—specific (per unit) volume kick,

$$\delta_\varepsilon = \beta_w\varepsilon_{wi} + (1-\beta_w)\varepsilon_g - \varepsilon_v \geq 0 \tag{15}$$

—specific (per unit) energy kick.

Introducing of hydrate system pressure capacity:

$$D_p = m\delta_\varepsilon \left\{ S_v \left[S_w \frac{(\rho_{wi})_p}{\rho_{wi}} + (1-S_w)\frac{(\rho_g)_p}{\rho_g} \right] + (1-S_v)\frac{(\rho_v)_p}{\rho_v} + \frac{(m)_p}{m} \right\}$$
$$+ \frac{\psi}{m\rho_v}\left\{ m\left[S_v\left[S_w\rho_{wi}(\varepsilon_{wi})_p + (1-S_w)\rho_g(\varepsilon_g)_p \right] + (1-S_v)\rho_v(\varepsilon_v)_p \right] + [(1-m)\rho_s\varepsilon_s]_p \right\}, \quad (16)$$

will rewrite Equation (11) in compact form:

$$D_p \frac{\partial P}{\partial t} + \delta_\varepsilon \text{DIG} + \frac{\psi}{m\rho_v}\text{DIG}_\varepsilon = 0. \quad (17)$$

For the thawed zone without hydrates the dissipative unit:

$$\frac{S_w}{\rho_{wi}}\frac{\partial}{\partial t}(m\rho_{wi}) + \frac{1-S_w}{\rho_g}\frac{\partial}{\partial t}(m\rho_g) + \text{DIG} = 0, \quad (18)$$

where

$$\text{DIG} = \frac{1}{\rho_{wi}}\text{div}(\rho_w \mathbf{V}_w) + \frac{1}{\rho_g}\text{div}(\rho_g \mathbf{V}_g) + \left(\frac{q_w}{\rho_{wi}} + \frac{q_g}{\rho_g}\right) \quad (19)$$

and

$$m\left[S_w \rho_{wi} \frac{\partial \varepsilon_{wi}}{\partial t} + (1-S_w)\rho_g \frac{\partial \varepsilon_g}{\partial t} \right] + \frac{\partial}{\partial t}[(1-m)\rho_s\varepsilon_s] + \text{DIG}_\varepsilon = 0, \quad (20)$$

where

$$\text{DIG}_\varepsilon = (\varepsilon_w - \varepsilon_{wi})\text{div}(\rho_w \mathbf{V}_w) + \rho_w \mathbf{V}_w \nabla \varepsilon_w + \rho_g \mathbf{V}_g \nabla \varepsilon_g + \text{div}[P(\mathbf{V}_w + \mathbf{V}_g)]$$
$$+ \text{div}\, \mathbf{W} + (q_\varepsilon - \varepsilon_{wi}q_w - \varepsilon_g q_g). \quad (21)$$

Therefore, complete physical processes splitting of problems of hydrate equilibrium and thawed zones is conducted using the following numerical solution of connected problems.

The derived system of equations is a generalization of the system obtained in the paper [4], for the processes related to gas hydrates in conditions allowing for the presence of ice.

3. Saturation Unit Analysis Using the Method of Characteristics

For simplification in this section $g = 0$.

3.1. Properties of Saturations Transfer Unit S_v, S_w if $0 \leq C_w \leq 1$

From the system of Equations (1) and (2) the following system is derived:

$$(S_v)'_t + \frac{1}{\psi}\frac{\rho_w}{\rho_{wi}}\frac{P'_x}{\mu_w}(k_i k_{rwi})'_x + \frac{1}{\psi}\frac{P'_x}{\mu_g}(k_i k_{rgi})'_x = <\ldots>, \quad (22)$$

$$(S_w)'_t - \frac{\rho_w}{\rho_{wi}}\frac{\psi_g}{mS_v\psi}\frac{P'_x}{\mu_w}(k_i k_{rwi})'_x + \frac{\psi_w}{mS_v\psi}\frac{P'_x}{\mu_g}(k_i k_{rgi})'_x = <\ldots>. \quad (23)$$

Taking only diagonal values of the spatial derivatives matrix for S_v and S_w:

$$(S_v)'_t + \left\{ \frac{(k_i)'_{S_{vi}}}{\psi}\left[\frac{\rho_w}{\rho_{wi}}\frac{k_{rwi}}{\mu_w} + \frac{k_{rgi}}{\mu_g} \right] P'_x (S_{vi})'_{S_v} \right\}(S_v)'_x + <\ldots> (S_w)'_x = <\ldots>, \quad (24)$$

$$
\begin{aligned}
&(S_w)'_t + <\ldots> (S_v)'_x \\
&+ \begin{cases} \dfrac{(k_i)'_{S_{vi}}}{mS_v\psi} \left[\dfrac{-\rho_w}{\rho_{wi}} \dfrac{k_{rwi}}{\mu_w} \psi_g + \dfrac{k_{rgi}}{\mu_g} \psi_w \right] P'_x (S_{vi})'_{S_w} - \\ -\dfrac{k_i}{mS_v\psi} \left[\dfrac{\rho_w}{\rho_{wi}} \dfrac{(k_{rwi})'_{S_{wi}}}{\mu_w} \psi_g - \dfrac{(k_{rgi})'_{S_{wi}}}{\mu_g} \psi_w \right] P'_x (S_{wi})'_{S_w} \end{cases} (S_w)'_x = <\ldots>. \quad (25)
\end{aligned}
$$

The notation $<\ldots>$ denotes an absence of spatial–time derivatives of values S_v and S_w in the matrix;

$$\dfrac{\psi_g}{m\rho_v} = \dfrac{1-\beta_w}{\rho_g} - \dfrac{1-S_w}{\rho_v} \quad \text{if} \quad S_{wi} > S_{w\min},$$

$$\dfrac{\psi_w}{m\rho_v} = \dfrac{\beta_w}{\rho_{wi}} - \dfrac{S_w}{\rho_v} \quad \text{if} \quad S_{wi} < S_{w\max}.$$

Clearly that: $\psi = \psi_w + \psi_g > 0$.

$$(S_{vi})'_{S_v} = (1 - C_i S_w) > 0, \quad (S_{vi})'_{S_w} = -C_i S_v < 0, \quad (S_{wi})'_{S_w} = \dfrac{C_w}{(1 - C_i S_w)^2} > 0. \quad (26)$$

Since the analysis of signs of the flow of a system of equations, which is similar to (1)–(4), but without hydrates ($S_v = 1$), gives for invariant S_w expressions, which are similar to $-P'_x \psi_g$ and $-P'_x \psi_w$, but without ψ_g and ψ_w functions—then the necessary condition required to cross-link hydrate and non-hydrate flow areas is the following requirements:

$$\dfrac{\psi_g}{m\rho_v} = \dfrac{1-\beta_w}{\rho_g} - \dfrac{1-S_w}{\rho_v} > 0 \quad \text{under the conditions} \quad S_{wi} > S_{w\min}, \quad (27)$$

$$\dfrac{\psi_w}{m\rho_v} = \dfrac{\beta_w}{\rho_{wi}} - \dfrac{S_w}{\rho_v} > 0 \quad \text{under the conditions} \quad S_{wi} < S_{w\max}. \quad (28)$$

The requirements (27) and (28), from the component-wise kicks of specific (per unit) volume along with phase transition point of view, can be interpreted as following. Under the condition of complete dissociation of hydrate, unit the volume of released gas must be greater than $(1 - S_w)$ (where S_w is the volume fracture in ice of hydrate) and unit of the volume of released water–ice mixture must be greater than S_w.

Hyperbolical analysis of saturation unit (1) and (2) demonstrates, that under difference approximation:

1. In fluid components of absolute permeability $k_i = k(S_{vi})$ it's necessary to take hydrate thawing S_v in the downward flow direction, since $\dfrac{\rho_w}{\rho_{wi}} \dfrac{k_{rwi}}{\mu_w} + \dfrac{k_{rgi}}{\mu_g} > 0$.
2. In fluid components of absolute permeability $k_i = k(S_{vi})$ water saturation S_w is taken in the upward flow direction, if $-\dfrac{\rho_w}{\rho_{wi}} \dfrac{k_{rwi}}{\mu_w} \psi_g + \dfrac{k_{rgi}}{\mu_g} \psi_w > 0$, and S_w is taken in the downward flow direction, if $-\dfrac{\rho_w}{\rho_{wi}} \dfrac{k_{rwi}}{\mu_w} \psi_g + \dfrac{k_{rgi}}{\mu_g} \psi_w < 0$.
3. In fluid components of relative permeability $k_{rwi} = k_{rw}(S_{wi})$ and $k_{rgi} = k_{rg}(1 - S_{wi})$ water saturation S_w is taken in the upward flow direction considering $\dfrac{\rho_w}{\rho_{wi}} \dfrac{(k_{rwi})'_{S_{wi}}}{\mu_w} \psi_g - \dfrac{(k_{rgi})'_{S_{wi}}}{\mu_g} \psi_w > 0$.

Grid approximation (upward/downward flow direction) for C_w and C_i will be clarified further.

3.2. Properties of Water–Ice Phase Transfer ($0 < C_w < 1$, $P'_t = T'_t = 0$) under Hydrate Equilibrium Conditions

In spatial areas, where the phase equilibrium of the water–ice mixture is presented ($0 < C_w < 1$), phase transition temperature T_0 and pressure P are considered constant and given. With that, piezoconductivity Equation (11) is used for calculation of volume water–ice phase fracture transferring C_w. In the areas where there are constant and given $C_w = 1$ (i.e., water if $T \geq T_0$) or $C_w = 0$ (ice if $T \leq T_0$), the same equation is applied for calculation of evolution of thermodynamic parameters T and P. Related areas are changed dynamically in time with optional phase transition surface boundary (Stefan's problem [21]), and this phenomenon is supposed to be analyzed with specific numerical algorithms. In the present section we study hyperbolic properties of water–ice phase transfer ($0 < C_w < 1$, $P'_t = T'_t = 0$) considering hydrate equilibrium.

In the case of four phases (hydrate, gas, water–ice mixture) being in thermodynamic equilibrium the piezoconductivity Equation (11) will take the form of:

$$m\delta_\varepsilon\left\{S_v\left[S_w\frac{1}{\rho_{wi}}\frac{\partial \rho_{wi}}{\partial t}\right]\right\} + \frac{\psi}{m\rho_v}\left\{m\left[S_v\left[S_w\rho_{wi}\frac{\partial \varepsilon_{wi}}{\partial t}\right]\right]\right\} + \delta_\varepsilon \text{DIG} + \frac{\psi}{m\rho_v}\text{DIG}_\varepsilon = 0, \quad (29)$$

where

$$\text{DIG} = \frac{1}{\rho_{wi}}\text{div}(\rho_w \mathbf{V}_w) + \frac{1}{\rho_g}\text{div}(\rho_g \mathbf{V}_g) + \left(\frac{q_w}{\rho_{wi}} + \frac{q_g}{\rho_g}\right), \quad (30)$$

$$\begin{aligned}\text{DIG}_\varepsilon &= [\text{div}(\rho_w \varepsilon_w \mathbf{V}_w) - \varepsilon_w \text{div}(\rho_w \mathbf{V}_w)] + (\varepsilon_w - \varepsilon_{wi})\text{div}(\rho_w \mathbf{V}_w) + \\ &+ [\text{div}(\rho_g \varepsilon_g \mathbf{V}_g) - \varepsilon_g \text{div}(\rho_g \mathbf{V}_g)] + \text{div}[P(\mathbf{V}_w + \mathbf{V}_g)] + \text{div}\,\mathbf{W} + \\ &+ (q_\varepsilon - \varepsilon_{wi}q_w - \varepsilon_g q_g).\end{aligned} \quad (31)$$

Considering that

$$(\rho_{wi})'_t = (\rho_w - \rho_i)(C_w)'_t, \quad \rho_w > \rho_i, \quad (32)$$

$$\begin{aligned}(\varepsilon_{wi})'_t &= [(C_w \rho_w \varepsilon_w + C_i \rho_i \varepsilon_i)/(C_w \rho_w + C_i \rho_i)]'_t = \\ &= \frac{1}{\rho_{wi}^2}[\rho_{wi}(\rho_w \varepsilon_w - \rho_i \varepsilon_i)(C_w)'_t - \rho_{wi}\varepsilon_{wi}(\rho_w - \rho_i)(C_w)'_t] = \\ &= \frac{1}{\rho_{wi}}[\rho_w(\varepsilon_w - \varepsilon_{wi}) + \rho_i(\varepsilon_{wi} - \varepsilon_i)](C_w)'_t, \quad \varepsilon_w > \varepsilon_{wi} > \varepsilon_i,\end{aligned} \quad (33)$$

the equation will reach the following form:

$$mS_v S_w\left\{\delta_\varepsilon\frac{(\rho_w - \rho_i)}{\rho_{wi}} + \frac{\psi}{m\rho_v}[\rho_w(\varepsilon_w - \varepsilon_{wi}) + \rho_i(\varepsilon_{wi} - \varepsilon_i)]\right\}(C_w)'_t \\ + \delta_\varepsilon \text{DIG} + \frac{\psi}{m\rho_v}\text{DIG}_\varepsilon = 0. \quad (34)$$

Assuming

$$C_{wi} = mS_v S_w\left\{\delta_\varepsilon\frac{(\rho_w - \rho_i)}{\rho_{wi}} + \frac{\psi}{m\rho_v}[\rho_w(\varepsilon_w - \varepsilon_{wi}) + \rho_i(\varepsilon_{wi} - \varepsilon_i)]\right\} > 0, \quad (35)$$

we get a more compact form of the piezoconductivity equation:

$$C_{wi}(C_w)'_t + \delta_\varepsilon \text{DIG} + \frac{\psi}{m\rho_v}\text{DIG}_\varepsilon = 0. \quad (36)$$

Next we will modify (30) and (31):

$$\text{DIG} = -\left\{\frac{\rho_w}{\rho_{wi}}\frac{1}{\mu_w}(k_ik_{rwi})'_{C_w} + \frac{1}{\mu_g}(k_ik_{rgi})'_{C_w}\right\}P'_x(C_w)'_x + <\ldots>, \tag{37}$$

$$\text{DIG}_\varepsilon = -\left\{\left\{[\rho_w(\varepsilon_w - \varepsilon_{wi}) + P]\frac{1}{\mu_w}(k_ik_{rwi})'_{C_w} + P\frac{1}{\mu_g}(k_ik_{rgi})'_{C_w}P'_x\right\} \right. \\ \left. + mS_vS_w(\lambda_w - \lambda_i)T'_x\right\}(C_w)'_x + <\ldots>. \tag{38}$$

Here the expressions $<\ldots>$ do not contain derivatives of C_w with respect to t and x. It is also clear that for thermal conductivity coefficient of water–ice mixture $\lambda_{wi} = C_w\lambda_w + (1-C_w)\lambda_i$ it is true that $(\lambda_{wi})'_{C_w} = \lambda_w - \lambda_i$. Thus, the value C_w in the expression $\lambda_{wi}(C_w)$ is being approximated in the upward flow direction $(-\lambda_{wi}T'_x)$, if $\lambda_w > \lambda_i$. Furthermore, otherwise—in the downward flow direction if $\lambda_w < \lambda_i$.

For absolute permeability in expressions (37) and (38) the following evaluation is true:

$$k_i = k(S_{vi}), \quad S_{vi} = S_v(1 - C_iS_w), \quad (S_{vi})'_{C_w} = S_vS_w > 0, \quad (k_i)'_{C_w} = (k(S_{vi}))'_{S_{vi}}(S_{vi})'_{C_w} > 0.$$

For relative permeability of water, we have:

$$k_{rwi} = k_{rw}(S_{wi}), \quad S_{wi} = \frac{C_wS_w}{1 - C_iS_w}, \quad (S_{wi})'_{C_w} = \frac{S_w(1-S_w)}{(1-C_wS_w)^2}, \quad (k_{rwi})'_{C_{wi}} = (k_{rw}(S_{wi}))'_{S_{wi}}(S_{wi})'_{C_w} > 0.$$

Therefore we get $(k_ik_{rwi})'_{C_w} > 0$, i.e., in (37) and (38) in expressions (k_ik_{rwi}) the values C_w and C_i are approximated in the upward filtration flow direction. Similarly, for relative permeability of gas we have following evaluation:

$$k_{rgi} = k_{rg}(1 - S_{wi}), \quad (k_{rgi})'_{C_{wi}} = (k_{rg}(1 - S_{wi}))'_{S_{wi}}(S_{wi})'_{C_w} < 0.$$

Hence:

$$(k_ik_{rgi})'_{C_w} = (k_i)'_{C_w}k_{rgi} + k_i(k_{rgi})'_{C_w}.$$

In other words, in (37) and (38) in expressions (k_ik_{rgi}) the values C_w, C_i, included in k_i, are approximated in the upward flow direction. Otherwise these values C_w, C_i, included in relative gas permeability k_{rgi}, are approximated in the downward flow direction.

3.3. Properties of Saturation Transfer S_w if $0 \leq C_w \leq 1$ in Hydrate-Thawed Zone ($S_v = 1$)

From Equation (12) we get following form of water saturation transfer equation:

$$m\rho_{wi}(S_w)'_t - \rho_w\frac{1}{\mu_w}(k_ik_{rwi})'_{S_w}P'_x(S_w)'_x = <\ldots>.$$

Here $<\ldots>$ does not contain any derivative of S_w with respect to t and x, and $S_v = 1$. For permeabilities it is true that

$$(k_ik_{rwi})'_{S_w} = k_i(k_{rwi})'_{S_w} + (k_i)'_{S_w}k_{rwi} = k_i(k_{rw})'_{S_{wi}}(S_{wi})'_{S_w} + (k_i)'_{S_{vi}}(S_{vi})'_{S_w}k_{rwi}.$$

Furthermore, the following evaluations are true: (see Section 3.2):

$$(k_{rw})'_{S_{wi}} > 0, \quad (S_{wi})'_{S_w} > 0, \quad (k_i)'_{S_{vi}} > 0, \quad (S_{vi})'_{S_w} < 0.$$

Hence in $k_{rwi} = k_{rw}(S_{wi})$ considering $S_{wi} = C_wS_w/(1 - C_iS_w)$ S_w is approximated in the upward flow direction. In $k_i = k(S_{vi})$ if $S_{vi} = 1 - C_iS_w$ and $S_v = 1$ take S_w in the downward direction.

3.4. Properties of Water–Ice Phase Transfer ($0 < C_w < 1$, $T'_t = 0$) in Hydrate-Thawed Zone ($S_v = 1$)

The equations of piezoconductivity (18) and energy (20) are being solved simultaneously related to increments ∂P and ∂C_w considering $T_0 = \text{const}$ in water–ice transfer zone. Particularly, in approximation div $\mathbf{W} = 0$ from (20) we can derive ∂C_w through ∂P and substitute in (18). Analysis of water–ice phase transferring process C_w in thawed zone ($S_v = 1$) is the analogue of the hydrate equilibrium case (see Section 3.2).

Particularly, C_w, C_i are taken in the upward flow direction for k_i and k_{rwi}, and for k_{rgi} these values (C_w, C_i) are taken downward.

4. Difference Schemes on Non-Regular Grids

For grids of the support operators method, consisting of cells (Ω), formed by nodes (ω), faces (σ) and edges (λ), it is characteristic that there is an isolated conjugate grid ("shifted") consisting of domains $d(\omega)$ around nodes ω (see Figure 1).

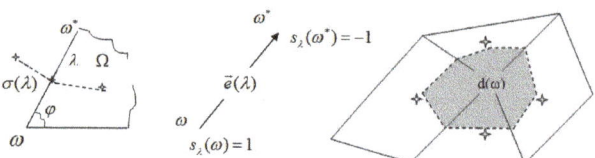

Figure 1. A basis building using the SOM algorithms. Solid lines determine cells created in modeling area and responsible for different sediment matter. Dashed lines serve to create a border at a homogeneous matter and to calculate the flow over the border.

Faces of the node domain are determined by the metric operator of the grid $\sigma(\lambda) = \sum_{\varphi(\lambda)} V_\varphi e'_\varphi(\lambda)$ (see also below). Here, the bases $\varphi(\lambda)$ are in pairs included in the cells $\Omega(\lambda)$, adjacent to the edge λ. The metric calibration of the difference grid involves choosing the volumes of bases (with natural normalization condition $\sum_{\varphi(\Omega)} V_\varphi = V_\Omega$). It determines a construction of an isolated conjugant mesh for various grids classes, such as triangular-quadrangular, tetrahedral, parallelepiped, prismatic, etc. 2D grids or 3D grids and their adaptation for vector analysis of continuous boundary value problems. The example of a triangular-quadrangular 2D grid illustrates the specific choice of local basis volumes V_φ.

We introduce a family of irregular difference grids in the region O. We consider the example when the grid consists of triangular and also quadrangular cells (Ω), edges (λ), nodes (ω), bases (φ), and related to them the boundaries ($\sigma(\lambda)$) of the node balance domains $d(\omega)$ (see Figure 1).

The system of initial (covariant) unit vectors $e(\lambda)$ created by the edges forms the bases φ. We accept the centers of cells Ω and edges λ like the arithmetic mean of radius vectors of their nodes ω. The curve is a surface that connects two adjacent cells through a cell or an edge:

$$\sigma(\lambda) = \sum_{\varphi(\lambda)} v_\varphi e'_\varphi(\lambda).$$

It is also oriented like the unit vector $e(\lambda)$. Here $e'_\varphi(\lambda)$ are the unit vectors of the reciprocal bases with respect to the initial bases. The expression $v_\varphi = \frac{1}{6}|e(\lambda_1) \times e(\lambda_2)|$ represents the base volume for a triangular cell Ω, containing as basis φ and $v_\varphi = \frac{1}{4}|e(\lambda_1) \times e(\lambda_2)|$ for a quadrangular cell, if $\lambda_1(\varphi)$ and $\lambda_2(\varphi)$ are the edges forming the basis φ. In a last step, $\sum_{\varphi(\lambda)}$ is summation over all bases φ, in the configuration of which the edge λ had place. The nodal domains $d(\omega)$ are formed by the surfaces $\sigma(\lambda(\omega))$ closed around the node ω.

The internal divergence of a vector field DIN : $(\varphi) \to (\omega)$ is defined by approximating of the Gauss's theorem on $d(\omega)$:

$$\text{DIN}\,X = \sum_{\lambda(\omega)} s_\lambda(\omega)\tau_X(\lambda), \quad \tau_X(\lambda) = \sum_{\varphi(\lambda)} v_\varphi(e'_\varphi(\lambda), X_\varphi).$$

Here $\sum_{\lambda(\omega)}$ is the summation over all edges λ having a common node ω.

The grid vector field X is given by its representations in the bases X_φ. We use $(\ )_\Delta$ to denote the approximation of the corresponding differential expressions and have:

$$\left(\int_O (\mathbf{X}, \nabla u) dv\right)_\Delta = -\left(\int_O u \operatorname{div} \mathbf{X} dv - \int_{\partial O} u(\mathbf{X}, \mathbf{ds})\right)_\Delta = -\sum_\omega (u_\omega, \operatorname{DIN} \mathbf{X}) = \sum_\varphi v_\varphi (\mathbf{X}_\varphi, \operatorname{GRAD} u).$$

Gradient vector field $\operatorname{GRAD} : (\omega) \to (\varphi)$ is given by its representations in bases:

$$\operatorname{GRAD} u = \sum_{\lambda(\varphi)} \Delta_\lambda u \mathbf{e}'_\varphi(\lambda), \quad \Delta_\lambda u = -\sum_{\omega(\lambda)} s_\lambda(\omega) u_\omega = u_{\omega^*} - u_\omega.$$

We assume a vector field $\mathbf{X}_\varphi = K_\varphi \operatorname{GRAD} u$ as $\mathbf{X}_\varphi$ in the bases φ and we obtain a self-adjoint nonnegative operator $-\operatorname{DIN} \mathbf{X} : (\omega) \to (\omega)$ or $-\operatorname{DIN} K \operatorname{GRAD} : (\omega) \to (\omega)$. The flow vector field $\mathbf{X}$ here is given by its components in the bases $\mathbf{X}_\varphi$. This flow vector field is determined by the gradient properties of the scalar grid function u given at the nodes ω and the grid symmetric positive definite tensor field of conductivity K, that is given by their representations in the bases K_φ. This operator will be strictly positive if the first boundary value problem is specified at least in one boundary node of a connected difference grid, i.e., the scalar grid function becomes zero in this boundary node.

Water and ice saturations, its volume fractions and hydrate thawing are taken in absolute and relative permeabilities in the upward or downward flow direction in according to analysis in Section 3. Particularly, in the absence of ice volume fracture the absolute permeability $k(S_v)$ in bases φ at edges $(\lambda(\varphi))$, forming these bases, always is taken in the downward flow direction (as thawing). Relative permeabilities $k_{rw}(S_w)$ and $k_{rg}(1 - S_w)$ are taken in the upward flow direction (as water- and gas saturations), i.e., as in the case of 2 phases thawed zone with the absence of hydrates.

5. Approximation of Divergent-Piezoconductive Difference Schemes in the Thawed Zone in the Medium with Gas Hydrate Inclusions and Water–Ice Phase

5.1. Hydrate-Equilibrium Zone with Water–Ice Phase

We introduce some notations for the grid functions of the support operator method (Section 4, see Figure 1) as well. We will refer to its nodes ω previously employed in the continuum model values

$$\overline{m}, S_v, S_{vi}, S_w, S_{wi}, C_w, C_i, \rho_v, \rho_w, \rho_i, \rho_{wi}, \rho_g, \rho_s, P, T, \varepsilon_v, \varepsilon_w, \varepsilon_i, \varepsilon_{wi}, \varepsilon_g, \varepsilon_s, \mu_w, \mu_g, k_{rwi}, k_{rgi}, q_w, q_g, q_\varepsilon.$$

We assign the vector functions to the grid bases φ in accordance with Section 4

$$\mathbf{V}_w, \mathbf{V}_g, \nabla \varepsilon_w, \nabla \varepsilon_g, \nabla P, \nabla T, \mathbf{W}.$$

We assign the grid functions that represent the discontinuous material properties of substances to cell Ω

$$m, k, \lambda_v, \lambda_w, \lambda_g, \lambda_s.$$

The relations are clear

$$\overline{m}_\omega = \sum_{\varphi(\omega)} V_\varphi m_{\Omega(\varphi)}, \quad \overline{(1-m)}_\omega = \sum_{\varphi(\omega)} V_\varphi (1 - m_{\Omega(\varphi)}) = V_\omega - \overline{m}_\omega, \quad V_\omega = \sum_{\varphi(\omega)} V_\varphi,$$

i.e., $\overline{m}_\omega$ and $\overline{(1-m)}_\omega$ perform the volume of the pore domain $d(\omega)$ (see Figure 1) and its frame part, respectively.

Then, we introduce the difference derivatives on time and the space-point (in the grid nodes ω) time interpolations $a_t = (\hat{a} - a)/\tau$, $a^{(\delta)} = \delta \hat{a} + (1 - \delta) a$ on the time layers t and $\hat{t} = t + \tau$ ($\tau > 0$ is the time step). Here the interpolation weight δ may depend on the spatial grid node ω. Under the value

$$\delta_v = \sqrt{(\overline{m}S_v)\hat{}} \Big/ \left(\sqrt{(\overline{m}S_v)\hat{}} + \sqrt{(\overline{m}S_v)\check{}}\right), \quad 0 < S_v < 1.$$

we will understand the free-volume time approximation of the grid functions given at the nodes ω. The proportion of the pore volume, intended for free movement of the liquid and gas will determine the interpolation weight δ_v. The result of such an approximation allows us to conduct discrete transformations of equations related to their splitting by physical processes, which will be similar to continual ones. Other arbitrary interpolations with respect to time will be denoted [ ]~. They can relate to different elements, such as grid nodes ω, bases φ etc.

We express the approximation of Equations (1) and (2) in the following form.

Conservation equations which are representing by themselves balance of water and gas components

$$\{\overline{m}[S_v S_w \rho_{wi} + (1 - S_v)\rho_v \beta_w]\}_t + \text{DIN}(\rho_w \mathbf{V}_w)\tilde{} + \tilde{q}_w = 0, \tag{39}$$

$$\{\overline{m}[S_v(1 - S_w)\rho_g + (1 - S_v)\rho_v(1 - \beta_w)]\}_t + \text{DIN}(\rho_g \mathbf{V}_g)\tilde{} + \tilde{q}_g = 0. \tag{40}$$

By the means of GRAD operator flow of water $(\rho_w \mathbf{V}_w)\tilde{}$ and gas $(\rho_g \mathbf{V}_g)\tilde{}$ are approximated in the grid bases φ considering discretization of Darcy's law (4) on implicit time layer by any of the standard methods [6,22]:

$$(\rho_w \mathbf{V}_w)_\varphi^{\tilde{P}} = -\left(\rho_w \frac{k_i k_{rwi}}{\mu_w}\right)_{\Delta\varphi}^{\tilde{}} \text{GRAD } \tilde{P} + \left(\rho_w^2 \frac{k_i k_{rwi}}{\mu_w}\right)_{\Delta\varphi}^{\tilde{}} g\mathbf{k},$$

$$(\rho_g \mathbf{V}_g)_\varphi^{\tilde{P}} = -\left(\rho_g \frac{k_i k_{rgi}}{\mu_g}\right)_{\Delta\varphi}^{\tilde{}} \text{GRAD } \tilde{P} + \left(\rho_g^2 \frac{k_i k_{rgi}}{\mu_g}\right)_{\Delta\varphi}^{\tilde{}} g\mathbf{k}.$$

Under $(\ )_{\Delta\varphi}^{\tilde{}}$ are considered approximation of corresponding expressions in the grid bases φ with some time interpolation.

However, in the presence of thermobaric relationship in the form of (5), for conservation of continuum properties of quadratic forms legitimacy of thermodynamic values gradients in the form of $\int \varepsilon \, \text{div}(\rho \mathbf{V}) dV$ (see also (43) below) it's more appropriate to have the Darcy's law energetic form. We will get one from the assumptions below.

Considering pressure–temperature relationships (5) in three phase equilibrium zone hydrate–water–gas it's allowed to write

$$d\varepsilon_w = \varepsilon'_{wp} dP, \quad d\varepsilon_g = \varepsilon'_{gp} dP,$$

where ε'_{wp} and ε'_{gp}—full derivatives from internal energy with respect to pressure.

That way Darcy's law (4) in the grid bases φ (that is formed by nodes, in which is fulfilled the thermobaric relationship (5)) we present in the energetic form:

$$(\rho_w \mathbf{V}_w)_\varphi^\varepsilon = -\left(\rho_w \frac{k_i k_{rwi}}{\mu_w \varepsilon'_{wp}}\right)_{\Delta\varphi}^{\tilde{}} \text{GRAD } \varepsilon_w^{(\delta_v)} + \left(\rho_w^2 \frac{k_i k_{rwi}}{\mu_w}\right)_{\Delta\varphi}^{\tilde{}} g\mathbf{k},$$

$$(\rho_g \mathbf{V}_g)_\varphi^\varepsilon = -\left(\rho_g \frac{k_i k_{rgi}}{\mu_g \varepsilon'_{gp}}\right)_{\Delta\varphi}^{\tilde{}} \text{GRAD } \varepsilon_g^{(\delta_v)} + \left(\rho_g^2 \frac{k_i k_{rgi}}{\mu_g}\right)_{\Delta\varphi}^{\tilde{}} g\mathbf{k}.$$

Thus

$$(\rho_w \mathbf{V}_w)_\varphi^{\tilde{}} = \left\{(\rho_w \mathbf{V}_w)_\varphi^{\tilde{P}} \Big| (\rho_w \mathbf{V}_w)_\varphi^\varepsilon\right\}, \quad (\rho_g \mathbf{V}_g)_\varphi^{\tilde{}} = \left\{(\rho_g \mathbf{V}_g)_\varphi^{\tilde{P}} \Big| (\rho_g \mathbf{V}_g)_\varphi^\varepsilon\right\}.$$

Internal energy balance equation that is approximating (3) has the form of:

$$\{\overline{m}[S_v(S_w\rho_{wi}\varepsilon_{wi} + (1-S_w)\rho_g\varepsilon_g) + (1-S_v)\rho_v\varepsilon_v] + \overline{(1-m)}\rho_s\varepsilon_s\}_t$$
$$+ \text{DIN}\left[\left(\varepsilon_w^{(\delta_v)}\right)_{\text{up}}(\rho_w\mathbf{V}_w)^{\sim}\right] + \text{DIN}\left[\left(\varepsilon_g^{(\delta_v)}\right)_{\text{up}}(\rho_g\mathbf{V}_g)^{\sim}\right] \quad (41)$$
$$+ \text{DIN}\{[P(\mathbf{V}_w + \mathbf{V}_g)]^{\sim}\} + \text{DIN}\,\mathbf{W}^{\sim} + q_{\varepsilon}^{\sim} = 0.$$

Index "up" in the expression for water energy $(\varepsilon_w^{(\delta_v)})_{\text{up}}$ denotes, that corresponding values are taken in the upward direction of flow $(\rho_w\mathbf{V}_w)^{\sim}$ in earlier determined divergence $\text{DIN}(\rho_w\mathbf{V}_w)^{\sim}$. The index "up" is understood similarly in the expression for gas energy $(\varepsilon_g^{(\delta_v)})_{\text{up}}$.

Energy from pressure forces work $[P(\mathbf{V}_w + \mathbf{V}_g)]^{\sim}$ and full heat flow $\mathbf{W}^{\sim}$ in the media are approximated in the grid basis φ, for example, at the implicit time layer by standard method [6,22]:

$$[P(\mathbf{V}_w + \mathbf{V}_g)]_{\varphi}^{\sim} = \left(\frac{P}{\rho_w}\right)_{\varphi}^{\sim}(\rho_w\mathbf{V}_w)_{\varphi}^{P\sim} + \left(\frac{P}{\rho_g}\right)_{\varphi}^{\sim}(\rho_g\mathbf{V}_g)_{\varphi}^{P\sim}.$$

Next, discrete analogue of piezoconductivity dissipative Equation (11), disintegrated by physical processes with saturation processes transfer unit, (39) and (40), but differentially equal to system of the model initial conservation law (39)–(41), has the form of:

$$\delta_{\varepsilon}^{(\delta_v)}\left\{[(\overline{m}S_v)S_w]^{(1-\delta_v)}\frac{(\rho_{wi})_t}{(\rho_{wi})^{(\delta_v)}} + [(\overline{m}S_v)(1-S_w)]^{(1-\delta_v)}\frac{(\rho_g)_t}{(\rho_g)^{(\delta_v)}} + [\overline{m}(1-S_v)]^{(1-\delta_v)}\frac{(\rho_v)_t}{(\rho_v)^{(\delta_v)}} + (\overline{m})_t\right\}$$
$$+ [\psi/(m\rho_v)]^{\sim}\left\{[(\overline{m}S_v)S_w\rho_{wi}]^{(1-\delta_v)}(\varepsilon_{wi})_t + [(\overline{m}S_v)(1-S_w)\rho_g]^{(1-\delta_v)}(\varepsilon_g)_t\right.$$
$$\left.+ [\overline{m}(1-S_v)\rho_v]^{(1-\delta_v)}(\varepsilon_v)_t + \overline{(1-m)\rho_s\varepsilon_s}\right]_t\right\} + \delta_{\varepsilon}^{(\delta_v)}\text{DIG}^{\sim} + [\psi/(m\rho_v)]^{\sim}\text{DIG}_{\varepsilon}^{\sim} = 0, \quad (42)$$

$$\delta_{\varepsilon} = [\beta_w\varepsilon_{wi} + (1-\beta_w)\varepsilon_g] - \varepsilon_v, \quad [\psi/(m\rho_v)]^{\sim} = \left[\beta_w/(\rho_{wi})^{(\delta_v)} + (1-\beta_w)/(\rho_g)^{(\delta_v)}\right] - 1/(\rho_v)^{(\delta_v)},$$

$$\text{DIG}^{\sim} = \frac{1}{(\rho_{wi})^{(\delta_v)}}\text{DIN}(\rho_w\mathbf{V}_w)^{\sim} + \frac{1}{(\rho_g)^{(\delta_v)}}\text{DIN}(\rho_g\mathbf{V}_g)^{\sim} + \frac{q_w^{\sim}}{(\rho_{wi})^{(\delta_v)}} + \frac{q_g^{\sim}}{(\rho_g)^{(\delta_v)}},$$

$$\text{DIG}_{\varepsilon}^{\sim} = \left[\text{DIN}\{(\varepsilon_w^{(\delta_v)})_{\text{up}}(\rho_w\mathbf{V}_w)^{\sim}\} - (\varepsilon_{wi})^{(\delta_v)}\text{DIN}(\rho_w\mathbf{V}_w)^{\sim}\right] \quad (43)$$
$$+ \left[\text{DIN}\{(\varepsilon_g^{(\delta_v)})_{\text{up}}(\rho_g\mathbf{V}_g)^{\sim}\} - (\varepsilon_g)^{(\delta_v)}\text{DIN}(\rho_g\mathbf{V}_g)^{\sim}\right]$$
$$+ \text{DIN}\{[P(\mathbf{V}_w + \mathbf{V}_g)]^{\sim}\} + \text{DIN}\,\mathbf{W}^{\sim} + \left(q_{\varepsilon}^{\sim} - \varepsilon_{wi}^{(\delta_v)}q_w^{\sim} - \varepsilon_g^{(\delta_v)}q_g^{\sim}\right).$$

5.2. Two-Phase Thawed Zone

Similarly to Section 5.1, considering the grid function $S_v = 1$ in nodes ω, we get two-phase series of completely conservative differential schemes in the thawed zone. Instead of using an interpolation weight δ_v, we here consequently introduce the weight

$$\delta_1 = \sqrt{(\overline{m})^{\hat{}}}\bigg/\left(\sqrt{(\overline{m})^{\hat{}}} + \sqrt{(\overline{m})}\right)$$

in the grid nodes ω.

Conservation equations, representing by themselves mass balance of water and gas components in the thawed zone will have the form of:

$$\{\overline{m}S_w\rho_{wi}\}_t + \text{DIN}(\rho_w\mathbf{V}_w)^{\sim} + q_w^{\sim} = 0, \quad (44)$$

$$\{\overline{m}(1-S_w)\rho_g\}_t + \text{DIN}(\rho_g\mathbf{V}_g)^{\sim} + q_g^{\sim} = 0. \quad (45)$$

In the thawed zone by means of GRAD operator the flows of water $(\rho_w \mathbf{V}_w)^\sim$ and gas $(\rho_g \mathbf{V}_g)^\sim$ are determined in non-energetic form, i.e., are approximated in the grad bases φ by values $(\rho_w \mathbf{V}_w)_\varphi^{\tilde{P}}$ and $(\rho_g \mathbf{V}_g)_\varphi^{\tilde{P}}$ accordingly (see Section 5.1).

Internal energy balance in the thawed zone approximating (10), has the form of:

$$\left\{\overline{m}\left(S_w \rho_{wi} \varepsilon_{wi} + (1 - S_w)\rho_g \varepsilon_g\right) + \overline{(1-m)}\rho_s \varepsilon_s\right\}_t + \text{DIN}\left[\left(\varepsilon_w^{(\delta_1)}\right)_{up}(\rho_w \mathbf{V}_w)^\sim\right]$$
$$+ \text{DIN}\left[\left(\varepsilon_g^{(\delta_1)}\right)_{up}(\rho_g \mathbf{V}_g)^\sim\right] + \text{DIN}\{[P(\mathbf{V}_w + \mathbf{V}_g)]^\sim\} + \text{DIN}\,\mathbf{W}^\sim + q_\varepsilon^\sim = 0. \tag{46}$$

Definition of differential objects (indexes "up", pressure forces, heat flow) are the same as in Section 5.1.

Further excluding the S_w function, which is determined in the grid nodes ω, from the differential derivative sign with respect to time, from (44)–(46), we get completely conservative differential equations determining non-isothermal process of piezoconductivity in thawed zone:

$$\frac{(S_w)^{(\delta_1)}}{(\rho_{wi})^{(\delta_1)}}[\overline{m}\rho_{wi}]_t + \frac{(1-S_w)^{(\delta_1)}}{(\rho_g)^{(\delta_1)}}[\overline{m}\rho_g]_t + \text{DIG}^\sim = 0, \tag{47}$$

$$(\overline{m})^{(1-\delta_1)}\left\{[S_w \rho_{wi}]^{(\delta_1)}(\varepsilon_{wi})_t + [(1-S_w)\rho_g]^{(\delta_1)}(\varepsilon_g)_t\right\} + \left[\overline{(1-m)}\rho_s \varepsilon_s\right]_t + \text{DIG}_\varepsilon^\sim = 0. \tag{48}$$

The combination of difference mass $\text{DIG}^\sim$ and energy $\text{DIG}_\varepsilon^\sim$ divergences in the grid nodes ω along with operation of active sources $q_w^\sim$, $q_g^\sim$, $q_\varepsilon^\sim$ are determined similarly to (43), but with change of interpolation weight δ_ν to weight δ_1.

5.3. On the Expediency of Using Numerical Simulation of One-Dimensional Problems of Dissociation of Gas Hydrates in a Porous Media: A Vertical Fault in a Large Strike Formation

Building non-one-dimensional models requires very large geological and geophysical information, which, especially in hard-to-reach northern regions or on the seabed, is difficult, costly, and sometimes impossible to obtain. The results of the calculations are not always easily visible, behind the details one cannot see the main defining characteristics of the process. Conducting a large number of calculations to compare the results and obtain final conclusions can require a significant amount of time. Therefore, the study of one-dimensional problems that require much less initial information and are much easier and faster to solve can be useful in many cases. In addition, downsizing of the models is possible if one of the scales is much larger than the others (for example, the case of a thin layer), and if the area under consideration is much larger than the size of the inhomogeneities.

One of these problems is to study the dissociation of gas hydrate from a vertical fault at the boundary of a large strike area along a plane whose vertical dimensions are small compared to the horizontal ones. Problems of this kind may correspond to the structure of observed areas of degassing in several seas often associated with fault systems.

To illustrate, consider a typical geological profile (Figure 2) and its discretization in 2D modeling [4]:

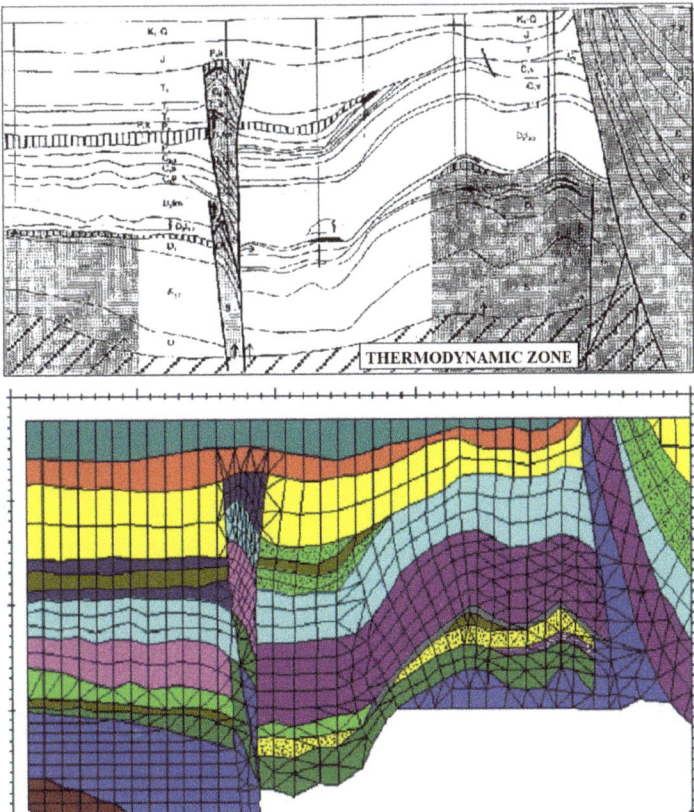

Figure 2. Geological profile of the Varandey–Adzvinskaya structure zone (above): K1–Q—Lower Cretaceous–Quaternary, J—Jurassic, T3—Upper Triassic, P2—Upper Permian, P1—Lower Permian, C1–P1—Lower Carboniferous–Lower Permian, D3—Upper Devonian, D2—Mid Devonian, S1—Lower Devonian Ordovician, D—Devonian, S—Silurian, T–P—Triassic–Permian; grid approximation of the upper profile (bottom).

With a good knowledge of the reservoir, knowledge of its properties, water, and hydrate saturation in each grid node, two-dimensional numerical modeling can be used. However, if there is little initial information and it is inaccurate, which is natural in this kind of problems, the use of high-precision methods is impractical. A model that matches the accuracy of the available data is more likely to be a one-dimensional vertically averaged model.

Models of this kind are widely used in problems associated with gas hydrates in a porous medium.

6. Test Calculation for the Problem of Interaction of Vertical Fault and Horizontal Seam Containing Gas Hydrates

We consider the problem of interaction of vertical fault and horizontal seam containing gas hydrate, that in initial approximation can be considered as one-dimensional horizontal problem in Cartesian coordinates $x \in [0, L]$, L is the length of calculation area. Herewith, gravity, due to the horizontal geometry, does not affect the process. We are interested in the region near the fault $x \in [0, L_1]$ (L_1 is about few meters). Note that, due to the parabolic nature of the pressure problem, the computational domain must greatly exceed the region of interest, $L_1 \ll L$, so that the solution in the vicinity of the fault (at a distance of about a meter from it) is practically independent of the boundary conditions at the other boundary of the area. L is taken about 300 m.

It is assumed that the depth of the formation corresponds to the conditions for the existence of methane hydrates, and initially the pore space of the formation is uniformly filled with water, gas, and gas hydrate. Thus, for initial time moment we set:

$$S_w(x, t = 0) = S_w^* = 0.6, \quad S_v(x, t = 0) = S_v^* = 0.7,$$
$$P(x, t = 0) = P_0 = 30 \text{ bar}, \quad T(x, t = 0) = T_0 = T_{\text{dis}}(P_0).$$

The initial pressure corresponds to a depth of 300 m, at which the existence of thermodynamically equilibrium methane hydrates is possible in the region of the permafrost.

The fault corresponds to the left boundary $x = 0$. The difference grid is uniform with a step $h = 0.01$ m at a distance of up to 1 m from the fault, and then increases exponentially with $q = 1.05$. The time steps are constant $\tau = 10$ sec. The condition $S_v = 1$ is set on the fault. For joining two-phase and three-phase regions, the overheated state method is used [23].

The problem of thermal influence of a fault is considered. On the left boundary, an increased temperature value is set, compared to the reservoir one:

$$T(x = 0, t) = T_1 = T_0 + 5 > T_0 = T_{\text{dis}}(P_0)$$

and non-flow conditions:

$$\nabla_x P(x = 0, t) = 0.$$

On the right (remote) boundary, unperturbed boundary conditions are set—the values of the variables coincide with their initial values:

$$S_w(x = L, t) = S_w^*, \quad S_v(x = L, t) = S_v^*, \quad P(x = L, t) = P_0, \quad T(x = L, t) = T_0.$$

Due to the zero flow velocity on the fault wall (due to the no-flow condition), the saturation values at $x = 0$ do not affect the process.

For the calculation, values of the parameters characteristic of the Messoyakha gas hydrate field were chosen [4].

Figures 3–6, below show the results of numerical calculations for a number of time points: pressure, temperature, thawing, water saturation profiles.

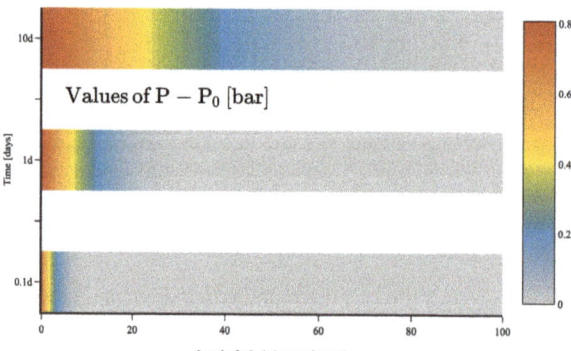

Figure 3. Pressure profile of deviation from initial pressure value $P - P_0$, $P_0 = 30$ bar (P_0—initial value, P—instantaneous value), for time moments $t = 0.1, 1, 10$ days. X-axis: calculation length in horizontal direction of the reservoir is taken long way from the fault (up to 100 m), where 0 X-value represents the fault.

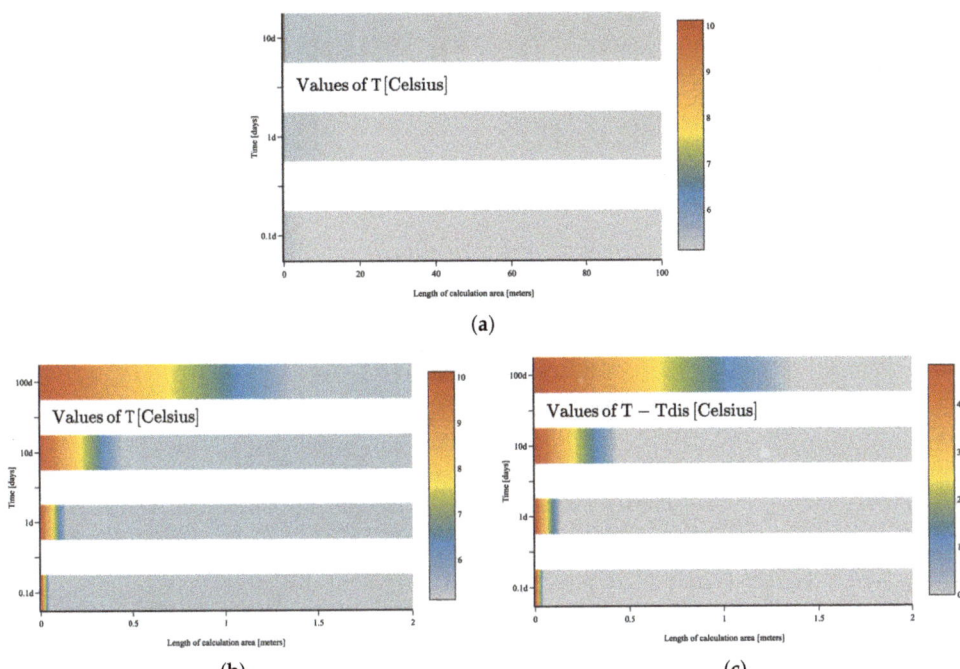

Figure 4. (**a**) Temperature profile T for time moments $t = 0.1, 1, 10$ days. X-axis: calculation length in horizontal direction of the reservoir is taken long way from the fault (up to 100 m), where 0 X-value represents the fault. (**b**) Temperature profile T in the nearest area around the fault for time moments $t = 0.1, 1, 10, 100$ days. X-axis: calculation length in horizontal direction of the reservoir is taken close to the fault (up to 2 m), where 0 X-value represents the fault. (**c**) Temperature increasing profile $T - T_{\text{dis}}(P)$ ($T_{\text{dis}}(P)$ is the temperature of the dissociation that is a function of pressure instantaneous value) in the area around the fault for time moments $t = 0.1, 1, 10, 100$ days. X-axis: calculation length in horizontal direction of the reservoir is taken close to the fault (up to 2 m), where 0 X-value represents the fault.

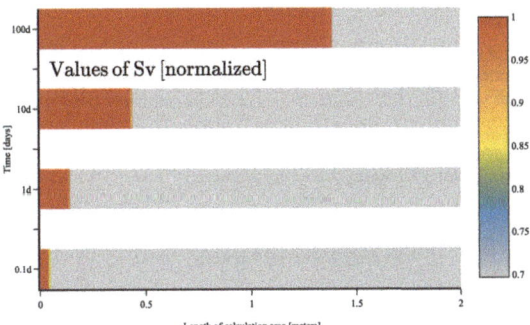

Figure 5. Hydrate thawing profile S_v in the area of the fault for the time moments $t = 0.1, 1, 10, 100$ days. X-axis: calculation length in horizontal direction of the reservoir is taken close to the fault (up to 2 m), where 0 X-value represents the fault.

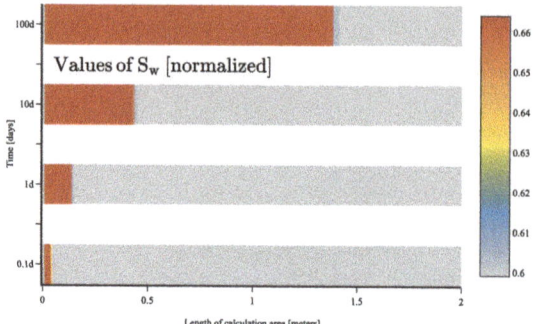

Figure 6. Water saturation profile S_w in the area of the fault for the time moments $t = 0.1, 1, 10, 100$ days. X-axis: calculation length in horizontal direction of the reservoir is taken close to the fault (up to 2 m), where 0 X-value represents the fault.

7. Conclusions

Two-dimensional modeling algorithms elaborated in the paper are useful for a problem of filtering multiphase and multicomponent flows for porous media with joint solid-phase inclusions from hydrates and water-ice mixture. A two-units mathematical model is implemented, which makes it possible to single out hyperbolic and dissipative subsystems in the corresponding system of equations and allows to build effective numerical algorithms for solving fluid dynamic problems in multi-component and multi-phase system. The Gibbs phase rule is used for systems with one thermodynamic degree of freedom in the hydrate-equilibrium zone to determine types of dissociative bonds between thermodynamic variables. The calculations performed show the interaction dynamic of a three-phase zone containing hydrate, gas and water, and a two-phase zone containing only gas and water. The results show the possibility of applying the developed methods to real problems related to gas hydrates. The approach can be successfully applied for study of natural gas hydrates in frozen-susceptible rocks.

Author Contributions: Conceptualization, N.A., R.C. and I.P.; methodology, P.R.; software, V.P.; formal analysis, P.R.; investigation, N.A., V.P. and P.R.; writing—original draft preparation, N.A., V.P. and P.R.; writing—review and editing, N.A., R.C. and I.P.; visualization, V.P.; supervision, R.C.; project administration, N.A. and I.P.; funding acquisition, V.P. and P.R. All authors have read and agreed to the published version of the manuscript.

Funding: The work of Rahimly P. (mathematical model, analysis) was supported by the Russian Science Foundation (project № 22-71-10109). The work of Podryga V. (numerical calculations) was carried out within the framework of the state assignment of KIAM RAS.

Institutional Review Board Statement: Not applicable.

Informed Consent Statement: Not applicable.

Data Availability Statement: Not applicable.

Conflicts of Interest: The authors declare no conflict of interest.

References

1. Makogon, Y.F. *Natural Gas Hydrates*; PennWell Publishing Co.: Tulsa, OK, USA, 1997.
2. Sloan, E.D. *Clathrate Hydrates of Natural Gases*; Marcel Dekker: New York, NY, USA, 1990.
3. Marchuk, G.I. Splitting and Alternating Direction Methods. In *Handbook of Numerical Analysis*; Ciarlet, P., Lions, J., Eds.; North-Holland: Amsterdam, The Netherlands, 1990; Volume 1, pp. 197–462.
4. Poveshchenko, Y.A.; Rahimly, P.I.; Rahimly, O.R.; Podryga, V.O.; Gasilova, I.V. A Numerical Approach to Study the Thermal Influence on Gas Hydrates by Physical Process Splitting. *Int. J. Numer. Anal. Model.* **2020**, *17*, 404–433.
5. Lipnikov, K.; Manzini, G.; Shashkov, M. Mimetic finite difference method. *J. Comput. Phys.* **2014**, *257*, 1163–1227. [CrossRef]

6. Samarskii, A.A.; Koldoba, A.V.; Poveshchenko, Yu.A.; Tishkin, V.F.; Favorskii, A.P. *Difference Schemes on Irregular Grids*; ZAO "Kriterii": Minsk, Belarus, 1996. (In Russian)
7. Zatsepina, O.Y.; Buffet, B.A. Phase equilibrium of gas hydrate: Implications for the formation of hydrate in the deep sea floor. *Geophys. Res. Lett.* **1997**, *24*, 1567–1570. [CrossRef]
8. Xu, W.; Ruppel, C. Predicting the occurrence, distribution, and evolution of methane gas hydrate in porous marine sediments. *J. Geophys. Res. Solid Earth* **1999**, *104*, 5081–5095. [CrossRef]
9. Liu, X.; Flemings, P.B. Dynamic multiphase flow model of hydrate formation in marine sediments. *J. Geophys. Res. Solid Earth* **2007**, *112*, B03101:1–B03101:23. [CrossRef]
10. White, M.D. *STOMP-HYDT-KE A Numerical Simulator for the Production of Natural Gas Hydrate Using Guest Molecule Exchange with CO_2 and N_2*; Pacific Northwest National Laboratory PNNL-22130: Richland, WA, USA, 2012.
11. Moridis, G.J.; Kowalsky, M.B.; Pruess, K. *TOUGH+HYDRATE v1.2 User's Manual: A Code for the Simulation of System Behavior in Hydrate-Bearing Geologic Media*; Lawrence Berkeley National Laboratory Report LBNL-0149E: Berkeley, CA, USA, 2012.
12. Qorbani, K.; Kvamme, B. Non-equilibrium simulation of CH4 production from gas hydrate reservoirs through the depressurization method. *J. Nat. Gas Sci. Eng.* **2016**, *35 Part B*, 1544–1554. [CrossRef]
13. Qorbani, K.; Kvamme, B. Olsen, R. Non-equilibrium simulation of hydrate formation and dissociation from CO_2 in the aqueous phase. *J. Nat. Gas Sci. Eng.* **2016**, *35*, 1555–1565. [CrossRef]
14. Gupta, S.; Wohlmuth, B.; Haeckel, M. An All-At-Once Newton Strategy for Marine Methane Hydrate Reservoir Models. *Energies* **2020**, *13*, 503. [CrossRef]
15. Yin, Z.; Chong, Z.R.; Tan, H.K.; Linga, P. Review of gas hydrate dissociation kinetic models for energy recovery. *J. Nat. Gas Sci. Eng.* **2016**, *35*, 1362–1387. [CrossRef]
16. Linga, P.; Clarke, M.A.; Englezos, P. Gas Hydrates and Applications. *J. Nat. Gas Sci. Eng.* **2016**, *35*, 1353–1608. [CrossRef]
17. White, M.D.; Kneafsey, T.J.; Seol, Y.; Waite, W.F.; Uchida, S.; Lin, J.S.; Myshakin, E.M.; Gai, X.; Gupta, S.; Reagan, M.T.; et al. An international code comparison study on coupled thermal, hydrologic and geomechanical processes of natural gas hydrate-bearing sediments. *Mar. Pet. Geol.* **2020**, *120*, 104566:1–104566:55. [CrossRef]
18. Istomin, V.A.; Yakushev, V.S. *Gas Hydrates in Natural Conditions*; Nedra: Moscow, Russia, 1992. (In Russian)
19. Bondarev, E.A.; Babe, G.D.; Groisman, A.G.; Kanibolotsky, M.A. *Mechanics of Hydrate Formation in Gas Flows*; Nauka: Novosibirsk, Russia, 1976. (In Russian)
20. Rahimly, P.I.; Poveshchenko, Yu.A.; Rahimly, O.R.; Podryga, V.O.; Kazakevich, G.I.; Gasilova, I.V. The use of splitting with respect to physical processes for modeling the dissociation of gas hydrates. *Math. Models Comput. Simul.* **2018**, *10*, 69–78. [CrossRef]
21. Grzymkowski, R.; Pleszczynski, M.; Slota, D. The Two-Phase Stefan Problem Solved by the Adomian Decomposition Method. In Proceedings of the 15th IASTED International Conference on Applied Simulation and Modelling, Rhodes, Greece, 26–28 June 2006; pp. 511–516.
22. Koldoba, A.V.; Poveshchenko, Y.A.; Samarskaya, E.A.; Tishkin, V.F. *Methods of Mathematical Modeling of the Environment*; Nauka: Moscow, Russia, 2000. (In Russian)
23. Rahimly, P.I.; Poveshchenko, Yu.A.; Podryga, V.O.; Rahimly, O.R.; Popov, S.B. Modeling the processes of joint filtration in melted zone and piezocunductive medium with gas hydrate inclusions. *Prepr. Keldysh Inst. Appl. Math.* **2018**, *40*, 1–32. [CrossRef]

Article

On Convergence of Support Operator Method Schemes for Differential Rotational Operations on Tetrahedral Meshes Applied to Magnetohydrodynamic Problems

Yury Poveshchenko, Viktoriia Podryga * and Parvin Rahimly

Keldysh Institute of Applied Mathematics of Russian Academy of Sciences, 125047 Moscow, Russia
* Correspondence: pvictoria@list.ru

Citation: Poveshchenko, Y.; Podryga, V.; Rahimly, P. On Convergence of Support Operator Method Schemes for Differential Rotational Operations on Tetrahedral Meshes Applied to Magnetohydrodynamic Problems. *Mathematics* **2022**, *10*, 3904. https://doi.org/10.3390/math10203904

Academic Editor: Nikolai A. Kudryashov

Received: 19 August 2022
Accepted: 17 October 2022
Published: 20 October 2022

Publisher's Note: MDPI stays neutral with regard to jurisdictional claims in published maps and institutional affiliations.

Copyright: © 2022 by the authors. Licensee MDPI, Basel, Switzerland. This article is an open access article distributed under the terms and conditions of the Creative Commons Attribution (CC BY) license (https://creativecommons.org/licenses/by/4.0/).

Abstract: The problem of constructing and justifying the discrete algorithms of the support operator method for numerical modeling of differential repeated rotational operations of vector analysis (*curl curl*) in application to problems of magnetohydrodynamics is considered. Difference schemes of the support operator method on the unstructured meshes do not approximate equations in the local sense. Therefore, it is necessary to prove the convergence of these schemes to the exact solution, which is possible after analyzing the error structure of their approximation. For this analysis, a decomposition of the space of mesh vector functions into an orthogonal direct sum of subspaces of potential and vortex fields is introduced. Generalized centroid-tensor metric representations of repeated operations of tensor analysis (*div*, *grad*, and *curl*) are constructed. Representations have flux-circulation properties that are integrally consistent on spatial meshes of irregular structure. On smooth solutions of the model magnetostatic problem on a tetrahedral mesh with the first order of accuracy in the rms sense, the convergence of the constructed difference schemes is proved. The algorithms constructed in this work can be used to solve physical problems with discontinuous magnetic viscosity, dielectric permittivity, or thermal resistance of the medium.

Keywords: self-gravitation; magnetohydrodynamic forces; support operator method; mathematical modeling

MSC: 65N12; 76W05; 00A71; 65M06

1. Introduction

Support operator method (SOM) [1–3] in the construction of the difference schemes is used for a consistent approximation (in the sense of some integral identities) of the conjugate operations of vector analysis (*div*, *grad*, *curl*, etc.) and their combinations that are necessary for the numerical modeling of mathematical physics problems. The SOM allows for constructing the difference schemes on irregular meshes for many equations of this class, including nonlinear ones, in particular, with the fulfillment of the principle of complete conservatism [4]. In particular, to solve the problems of magnetic gas dynamics and for the development of hydrodynamic instabilities, the computational schemes should ensure conservation laws with an error that must be time-limited in order to be able to consider asymptotic solutions for the problems. These requirements together led to the development of integrally consistent approximations of systems of partial differential equations that arise in continuum mechanics.

The construction of consistent approximations is subjected to the multiphysical nature of most practical problems in continuum mechanics and magnetic gas dynamics. This branch of the theory of mesh methods for solving initial-boundary value problems for systems of partial differential equations has a long history and has turned out to be very productive. A classic example is the construction of completely conservative difference schemes for gas dynamics [4]. Matching the approximations for the momentum balance equations, gas internal energy, and magnetic energy makes it possible to obtain their difference analogs. From these analogs, one can obtain the total energy balance equation which is free of "nonphysical" terms, i.e., those that do not have a physical nature, but occur only as a result of the chosen method of approximation. Thus, completely conservative schemes can be used in two basic equivalent forms, obtained one from another by algebraic transformations, either one that includes the total energy balance equation, or component-by-component balances of the kinetic, internal energy of the gas and magnetic energy. The latter form is important in such applications as, for example, calculations of high-velocity flows of gas mixtures, in cases where the characteristic energy relaxation time is longer than the characteristic momentum relaxation time, and the temperatures of individual components can differ markedly during the motion. Integral-consistent approximations are important in multiphysics calculations with a complicated description of energy exchange: gas dynamics of chemically reacting flows, radiation gas dynamics, magnetic gas dynamics, hydro-gasdynamic processes with energy flows to condensed matter, etc.

The SOM under consideration is actively studied and applied to practice problems. Let us take a look at some of them. Ref. [5] presents a comprehensive workflow for modeling integrally consistent single-phase flow and transport in a fractured porous medium using a discrete fracture matrix approach. In [6], the relationship between surface and underground flows was studied on completely unstructured meshes corresponding to complex soil structures. To accommodate the distorted grids that inevitably result from the explicit representation of complex soil structures, a mimetic finite-difference scheme structure (which is analogous to SOM) of spatial sampling is used to connect surface and underground flows. The Ref. [7] presents a mimetic finite-difference discretization of an arbitrary order for the diffusion equation with asymmetric positive definite tensor diffusion coefficient in a mixed formulation on general polygonal meshes. This scheme was tested on a non-stationary problem of modeling the Hall effect in resistive magnetohydrodynamics (MHD). In [8], the convergence of a new family of mimetic difference schemes for linear diffusion problems was studied. In contrast to the traditional approach, the diffusion coefficient enters both into the primary mimetic operator, i.e., into discrete divergence, and into the scalar product in the space of gradients. The diffusion coefficient is evaluated at different locations in the mesh, i.e., inside the mesh cells and on the mesh faces.

In Ref. [9], the explicit and implicit mimetic finite-difference schemes for the Landau–Lifshitz equation describing the dynamics of magnetization inside ferromagnetic materials were developed and analyzed. These schemes operate on common polyhedral meshes, which provide the flexibility to model magnetic devices of various shapes. The Ref. [10] presents a new family of mimetic difference schemes for solving elliptic partial differential equations in direct form on unstructured polyhedral meshes. Higher-order schemes are constructed using higher-order moments. The developed schemes are verified numerically on diffusion problems with constant and spatially variable tensor coefficients. In [11], the stability and convergence properties of the mimetic finite-difference method for diffusion-type problems on polyhedral meshes were studied. The optimal rates of convergence of scalar and vector variables in a mixed formulation of the problem are proved.

In Ref. [12], two new numerical methods for spatial discretization are presented, based on a mimetic finite-difference method for a degenerate partial differential equation in one dimension known as the Black–Scholes partial differential equation, which governs option pricing. To deal with partial differential equation degeneracy, a new customized finite-difference mimetic scheme is proposed along with the standard finite-difference mimetic method. Temporal discretization is performed according to the standard implicit scheme. In addition, rigorous proofs of convergence in the corresponding normed spaces are proposed. In [13], a systematic approach was developed to obtain mimetic finite-difference discretizations for the divergence and gradient operators, which provides the same order of accuracy at the boundary and internal mesh nodes. In Ref. [13], a second-order version of these operators is used to develop a new mimetic finite-difference method for the stationary diffusion equation. A theoretical and numerical analysis of this new method is presented, including an original and non-standard proof of the quadratic convergence rate of this new method.

In Ref. [14], a numerical analysis was performed to study the heat transfer in a three-dimensional magnetohydrodynamic flow of a magnetic nanofluid (ferrofluid) through a bidirectional exponentially stretching sheet of a hybrid nanofluid. The research results showed that, with an increase in the shape factor and generation/absorption parameters, the temperature above the surface increased. The obtained data prove that the skin friction coefficient corresponds to the magnetic parameters and the suction/injection parameters. Ref. [15] considers the magneto-hyperbolic-tangent liquid model taking into account magnetohydrodynamic processes. MHD has several applications in heat exchanger manufacturing, spacecraft strength, thermal enrichment, polymer technology, power generators, petroleum industry, and crude oil refining. In [15], hydromagnetic characteristics were studied under convective and stratified model constraints. Ref. [16] considers the magnetohydrodynamic flow and heat transfer of a non-Newtonian micropolar dusty liquid, suspended $Cu-Al_2O_3$ hybrid nanoparticles, past a stretching sheet in the presence of non-linear thermal radiation, variable thermal conductivity, and various shapes of nanoparticles (bricks, cylinders, platelets, and blades). H_2O is used as base fluid. The effect of various parameters on the velocity and temperature profiles is analyzed for a given heat flux and a given surface temperature. An increase in the Hartmann number led to a decrease in speed due to the Lorentz force. The temperature also increased as a result of the increase in the Hartmann number due to the Joule heating effect.

In Ref. [17], the entropy generation of nanofluids between two stretching rotating disks under the action of magnetohydrodynamic and thermal radiation is considered. In [17], ethylene glycol $(CH_2OH)_2$ is used as the base liquid, and carbon nanotubes, which include both single-walled carbon nanotubes and multi-walled nanotubes, are used as nanoparticles. The effect of the radiation parameter, magnetic field, porosity, suction/injection, and Brinkmann number on the skin friction coefficient and Nusselt number are studied. In [18], a magnetohydrodynamic flow is studied in the presence of microorganisms and nanoparticles on the surface. The desired results are the number of motile microorganisms, the Nusselt number, the coefficient of friction of the skin, and the Sherwood number. The influence of Brownian motion, thermal radiation, Schmidt number, thermophoresis, Peclet number, magnetic field, and bioconvection Schmidt number on the desired results have been studied. In [19], a three-dimensional estimate of the convective heat transfer properties of a magnetohydrodynamic flow of a nanofluid consisting of mobile oxytactic microorganisms and nanoparticles passing through a rotating cone was obtained. The influence of various factors on the distribution of velocity, temperature, and concentration is studied, taking into account the addition of a magnetic field, thermal radiation, and viscous dissipation to the calculations. Changing the magnetic parameter from 0 to 1 led to a decrease in the temperature distribution by approximately 3.11%.

The expansion of the practice of using grids of irregular structure is due to the need to solve applied problems of mathematical physics in geometrically nontrivial areas. One such very effective method for constructing consistent approximations is the method of support or integrally consistent operators. The idea of constructing integrally consistent approximations of differential operators was realized in [20,21], where approximations on rectangular grids were obtained. Generalizations of this method to the case of irregular grids appeared as a result of the analysis of the development of projection-grid and variational-difference schemes for equations of elliptic type [22], as well as variational-difference schemes for equations of gas and magnetic gas dynamics [23]. In the works of this direction, in particular, the possibilities of constructing difference schemes without assumptions about the structure of the difference grid were studied [24–26]. It turned out that the natural basis for the corresponding difference constructions approximating differential operators is the integral identities of vector and tensor analysis [27]. Since these identities connect vector analysis operators in an invariant form, for their use in constructing grid approximations, the natural form of representation of the original differential equations (and the corresponding boundary value problems) is invariantly defined operators. In this case, it turns out to be possible to construct an approximation of any one of the operators, for example, the gradient. Some integral identities link operators of different types, i.e., acting on scalar and vector functions, which allows, for example, to obtain an approximation of the divergence of a vector field as a generated operator [28,29], which, together with the gradient difference operator, satisfies the difference analogue of the corresponding integral identity.

The problems of research and justification for these schemes are less developed. In this work, on the classical solutions of the model magnetostatic problem on tetrahedral irregular meshes, the convergence of SOM difference schemes for repeated rotational operations of vector analysis (curl curl) with zero eigenvalues of the spectral problem is proved. All equations are linear and, moreover, with constant coefficients. This choice is explained by the desire to highlight the problems associated exclusively with the irregularity of the mesh and to show the commonality of approaches to their solution. Convergence is proved at the geometric level, i.e., depending on the degree of coordination of the geometry of the mesh and its metric properties with template functionals that determine the specific form of the difference scheme. In this case, the sufficient smoothness of the solution of the original differential problem is assumed.

The considered difference schemes generally do not approximate the equations in the local sense; therefore, the proof of convergence is possible after analysis of the structure of the approximation error. An investigation of this problem leads to a splitting of the space of vector mesh functions into an orthogonal direct sum of the subspaces of potential and vortex ones. As applied to the SOM difference scheme for the magnetostatic problem, the difference rotor of the circulations calculation error is zero. Therefore, this error is the difference gradient of some mesh function $grad\xi$. The norm of circulation error $grad\xi$ is determined by the energy of the metric mesh operator G [30]. The action of the metric operator G on the area of the faces of the cells $\vec{S}$, in turn, is consistent with the sizes of the cells (the location of the centers of gravity of the cells, faces, and edges). We introduce a decomposition of the space of mesh vector functions into the orthogonal direct sum of the subspaces of potential and vortex fields, so that the error in computing the circulations is a potential function.

Thus, in the present work, on sufficiently smooth solutions of the differential problem on tetrahedral meshes with the first order of accuracy in the mean-square sense, the convergence of SOM difference schemes for repeated rotational operations (curl curl) with zero eigenvalues of the spectral problem is proved. There are no restrictions on the tetrahedral mesh, except for its non-degeneracy.

2. Covariant Representation of a Mesh Dot Product on the Mesh $(\sigma) \cdot (\phi)$

Cells (Ω) are made up of faces (σ) and nodes (ω). The bases $\varphi(\Omega)$ are formed by the unit normal $\vec{e}(\sigma)$ of the faces σ forming the given basis. Its central node $\omega(\Omega)$ corresponds to such a basis $\varphi(\Omega)$. In the bases $\varphi(\Omega)$, their volumes $V_\varphi > 0$ are selected with the normalization condition in the cell $\sum_{\varphi(\Omega)} V_\varphi = V_\Omega$. Spatial meshes with the above-described structural elements were introduced in [1,30] and are shown in Figure 1a. The strengths of the magnetic field are componentwise related to the normals $\vec{e}(\sigma)$ of which the bases $\varphi(\Omega)$ are composed.

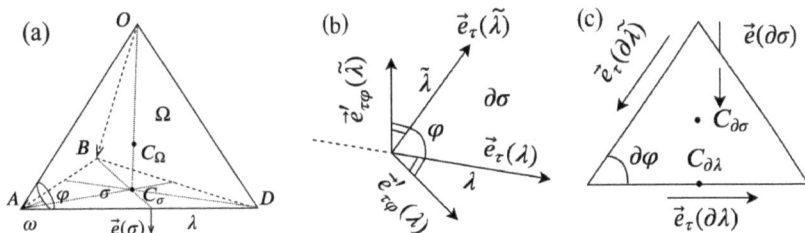

Figure 1. Mesh and mesh bases: (**a**) tetrahedron; (**b**) boundary approximation of the Poynting flux; (**c**) magnetic circulation on the boundary contour $\overrightarrow{C_{\partial\sigma}C_{\partial\lambda}}$, $s_\sigma(\lambda) = -1$, $s_{\partial\sigma} = -1$. Beyond the face $\partial\sigma$, the cell $\partial\Omega$ is located.

Using the facet weight volume $V_\sigma = \sum\limits_{\varphi(\sigma)} V_\varphi > 0$, we introduce the mesh dot product approximating the integral $\int\limits_O (\vec{h}, \vec{g})dV$ in the domain O in its covariant representation

$$(\hbar, g')_\sigma = \sum_\varphi V_\varphi \sum_{\sigma(\varphi), \tilde{\sigma}(\varphi)} Gr'_\varphi(\sigma, \tilde{\sigma})\hbar'(\tilde{\sigma}) g'(\sigma).$$

Here, by the definition,

$$(\hbar_1, \hbar_2)_\sigma = \sum_\sigma V_\sigma \hbar_1(\sigma)\hbar_2(\sigma).$$

Thus, the metric operator G, including $\tilde{\hbar} = G\hbar'$, is actually introduced according to the formula

$$\tilde{\hbar}(\sigma) = \frac{1}{V_\sigma} \sum_{\varphi(\sigma)} V_\varphi \sum_{\tilde{\sigma}(\varphi)} Gr'_\varphi(\sigma, \tilde{\sigma})\hbar'(\tilde{\sigma}).$$

We have constructed a positive definite self-adjoint operator $G : (\sigma) \to (\sigma)$, $G = G^* > 0$ on the mesh. It is given by a family of Gram matrices $Gr'_\varphi(\sigma, \tilde{\sigma}) = (\vec{e}'_\varphi(\sigma), \vec{e}'_\varphi(\tilde{\sigma}))$ in local bases φ. Here, $\vec{e}'_\varphi(\sigma)$ are the vectors of the mutual basis φ with respect to the initial one formed by the vectors $\vec{e}(\sigma)$. This operator G connects the covariant $h'(\sigma)$ and contravariant $\tilde{\hbar}(\sigma)$ representations of the magnetic field strength. For triangular 2d cells Ω according to [1], the base volume is defined as $V_\varphi = \frac{1}{6}|\vec{e}_1 \times \vec{e}_2|$. Here, $\vec{e}_1$ and $\vec{e}_2$ are sides of the triangle forming the basis φ.

Likewise in a quadrangular cell, it is $V_\varphi = \frac{1}{4}|\vec{e}_1 \times \vec{e}_2|$. For tetrahedral 3D cells Ω, it is selected as $V_\varphi = \frac{1}{4}V_\Omega$, $\varphi \in \Omega$.

What has been described in this section is generalized to non-unit normals $\vec{e}(\sigma)$ to cell faces σ.

Mesh divergence $DIV : (\sigma) \to (\Omega)$ is given as:

$$DIV\,\vec{g} = \frac{1}{V_\Omega} \sum_{\sigma(\Omega)} s_\nu(\Omega)g'(\sigma)S(\sigma). \tag{1}$$

Here, $S(\sigma)$ is the area of the face σ divided by the length $\vec{e}(\sigma)$ of the ort $\sqrt{(\vec{e}(\sigma), \vec{e}(\sigma))}$, i.e., the specific area. If the normal $\vec{e}(\sigma)$ to the cell Ω is external, then $s_\sigma(\Omega) = +1$. For the inner normal, this sign function is equal to minus one.

The cell scalar product is defined as

$$(F_1, F_2)_\Omega = \sum_\Omega V_\Omega F_{1\Omega} F_{2\Omega}.$$

Using (1) from the difference analogue of the integral identity [3]:

$$\int_O \text{grad} F \vec{\hbar} dV + \int_O F \text{div} \vec{\hbar} dV = \int_\Sigma F \vec{\hbar} d\vec{S}$$

in the area O closed by the surface Σ, we obtain the mesh operator $GRAD : (\Omega) \to (\sigma)$

$$(\overline{GRADF}, \hbar')_\sigma + (F, DIV\vec{\hbar})_\Omega = \sum_{\partial \sigma} s_{\partial \sigma} F_{\partial \sigma} \hbar'(\partial \sigma) S(\partial \sigma). \quad (2)$$

On the boundary faces $\partial \sigma$ in this identity, $S(\partial \sigma)$ is the specific area. $s_{\partial \sigma} = +1$ for the outer surface normal $\vec{e}(\partial \sigma)$ and $s_{\partial \sigma} = -1$ if otherwise. In addition, the function $F_{\partial \sigma}$ is defined on the boundary faces $\partial \sigma$. The quantities $\bar{\hbar} = G\hbar'$ and F are arbitrary mesh functions; therefore, on the faces σ, we obtain

$$\overline{GRADF} = \frac{\Delta F}{\hbar'}, h' = \frac{V_\sigma}{S(\sigma)},$$

where

$$\Delta F = -\sum_{\Omega(\sigma)} s_\sigma(\Omega) F(\Omega) + s_{\partial \sigma} F_{\partial \Omega}.$$

The last term in the expression for ΔF on the face σ is added at the boundary of the region (i.e., $\sigma = \partial \sigma$).

3. Difference Evolution Model of the Magnetic Energy of the System

3.1. Metric Support-Operator Meshes for MHD Processes

$h_\tau(\lambda) > 0$ is the length of the oriented edge λ divided by the length of the ort vector $\sqrt{(\vec{e}_\tau(\lambda), \vec{e}_\tau(\lambda))}$. This is the specific length of the edge. The oriented area $\vec{S}_{\partial \sigma}$ of the boundary face $\partial \sigma$ is divided into the sum of the areas of the surface bases $\vec{S}_{\partial \varphi}$ inside this face $\vec{S}_{\partial \sigma} = \sum_{\partial \varphi(\partial \sigma)} \vec{S}_{\partial \varphi}$. The boundary edge $\partial \lambda$ has a superficial near edge area $S_{\partial \lambda} = \sum_{\partial \varphi(\partial \lambda)} S_{\partial \varphi}$ and a transverse length $h'_\Sigma(\partial \lambda) = S_{\partial \lambda}/h_\tau(\partial \lambda)$. The mesh $(\lambda).(\varphi)$ is formed by local bases φ of edges λ with oriented vectors $\vec{e}_\tau(\lambda)$. Electric field strengths $\vec{e}$ are componentwise related to the edges of a given mesh. To define the metric operator G_τ on $(\lambda).(\varphi)$, we consider the dot product: $(e_1, e_2)_\lambda = \sum_\lambda V_\lambda e_1(\lambda) e_2(\lambda)$ with near-edge volume $V_\lambda = \sum_{\varphi(\lambda)} V_\varphi > 0$. The continual scalar product $\int_O (\vec{e}, \vec{b}) dV$ in the entire region O is approximated by the representation

$$(\vec{e}, b')_\lambda = \sum_\varphi V_\varphi \sum_{\tilde{\lambda}(\varphi), \lambda(\varphi)} Gr'_{\tau \varphi}(\lambda, \tilde{\lambda}) e'(\tilde{\lambda}) b'(\lambda).$$

Thus, the metric operator G_τ, including $\vec{e} = G_\tau e'$, is actually introduced by the formula

$$\vec{e}(\lambda) = \frac{1}{V_\lambda} \sum_{\varphi(\lambda)} V_\varphi \sum_{\tilde{\lambda}(\varphi)} Gr'_{\tau \varphi}(\lambda, \tilde{\lambda}) e'(\tilde{\lambda}).$$

In the sense of the scalar product $(e_1, e_2)_\lambda$, we have constructed a positive definite self-adjoint operator $G_\tau : (\lambda) \to (\lambda)$, $G_\tau = G_\tau^* > 0$. It is given by a family of Gram matrices in local mutual basis φ. Here, $\vec{e}_{\tau \varphi}(\lambda)$ are the vectors of the mutual basis φ with respect to the initial one formed by the vectors $\vec{e}_\tau(\lambda)$. The index τ determines the object relation to the mesh $(\lambda).(\varphi)$. This operator G_τ connects the covariant $e'(\lambda)$ and contravariant $\vec{e}(\lambda)$ representations of the electric field intensity. Approximating Stokes' theorem on the cell face σ, we obtain a mesh rotor $ROD : (\lambda) \to (\sigma)$ (see Figure 2a) acting on an electric field $\vec{e}$:

$$(ROD\vec{e})' = \frac{1}{S(\sigma)} \sum_{\lambda(\sigma)} s_\lambda(\sigma) e'(\lambda) h_\tau(\lambda). \quad (3)$$

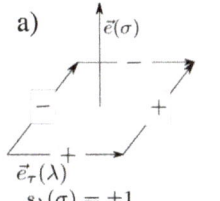 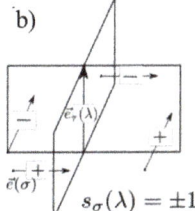

Figure 2. Circular matching of oriented normals to faces σ on the left and tangents along mesh edges λ on the right. The sign function $s_\lambda(\sigma) = \pm 1$ (**a**) takes values according to whether the orientation of the edge $\vec{e}_\tau(\lambda)$ coincides with the direction of rotation about the normal $\vec{e}(\sigma)$. The sign function $s_\sigma(\lambda) = \pm 1$ (**b**) is defined similarly, but the contour is made up of oriented face normals $\vec{e}(\sigma)$, and the rotation is around the tangent along the edges $\vec{e}_\tau(\lambda)$.

Here, $S(\sigma)$ is the area of the face σ divided by the length of the ort $\sqrt{(\vec{e}(\sigma), \vec{e}(\sigma))}$. From Figure 2, sign functions $s_\lambda(\sigma) = \pm 1$, $s_\sigma(\lambda) = \pm 1$ are set (including $s_\lambda(\sigma) = s_\sigma(\lambda)$). The boundary sign function $s_{\partial\lambda(\partial\varphi)}$ is equal to plus one if in the surface basis $\partial\varphi(\partial\sigma)$ the rotation from the unit vector $\vec{e}_\tau(\partial\lambda)$ to the complementary to it in $\partial\varphi(\partial\sigma)$ determines the outward normal to the region. Otherwise, $s_{\partial\lambda(\partial\varphi)} = -1$.

On the edges $\partial\lambda$ of the boundary of the region O, as well as an electric field $e'(\partial\lambda)$, we consider a magnetic field $\vec{\hbar}_\tau$ with components $\hbar'_\tau(\partial\lambda)$ tangential to the surface of the region. Using (3) from the difference analog of the integral identity [3]:

$$\int_O \vec{e}\; curl\; \vec{\hbar}dV - \int_O \vec{\hbar}\; curl\; \vec{e}dV = \int_\Sigma [\vec{\hbar}_\tau \times \vec{e}]d\vec{s} \quad (4)$$

in the area O, closed by the surface Σ, we obtain the mesh operator

$$(e', \overline{ROG\vec{\hbar}})_\lambda - (\vec{\hbar}, (ROD\vec{e})')_\sigma = \sum_{\partial\lambda} e'(\partial\lambda) h_\tau(\partial\lambda)(\vec{\hbar}d\vec{h})_\Sigma(\partial\lambda). \quad (5)$$

The operator ROG acts on magnetic field $\vec{\hbar}$.

From the approximation in the surface basis $\partial\varphi$ of the mixed product $[\vec{\hbar}_\tau \times \vec{e}]d\vec{s}$ in (4), the magnetic circulation transverse to the edge $\partial\lambda$ is determined on the surface of the region (see Figure 1b)

$$(\vec{\hbar}d\vec{h})_\Sigma(\partial\lambda) = -\frac{1}{h_\tau(\partial\lambda)} \sum_{\partial\varphi(\partial\lambda)} \frac{s_{\partial\lambda(\partial\varphi)} S_{\partial\varphi}}{\sqrt{det\|Gr_{\tau\partial\varphi}\|}} \hbar'_\tau(\partial\tilde\lambda)|_{\partial\tilde\lambda(\partial\varphi) \neq \partial\lambda}. \quad (6)$$

$Gr_{\tau\partial\varphi}$ is Gram matrix composed of orts $\vec{e}_\tau(\partial\lambda)$ and $\vec{e}_\tau(\partial\tilde\lambda)$ in a surface basis $\partial\varphi$. Its determinant is:

$$det\|Gr_{\tau\partial\varphi}\| = (\vec{e}_\tau(\partial\lambda), \vec{e}_\tau(\partial\lambda)) \cdot (\vec{e}_\tau(\partial\tilde\lambda), \vec{e}_\tau(\partial\tilde\lambda)) \cdot sin^2 \widehat{\vec{e}_\tau(\partial\lambda)\vec{e}_\tau(\partial\tilde\lambda)}|_{\partial\lambda(\partial\varphi) \neq \partial\tilde\lambda(\partial\varphi)}. \quad (7)$$

For the angle $\varphi = \widehat{\vec{e}_\tau(\partial\lambda)\vec{e}_\tau(\partial\tilde\lambda)}$ between the vectors of the surface basis $\partial\varphi$, the identity is fulfilled

$$|[\vec{e}'_{\tau\varphi}(\lambda) \times \vec{e}'_{\tau\varphi}(\tilde\lambda)]| = sin(\pi - \varphi)/\{|\vec{e}_\tau(\lambda)| \cdot |\vec{e}_\tau(\tilde\lambda)| cos^2(\pi/2 - \varphi)\} = 1/\sqrt{det\|Gr_{\tau\partial\varphi}\|}.$$

Hence, the integral conjugate to the operator ROD, the operator ROG of interest to us, will be obtained from (5):

$$\overline{ROG\vec{\hbar}} = 1/S'_\tau [\sum_{\sigma(\lambda)} s_\sigma(\lambda) \vec{\hbar}(\sigma) h'(\sigma) + (\vec{\hbar}d\vec{h})_\Sigma(\partial\lambda)], \quad S'_\tau = V_\lambda / h_\tau. \tag{8}$$

If the magnetic circulation $(\vec{\hbar}d\vec{h})_\Sigma(\partial_1 \lambda)$ is used to close the contour around the surface edge $\partial_1 \lambda$ in the ROG operator, then the first boundary value problem (Dirichlet) is considered to be posed on this edge $\partial_1 \lambda$. The edge $\partial \lambda = \{\partial_1 \lambda | \partial_0 \lambda\}$, in other words, we will understand as $\sigma(\partial_0 \lambda)$, and we will put on it the second boundary value problem (Neumann), if the electric circulation $e'(\partial_0 \lambda) \cdot h_\tau(\partial_0 \lambda)$ along the surface edge $\partial_0 \lambda$ is defined. This edge closes the contours of the faces $\sigma(\partial_0 \lambda)$ in (3) for the operator ROD. In this case, the operation $ROD\ ROG : (\sigma) \to (\sigma)$, including $ROD\ ROG = (ROD\ ROG)^* \geq 0$ turns out to be self-adjoint and non-negative according to (5) in the sense of the scalar product $(\cdot, \cdot)_\sigma$. For the operation $ROG\ ROD : (\lambda) \to (\lambda)$, we similarly have $ROG\ ROD = (ROG\ ROD)^* \geq 0$, in the sense of the scalar product $(\cdot, \cdot)_\lambda$. Due to the metric properties of the meshes $(\sigma).(\varphi)$ and $(\lambda).(\varphi)$, as well as mesh-oriented flow-circulation relationships (see Figure 2), the properties of operations $DIV\ ROD\ \vec{e} = 0$ in the mesh cells Ω are fulfilled.

3.2. Metric Properties of Rotary Operations on Tetrahedral Meshes

Let us justify the approximation of the operation $\overline{ROG\vec{\hbar}}$ (see (5), (8)) and its circulation properties.

On the tetrahedral mesh, we also set the form of a closed conjugate magnetic contour $(\sigma(\lambda))$ with an axis around the edge λ. For the surface edges $\partial \lambda$, the contribution to the spatial closure of the contour will be made taking into account the approximation of the Poynting vector on the faces $\partial \sigma$.

Consider the contour of magnetic circulation around the edge λ, formed by adjacent tetrahedra (see Figure 1a). We introduce the centroid points of the tetrahedron (for Ω, σ and λ):

$$\vec{c}_\Omega = \frac{1}{4} \sum_{\omega(\Omega)} \vec{r}_\omega, \quad \vec{c}_\sigma = \frac{1}{3} \sum_{\omega(\sigma)} \vec{r}_\omega, \quad \vec{c}_\lambda = \frac{1}{2} \sum_{\omega(\lambda)} \vec{r}_\omega.$$

Here, $\vec{r}_\omega$ are vectors defining the spatial arrangement of nodes forming cells Ω, faces σ and edges λ. Deferring these vectors from the node O (see Figure 1a), we obtain

$$\overrightarrow{OC_\Omega} = \frac{1}{4}(\overrightarrow{OA} + \overrightarrow{OB} + \overrightarrow{OD}), \quad \overrightarrow{OC_\sigma} = \frac{1}{3}(\overrightarrow{OA} + \overrightarrow{OB} + \overrightarrow{OD}),$$

$$\overrightarrow{OC_\lambda} = \frac{1}{2}(\overrightarrow{OA} + \overrightarrow{OD}), \quad \overrightarrow{C_\Omega C_\sigma} = \vec{C}_\sigma - \vec{C}_\Omega.$$

We transform the expression from (8)

$$S'_\tau \overline{ROG\vec{\hbar}} - (\vec{\hbar}d\vec{h})_\Sigma(\partial\lambda) = \sum_{\sigma(\lambda)} s_\sigma(\lambda) \vec{\hbar}(\sigma) h'(\sigma) = \sum_{\sigma(\lambda)} s_\sigma(\lambda)(G\vec{\hbar}')(\sigma) h'(\sigma) =$$

$$= \sum_{\sigma(\lambda)} s_\sigma(\lambda) \frac{1}{V_\sigma} \sum_{\varphi(\sigma)} V_\varphi \sum_{\tilde{\sigma}(\varphi)} Gr'_\varphi(\sigma, \tilde{\sigma}) \hbar'(\tilde{\sigma}) \frac{V_\sigma}{S(\sigma)} = \sum_{\sigma(\lambda)} \frac{s_\sigma(\lambda)}{S(\sigma)} \sum_{\Omega(\sigma)} \sum_{\varphi(\sigma) \in \Omega} V_\varphi \vec{e}'_\varphi(\sigma) \cdot \vec{\hbar}_\varphi$$

$$= \sum_{\sigma(\lambda)} s_\sigma(\lambda) \sum_{\Omega(\sigma)} \frac{1}{4}\frac{1}{3} h_{\Omega \perp \sigma} \sum_{\varphi(\sigma) \in \Omega} \vec{e}'_{1\varphi}(\sigma) \cdot \vec{\hbar}_\varphi.$$

The vector of the magnetic field intensity in the basis φ is $\vec{\hbar}_\varphi = \sum_{\tilde{\sigma}(\varphi)} \hbar'(\tilde{\sigma}) \vec{e}'_\varphi(\tilde{\sigma})$. The height in the tetrahedron Ω drawn to the face σ is denoted as $h_{\Omega \perp \sigma}$. In addition, on the φ-basis, $\vec{e}'_{1\varphi}(\sigma)$ is the mutual (contravariant) vector corresponding to the unit normal to the face σ. The representation takes place (see Figure 1a)

$$\frac{1}{12} h_{\Omega \perp \sigma} \sum_{\varphi(\sigma) \in \Omega} \vec{e}_{1\varphi}(\sigma) = s_\sigma(\Omega) \overrightarrow{C_\Omega C_\sigma}.$$

This identity constructs the circulation of the magnetic field intensity between the gravity centers of the cell Ω and one of its faces σ as

$$s_\sigma(\Omega) \left(\int_{C_\Omega}^{C_\sigma} \vec{\hbar} d\vec{e} \right)_\Delta = \frac{1}{12} h_{\Omega \perp \sigma} \sum_{\varphi(\sigma) \in \Omega} \vec{e}_{1\varphi}(\sigma) \vec{\hbar}_\varphi.$$

Because of this, (8) can be represented in the form

$$S'_\tau \overline{ROG\vec{\hbar}} - (\vec{\hbar}d\vec{\hbar})_\Sigma(\partial \lambda) = \sum_{\sigma(\lambda)} s_\sigma(\lambda) \sum_{\Omega(\sigma)} s_\sigma(\Omega) \cdot \left(\int_{C_\Omega}^{C_\sigma} \vec{\hbar} d\vec{e} \right)_\Delta.$$

The Pointing electromagnetic energy flux approximated on the surface of the region Σ on the right-hand side of (4) is consistent with the discrete representation of the boundary magnetic circulation (5), (6) between the gravity centers of the surface faces $\partial \sigma$ and the midpoints of their edges $\partial \lambda(\partial \sigma)$ (see Figure 1c). The corresponding contours have a geometric representation (see (6))

$$s_\sigma(\lambda) s_{\partial \sigma} \overrightarrow{C_{\partial \sigma} C_{\partial \lambda}} = -1/h_\tau(\partial \lambda) \sum_{\partial \varphi(\partial \lambda) \in \partial \sigma} \frac{s_{\partial \lambda(\partial \varphi)} \cdot S_{\partial \varphi}}{\sqrt{det \|Gr_{\tau \partial \varphi}\|}} \vec{e}_\tau(\partial \tilde{\lambda})|_{\partial \tilde{\lambda}(\partial \varphi) \neq \partial \lambda}.$$

The intersection point of the medians $C_{\partial \sigma}$ in the triangle $\partial \sigma$ is connected to vectors $\overrightarrow{C_{\partial \sigma} C_{\partial \lambda}}$ by the midpoint of one of its edges $\partial \lambda(\partial \sigma)$. $\partial \varphi$ are surface bases in the triangle $\partial \sigma$. Their area can be represented as $S_{\partial \varphi} = \frac{1}{3} S_{\partial \sigma \supset \partial \varphi}$ through the area of the triangle $S_{\partial \sigma \supset \partial \varphi}$ containing this basis $\partial \varphi$. $s_{\partial \sigma} = +1$ is true for the outer surface normal $\vec{e}(\partial \sigma)$ and $s_{\partial \sigma} = -1$, if otherwise.

By virtue of the above geometric reasoning, we see that the discrete magnetic circulation on $\overrightarrow{C_{\partial \sigma} C_{\partial \lambda}}$ can be represented as

$$s_\sigma(\lambda) s_{\partial \sigma} \left(\int_{C_{\partial \sigma}}^{C_{\partial \lambda}} \vec{\hbar} d\vec{e} \right)_\Delta = -\frac{1}{h_\tau(\partial \lambda)} \sum_{\partial \varphi(\partial \lambda) \in \partial \sigma} \frac{s_{\partial \lambda(\partial \varphi)} \cdot S_{\partial \varphi}}{\sqrt{det \|Gr_{\tau \partial \varphi}\|}} \hbar'_\tau(\partial \tilde{\lambda})|_{\partial \tilde{\lambda}(\partial \varphi) \neq \partial \lambda}.$$

Finally,

$$S'_\tau \overline{ROG\vec{\hbar}} = \sum_{\sigma(\lambda)} s_\sigma(\lambda) \sum_{\Omega(\sigma)} s_\sigma(\Omega) \left(\int_{C_\Omega}^{C_\sigma} \vec{\hbar} d\vec{e} \right)_\Delta + \sum_{\partial \sigma(\partial \lambda)} s_\sigma(\lambda) s_{\partial \sigma} \left(\int_{C_{\partial \sigma}}^{C_{\partial \lambda}} \vec{\hbar} d\vec{e} \right)_\Delta. \quad (9)$$

Equality (9) means that the rotor of the magnetic field (see (8)) can be represented by a spatially closed centroid contour circulation around the axis of the edge λ. A spatial contour connects the gravity centers of cells Ω and faces σ around the edge λ. On the boundary face $\partial \sigma$, the intersection point of its medians is connected to the middle of the axial edge $\partial \lambda(\partial \sigma)$, on which $S'_\tau \overline{ROG\vec{\hbar}}(\lambda)$ is defined. From the spatial closeness of the circulation representation (9) on the mesh, it follows that

$$\overline{ROG\vec{\hbar}} \equiv 0 \text{ at } \vec{\hbar} = const.$$

4. Convergence of Difference Schemes of the Support Operator Method for Rotational Operations of Vector Analysis on Tetrahedral Meshes

4.1. Formulation of the Problem

On sufficiently smooth solutions, the approximation by difference schemes of support operator method [31]

$$\text{curl } \vec{H} = \vec{f}(\vec{r}), \tag{10}$$

$$\vec{H} = \text{curl } \vec{E} \tag{11}$$

with solenoidal magnetic field ($div \vec{H} = 0$) is considered, for which with necessity [32] a certain field $\vec{E}$ exists, incl. (11) holding. It is also assumed that a certain distribution of current densities $\vec{f}(\vec{r})$, for which (10) holds, and boundary tangential components of magnetic field $\vec{H}_\tau|_\Sigma$ are explicitly given. Obviously, "electric" field $\vec{E}$ is determined to be accurate for a constant and homogeneous spectral problem (with $\vec{f}(\vec{r}) = 0$ and $\vec{H}_\tau|_\Sigma = 0$) having zero eigenvalue.

For the solenoidality of the function $\vec{f}$ (i.e., $div \vec{f} = 0$), the existence of the function $\vec{F}$, incl. $\vec{f} = \text{curl } \vec{F}$ is necessary and sufficient [32]. For Equations (10) and (11), we consider the boundary-value problem with the tangential components of the magnetic field defined on the boundary Σ of the region O

$$\vec{H}_\tau|_\Sigma = \vec{F}_\tau|_\Sigma. \tag{12}$$

In addition, obviously, for any closed loop Γ bounding the surface Σ_Γ the following will be satisfied:

$$\int_\Gamma \vec{H} d\vec{h} = \int_{\Sigma_\Gamma} \vec{f} d\vec{S}.$$

The difference scheme of the support operator method will have the form

$$V_\lambda \overline{ROG\vec{h}} = f_\lambda, \tag{13}$$

$$\hbar' = (ROD\vec{e})'. \tag{14}$$

Hereinafter, when investigating the convergence of this difference scheme (13) and (14), the specific lengths of the edges $h_\tau(\lambda)$ and the areas of faces $S(\sigma)$ are considered to be unit (see (3), (1)). We represent the electric flow f_λ through the area

$$\vec{S}_\lambda = \bigcup_{(\Omega(\lambda), \sigma(\lambda)) \in \Omega} \vec{S}_{\Omega \sigma \lambda}$$

penetrated by the vector $\vec{e}_\tau(\lambda)$ in the form

$$f_\lambda = \sum_{\Omega(\lambda)} \sum_{\sigma(\lambda) \in \Omega} \int_{\vec{S}_{\Omega \sigma \lambda}} \vec{f}(\vec{r}) d\vec{S} =$$

$$= \sum_{\sigma(\lambda)} s_\sigma(\lambda) \sum_{\Omega(\sigma)} s_\sigma(\Omega) \left(\int_{C_\Omega}^{C_\sigma} \vec{F} d\vec{e} \right) + \sum_{\partial \sigma(\partial \lambda)} s_\sigma(\lambda) s_{\partial \sigma} \left(\int_{C_{\partial \sigma}}^{C_{\partial \lambda}} \vec{F} d\vec{e} \right). \tag{15}$$

Here, $\vec{S}_{\Omega \sigma \lambda}$ is the area vector of the triangle connecting the gravity center of cell C_Ω, face C_σ, edge C_λ and oriented towards the vector $\vec{e}_\tau(\lambda)$ (see Figure 1a). Equality (15) is obtained using the Stokes theorem for a joint contour of triangles $\vec{S}_\lambda$ around an edge λ.

By reasoning of Section 3.2 (see also (8), (9)), we can assume

$$f_\lambda = V_\lambda \overline{ROG\vec{F}} \tag{16}$$

believing

$$\bar{F}(\sigma)h'(\sigma) = \sum_{\Omega(\sigma)} s_\sigma(\Omega)(\int_{C_\Omega}^{C_\sigma} \vec{F}d\vec{e}), \qquad (17)$$

$$(\vec{F}d\vec{h})_\Sigma(\partial\lambda) = \sum_{\partial\sigma(\partial\lambda)} s_\sigma(\lambda)s_{\partial\sigma}(\int_{C_{\partial\sigma}}^{C_{\partial\lambda}} \vec{F}d\vec{e}). \qquad (18)$$

By virtue of condition (12), when studying the convergence of the difference scheme (13), (14), we will also instead of (6) assume

$$(\vec{\hbar}d\vec{h})_\Sigma(\partial\lambda) = \sum_{\partial\sigma(\partial\lambda)} s_\sigma(\lambda)s_{\partial\sigma}(\int_{C_{\partial\sigma}}^{C_{\partial\lambda}} \vec{H}d\vec{e}), \qquad (19)$$

$$\int_{C_{\partial\sigma}}^{C_{\partial\lambda}} \vec{H}d\vec{e} = \int_{C_{\partial\sigma}}^{C_{\partial\lambda}} \vec{F}d\vec{e}. \qquad (20)$$

4.2. Solvability of the Difference Problem

We study the solvability conditions for problems (13), (14), and (20). Introduce internal rotation $RNG : (\sigma) \to (\lambda)$ as

$$S'_\tau\overline{RNG\vec{\hbar}} = \sum_{\sigma(\lambda)} s_\sigma(\lambda)\vec{\hbar}(\sigma)h'(\sigma) = S'_\tau\overline{ROG\vec{\hbar}} - (\vec{\hbar}d\vec{h})_\Sigma(\partial\lambda),$$

$$S'_\tau(\lambda) = V_\lambda/h_\tau(\lambda), \quad h'(\sigma) = V_\sigma/S(\sigma).$$

Obviously, by virtue of (5),

$$(e', \overline{RNG\vec{\hbar}})_\lambda = (\vec{\hbar}, (ROD\vec{e})')_\sigma.$$

The homogeneous system of equations corresponding to the problems (13), (14), and (20) has the form

$$V_\lambda \overline{RNG\vec{\hbar}} = 0, \quad \vec{\hbar}' = (ROD\vec{e})', \qquad (21)$$

$$(e', \overline{RNG\vec{\hbar}})_\lambda = (\vec{\hbar}, (ROD\vec{e})')_\sigma = (G(ROD\vec{e})', (ROD\vec{e})')_\sigma \geq 0.$$

Hence, we see that the operator of homogeneous system $RNGROD : (\lambda) \to (\lambda)$ is self-adjoint and non-negative. Thus, the solution of a conjugate homogeneous system has the property $(ROD\vec{e})' = 0$ (for example, $\vec{e} = const$). The orthogonality condition on the right-hand side in (13) according to (8) has the form

$$\sum_\lambda e'(\lambda)[f_\lambda - (\vec{\hbar}d\vec{h})_\Sigma(\partial\lambda)] = 0$$

or, taking into account (16)–(20), we have

$$(e', \overline{RNG\vec{F}})_\lambda = (\vec{F}, (ROD\vec{e})')_\sigma = 0.$$

Thus, since $(ROD\vec{e})' = 0$, for any $\vec{F}$ in the solenoidal representation $\vec{f} = \text{curl}\,\vec{F}$ in accordance with (17), the condition of orthogonality of the solution of the homogeneous conjugate system of Equation (21) and the right-hand side (13) under condition (20) is fulfilled. This is the condition for the solvability of problem (13), (14), (20) by the Fredholm matrix theorem [33].

4.3. Accuracy of the Difference Scheme

Now, consider the question of accuracy of difference scheme (13), (14), (20).

Integrating (10) over the area $\vec{S}_\lambda$ around the edge λ, we find

$$V_\lambda \overline{ROG\vec{H}} = f_\lambda$$

where

$$\overline{H}(\sigma)h'(\sigma) = \sum_{\Omega(\sigma)} s_\sigma(\Omega)\left(\int_{C_\Omega}^{C_\sigma} \vec{H}d\vec{e}\right), \qquad (22)$$

$$(\vec{H}d\vec{h})_\Sigma(\partial\lambda) = \sum_{\partial\sigma(\partial\lambda)} s_\sigma(\lambda)s_{\partial\sigma}\left(\int_{C_{\partial\sigma}}^{C_{\partial\lambda}} \vec{H}d\vec{e}\right) \qquad (23)$$

and, subtracting (13) from this equation, we obtain

$$V_\lambda \overline{RGN(\vec{H}-\vec{\hbar})} = 0. \qquad (24)$$

Conditions (24) mean that, in the cell Ω, there is a grid function ξ_Ω such that

$$\overline{H}-\hbar = \overline{GRAD\xi} = \frac{\Delta\xi}{h'}$$

and constant on the boundary faces $\partial\sigma$, i.e., $\xi_{\partial\sigma} = const$. This constant will be considered equal to zero, $const = 0$. We obtain the equation that the function ξ satisfies. We have

$$G^{-1}\overline{GRAD\xi} = H'-\hbar', \quad GH' = \overline{H}.$$

Summing up this equality over the cell faces Ω, taking into account $DIV\vec{\hbar}=0$ (see (14)), we obtain

$$DIV\overrightarrow{GRAD\xi} = DIV\vec{H}$$

by (2); taking into account $\xi_{\partial\sigma} = 0$, we have

$$(G(GRAD\xi)', (GRAD\xi)')_\sigma = (G(GRAD\xi)', H')_\sigma \geq 0.$$

From identity (2) for $\xi_{\partial\sigma} = 0$, for any difference solenoidal function $\overrightarrow{ROD\vec{E}}$ (i.e., $DIV\overrightarrow{ROD\vec{E}} = 0$), by virtue of its orthogonality to $\overrightarrow{GRAD\xi}$, we have

$$\|GRAD\xi\|_\sigma^2 = (G(GRAD\xi)', H'-(ROD\vec{E})')_\sigma \leq \|GRAD\xi\|_\sigma \cdot \|H-ROD\vec{E}\|_\sigma.$$

Here, as applied (3), which determines $(ROD\vec{E})'$, we have

$$E'(\lambda)h_\tau(\lambda) = \int_\lambda \vec{E}d\vec{e} \qquad (25)$$

and the integrals of the exact solution $\vec{E}$ (see (11)) are taken along the edges λ oriented by $\vec{e}_\tau(\lambda)$. The norms of grid vectors on the faces σ here are understood $\|X\|_\sigma = \sqrt{(GX', X')_\sigma}$, as well as $\|X\|_* = \sqrt{(X,X)_*}$, $(X,Y)_* = \sum_\sigma X(\sigma)Y(\sigma)$.

The boundaries of the spectrum of a self-adjoint, positive definite operator $V_\sigma G$: $(\sigma) \to (\sigma)$ consisting of Gram matrices $Gr'_\sigma(\sigma, \tilde{\sigma})$ in mutual bases (see Section 2), provided that tetrahedral mesh is non-degenerate, can be estimated as

$$0 < \frac{\gamma_1}{h}(X,X)_* \leq (V_\sigma GX, X)_* \leq \frac{\gamma_2}{h}(X,X)_*.$$

The corresponding estimate for the inverse operator has the form

$$0 < \frac{h}{\gamma_2}(X,X)_* \leq ((V_\sigma G)^{-1}X,X)_* \leq \frac{h}{\gamma_1}(X,X)_*.$$

Here, γ_1 and γ_2 are bounded ($O(1)$) quantities that do not tend to zero and do not depend on the grid step $h > 0$.

A mesh is considered non-degenerate if:

1. There is a parameter $h > 0$ characterizing the partition detail of computational domain O and having the meaning of linear dimensions of grid elements.

2. The unreasonable sizes of grid elements are uniformly evaluated for the entire grid family:

$$a_1 h^3 \leq V_\Omega \leq a_2 h^3, \quad b_1 h^2 \leq S(\sigma) \leq b_2 h^2, \quad c_1 h \leq h_\tau(\lambda) \leq c_2 h.$$

3. The ratio of nonspecific areas of faces $S(\sigma)$, as well as the lengths of edges $h_\tau(\lambda)$ included in one basis ϕ, uniformly across h, does not tend to zero and is bounded above by the number $O(1)$.

4. Among the dihedral and flat corners of the cells Ω, there are no very sharp and very obtuse ones, i.e., they are all uniformly across h enclosed in the range from Θ to $\pi - \Theta$ with a non-zero angle $\Theta = O(1)$.

Next, we obtain

$$\|GRAD\xi\|_\sigma^2 \leq \|H - RO D\vec{E}\|_\sigma^2 =$$
$$= ((H' - (RO D\vec{E})'), (V_\sigma G)(H' - (RO D\vec{E})'))_* \leq \frac{h}{\gamma_1}\|(V_\sigma G)(H' - (RO D\vec{E})')\|_*^2.$$

On the face σ according to (22), we have

$$[(V_\sigma G) H'](\sigma) = \overline{H}(\sigma) h'(\sigma) = \sum_{\Omega(\sigma)} s_\sigma(\Omega) [\vec{H}_{C\sigma} \cdot \overrightarrow{C_\Omega C_\sigma} + O(h^2)].$$

Here, $\vec{H}_{C\sigma}$ is the magnetic field for solving problems (10), (11), and (20) at the gravity center C_σ of face σ (see Figure 1a).

According to (3) and (25), on face σ, we estimate

$$(RO D\vec{E})'(\tilde{\sigma}) = \frac{1}{S(\tilde{\sigma})} \sum_{\lambda(\tilde{\sigma})} s_\lambda(\tilde{\sigma}) \int_\lambda \vec{E} d\vec{e} =$$
$$= \frac{1}{S(\tilde{\sigma})} \int_{\tilde{\sigma}} curl\, \vec{E} d\vec{S} = \frac{1}{S(\tilde{\sigma})} \int_{\tilde{\sigma}} \vec{H} d\vec{S} = [\vec{H}_{C\sigma} + O(h)]\vec{e}(\tilde{\sigma}).$$

The last integral is taken over the oriented area of the face $S(\tilde{\sigma})\vec{e}(\tilde{\sigma})$ from the operator template $V_\sigma G$ on the face σ. $S(\tilde{\sigma})$ is a specific area of the face $\tilde{\sigma}$. Obviously on the face σ,

$$[(V_\sigma G)\vec{e}](\sigma) = \sum_{\Omega(\sigma)} \sum_{\phi(\sigma)\in\Omega} \sum_{\tilde{\sigma}(\phi)} V_\phi Gr'_\phi(\sigma,\tilde{\sigma})\vec{e}(\tilde{\sigma}) = \sum_{\Omega(\sigma)} \sum_{\phi(\sigma)\in\Omega} V_\phi \vec{e}'_\phi(\nu) -$$
$$= \sum_{\Omega(\sigma)} s_\sigma(\Omega) \cdot \overrightarrow{C_\Omega C_\sigma}.$$

Hence,

$$[(V_\sigma G)(RO D\vec{E})'](\sigma) = \sum_{\Omega(\sigma)} \sum_{\phi(\sigma)\in\Omega} \sum_{\tilde{\sigma}(\phi)} V_\phi Gr'_\phi(\sigma,\tilde{\sigma})[\vec{H}_{C\sigma} +$$
$$O(h)]\vec{e}(\tilde{\sigma}) = \vec{H}_{C\sigma} \sum_{\Omega(\sigma)} s_\sigma(\Omega) \overrightarrow{C_\Omega C_\sigma} + O(h^2).$$

We see
$$[(V_\sigma G)(H' - (ROD\vec{E})')](\sigma) = O(h^2),$$
i.e.,
$$\|H - \hbar\|_\sigma^2 \leq \frac{h}{\gamma_1} \sum_\sigma O(h^4) = O(h^2),$$

because in total, the summation $\sum_\sigma$ contains $O(h^{-3})$ terms.

Finally, we obtain an estimation
$$\|H - \hbar\|_\sigma = O(h)$$

which shows the convergence of the considered difference problems (13), (14), and (20) to the continuum problems (10) and (11) with the boundary condition $\vec{H}_\tau|_\Sigma$ with the first order of accuracy on smooth solutions.

5. Evolution of Electromagnetic Energy

In the numerical modeling of astrophysical problems with consideration of the magnetohydrodynamic phenomena, the processes of matter supercompression may occur (the density changes by several orders of magnitude). Thus, it is important to take into account the corresponding energy transformations of magnetohydrodynamic, as well as kinetic, and internal energy during the evolution of a star at a discrete level. This problem is solved by constructing a completely conservative difference transformation [4] of the magnetic energy of the medium, which considers these magnetohydrodynamic processes.

Accounting for magnetohydrodynamic forces in the construction of completely conservative difference schemes is associated with significant difficulties [4]. Using the method of support operators [1], an integrally consistent difference scheme is proposed in this work, which makes it possible to match the change in the kinetic, internal, and magnetohydrodynamic energies [30]. As a basic operator, this method uses the result of varying the magnetohydrodynamic energy of the system, which is a discrete convolution of two tensors. The first tensor is the Maxwell tensor in the difference medium under study, which is fully responsible for all magnetohydrodynamic processes unfolding against the background of the hydrodynamic motion of matter. The second tensor is the symmetrized strain rate tensor, which represents kinematic motions in this system. The operator conjugate to the convolution of these tensors, due to the technology of the support operator method, automatically gives a magnetic force (the divergence of the Maxwell tensor) acting on the nodal balance domains of the difference medium.

In conclusion, let us consider the issue of applying the developed tools for discrete integrally consistent modeling of rotational operations of vector analysis in application to magnetohydrodynamic problems.

Let O be a flux region with a surface Σ ($d\vec{s}$ is the externally oriented area) and a mass M concentrated in it. dM is the constant mass of Lagrangian particles of the medium occupying the volume dV. In the magnetohydrodynamic approximation, the integral balance of magnetic energy in a medium has the form [31]:

$$\frac{c^2}{8\pi} \int_{O(\hat{t})} \hat{\vec{\hbar}}^2 d\hat{V} = \frac{c^2}{8\pi} \int_{O(t)} \vec{\hbar}^2 dV + \int_t^{\hat{t}} d\tau \left(\int_{O(\tau)} (D_\hbar - D) dV - \int_{\Sigma(\tau)} \vec{q} d\vec{s} \right). \quad (26)$$

The Maxwell tensor is given by the representation $t_\hbar = (c^2/4\pi)(\vec{\hbar} \cdot \vec{\hbar} - 0.5\vec{\hbar}^2 \delta)$ where δ is the metric tensor, $\vec{\hbar}$ is the magnetic field strength divided by the speed of light c, and $\vec{e}$ is the electric field strength in the coordinate system associated with the moving particle. $D = (c^2/4\pi)\vec{e}curl\vec{\hbar}$ is the Joule heating per unit volume of the medium. $D_\hbar = tr(t_\hbar t_v)$ is the magnetic dissipative function. The kinematic tensor is given by the representation

$t_v = 0.5(d\vec{v}/d\vec{r} + grad\vec{v})$, where $\vec{v}$ is the velocity of the medium particles. $\vec{q} = (c^2/4\pi)[\vec{e} \times \vec{h}]$ is the Poynting vector, which determines the external flux of electromagnetic energy.

The corresponding Maxwell equations for the electromagnetic field in the circulation circuits H_τ and H limiting the surface Σ are written as [31]:

$$d\left(\int_\Sigma \vec{h}d\vec{s}\right)/dt = \oint_{H_\tau} \vec{e}d\vec{h}_\tau, \quad \int_\Sigma X_\tau^{-1}\vec{e}d\vec{s} = \oint_H \vec{h}d\vec{h}. \tag{27}$$

Here, d/dt is the substantial derivative. X_τ is the positive definite tensor of magnetic viscosity in the medium ($X_\tau = c^2/(4\pi\sigma)$). For the current density in a medium with conductivity σ, Ohm's law is also valid in the form: $\vec{j} = \sigma\vec{e} = (c^2/4\pi)curl\vec{h}$, $\vec{e} = X_\tau curl\vec{h}$. On a closed surface Σ, the relation $\int_\Sigma \vec{h}d\vec{s} = 0$ follows from the condition of the absence of magnetic charges.

Passing to discretization, we represent the evolution of the magnetic field on the faces of the mesh $(\sigma).(\varphi)$ (the first Maxwell equation from (27)) in the form

$$d(\hbar'S)/dt = -S(ROD\,\vec{e})'. \tag{28}$$

From (28), we see that, in the absence of magnetic charges in the mesh cell Ω at the initial moment, the condition of their absence is always satisfied in this cell. The normal components of the magnetic field $\hbar'(\sigma)$ are assumed to be continuous on the mesh faces.

Furthermore, on the mesh $(\lambda).(\varphi)$, analogous with the metric operator $G_\tau : (\lambda) \to (\lambda)$ (see Section 3.1), for a self-adjoint, positive-definite magnetic conductivity tensor $\rho_{\tau\varphi} = (X_\tau^{-1})_\varphi$, which approximates the reciprocal magnetic viscosity in the medium in the mesh bases φ, we introduce the metric conductivity operator $G_{\rho\tau} : (\lambda) \to (\lambda)$ and the second Maxwell equation from (27) for the electric field flux can be represented as

$$G_{\rho\tau}e' = \overline{ROG\hbar}, \quad G_{\rho\tau}e' = 1/V_\lambda \sum_{\varphi(\lambda)} V_\varphi \sum_{\tilde\lambda(\varphi)} Gr'_{\rho\tau\varphi}(\lambda,\tilde\lambda)e'(\tilde\lambda). \tag{29}$$

Here, the Gram matrices of the conductivity of the medium are defined as

$$Gr'_{\rho\tau\varphi}(\lambda,\tilde\lambda) = (\vec{e}'_{\tau\varphi}(\lambda), \rho_{\tau\varphi}\vec{e}'_{\tau\varphi}(\tilde\lambda)).$$

Obviously, the operator $G_{\rho\tau} = (G_{\rho\tau})^* > 0$ is also self-adjoint and positive definite on the mesh $(\lambda).(\varphi)$. The tangential components $e'(\lambda)$ of the electric field are considered continuous on the mesh $(\lambda).(\varphi)$.

From (28), taking into account (3) from Section 3.1, it follows

$$(c^2/4\pi) \sum_\sigma V_\sigma \hbar(\sigma)[1/S(\sigma)][d(\hbar'(\sigma)S(\sigma))/dt] = -\left(\int_O DdV\right)_\Delta - \left(\int_\Sigma \vec{q}d\vec{s}\right)_\Delta.$$

Here, the Joule heating of the entire volume of the medium

$$\left(\int_O DdV\right)_\Delta = (c^2/4\pi)(G_{\rho\tau}e', e')_\lambda = \sum_\varphi D_\varphi V_\varphi \geq 0$$

is defined as its sum in local bases φ

$$D_\varphi = (c^2/4\pi) \sum_{\lambda(\varphi),\tilde\lambda(\varphi)} Gr'_{\rho\tau\varphi}(\lambda,\tilde\lambda)e'(\lambda)e'(\tilde\lambda) = (c^2/4\pi)(\vec{e}_\varphi, \rho_{\tau\varphi}\vec{e}_\varphi) \geq 0$$

with electric field strengths in these bases $\vec{e}_\varphi = \sum_{\lambda(\varphi)} e'(\lambda) \vec{e}'_{\tau\varphi}(\lambda)$. It is also obvious that, for the flux of the Poynting vector $\vec{q} = \frac{c^2}{4\pi}[\vec{e} \times \vec{h}]$ through the surface Σ, bounding the required area O, the representation follows

$$\left(\int_\Sigma \vec{q} d\vec{s}\right)_\Delta = -(c^2/4\pi)\sum_{\partial \lambda} e'(\partial\lambda) h_\tau(\partial\lambda)(\vec{h}dh)_\Sigma(\partial\lambda).$$

Let us now transform the expression for changing the magnetic energy (see (26)) on the mesh $(\sigma).(\varphi)$ with the metric operator G

$$(c^2/8\pi)d[(\bar{h}, \bar{h}')_\sigma]/dt = (c^2/4\pi)\sum_\sigma V_\sigma \bar{h}(\sigma)[1/S(\sigma)][d(\bar{h}'(\sigma)S(\sigma))/dt] + \sum_\varphi D_{\hbar\varphi} V_\varphi,$$

$$D_{\hbar\varphi} = (c^2/4\pi) \sum_{\sigma(\varphi),\tilde{\sigma}(\varphi)} \hbar'(\sigma)\hbar'(\tilde{\sigma})(t^{\hbar}_{\nu(-1/2)\varphi})^{\sigma\tilde{\sigma}},$$

$$(t^{\hbar}_{\nu(-1/2)\varphi})^{\sigma\tilde{\sigma}} = \frac{V_\varphi}{2h'_\varphi(\sigma)h'_\varphi(\tilde{\sigma})} \frac{d}{dt}\left(\frac{h'_\varphi(\sigma)h'_\varphi(\tilde{\sigma})Gr'_\varphi(\sigma,\tilde{\sigma})}{V_\varphi}\right),$$

$$(t^{\hbar}_{\nu\varphi})^{\sigma\tilde{\sigma}} = 1/[2h'_\varphi(\sigma)h'_\varphi(\tilde{\sigma})]\frac{d}{dt}\left(h'_\varphi(\sigma)h'_\varphi(\tilde{\sigma})Gr'_\varphi(\sigma,\tilde{\sigma})\right), \quad h'_\varphi(\sigma) = V_\varphi/S(\sigma).$$

Finally, we have the law of conservation of magnetic energy:

$$(c^2/8\pi)d[(Gh', h')_\sigma]/dt = \sum_\varphi D_{\hbar\varphi} V_\varphi - \left(\int_O DdV\right)_\Delta - \left(\int_\Sigma \vec{q}d\vec{s}\right)_\Delta.$$

Since $D_\hbar = (c^2/4\pi)tr(\vec{\bar{h}} \cdot \vec{\bar{h}}(t_\nu - 0.5tr(t_\nu)\delta))$, we conclude that the quantities $(t^{\hbar}_{\nu(-1/2)\varphi})^{\sigma\tilde{\sigma}}$ and $(t^{\hbar}_{\nu\varphi})^{\sigma\tilde{\sigma}}$ approximate on the mesh $(\sigma).(\varphi)$ the magnetically consistent contravariant tensor $(t_\nu - 0.5tr(t_\nu)\delta)^{\sigma\tilde{\sigma}}$ and contravariant symmetrized strain velocity tensor $(t_\nu)^{\sigma\tilde{\sigma}}$, respectively.

6. Conclusions

The work is devoted to the construction and justification of difference schemes of the support operator method in relation to the modeling of repeated rotational operations of vector analysis (*curl curl*) for problems of magnetohydrodynamics. Discrete algorithms of the method of support operators on spatial grids of irregular structure do not approximate equations in the local sense. Because of this, it becomes necessary to prove the convergence of these schemes to the exact solution. The solution to this problem is possible after analyzing the structure of the approximation error of the schemes under consideration. In this work, the convergence of difference schemes of the support operator method is proved for repeated rotational operations of vector analysis based on classical solutions of a model magnetostatic problem. Convergence is proved in the root-mean-square sense with the first order of accuracy on irregular tetrahedral meshes. The case of zero eigenvalues of the spectral problem is considered. The proof is carried out in mesh-dependent norms related to the energy of the metric operator of the mesh, which is not subject to any restrictions, except for its non-degeneracy. For the research carried out, generalized centroid-tensor metric representations of repeated operations of tensor analysis (*div*, *grad*, and *curl*) have been developed. Metric representations have flux-circulation properties and are integrally consistent on meshes of irregular structure. The developed mesh centroid-tensor metric formalism is also used in this work to analyze the time evolution of electromagnetic energy on a mesh in the magnetohydrodynamic approximation. Generalized centroid-tensor metric transformations can also be used in other problems in the theory of the support operator method. In addition, an algorithm for the evolution of electromagnetic energy, integrally consistent with the kinetic and internal energies of the medium, has been developed in the work. As a result, a completely conservative difference transformation of the magnetic energy of the medium was constructed, which takes into account these magnetohydrodynamic processes. Accounting for magnetohydrodynamic forces in the construction of completely conservative difference schemes is associated with significant difficulties. Integral matching of kinetic and magnetohydrodynamic energies due to the methodology of support operators automatically gives the magnetic force acting on the nodal balance domains of the difference medium.

Author Contributions: Conceptualization, Y.P.; methodology, P.R.; formal analysis, V.P.; investigation, Y.P., V.P. and P.R.; writing—original draft preparation, Y.P. and P.R.; writing—review and editing, Y.P. and V.P.; supervision, Y.P. and V.P. All authors have read and agreed to the published version of the manuscript.

Funding: This research was carried out within the framework of the state assignment of KIAM RAS.

Data Availability Statement: Not applicable.

Conflicts of Interest: The authors declare no conflict of interest.

References

1. Samarskii, A.A.; Koldoba, A.V.; Poveshchenko, Y.A.; Tishkin, V.F.; Favorskii, A.P. *Different Schemes on the Non-Regulated Grids*; CJSC "Criterion": Minsk, Belarus, 1996.
2. Shashkov, M. *Conservative Finite-Difference Methods on General Grids*; CRC Press: Boca Raton, FL, USA, 1996.
3. Lipnikov, K.; Manzini, G.; Shashkov, M. Mimetic finite difference method. *J. Comput. Phys.* **2014**, *257*, 1163–1227. [CrossRef]
4. Samarskii, A.A.; Popov, Y.P. *Difference Methods for Solving Problems of Gas Dynamics*; Nauka: Moscow, Russia, 1992.
5. Hyman, J.D.; Sweeney, M.R.; Gable, C.W.; Svyatsky, D.; Lipnikov, K.; Moulton, J.D. Flow and transport in three-dimensional discrete fracture matrix models using mimetic finite difference on a conforming multi-dimensional mesh. *J. Comput. Phys.* **2022**, *466*, 111396. [CrossRef]
6. Coon, E.T.; Moulton, J.D.; Kikinzon, E.; Berndt, M.; Manzini, G.; Garimella, R.; Lipnikov, K.; Painter, S.L. Coupling surface flow and subsurface flow in complex soil structures using mimetic finite differences. *Adv. Water Resour.* **2020**, *144*, 103701. [CrossRef]
7. Gyrya, V.; Lipnikov, K. The arbitrary order mimetic finite difference method for a diffusion equation with a non-symmetric diffusion tensor. *J. Comput. Phys.* **2017**, *348*, 549–566. [CrossRef]
8. Manzini, G.; Lipnikov, K.; Moulton, J.D.; Shashkov, M. Convergence analysis of the mimetic finite difference method for elliptic problems with staggered discretizations of diffusion coefficients. *SIAM J. Numer. Anal.* **2017**, *55*, 2956–2981. [CrossRef]
9. Kim, E.; Lipnikov, K. The mimetic finite difference method for the Landau–Lifshitz equation. *J. Comput. Phys.* **2017**, *328*, 109–130. [CrossRef]
10. Lipnikov, K.; Manzini, G. A high-order mimetic method on unstructured polyhedral meshes for the diffusion equation. *J. Comput. Phys.* **2014**, *272*, 360–385. [CrossRef]
11. Brezzi, F.; Lipnikov, K.; Shashkov, M. Convergence of the mimetic finite difference method for diffusion problems on polyhedral meshes. *SIAM J. Numer. Anal.* **2005**, *43*, 1872–1896. [CrossRef]
12. Attipoe, D.S.; Tambue, A. Convergence of the mimetic finite difference and fitted mimetic finite difference method for options pricing. *Appl. Math. Comput.* **2021**, *401*, 126060. [CrossRef]
13. Guevara-Jordan, J.M.; Rojas, S.; Freites-Villegas, M.; Castillo, J.E. Convergence of a mimetic finite difference method for static diffusion equation. *Adv. Differ. Equ.* **2007**, *2007*, 012303. [CrossRef]
14. Zangooee, M.R.; Hosseinzadeh, K.; Ganji, D.D. Investigation of three-dimensional hybrid nanofluid flow affected by nonuniform MHD over exponential stretching/shrinking plate. *Nonlinear Eng.* **2022**, *11*, 143–155. [CrossRef]
15. Gulzar, M.M.; Aslam, A.; Waqas, M.; Javed, M.A.; Hosseinzadeh, K. A nonlinear mathematical analysis for magneto-hyperbolic-tangent liquid featuring simultaneous aspects of magnetic field, heat source and thermal stratification. *Appl. Nanosci.* **2020**, *10*, 4513–4518. [CrossRef]
16. Ghadikolaei, S.S.; Hosseinzadeh, K.; Hatami, M.; Ganji, D.D. MHD boundary layer analysis for micropolar dusty fluid containing hybrid nanoparticles ($Cu'Al_2O_3$) over a porous medium. *J. Mol. Liq.* **2018**, *268*, 813–823. [CrossRef]
17. Hosseinzadeh, K.; Asadi, A.; Mogharrebi, A.R.; Khalesi, J.; Mousavisani, S.; Ganji, D.D. Entropy generation analysis of ($CH_2OH)_2$ containing CNTs nanofluid flow under effect of MHD and thermal radiation. *Case Stud. Therm. Eng.* **2019**, *14*, 100482. [CrossRef]
18. Hosseinzadeh, K.; Salehi, S.; Mardani, M.R.; Mahmoudi, F.Y.; Waqas, M.; Ganji, D.D. Investigation of nano-bioconvective fluid motile microorganism and nanoparticle flow by considering MHD and thermal radiation. *Inf. Med. Unlocked* **2020**, *21*, 100462. [CrossRef]
19. Mogharrebi, A.R.; Ganji, A.R.D.; Hosseinzadeh, K.; Roghani, S.; Asadi, A.; Fazlollahtabar, A. Investigation of magnetohydrodynamic nanofluid flow contain motile oxytactic microorganisms over rotating cone. *Int. J. Numer. Method Heat Fluid Flow* **2021**, *31*, 3394–3412. [CrossRef]
20. Lebedev, V.I. Difference analogues of orthogonal decompositions of basic differential operators and some boundary value problems of mathematical physics, Part I. *USSR Comput. Math. Math. Phys.* **1964**, *4*, 69–92. [CrossRef]

21. Lebedev, V.I. Difference analogues of orthogonal decompositions of basic differential operators and some boundary value problems of mathematical physics, Part II. *USSR Comput. Math. Math. Phys.* **1964**, *4*, 36–50. [CrossRef]
22. Samarskii, A.A.; Lazarov, R.L.; Makarov, V.L. *Difference Schemes for Differential Equations with Generalized Solutions*; Nauka: Moscow, Russia, 1987.
23. Goloviznin, V.M.; Samarskii, A.A.; Favorskii, A.P. A variational approach to constructing finite difference mathematical models in hydrodynamics. *Proc. USSR Acad. Sci.* **1977**, *235*, 1285–1288.
24. Mikhailova, N.V.; Tishkin, V.F.; Tyurina, N.N.; Favorskii, A.P.; Shashkov, M.Y. Numerical modelling of two-dimensional gas-dynamic flows on a variable-structure mesh. *Comput. Math. Math. Phys.* **1986**, *26*, 74–84. [CrossRef]
25. Solov'ev, A.V.; Solov'eva, E.V.; Tishkin, V.F.; Favorskii, A.P.; Shashkov, M.Y. Investigation of the approximation of difference operators on a grid of dirichlet cells. *Differ. Equ.* **1986**, *22*, 1227–1237.
26. Solov'ev, A.V.; Solov'eva, E.V.; Tishkin, V.F.; Favorskii, A.P.; Shashkov, M.Y. Difference schemes of the method of "Dirichlet particles", which preserve the one-dimensionality of gas dynamic flows in Cartesian, cylindrical and spherical coordinates. *Differ. Equ.* **1987**, *23*, 2133–2147.
27. Krasnov, M.L.; Kiselev, A.I.; Makarenko, G.I. *Vector Analysis*; Mir Publishers: Moscow, Russia, 1983.
28. Samarskii, A.A.; Tishkin, V.F.; Favorskii, A.P.; Shashkov, M.Y. Operator difference scheme. *Differ. Equ.* **1981**, *17*, 1317–1327.
29. Koldoba, A.V.; Poveshchenko, Y.A.; Gasilova, I.V.; Dorofeeva, E.Y. Numerical schemes of the support operators method for elasticity theory equations. *Math. Model.* **2012**, *24*, 86–96.
30. Poveshchenko, Y.A.; Podryga, V.O.; Sharova, Y.S. Integral-consistent methods for calculating self-gravitating and magnetohydro-dynamic phenomena. *KIAM Prepr.* **2018**, *160*, 1–21. [CrossRef]
31. Kulikovskii, A.G.; Lyubimov, G.A. *Magnetic Hydrodynamics*, 3rd ed.; Logos: Moscow, Russia, 2011.
32. Korn, G.; Korn, T. *Handbook of Mathematics*; Nauka: Moscow, Russia, 1973.
33. Voevodin, V.V.; Kuznetsov, Y.A. *Matrices and Computing*; Nauka: Moscow, Russia, 1984.

Article

Modeling of Mechanisms of Wave Formation for COVID-19 Epidemic

Alexander Leonov, Oleg Nagornov * and Sergey Tyuflin

Department of High Mathematics, National Research Nuclear University MEPhI, Kashirskoe Shosse, 31, 115409 Moscow, Russia
* Correspondence: nagornov@yandex.ru

Abstract: Two modifications with variable coefficients of the well-known SEIR model for epidemic development in the application to the modeling of the infection curves of COVID-19 are considered. The data for these models are information on the number of infections each day obtained from the Johns Hopkins Coronavirus Resource Center database. In our paper, we propose special methods based on Tikhonov regularization for models' identification on the class of piecewise constant coefficients. In contrast to the model with constant coefficients, which cannot always accurately describe some of infection curves, the first model is able to approximate them for different countries with an accuracy of 2–8%. The second model considered in the article takes into account external sources of infection in the form of an inhomogeneous term in one of the model equations and is able to approximate the data with a slightly better accuracy of 2–4%. For the second model, we also consider the possibility of using other input data, namely the number of infected people per day. Such data are used to model infection curves for several waves of the COVID-19 epidemic, including part of the Omicron wave. Numerical experiments carried out for a number of countries show that the waves of external sources of infection found are ahead of the wave of infection by 10 or more days. At the same time, other piecewise constant coefficients of the model change relatively slowly. These models can be applied fairly reliably to approximate many waves of infection curves with high precision and can be used to identify external and hidden sources of infection. This is the advantage of our models.

Keywords: COVID-19 pandemic; inverse problems; time-dependent SEIR model

MSC: 34A55

Citation: Leonov, A.; Nagornov, O.; Tyuflin, S. Modeling of Mechanisms of Wave Formation for COVID-19 Epidemic. *Mathematics* **2023**, *11*, 167. https://doi.org/10.3390/math11010167

Academic Editor: Jiancang Zhuang

Received: 16 November 2022
Revised: 24 December 2022
Accepted: 26 December 2022
Published: 29 December 2022

Copyright: © 2022 by the authors. Licensee MDPI, Basel, Switzerland. This article is an open access article distributed under the terms and conditions of the Creative Commons Attribution (CC BY) license (https://creativecommons.org/licenses/by/4.0/).

1. Introduction

The mathematical modeling of epidemics has a long history (see, for example, [1]). However, the spread of COVID-19 has given this area of research a significant expansion and advancement. Due to the avalanche of publications on this topic, we cannot discuss all areas in detail here. We only note that along with the classical SIR-type models based on ordinary differential equations and improved recently (see, for example, [2,3]), models have appeared that include partial differential equations (see, for example, [4]), models with stochastic differential equations (e.g., [5]), agent-based models [6], etc. In turn, each of these areas has received internal development and generalization. For example, in SIR models, a direction associated with the use of fractional derivatives has emerged (see, e.g., [7], etc.). In our work, we study some extension of the classical SIR-type model and do not use other approaches.

SIR models have the form of specific systems of ordinary differential equations and contain coefficients that have an important epidemiological meaning. However, some of the coefficients, and sometimes all, are unknown. Therefore, the question of finding them is very relevant, using, for example, data on the dynamics of the number of infected people and, possibly, other data. Thus, an inverse coefficient problem arises for the corresponding SIR system. Methods for solving such inverse problems are well developed. An overview of such methods can be found, for example, in [8]. Specific implementations of the methods, based mainly on various optimization algorithms, are detailed in numerous works (see, for example, [9–15] and others). A detailed analysis of these approaches and a block diagram of their connection are given, for example, in [16].

In the classical formulation of inverse problems for SIR models, the coefficients are assumed to be constant. However, it turned out that such models are not always adequate to epidemiological data, and, as a rule, do not explain the emergence of pandemic waves. In this regard, we note a recent publication [17], which proposes a new multi-wave SIR model that can explain the generation of pandemic waves. The principal feature of this model is a new form of differential equations and the use of functions with a retarded argument, while the coefficients of the model are constant.

In our work, we use two other approaches within the framework of SIR models. Our goal is rather modest: an adequate description of the data of the inverse problem, namely, the dynamics of the number of infected for some countries. The first approach uses time-varying coefficients in our SIR model, and here we develop the results of work [18]. To adequately reproduce the data, we solve the inverse coefficient problem for the model on the class of piecewise constant coefficients with some additional restrictions on the latter. This makes it possible to model inverse problem data with sufficiently high accuracy for a number of countries, but does not describe the generation of epidemic waves. This feature can be explained by the fact that standard SIR models, as a rule, are written for closed systems that do not take into account the external flow of infections. Therefore, to describe the emergence of epidemic waves, we supplement the modeling with variable coefficients by assuming that there are unknown external sources of infection that change over time. These can be in the aggregate latent carriers of the infection, which are activated at different times of the year due to weather conditions, as well as carriers of the infection arriving from other countries and other sources. Mathematically, these sources are modeled by including an additional term, represented by an unknown function of time, in one of the equations of our SIR-type model. To find this term and the coefficients, the problem of minimizing the discrepancy between the data and their analogs calculated from the model is solved under restrictions on piecewise constant coefficients and on the source. Based on the coefficients and sources found, it is possible to fairly accurately reproduce data on infections from several waves of the epidemic for a number of countries. We solved this problem using data from The Johns Hopkins Coronavirus Resource Center (CRC) [19] for Austria, the Czech Republic, Germany, France, Italy and Russia. The time of the receipt of data is 10 February 2022. Comparison of COVID-19 cases from different sources has been studied [20]. Due to the size of the article, we are unable to give all these results in detail, so we include figures in the article that correspond only to the calculations for Austria and Russia. For the rest of the countries, we confine ourselves to presenting some numerical data.

2. Modeling of Individual Waves of Epidemic

The SEIR model is widely used in mathematical epidemiology. In this section, we use its modification with variable coefficients from [18]. The model has the following form:

$$\begin{cases} \dot{S} = -\beta(t)S(I+E) \\ \dot{E} = \beta(t)S(I+E) - (\gamma(t) + \delta(t))E, \quad t_0 < t < t_1 \\ \dot{I} = \delta(t)E - \gamma(t)I \end{cases} \quad (1)$$

$$S(t_0) = \alpha, \ E(t_0) = 0, \ I(t_0) = I_0$$

It will be used for different countries with different values for number N of people included in epidemic process. The main variables of the model are defined as follows: $S(t)$ is the proportion of people who can be infected at time t; $E(t)$ is proportion of infected people in whom illness is not identified yet at time t, but they are able to infect surrounding people; and $I(t)$ is the proportion of ill people with confirmed diagnoses at time t. One can calculate the number of people from the entered relative values by multiplying by N. The choice of total number N of people for considered countries is discussed [9]. Moreover, the proportion $R(t)$ of recovered people at time t can be determined from system (1) by using the equation: $\dot{R} = \mu E + \nu I$, $R(t_0) = R_0$. However, we do not use this equation, because our goal is an adequate modeling of the quantity $I(t)$. So, we consider in this section the SEI model (1).

Note that we assume that coefficients of Equation (1) can be variable unlike the standard SEIR model. The time t was measured in days. The coefficients of system (1) have the following meaning: $\beta(t)$ is proportional to probability of infection and is measured in 1/days; $\gamma(t)$ is the reciprocal of the mean time to diagnosis of infection, 1/days; $\delta(t)$ is the inverse value of the average time to cure the patient from the moment of diagnosis, 1/days.

The coefficients can vary due to health measures in specific country. For example, a decrease in $\beta(t)$ can consider the response to introduced restricted measures. A weakening of these measures can result in an increase in $\beta(t)$. An Increase in $\gamma(t)$ can be interpreted as a decrease in the average time of the determination of illness, while an increase in $\delta(t)$ reflects a decrease in the average time of recovering.

Previously, in [18], the inverse problem of finding α, $\beta = \beta(t)$, $\gamma = \gamma(t)$, $\delta = \delta(t)$ from the data $I_{dat}(t)$, I_0 was posed. Similar to [19], the input data for the inverse problem were taken from the statistics of C = confirmed, R = recovered, D = died given in the database of The Johns Hopkins CRC [19] and were computed as $I_{dat}(t) = C - R - D$ for some countries. To model piecewise constant coefficients, we divide the time axis into segments of the form $[t_n, t_{n+1}]$ with constant length $\Delta t = 7$. Then, we solve the inverse problem with constant values α, β, γ, δ separately at each segment. The corresponding solution is found out by the minimization of the following discrepancy functional at $t \in [t_n, t_{n+1}]$:

$$\Phi(\alpha, \beta, \gamma, \delta) = \frac{\|I(t; \alpha, \beta, \gamma, \delta) - I_{dat}(t)\|_{L_2[t_n, t_{n+1}]}}{\|I_{dat}(t)\|_{L_2[t_n, t_{n+1}]}}$$

under a priori constraints of the form $K = \{0 \leq \alpha \leq \alpha_0, 0 \leq \beta \leq \beta_0, 0 \leq \gamma \leq \gamma_0, 0 \leq \delta \leq \delta_0\}$ with estimates $\alpha_0, \beta_0, \gamma_0, \delta_0$ known from the literature. Here, $I(t; \alpha, \beta, \gamma, \delta)$ is the solution of (1) for given α, β, γ, δ. Collecting the results of such minimization for all segments, we obtain a solution in the form of piecewise constant functions $\beta = \beta^*(t)$, $\gamma = \gamma^*(t)$, $\delta = \delta^*(t)$ and of a set $\{\alpha_n\}$. However, such a problem can be ill-posed for each segment, and this is expressed in an ambiguous solution to the discrepancy minimization problem. To isolate a single solution, we used a special variant of Tikhonov regularization [21]. We present it in the form of computation method 1.

Method 1.

Step 1. Set the values of the regularization parameter $\lambda_m = \lambda_0 10^{-m}$ $(m = 0, 1, \ldots)$.

Step 2. For each parameter λ_m and for each segment $[t_n, t_{n+1}]$, $n = 0, 1, \ldots, n_{max}$, we minimize on the set K the Tikhonov functional of the form

$$M^{\lambda_m}(\alpha, \beta, \gamma, \delta) = \lambda_m \Omega(\alpha, \beta, \gamma, \delta) + \Phi^2(\alpha, \beta, \gamma, \delta)$$

where the functional

$$\Omega(\alpha, \beta, \gamma, \delta) = \frac{(\alpha - \alpha_n)^2 + (\beta - \beta_n)^2 + (\gamma - \gamma_n)^2 + (\delta - \delta_n)^2}{\alpha_n^2 + \beta_n^2 + \gamma_n^2 + \delta_n^2}. \quad (2)$$

determines the relative deviation of the parameters from their values α_n, β_n, γ_n, δ_n obtained at the previous minimization on the segment $[t_{n-1}, t_n]$. For $n = 0$, these quantities are equal to zero. So, at step 2 we obtain the coefficients $\alpha_{n+1}(\lambda_m)$, $\beta_{n+1}(\lambda_m)$, $\gamma_{n+1}(\lambda_m)$, $\delta_{n+1}(\lambda_m)$, and solving problem (1) for these coefficients, we then find the functions

$$N_{n+1}(\lambda_m) = \Phi(\alpha_{n+1}(\lambda_m), \beta_{n+1}(\lambda_m), \gamma_{n+1}(\lambda_m), \delta_{n+1}(\lambda_m)),$$
$$\Omega_{n+1}(\lambda_m) = \Omega(\alpha_{n+1}(\lambda_m), \beta_{n+1}(\lambda_m), \gamma_{n+1}(\lambda_m), \delta_{n+1}(\lambda_m)).$$

Step 3. Choice of the regularization parameter $\lambda = \lambda^*$. To calculate it, we first find the averages $N(\lambda_m) = \overline{N_n(\lambda_m)}$, $\Omega(\lambda_m) = \overline{\Omega_n(\lambda_m)}$ across all segments for each λ_m. Next, we build a Pareto curve, $N(\lambda_m)$ vs. $\Omega(\lambda_m)$, which in the theory of regularization is called an L-curve, and next find on it the point closest to the origin. The value of the parameter λ_m corresponding to this point is taken as the optimal value of the regularization parameter λ^*.

Step 4. We repeat step 2 for $\lambda = \lambda^*$ and for each segment $[t_n, t_{n+1}]$ and find out the optimal coefficients α^*_{n+1}, β^*_{n+1}, γ^*_{n+1}, δ^*_{n+1}. Combining these coefficients for all intervals, we obtain the regularized piecewise coefficients

$$\beta = \beta^*(t), \gamma = \gamma^*(t), \delta = \delta^*(t): \quad \beta^*(t) = \beta^*_{n+1}, \gamma^*(t) = \gamma^*_{n+1}, \delta^*(t) = \delta^*_{n+1}, \ t \in [t_n, t_{n+1}], n = 0, 1, \ldots, n_{\max}.$$

Step 5. At the end, we solve system (1) for each interval $[t_n, t_{n+1}]$ with the found coefficients $\alpha^*_{n+1}, \beta^*_{n+1}, \gamma^*_{n+1}, \delta^*_{n+1}$, and so we find the function $I_{calc}(t)$, which is an approximation for $I_{dat}(t)$. At the same time, we find the functions $S_{calc}(t)$, $E_{calc}(t)$.

The procedure described in Method 1 has the following meaning. We try to simultaneously minimize two functionals for each time interval, namely the discrepancy $\Phi(\alpha, \beta, \gamma, \delta)$ and $\Omega(\alpha, \beta, \gamma, \delta)$. This means the best approximation of the problem data using the model while ensuring the smallest change in the model parameters when moving from the previous time interval to the next. To do this, we use a combination of $\Phi(\alpha, \beta, \gamma, \delta)$ and $\Omega(\alpha, \beta, \gamma, \delta)$ in the form of the Tikhonov functional. The weight parameter λ_m shows what is more important for us, to accurately approximate the data or to provide small changes in the model parameters. At step 3, the weight selection procedure gives a compromise value $\lambda = \lambda^*$ for all time intervals at once. So, we provide the smallest deviation of the calculated value $I_{calc}(t)$ from the data $I_{dat}(t)$ for all points in time with the smallest change in the model parameters.

A result of such a procedure for solving the inverse problem is shown in Figure 1 for Russia. All calculations were carried out in MATLAB. The top subplot shows the initial data $I_{dat}(t)$ and calculated approximation $I_{calc}(t)$. The values are converted to the number of people. These curves almost do not differ graphically. The middle subplot shows calculated piecewise coefficients $\beta = \beta^*(t)$, $\gamma = \gamma^*(t)$, $\delta = \delta^*(t)$. The bottom subplot shows the residual values (discrepancy), $\Phi_{\min}(\alpha, \beta, \gamma, \delta)$, when minimizing at each time interval. An important characteristic of Method 1 is the average value for $\Phi_{\min}(\alpha, \beta, \gamma, \delta)$ over all time intervals, $\overline{\Phi}_{\min}$, which characterizes the quality of the approximation of data $I_{dat}(t)$ by the found approximate function $I_{calc}(t)$. For Russia, we obtain $\overline{\Phi}_{\min} = 0.02$. For other countries, these values are presented in Table 1.

Table 1. Accuracy of the approximation of data for Method 1.

Country	Austria	Czech Rep.	Germany	France	Italy
$\overline{\Phi}_{\min}$	0.040	0.071	0.050	0.081	0.077

Thus, the presented procedure for solving the inverse problem makes it possible to approximate the data for model (1) with good accuracy (2–8%). It is interesting to note that the coefficients $\beta = \beta^*(t)$, $\gamma = \gamma^*(t)$, $\delta = \delta^*(t)$ calculated in solving the inverse problem generally change slowly, and this is what we wanted by applying Method 1.

Unfortunately, model (1) does not describe well all waves of the COVID-19 epidemic. Such sharply growing waves as for the Omicron strain are approximated by this model with a significant error. For such waves, the model needs to be corrected by including a mechanism for generating successive waves.

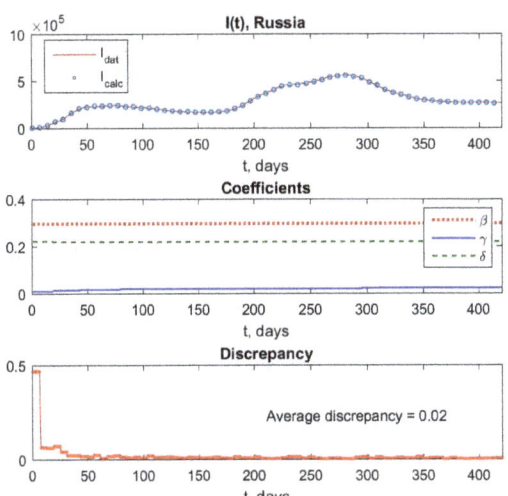

Figure 1. The input and calculated data, the coefficients of the model and discrepancy for epidemic in Russia.

3. A mechanism of Successive Waves Simulation in SEI Model

Some models are known from the literature that describe the mechanism of the generation of epidemic waves (see, e.g., [17]). In this article, we consider one of the possibilities for changing the SEI model (1) so that such generation occurs in it as well. Formally, we ensure this by including an additional term $f(t)$ in the third equation of system (1). After multiplying by N, the function $f(t)$ represents the additional number of infected people per day. Therefore, the new modification of the SEI model has the form

$$\begin{cases} \dot{S} = -\beta(t)S(I+E) \\ \dot{E} = \beta(t)S(I+E) - (\gamma(t) + \delta(t))E, \quad t_0 < t < t_1 \\ \dot{I} = \delta(t)E - \gamma(t)I + f(t) \end{cases} \quad (3)$$

with the same initial conditions $S(t_0) = \alpha$, $E(t_0) = 0$, $I(t_0) = I_0$. This additional term can, for example, be considered as a source of infections associated with hidden carriers that are seasonally activated due to weather changes. Moreover, this term may include the transition of infection into the country in question from abroad. For model (3), we first set the inverse problem of finding the values α, $\beta = \beta(t)$, $\gamma = \gamma(t)$, $\delta = \delta(t)$ and the function $f(t)$ using the same data $I_{dat}(t) = C - R - D$ as in Section 2. We again assume piecewise constancy of the quantities $\beta(t), \gamma(t), \delta(t), f(t)$ on time intervals $[t_n, t_{n+1}]$ and try to minimize a new discrepancy of the form

$$\Phi_1(\alpha, \beta, \gamma, \delta, f) = \frac{\|I(t; \alpha, \beta, \gamma, \delta, f) - I_{dat}(t)\|_{L_2[t_n, t_{n+1}]}}{\|I_{dat}(t)\|_{L_2[t_n, t_{n+1}]}}.$$

for such interval under restrictions $(\alpha, \beta, \gamma, \delta) \in K$ and $f \geq 0$. Here, $I(t; \alpha, \beta, \gamma, \delta, f)$ is the solution to system (3) for given quantities $\alpha, \beta, \gamma, \delta, f$.

Again, taking into account the ambiguity of the solution of such an inverse problem, we apply for its solution **Method 2**, a modification of Method 1. It is based on introduction of the external source of infection $f(t)$. In this modification, we replace the quantities

α, $\beta(t)$, $\gamma(t)$, $\delta(t)$ with their analogs α, $\beta(t)$, $\gamma(t)$, $\delta(t)$, $f(t)$ and use the discrepancy of the form Φ_1 instead of Φ. Moreover, the functional (2) is replaced by the following:

$$\Omega_1(\alpha, \beta, \gamma, \delta, f) = \frac{(\alpha - \alpha_n)^2 + (\beta - \beta_n)^2 + (\gamma - \gamma_n)^2 + (\delta - \delta_n)^2 + (f - f_n)^2}{\alpha_n^2 + \beta_n^2 + \gamma_n^2 + \delta_n^2 + f_n^2}.$$

As a result of applying Method 2, we obtain another approximate counterpart $I_{calc}(t)$ of the data $I_{dat}(t)$ and corresponding piecewise constant optimal coefficients of model (3), $\beta^*(t)$, $\gamma^*(t)$, $\delta^*(t)$, $f^*(t)$.

Now we present the results of numerical experiments on modeling epidemic waves using model (3) and Method 2 for some countries. Figure 2 refers to Russia. The top subplot represents the curves $I_{dat}(t)$ and $I_{calc}(t)$. One can see their practical coincidence. This subplot also shows a curve representing the dynamics of the changes in external sources of infection, $f^*(t)$. Since curves $I_{calc}(t)$ and $f^*(t)$ are very different in scale, graph $10f^*(t)$ is given instead of $f^*(t)$. All values are converted to the number of people.

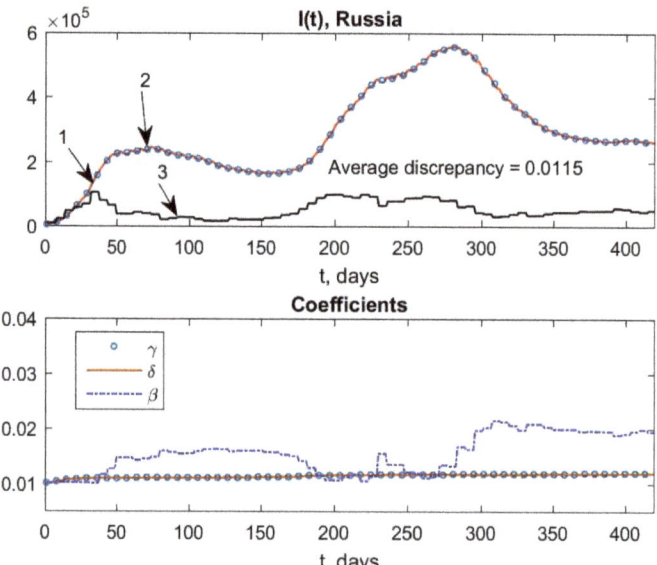

Figure 2. Results of modeling of epidemic for Russia: 1—$I_{dat}(t)$, 2—$I_{calc}(t)$, 3—$10f^*(t)$.

The lower subplot demonstrates the found dynamics of the coefficients. Next, Figure 3 refers to Austria. Again, we present in the upper subplot the quantity $5f^*(t)$ instead of $f^*(t)$ along with $I_{dat}(t)$ and $I_{calc}(t)$.

Similar calculations for other countries show that data approximations, that is the average discrepancies $\overline{\Phi}_{1,\min}$, for model (3) are generally better than those for model (2), and this is due to using the source $f(t)$. This is presented in the Table 2.

Table 2. Accuracy of the approximation of data for Method 2.

Country	Czech Rep.	Germany	France	Italy
$\overline{\Phi}_{1,\min}$	0.0438	0.0327	0.0248	0.0155

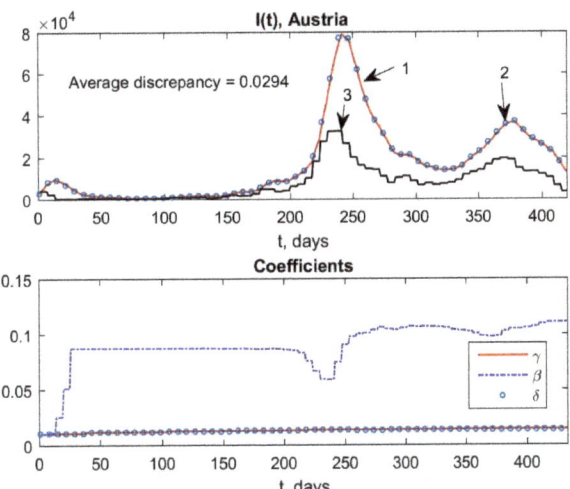

Figure 3. Results of modeling of epidemic for Austria: 1—$I_{dat}(t)$, 2—$I_{calc}(t)$, 3—$5f^*(t)$.

At the same time, the coefficients $\gamma(t)$, $\delta(t)$ vary insignificantly, while the coefficient $\beta(t)$ changes more markedly. In all numerical experiments, it turned out that the found waves of external sources of infection, $f(t)$, were ahead of the wave of infection $I(t)$ by 10 or more days.

4. Applying Other Data

Unfortunately, data provided by Hopkins Coronavirus Resource Center database do not contain information about recovered persons $R = R(t)$ for several recent waves of the epidemic. Therefore, we cannot use, for example, input values $I_{dat}(t) = C - R - D$ dated 10 February 2022 in our models. In this situation, we use the number of infected people per day, that is the quantity $\dot{I}(t)$, as a new type of data for the inverse problem. Accordingly, the inverse problem here is related to the minimization of the residual of the form

$$\Phi_2(\alpha, \beta, \gamma, \delta, f) = \frac{\|\dot{I}(t; \alpha, \beta, \gamma, \delta, f) - \dot{I}_{dat}(t)\|_{L_2[t_n, t_{n+1}]}}{\|\dot{I}_{dat}(t)\|_{L_2[t_n, t_{n+1}]}}.$$

Here, $\dot{I}_{dat}(t)$ is the data presented in [19] and the value of $\dot{I}(t; \alpha, \beta, \gamma, \delta, f)$ can be found from the equation $\dot{I} = \delta(t)E - \gamma(t)I + f(t)$ after solving problem (3) with given coefficients α, $\beta = \beta(t)$, $\gamma = \gamma(t)$, $\delta = \delta(t)$, $f = f(t)$. In this case, we use a modification of Method 2 with Φ_1 replaced by Φ_2 to approximate data $\dot{I}_{dat}(t)$ by $\dot{I}(t; \alpha, \beta, \gamma, \delta, f)$.

The results of such numerical experiments are shown in Figures 4 and 5 again for Russia and Austria. In these calculations, the initial conditions are taken at points t_0 other than 0, due to the small value of data $\dot{I}_{dat}(t)$ for $t < t_0$, where values are compared with background.

We have to note that the accuracy of the approximation of data $\dot{I}_{dat}(t)$ is 5–10 times worse here than for data $I_{dat}(t) = C - R - D$ in Section 3. The Table 3 confirms this.

Table 3. Accuracy of approximation for other data.

Country	Czech Rep.	Germany	USA	Italy
$\overline{\Phi}_{2,\min}$	0.294	0.268	0.183	0.245

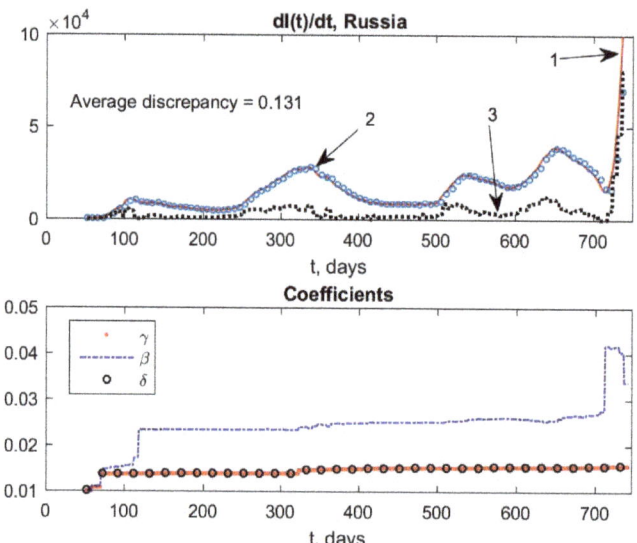

Figure 4. Results of modeling with new data for Russia: 1—$I_{dat}(t)$, 2—$I_{calc}(t)$, 3—$8f^*(t)$.

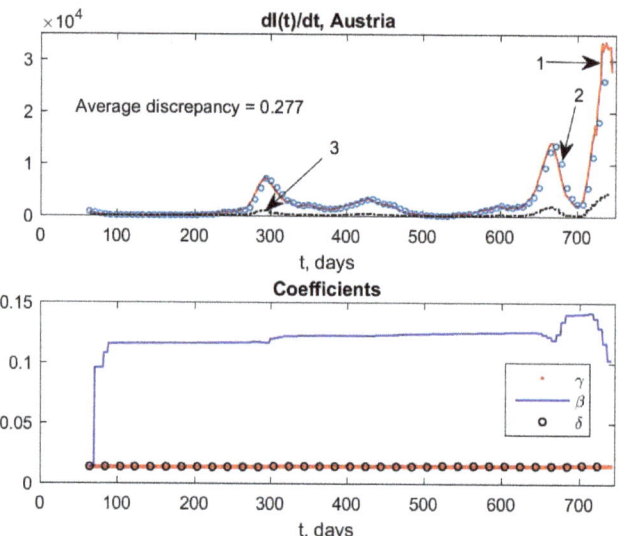

Figure 5. Results of modeling with new data for Austria: 1—$I_{dat}(t)$, 2—$I_{calc}(t)$, 3—$f^*(t)$.

Thus, the use of $I_{dat}(t) = C - R - D$ seems to be preferable if such data are available. Nonetheless, we can observe for data $\dot{I}_{dat}(t)$ the same effect that the peak of source $f(t)$ precedes the peak of infection $I(t)$.

5. Discussion and Conclusions

Numerical experiments with the identification of model (1), which includes piecewise constant coefficients, show that for a number of countries the data to the inverse problem, i.e., infection curves, can be approximated with a high accuracy of 2–8%. This is true for modeling both an isolated wave of an epidemic and a sequence of waves that do not rise sharply. In this case, the found piecewise constant coefficients generally change slightly. For example, the coefficient $\gamma(t)$ (see Figure 1) approximately changes by 3%. Identification is carried out here using the proposed Method 1 based on Tikhonov regularization. However, for infection waves with a sharp increase, the approximation errors grow tenfold.

To overcome this trouble, we introduce an additional term $f(t)$ into model (1). The term takes into account external and latent sources of infection. For model (3), an identification process similar to Method 1 can be proposed. Then, for the data at our disposal, the model makes it possible to approximate all successive infection peaks, up to the Omicron peak, with an accuracy of about 2–4% for different countries. This is somewhat better than for model (1). This is significantly better (by a factor of 2 to 5) than the results that can be obtained using the algorithm from [18] when trying to approximate several epidemic waves without the term $f(t)$ using spline variable coefficients.

When modeling the Omicron peak, we encountered the lack of a series of data in the Hopkins Coronavirus Resource Center database. Therefore, we had to use other data that can be extracted from this database, namely the number of infected people per day. Applying another modification of our Method 1 for the identification of model (3) with such input data for some countries, we approximated the infection curves for all waves, including the Omicron wave, with an accuracy of about 10–30%.

The three parts of our work noted here also show the degree of applicability of the SEI models used to describe the COVID epidemic. These models can be applied fairly reliably to approximate many waves of infection curves with high precision and can be used with a certain degree of confidence to identify external and hidden sources of infection. It distinguishes our models from other models with variable coefficients known in the literature.

Author Contributions: Software, O.N.; Formal analysis, A.L. and S.T.; Investigation, O.N.; Writing—original draft, A.L., O.N. and S.T.; Writing—review–editing, A.L., O.N. and S.T. All authors have read and agreed to the published version of the manuscript.

Funding: The work was partially supported by the Ministry of Science and Higher Education of the Russian Federation (State Task Project No. FSWU-2023-0031).

Institutional Review Board Statement: Not applicable.

Informed Consent Statement: Not applicable.

Data Availability Statement: Not applicable.

Conflicts of Interest: The authors declare no conflict of interest.

References

1. Kermack, W.O.; McKendrick, A.G. A contribution of the mathematical theory of epidemics. *Proc. R. Soc. Lond. A* **1927**, *115*, 700–721. [CrossRef]
2. Zhu, W.J.; Shen, S.F. An improved SIR model describing the epidemic dynamics of the COVID-19 in China. *Results Phys.* **2021**, *25*, 104289. [CrossRef] [PubMed]
3. Quintero, Y.; Ardila, D.; Camargo, E.; Rivas, F.; Aguilar, J. Machine learning models for the prediction of the SEIRD variables for the COVID-19 pandemic based on a deep dependence analysis of variables. *Comput. Biol. Med.* **2021**, *134*, 104500. [CrossRef] [PubMed]
4. Habtemariam, T.; Tameru, B.; Nganwa, D.; Beyene, G.; Ayanwale, L.; Robnett, V. Epidemiologic Modeling of HIV/AIDS: Use of Computational Models to Study the Population Dynamics of the Disease to Assess Effective Intervention Strategies for Decision-making. *Adv. Syst. Sci. Appl.* **2008**, *8*, 35–39. [PubMed]
5. Lee, W.; Liu, S.; Tembine, H.; Li, W.; Osher, S. Controlling propagation of epidemics via mean-field games. *arXiv* **2020**, arXiv:2006.01249.
6. Wolfram, C. An agent-based model of COVID-19. *Complex Syst.* **2020**, *29*, 87–105. [CrossRef]
7. Zhou, J.C.; Salahshour, S.; Ahmadian, A.; Senu, N. Modeling the dynamics of COVID-19 using fractal-fractional operator with a case study. *Results Phys.* **2022**, *33*, 105103. [CrossRef] [PubMed]
8. Engl, H.W.; Flamm, C.; Kugler, P.; Lu, J.; Muller, S.; Schuster, P. Inverse Problems in systems biology. *Inverse Probl.* **2009**, *25*, 123014. [CrossRef]
9. Kabanikhin, S.I.; Krivorotko, O.I.; Ermolenko, D.V.; Kashtanova, V.N.; Latyshenko, V.A. Inverse problems of immunology and epidemiology. *Eurasian J. Math. Comput. Appl.* **2017**, *5*, 14–35. [CrossRef]

10. Sarkar, K.; Khajanchi, S.; Nieto, J.J. Modeling and forecasting the COVID-19 pandemic in India. *Chaos Solitons Fractals* **2020**, *139*, 110049. [CrossRef] [PubMed]
11. Martelloni, G.; Martelloni, G. Modelling the downhill of the Sars-Cov-2 in Italy and a universal forecast of the epidemic in the world. *Chaos Solitons Fractals* **2020**, *139*, 110064. [CrossRef] [PubMed]
12. Ala'raj, M.; Majdalawieh, M.; Nizamuddin, N. Modeling and forecasting of COVID-19 using a hybrid dynamic model based on SEIRD with ARIMA corrections. *Infect. Dis. Model.* **2021**, *6*, 98–111. [CrossRef] [PubMed]
13. Comunian, A.; Gaburro, R.; Giudici, M. Inversion of a SIR-based model: A critical analysis about the application to COVID-19 epidemic. *Phys. D Nonlinear Phenom.* **2020**, *413*, 132674. [CrossRef] [PubMed]
14. Margenov, S.; Popivanov, N.; Ugrinova, I.; Hristov, T. Mathematical Modeling and Short-Term Forecasting of the COVID-19 Epidemic in Bulgaria: SEIRS Model with Vaccination. *Mathematics* **2022**, *10*, 2570. [CrossRef]
15. Kudryashov, N.A.; Chmykhov, M.A.; Vigdorowitsch, M. Analytical features of the SIR model and their applications to COVID-19. *Appl. Math. Model.* **2021**, *90*, 466–473. [CrossRef] [PubMed]
16. Kabanikhin, S.I.; Krivorotko, O.I. Mathematical Modeling of the Wuhan COVID-2019 Epidemic and Inverse Problems. *Comput. Math. Math. Phys.* **2020**, *60*, 1889–1899. [CrossRef]
17. Ghosh, K.; Ghosh, A.K. Study of COVID-19 epidemiological evolution in India with a multi-wave SIR model. *Nonlinear Dyn.* **2022**, *109*, 47–55. [CrossRef] [PubMed]
18. Leonov, A.S.; Nagornov, O.V.; Tyuflin, S.A. Inverse problem for coefficients of equations describing propagation of COVID-19 epidemic. *J. Phys. Conf. Ser.* **2021**, *2036*, 012028. [CrossRef]
19. The Johns Hopkins Coronavirus Resource Center (CRC). Available online: https://coronavirus.jhu.edu (accessed on 15 November 2022).
20. Dong, E.; Du, H.; Gardner, L. An interactive web-based dashboard to track COVID-19 in real time. *Lancet Inf. Dis.* **2020**, *20*, 533–534. [CrossRef] [PubMed]
21. Tikhonov, A.N.; Leonov, A.S.; Yagola, A.G. *Nonlinear Ill-Posed Problems*; Chapman and Hall: London, UK, 1998; Volume 1 and 2.

Disclaimer/Publisher's Note: The statements, opinions and data contained in all publications are solely those of the individual author(s) and contributor(s) and not of MDPI and/or the editor(s). MDPI and/or the editor(s) disclaim responsibility for any injury to people or property resulting from any ideas, methods, instructions or products referred to in the content.

MDPI
St. Alban-Anlage 66
4052 Basel
Switzerland
Tel. +41 61 683 77 34
Fax +41 61 302 89 18
www.mdpi.com

Mathematics Editorial Office
E-mail: mathematics@mdpi.com
www.mdpi.com/journal/mathematics